D0203932

SOCIETY FOR NEW TESTAMENT STUDIES
MONOGRAPH SERIES

GENERAL EDITOR
MATTHEW BLACK, D.D., F.B.A.

20

THE MEANING OF RIGHTEOUSNESS IN PAUL

THE MEANING OF RIGHTEOUSNESS IN PAUL

A LINGUISTIC AND THEOLOGICAL ENQUIRY

J. A. ZIESLER

Tutor in New Testament at Trinity College, Auckland

CAMBRIDGE
AT THE UNIVERSITY PRESS
1972

Published by the Syndics of the Cambridge University Press
Bentley House, 200 Euston Road, London NW1 2DB
American Branch: 32 East 57th Street, New York, N.Y. 10022

Library of Congress Catalogue Card Number: 75-164455

ISBN: 0 521 08316 8

Printed in Great Britain
at the University Printing House, Cambridge
(Brooke Crutchley, University Printer)

CONTENTS

PREFACE

This study was begun in New Zealand, but I very quickly ran into difficulty because of the lack of source material. At this stage I was unexpectedly given the opportunity to spend two years in Cambridge, at Wesley House, where the bulk of the work was done. I shall always be immeasurably grateful to Professor E. G. Rupp for his initiative in getting me to Cambridge, to the Methodist Ministerial Training Department, and to the Governors of Wesley House. I also owe a debt to the Robert Gibson Methodist Trust Board which gave me a grant.

The substance of the book was read in manuscript by Dr Marcus Ward of Richmond College, Professor C. F. Evans of London University, Professor R. McL. Wilson of St Andrews, and Professor C. F. D. Moule of Cambridge. To all these I am grateful for comments and criticisms, though naturally whatever errors and omissions remain are my responsibility, not theirs. I am particularly indebted to Professor Moule, not only for his invaluable advice, criticism, and encouragement, but also for his characteristic kindness, and to my colleague Dr J. J. Lewis of Trinity College, Auckland, who first put the idea into my head that has developed into this book.

The literature on this subject is so vast that it is inevitable that I have done less than justice to many scholars, past and present, and I crave their pardon for apparently ignoring their work, or else giving it only a cursory mention. To do justice to them all, several large volumes would be necessary, or a book consisting of more footnotes than text. Instead, I have concentrated on my own linguistic investigation which has necessitated a good deal of attention to detail. As this can be tiresome to read, I have tried to summarise the results at the end of each chapter or main section, but the evidence had to be included, tiresome or not, because my case stands or falls with it.

To my colleagues at Wesley House, Professor Gordon Rupp, the Revd Michael Skinner, and the Revd Brian Beck, I owe a heavy debt of affection for seven very happy terms, and to Professor Moule I owe an equal debt. My wife and children bore patiently with a preoccupied husband and father for several years, and eased my path greatly.

The book originated as a Ph.D. thesis at London University, and was presented in 1969.

Trinity College,
Auckland, N.Z.
November 1970

J. A. ZIESLER

ABBREVIATIONS

AJT	*American Journal of Theology* (Chicago, 1897–1920).
APOT	*Apocrypha and Pseudepigrapha of the Old Testament*, ed. R. H. Charles (2 vols., Oxford, 1913).
BIB	*Biblica* (Rome, 1920–).
BJRL	*Bulletin of the John Rylands Library* (Manchester, 1903–).
BKW	Bible Key Words, translations of articles in *TWNT*.
DBS	*Dictionnaire de la Bible, Supplément*, ed. L. Pirot and A. Robert (Paris, 1928 onwards; vol. IV in 1949).
EQ	*Evangelical Quarterly* (London, 1929–).
ERE	*Encyclopaedia of Religion and Ethics*, ed. J. Hastings (Edinburgh, 1908–26).
ET	*Expository Times* (Edinburgh, 1889–).
E.Tr.	English Translation.
EV(V)	English Version(s).
HDB	*Dictionary of the Bible*, ed. J. Hastings (Edinburgh, 1898–1904).
HJ	*Hibbert Journal* (London, 1902–).
HTR	*Harvard Theological Review* (Cambridge, Mass., 1908–).
HzNT	*Handbuch zum Neuen Testament* (Tübingen).
IB	*Interpreter's Bible*, general ed. G. A. Buttrick (New York and Nashville, 1952–7).
ICC	International Critical Commentary.
IDB	*Interpreter's Dictionary of the Bible*, ed G. A. Buttrick (New York and Nashville, 1962).
INTERP	*Interpretation* (Richmond, Va., 1947–).
JBL	*Journal of Biblical Literature* (New Haven; Boston; Philadelphia, 1881–).
JE	*Jewish Encyclopedia*, ed. I. Singer (New York and London, 1901–6).
JQR	*Jewish Quarterly Review* (London, 1889–1908; Philadelphia, 1910–).
JSS	*Journal of Semitic Studies* (Manchester, 1956–).
JThCh	*Journal for Theology and the Church* (Tübingen, 1965–).
JTS	*Journal of Theological Studies* (Oxford, 1899–).
LQHR	*London Quarterly and Holborn Review* (London, 1932–68).
LXX	Septuagint.
MM	Moulton and Milligan, *Vocabulary of the Greek Testament* (London, 1914–29).
MNTC	Moffatt New Testament Commentary.

MT	Masoretic Text.
NEB	New English Bible.
NT	*Novum Testamentum* (Leiden, 1956–).
NTD	Das Neue Testament Deutsch (Göttingen).
NTS	*New Testament Studies* (Cambridge, 1954–).
RB	*Revue Biblique* (Paris, 1892–).
[3]*RGG*	*Die Religion in Geschichte und Gegenwart*, ed. K. Galling and others (3rd edn, Tübingen, 1957–65).
RSV	Revised Standard Version.
S–B	H. L. Strack and P. Billerbeck, *Kommentar zum Neuen Testament aus Talmud und Midrasch* (Munich, 1922–56).
TDNT	*Theological Dictionary of the New Testament*, ed. and trans. from *TWNT* by G. W. Bromiley (Grand Rapids, 1964–).
Th	Theodotion.
ThLZ	*Theologische Literaturzeitung* (Leipzig, 1876–).
ThQ	*Theologische Quartalschrift* (Tübingen, Ravensburg, 1819–).
ThStKr	*Theologische Studien und Kritiken* (Hamburg; Gotha, 1828–1938).
ThZ	*Theologische Zeitschrift* (Basel, 1945–).
TWNT	*Theologisches Wörterbuch zum Neuen Testament*, ed. G. Kittel (Stuttgart, 1933–).
VT	*Vetus Testamentum* (Leiden, 1951–).
ZNW	*Zeitschrift für die neutestamentliche Wissenschaft und die Kunde des Urchristentums* (Giessen; Berlin, 1900–).
ZSystTh	*Zeitschrift für systematische Theologie* (Gütersloh, 1923–55).
ZThK	*Zeitschrift für Theologie und Kirche* (Freiburg i. B., 1891–).

INTRODUCTION

Of the many problems connected with Paul's use of δικαιόω and its cognates, few, unfortunately, can be regarded as solved. This study is limited to one problem, namely how far the words are used purely relationally (whether the relation is understood forensically or not), and how far ethically. Two main questions are obvious. First, does δικαιόω mean 'declare righteous' or 'make righteous'? Second, does the noun δικαιοσύνη refer to a relationship, or a way of living, or both?

The heart of the present study is the contention that the verb 'justify' is used relationally, often with the forensic meaning 'acquit', but that the noun, and the adjective δίκαιος, have behavioural meanings, and that in Paul's thought Christians are both justified by faith (i.e. restored to fellowship, acquitted), and also righteous by faith (i.e. leading a new life in Christ). These two are not identical, yet they are complementary and inseparable. This view, which will be amplified and supported with evidence in what follows, is at odds with the usual Protestant understanding, and was certainly not foreseen when the study was begun. Nevertheless it appears to be demanded by the linguistic and exegetical data which will be presented.

THE STATE OF THE QUESTION

The quantity of literature on the subject is immense,[1] and here we attempt only to summarise the various positions which are held, without trying to give an adequate account of the total contribution to research made by the scholars concerned. Unfortunately there is little sign of an emerging consensus.

The Meaning of δικαιόω

Is the Christian made righteous by Christ, and if so what does 'righteous' mean? Or is he declared righteous, i.e. acquitted or

[1] See the bibliography in H. Küng, *Justification*, E.Tr. (London, 1966); the survey of nineteenth-century discussion in A. Schweitzer, *Paul and his Interpreters*, E.Tr. (London, 1912), 10–19; also P. Stuhlmacher, *Gottes Gerechtigkeit bei Paulus* (Göttingen, 1965), 11–70, though he is not adequate for other than German Protestant literature.

brought into a right relationship? The traditional Roman Catholic view is that of the Council of Trent, that justification is both an acquittal and a making righteous in the full ethical sense, thus embracing both relational and behavioural renewal. It means the sinner's forgiveness *and* his moral regeneration, i.e. his sanctification.[1] We may speak of the 'increase' of this justification because it is a process as well as an act.[2] Although expressed and defended in various ways, essentially this view is held by most Catholic biblical scholars.[3] The stress may tend to be placed on the effective rather than the declaratory aspect, because the final declaration is still awaited:

> Clearly, God considers just those whom he has rendered just, and implicitly declares them to be so. But he does not, strictly speaking, pronounce a judgment. The judgment is reserved for the day of the appearance before the judgment seat of Christ... Then it is that God will finally declare just those who are just, having remained faithful to the end.[4]

Meanwhile, justification is the communication of new life in Christ, the radical putting-away of the life of sin, and the inner transformation of the believer, understood to include God's forgiveness. It is forensic, but not merely forensic, and has to do with 'real' rather than 'imputed' righteousness.[5] Some Protestant and Anglican scholars have maintained the same position, including E. J. Goodspeed who argues that the plain meaning of the Greek verb is 'make upright', and that because of the new being in Christ, the believer really is righteous. When God declares him so, the declaration fits the facts.[6] It has been claimed

[1] Session VI, vii; 799 in H. Denzinger, *Enchiridion Symbolorum et Definitionum* (Freiburg, 1922).

[2] Session VI, Canon 24 (Denzinger, 834).

[3] E.g. M. J. Lagrange, *Saint Paul: Épître aux Romains* (Paris, 1931), especially 119–33; F. Amiot, *The Key Concepts of St Paul*, E.Tr. (Freiburg, 1962), 120–5; O. Kuss, *Der Römerbrief* (Regensburg, 1957), 121–31.

[4] Amiot, *Key Concepts*, 124.

[5] Thus K. Kertelge, '*Rechtfertigung*' *bei Paulus* (Münster, 1967), 115–20.

[6] 'Some Greek Notes: III Justification', *JBL*, 73 (1954), 86–91; also *Problems of New Testament Translation* (Chicago, 1945), 143–6. He had many predecessors, e.g. M. R. Vincent, *The Epistles to the Philippians and to Philemon*, ICC (Edinburgh, 1902), 123–8.

that even Luther allowed for a more than declaratory justification.[1]

R. Bultmann, followed by C. K. Barrett, holds that the verb does mean 'make righteous' because it regularly renders the Hebrew hiph'il and therefore must be causative. Yet he takes 'righteous' to mean simply 'in a right relationship' rather than 'ethically upright', and the resulting position is thus very similar to the usual Protestant one.[2] We shall have to enquire whether either verb or adjective can have the meaning suggested.

The main-line Catholic view rests upon a number of supports which are usually presented so as to be cumulative, and not alternative. First, though now rarely, δικαιόω is held to mean 'make righteous' in an ethical sense.[3] Secondly, and more commonly, stress is laid on passages where the noun rather than the verb occurs, passages which do very probably refer to the new life of Christians, e.g. 1 Cor. 1. 30, 2 Cor. 5. 21, so that the verb is interpreted by the noun.[4] We shall see that the Protestant tendency is to do the reverse. Thirdly, and somewhat inferentially, God's word in justification is understood to be a creative word: to say God declares someone righteous is to say that he makes him righteous.[5] Rather similarly, K. Kertelge sees the declaration as first establishing a new relation, and consequently a new being – the latter being implied in the former.[6] Fourthly, just as forgiveness is particularly connected with the Cross, so

[1] G. W. Bromiley, 'The Doctrine of Justification in Luther', *EQ*, 24 (1952), 91–100. On the debate about this, E. G. Rupp, *The Righteousness of God* (London, 1953), 177–83, 221, 254.

[2] R. Bultmann, *Theology of the New Testament* (2 vols., London, 1952 and 1955), I, 271ff; C. K. Barrett, *The Epistle to the Romans*, Black's N.T. Commentaries (London, 1957), 75f.

[3] E.g. Amiot, *Key Concepts*, 120–5, Goodspeed, 'Greek Notes', 86–91. The question is whether an -όω verb must be causative. However, analogies with other verbs are less important than usage in LXX etc. – not what *ought* to occur but what *does* occur. Cf. below, p. 48.

[4] See L. Cerfaux, *Christ in the Theology of St Paul*, E.Tr. (2nd edn, New York and Edinburgh, 1959) in his stress on the communication of Christ's justice to men, Book 2, Ch. 2, especially on Rom. 5; also *The Christian and the Theology of St Paul*, E.Tr. (London, 1967), 392, where he regards the realistic meaning of δικαιοσύνη as governing δικαιοῦν in Rom. 3. 24.

[5] Thus J. H. Newman, *Lectures on the Doctrine of Justification* (4th edn, London, 1885), 78–84; Cerfaux, *The Christian*, 392, 422f.

[6] '*Rechtfertigung*', 115f, 120, 158f, 282.

justification is particularly connected with Christ's resurrection, which means new life in every sense.[1] Fifthly, and most commonly, when one is justified one is therefore in Christ, and so a new creature. This is represented by baptism, which is closely linked with justification, and the whole baptism–union-with-Christ circle of ideas is used to show that more than status is involved.[2] Thus the believer's justice (or righteousness) and his justification are identical, and equivalent to sanctification.[3]

The relation of this justification to the Judgment is variously conceived. F. Amiot sees the sentence as pronounced only at the Judgment.[4] Kertelge sees it as a verdict which the believer hears now, but which awaits its final confirmation at the Judgment, whereas S. Lyonnet suggests a complete dissociation of justification from judgment which have, he argues, nothing to do with one another.[5]

In general it may be objected against the usual Catholic exegesis that it confuses the verb and the noun, and that by transferring quite correct observations from noun passages to verb passages, it renders itself open to attack.[6] On the other hand, traditional Protestant exegesis starts by emphasising that the verb can be only declaratory and that justification is therefore a matter of status only. We shall try to show that on linguistic grounds this is basically correct. There is nevertheless variety in how it is understoood. Some take it forensically, to mean 'acquit' at the tribunal of God.[7] Others see the forensic dress as subsidiary and relatively unimportant; what matters is that 'justify' means 'to restore to right relationship';[8] similarly T. W.

[1] Cerfaux, *Christ*, 140–2.

[2] Cerfaux, *Christ*, 220–44; especially on baptism as modifying a strictly juridical approach, R. Schnackenburg, *Baptism in the Thought of St Paul*, E.Tr. (Oxford, 1964), 122ff.

[3] Cerfaux, *Christ*, 244, 311f; F. Prat, *The Theology of Saint Paul*, E.Tr. (London, 1926–7), I, 171f.

[4] *Key Concepts*, 124.

[5] Kertelge, '*Rechtfertigung*', 158f; S. Lyonnet, 'Justification, Jugement, Rédemption, principalement dans l'épître aux Romains', *Recherches Bibliques*, v (1960), 166–84.

[6] Thus Prat, *Saint Paul*, 168–81; Lagrange, *Romains*, 119–41.

[7] E.g. L. Morris, *The Apostolic Preaching of the Cross* (London, 1955), especially 234, 259–63.

[8] E.g. D. E. H. Whiteley, *The Theology of St Paul* (Oxford, 1964), 159ff; E. K. Lee, *A Study in Romans* (London, 1962), 90.

Manson regards the vocabularly as more regal than legal, with the verb meaning 'pronounce an amnesty' rather than 'acquit' (juridically).[1] Some prefer to speak simply in soteriological terms: 'justification' is another word for salvation, normally understood relationally.[2] Commonly it is said that in the end justification amounts to free unmerited forgiveness, the acceptance of the unacceptable.[3] These are not really alternatives, of course, but different ways of approaching the same fact that in justification Christ receives sinful men. There are also now some Roman Catholic scholars who express remarkably similar views, the most notable of whom is Hans Küng, who shows that on linguistic grounds the verb must be declaratory. The theologian may argue that justification is more than this, and be right in so arguing, but he must recognise that Paul does not include this 'more' in his use of the verb.[4] Much earlier, E. Tobac had maintained the view that justification is declaratory, but subsequent to God's gift of righteousness to those who are united to Christ, so that it is an acknowledgement of what exists. Being made righteous and being acknowledged righteous are logically distinct, but in practice simultaneous. This is not unlike the position of V. Taylor, who argues that God declares man righteous because man is righteous *in Christ*, though at the time of the declaration the righteousness is a matter of will and intention rather than achievement.[5]

A common criticism of the main-line Protestant view is that there is no road from it to ethics, that it represents a cul-de-sac.[6] Equally commonly this criticism has been answered in terms

[1] *On Paul and John*, ed. M. Black (London, 1963), 54–6, 122.

[2] Thus C. H. Dodd, *The Epistle to the Romans*, MNTC (London, 1932), 51f; N. H. Snaith, *The Distinctive Ideas of the Old Testament* (London, 1944), 168–73.

[3] E.g. H. Cremer, *Die paulinische Rechtfertigungslehre im Zusammenhange ihrer geschichtlichen Voraussetzungen* (Gütersloh, 1899), 448; Barrett, *Romans*, 75f.

[4] *Justification*, 200–4, though he also stresses the creativeness of God's word.

[5] E. Tobac, *Le Problème de la Justification dans St Paul* (2nd edn, Louvain, 1941), especially 192–209; V. Taylor, *Forgiveness and Reconciliation* (London, 1941), 1–8, 30–59. Much of Taylor's argument rests on a rejection of 'fictional' justification, and on a view of forgiveness as less than full restoration to fellowship.

[6] Thus A. Schweitzer, *The Mysticism of Paul the Apostle*, E.Tr. (London, 1931), 225f; H. J. Schoeps, *Paul*, E.Tr. (London, 1961), 196; J. Knox, *The Ethic of Jesus in the Teaching of the Church* (London, 1961), 76.

reminiscent of the arguments used in Catholic exegesis for a 'real' rather than a 'juridical' or 'fictional' justification. This similarity must not obscure the fact that the arguments are used differently, for in the Catholic tradition they explicate the nature of justification, but in the Protestant tradition they are its complement (i.e. justification is not the whole of Paul's gospel, and these other things must be kept in mind). The following answers to the 'cul-de-sac' criticism are not alternatives, as many exegetes appeal to several of them.

First, some have argued that in Romans 1–5, Paul deals with God's righteousness as conferring a new status, and in 6–8 he deals with it as energising man and leading to a new life.[1] Somewhat similar is the nineteenth-century view that Paul has two doctrines of redemption, one that is juridical (justification) and one of a really new creation by the Spirit, with the first based largely on the Cross, the second largely on the resurrection.[2] The idea of two distinct soteriologies is now widely rejected,[3] and we also find it unacceptable. Second, it is held that God's word is creative, that it effects what it declares, and that though justification itself is simply declaratory, it yet carries within itself consequences which are in the ethical realm.[4] A like view is that forgiveness (justification) is by nature regenerative, and necessarily leads to a new life.[5] Third, the importance and centrality of justification is minimised (this is perhaps a variation of the first argument). Sometimes the fact is appealed to that the teaching appears explicitly in only two letters, and sometimes the related fact (if it is a fact) that it appears mainly in the context of anti-Judaising polemic. However, while some have agreed

[1] See H. P. Liddon, *Explanatory Analysis of St Paul's Epistle to the Romans* (4th edn, London, 1899), vii and passim, followed with hesitation by W. Sanday and A. C. Headlam, *The Epistle to the Romans*, ICC (Edinburgh, 1902), 38f.

[2] H. Lüdemann, *Die Anthropologie des Apostels Paulus* (Kiel, 1872), 170–3; on the debate, see Schweitzer, *Interpreters*, 29ff, and E. E. Ellis, *Paul and his Recent Interpreters* (Grand Rapids, Mich., 1961), 24. Lüdemann saw the first soteriology as basically Jewish, and the second as Hellenistic.

[3] See especially W. Grundmann, 'Gesetz, Rechtfertigung und Mystik bei Paulus', *ZNW*, 32 (1933), 52–65; H. D. Wendland, *Die Mitte der paulinischen Botschaft* (Göttingen, 1935), 35ff.

[4] E.g. J. Jeremias, *The Central Message of the New Testament* (London, 1965), 64.

[5] E.g. R. N. Longenecker, *Paul, Apostle of Liberty* (New York, 1964), 179.

with A. Schweitzer that justification is 'a subsidiary crater', many others have pressed for its centrality in Paul.[1] Fourth, the inseparability of justification and sanctification has been stressed – not that they are identified or confused, but that to discuss the first without immediately mentioning the second is to make a serious distortion.[2] Fifth, the inseparability of the doctrines of justification and of the Spirit has been underlined, so that in speaking of the first, one needs to go on to mention walking by the Spirit.[3] Lastly, and perhaps chiefly, justification is held to be inseparable from the being-in-Christ which demands and empowers a quite radically new way of living, and which is represented in baptism. This complement to justification is held to provide the way out of the cul-de-sac into Christian ethics, and explains why one sometimes hears the expression, 'baptismal justification'.[4]

In view of the above, it is inaccurate to suggest that the proponents of the declaratory view of justification are unconcerned about its relation to ethics, any more than the proponents of the 'real justification' view are unconcerned about acquittal or forgiveness. The debate centres on the question of how much may properly be attached to the verb δικαιόω. One ought perhaps to add that in the usual Protestant view, the declaration of acquittal, though really belonging to the Last Judgment, is heard by the believer here and now as an anticipation of the final verdict, just as other eschatological realities are already realised or anticipated.[5]

The Meaning of δικαιοσύνη

As in the case of the verb, there are two main conceptions of the meaning of the noun. It is usually assumed without argument by

[1] Schweitzer, *Mysticism*, 219–26, especially 225, followed by Schoeps, *Paul*, 196f, and W. D. Davies, *Paul and Rabbinic Judaism* (London, 1948), 221f; contra, Wendland, *Die Mitte*; E. von Dobschütz, 'Die Rechtfertigung bei Paulus, eine Rechtfertigung des Paulus', *ThStKr*, 85 (1912), 38–67; E. Jüngel, *Paulus und Jesus* (2nd edn, Tübingen, 1964), 17–32.

[2] E.g. J. Calvin, *Institutes of the Christian Religion*, ed. J. T. McNeill (London, 1961), III xiv 9. On the relation between the two, Küng, *Justification*, Excursus II.

[3] Thus Bultmann, *Theology*, I, 332.

[4] E.g. A. Richardson, *An Introduction to the Theology of the New Testament* (London, 1958), 235–43. Cf. also W. F. Flemington, *The New Testament Doctrine of Baptism* (London, 1948), 55–61, 69; Wendland, *Die Mitte*, 46ff.

[5] Cf. Barrett, *Romans*, 30, 75.

Roman Catholic exegetes that it means 'justice' in the sense of uprightness, rather than strict distributive justice or even forensic justice in general. The word is part of ethical vocabulary, a 'common-sense' view that has not been without Protestant support.[1] The usual Protestant position however has been that righteousness as imputed in justification is real righteousness, which comes from God to man, but *for forensic purposes only*. Man is not righteous, but he is treated by God as if he were, because he stands clothed in the righteousness of Christ.[2] More commonly today, the language of imputation is avoided, partly because of the difficulties to which it has led, and partly because its use in Rom. 4 and Gal. 3 seems very much due to the exigencies of polemic. Instead, it is widely considered that 'righteousness' belongs to the language of relationships, and denotes a right relation to God which is not imputed by anyone but really exists. It is a real righteousness, with no 'as if' about it, but is purely relational.[3] Because of this, the noun can be taken to mean 'acceptance' (of man, by God), or to mean 'forgiveness'.[4]

Thus righteousness from God and justification are the same thing. Both are to do with the granting of a status before God, an undeserved status which *in itself* is not concerned with ethics, but which has ethical consequences. The indicative of justification implies an ethical imperative, but this is subsequent, and the Christian is always *simul iustus et peccator*. Now the advantage of this interpretation is that any fictional view of justification is avoided: the sinner is declared righteous, but as 'righteous' is a relationship, not an ethical, term, nothing untrue is declared. God may put whom he pleases into a right relationship with himself. Clearly, in these terms there is no difference between 'make' and 'declare' righteous, for it is simply a matter of bringing sinners into a new relationship.[5]

[1] Thus Cerfaux, *Christ*, 220–35; J. Drummond, 'On the Meaning of "Righteousness of God" in the Theology of St Paul' (I), *HJ*, I (1902), 83–95, cf. (II), 272–93.

[2] Cf. Calvin, *Institutes*, II xvi 6.

[3] Bultmann, *Theology*, I, 271f, 277; Whiteley, *St Paul*, 160, among many others.

[4] So Morris, *Apostolic Preaching*, 235, 246, 249, 256; A. Ritschl, *Die christliche Lehre von der Rechtfertigung und Versöhnung dargestellt* (2nd edn, Bonn, 1882), II, 303–8.

[5] Bultmann, *Theology*, I, 276.

A. Richardson contends that the Christian's righteousness from God is entirely real, so that he stands before God as the righteous man he actually is, but *only eschatologically*. What is acquitted is presumably not the self that is, but the one that is to be. What matters is what he is to be, and therefore it is proper and no fiction when God acquits him.[1] The usual weakness of the 'imputation' approach, that it makes an un-Jewish separation of righteousness in God's sight, from righteousness in life and society,[2] is here avoided, but one cannot see that the texts support Richardson's solution.

Although it is often acknowledged that elsewhere δικαιοσύνη may have an ethical meaning,[3] in 'justification' contexts a relational meaning is then widely accepted. If we ask what is the basis on which this non-ethical meaning has been given to it, two answers are found. First, it is said that the meaning in Paul has been influenced by the meaning of the cognate verb, which means that this 'relational' meaning is a peculiarly Pauline one.[4] Second, it is argued that the ethical meaning is essentially Greek, and the relational meaning characteristically Hebraic, representative of the tradition to which Paul belongs.[5] In any case, the result is a general tendency to interpret the noun by the verb, in exact opposition to the tendency of the Catholic tradition. We shall have to question whether either of these procedures is correct.

The Expression δικαιοσύνη θεοῦ

Especially because this expression is used in connection with justification in Romans (cf. 3. 21–6, and pp. 169f below), its correct interpretation is widely seen as the clue to the meaning

[1] *Theology*, 236ff. Richardson's view is distinct from that of Bultmann, who sees righteousness as forensic–eschatological in the sense that the verdict is partly now, partly in the future, cf. 'ΔΙΚΑΙΟΣΥΝΗ ΘΕΟΥ', *JBL*, 83 (1964), 12–16.

[2] Cf. Kertelge's criticism of the separation of inner from outer in 'imputation': '*Rechtfertigung*', 118f.

[3] E.g. Ritschl, *Rechtfertigung*, II, 340; D. Hill, *Greek Words and Hebrew Meanings* (Cambridge, 1967), 153.

[4] E.g. W. A. Stevens, 'The Forensic Meaning of δικαιοσύνη', *AJT*, I (1897), 443–50, especially 445f.

[5] E.g. Hill, *Greek Words*, 152.

of justification. It is often treated as a formula, i.e. a set phrase with a stereotyped meaning and often or regularly used for that meaning – in effect a technical term. It is debated whether Paul adopted a formula from the Old Testament and late Judaism, and adapted it to his own purposes,[1] or whether he newly minted it himself.[2] Unfortunately, even if it is a formula, which may be doubted on the grounds that the instances of it do not clearly all bear the same meaning, and that the main meanings it conveys are more frequently conveyed in other words, there is disagreement on what it means.[3] We shall have to revert to this question after our own investigation of the texts.

The traditional Protestant view (and Luther's) was that the term is an 'objective genitive' (an infelicitous use of the term). That is to say, the righteousness of God of which it speaks is indeed the righteousness God grants, but is granted by him because it is that which 'vor Gott gilt' (Luther's rendering in Rom. 1. 17, 3. 21, 25f). It is *iustitia aliena*, external to man, imputed.[4] Since the middle of the nineteenth century, this view has found relatively little support among exegetes. In the latter part of last century, and the beginning of the present one,

[1] Thus A. Oepke, 'Δικαιοσύνη Θεοῦ bei Paulus in neuer Beleuchtung', *ThLZ*, 78 (1953), 257–64; also E. Käsemann, 'God's Righteousness in Paul' (E.Tr. of 'Gottesgerechtigkeit bei Paulus', *ZThK*, 58 (1961), 367–78), *Journal for Theology and the Church*, 1 (1965), 100–10, especially 102f. All references will be from the English.

[2] So Bultmann, 'ΔΙΚΑΙΟΣΥΝΗ ΘΕΟΥ', 16. The passages cited on both sides are: Deut. 33. 21; Sifre Deut. 33. 21; TDan 6. 10; 1 QS 11. 12; also Mt. 6. 33 and Jas 1. 20, but Bultmann considers the Pauline and late Judaistic meanings quite different.

[3] Thus Oepke thinks it means both God's activity and a predicate conferred on man by God, the righteousness which 'vor Gott gilt', 'Δικαιοσύνη Θεοῦ', 260, but Bultmann sees it strictly as God's gift, that of right standing, 'ΔΙΚΑΙΟΣΥΝΗ ΘΕΟΥ', 13ff. Käsemann's very rich conception is that it is and remains God's own, and has the character of power, yet is also a gift to the believer, a gift which nevertheless is inseparable from the Giver, 'God's Righteousness,' 103 f. On the question of 'formula', we accept the dictum that 'A formula is only present when there is a clear tendency to express an idea by a set phrase', R. C. Tannehill, *Dying and Rising with Christ*, Beiheft zur *ZNW* (Berlin, 1967), 6.

[4] Oepke, 'Δικαιοσύνη Θεοῦ', especially 263, sees it as a genitive of origin approaching an objective genitive. He made an unsuccessful attempt to distinguish different meanings or nuances in the expression by the presence or absence of the article.

intensive research into Paul's teaching on justification, and particularly into the meaning of 'righteousness of God', produced a strong emphasis on θεοῦ as a 'subjective genitive', meaning in this case that it is God's own righteousness, not as a static attribute, but as an expression for the activity of the living God. A whole galaxy of German scholars held this position.[1] Specifically, the activity of God was as Judge and Saviour, but different scholars gave different emphases to judging and saving aspects,[2] though the stress was more usually on the latter. More recently, J. A. Bollier has supported a subjective genitive, but with the rider that it has 'a transeunt as well as an immanent aspect, for man is directly affected by the manifestation of this righteousness'.[3] Man may experience this righteousness as wrath, when he seeks God's favour through law-fulfilment, but as acceptance when he responds to Christ in faith. E. Käsemann also of course represents the subjective genitive view, and for him it is God's own saving power.[4]

The third main interpretation of the expression, that it is a genitive of origin, is the usual view today. The righteousness is God's, it proceeds from him to man, thus creating a relation to God. This view is held by both Roman Catholic and Protestant exegetes.[5] Nevertheless, not surprisingly, this righteousness from God to man is variously understood. For Bultmann it is a right standing,[6] but for Cerfaux it is real righteousness of life.[7] Yet this

[1] E.g. Ritschl, *Rechtfertigung*, II, 113–19; Th. Häring, ΔΙΚΑΙΟΣΥΝΗ ΘΕΟΥ *bei Paulus* (Tübingen, 1896), 38, 45, 63.

[2] Thus Ritschl, *Rechtfertigung*, II, 102–19, considers it invariably saving; for Häring, ΔΙΚΑΙΟΣΥΝΗ ΘΕΟΥ, 38, it is God's judicial but acquitting righteousness; O. Zanker, 'Δικαιοσύνη Θεοῦ bei Paulus', *ZSystTh*, 9 (1931–2), 398–420, finds it either judging or saving, depending on man's response.

[3] J. A. Bollier, 'The Righteousness of God', *INTERP*, 8 (1954), 404–13, the quotation being from 413.

[4] 'God's Righteousness', especially 100f.

[5] E.g. Lagrange, *Romains*, 19; Cerfaux in L. Cerfaux and A. Descamps, 'Justice, Justification', *Dictionnaire de la Bible, Supplément* IV (Paris, 1949), cols 1417–510, and especially cols 1478f; Bultmann, *Theology*, I, 280–5; Jüngel, *Paulus und Jesus*, 39–48. H. Lietzmann, *An die Römer*, *HzNT*, 8 (4th edn, Tübingen, 1933), 30f, 95, sees a 'schillernde Doppelbedeutung' – a genitive both subjective and of origin.

[6] 'ΔΙΚΑΙΟΣΥΝΗ ΘΕΟΥ', 13ff.

[7] 'Justice, Justification', cols 1478f; cf. Lagrange, *Romains*, 120f.

is not simply a Catholic–Protestant disagreement, for G. Schrenk most notably sees the power of a new life involved.[1]

Much fuller accounts of the various interpretations of the expression are available;[2] the above merely outlines the main varieties.

In the last few years there have been two interesting developments, one (Roman Catholic) largely associated with S. Lyonnet, and one (Protestant) largely associated with E. Käsemann. Lyonnet's position is that in the Bible in general, 'the righteousness of God' always refers to God's saving activity.[3] This is especially true for Paul, and Lyonnet finds a double dissociation in the epistles, of salvation (future) from justification (past), and of Judgment (future, and necessarily forensic) from justification (which is not forensic at all).[4] God's righteousness saves precisely in that it justifies here and now, and there is no relation to future judgment. His scheme is beautifully simple, but it must be questioned whether 'God's righteousness' does universally have this meaning in the Bible, and whether the double dissociation can be successfully carried through, both in view of biblical usage generally, which as we shall see, does associate justification with judgment, and in view of such a passage as Rom. 3. 20–2.[5]

[1] In G. Quell and G. Schrenk, *Righteousness*, BKW, E.Tr. from TWNT (London, 1951), especially 43–55, 72f; righteousness is communicated to believers by God (though it remains his) and this both acquits the sinner and breaks sin's bondage.

[2] Häring, ΔΙΚΑΙΟΣΥΝΗ ΘΕΟΥ, 14–71, tabulates eleven different interpretations; recently Stuhlmacher, *Gottes Gerechtigkeit* (11–70), has given a good survey mainly of German works.

[3] His work is most readily available in pp. 820–65 of *Introduction to the New Testament*, ed. A. Robert and A. Feuillet, E.Tr. (New York – Rome – Paris – Tournai, 1965) and in 'Justification, Jugement, Rédemption'.

[4] 'Justification, Jugement, Rédemption'; Lyonnet was not the first Catholic exegete to stress the saving nature of God's righteousness; see Tobac, *Le Problème*, 107–21, nor the last, see Kertelge, '*Rechtfertigung*', 107–9 and Kuss, *Römerbrief*, 158f, though Kuss does not find the same meaning everywhere.

[5] H. Cazelles has tried to remove some of the more difficult objections to the Lyonnet position: 'À propos de quelques textes difficiles relatifs à la Justice de Dieu dans l'Ancien Testament', *RB*, 58 (1951), 169–88. However, Lyonnet's pupil, S. Schmidt, modifies Lyonnet's position. He gives an account of his dissertation in *Verbum Domini*, 37 (1959), 96–105, 'S. Pauli "iustitia Dei" notione iustitiae quae in VT et apud S. Paulum habetur, dilucidata', and concludes (101): 'God's righteousness in the Old Testament is not to be

About this latter, Lyonnet would argue that v. 20 represents the Jewish point of view rejected by Paul, but its close juxtaposition with vv. 21f suggests that although Paul rejects legalism as a means of justification, yet he does not reject the link between justification and judgment.

Käsemann's interpretation is that God's righteousness is a power (cf. Rom. 1. 17, 10. 3ff) which is a gift to the believer and which both obliges us to obedience and also makes that obedience possible. It possesses us, we do not possess it, because the gift is inseparable from the Giver. This power–gift unites justification and sanctification, present and future, and to describe it Paul uses a formula which was known in late Judaism, especially in apocalyptic.[1] Käsemann's thesis has been followed up by his pupils Müller and Stuhlmacher.[2] Stuhlmacher regards God's righteousness as essentially his loyalty to his creation (thus more universal than loyalty to his covenant), and makes it the key to Paul's theology. In relation to justification, like Käsemann he thinks it enables a synthesis to be made of forensic declaration and creative act, though all stands under the 'eschatological reservation'.[3] He concludes that it means 'Gottes befreiende Recht'.[4] We shall have to dispute many individual points with

described as exclusively or essentially salvific, nor to be identified with his kindness and mercy, but consists in the correspondence of God's activity to his divine Esse.' I have been unable to consult Schmidt's article, and have relied on the account of it in Kertelge, '*Rechtfertigung*', 13f.

[1] 'God's Righteousness.' Käsemann was not the first to see God's righteousness as power, cf. A. Schlatter, *Gottes Gerechtigkeit; ein Kommentar zum Römerbrief* (4th edn, Stuttgart, 1965), 36ff, and A. Nygren, *A Commentary on Romans*, E.Tr. (London, 1952), 146, 152. Käsemann's interpretation is not necessarily invalid if, with Bultmann, we reject his view that Paul takes over a technical term, nor if we reject apocalyptic as *the* context of that term.

[2] Stuhlmacher, *Gottes Gerechtigkeit*; C. Müller, *Gottes Gerechtigkeit und Gottes Volk* (Göttingen, 1964). Müller relates Käsemann's insights particularly to Rom. 9–11: because we must think of creation-righteousness rather than covenant-righteousness, we may see the relation of the *sola gratia* to the universality of God's new people.

[3] *Gottes Gerechtigkeit*, especially 217–36.

[4] *Gottes Gerechtigkeit*, 236 and passim. Kertelge, '*Rechtfertigung*', 307–9, criticises Stuhlmacher on the grounds that faithfulness to the creation is not a prominent Pauline theme, that God's creative activity is not suggested by 'God's righteousness' as unequivocally as Stuhlmacher thinks, and that

Stuhlmacher and Käsemann, and we may doubt whether creation-loyalty has the support in the texts adequate for the building erected upon it, yet much of what is said, especially in Käsemann's original article, is supported by our own independent investigation, despite a great difference in approach.

We may summarise the present position thus:

i. There is little sign of an emerging consensus.

ii. With exceptions, the Protestant tradition tends to interpret the noun by the verb, i.e. make it purely relational, while the Catholic tradition tends to do the reverse, i.e. speak of a 'real' justification.

iii. There is a widely held belief that δικαιοσύνη θεοῦ holds the key to the meaning of justification, but some disagreement about its meaning.

THE METHOD OF THE PRESENT STUDY

In view of the absence of consensus, it seems essential to go back to the beginning, and try to determine the meaning, or rather the possible varieties of meaning, of the crucial words. This has required an investigation of the occurrences of δικαιόω, δίκαιος, and δικαιοσύνη, which are the chief words concerned. The meanings of δικαίωμα are not disputed and will be dealt with summarily later; the noun δικαίωσις is important, but rare; δίκη is not important, for it occurs in Paul only in 2 Thess. 1. 9, where it means 'punishment'. All the literature which is likely to have a bearing on Pauline usage has been examined, and a study has been made of Hebrew equivalents, notably the root צדק, in the Old Testament and elsewhere. As far as possible the analysis has been exhaustive, all cases being examined, but in one or two instances this has proved impracticable: in the Rabbinic writings, because of the sheer volume of the material; and in Josephus, partly because of the lack of an exhaustive index, and partly because of the relatively minor importance of the material. Instead, what one hopes is a fair sample has been taken. Wearisome though this exhaustive method may be, it seems necessary if one is to escape from the danger of citing one

Stuhlmacher overestimates the role of 'God's righteousness' in universal history, not allowing enough for the new history it inaugurates.

case, or even a string of cases, without any indication of how far these represent, or are deviations from, normal usage. Necessarily then, this is a linguistic study more than a study in the history of ideas, yet the theological framework within which the words are used cannot be ignored, and some account has had to be taken of it.

Considerable compression has been necessary, and as a consequence the views of other investigators have at times been barely mentioned and seldom given the attention they merit. Consequently also, when we come to Paul, only an adumbration of an exegesis has been possible. Priority has been given to the attempt to determine what the words are likely to have meant to Paul and his correspondents.

It is sometimes said that Paul used 'righteousness' in a highly idiosyncratic way, different certainly from its usual Greek meaning, but different also from its meaning in Jewish contexts.[1] This is possible, but such a view must be a last resort and is legitimate only when we have failed to make sense of Paul's vocabulary in terms of either its Greek or Hebrew background, or both.[2] It is not easy to imagine Paul trying to communicate with his churches, and using familiar words in a new way, without some explanation. His use of σάρξ does not tell against this contention, for there the Hebrew background is in the ascendant.

James Barr has given a healthy warning to all who deal with meanings of biblical words.[3] We have tried to heed that warning and to avoid such errors as the etymological fallacy and the adding of significances; particularly in examining δίκαιος and its cognates, we have rejected the assumption that what is true of one word is also necessarily true of a cognate. The existence of 'awe' and 'awful' in English is sufficient reminder of the dangers of this, at least without due testing. The path suggested by Barr which has recently been examined and largely put into practice by David Hill, is that of examining words within larger linguistic

[1] E.g. B. S. Easton, *The Pastoral Epistles* (London, 1948), 218–20, note on δίκαιος.

[2] Cf. J. B. Skemp, *The Greeks and the Gospel* (London, 1964), 63: 'Theologians should...use the general lexicon before making any special ones.'

[3] *The Semantics of Biblical Language* (Oxford, 1961).

complexes, i.e. contextually.[1] We have also tried to make this a basic method.

Finally, in what follows no attempt has been made to give a complete coverage of all the problems involved in this word-group. The concentration is on the question of whether any given occurrence is behavioural, or relational, or some combination of the two.

[1] Barr, *Semantics*, especially 263ff, and Hill, *Greek Words*, 1–14.

CHAPTER I

THE OLD TESTAMENT

THE NATURE OF HEBREW JUSTICE

Our conception of the functions of a judge must be modified somewhat if we are correctly to understand the use of words like מִשְׁפָּט and צְדָקָה in forensic settings. This point is frequently made.[1] In Israel, the judge was normally the king, and his legal and regal functions were not to be separated. Further, all human judgment was seen as subject to that of God the King, who was *the* Judge, and human justice was justice only in so far as it truly reflected God's.[2] Again, for both human and divine justice, *mishpat* meant much more than the passing of sentence, as did also the associated terms *tsedeq* and *tsedaqah*. They could mean the vindicating of the falsely accused and the downtrodden, the rescue of the oppressed (hence the close connection with salvation), as well as the punishment of the wicked. To 'judge the fatherless' is not to condemn him, but to see that he gets his rights, and when the Psalmist asks God to judge him, it is a cry for help (Ps. 7. 8; 26. 1; 35. 24; 43. 1). The Judges in the pre-monarchy period are men who by military means help Israel to achieve justice – almost in the sense of civil rights.[3] This means that the judge exercised 'a positive energy on the side of right',[4] that his task was nothing less than the maintenance of the community, and that his righteousness consisted in his will and power to maintain the covenant. He did this not only by curbing the actions of those who transgressed the proper limits, but also by giving support to those who needed it.[5] All this entails much

[1] E.g. by L. Köhler, *Hebrew Man*, E.Tr. (London, 1956), Appendix on 'Justice in the Gate', and by J. Muilenburg, *The Way of Israel* (London, 1962), 87ff.

[2] See A. R. Johnson, *Sacral Kingship in Ancient Israel* (Cardiff, 1955), 6.

[3] Köhler, *Hebrew Man*, 156; Muilenburg, *Way of Israel*, 36f, 76.

[4] The phrase used by J. Skinner, 'Righteousness in O.T.', *HDB*, IV, 274.

[5] Cf. J. Pedersen, *Israel, Its Life and Culture*, E.Tr. (4 parts in 2 vols., London–Copenhagen, 1926–40), vol. I, 348: 'He is to uphold the covenant both outwardly and inwardly and the inward equilibrium he maintains by supporting those who are about to fall and by checking those who want to

more than making a forensic declaration about guilt or innocence, cf. Isa. 1. 17; 11. 4; Jer. 22. 15f; Deut. 24. 17; Ps. 82. 3. It is therefore not surprising that in our examination of the root צדק we cannot easily distinguish the forensic from the ethical, nor that we discover some meanings which are clearly forensic, but others which have nothing to do with legal processes. The point is that, at least in the early period, the forensic as a self-contained sphere simply did not exist.

ANALYSIS OF VOCABULARY

The extent of semantic overlap of δίκαιος and cognates with the root צדק is so considerable that we must give close attention to the latter. It is in the Septuagint that this overlap is encountered most strikingly, and although counts vary, ours is that in the Kittel edition of the Old Testament there are 504 cases of some form of צדק; of these only about 50, i.e. 10 per cent, are not rendered in the LXX by δίκαιος or a cognate.

The Verb

1. *Hiph'il*

We start here because it is sometimes stated that δικαιοῦν normally renders the hiph'il of צָדַק. The hiph'il occurs twelve times and the dominant meaning is the forensic one, 'declare to be in the right, not guilty, innocent'. Nine cases have a judicial setting, viz. Deut. 25. 1; 2 Sam. 15. 4; Isa. 5. 23; and Prov. 17. 15 (all involving human legal processes); and Ex. 23. 7; 1 Kgs 8. 32 and 2 Chron. 6. 23; Ps. 82. 3; Isa. 50. 8 (all to do with divine justice). In three of these the point is that men must not (Isa. 5. 23; Prov. 17. 15) and God does not (Ex. 23. 7) acquit the wicked.

In each case, men are declared to be in the right *on the facts*, i.e. because in general or in a specific matter they *are* upright, and innocent. However, these nine forensic cases are not merely forensic: the note of vindication in rewarding the righteous is present in 1 Kgs 8. 32 and 2 Chron. 6. 23; seeing to it that people get their rights, even their civil rights, is involved in 2 Sam. 15. 4,

take too much.' Cf. 1 Sam. 3. 13; Isa. 1. 17, 23; 11. 4; Jer. 5. 28; Ps. 10. 18; 82. 3; Prov. 29. 14.

Ps. 82. 3, and perhaps Isa. 5. 23 and 50. 8. This supports the contention of Pedersen that the hiph'il means 'put in the right' in the sense of 'restore to proper position within the covenant'.[1] This fits the nature of Hebrew justice.

There remain three instances of the hiph'il which are not so certainly forensic:

Job 27. 5: חָלִילָה לִּי אִם־אַצְדִּיק אֶתְכֶם
(RSV: Far be it from me to say that you are right)

Contention is the context, and, remotely, so is judgment, if we take the whole of Job to be the hearing of a case about a man's righteousness. Yet here the forensic note is weak, and in any case it is Job, not Bildad, who is on trial, and thus for him to be in the right is simply to have the correct view of the matter.

Isa. 53. 11: בְּדַעְתּוֹ יַצְדִּיק צַדִּיק עַבְדִּי לָרַבִּים

MT appears not to require the RSV 'make many to be accounted righteous'. Clearly, in some sense others become righteous through the Righteous One, but it is improbable that as early as this there is any notion of acquiring merit for others.[2] Rather do others become righteous when they are cleansed by his sacrifice, 'when they bring to it the spirit that validates it for them by making it the organ of their approach to God'.[3] Thus while conceivably this is an anticipation of 'justify the ungodly',[4] particularly in view of the following clause 'he shall bear their iniquities', it is also possible that because of the vicarious action of the Servant, and in so far as others recognise him as their representative, they *are* righteous. A further difficulty about a forensic sense is that only God can acquit in the divine court, and if this is set in that court, it is odd to find the Servant taking God's place. Therefore, despite the nine other cases where the hiph'il is forensic, there is doubt here. The Servant may be the cause not of the accounting righteous, but of the actual being righteous, of many.[5]

[1] *Israel*, I, 346; cf. Schrenk, *Righteousness*, 30, 58.

[2] As is suggested by R. A. Rosenberg, 'Jesus, Isaac, and the "Suffering Servant"', *JBL*, 84 (1965), 381–8.

[3] H. H. Rowley, *From Moses to Qumran* (London, 1964), 102.

[4] So J. Muilenburg, *Isaiah, IB*, v (New York–Nashville, 1962), 630.

[5] So G. A. F. Knight, *Deutero-Isaiah* (New York, 1965), 242f, and Skinner, 'Righteousness in O.T.', 276.

Dan. 12. 3: וּמַצְדִּיקֵי הָרַבִּים
(RSV: those who turn many to righteousness)

The context here gives too little indication for certainty; this could be forensic, but more plausibly belongs with Isa. 53. 11 and means 'make many righteous'.[1]

To summarise the hiph'il: the tendency is strongly forensic, but with important probable exceptions. Even the clearly forensic cases are forensic in the Hebrew sense, i.e. they represent restoration of the community or covenant relationship, and thus cannot be separated from the ethical altogether. The restoration is not merely to a standing, but to an existence in the relationship.[2]

2. *Qal*

There are twenty-two occurrences. As in the hiph'il, we find a forensic note, but at times this is almost metaphorical. Broadly forensic are: Gen. 38. 26; Ps. 143. 2; Isa. 43. 9, 26; Ezek. 16. 52. Also forensic, but referring to edicts or ordinances, are Ps. 19. 9 and probably 51. 4. Once it means 'be vindicated' in a somewhat remotely forensic sense, Isa. 45. 25. The remaining 14 instances are in the book of Job, and whether or not they are forensic is arguable. If we take the whole book to be forensic, then most of these 14 are forensic too. Some are in any case. All have a strong note of innocence, which is a fusion of the forensic and the ethical. An interesting example is 9. 15:

> 'Though I am innocent, I cannot answer him, I must appeal for mercy to my accuser' (RSV).

There seems to be no doubt of his ethical uprightness, yet there *is* doubt about its forensic recognition. Similar are: 9. 20; 10. 15; 22. 3; 34. 5; 35. 7. In other cases, while this ethical stress is present, the stronger note is that of rightness before God: 4. 17; 9. 2; 15. 14; 25. 4, and perhaps 40. 8. In 33. 12 it simply means being right and not wrong. In 11. 2 and 13. 18 we have a note of vindication where again ethical and forensic are united.

To summarise the Qal: it means 'be righteous' in an ethical or a forensic sense, or both together.[3] Forensic rightness normally

[1] So R. H. Charles, *Commentary on Daniel* (Oxford, 1929), 331.

[2] A somewhat similar summary to the above is given by N. M. Watson, 'Some Observations on the use of ΔΙΚΑΙΟω in the Septuagint', *JBL*, 79 (1960), 255–66.

[3] As against C. H. Dodd, *The Bible and the Greeks* (London, 1935), 46, who opts for 'being in the right'. This is true, but not the whole picture.

is rightness in God's sight, i.e. by his definition of rightness, and so it is not surprising that it is often hard to disentangle this from the ethical meaning. It is precisely rightness in God's sight that is the basis of ethics.

3. *Pi'el*

There are five instances: Jer. 3. 11; Ezek. 16. 51, 52; Job 32. 2, 33. 32. All denote the demonstration of an already existing righteousness. As the demonstration is usually forensic, and vindicatory, we meet here the same duality which we found in the qal. Both ethical and forensic notes are here.[1] In Job 32. 2, Job is certainly trying to put himself in the right (he 'justified himself rather than God'), but he is also trying to prove his own righteousness. Similarly in 33. 32 we have God's desire to find Job righteous, i.e. prove his innocence, demonstrate his righteousness. To summarise the pi'el: all the cases combine forensic and ethical elements in that they all denote the demonstration of an existing righteousness.

4. *Niph'al*

The sole instance, Dan. 8. 14 ('the sanctuary shall be restored to its rightful state') (RSV), is important. Without doubt נִצְדַּק means 'make right' both in the sense of 'put into proper order' and also with the recognition that the proper order is defined by God.[2] By analogy with the personal uses, we may say that here again we find the ethical inseparable from the forensic.

5. *Hithpa'el*

The sole case, Gen. 44. 16, is parallel to the pi'el cases, 'how can we clear ourselves', i.e. show our righteousness? Ethical and forensic are again united.

No attempt has been made to give a full account of the meaning of the various forms of the verb, and only what seems to bear on

[1] By 'ethical' we mean throughout not some moralistic notion, but behaviour in general, including liturgical behaviour. A sharp division between different realms of behaviour is not possible in the Bible.

[2] A. B. Davidson, *The Theology of the Old Testament*, ed. S. D. F. Salmond (Edinburgh, 1904), 267, thinks this is the only place where the verb means 'make ethically pure'. N. Snaith, *The Distinctive Ideas of the Old Testament*, 74, renders 'put into proper order'.

the matter in hand has been dealt with. To speak of the verb as 'forensic' is only partly correct. Sometimes the forensic note is very weak indeed, and the 'making righteous' note dominates. Even in the majority of cases, where the forensic note is heavy, it is seldom the only note.[1] Usually forensic and ethical are inseparable, though there is a distinction between them in some of the Job cases of the qal. Generally, however, this duality exists in all forms of the verb, and therefore a sharp forensic–ethical distinction seems to find no basis in the usage of the verb צדק. How much stress is on each depends on context and circumstances.

The Nouns צֶדֶק *and* צְדָקָה *and the Adjective* צַדִּיק

There are in the Kittel edition of the Hebrew Old Testament about 481 cases of these three words.[2] They have all been examined in their context with certain questions chiefly in mind:

1. Is this forensic, and if so, in what sense? The first part of the question is not enough. When we speak of the forensic righteousness of an accused person, we mean he is innocent, not guilty, acquitted, i.e. his rightness or righteousness is a matter of status in, or relationship to the court. When a judge, however, is righteous or just, the reference is not so much to his status as to the way in which he acts in court. This difference is important, and the word 'forensic' may conceal this distinction between status and behaviour. Therefore it must be used cautiously, and not in a misleadingly general way.[3] We shall normally reserve it for the status use.

2. If this instance refers to activity or behaviour rather than status, is there also an explicit or clearly implicit reference to God? That is, is man's righteousness approved or commanded or rewarded or even caused, by God? In other words, is there a double reference, to man's behaviour, but also to that behaviour as seen before God?

The examination is contextual, not etymological, and its aim

[1] Cf. Pedersen, *Israel*, I, 408, 428.

[2] Of these, 115 are *tsedeq*, 158 are *tsedaqah*, and 208 are *tsaddiq*. Isa. 49. 24 is omitted because the text is probably corrupt and *tsaddiq* not the correct reading, cf. LXX, Vulgate, etc.

[3] The point is also made by Drummond, '"Righteousness of God"', especially 87f, and noted by Skinner, 'Righteousness in OT', 272f.

is not to give a thorough account of the nuances of meaning, but to determine the use of the words in relation to the above two questions. Nevertheless some attention must be given to more precise meaning, and if it is often hard to determine this, yet there is usually reasonable certainty. It is likely, for instance, that if in a passage about a king, *mishpat* is juxtaposed with *tsedeq*, what is meant by the latter is to do with his activity as judge and ruler. In poetic passages the parallelism may make the task easier, and in general other words used with our word-group give considerable aid.

Each of the 481 cases has been examined in detail. That examination ought ideally to be recorded in full, but as this would be tedious, repetitive, and often the laborious delineation of the obvious, instead a random sample is given at the beginning of each category. A rough division has been made between different sorts of activity, but its roughness must be emphasised; the categories will often overlap. Where references are in italics, this means that in the case of 'man's activity' we can detect no explicit or implicit relation to God. In the case of forensic rightness, it means there is no double reference, i.e. to actual rightness as well as to forensic (or 'purely forensic') rightness. All references are to the enumeration of Kittel's Hebrew text.

Man's Activity or Behaviour

Certainly behaviour springs from character, but in the OT the stress is concrete, on actions rather than the character behind them. This activity takes various forms.

Legal Activity. By this we mean the activities of judging and establishing justice in the community, as against the *status* of being in the right. This category is often impossible to separate from the immediately following one. Sample, Isa. 5. 7

> and he looked for justice (מִשְׁפָּט),
> but behold, bloodshed;
> for righteousness (צְדָקָה),
> but behold, a cry! (RSV)

In response to God's graciousness towards Israel and Judah, the people have not practised that justice and righteousness towards one another which God wants. The parallel with the juridical *mishpat* suggests that it is largely bad justice that is in mind here, but of course social injustice as a whole is included. In this category are 14 cases of צֶדֶק,[1] also 14 of צְדָקָה,[2] and none of צַדִּיק.

Governing, Ruling Activity. This is very similar to the first category, but with the emphasis less on legal than on administrative functions. The sample illustrates the closeness of regal and legal aspects:

> Jer. 23. 5: I will raise up for David a righteous Branch, and he shall reign as king and deal wisely, and shall execute justice and righteousness (מִשְׁפָּט וּצְדָקָה) in the land (RSV).

It is placed here because the context is the reign of the coming king, and the passage is more about this than about his specifically judicial functions. In this category there are 3 cases of צֶדֶק,[3] 10 of צְדָקָה,[4] and 5 of צַדִּיק.[5]

General or Undefined Ethical Uprightness. Here the words are used as the opposite of a word for 'wickedness, evil, wicked' or as general terms for doing what is right in God's eyes, being faithful to him, not in some 'spiritual' sense, but in the conduct of life and society. This of course includes liturgical behaviour, cf. Ezek. 18. 5, 9; 23. 45; Ps. 97. 11, 12; Eccl. 9. 1, 2 (all using the adjective). The sample is Gen. 6. 9:

> Noah was a righteous (צַדִּיק) man, Blameless in his generation; Noah walked with God (RSV).

Clearly Noah was upright, but equally clearly his uprightness was 'before God' and in relation to him. In this category there are

[1] Lev. 19. 15; Deut. 1. 16; 16. 18, 20, 20; Isa. 11. 4, 5; 16. 5; 59. 4; Ps. *58. 2*; 72. 2; Prov. 8. 15; *31. 9*; Eccl. 5. 7; Ps. 58. 2 is unusual in that it refers to the gods, not to men or Yahweh.

[2] 2 Sam. 8. 15; 1 Kgs 10. 9; Isa. 5. 7; 59. 9; Jer. 22. 3, 15; Amos 5. 7, 24; 6. 12; Ps. 72. 1, 3; Prov. 8. 20; 1 Chron. 18. 14; 2 Chron. 9. 8. In the case of Amos 5. 24 it is possible that this refers to the effect of God's beneficent righteousness in the life of human society, cf. Cazelles, 'À propos de quelques textes', 173–6.

[3] Isa. 32. 1; Ps. 45. 5; Prov. *25. 5*.

[4] Isa. 9. 6; 59. 9, 14; 60. 17; Jer. 23. 5; 33. 15, 15; Ezek. 45. 9; Prov. 14. 34; 16. 12.

[5] 2 Sam. 23. 3; Jer. 23. 5; Zech. 9. 9 (probably, despite RSV); Ps. 72. 7; Prov. *29. 2*.

22 cases of *tsedeq*,[1] 56 of *tsedaqah*,[2] and 108 of *tsaddiq*.[3] In a few cases what is meant is possibly not so much the active righteousness of man as the vindicated existence conferred on man by a gracious God, thus possibly Hos. 10. 12; Isa. 33. 5; 48. 18. What this means is that men live together in freedom, possessing their civil rights, in a good society. It is not just a vindicated status, but a vindicated life.

Referring to the Life of the Covenant People. This is a category whose importance is considerable in later literature, and which refers not to the perfect moral uprightness of the people, but essentially to their keeping the covenant. The 'righteous' then, for this is largely an adjectival category, are the 'poor', humble, faithful, law- and covenant-keeping people of Yahweh, as against the rich and arrogant oppressors. Ethical and relational are com-

[1] Isa. 1. 21, 26; 26. 9, 10; 51. 1; 64. 4; Jer. 22. 13; Ezek. 3. 20; Hos. 10. 12; Zeph. 2. 3; Job 29. 14; Ps. 7. 9; 15. 2; 18. 21, 25; 45. 8; 119. 121; Prov. *1. 3*; *2. 9*; Eccl. 3. 16; 7. 15; Dan. 9. 24. For Isa. 51. 1 we follow C. R. North, *The Second Isaiah* (Oxford, 1964), 208, against RSV 'deliverance'.

[2] Gen. 15. 6; 18. 19; 30. 33; Deut. 9. 4, 5, 6; 1 Sam. 26. 23; 1 Kgs 3. 6; 8. 32; Isa. 28. 17; 33. 5, 15; 48. 18; 56. 1; 57. 12; 58. 2; 64. 5; Ezek. 3. 20; 14. 14, 20; 18. 5, 20, 22, 24, 24, 26, 27; 33. 12, 13, 13, 14, 16, 18, 19; Hos. 10. 12; Mal. 3. 3; Job 27. 6; 35. 8; Ps. 11. 7; 106. 3, 31; Prov. 10. 2; 11. 4, 5, 6, 18, 19; 12. 28; 13. 6; 15. 9; 16. 8; *16. 31*; 21. 3; Dan. 9. 18; 2 Chron. 6. 23. Also possibly Dan. 4. 24, the Aramaic צִדְקָה, which may however have the later meaning 'charity', cf. G. von Rad, *Old Testament Theology*, E.Tr. (2 vols., Edinburgh, 1962), I, 383. Gen. 15. 6 is difficult, and will be examined later, but briefly, we consider 'righteousness' here to be 'real', and 'faith' to be 'faithfulness', which is naturally reckoned as righteousness. Similarly Ps. 106. 31, see von Rad, *Theology*, I, 379. Mal. 3. 3, despite RSV, refers to the character of those who offer, not of the offerings themselves.

[3] Gen. 6. 9; 7. 1; 18. 23, 24, 24, 25, 25, 26, 28; 1 Sam. 24. 18; 2 Sam. 4. 11; 1 Kgs 2. 32; Isa. 57. 1, 1; Ezek. 3. 20, 21, 21; 13. 22; 18. 5, 9, 20, 24, 26; 21. 8, 9; 23. 45; 33. 12, 12, 13, 18; Hab. 1. 13; 2. 4; Mal. 3. 18; Job 12. 4; 17. 9; 22. 19; 27. 17; 36. 7; Ps. 1. 5, 6; 141. 5; Prov. *2. 20*; 3. 33; *4. 18*; 10. 3, 6, 7, *11*, 16, *20, 24, 25, 28, 30, 32*; 11. *8*, 9, *10*, 21, 23, *28, 30, 31*; 12. 3, *5, 7, 10, 12, 13, 21, 26*; 13. *5, 9, 21, 22, 25*; 14. *19, 32*; 15. *6, 28*, 29; 18. 10; *20. 7*; *21. 12, 18, 26*; *24. 15, 16*; *25. 26*; *28. 1, 12, 28*; *29. 6, 7, 16, 27*; Eccl. 3. 17; 7. 15, 16; 7. 20; 8. 14, 14; 9. 1, 2. Also, Prov. *9. 9*; *10. 21, 31*; *23. 24*, where there is an equivalence, if not an identity, between the righteous and the wise. We may note that between them Hab. 2. 4 and Mal. 3. 18 offer a good definition of 'righteous': 'the righteous shall live by his faith' and 'you shall distinguish between the righteous and the wicked, between one who serves God, and one who does not serve him'.

bined here: the righteous are those who live in a proper relation to Yahweh, but they do this by keeping the law and holding to the covenant and by living uprightly before God. They will finally be vindicated by God.

> Sample, Ps. 37. 12: The wicked plots against the righteous (לַצַּדִּיק) and gnashes his teeth at him; but the Lord laughs at the wicked, for he sees that his day is coming (RSV).

This is not just good men versus bad men; the category is almost political, 'nationalist', yet still both ethical and relational. There is one case of *tsedeq* (Ps. 17. 15), none of *tsedaqah*, and 51 cases of *tsaddiq*.[1]

Obedience to the Law. The stress here is more markedly on righteousness as law-obedience than in the preceding category, to which it is similar.

> Sample, Isa. 51. 7: Hearken to me, you who know righteousness (יֹדְעֵי צֶדֶק), the people in whose heart is my law (RSV).

In this category there is one case of *tsedeq* (Isa. 51. 7), 5 cases of *tsedaqah* (Deut. 6. 25; 2 Sam. 22. 21, 25; Ezek. 18. 19, 21), and one case of *tsaddiq* (Hos. 14. 10). It is not only in this category, of course, that righteousness includes keeping the Torah, on the contrary. It does mean that here Torah-keeping is expressly in the foreground.

Gracious Activity, Reflecting God's Own. More cases of this may have been included in the 'undefined' category, but if so they do not display this connotation very clearly.

> Sample, Isa. 58. 8 (God speaks of the kind of fasting that pleases him): Then shall your light break forth like the dawn, and your healing shall spring up speedily; your

[1] Isa. 3. 10; 26. 2, 7, 7; 33. 15; 53. 11; 60. 21; Jer. 20. 12; Amos 2. 6; 5. 12; Ps. 5. 12; 7. 9; 11. 3, 5; 14. 5; 31. 18; 32. 11; 33. 1; 34. 16, 20, 22; 37. 12, 16, 17, 21, 25, 29, 30, 32, 39; 52. 8; 55. 23; 58. 11, 12; 64. 11; 68. 4; 69. 29; 75. 11; 92. 13; 94. 15, 21; 97. 11, 12; 118. 15, 20; 125. 3, 3; 140. 14; 142. 8; 146. 8; Lam. 4. 13. In Isa. 53. 11 the 'Righteous One' is of course the Servant. In Ps. 94. 15 we read *tsaddiq* instead of *tsedeq*. In Isa. 60. 21 the righteousness of the people is seen as the result of God's action.

righteousness (צִדְקֶךָ) shall go before you, the glory of the Lord shall be your rear guard (RSV).

It seems likely that the precise nature of this righteousness is defined by what precedes this verse, in vv. 6, 7, i.e. it consists in freeing the oppressed, feeding the hungry, and so on. Despite the small number of cases, this category is of special interest, because it reflects one of the common uses of the noun when applied to God, and because of the common meaning of 'almsgiving' or 'benevolence' for *tsedaqah* among the Rabbis. There is one case of *tsedeq* (Isa. 58. 8), one of *tsedaqah* (Prov. 21. 21), and one of *tsaddiq* (Ps. 112. 6).

Good Speaking, Telling the Truth.

Sample, Ps. 52. 5: You love evil more than good, and lying more than speaking the truth (שֶׁקֶר מִדַּבֵּר צֶדֶק) (RSV).

This is that aspect of righteousness involving speech, but otherwise is no different from righteousness in general. There are 4 cases of *tsedeq* (Ps. 52. 5; Prov. 8. 8; *12. 17*; *16. 13*), 2 of *tsedaqah* (Isa. 48. 1; Jer. 4. 2), and there is one of *tsaddiq* (Isa. 41. 26).

In passing from this use of *ts-d-q* for some form of human activity, we may quote Ezek. 18. 5–9:

If a man is righteous and does what is lawful and right, if he does not eat upon the mountains or lift up his eyes to the idols of the house of Israel, does not defile his neighbour's wife or approach a woman in her time of impurity, does not oppress anyone, but restores to the debtor his pledge, commits no robbery, gives his bread to the hungry and covers the naked with a garment, does not lend at interest or take any increase, withholds his hand from iniquity, executes true justice between man and man, walks in my statutes, and is careful to observe my ordinances – he is righteous, he shall surely live, says the Lord God (RSV).

If this is a pre-Ezekiel liturgical passage, with a declaratory formula at the end,[1] then we have a classic expression of the

[1] Cf. von Rad, *Theology*, I, 378f, also his *The Problem of the Hexateuch and Other Essays*, E.Tr. (London, 1966), 128f, 245.

inseparability of the ethical and the forensic. In any case, this passage sums up most neatly the connotations attached to the word.

Man's Forensic or Relational Righteousness

This is to do with man as not guilty before, or in a right relationship to, a human or divine tribunal, or else in a right relationship that is not specifically forensic. Usually, being not guilty is inseparable from actually being righteous, for 'innocence' blends ethical and forensic rightness.[1] The 'purely forensic' cases are in italics.

> Sample, Isa. 5. 23: Woe to those...who acquit the guilty for a bribe, and deprive the innocent of his right (וְצִדְקַת צַדִּיקִים יָסִירוּ מִמֶּנּוּ) (RSV).

The context is forensic, yet it is evident that the righteous ought to be acquitted because they really are righteous, i.e. innocent (in Prov. 24. 24, to say 'you are righteous' forensically, to a man who patently is not, is seen as a great evil). Now being in the right is related to having a right, and there are three places where one of the nouns means 'right' in this sense: Job 35. 2; 2 Sam. 19. 29; Neh. 2. 20. These are classed as 'purely forensic', though with misgivings. At any rate, the stress is so heavily forensic that it seems the wiser course. In this category then there are 3 cases of *tsedeq*,[2] 5 of *tsedaqah*,[3] and 19 of *tsaddiq*.[4]

It is clear that just as nearly all 'activity' cases have some explicit or implicit relation to God, so also nearly all forensic cases imply ethical righteousness in general, or innocence in a particular.

God's Activity

Legal Activity. By this is meant judging and lawgiving, but not God's status of being 'in the right'. The execution of the judgment is often included.

[1] Cf. the parallel situation in the case of רשע, and Pedersen, *Israel*, I, 418f.

[2] Job 6. 29 (probably, despite RSV); *35. 2*; Ps. 17. 1.

[3] Deut. 24. 13; 2 Sam. *19. 29*; Isa. 5. 23; Ps. 69. 28; Neh. *2. 20*.

[4] Gen. 20. 4; Ex. 23. 7, 8; Deut. 16. 19; 25. 1; 1 Kgs 8. 32; 2 Kgs 10. 9; Isa. 5. 23; 29. 21; Hab. 1. 4; Ps. 69. 29; Job 32. 1; Prov. 17. 15, 26; 18. 5, 17; 21. 15; 24. 24; 2 Chron. 6. 23.

> Sample, Ps. 119. 7: I will praise thee with an upright heart, when I learn thy righteous ordinances (מִשְׁפְּטֵי צִדְקֶךָ) (RSV).

It makes little difference whether we argue that the ordinances or the Lord behind the ordinances has the righteousness, for in any case the reference is finally to God the lawgiver. A rather different sample is Ps. 9. 5:

> For thou hast maintained my just cause, thou hast sat on the throne giving righteous judgment (שׁוֹפֵט צֶדֶק) (RSV).

Here it is judging rather than lawgiving, but the whole psalm shows that giving righteous judgment involves defeating enemies and upholding the faithful. This shows how difficult it is to draw definite lines in classifying. There are 18 cases of *tsedeq*,[1] 4 of *tsedaqah*,[2] and 6 of *tsaddiq*.[3]

Gracious, Saving Activity. Here the nouns are virtually equivalent to 'salvation' and are often so rendered in RSV. This class cannot be sharply distinguished from the next one, but generally there is a stress here on graciousness, and in the next, on the victorious strength of a God who vindicates his own.

> Sample, Isa. 51. 5: My deliverance (צִדְקִי) draws near speedily, my salvation (יִשְׁעִי) has gone forth (RSV).

There are 14 cases of *tsedeq*,[4] 34 of *tsedaqah*,[5] and 5 of *tsaddiq*.[6]

[1] Isa. 42. 21; 58. 2; Jer. 11. 20; Ps. 9. 5, 9; 50. 6; 96. 13; 98. 9; 119. 7, 62, 75, 106, 138, 142, 144, 160, 164, 172.

[2] Deut. 33. 21; Ps. 99. 4; 119. 40, 142. Cazelles, 'À propos de quelques textes', 173, sees Deut. 33. 21 as the fulfilment of the promise of a kindly providence. We are convinced, with RSV, that it belongs here, and does not help in elucidating δικαιοσύνη θεοῦ in Paul, but see Oepke, 'ΔΙΚΑΙΟΣΥΝΗ ΘΕΟΥ', 263; Kertelge, '*Rechtfertigung*', 10f, and Stuhlmacher, *Gottes Gerechtigkeit*, 182f, 142–5.

[3] Deut. 4. 8; Job 34. 17; Ps. 7. 10, 12; 119. 137; 2 Chron. 12. 6.

[4] Isa. 42. 6; 45. 8, 13; 51. 5; Jer. 23. 6; 33. 16; probably 50. 7; Hos. 2. 21; Ps. 40. 10; 65. 6; 85. 11, 12, 14; 119. 123. Ps. 85. 11, 12, 14, and 89. 15 (next category) may reflect an hypostatisation of *tsedeq*, or the persistence of an ancient god *Tsedeq* – see E. Jacob, *Theology of the Old Testament*, E.Tr. (London, 1958), 98, and von Rad, *Theology*, I, 376, for righteousness as a force.

[5] 1 Sam. 12. 7; Isa. 1. 27; 5. 16; 45. 8; 46. 12, 13; 51. 6, 8; 56. 1; 61. 10 and perhaps 61. 11; 63. 1; Mic. 6. 5; 7. 9; Zech. 8. 8; Mal. 3. 20 (4. 2 in EVV); Job 33. 26; Ps. 22. 32; 31. 2; 36. 7, 11; 40. 11; 51. 16; 71. 2, 15, 16, 24; 88. 13; 103. 17; perhaps 111. 3; 112. 9; 143. 11; 145. 7; Dan. 9. 16.

[6] Isa. 45. 21; Ps. 112. 4; 116. 5; 145. 17; Ezra 9. 15.

Vindication, Giving Victory or Prosperity. God works effectively against the wicked and for the faithful. There may be no stress on vindictiveness, but always on the positive benefits of the powerful activity of God. Sometimes it is hard to tell whether the stress is on God's activity itself, or on the life of the people which ensues, a life of freedom, prosperity, good government, and true justice. God's righteousness produces not only a status of being vindicated, but positively a new corporate life.[1]

> Sample, Judg. 5. 11, 11: they repeat the triumphs of the Lord, the triumphs of his peasantry in Israel (RSV) ['triumphs' is צִדְקוֹת both times].

This is part of the Song of Deborah, and RSV surely renders correctly. The reference is to the mighty and victorious action of God. In this category are 18 cases of *tsedeq*,[2] 21 of *tsedaqah*,[3] and only one of *tsaddiq*.[4]

Acting Reliably, Trustworthily, Faithfully. This is really in distinction from man's wickedness!

> Sample, Dan. 9. 7: To thee, O Lord, belongs righteousness (הַצְּדָקָה) but to us confusion of face...because of the treachery which they have committed against thee (RSV). [Cf. also 9. 14 (*tsaddiq*).]

Porteous,[5] though without full discussion, considers this forensic, God being 'in the right', as against men who are 'in the wrong'. This is possible, but the contrast seems rather to be between what men have done and what God has done, and therefore, while we cannot deny the presence of a forensic element, it

[1] So Cazelles, 'À propos de quelques textes', especially 188.

[2] Isa. 41. 2, 10; 62. 1, 2; Jer. 31. 23; Job 8. 6; Ps. 4. 2; 7. 18; 35. 24, 27, 28; 37. 6; 48. 11; 89. 15; 97. 2, 6; 118. 19; 132. 9.

[3] Judg. 5. 11, 11; Isa. 10. 22; 32. 16, 17, 17; 45. 24; 54. 14; 59. 16, 17; Jer. 51. 10; Joel 2. 23; Ps. 5. 9; 24. 5; 71. 19; 89. 17; 98. 2; 103. 6; 112. 3, and perhaps Prov. 8. 18 and 21. 21 (2nd). We include Prov. 8. 18 on the assumption that 'wisdom' acts on God's behalf.

[4] Ps. 129. 4. The note of vindicated existence is probable at least in Ps. 24. 5; 112. 3; Isa. 32. 16, 17, 17; 45. 24; 54. 14.

[5] N. W. Porteous, *Daniel* (London, 1965), 137f.

appears to be subsidiary. There are no cases of *tsedeq*, 5 of *tsedaqah*,[1] and 7 of *tsaddiq*.[2]

Right Speaking. God is the source, and the speaker, of the truth.

> Sample, Isa. 45. 19: I the Lord speak the truth (דֹּבֵר צֶדֶק), I declare what is right (RSV).

There are 2 cases of *tsedeq* (Isa. 45. 19, and probably Job 36. 3), one of *tsedaqah* (Isa. 45. 23), none of *tsaddiq*.

The total number of cases is noticeably smaller than for man, and the cases of God's legal activity are in a distinct minority.

God's Forensic or Relational Righteousness

There are remarkably few cases, and all are adjectival, only 3 in all.

> Sample, Ex. 9. 27: Then Pharaoh sent and called Moses and Aaron, and said to them, I have sinned this time; the Lord is in the right (יהוה הַצַּדִּיק), and I and my people are in the wrong (RSV).

This is difficult, for it makes equally good sense whether one takes it forensically, as above, or ethically:

> I have sinned this time; the Lord has done right, and I and my people have done wrong.

Certainly it is about what Pharaoh and his people have *done*. Yet we give the benefit of the doubt to the forensic, because the meaning probably is that by their respective actions the Egyptians have put themselves in the wrong, and Yahweh in the right. The instances (all *tsaddiq*) are Ex. 9. 27; Jer. 12. 1; Lam. 1. 18.

One ought here to add a note about the 'righteousness of things'. We have included the cases where God's ordinances or judgments are righteous under God's Legal Activity, but there are a further 14 cases, all of *tsedeq*, where other things are involved. In 10 cases *tsedeq* refers to correct weights and measures,[3]

[1] Jer. 9. 23; Job 37. 23; Ps. 33. 5; 143. 1; Dan. 9. 7.

[2] Deut. 32. 4; Isa. 24. 16; Zeph. 3. 5; Ps. 11. 7; Dan. 9. 14; Neh. 9. 8, 33.

[3] Lev. 19. 36 (4 times); Deut. 25. 15 (twice); Ezek. 45. 10 (3 times); Job 31. 6.

3 where it refers to peace-offerings,[1] and one where the probable reference is to right paths, i.e. the correct ones to lead to the destination.[2] All these imply conformity to a norm, or being of the proper character. They do not fit neatly into any category.

Summary of the Analysis

1. Use of the nouns for God and man: it has been suggested[3] that *tsedeq* is used more for God's righteousness, and *tsedaqah* more for its effect among men. Our analysis does not support this. Leaving out the 14 cases referring to things, *tsedeq* refers to man 49 out of 111 times, i.e. approximately 44 per cent, and to God approximately 56 per cent of the cases. *Tsedaqah* refers to man 93 out of 158 times (nearly 59 per cent) and to God a little over 41 per cent of the cases. There is a difference, but hardly a significant one.[4]

2. Relation of purely forensic to activity cases: the total picture (nouns and adjective, God and man, except the cases referring to things) is thus: purely forensic, 30 out of 467 (6.4 per cent); activity, 437 out of 467 (93.6 per cent). If we put together legal activity and purely forensic, i.e. legal as a whole, the figures are, legal, 86 out of 467 (18.4 per cent), non-legal, 381 out of 467 (81.6 per cent). On the basis of these figures, it is not correct to say that *ts-d-q* in its noun and adjective forms is particularly forensic, or even legal. In Tables 1 and 2 we now break these figures down for each noun and the adjective, for man and for God, and for the sections of the Canon.

We see from Table 1 that both nouns and the adjective are used predominantly as activity words rather than as status or relationship words, when applied to God. Further, apart from the Pentateuch, where the total number of cases is very small, they are used mainly in non-legal contexts. *Tsaddiq* is used in legal contexts more often than either noun, but of the nouns, *tsedeq* is

[1] Deut. 33. 19; Ps. 4. 6; 51. 21.

[2] Ps. 23. 3. A. Weiser, *The Psalms*, E.Tr. (London, 1962), 229, takes it to mean 'salvation'; W. O. E. Oesterley, *The Psalms* (2 vols., London, 1939), I, 183, seems to take it as man's behaviour. We follow C. A. Briggs, *Psalms*, ICC (2 vols., Edinburgh, 1906), I, 209.

[3] So G. A. F. Knight, *A Christian Theology of the Old Testament* (London, 1959), 245.

[4] Cf. Snaith, *Distinctive Ideas*, 72.

TABLE 1

God	*Tsedeq*	*Tsedaqah*	*Tsaddiq*
Purely forensic	– (0%)	– (0%)	3 (13.6%)
Activity	52 (100%)	65 (100%)	19 (86.4%)
Legal as a whole	18 (34.6%)	4 (6.15%)	9 (40.9%)
Non-legal activity	34 (65.4%)	61 (93.85%)	13 (59.1%)

Sections of the Canon (all three words together):

	Law	Prophets	Writings
Purely forensic	1 (25%)	1 (2%)	1 (1.2%)
Activity	3 (75%)	50 (98%)	83 (98.8%)
Legal as a whole	3 (75%)	4 (7.85%)	24 (28.57%)
Non-legal activity	1 (25%)	47 (92.15%)	60 (71.43%)

God's righteousness as a whole:

Purely forensic	3 (2.16%)
Activity	136 (97.84%)
Legal as a whole	34 (24.5%)
Non-legal activity	105 (75.5%)

so used more often by far than *tsedaqah*.[1] Legal use is much more frequent in the Writings than in the Prophets, but the purely forensic use is rare everywhere.

Of the 301 'activity' instances noted in Table 2, only 57 (18.9 per cent) have no clear relation to God as approving, rewarding, commanding, or creating man's righteousness, and all but one of this minority are in the book of Proverbs. Of the purely forensic cases, all but three (i.e. 11 per cent) are also ethical, and those three all refer to 'having a right'. As in the case of the words as applied to God, we see that nouns and adjective are nearly always *activity* words, and in the majority of cases in each category, that activity is not of a legal character. Moreover, because only 11 per cent of the purely forensic cases lack an ethical

[1] Jacob, *Theology*, 98, suggests that the norm of God's action is *tsedeq*, and 'the visible manifestation of that norm is *tsedaqah*', but this is probably much too precise.

TABLE 2

Man	*Tsedeq*	*Tsedaqah*	*Tsaddiq*
Purely forensic	3 (6.12%)	5 (5.37%)	19 (10.2%)
Activity	46 (93.88%)	88 (94.63%)	167 (89.8%)
Legal as a whole	17 (34.7%)	19 (20.43%)	19 (10.2%)
Non-legal activity	32 (65.3%)	74 (79.57%)	167 (89.8%)

Sections of the Canon (all three words together):

	Law	Prophets	Writings
Purely forensic	6 (22.2%)	7 (6%)	14 (7.57%)
Activity	21 (77.7%)	109 (94%)	171 (92.43%)
Legal as a whole	11 (40.74%)	20 (17.24%)	24 (13%)
Non-legal activity	16 (59.26%)	96 (82.76%)	161 (87%)

Man's righteousness as a whole:

Purely forensic	27 (8.23%)
Activity	301 (91.77%)
Legal as a whole	55 (16.77%)
Non-legal activity	273 (83.23%)

accent as well, the activity category is really much more dominant than the figures suggest.

As in the case of God's righteousness, *tsedeq* tends to be used in legal contexts more often than *tsedaqah*, but *tsaddiq* less often than either noun, so differing from the situation when God is described as righteous. The proportion of legal uses is higher in the Pentateuch than elsewhere, but not as high as for God's righteousness there.

While it is true that the words are almost entirely activity words, and not primarily status or relational words, they are not merely ethical. We have noted that all but 18.9 per cent of the man's activity cases are also in some relation to God, that is to say, the activity is understood as being righteous only as it is seen in relation to him. In this sense it is true that in the OT righteousness is a *Verhältnisbegriff*, a relationship term, and quite apart from the fact that it normally refers to behaviour within relationship, a relationship to Yahweh is nearly always added. This relational stress is especially clear in Ezek. 33. 10ff, where righteousness is seen to exist from moment to moment, depending on one's present relation to God and his will. How a man stands *now* determines whether he lives or dies, this is the forensic side. But how he stands before God is determined by how he stands in relation to God's will, this is the ethical side.[1]

The 18.9 per cent of cases where this reference to God is absent present a peculiar difficulty simply because they are in all but one instance in Proverbs. Two possible explanations offer themselves. First, this apparent detachment of ethics from an explicit relation to God reflects a spirit of secularism which may be accounted for at least partly in terms of Hellenisation. Righteousness thus becomes a self-contained human, even humanistic, ideal. Thus J. C. Rylaarsdam speaks of Proverbs as looking 'at man *qua* man, rather than in the light of God'.[2] Others would suggest that this is an oversimplification, that behind all the ethical teaching is the recognition that the fear of the Lord is the beginning of wisdom, and that God's will is the final arbiter of righteousness. The apparent independence from God, it is suggested, is only apparent, and is due to the practical concern to make the call to righteousness concrete and detailed.[3] This means that though the relation to God is often unstated, it is nonetheless present as a basic assumption. Second, it is possible that the at times rather disjointed nature of the book means that it is unreasonable to look for illumination from context which we find elsewhere. If one takes into account the whole context, as suggested immediately above, and not just contiguous passages, which may not be relevant at all, then it is arguable that even these instances of the root are really in relation to God.

[1] Cf. Ezek. 18. 20ff. On the inseparability of ethics and religion in Israel, see Snaith, *Distinctive Ideas*, 59ff. Von Rad, *Theology*, I, 378, argues from the 'liturgies of the gate' (cf. Pss. 15 and 24) that 'those who came to worship were asked for something like a declaration of loyalty to Yahweh's will for justice', hence the expression, 'gates of righteousness'. If this is right, *tsedeq* in Ps. 118. 19 should be classed under man's, and not God's, righteousness. On the link between the cult, covenant-renewal, and the renewal of righteousness, see von Rad, *Hexateuch*, 243–53.

[2] 'Proverbs', in M. Black and H. H. Rowley, editors, *Peake's Commentary on the Bible* (new edition, London, 1962), 444.

[3] So, among others, T. Henshaw, *The Writings* (London, 1963), 70, 141f.

Generally it remains true that while the verb is strongly declaratory, forensic, or better, relational, because 'to justify' is to restore to a position in the covenant or the community, on the other hand the nouns and adjective are ethical-in-relation-to-God. It must be stressed, however, that to proceed from this to say that they are therefore relationship words, is not correct if we mean that they *denote* a relationship. They denote rather activity within a relationship. Thus, if we bring together our examination of the verb with that of the nouns and adjective, we come to the conclusion that whereas the verb is used mainly, if not quite entirely, forensically (or for restoration into fellowship), the nouns and adjective are used mainly, if not quite entirely, for behaviour, behaviour seen in the light of Yahweh and his will, and more often than not, for behaviour which is not specifically in a legal context.[1]

THE MEANING OF RIGHTEOUSNESS

Is there a single 'concept' which contains and explains all the uses of the root *ts-d-q* which we have noted? Nearly a century ago Kautzsch concluded that the root meaning is conformity to a norm.[2] This basic idea is elaborated in terms of objects, men, and God, and takes account of inward disposition as well as outward acts. Thus righteous paths are paths which go the right way (Ps. 23. 3), and righteous measures are those which conform to the norm (Lev. 19. 36, etc.). There has been some disagreement about what lies behind the idea of a norm, whether the basic idea is straightness[3] or hardness.[4] Mostly however, in recent times, there has been scepticism about the value of this etymological approach,[5] and it is generally regarded as peripheral. In any

[1] This examination has obvious limitations. One could take it further by examining different strata of tradition, or by taking books in order of probable date. A. Descamps in Cerfaux and Descamps, 'Justice, Justification', cols 1422–59, relates the instances to the context of their literary genre.

[2] E. Kautzsch, *Über die Derivate des Stammes* צדק *im alttestamentlichen Sprachgebrauch* (Tübingen, 1881), followed by many other scholars, e.g. S. A. Cook, in W. R. Smith, *The Religion of the Semites* (3rd edn by S. A. Cook, London, 1927), 655ff, and Jacob, *Theology*, 94ff.

[3] Snaith, *Distinctive Ideas*, 73f.

[4] Skinner, 'Righteousness in OT', 274.

[5] Thus in general, Barr, *Semantics*, 107–60; here in particular, E. R. Achtemeier, 'Righteousness in the O.T.', *IDB*, IV, 80–5, especially 80.

case, the 'norm' idea fits things much better than people or situations, and it is now either rejected or carefully qualified.

Some scholars have considered the root to be basically forensic, with all other uses derived from this.[1] Wheeler Robinson thinks the basic idea quite separable from morality and holiness, and to be primarily acquittal at the bar of God. This acquittal is demonstrated by a man's prosperity and general well-being (cf. Ps. 32 and the book of Job), though of course in the prophets it comes to have a moral connotation.[2] Yet we have seen that in the OT as we have it, only a minority of occurrences are forensic, and even if the nouns' origins were juridical, it does not follow that they remain in some sense 'basically forensic' for all time. Again, L. Köhler thinks that in the case of man's righteousness, the primary meaning was 'innocence', the state of being 'not guilty', but that it developed into a term for the loyal carrying-out of the demands of community life, then of the demands of God, and so became a term for practical piety.[3] Now the origins of the words may have been forensic, though to trace these is not relevant to the present enquiry. Certainly some things point in that direction: the use of the verb, and the occurrence of the root meaning 'in the right' in the Tell el-Amarna correspondence, and meaning 'legitimate' in the Ugaritic texts.[4] Yet, apart from the verb, the usage in the OT is not predominantly forensic, and we cannot assume that semantic background determines the meaning of words. In any case the Hebrew understanding of justice was such that to use the word 'forensic' is liable to be more misleading than illuminating. Indeed (as we shall shortly see) righteousness is a covenant word, and sometimes the covenant is spoken of in terms of a lawsuit between Yahweh and Israel (cf. Isa. 1; Mic. 6; Jer. 2), but this is not dominant. Indeed also, part of God's demand for covenant behaviour is a demand for

[1] E.g. G. Dalman, *Die richterliche Gerechtigkeit im Alten Testament* (Berlin, 1897). He sees two aspects of it, 'eine vergeltende und eine rettende', 18.

[2] *The Religious Ideas of the Old Testament* (London, 1913), 168f, also *Inspiration and Revelation in the Old Testament* (ed. L. H. Brockington and E. A. Payne, Oxford, 1946), 57.

[3] *Hebrew Man*, 174. Dodd, *Bible and Greeks*, 47, also holds the 'basically forensic' view, but against this position see W. F. Lofthouse, 'The Righteousness of Jahveh', *ET*, 50 (1938–9), 341–5.

[4] Cf. R. Davidson, *The Old Testament* (London, 1964), 78f, and the references there given, and Johnson, *Sacral Kingship*, 31f.

true justice which on the one hand is fair, impartial, and not for sale, and on the other hand sees to the needs of the weak, helpless, and oppressed. Yet this is part of the idea, rather than the leading note. While the meanings of 'righteousness' that belong to the salvation vocabulary may derive ultimately from this aspect of a good judge's activity, in the large majority of cases they have gained their independence from their origin. We cannot interpret such instances as if they were still emerging from their origin, any more than we can interpret 'silly' in English as if it still carried overtones of 'blessed'.

Particularly since the work of H. Cremer,[1] most scholars regard righteousness as fundamentally concerned with relationships. Sometimes this is seen as compatible with the 'norm' idea, so that we hear of 'norms of relationship'.[2] Sometimes the norm approach is rejected altogether: thus von Rad says that righteousness is 'about acts, not norms' and goes direct to the relationship idea.[3] In the end, the difference is not great, for it is generally agreed that righteousness is behaviour proper to some relationship, but we must be careful to state precisely what we mean here. The acts appropriate to a relationship are not the relationship itself, and righteousness is the first, not the second. If we slide imperceptibly from one to the other, we fall into confusion.

In the OT the relationship above all others within which behaviour occurs which may be called 'righteous' is the covenant. Several scholars, working from different points, have shown that the notion of covenant is basic to OT religion. Israel's awareness of God, and her consciousness of herself, her worship, justice, law, social relationships, history and nationhood, are all centred in this notion.[4] When Israel thought of relationship (our term) she thought of covenant (her term). It is true that the covenant was primarily what Yahweh had done and was doing, that is, it was a matter of grace, but it was also a reciprocal thing. The act of grace required a continuing response, and that response

[1] *Rechtfertigungslehre*, especially 23, 33ff. It was he who first described righteousness as a 'Verhältnisbegriff'. See also K. Hj. Fahlgren, *Sedāḳā, nahestehende und entgegengesetzte Begriffe im Alten Testament* (Uppsala, 1932), 78–109.

[2] Jacob, *Theology*, 95.

[3] *Theology*, I, 370–4, cf. Achtemeier, 'Righteousness in the O.T.', 80.

[4] Notably the sociologist M. Weber, *Ancient Judaism*, E.Tr. of *Religionssoziologie*, III (Glencoe, Ill., 1952), 75–7 and passim.

was to a large extent righteousness, the behaviour proper to the covenant. Thus J. Pedersen despite his erroneous (so von Rad) identification of *nephesh* as the seat of *tsedaqah*, and his consequent definition of righteousness as the 'health of the soul', rightly saw that the Hebrew could not conceive of the soul except in relationship, as a 'link in a covenant'. Health or wholeness was no individual thing. He therefore understood *ts-d-q* as primarily loyal activity within a relationship rather than in terms of some norm.[1]

Despite divergence on details, and on the history of the root, there is something of a consensus that righteousness is covenant-behaviour, or loyalty to the covenant.[2] Skinner does not agree;[3] he accepts that covenant faithfulness is part of Yahweh's righteousness, but denies that the word is essentially a covenant one. Rather is it essentially as well as originally forensic. Our point is that whatever the origins may have been, in the OT as we have it, it has become a covenant word. Now as a covenant word, it may in the case of man's righteousness have a double reference, i.e. both to community relationships and also to Yahweh who is Lord over those relationships and over the whole people. We have already seen that almost without exception the cases of man's righteousness have some relation to God. In view of this, righteousness is related naturally to חסד and also to 'love', 'good', and 'truth' (cf. 2 Kgs 10. 3; Ps. 17. 15; 25. 8; 85. 11; 103. 17; Mic. 6. 8; Hos. 12. 7).

We have said nothing about righteousness as corporate or individual. Von Rad is correct in saying that it is in the later literature that righteousness becomes a matter between the individual and God, whereas earlier it was usually between a society and God.[4] The later, more individual concern is reflected in Pss. 1, 73, 119; Jer. 31. 29ff; Ezek. 13. 22; 14. 14; 18. 2–5, and of

[1] Pedersen, *Israel*, I, 336–8, 340–2, and passim; von Rad, *Theology*, I, 376.

[2] Thus among many, Schrenk, *Righteousness*, 30; Hill, *Greek Words*, 85–96; von Rad, *Theology*, I, 373; F. Horst, *Gottes Recht; gesammelte Studien zum Recht im Alten Testament* (Munich, 1961), 256f.

[3] 'Righteousness in OT', 280. The learned study by H. H. Schmid *Gerechtigkeit als Weltordnung* (Tübingen, 1968) came to my notice too late for adequate consideration here. The title indicates the basic thesis, which does not ignore the covenant aspect, but starts rather from the general background in the Ancient East than from Israel's peculiar situation.

[4] *Theology*, I, 379ff.

course in Job.[1] We must also mention the question of outward behaviour and inward disposition: Pedersen stresses the outward acts as the expression of the inner disposition, while Jacob stresses the outward act much more than the inner disposition,[2] but it is preferable not to elevate one above the other, rather take them both together while recognising that in general the OT is more concerned with concrete acts.[3]

On what grounds do we take loyalty to the covenant as the meaning of righteousness? First, it has explicit warrant in the text: we note the occurrence of *ts-d-q* in the covenantal passage Gen. 18. 19, and also the close connection between *ts-d-q* and the covenant in Ps. 15; in Ezek. 18 where we have a full description, even a definition, of the righteous man, the setting is the covenant relation between God and Israel. Second, it accords well with the view that the verb, especially the hiph'il, denotes restoration to relationship, and the covenant relationship in particular. Third, a fair test of any hypothesis is the degree to which it explains the facts, and this hypothesis makes very good sense of disparate and sometimes almost contradictory facts, for it means that righteousness is a situational word, its precise meaning to be determined by the circumstances. This does not mean that it can denote anything, certainly not anything we please. It does mean that the denotation is always to be determined by God, and in terms of a given situation. Righteousness is neither a virtue nor the sum of the virtues, it is activity which befits the covenant. Similarly, on God's side it is not an attribute but divine covenant-activity. If we must speak of norms, then the norm is the covenant and whatever is appropriate to it. Everything (including inward disposition) which fits the requirements of the covenant in a given situation is then 'normal' or righteous.[4]

We must recognise that on this view, God's righteousness may take many forms. Sometimes indeed it may take the form of

[1] See E. G. Hirsch, 'Right and Righteousness', *JE*, x, 420–4, especially 421, on 'the individualization of righteousness after the Exile'.

[2] Pedersen, *Israel*, I, 336f, 358; II, 565; Jacob, *Theology*, 95.

[3] Cf. S. Mowinckel, *The Psalms in Israel's Worship*, E.Tr. (2 vols., Oxford, 1962), II, 12. Note Pss. 1; 119; Isa. 29. 13; 54. 13; 60. 21; Jer. 12. 2. C. R. Smith, *The Bible Doctrine of Salvation* (London, 1941), 142, argues that this distinction was never fully thought out by the Hebrews.

[4] Snaith, *Distinctive Ideas*, 77; W. Eichrodt, *Theology of the Old Testament*, E.Tr. (2 vols., London, 1961–7), I, 241f.

gracious, merciful, saving action, but it is too simple to say that it is always this and that severity is never meant by the term.[1] In a situation where the covenant people are being oppressed, it may take the form of harsh judgment and punishment, cf. Judg. 5. 11 where Israel's victories over Canaan are called not the wrath but the 'righteousness' of Yahweh, and Isa. 5. 16; Ps. 7. 9f. At times indeed it is the covenant people who experience God's righteousness as severity, thus probably Isa. 10. 22. So it is too much to say that his righteousness *means* his salvation (unless one makes 'salvation' virtually synonymous with the establishment and maintenance of the covenant). Certainly commandments are seen as part of God's mercy (cf. Ps. 50. 6) along with his mighty saving acts, but righteousness was always faithfulness, and Israel could even think of God as bound by his own covenant obligations though they are obligations he has imposed upon himself by reason of the covenant he has made (cf. Job; Gen. 18. 23, 25; Jer. 18). This does have its legal side, especially when God is thought of as Judge, but this is an aspect, not the whole: 'It is incidental that *tsedeq* stands for justice...because *tsedeq* actually stands for the establishment of God's will in the land, and secondarily for justice, because that in part is God's will.'[2] So God's righteousness means mercy in one situation, triumph in another, judgment in another, the establishment of good government and good justice in another. In this last, the king (present or to come) is often seen as God's agent, cf. Pss. 45. 4–7; 72. 1–4. He rules righteously by saving the covenant people from their enemies, giving them peace and prosperity, and by establishing justice and civil rights (cf. 1 Sam. 9. 16; 10. 1).[3]

In view of all this, it is not quite accurate to say that in Deutero-Isaiah, for instance, righteousness 'comes to mean salvation'.[4] Given the right situation, it could mean something like this as early as the Song of Deborah (Judg. 5. 11), and at the time of the second Isaiah the situation was such that God's

[1] As does Ritschl, *Rechtfertigung*, II, 102–13.

[2] Snaith, *Distinctive Ideas*, 70.

[3] On this see S. Mowinckel, *He That Cometh*, E.Tr. (Oxford, 1956), 67f, 178f, 308f. Von Rad, *Theology*, I, 375f, sees the monarchy as a focus in the matter of righteousness.

[4] So Smith, *Bible Doctrine of Salvation*, 68.

covenant loyalty meant the rescue of his people; hence, his righteousness becomes his salvation. Certainly, in second Isaiah this use achieves prominence, but it is more correct to say that salvation is the form God's righteousness took in these circumstances than to say that it comes to mean salvation.[1]

When we turn to man's righteousness, it is clearly a possibility only within the covenant. Those outside the covenant, and therefore not in relation to Yahweh, cannot be righteous.[2] Being within the covenant involves doing God's will, whether or not this is seen specifically in terms of law-obedience, and it is loyalty to the covenant and therefore righteousness. So also right judging, right governing, right worshipping, and gracious activity, are all covenantal and righteous, despite their diversity. The forensic instances are not a problem, especially if we recall inseparability of ethical and forensic, for while *ts-d-q* usually refers to acting loyally, those who so act are in a state of loyalty, and will be adjudged thus at the bar of man or God. A verdict about guilt or innocence was really a verdict about loyalty or disloyalty, for both human and divine justice. That is, within a relationship between men, or between God and men, he is righteous who renders what is due from him, this understood more in terms of loyalty than of legality. As the external or internal situation of Israel varies, so does the meaning of righteousness. In our 'covenant keeping' category, especially in the Psalms, 'righteous' becomes almost a synonym for 'poor, oppressed', simply because at the time the two were so often identical. Some see the righteous–wicked opposition here as basically between Israel and her enemies,[3] but others see 'the righteous' as a party within Israel;[4] it is possible that the distinction is between the covenant people and those outside the covenant, so that not only national enemies, but also apostate elements within Israel are included.[5] Whatever view is right, we still have the righteous as the keepers of the covenant, and the wicked (oppressors) as those who do not keep it.

[1] Discussions of the varying meaning of righteousness at different times are in Hirsch, 'Right and Righteousness', 420–2, and Eichrodt, *Theology*, I, 242–8.

[2] Cf. Mowinckel, *Psalms*, I, 209.

[3] Thus Mowinckel, *Psalms*, I, 207f.

[4] Thus Hirsch, 'Right and Righteousness', 422.

[5] Thus H. Ringgren, *The Faith of the Psalmists* (London, 1963), 37–46.

In the light of the above, it may be helpful to look again at two notoriously difficult passages.

Gen. 15. 6: And he believed the Lord, and he reckoned it to him as righteousness (RSV) (וַיַּחְשְׁבֶהָ לּוֹ צְדָקָה).

The passage may well be understood in loyal behaviour terms. Abraham's trust in God amounted to faithfulness, or loyal behaviour, and God naturally therefore reckoned it as righteousness. There is then no complicated process of reckoning one thing in place of another. It is not reckoned *in lieu of* righteousness. Of course, the normal way of understanding loyal behaviour was obedience to God's commandments, in the Pentateuch, cf. Deut. 6. 25; 24. 13, but the possibility of a case like this is not precluded.[1] Something like this was the later Jewish view.[2]

Gen. 38. 26 (the words of Judah about Tamar): she is more righteous than I (RSV) (צָדְקָה מִמֶּנִּי).

The story is too long to quote, but this instance is of special interest because it involves the verb. In view of the general understanding of family obligations which underlines the story, the meaning is probably not simply 'she is more in the right than I am' – though this is present – but rather, 'she has fulfilled the community obligations better than I have' and therefore is more righteous.[3] The standing is consequent. In our discussion of the qal, we included this as 'broadly forensic', but concluded the section by saying that usually the forensic and ethical are inseparable. This is borne out here, if we understand 'ethical' in terms of maintenance of the community. The hiph'il, on the other hand, stands for the re-establishment of the community or covenant relationship.

[1] See Pedersen, *Israel*, I, 348, 530, who renders: 'Abraham showed Yahweh confidence, and therefore Yahweh considered him righteous.' He adds (530): 'That this is the meaning of ḥāshabh le appears abundantly from Gen. 38. 15; 1 Sam. 1. 13.' See also von Rad, *Theology*, I, 379.

[2] Cf. 1 Macc. 2. 52, where Abraham's faith is the first of the *works* of the fathers. See below pp. 103f.

[3] Cf. von Rad, *Theology*, I, 374, and Snaith, *Distinctive Ideas*, 73f.

APPENDED NOTE I

The Connection Between God's and Man's Righteousness

There are several passages where a link is made clear.

Isa. 32. 16, 17, 17. The three instances of *tsedaqah* in these verses have been classed under God's vindicating righteousness, but the position is really more complex. The existence of righteousness and justice among men is to be the direct outcome of the outpouring of the Spirit in the last days, so that while we are dealing with God's activity, this activity is a new creation in the realm of community life and behaviour which corresponds to the new creation in the realm of nature (v. 15). This new creation in righteousness makes possible that measure of peace and security which the nation desires, for it has the character (to judge by the context) of good government. It is God's gift, yet also something which men practise. There is thus more than a hint that righteousness will be God's creation in and among men.

Jer. 23. 5f and 33. 15f. God will raise up a righteous (*tsaddiq*) Branch, who as king will carry out justice and *tsedaqah* in the land, and this will mean salvation and security for Israel and Judah. This king will be called 'the Lord is our righteousness' (*tsedeq*), 23. 5f (33. 15f is similar). In our analysis all the instances except in this title are classified under man's activity of government; *tsedeq* in the title in both instances is classified under God's gracious, saving activity. It is hard to avoid the conclusion that while *tsedeq* in the title refers first to God's activity, it refers secondarily to this *as the cause* of the righteousness of the Davidic king, and so of the people's good government, peace, and security. The juxtaposition makes this at least very likely.[1] If God is to raise up a Messiah to rule righteously, then God is the cause of the resulting righteousness, cf. Isa. 11. 4f and perhaps Zech. 9. 9. Similarly, Mowinckel speaks of Yahweh's endowment of righteousness on the king, a righteousness which includes his ability to save his people militarily, to judge rightly, to maintain

[1] Cf. J. P. Hyatt, *Jeremiah, IB*, v, 989, who suggests that *tsedeq* in the title has the double meaning, 'righteousness and salvation', as in Isa. 46. 13; 51. 1; 51. 6–8.

civil rights, and to bring good fortune to the nation.[1] On the king's side, of course, this means ruling 'in the fear of God' (2 Sam. 23. 2f).

Ps. 72. 1–4. This supports the contention just made, and is also appealed to by Mowinckel. The king's righteousness as ruler, judge, and deliverer comes from Yahweh. To be sure, the king is not just any man, but this passage with the others shows that it was possible to think of man's righteousness as having been given or created by God.[2]

There is less substantial evidence. Von Rad thinks that *tsedaqah*, especially with the prefix בְּ, may represent some kind of spatial notion, a power-charged sphere in which man may live or into which he may be drawn (cf. Ps. 69. 28; 72. 3; 89. 17).[3] Jacob suggests that Yahweh's righteousness is the grace which puts an end to sin, and therefore creates man's righteousness.[4] At any rate, especially in connection with the monarchy, man's righteousness can be seen as created by God.

APPENDED NOTE 2

Wisdom and Righteousness

Although it cannot be treated fully, the notion of wisdom must be given some attention because of its bearing on the relation between God's righteousness and man's.[5] Whether we think of it as the wisdom which man has, or as that which is at the side of God, wisdom is very much concerned with righteousness. This is evident in the texts, especially in Proverbs. For example, in Prov. 10. 2, 3, 6, 7, 11, 20, 21, 24, 25, 28, 30, 31, 32, wisdom involves the righteousness 'of a man who organizes his life properly and who takes his place in a helpful way within the community, who does justice to the claims of others (and also of

[1] *He That Cometh*, 67ff.

[2] Cf. Johnson, *Sacral Kingship*, 6f, 11; Muilenburg, *Way of Israel*, 70, who says 'The justice of God is to evoke Israel's justice'.

[3] Von Rad, *Theology*, 1, 376f.

[4] Jacob, *Theology*, 101. He cites Mic. 7. 9ff; Ps. 51. 16; 85. 10f; 143. 1f; Zech. 9. 9; Joel 2. 23, but of these Ps. 51. 16 is the most convincing.

[5] See especially J. W. Montgomery, 'Wisdom as Gift', *INTERP*, 16 (1962), 43–54.

course to those of God)'.[1] This is an implication of 'practical wisdom'.

The idea of wisdom, however, developed into 'theoretical' or 'theological' wisdom, i.e. that which is at the side of God, whether we think of it as a personification, or personalisation, or hypostatisation. It is something God is, or has, and not man's possession. Is there then any link between the two? They may have been originally separate conceptions, so that one is not the source of the other, yet in the wisdom literature as we have it (and more important, as Paul had it), they are joined together with no apparent sense of incompatibility. Thus wisdom is both something man practises and something God is, and there is evidence that the divine Wisdom was at least sometimes thought of as creating in men, or in some men, a like wisdom, so that the gap between the 'theological' wisdom of Prov. 1–9 and the 'practical' wisdom of 10–29 is bridged. There are specific hints. Wisdom is described as having been created in the faithful in their mother's womb (Sir. 1. 14, also 1. 9f). Man's wisdom may consist mainly in humility and awe before God's Wisdom (Prov. 1. 7; 9. 10; Ps. 111. 10; Job 28. 28), but it can be given to men by God (cf. Isa. 11. 2), especially to the wise men, who are 'one of the channels through which God's presence is communicated to men'.[2] This seems to imply that their wisdom is a reflection or representation of the divine, and a communication of it.

Wisdom and righteousness are closely related not only in the 'practical' Prov. 10–29, but also in 1–9, where wisdom gives understanding of righteousness (2. 9), and keeps men in righteous ways (2. 20; 8. 20). The double nature of wisdom in the literature as it has come down to us thus provides a setting in which righteousness may be God's, and yet granted to man.

[1] Von Rad, *Theology*, 1, 436; cf. H. Ranston, *The Old Testament Wisdom Books* (London, 1930), 14, 23.

[2] Jacob, *Theology*, 120; cf. also 253.

CHAPTER 2

GREEK USAGE OF ΔΙΚΑΙΟΣ AND COGNATES

We can no longer talk about the Greek and Hebrew 'thought worlds' as if they were utterly different.[1] Paul and other early Christians used the Greek tongue, and Paul wrote to people living amidst, and many of them native to, Greek culture. Even Palestinian Judaism was influenced by Greece. In our study, then, we must look at contemporary Hellenistic use of δίκαιος etc., as well as at *ts-d-q* in the Hebrew OT. In the Greek OT there is a high degree of overlap of *ts-d-q* with δίκαιος and cognates, and this may be partly due to the influence of the Hebrew on the Greek used to render it, a sort of backlash effect. Yet the LXX translators must have thought δίκαιος etc. the appropriate word-group to use, and in fact, as we shall see, they used it with some consistency and sensitivity. This means that what Gentile as well as Jewish readers understood by it must be considered, unless we are to assume that when the early Christians entered their assemblies or read their literature, they put away the normal associations of words, and adopted another set.

THE VERB

It has been claimed that to a contemporary Greek-speaker the most natural meaning of 'God who justifies the ungodly' would be 'God who condemns the ungodly',[2] because when the verb is used with a personal object it means 'to treat justly' (the opposite of ἀδικεῖν). However, Aristotle's use of the passive suggests that the verb may have a neutral sense, though in fact it is mainly used of meting out justice to wrongdoers.[3] Even so, however, there is no clear link with the Pauline use, or with the

[1] Cf. Barr, *Semantics*, especially Ch. 2.

[2] Dodd, *Bible and Greeks*, 52.

[3] Aristotle, *Eth. Nic.* v ix 1136*a*. Schrenk, *Righteousness*, 57, points out that in Polyb. III 31 seeing that justice is done involves 'defending'. Half the trouble lies in the rarity of the word.

LXX's vindicatory use. Rather oddly, it is the verb's use with an impersonal object that is more promising. Here, the meaning is 'to think or deem (something) right'.[1] Moulton and Milligan[2] quote from a papyrus in the John Rylands Library (II 119. 14) where the form ἐδικαίωσεν refers to the award of a verdict in court, and from another papyrus (PTebt. II 444) where the perfect participle passive means 'fixed' or 'declared just' (in fixing a contract). Both are first-century papyri. Perhaps the verb has been employed in biblical Greek with this usage in mind, but substituting a personal for an impersonal object. Dodd thinks this did happen, but that another process went on also: in certain circumstances 'doing justice' to a person would mean vindicating him, seeing that he got his rights, and these circumstances were so common in the OT period that this use became common in the LXX.[3] However this does not explain the rise of the meaning 'acquit' as readily as the impersonal–personal shift does.

The debate about whether on *a priori* grounds δικαιόω can mean 'declare righteous' must surely be regarded as closed. Not only is it clear that it *does* mean this in Biblical Greek, but the parallel with ἀξιόω,[4] and the fact that in secular Greek there is only one place where it has been discovered to mean 'make righteous',[5] show that a declaratory force ought to be given to it unless there are strong reasons to the contrary.

Paul's use, therefore, while a little unusual to anyone not raised on the LXX, was not impossible Greek in its day.

δικαιοσύνη AND δίκαιος

Much is sometimes made of the view that the Greek meaning of these words is a barrier to a correct understanding of St Paul's

[1] H. G. Liddell and R. Scott, *Greek–English Lexicon* (new edition by H. S. Jones, Oxford, 1940).

[2] J. H. Moulton and G. Milligan, *The Vocabulary of the Greek Testament* (London, 1914–29), 162f.

[3] *Bible and Greeks*, 50–3.

[4] See Sanday–Headlam, *Romans*, 30f; J. H. Moulton, *Grammar of New Testament Greek*, II (with W. F. Howard) (Edinburgh, 1913), 397.

[5] *Corp. Herm.* XIII 9. On this see Moulton and Milligan, Dodd, *Bible and Greeks*, 58f, and Hill, *Greek Words*, 102.

meaning.[1] If pressed, this means that Paul was quite incompetent in having used the words at all. There must have been effective points of contact. Moulton and Milligan found very few cases of the words occurring in the papyri, but many in inscriptions, where the meaning is 'justice', 'just'. In the case of the adjective, there is special reference to social and legal, but also religious, duties.[2] This is interesting, as it continues certain uses in Classical Greek.

First, the noun could be used for 'justice' in the strict judicial sense, as of course could *tsedeq*, and in saying this we do not forget that justice was rather differently conceived in Greece and Israel, but the difference was not entire. Nevertheless, δικαιοσύνη becomes something more. As early as Theognis, it is not just the judicial virtue, but the proper behaviour of the citizen within social relationships, 'In justice all virtue is comprehended'.[3] By the time of Aristotle the two meanings, justice in the narrow sense, and more widely, the performance of all social duties, are both firmly established and exist side by side. The comprehensive meaning is more dominant than the judicial one,[4] even if, perhaps, the latter coloured the wider meaning.[5] With courage, wisdom, and temperance, it was one of the cardinal virtues from Plato onwards, and as such it usually meant more than judicial justice, in fact doing what was right to one's neighbour, however that 'right' was defined. It is in Plato that we find the most fruitful material, especially in the *Republic*. He sees δικαιοσύνη as primarily a quality of soul (*Gorgias* 477, 509b–d, both in terms of the negative) and the same thing as piety (*Protagoras* 330b–333e). In the *Republic*, it is still a matter of the soul, but is also that condition of a society or state in which each plays his appropriate part, does his own job. It is the activity within the society proper to a man (*Republic* II 368e–372a; IV 433a–434c). This is far from the same thing as covenant behaviour, yet it is not entirely inappropriate that the same word should be used for it as for *ts-d-q* in the LXX. With Epicurus we

[1] E.g. Snaith, *Distinctive Ideas*, 161ff.

[2] Moulton and Milligan, *Vocabulary*, 162.

[3] Theognis 147, cited from E. Harrison, *Studies in Theognis, Together with a Text of the Poems* (Cambridge, 1902), 7. Cf. W. Jaeger, *Paideia*, E.Tr. (3 vols., Oxford, 1939–47), I, 103.

[4] Cf. Aristotle, *Eth. Nic.* V iii–v; Schrenk, *Righteousness*, 26f.

[5] So Dodd, *Bible and Greeks*, 43.

may go even farther, for he associates covenant (συνθήκη)[1] with justice (τὸ δίκαιον, but once δικαιοσύνη), which also involves an inward attitude.[2] Of course both terms were understood differently from Judaism, and more in terms of social contract, yet there are similarities or analogies once we grant different thought worlds. In both places we have activity within a relationship, represented by a situational word whose precise meaning must be determined by the given circumstances. Aristotle also stresses that δικαιοσύνη is not something absolute, but 'in relation to our neighbour' (*Eth. Nic.* v i, 1129*b* 25f, also v i, 1130*a* 3–5).

Dodd maintains that the Hebrew conception always tended to be 'more inward, more humane, and more inclusive', and of course much more related to a personal God than to abstract principles.[3] Yet Greek usage, like Greek thought, was not monochrome, and Dodd himself recognises that much of what is said about the Hebrew conception could also be said about Plato, indeed he regards Plato as nearer the Hebrew understanding than either is to the usual Greek view of righteousness. At all events, the greatest of the Greeks is enough to warn us against supposing that there is an unbridgeable gap between Hebrew *tsedaqah* and secular Greek δικαιοσύνη.

Throughout Classical Greek, the adjective is applicable not only to judicial situations, but to all matters involving society and the gods.[4] It can be used to denote the observance of legal norms as in Aristotle, but also to denote the whole of the activities of life, including at times a reference to the inward nature as well as the outward social behaviour (cf. Aristotle, *Eth. Nic.* v i 1129*a*; Epictetus, *Diss.* I xxii 1; II xvii 6; Plato, *Republic* IV 433a–c). It often has a perceptibly religious background.[5]

[1] This is not the usual LXX word, though it does occur a handful of times, e.g. for בְּרִית in 2 Kgs 17. 15.

[2] Cf. N. W. De Witt, *Epicurus and his Philosophy* (Minneapolis, 1954), 294–7, and Epicurus, *Doctrines* 31–8, in C. Bailey, *Epicurus, the Extant Remains* (Oxford, 1926), 102f.

[3] *Bible and Greeks*, 44f.

[4] Cf. Liddell and Scott, also Hill, *Greek Words*, 99f: the man who is δίκαιος conforms to δίκη, i.e. 'he does what is right, according to the traditions of society...he renders to others their rights and exacts his own'. This includes obligation to the gods.

[5] H. Cremer and J. Kögel, *Biblisch-theologisches Wörterbuch der Neutestamentlichen Gräzität* (10th edn, Gotha, 1911–15), 297–9.

We conclude that while in the LXX and the NT the influence of Hebrew has been strong, this word-group would have quite successfully communicated to an ordinary non-Jewish Christian. The real difference lies less in the use of the words themselves than in accompanying ideas of God and of man's relation to him. Allowing for this, these words are proper and comprehensible. What is abundantly clear is that neither noun nor adjective is used in a purely forensic way, i.e. to refer to a status alone. The closest we get to this is where τὸ δίκαιον is used for 'a right' or 'one's due' in a way strikingly similar to Job 35. 2, 2 Sam. 19. 29, and Neh. 2. 20 (see above, p. 28). If Paul did use the words primarily for one's standing before God, we must seriously question whether any of his readers, and especially his Gentile readers, would understand him at all. It is not enough to say that in Biblical Greek they are fundamentally religious words, and not basically secular as in ordinary Greek.[1] In the first place, it is doubtful whether they always are purely secular in non-biblical Greek. In the second place, behaviour words do not stop being behaviour words because they have a religious orientation as well, even when the religion is that of the God of Israel.

[1] Cf. Schrenk, *Righteousness*, 16f.

CHAPTER 3

LATER JUDAISM I: THE SEPTUAGINT

As the LXX was the OT Greek version which the Church made peculiarly its own, it has relevance in a study of Paul's use of Greek. It contained, of course, more than the OT books, but it is to these we confine our attention until later.

There were probably varieties of text in the first century which are not represented in our few surviving chief manuscripts,[1] and we must therefore not be over-precise in detail when examining its relevance to Paul, yet it is an invaluable guide to his usage, particularly as he so often uses its text when quoting,[2] and it also shows us how biblical ideas were expressed by Greek-speakers.

THE VERB

Of the 45 times δικαιοῦν is used, 15 are in the Apocrypha and therefore outside our concern at the moment. Thirty remain.

δικαιοῦν *and the Hiph'il of* צָדַק

There are 12 instances, in the Hebrew, of the hiph'il, and of these 9 are rendered by the active of δικαιοῦν: Ex. 23. 7; Deut. 25. 1; 2 Sam. 15. 4; 1 Kgs 8. 32 – 2 Chron. 6. 23; Ps. 81 (82). 3; Isa. 5. 23; 50. 8; 53. 11. With the exception of the last, they are all clearly forensic in Hebrew, though of course as much regal as legal, and involve more than the pronouncing of a verdict. In LXX as in the Masoretic Text, a sharp distinction between

[1] See B. J. Roberts, *The Old Testament Text and Versions* (Cardiff, 1951), 101–87.

[2] H. B. Swete, *An Introduction to the Old Testament in Greek* (2nd edn, Cambridge, 1914), 400–2, concluded that Paul used LXX 'without material change' for more than half his quotations. Recently, E. E. Ellis, *Paul's Use of the Old Testament* (Edinburgh, 1957), 12–16, finds LXX predominating: 51 out of 93 quotations are 'in absolute or virtual agreement with the LXX. In four passages Paul follows the Hebrew against the LXX; 38 times he diverges from both.'

ethical and forensic is not possible, and the implication of 'declare in the right' is 'because really so'. In all 9 cases, the Greek verb appears to render the hiph'il satisfactorily.

This is confirmed when we examine the 3 places where δικαιοῦν is not used. In Prov. 17. 15 δίκαιον κρίνει is used for מַצְדִּיק. Yet the setting is forensic enough, and δικαιοῦν would seem natural. The most likely explanation is stylistic (in the similar statement in Isa. 5. 23 the verb *is* used). Here, by using the adjective with κρίνειν an elegant parallel has been achieved without altering the meaning: δίκαιον...τὸν ἄδικον, ἄδικον δὲ τὸν δίκαιον. Moreover, it would be difficult to find an antonym to render מַרְשִׁיעַ, and it was better to use periphrastic forms for both Hebrew verbs. In Isa. 5. 23 there is no such problem, and δικαιοῦν is used. All this suggests that δικαιοῦν and δίκαιον κρίνειν mean the same, 'declare (or adjudge) righteous, acquit'.[1]

In Job 27. 5 אַצְדִּיק אֶתְכֶם is rendered by δικαίους ὑμᾶς ἀποφῆναι. This is important in view of our earlier (p. 19 above) discussion of the verse as being barely forensic. LXX apparently adopts the same view, avoids the forensic verb, and chooses the adjective which, as we shall see, is very much less forensic, and which here simply means 'you are right' (and not wrong). So RSV renders, 'Far be it from me to say that you are right'. The forensic use of the verb is so clear that in a context like this it is avoided.

The third place where δικαιοῦν does not render the hiph'il is Dan. 12. 3, but here LXX clearly represents a different text tradition from MT.[2] So then, in their different ways, both Prov. 17. 15 and Job 27. 5 suggest that we are correct in seeing δικαιοῦν as essentially forensic, and as adequately rendering the hiph'il. Indeed, in Isa. 53. 11 it is arguable that the use of the Greek verb makes the verse much more plainly forensic than in Hebrew, where there is a strong possibility that 'make righteous' is meant (cf. pp. 19f above). The Greek, δικαιῶσαι δίκαιον εὖ δουλεύοντα πολλοῖς, while not exactly the same text as MT, is more forensic, and can hardly mean anything but 'acquit'.[3] Our

[1] Cf. the same view taken by N. M. Watson, 'Some Observations on the Use of ΔΙΚΑΙΟΩ in the Septuagint', 259, also Hill, *Greek Words*, 107, against Snaith, *Distinctive Ideas*, 166, who concludes from this that δικαιοῦν is not particularly forensic.

[2] Cf. Charles, *Daniel*, 331.

[3] Ambiguity, however, is allowed for by R. R. Ottley, *The Book of Isaiah According to the Septuagint* (London, 1904), 279.

view of the use of δικαιοῦν in LXX is supported by the places where it translates something other than *tsadaq*.

These are Ps. 72 (73). 13; Isa. 1. 17; Mic. 7. 9; 1 Sam. 12. 7; and perhaps Ezek. 44. 24.

In Ps. 72 (73). 13, זִכִּיתִי לְבָבִי is rendered by ἐδικαίωσα τὴν καρδίαν μου. Now זכה, while in OT a term for being clean or pure, either literally or ritually, acquires in the literature of late Judaism strong forensic connotations in certain contexts, namely in connection with 'merits'. Perhaps the LXX translator has wrongly assumed a forensic meaning at this early stage, and so used δικαιοῦν. No clear forensic note is struck in the psalm; the theme is the psalmist's upright behaviour, and others' wicked behaviour, before God certainly, though this note is not dominant. Therefore, rather than say that the Greek verb is used ethically here, it seems better to see reflected the later forensic understanding of the Hebrew verb. In other words, it is a misunderstanding.[1]

In Isa. 1. 17 and Mic. 7. 9 it is important to note that δικαιοῦν renders the entirely forensic ריב, 'plead for'.[2]

The case of 1 Sam. 12. 7 is complicated. MT is straightforward: וְאִשָּׁפְטָה אִתְּכֶם לִפְנֵי יהוה, but LXX renders καὶ δικάσω ὑμᾶς ἐνώπιον κυρίου καὶ ἀπαγγελῶ ὑμῖν (quoting from text of Rahlfs). Codex Alexandrinus, however, instead of δικάσω reads δικαιώσω, which is a much more common verb, and therefore more likely to have been substituted for the former, than vice versa. In either case the meaning is forensic, of course. We note also that two Greek verbs translate one Hebrew verb. Watson argues, for once not quite convincingly,[3] that the two verbs are needed to render the complex notion, so neatly put in the Hebrew, 'that I may judge with you before Yahweh all the saving deeds...', i.e. 'that I may vindicate the saving deeds by successful pleading'. It is simpler to say that the niphʿal of שפט here is near the usual meaning, 'enter into judgment with you concerning all...' so that it is not a question of judging (or vindicating) God's saving acts, but rather of calling *Israel* to the bar in view of all God's saving acts. To express this idea in Greek, δικάσω is used

[1] Cf. Watson, 'Some Observations', 259.

[2] So also Watson, 'Some Observations', 258. Ottley, *Isaiah*, 63, on 1. 17, points out that B* and Clement of Rome take it as 'do justice for the widow'.

[3] 'Some Observations', 257f.

(perhaps later changed to the less appropriate δικαιώσω), but ἀπαγγελῶ is added to show that in the prosecution of the case there will be a rehearsal of the saving acts. Once δικαιώσω is read, the addition of the second verb becomes very puzzling, as the declaratory idea is already included in the first.

In Ezek. 44. 24 MT and LXX must represent different textual traditions, but δικαιοῦν seems to represent *shāphat*, and to be used forensically to mean something like 'they will declare (or show?) my ordinances to be righteous' – presumably by enforcing and so ratifying them.

We probably ought to include here the case of Mic. 6. 11 although the passive is used. It is a true passive, and its meaning is not (as when it renders the qal) 'be righteous, right', but 'be declared righteous, acquitted).[1] Thus it either renders an early instance of the forensic use of זכה, or if one argues that this is too early for such a use, then the same argument applies as was used for Ps. 72 (73). 13.[2]

Thus δικαιοῦν represents the hiph'il both widely and satisfactorily. Both are primarily forensic, and when the hiph'il is not particularly so, it is rendered by something other than δικαιοῦν. Similarly, when δικαιοῦν is used for something other than the hiph'il of *tsādaq*, it is for other forensic words.

δικαιοῦσθαι *and the Qal of* צָדַק

Out of 22 cases of the qal, only 8 are rendered by δικαοιῦν; the 14 that are not, are all in Job. All the 8 (Gen. 38. 26; Ps. 18 (19). 9; 50 (51). 4; 142 (143). 2; Isa. 43. 9, 26; 45. 26 (25); Ezek. 16. 52 (1st)) are rendered by the passive, except the last. We noted when discussing the qal (pp. 20f above) that the meaning is 'be righteous' in a forensic, or ethical sense, or usually both together. This applies here too. The passive is used presumably because of the forensic aspect, i.e. because of the declaration of righteousness which is not given, but received. The exception is Ezek. 16. 52, where the qal is rendered by the active: ἐδικαίωσας αὐτὰς ὑπὲρ σεαυτήν, cf. MT תִּצְדַּקְנָה מִמֵּךְ. The literal meaning of LXX must be 'you have declared (or shown) them to be more in

[1] We should probably read the pi'el of זכה, which is clearly forensic in later times, is plausible here, and has the support of the Vulgate, Kittel, and RSV.

[2] Cf. Watson, 'Some Observations', 258f.

the right (or righteous) than yourself', which is what the Hebrew means anyway, though rather cryptically. In being more explanatory, a different construction is used in LXX, in which the active is necessary. Therefore, this really belongs with LXX renderings of the hiph'il, for though it is actually the qal that is translated, the idea is more a hiph'il one. It is undoubtedly forensic, and as usual expresses the facts of the case.

The 14 cases in Job are twelve times rendered by the adjective δίκαιος (9. 2, 15, 20; 10. 15; 11. 2; 13. 18; 15. 14; 25. 4; 33. 12; 34. 5; 35. 7; 40. 8), once by the adjective καθαρός (4. 17) and once by ἄμεμπτος (22. 3). Is this preference for the adjective a translator's quirk? Certainly the simple adjective is a good rendering of the qal which mostly means 'be righteous', perhaps a better rendering than δικαιοῦσθαι which may introduce too complicated a notion. 'Be acquitted' may say too much. On the other hand, this avoidance of the verb raises again the question of the forensic nature of the book. Certainly the whole thing is forensic, yet in specific instances the discussion of Job's righteousness is usually about what Job has or has not *done*. Thus the emphasis may be ethical with the forensic subsidiary, and to be settled after the ethical question has been answered. We are again up against the inseparability of ethical and forensic, but it does look as if the verb has been avoided precisely in order to avoid too forensic a note. This is confirmed by 4. 17 (καθαρός) and 22. 3 (ἄμεμπτος), where words with a strong moral or ritual content have been used, but where there is no clear difference from the other 12 places where we find δίκαιος.

Moreover, if we examine the 12 (cf. pp. 20f above) we can understand the reluctance of the translators to commit themselves to the more forensic verb. In some the forensic note is stronger than in others, e.g. 4. 17; 9. 2; 25. 4, where some qualifier like 'before the Lord' is used, and 11. 2; 13. 18; 40. 8, where some verb such as ἀναφαίνεσθαι occurs. Others are much more ethical in emphasis, 9. 15, 20; 10. 15; 15. 14; 22. 3; 35. 7 and probably also 34. 5 and 33. 12, though in the last the Greek and Hebrew texts are different.

Out of all this, we see that in the 6 places where the forensic note is strong and where the verb might have been expected, some equivalent expression occurs. Where the adjective is used by itself, the LXX translators seem to see the passage as primarily ethical. The position is not as clear as for the hiph'il, but as there we find the verb or an equivalent used in forensic contexts, and avoided in non- or barely-forensic ones. The general avoidance of the verb in Job may be due to a desire to keep to the adjective because the basic question of the book is whether Job is δίκαιος, or to a failure to spot the forensic nature of the whole. At all events, the general observation holds, that the verb tends to be used in forensic contexts and avoided elsewhere.

δικαιοῦν *and the Pi'el of* צִדֵּק

Of 5 cases, 4 are rendered by δικαιοῦν (Jer. 3. 11; Ezek. 16. 51, 52 (2nd); Job 33. 32). The fifth, not surprisingly in Job (32. 2), is rendered by the cognate adjective with a qualifier, δίκαιον ἐναντίον κυρίου. We noted in our examination of the pi'el that the emphasis falls varyingly on the forensic and the ethical, but that both are always present, and that the meaning is the demonstration of an already existing righteousness (cf. p. 21 above). The exceptional case in Job 32. 2 is to be explained as for the qal. In Job 33. 32, oddly enough, the passive is used, but this is because the whole expression has been put in a passive form, presumably to avoid the anthropomorphism of having God acting directly.

δικαιοῦσθαι *and Other Forms*

The sole instance of the niph'al of *tsādaq*, Dan. 8. 14, is rendered not by δικαιοῦσθαι but by the passive of καθαρίζω. It is of course the sanctuary, not a person, that is to be 'made right', and it is not surprising that LXX seems to regard it as non-forensic and avoids using δικαιοῦσθαι, cf. p. 21 above, where it is pointed out that the verb must mean 'make right', in God's sight, of course.

The only instance of the hithpa'el, Gen. 44. 16, has been turned into a Greek passive, 'how are we to be cleared (δικαιωθῶμεν)?' Although not in a formally forensic context, it is nonetheless forensic, and it fits the pattern that the Greek verb should be used. It is similar to the pi'el cases: 'How are we to show ourselves (or be shown) to be righteous?'; i.e. it is a question of demonstrating an already existing righteousness, or of failing to do so.

In Isa. 42. 21 the noun is rendered by δικαιοῦσθαι. On p. 29

above we classified this as God's legal activity, lawgiving rather than judging. 'The Lord was pleased for his righteousness' sake to magnify his law and make it glorious' (RSV). The LXX κύριος ὁ θεὸς ἐβούλετο ἵνα δικαιωθῇ καὶ μεγαλύνῃ αἴνεσιν is hardly an appropriate rendering. This may be due to a difference in text, or perhaps to a misreading of לְמַעַן צִדְקוֹ, taking למען to mean 'in order that', which would necessitate taking צדקו as a verb.

The verb in the perfect also occurs in Ezek. 21. 18 (13) where there are considerable problems of text and translation.[1] Plainly, however, δεδικαίωται renders בֹּחַן the pu'al of בָּחַן, and refers to a testing, which will be in action and experience, not in a court. It is odd that δικαιοῦσθαι should be used, unless it is by analogy with forensic testing. Watson argues for a connection in the Hebrew meaning 'vindicated by successful testing' or 'examined and declared fit', so that the declaratory Greek verb is appropriate because of this emphasis on a declaration.[2] This is possible, but both Hebrew and Greek texts remain puzzling even if he is right.

Our conclusions on the use of the verb in LXX are, first, that it is primarily forensic or relational, largely rendering some form of *tsādaq*, and especially its forensic emphasis. When the forensic note is weak in *ts-d-q*, some other Greek rendering tends to appear, and when δικαιοῦν is used for something other than *ts-d-q*, it tends to be for some other forensic word.

Second, by 'forensic' we mean in the wider Hebrew sense.

Third, we conclude with Watson against Lagrange and Snaith that the LXX use of δικαιοῦν quite adequately represents the forensic–relational verb *tsādaq*.[3] The active is mainly declaratory, when rendering the hiph'il, or demonstrative, when rendering the pi'el, but never causative. As in the Hebrew, there is a close correspondence between what is, and what is declared or shown to be. The passive may be a true passive, meaning 'be declared righteous', but is largely used for 'be right, righteous, innocent', still in a mainly forensic sense.

[1] H. G. May, *Ezekiel*, *IB*, VI, 179, says the verse is 'obscure and doubtless corrupt'; G. A. Cooke, *Ezekiel*, ICC (Edinburgh, 1936), 229 says 'the text is, in fact, beyond hope of recovery'.

[2] 'Some Observations', 258.

[3] Watson, 'Some Observations'; Lagrange, *Romains*, 123ff; Snaith, *Distinctive Ideas*, 166ff.

THE NON-VERBAL FORMS

The overlap of *tsedeq*, *tsedaqah*, and *tsaddiq* with δικαιοσύνη and δίκαιος is not complete, but extensive. Of 481 cases in the Hebrew OT, only about 32 are not represented in LXX by some form of δικαι-. Conversely, about 100 instances of the latter in LXX represent something other than *ts-d-q*. The overlap is a little greater if we allow for places where different texts are obviously used, and in any case is great enough for us to regard overlap as the rule, and to concentrate on the exceptions in both directions.

צֶדֶק, צְדָקָה, *and* צַדִּיק *not Rendered by* δίκαιος *or* δικαιοσύνη

A few of these must be disregarded because the relevant verses do not occur in LXX (Jer. 33. 15, 16, where *tsedaqah* occurs twice, and *tsedeq*, once; Prov. 21. 21 where the second *tsedaqah* is missing in LXX). In some others, the difference is so great that a different Hebrew text must be behind the Greek: Isa. 49. 24 (*tsaddiq*); Jer. 23. 6 (*tsedeq*); 2 Sam. 23. 3 (*tsaddiq*); Ezek. 21. 8, 9 (3, 4 in EVV) where *tsaddiq* is rendered by ἄδικον – if not a different text, then an intentional 'correction'. If we now deduct from our total of 32 these where a rendering into δικαι- is scarcely possible, we find only 23 where it is not used. It seems from this that the LXX translators considered δικαι- to represent *ts-d-q* adequately.

When δίκαιος and cognates are not used, the most common rendering by far is ἐλεημοσύνη: it is used for *tsedaqah* 9 times (Deut. 6. 25; 24. 13; Ps. 24 (23). 5; 33 (32). 5; 103 (102). 6; Isa. 1. 27; 28. 17; 59. 16; also Dan. 4. 24, where it renders the Aramaic צִדְקָה). In 3 further cases, ἔλεος is used (Isa. 56. 1; Ezek. 18. 19, 21). We have now accounted for 12 of the 23 cases, and this is interesting as showing that the Rabbinic tendency to give *tsedaqah* the meaning 'benevolence', 'charity' or even 'almsgiving', was extant as early as this, and was not a purely Palestinian phenomenon. Do we also infer that δίκαιος and δικαιοσύνη, while they were regarded as adequate for righteous activity in general, were not considered suitable for this aspect of it – perhaps because in secular Greek the judicial meaning tended to colour the wider one, as Dodd thinks?[1] However

[1] *Bible and Greeks*, 43, 46; cf. Schoeps, *Paul*, 29.

rather decisively against this view must be put the fact to be noted below, that δικαιοσύνη can be used to render חֶסֶד. It would certainly be premature to conclude that when δίκαιος or δικαιοσύνη render *tsedaqah* with the meaning of graciousness, or salvation, a Hellenising misunderstanding is at work.

The next largest group is where some word for 'godliness' is used: πιστός for *tsaddiq*, probably on stylistic grounds, in Job 17. 9; some form of εὐσεβέω for *tsaddiq* in Isa. 24. 16; 26. 7, 7; Prov. 12. 12 – where the Hebrew is obscure; ἀληθῆ for *tsaddiq* in Isa. 41. 26; there is also one incomprehensible rendering of *tsedaqah* by εὐφροσύνη in Isa. 61. 10. These account for a further 7. There are 3 places where *ts-d-q* is rendered by some strictly forensic word: κρίσις for *tsedeq* in Isa. 11. 4; 51. 7; and κρίμα for *tsedaqah* in Jer. 51. 10 (LXX 28. 10). The last of the 23, δικαίωμα for *tsedaqah* in 2 Sam. 19. 29, also perhaps belongs in this group.

The total number of exceptions is small, and no trend is perceptible, except the very notable one of using ἐλεημοσύνη or ἔλεος instead of a δικαι- word. It would be precarious to say that δικαι- is avoided for strongly forensic uses, because whereas it is discarded for the more judicial κρίσις in Isa. 51. 7, it nevertheless translates *mishpat* in Ezek. 18. 19, 21, where twice מִשְׁפָּט וּצְדָקָה is rendered by δικαιοσύνη καὶ ἔλεος. This would almost suggest that it is exactly the legal word for which it was thought appropriate! It would also be precarious at this stage to conclude that δικαιοσύνη cannot bear the 'gracious' connotations of *tsedaqah*. We have as yet seen only part of the picture, and cannot yet make useful judgments about the overlap of connotations of the two word-groups.

δικαιοσύνη *and* δίκαιος *Rendering Words Other Than* צדק

Here the number of cases is very much larger, 28 for the noun, and 35 for the adjective, but on the other hand clearer trends are perceptible.

δικαιοσύνη

Only three words are rendered with any regularity, חֶסֶד, אֱמֶת, and מִשְׁפָּט. It is notable that the first two are characteristically covenant words. Thus in Gen. 24. 49 ἔλεος renders *chesed*, and δικαιοσύνη renders *'emeth*, but in Prov. 20. 28, *chesed* occurs twice with the same meaning, but once is rendered ἐλεημοσύνη and once δικαιοσύνη, while in the same verse *'emeth* is rendered ἀλήθεια! This apparent confusion suggests that the translators correctly saw that in using δικαιοσύνη regularly for *ts-d-q*, they were giving it the connotation of a covenant-behaviour word, which could then enable it to be used for other covenant words, even though its formal dictionary meaning was far removed from those of *chesed* and *'emeth*.

So then, the Greek noun 4 times renders *'emeth* when it refers to man's righteousness (Gen. 24. 49; Isa. 39. 8; Josh. 24. 14; Dan. 8. 12), and twice when referring to God's (Isa. 38. 19; Dan. 9. 13). It 4 times renders *chesed* when referring to man's righteousness (Gen. 19. 19; 20. 13; 21. 13; Prov. 20. 28), and 5 times when referring to God's (Gen. 24. 27; 32. 11 (10); Ex. 15. 13; 34. 7; Isa. 63. 7 – where *chesed* occurs twice, the first case being rendered by ἔλεος). It is possible that ἀλήθεια and ἐλεημοσύνη were regarded as insufficiently corporate words to convey the covenantal *'emeth* and *chesed*,[1] whereas δικαιοσύνη had acquired the right connotations. One must therefore question Dodd's view that the translators completely failed to understand the difference in meaning between δικαιοσύνη and *ts-d-q*.[2] It is true as we have seen, that some 'benevolent' cases of the latter are not rendered by δικαι-, but also true that some strictly legal ones are not either. Moreover, the use of δικαιοσύνη for *'emeth* and *chesed*, particularly the latter, shows that presumably because of the covenantal associations of the Hebrew equivalents, the meanings of ἐλεημοσύνη and δικαιοσύνη had 'interpenetrated each other'.[3]

The third word to be rendered is *mishpat*, 6 times, but it is always something one does, i.e. legal activity, and in relation to

[1] Cf. Schrenk, *Righteousness*, 31. Normally, of course, *chesed* was rendered by ἐλεημοσύνη or ἔλεος – more than 100 times, according to E. Hatch, *Essays in Biblical Greek* (Oxford, 1889), 49.

[2] *Bible and Greeks*, 54–7.

[3] Hatch, *Essays*, 50. Quell, *Righteousness*, 3, thinks LXX failed to understand *chesed*, for which δικαιοσύνη is really an excellent equivalent. At all events it is clear that δικαιοσύνη and ἐλεημοσύνη can be used interchangeably for *ts-d-q* and *ch-s-d*. Hatch, *Essays*, 49, notes that the Hexapla tends to change LXX renderings so that *ch-s-d* and *ts-d-q* are translated by ἐλεημοσύνη and δικαιοσύνη more uniformly, and that LXX MS disagreement points in the same direction.

God, with one exception: Prov. 8. 20, though the text is confused; 17. 23, the one exception, no clear reference to God; Isa. 61. 8; Ezek. 18. 17, 19, 21. There is one further place where it renders God's *mishpat*: Mal. 2. 17. The 6 cases of man's *mishpat* have a distinct tendency to mean social justice, rather than be purely juridical.

So far, then, the pattern emerging is that of rendering other covenant words and *mishpat*. There remain 6 cases out of 28 rendering some other word than *ts-d-q*. One, Prov. 16. 11, has δικαιοσύνη for *mishpat*, referring to scales and balances, but what is really in mind of course is man's fair dealing as he uses them, and this is seen as resting on God's 'norm'. Of the other five cases, each renders a different Hebrew word. In Dan. 6. 22 (23) – זָכוּ – it is forensic, but the meaning 'blameless' is actual as well. In two, Gen. 20. 5 and 1 Chron. 29. 17, the reference is to the right intention rather than to the right deed (נִקָּיוֹן in the first, and מֵישָׁרִים in the second; in the latter, intention and deed are congruous). In two more, Ps. 38 (37). 21 (20) – טוֹב, for good or right behaviour – and Prov. 21. 16 – שָׂכֵל[1] – the reference is to good action. From these 28 instances of rendering something other than *ts-d-q*, there emerges a strong tendency to translate other covenant words (15), and a distinct tendency to render *mishpat* in the sense of right legal behaviour. The other words rendered refer to right intention or action, except one which is forensic. There is nothing here to contradict the pattern so far noted for rendering *ts-d-q*.

There are 20 more cases which either have no parallel in Hebrew, or are in some other way doubtful. Of the 20, two are really renderings of *tsedaqah*: 1 Sam. 2. 10 is quite different from MT and almost exactly duplicates Jer. 9. 22f, so as there, δικαιοσύνη actually does render *tsedaqah*; Dan. 9. 8, Th only, not LXX, has in MS B a repetition of ἡ δικαιοσύνη at the beginning of v. 7, which does render *tsedaqah*. Four refer to legal activity: 1 Kgs 3. 9, where ἐν δικαιοσύνῃ is added to Solomon's prayer for wisdom in ruling, and seems to refer to legal as well as regal functions; Ps. 67 (66). 5 (4 in EVV), where MS א adds 'judge the world in righteousness'; Prov. 3. 16 where LXX adds a passage about the

[1] Quell, *Righteousness*, 2, thinks this is rendered δικαιοσύνη 'through carelessness'; but after all, wisdom is right acting as well as understanding. This is odd, but not impossible.

judge's judicial right speaking; Prov. 16. 5 (9), quite different from MT, where (i.e. in LXX) the reference is probably to God's judicial activity. Seven are concerned with ethical behaviour in general: Job 24. 13, where LXX and MT are quite different; Job 28. 4, MS A only, similarly; Prov. 1. 22, where the texts seem to differ,[1] Prov. 3. 9, where the addition of δικαιοσύνης probably refers to ethical behaviour in general, rather than to the fruit of God's vindicatory action, in view of the character of the book; Prov. 13. 2, where it is probably the fruit of his own, not God's, righteousness that the good man eats; Prov. 16. 17, and 17. 14, both of which are quite different from MT and probably refer to ethical behaviour in general, though the second is less clear than the first. It is clear in Prov. 13. 2 that the emphasis is on law-obedience. Five or six are to do with salvation or vindication: Isa. 33. 6, where MT is different; Isa. 42. 6 (2nd, εἰς δικαιοσύνην added by א indicating that Israel is to be God's agent in that righteousness which is salvation); possibly Isa. 49. 13 where it may mean almost prosperity;[2] Job 22. 28, different from MT; Ps. 71 (70). 21, where B א have δικαιοσύνην in place of μεγαλοσύνην, and where the former must mean God's saving or vindicating activity; and probably Dan. 9. 9 (LXX but not Th).[3] There remains only Job 33. 13 which may be purely forensic, but is rather obscure.[4]

[1] MT has פֶּתִי, and LXX δικαιοσύνη, though the former is pejorative, which the latter cannot be. Perhaps LXX misunderstood the text, giving פֶּתִי the meaning 'innocent' which it can bear, though not here.

[2] Instead of the familiar 'break forth O mountains into singing', LXX has: ῥηξάτωσαν τὰ ὄρη εὐφροσύνην καὶ οἱ βουνοὶ δικαιοσύνην. If the two abstract nouns are parallel, then δικαιοσύνην means something like rejoicing over victory or salvation. Probably, however, it means virtually prosperity, as the expression of salvation by the covenant God.

[3] LXX: τῷ κυρίῳ ἡ δικαιοσύνη καὶ τὸ ἔλεος
Th: τῷ κυρίῳ θεῷ ἡμῶν οἱ οἰκτιρμοὶ καὶ οἱ ἱλασμοί
MT: לַאדֹנָי אֱלֹהֵינוּ הָרַחֲמִים וְהַסְּלִחוֹת
If LXX follows MT, this is a remarkable case of God's righteousness being his gracious, even forgiving, activity. If the texts are different, then either (*a*) the meaning of δικαιοσύνη is similar to ἔλεος, or (*b*) the two are complementary, the former perhaps representing *mishpat* or even *dīn*. The second alternative however intrudes an alien note, and the first is therefore more likely.

[4] MS A has τῆς δικαιοσύνης μου instead of τῆς δίκης μου. Either word is an intrusion into MT, but A's reading replaces a less familiar by a more familiar and less appropriate word. It is probably to be rejected.

As for the Hebrew nouns, ethical behaviour is usually in relation to God: of the 11 cases which probably refer to man's righteousness (1 Sam. 2. 10; 1 Kgs 3. 9; Prov. 1. 22; 3. 9, 16; 16. 17; 17. 14; Job 24. 13; 28. 4; 33. 13; and also Prov. 13. 2), all are in relation to God except Prov. 1. 22, even Prov. 13. 2 where righteousness is to do with God's law, and Job 28. 4, for there it is to do with wisdom which begins with the fear of God (cf. v. 28). The one exception then is where we should from experience in the Hebrew bible expect to find it, in Proverbs.

Altogether, in our study of the use of δικαιοσύνη, we can see no reason to assume any different range of meaning from that of *ts-d-q*. The only marked tendency is for it to render other covenant words. This suggests that the two correspond even more than their statistical overlap shows. We may add that we have fresh hints of the communication of God's righteousness to man in Prov. 3. 16, where it is an aspect of wisdom which is both divine in origin and human as possessed and practised, and also in Isa. 42. 6 (2nd) where Israel is God's agent in his saving work and to this extent shares his righteousness.

δίκαιος

There are 35 cases where it renders something other than *ts-d-q*, and these fall into four main categories.

First, it renders some other covenant word, *'emeth* 5 times (Ex. 18. 21; Zech. 7. 9; Isa. 61. 8; Ezek. 18. 8, all used of men, also Jer. 42 (49). 5, used of God), and *chesed* once, Isa. 57. 1 (2nd).[1] Second, it renders some form of יָשָׁר 11 times: Num. 23. 10; Job 1. 1; Job 1. 8 (A and א^2 only); Job 2. 3 (A only); Prov. 3. 32; 4. 25 (used metaphorically to mean straight); Prov. 11. 3; 14. 9; 21. 2; 21. 18 (where δικαίου represents יָשָׁר and צַדִּיק together), and Prov. 17. 26 (2nd). In all the cases of *'emeth* there is a strong legal connotation, though it is not all of exactly the same kind. In all the cases of *yāshār*, which are all applied to man, the reference is to character as true or upright, but usually in God's sight.

Third, it renders נָקִי or נָקִיא 6 times (Job 9. 23; 17. 8; Prov. 1. 11; 6. 17; Joel 3 (4). 19; Jon. 1. 14), all of man, and all with a double reference to the character of the person and to a

[1] When one compares LXX with MT, *chesed* in the second part of the verse is clearly synonymous with *tsaddiq* in the first, and LXX correctly renders both by δίκαιος.

status matching the character. Fourth, it 5 times renders *mishpat*, mainly in a strict or else vague legal sense: Prov. 21. 7 and 29. 4 (man); Job 34. 12, Prov. 16. 33, and 29. 26 (God). There remain 7 instances, each of which renders a different word: Prov. 20. 8 (דין) – judging and ruling; Prov. 30. 12 (טָהוֹר) – ethical in general; Prov. 17. 7 (נָדִיב) – apparently for lofty character; Prov. 11. 1 (שָׁלֵם) – of a 'just weight', but really referring to man's fair dealing; Prov. 28. 18 (תָּמִים) – for a manner of life, א^1 only; Job 34. 10 (for the opposite of עָוֶל) – with a legal connotation; Isa. 47. 3 (rather oddly rendering נָקָם). These 7 are all concerned with man as righteous, except Isa. 47. 3 which is clearly legal but otherwise defies classification.

Apart from the 35 where something other than *ts-d-q* is rendered, there are about 40 which have no Hebrew equivalent. Of these, 5 are really renderings of *tsaddiq*, either because this obviously must have been in the text used by the translator (Ps. 34 (33). 18 – not only LXX but also Syriac and Targum require it), or because something occurring once in Hebrew is repeated in Greek: Gen. 18. 23; Isa. 45. 22; Ps. 37 (36). 26; Prov. 28. 28 (1st). We do not mean necessarily the repetition of a whole phrase, but simply that if the same word is used twice in a verse, one naturally assumes that both times it has the same meaning, and if we know the Hebrew equivalent for one, we infer it for the other. Obvious mistranslation accounts for perhaps another 4: Prov. 17. 15 (2nd, instead of ἄδικον, א only); Jer. 30 (37). 16 (instead of ἀδικιῶν, א only); Ps. 139 (138). 5 (the א^1 reading δίκαια for ἀρχαῖα), and Zech. 8. 16 (the A reading δίκαιον for εἰρηνικόν). Twice it seems to render טוב: Prov. 13. 11, where there seems to be an intrusion from Ps. 112 (111). 5, and Prov. 19. 22, where πτωχὸς δίκαιος represents טוב־רָשׁ, perhaps because of the common association of 'poor' with 'righteous'. The instance in Job 28. 4 is a variant of the noun, and has been dealt with above, p. 63. In Prov. 16. 11 we really have a duplicated rendering of *mishpat*.[1] We thus have 28 unaccounted for, and while these cannot be discussed in detail, a few general statements may be made.

The 28 are: 1 Sam. 2. 2, 9; Job 5. 5; 22. 15 (following Origen's text); 24. 4, 11; 36. 10, 17; Ps. 2. 11 (12); Prov. 2. 16; 3. 9;

[1] The first δικαιοσύνη renders *mishpat*, and the parallelism is clear.

10. 17, 18, 22; 11. 7, 15, 16; 12. 25; 13. 9, 23; 15. 28 (16. 7); 16. 7 (LXX); 15. 29 (16. 9); 16. 33 (1st); 17. 4; 23. 30; 28. 21; Ezek. 18. 11. None is purely forensic, and all describe ethical activity of some kind. One is probably legal (Prov. 28. 21). One is liturgico-ethical (Ezek. 18. 11). One means 'benevolent' (Prov. 13. 9). Only one refers to God, 1 Sam. 2. 2, and is vindicatory.[1] The other 24 denote good behaviour without being specific enough for us to be quite sure of its nature.[2]

One most interesting fact will already be apparent. In the total group of 76 cases rendering either something other than *ts-d-q* or no recoverable Hebrew equivalent, 41 (or 54 per cent) are in Proverbs, and a further 14 in Job, altogether 55 (or 72 per cent). This is such a high proportion that some special factor must be at work. We may note moreover, that all 6 cases of rendering other covenant words are outside Proverbs and Job. Yet to say that the overlap between the two word-groups breaks down is incorrect, for in the two books only 2 cases of *tsedeq*, *tsedaqah*, or *tsaddiq*, are not rendered by δικαι-, and there are special reasons in both cases (Job 17. 9 and Prov. 12. 12, cf. above p. 60). It seems that the LXX translators of these books had a special fondness for δίκαιος, and δικαιοσύνη also, because the same tendency to a smaller extent is perceptible for the noun as for the adjective.[3] It may be that at least in Proverbs, a weakened sense of the covenant is responsible,[4] but we can find no altogether satisfying explanation. However, the fact that the lack of overlap is mainly confined to two books, means that in the bulk of LXX the overlap is considerably greater than a first look suggests.

Other Forms of δικαι-[5]

The adverb δικαίως occurs only 5 times. Three times it renders *tsedeq*: Deut. 1. 16; 16. 20; Prov. 31. 9 (24. 77). In Prov. 28. 18,

[1] Cf. A. Descamps, 'La Justice de Dieu dans la Bible grecque', *Studia Hellenistica*, 5 (1948), 69–92, esp. 74.

[2] In Prov. 16. 7 (15. 28*a*) we note that δεκτός, not δίκαιος, expresses 'acceptable before God'.

[3] Out of 28 cases, 15 render other covenant words, only one of these (Prov. 20. 28) in Job or Proverbs. Of the 13 remaining, 4 are in Job or Proverbs, a high but not startling proportion.

[4] See R. E. Clements, *Prophecy and Covenant* (London, 1965), 17f.

[5] We have not included δικαίωμα, which is peripheral to the enquiry, but which will be discussed when we come to Rom. 1. 32.

MSS ABא[2] have it instead of δίκαιος for תָּמִים (cf. p. 65 above), and it renders הֲכִי, meaning 'correctly' (i.e. in accordance with the facts) in Gen. 27. 36. From so few cases, no clear conclusions can be drawn. The noun δικαίωσις occurs only once, Lev. 24. 22, where it renders *mishpat*, apparently in the sense of a legal process.

Summary of the Enquiry into LXX

1. The range of meaning of the two word-groups is substantially the same.

2. This is supported not only by the places where overlap occurs, but by an examination of the places where it does not occur. The only firm tendency in non-overlap places is to render legal words, and other covenant words.

3. Especially in Proverbs, and less so in Job, some special factor causes a relatively high use of δικαι- words.

4. The meaning of the Greek words seems to be dominated by the Hebrew words they render; this must be seen, however, in the light of our remarks on the use, particularly of the noun, in secular Greek, and especially in Plato and Epicurus. The LXX translators seem to have perceived that *ts-d-q* was basically covenantal, hence their rather astonishing rendering by δικαι- of other covenant words whose dictionary meaning is widely different.[1]

APPENDED NOTE 3

The Inadequacy of δικαιοσύνη

We have just noted our disagreement with Descamps in his contention that the Greek noun seriously distorts the meaning of the Hebrew, especially in Isa. 41. We conclude rather that the Greek noun has taken over the range of meanings of *tsedaqah*, and that this is shown by its use for *chesed*. If we examine the 53 cases where the Hebrew nouns or adjective describe God's gracious, saving activity (p. 29 and notes, above), we find that all but two are rendered by δικαι-, and that one of these (Jer. 33. 16) is missing

[1] We thus disagree with Descamps, 'Justice de Dieu dans la Bible grecque', 75ff, 88–91, who thinks that the use of δικαιοσύνη for *tsedaqah*, especially in Isa. 41, has distorted the meaning towards *iustitia distributiva*. Cf. Appended Note 3 below.

from LXX, and that the other (Isa. 61. 10) is rendered oddly by εὐφροσύνη. If we look at the 40 cases of God's vindicating activity (p. 30 and notes, above), we find that all but 4 are rendered by δικαι-. Of these, two (Ps. 24. 5 and 103. 6) are rendered by ἐλεημοσύνη, one is missing from LXX (Prov. 21. 21, 2nd), and one (Jer. 51. 10) is rendered by κρίμα. There are only three cases under 'man's gracious activity' (pp. 26f above), and all are rendered by δικαι-. Rightly or wrongly, then, these 'gracious, benevolent, vindicating' cases are nearly always translated by δικαι-. What evidence we have suggests that the translators knew what they were doing and proceeded with sensitivity and intelligence. For them, δικαι- had acquired the gracious (because covenantal) associations of the Hebrew words.

This brings us to Professor Dodd's view that LXX tends to use ἔλεος and ἐλεημοσύνη when the Hebrew clearly has the 'benevolent' meaning.[1] For man's *tsedaqah* rendered by ἐλεημοσύνη he cites only Dan. 4. 24; Ezek. 18. 19, 21; and Ps. 33 (32). 5, not a large amount of evidence, and indeed there are special circumstances in all except the last. In Dan. 4. 24, it is the Aramaic צִדְקָה, and if this does have the later meaning 'almsgiving', then certainly ἐλεημοσύνη is more suitable. In Ezek. 18. 19, 21, the expression is δικαιοσύνην καὶ ἔλεος for מִשְׁפָּט וּצְדָקָה: having used δικαιοσύνη for *mishpat* a translator could hardly use it again for *tsedaqah*. For God's *tsedaqah* he cites Ps. 24. 5,[2] Deut. 6. 25,[3] Deut. 24. 13, Ps. 103 (102). 6, Isa. 56. 1, and perhaps Ps. 33 (32). 5 if it does not refer to man. He maintains that 'two aspects of צדק are polarised into δικαιοσύνη and ἐλεημοσύνη. In place of the comprehensive virtue of צדקה, we have justice on the one hand, mercy on the other.'[4]

This must be doubted. It would be foolish to deny that sometimes there was such a tendency, but it is hardly a general rule. Like *tsedaqah* in MT, δικαιοσύνη in LXX can be used for a wide variety of ways of acting, but all within the covenant.

[1] *Bible and Greeks*, 45f, 55–7.

[2] Dodd is surely right in thinking the LXX has erred here, for the meaning is probably God's vindicating action, cf. p. 30, n. 3 above.

[3] Here again LXX may err, cf. Dodd, 56, and our p. 26 above, as also Deut. 24. 13, cf. p. 28, n. 3 above.

[4] *Bible and Greeks*, 56; against this is Hatch's view, *Essays*, 50, that in LXX the meanings of the two Greek words had 'interpenetrated each other'.

This includes legal uprightness in judging and lawgiving, and also graciousness, kindness, whether on God's part or man's.[1]

[1] Cf. Hill, *Greek Words*, 198f: 'The δίκαιος-words underwent considerable expansion and change of meaning through being consistently used to render the Hebrew root צדק.'

CHAPTER 4

LATER JUDAISM II: INTERTESTAMENTAL WRITINGS

There are several ways in which these could be classified. One is in terms of Palestinian and Alexandrian (or Hellenistic) origin, and some account of this must indeed be taken, but the dividing lines are not clear enough to be useful. There is probably no book without some debt to both Palestine and Hellas, whether acknowledged or not. Another method could be in terms of date, but this is sometimes quite uncertain, though most are probably pre-Pauline and all are early enough to be admissible evidence for usage of words. The method appropriate to this enquiry seems to be classifying by language, i.e. Hebrew, Greek, and Hebrew and Greek together. No account has been taken, in the vocabulary analysis, of books surviving only in languages other than Hebrew or Greek, though their teaching has been considered in the appropriate section. There is only one book whose Hebrew and Greek texts are both sufficiently well established for a useful examination of their relation to be made, and that is Sirach.[1] However, because of the surprising lack of overlap of our two word-groups in Sirach, the cases of δικαι- have also been included in the analysis of Greek books. It will be evident that the categories are not the same in every case as those used for the OT. This was not planned, but is how the pattern fell out, which may in itself be important.

[1] Although the value of the five Hebrew fragments (together about two-thirds of the whole) has been debated, the Qumran fragments seem to confirm that our text is substantially correct, and early. Cf. J. T. Milik, *Ten Years of Discovery in the Wilderness of Judaea*, E.Tr. (London, 1959), 32; B. M. Metzger, *An Introduction to the Apocrypha* (New York, 1957), 79. In the case of Tobit, extant Hebrew and Aramaic fragments are late, cf. F. Zimmerman, *The Book of Tobit* (New York, 1958), 32–5, 135ff. Fragments have been found at Qumran, cf. Milik, 31, and A. Dupont-Sommer, *The Essene Writings from Qumran*, E.Tr. (Oxford, 1961), 296f. Fragments of a Hebrew version of Jubilees have also been found at Qumran, cf. O. Eissfeldt, *The Old Testament, An Introduction*, E.Tr. (Oxford, 1965), 608, 641, 664.

GREEK AND HEBREW: SIRACH

δικαιόω

Of 11 cases, only 3 render *tsādaq*. Five have no Hebrew equivalent, because that part of the Hebrew text is lacking:[1] Sir. 1. 22; 18. 2, 22; 23. 11; 26. 29. The 3 cases where *tsādaq* is rendered are: 7. 5, where the hithpa'el is rendered by the middle, and where the context is plainly forensic; 10. 28 (29), where the active renders the hiph'il, and is forensic; and 42. 2, where again the active renders the hiph'il, and is forensic.

Two cases render נקה by the passive, 9. 12 and 31. 5. The first is clearly forensic in Hebrew and in Greek. The second is more difficult: נקה can refer to cleanliness in a literal, moral, or liturgical sense as well as a forensic one, and the two halves of this verse ('He who loves gold will not be justified, and he who pursues money will be led astray by it', RSV) suggest that a better parallel is obtained if לא ינקה is taken ethically. On balance, however, a forensic meaning is preferable in Hebrew as in Greek because of the forensic meaning of the same phrase in 9. 12, and the analogy with Prov. 28. 20. In the remaining case, 13. 22, the hoph'al participle of יפה is rendered by ἐδικαίωσαν. This is clearly a case of justifying the ungodly as a deplorable thing.[2] The forensic or declaratory pattern stands.

Working the other way, we find the only 3 clear cases of *tsādaq* all rendered by δικαιοῦν. There is a possible fourth, 42. 2, but it is likely that מִשְׁפָּט, which reads much more naturally in the line, is the correct reading, rather than מַצְדִּיק.

δικαιοσύνη

Of the 5 cases, 3 are missing from the Hebrew text: 26. 28; 38. 33; 45. 26. One – 16. 20 (22) – renders *tsedeq*, and both in

[1] The Hebrew text used is I. Lévi, *The Hebrew Text of the Book of Ecclesiasticus* (Leiden, 1904). For all the Apocrypha unless otherwise stated, we use the Greek text of A. Rahlfs, *Septuaginta* (2 vols., Stuttgart, 1935).

[2] Cf. RSV: 'If a rich man slips, his helpers are many; he speaks unseemly words, and they justify him.' The Hebrew is literally, 'they are made beautiful', but really they are only declared or regarded so. G. H. Box in R. H. Charles, *The Apocrypha and Pseudepigrapha of the Old Testament* (henceforth cited as *APOT*) (2 vols., Oxford, 1913), I, 365, suggests emendation, but this is probably unnecessary.

Greek and in Hebrew the meaning is covenant activity, though in Greek it is man's, and in Hebrew God's. In 44. 10, a different Hebrew text is probably used.[1] Working the other way, we find a marked lack of correspondence, at least for *tsedaqah*. There are 5 cases of *tsedeq*, and 3 are rendered by δικαι- words: 16. 20 (22) by δικαιοσύνη; 9. 16 by δίκαιος; 35. 17 (18) by δικαίως – MS A has δικαίοις, but the B א reading fits *tsedeq* better. The 2 remaining cases are rendered by ἀλήθεια (4. 28) and ἐλεημοσύνη (40. 24 – reading *tsedeq* rather than *tsedaqah*). This last reflects the 'interpenetration' of δικαιοσύνη and ἐλεημοσύνη, and both the last two reflect the merging of the three covenant words, *tsedeq*, *chesed*, and *'emeth*. Of course, in 40. 24 ἐλεημοσύνη is explained if 'almsgiving' is the meaning.

Of the 8 cases of *tsedaqah*, not one is rendered by a δικαι- word. One (51. 30) is not in the Greek text; one is rendered δόξα (44. 13 – where it must mean 'reputation for righteousness'); and the other 6 are all rendered by ἐλεημοσύνη (3. 14, 30 (28); 7. 10; 12. 3; 16. 14; 40. 17). In each case the rendering is clearly appropriate and reflects the tendency for *tsedaqah* in late Hebrew to mean 'charitableness' in general, or 'almsgiving' ('charity') in particular.[2] While, to judge by LXX usage, δικαιοσύνη was possible for this, it was not natural.

δίκαιος

There are 7 instances, if we take the adverb and not the adjective as the right reading in 35. 17 (18), of which 3 are missing from the Hebrew text: 27. 8; 35. 6, 7. One (33. 3) either represents a different Hebrew text, or else hides the embarrassment of a translator who had no idea how to render 'Urim'. One – with the negative – renders אין (10. 22 (23); 'one is not to' becomes 'it is not right to'). The two remaining render *ts-d-q*. In 9. 16 the word is *tsedeq* (see above) and this is straightforward, both in Greek and in Hebrew the reference being to ethical rightness in

[1] As it stands, αἱ δικαιοσύναι represents ותקותם, presumably 'their hope'. Box, *APOT*, I, 481, suggests emending to וצדקתם.

[2] On ἐλεημοσύνη as both general benevolence and specific almsgiving, H. L. Strack and P. Billerbeck, *Kommentar zum Neuen Testament aus Talmud und Midrasch* (henceforth cited as S–B) (5 vols. in 6, Munich, 1922–56), I, 387f.

relation to God. In 44. 17 the word is *tsaddiq*, and again it is straightforwardly ethical in relation to God.

Working the other way, we find an almost complete lack of correspondence. Of 6 cases of *tsaddiq*, only one (44. 17) is rendered by δίκαιος, the other 5 all being translated by εὐσεβής: 11. 15 (17), 20 (22); 12. 2; 13. 16 (17); 16. 13. This is distinctly odd, and is a situation similar to that in the Qumran texts (and it is noteworthy that fragments of Sirach have been found at Qumran). In the Scrolls *tsaddiq* and its plural have an almost political sense as the party of the righteous, really carrying on and developing our covenant-keeping category for the OT. The term 'righteous' is compounded almost equally of relationship to God, and of an appropriate manner of life. It is just this meaning of *tsaddiq* that δίκαιος often bears in the Apocrypha and Pseudepigrapha generally, and one wonders why it could not have been used here also. Perhaps both εὐσεβής and δίκαιος are needed to bring out the full meaning of *tsaddiq*, especially if Sirach's grandson is less than normally influenced by the broadening effect of *ts-d-q* on δικαι- words.

The adverb occurs only in the B א reading at 35. 17 (18), for *tsedeq*, referring to God's judging activity.

To conclude on Sirach, the degree of overlap of the two word-groups is not impressive, only 7 cases in all. However, out of 24 cases of δικαι-, 11 are not in the Hebrew text, 2 probably represent a different text, and only 4 render something other than *ts-d-q*, whereas 7 do render *ts-d-q*. Thus it renders *ts-d-q* more often than not. The reverse, however, is not true: out of 22 cases of *ts-d-q*, one is not in the Greek, 7 are rendered by ἐλεημοσύνη, 5 by εὐσεβής, 2 by something else, and only 7 by δικαι-. We must conclude that Sirach does not exhibit that degree of overlap which we generally find between the word-groups in LXX and MT. This may be because it shows greater sensitivity in translation, or because it denies to δικαι- the wide range of meaning of *ts-d-q*.

THE GREEK BOOKS OF THE APOCRYPHA AND PSEUDEPIGRAPHA

Some books do not appear in the lists which follow, either because instances of δικαι- are lacking, as in the case of Judith, or because there is no satisfactory Greek text: thus Jubilees, the

Martyrdom and Ascension of Isaiah, Slavonic Enoch, Assumption of Moses, 2 Baruch (the Syriac Apocalypse of Baruch), II (IV) Esdras. The few Greek fragments of 2 Baruch contain no form of δικαι-.[1]

δικαιόω

This occurs 25 times.

It occurs with God as object 9 times, always with a forensic–declaratory meaning. God is found or declared righteous because in fact he is, 6 times: Sir. 18. 2; Pss. Sol. 2. 15; 3. 5; 8. 23, 26; 9. 2. God's judgments are found or declared righteous, again because they are, 3 times: Pss. Sol. 3. 3; 4. 8; 8. 7.

It is used once, Esth. 10. 3*i*, of God as vindicator, 'And God remembered his people and vindicated his inheritance' (RSV, 10. 12). Because the passage is about God's vindication in action, the meaning is probably tantamount to 'saved', rather than to a merely forensic declaration. This is unusual, but not impossible.

Three times it means man 'has a right' or 'is entitled to...', and all are forensic (and all the middle of the verb): Tob. 6. 12, א only; 6. 13, א only; 12. 4 (in terms of desert).

It occurs with man as object 12 times, and all are forensic: Sir. 1. 22; 7. 5; 9. 12; 10. 29; 13. 22; 18. 22; 23. 11; 26. 29; 31. 5; 42. 2; TSim. 6. 1; TDan 3. 3.[2] This means that all 25 cases are forensic, except perhaps Esth. 10. 3*i*, and all accord with the real state of affairs, except apparently TDan 3. 3. However the exception is only apparent, for although ungodly deeds are

[1] Printed in Charles, *APOT*, II, 487–90.

[2] Sir. 26. 29 is difficult: μόλις ἐξελεῖται ἔμπορος ἀπὸ πλημμελείας καὶ οὐ δικαιωθήσεται κάπηλος ἀπὸ ἁμαρτίας. RSV: 'A merchant can hardly keep from wrongdoing, and a tradesman will not be declared innocent of sin.' A non-forensic meaning in the second half of the verse would make a better parallel, and this is supported by W. F. Arndt and F. W. Gingrich, *A Greek–English Lexicon of the New Testament and Other Early Christian Literature* (Cambridge, 1957). If we reject this view, it is not only because of the verb's prevailing meaning, but also because 'from sin' makes better sense when the verb is taken forensically, cf. W. O. E. Oesterley in Charles, *APOT*, I, 405. On Sir. 31. 5 see p. 71 above. In Sir. 42. 2, 'of the following things do not be ashamed...περὶ κρίματος δικαιῶσαι τὸν ἀσεβῆ' – is ἀσεβῆ written in error for εὐσεβῆ? The only other plausible explanation is that of Box in Charles, *APOT*, I, 469, who says it means 'not to hesitate to acquit the ungodly man when he is proved innocent of a particular charge'. But why was this not made plainer?

justified, the justification is in accordance with what are believed to be the facts. All the cases except Esth. 10. 3*i* are in books which are probably Palestinian in character.

δικαιοσύνη

There are 112 cases altogether.

God's Righteousness (28 cases)

God's Activity of Judging and Lawgiving. 12 cases.

> Sample, Pss. Sol. 2. 15: ἐγὼ δικαιώσω σε, ὁ θεός, ἐν εὐθύτητι καρδίας, ὅτι ἐν τοῖς κρίμασίν σου ἡ δικαιοσύνη σου, ὁ θεός.

The following verses make it clear that this is God's judicial righteousness, almost his *iustitia distributiva*. One of the 12 cases is to do with lawgiving, 1 Bar. 4. 13, and the rest with judging: Pss. Sol. 2. 15; 4. 24; 8. 24, 25, 26; 9. 4, 5; Wisd. 5. 18; 12. 16; 1 En. 13. 10; 14. 1 (in this last, God's judgment is carried out through Enoch).[1] Wisd. 12. 16 is notable in that it refers to God's *merciful* judgment, cf. vv. 15, 18, and especially v. 16*b*.

God's Covenant-Keeping, Reliable Activity. 7 cases.

This is really God's own ethical behaviour, in a variety of contexts, but excluding both his judicial and his saving work. It is often set in opposition to man's sin, or unfaithfulness, or covenant-breaking.

> Sample, Sir. 16. 22: ἔργα δικαιοσύνης τίς ἀναγγελεῖ; ἢ τίς ὑπομενεῖ; μακρὰν γὰρ ἡ διαθήκη.

Almost certainly *God's* acts of righteousness are meant. The 7 cases are: 1 Bar. 1. 15; 2. 6, 18; Sir. 16. 22; Pss. Sol. 9. 2; 1 En. 22. 14; TDan 6. 10. In view of the current discussion about δικαιοσύνη θεοῦ, TDan 6. 10 is of special interest. The opposition, between man's ἀδικία and ἡ δικαιοσύνη τοῦ θεοῦ, makes a 'saving' interpretation unlikely; the saving idea is in the verse,

[1] For Pss. Sol. 9. 4, 'in thy righteousness dost thou visit the sons of men', H. E. Ryle and M. R. James, *Psalms of the Pharisees* (Cambridge, 1891), 91, suggest the meaning 'salvation', but the drift of the passage rather favours 'judgment', cf. G. B. Gray in Charles, *APOT*, II, 642.

but is subsequent to and not included in κολλήθητε τῇ δικαιοσύνῃ τοῦ θεοῦ. The opposition suggests that it is either man's righteousness as defined and required by God, or God's own righteousness as distinct from man's unrighteousness. Oepke adopts the first of the alternatives, and though this is entirely possible, we prefer the second, as making a clearer contrast.[1]

God's Saving Activity. 9 cases.

Sample, 1 Bar. 5. 2: περιβαλοῦ τὴν διπλοΐδα τῆς παρὰ τοῦ θεοῦ δικαιοσύνης.

The full context is:

> Take off the garment of your sorrow and affliction, O Jerusalem, and put on for ever the beauty of the glory from God. Put on the robe of the righteousness from God; put on your head the diadem of the glory of the Everlasting (vv. 1, 2, RSV).

This is God's righteousness, cf. vv. 4, 9, which replaces man's sorrow and affliction, and is linked to his mercy, vv. 2, 9. It seems then to refer to his saving, vindicating, gracious action. The 9 cases are: 1 Bar. 5. 2, 4, 9; Wisd. 14. 7; Tob. 13. 7 ('merciful', but in a legal context); TLev. 18. 14; TJud. 22. 2; 24. 1; TZeb. 9. 8.[2]

Man's Righteousness

There are 84 cases.

Man's Legal Activity. There are 3 cases: 1 Macc. 2. 29; Sir. *38. 33* (B text); 45. 26. Italics here, as for the OT, mean that there is no

[1] Oepke, 'ΔΙΚΑΙΟΣΥΝΗ ΘΕΟΥ', 262. Kertelge, '*Rechtfertigung*', 25–8, thinks the basic contrast is between two kinds of human behaviour, but the second, 'righteousness of God', has the character of power from God, so making possible the righteousness he requires – hence κολλήθητε.

[2] In Wisd. 14. 7, the meaning could be 'the carrying-out of God's will' (so W. J. Deane, *The Book of Wisdom* (Oxford, 1881), 185*a*), or it could refer to 'righteous seed' (so A. T. S. Goodrick, *The Book of Wisdom* (London, 1913), 292), but the point seems to be that the ark was the instrument of God's salvation. In TJud. 24. 1 'sun of righteousness' could mean God or the Messiah. We take the first part of the verse to refer to God, and the second to the Messiah. In TZeb. 9. 8 it is clearly God, cf. Mal. 3. 20 (4. 2 in EVV).

clear relationship to God. In 1 Macc. 2. 29 we take δικαιοσύνη and κρίμα as virtually synonymous, and not as foils to one another.

Sample, Sir. 38. 33 (B text only, and not in Hebrew): διαθήκη κρίματος οὐ διανοηθήσονται οὐδὲ μὴ ἐκφάνωσιν δικαιοσύνην καὶ κρίμα.

The other reading (παιδείαν) is perhaps to be preferred, but this one, if read, must in its context be legal, even though the next line moves beyond the purely legal realm.

Man's Ruling Activity. There are 18 cases: 1 Macc. *14. 35*; Pss. Sol. 17. 23, 26, 29, 37, 40; 18. 7 (all in Pss. Sol. are of the Messiah); TJud. 24. 1, 6 (both of the Messiah, and the latter combining the notions of judging and saving in governing); Wisd. 1. 1; 9. 3; Arist. 209, *232*; 259; 267; 278; 280; 281.[1]

Sample, 1 Macc. 14. 35: καὶ ἔθεντο αὐτὸν ἡγούμενον αὐτῶν καὶ ἀρχιερέα διὰ τὸ αὐτὸν πεποιηκέναι...τὴν δικαιοσύνην καὶ τὴν πίστιν ἣν συνετήρησεν τῷ ἔθνει αὐτοῦ...

RSV renders 'justice',[2] but the point surely is that in his military command his righteousness was seen.

Man's Ethical Behaviour – Unspecified. This tends to be a very broad category. In some cases the emphasis is strongly on the relationship to God out of which the activity springs, or within which it occurs, viz. 1 Macc. 2. 52; Tob. 14. 7; TLev. 8. 2; TAsh. 6. 4. Most are in some degree in relation to God, and many which are not explicitly so, are probably so implicitly, though one cannot be sure. In Aristeas there is great trouble in deciding; in the Table-Talk section it is repeatedly stated that righteousness is in relation to God, so that one's first impression of a thoroughgoing Hellenism needs to be corrected.[3] A different problem arises in Tobit, where δικαιοσύνη and ἐλεημοσύνη are often juxtaposed: are they equivalent, or complementary? It is

[1] In Arist. 280 I have followed H. G. Meecham, *The Letter of Aristeas* (Manchester, 1935), 298f, in taking 'crown of righteousness' to mean 'crown consisting in righteousness'.

[2] Cf. also Oesterley in Charles, *APOT*, 1, 119.

[3] We have refrained from assuming this reference to God where it is not explicit, though its presence is arguable.

usually impossible to be sure, but in 4. 5, 7 it is clear that δικαιοσύνη cannot mean 'almsgiving' or 'benevolence', but must mean 'upright behaviour'. It seems a reasonable inference, in the absence of other evidence, that it has this meaning elsewhere too.

Sample, Tob. 4. 5: δικαιοσύνην ποίει πάσας τὰς ἡμέρας τῆς ζωῆς σου, καὶ μὴ πορευθῇς ταῖς ὁδοῖς τῆς ἀδικίας.

'Doing righteousness' is contrasted with 'walking in the ways of wrongdoing', and so is 'doing the truth', v. 6. Moreover, in v. 7 'give alms to those who live righteously' is more likely than 'give alms to those who give alms', and therefore we take it that here, and probably elsewhere in Tobit, the word refers to ethical behaviour in general rather than to charitable behaviour in particular, though perhaps sometimes including it. There are 37 cases.[1]

The Greek Virtue. There are a few places in strongly Hellenistic books where 'righteousness' is used in this sense. The clearest case, where it occurs twice, first in the inclusive and then in the narrower sense, is

Wisd. 8. 7: καὶ εἰ δικαιοσύνην ἀγαπᾷ τις, οἱ πόνοι ταύτης εἰσὶν ἀρεταί· σωφροσύνην γὰρ καὶ φρόνησιν ἐκδιδάσκει, δικαιοσύνην καὶ ἀνδρείαν, ὧν χρησιμώτερον οὐδέν ἐστιν ἐν βίῳ ἀνθρώποις.

There is no doubt that the second instance is the cardinal virtue, and little doubt that the first is inclusive. The wider setting of course is Hebraic, and we cannot call this purely Greek, but it is as near as it can be. There are 8 cases.[2]

[1] Tob. 1. 3; 2. 14; 4. 5, 7; 12. 8, 8, 9; 13. 8; 14. 7, 9, 11; 1 Macc. 2. 52; Sir. 26. 28; TLev. 8. 2; 13. 5; TGad 3. 1; TAsh. 1. 6; 6. 4; TBenj. 10. 3; Wisd. 1. 15; 2. 11; 5. 6; 15. 3; Arist. 18; *43*; 131; *144*; *147*; *151*; 159, 168; 168; *169*; 306; Sib. Or. 3. 580; 3. 630; Apoc. Mos. 20. 1. In TLev. 13. 5, TGad 3. 1, Sib. Or. 3. 580, there is a stress on keeping the Law. In Arist. 43, 144, the accent is on character rather than actions. About Wisd. 1. 15 there is uncertainty – there may be textual corruption, cf. S. Holmes in Charles, *APOT*, I, 536. We in effect follow RSV: 'righteous living leads to immortality'.

[2] Wisd. 8. 7, 7 (RSV preserves the distinction by rendering the first 'righteousness' and the second 'justice'); 4 Macc. *1. 4*, *6*, *18*; 2. 6; 5. 24; perhaps Sib. Or. *3. 234*. Some of the Aristeas cases from the previous group may belong here.

Graciousness, *Charity*, *Almsgiving* (cf. the 'benevolence' and 'almsgiving' use of *tsedaqah* in Rabbinic writings).

Sample, Sir. 44. 10: οὗτοι ἄνδρες ἐλέους, ὧν αἱ δικαιοσύναι οὐκ ἐπελήσθησαν.

The second clause probably explains the first, so that a 'merciful' connotation attaches to δικαιοσύναι. There are only 3 cases: Sir. 44. 10; TNaph. 4. 5 (used of the Messiah); TGad 5. 3.

Covenant Behaviour (a category strongly represented in the Qumran Scrolls). Righteousness in this sense means the life and activity of those who are loyal to God, who live within the covenant, and who may also be the poor and oppressed. The connotations are thus ethical, relational, and political. Selecting a sample would be pointless, as a large amount of context is needed to reveal the point. There are 13 cases: Pss. Sol. 1. 2, 3; 5. 17, 17; 8. 6; 9. 3, 4, 5; 14. 2; 17. 19; 18. 8; 1 En. 10. 16; 12. 4.

Vindication (as received by man, rather than as given by God). The meaning is thus peace, prosperity, or even the final state of vindication.

Sample, 1 En. 10. 18: τότε ἐργασθήσεται πᾶσα ἡ γῆ ἐν δικαιοσύνῃ καὶ καταφυτευθήσεται δένδρον ἐν αὐτῇ, καὶ πλησθήσεται εὐλογίας.

There are only two clear cases, this one, and 1 En. 32. 3 (where it is used of the final state in Paradise), but very similar are 1 Bar. 5. 2, 4, 9, which are classified above under God's saving activity. This is because in them the stress is on what God does, whereas here it is on the outcome for men.

There appear to be no purely forensic cases.

δίκαιος

The question arises of the precise meaning in a group of neuter adjectives, usually having the article, and either singular or plural, but sometimes attached to the noun κρίμα, singular or plural. These have been treated in no one way. God's righteous judgments are classified as God's legal activity, but where τὸ δίκαιον means abstract justice, it is classed under 'Things', as also is the meaning 'It is right to...'.

There are 26 cases where it refers to 'things'. There are 15 of these which have the meaning 'justice', usually with the article, but sometimes not, and either singular or plural: 1 Macc. *7. 12*; *11. 33* (meaning 'obligations'?); Wisd. 14. 30 (just penalties); 2 Macc. *4. 34*; 7. 36 (just penalties); *10. 12*; *11. 14*; 3 Macc. *2. 25*; Arist. *24*, *24*, 189, 212, *215*, 291; Sib. Or. *3. 116* (just shares). There are 3 cases where it means 'It is right to...': Sir. *10. 23*; 2 Macc. 9. 12; 4 Macc. *6. 34*. In two places it means 'Rights': Wisd. *19. 16*; 2 Macc. 13. 23. In addition there are 6 miscellaneous cases: Sir. 33. 3 (rendering 'Urim', and almost nonsensical); Esth. 8. 12*p* (RSV 16. 15, referring to laws); 2 Macc. *4. 44* (δικαιολογία, meaning an accusation, or case, or legal matter); Sib. Or. *3. 237* (measures); 257 (ordinances); 783 (wealth).

If one wished to push all these into either forensic or ethical categories, the two cases meaning 'Rights' would be forensic, perhaps the 'It is right to...' cases, some of those meaning 'Justice', and some of the miscellaneous cases, would be ethical, but some would resist such pushing, particularly the cases of justice in the abstract, which may be expressed forensically, or ethically, or both at once.

God as Righteous

Samples are omitted because the categories follow those for the noun, except for 'God as Ruler'. There are only 28 cases. Of these, 20 are used of God as Judge and Lawgiver: twice it is used of God as Lawgiver, 1 Bar. 2. 9; Sib. Or. 3. 720; 7 times it is used of God as Judge, Tob. 3. 2 (3rd, BA text); III (1) Esdr. 4. 39 (used of 'truth', but really about God); Esth. 4. 17*n* (RSV 14. 7); 2 Macc. 12. 6, 41 (δικαιοκρίτης); Sib. Or. 3. 704 (δικαιοκρίτης); Apoc. Mos. 27. 5. It is also used 11 times for God's righteous judgments: 2 Macc. 9. 18; 3 Macc. 2. 22; Pss. Sol. 2. 10, 18, 32; 5. 1; 8. 8; 9. 2; 10. 5; TLev. 3. 2; 15. 2 (both the last are δικαιοκρισία).

A further two cases are used of 'God as Ruler'. This category is very difficult to separate from the previous one, but the stress is on regal rather than legal functions.

Sample, Wisd. 12. 15: δίκαιος δὲ ὢν δικαίως τὰ πάντα διέπεις.

Here, while a legal note is present, a governing one is also clear. The other case is 3 Macc. 2. 3.

Finally, there is one case of God as saving or vindicating, 4 Macc. 9. 24, and there are 5 where it is God as covenant-keeping, reliable: 2 Macc. 1. 24, 25; Tob. 3. 2, 2 (2nd in א only; both are associated with mercy, but probably are complementary); Dan. (Song) 3. 27 (RSV v. 4).

Man as Righteous

The categories are again as for the noun, and therefore no samples are given. There are 140 cases.

There is one case of man's legal activity, where it refers to judgments (Susanna 9). There are 8 cases of man as ruling;[1] and there are 41 cases of man as behaving ethically, though the precise nature of the action is not specified.[2] In these last, we have the same problem with the Tobit instances that we had in the noun. As there, we take 'righteous' to be complementary, not equivalent, to 'merciful' etc. In some instances, the relation to God is especially clear,[3] and it is perhaps worth noting that in Sir. 35. 6 there is a distinction between being righteous (δίκαιος) and being acceptable (δεκτός) to God.

There are three cases where it seems to represent the Greek virtue, 4 Macc. *2. 23*; 13. 24; 15. 10, and these illustrate the difficulty of making a hard and fast distinction between Jewish and Hellenistic. Although these three are clearly in this category, yet they are in each case related to the Law which teaches the virtue, and once we bring a Greek virtue under the hegemony of the Law, it is no longer what it was.

There are no instances of the 'Gracious, Charitable' use, but

[1] Pss. Sol. 17. 32 (referring to Messiah); Arist. *46*; 209 (φιλοδίκαιος); 212; 231 (δικαιοπραγεῖν); 279 (δικαιοπραγεῖν); 280, Sib. Or. 3. 782.

[2] Tob. 4. 17; 7. 6; 9. 6; 13. 10, 15, 15; 14. 9 (BA); Sir. 9. 16; Sir. *27. 8*; 35. 5, 6; 44. 17; 3 Bar. (the Greek Apocalypse of Baruch) 10. 5; 11. 9; 12. 5; TLev. 3. 5; TGad 5. 3; TAsh. 1. 7; 4. 1; 5. 2, 3; TJos. 10. 6; TDan 1. 3 (δικαιοπραγία); Arist. *125*, 147, 169; 4 Macc. 9. 6; Sib. Or. 3. 214, *219*, *233*, 312; 4. 153; 5. 154, 226, 270, 283, 357, 426, 331; Apoc. Mos. 43. 3; 3 Macc. 3. 5.

[3] Tob. 13. 15, 15; TLev. 3. 5; TAsh. 4. 1; Sib. Or. 5. 283, 357, 426.

in the Covenant-Loyalty category there are 86 cases.[1] We see relatively more instances here than for the noun; there, out of 84 cases referring to man, 13 were 'covenant behaviour', i.e. 15.5 per cent. Here, the figure is 86 out of 140, or just over 61 per cent. This makes it all the more strange that in Sirach δίκαιος is avoided for *tsaddiq* in this sense. In some of the 86 cases there is a strong emphasis on law-obedience (especially Susanna 3 and TGad 3. 2); in some, on true worshipping as against idolatry (cf. Ep. Jer. 72; Wisd. 16. 17, 23; 18. 7, 20; 4 Macc. 16. 21; 18. 6, 15; Or. Man. 1, 8, 8). In some, e.g. Pss. Sol. 15. 3, the relation to God is particularly important. Yet despite varieties of emphasis, all are roughly equivalent to the poor, perhaps oppressed, godly, faithful, covenant-keeping people, as in the OT.[2]

There are no instances of the 'Vindication' use, and only one forensic case, Susanna 53 in a quotation from Ex. 23. 7, where the forensic note dominates, but where forensic and ethical notes are both present and inseparable, as in Ex. 23. 7 itself, cf. above, p. 28, n. 4.

Thus, of 194 cases of the adjective, 140 refer to man.

δικαίως

We have discovered only 14 cases. There are 4 cases of God's acting rightly, of which three are in legal contexts (Wisd. 19. 13; 2 Macc. 7. 38; Sir. 35. 18), and one in a regal context (Wisd. 12. 15). There are 8 cases of man's acting rightly, of which three are in legal contexts (TSim. *4. 3*; TDan *4. 4*; 3 Macc. *7. 7*); three are in ruling contexts (Wisd. 9. 12 – with strong legal associations

[1] Wisd. 2. 10, 12, 16, 18; 3. 1, 10 (so RSV, but Deane, *Wisdom*, 126*a*, and Goodrick, *Wisdom*, 129, both take it to mean 'what is right' or 'justice'); 4. 7, 16; 5. 1, 15; 10. 4, 5, 6, 10, 13, 20; 11. 14; 12. 9, 19 (Goodrick, 269, says it here means the fulfilment of the ceremonial law, yet a covenant meaning seems preferable); 16. 17, 23; 18. 7, 20; 19. 17; 4 Macc. 16. 21; 18. 6, 15; Or. Man. 1, 8, 8; Esth. 1. 1*f* (RSV 11. 7); 1. 1*h* (RSV 11. 9); Dan. (Song) 3. 86 (RSV v. 64); Susanna 3 (probably); Ep. Jer. 72; Pss. Sol. 2. 34, 35, 35; 3 title; 3. 3, 4, 5, 6, 6, 7, 11; 4. 8; 10. 3; 13 title; 13. 6, 7, 8, 8, 9, 11; 14. 9; 15. 3, 6, 7; 16. 15; 1 En. 1. 1, 1, 2, 8; 5. 6; 10. 17; 22. 9; 25. 4, 7; 27. 3; TLev. 5. 7; 10. 5; 16. 2; TJud. 18. 1; 21. 6, 9; TDan 2. 3; 5. 6, 12; TNaph. 8. 3; TGad 3. 2 (probably); TBenj. 4. 3; 5. 5, 5; 7. 4; 9. 1.

[2] On this 'political use' in Pss. Sol., cf. Gray in Charles, *APOT*, II, 628f. Here the righteous may be the Pharisees.

also; Arist. 193; 292); two are about ethical acting in general (Sib. Or. *5. 151*; *182*). There are two more cases where it is unclear whether the reference is divine or human, 2 Macc. 9. 6; 13. 8. In the first, punishment, and in the second, fate, come justly. The first is clearly legal.

Summary of Analysis

The books which are generally agreed to be mainly Palestinian and those which are generally agreed to be Hellenistic or Alexandrian are separated out. It has not been possible to argue the provenance of the books, and in some cases an arbitrary decision has had to be made, though always in accordance with what appears to be prevailing opinion.[1]

To take the verb first, out of 25 cases, 24 are clearly forensic. The one exception is Esth. 10. 3*i* (cf. p. 74 above), which is

[1] Considered entirely or mainly Palestinian are: 1 Macc.; Tobit (several places of origin have been suggested: Jerusalem, Antioch, Alexandria, and Babylon, but the finding of some Aramaic and Hebrew fragments at Qumran makes a Palestinian provenance likely); Or. Man. (following Metzger, *Introduction to the Apocrypha*, 125, rather than H. E. Ryle in Charles, *APOT*, I, 612, but the point is moot); Extra Dan.; 1 Bar.; Ep. Jer. (this may have originated in Babylon, so Ball in Charles, *APOT*, I, 596, and Eissfeldt, *Introduction*, 595); Sirach (there are, however, Hellenistic elements, cf. Oesterley in Charles, *APOT*, I, 269); Pss. Sol.; 1 En. (Ethiopian Enoch – Eissfeldt thinks it came from Qumran, *Introduction*, 619, with both Essene and Pharisaic influences, against H. M. Hughes, *The Ethics of Jewish Apocryphal Literature* (London, 1909), 76, who stresses Pharisaism); Test. XII Patriarchs – concerning these, the debate continues about the degree of Christian authorship or editing. Because of the Qumran discoveries, we follow Dupont-Sommer, *Essene Writings*, 301–5, in minimising this, cf. E. J. Bickerman, 'The Date of the Testaments of the Twelve Patriarchs', *JBL*, 69 (1950), 245–60 (first quarter of Second Century B.C.). The 'Christian' view is notably associated with M. de Jonge, *The Testaments of the Twelve Patriarchs* (Assen, 1953), who now thinks that basically Jewish documents underwent a thorough Christian revision, 'Christian Influence in the Testaments of the Twelve Patriarchs', *NT*, 4 (1960), 182–235. See also J. T. Milik, 'Le Testament de Lévi en Araméen', *RB*, 62 (1955), 392–406, especially 405f.

Considered as entirely or mainly Hellenistic/Alexandrian are: 1 (III) Esdr. (the sole case, 4. 39, is in the part which seems not to have a Hebrew or Aramaic original, and is not a re-writing of an OT book); 2, 3, and 4 Macc.; Extra Esther; Wisdom of Solomon; Letter of Aristeas; Sibylline Oracles; 3 Bar. (Greek Apocalypse of Baruch); Apocalypse of Moses, probably. In the case of 3 Bar. we again have a possible Christian origin, and its date is late.

vindicatory in a possibly non-forensic sense. The pattern thus continues, the verb is normally forensic. Once again, however, this cannot be divorced from an element of 'real' righteousness.

To turn to the noun, out of 112 cases, 74 are in Palestinian and 38 in Hellenistic books; 28 refer to God's righteousness, i.e. 25 per cent, and 84 to man's, i.e. 75 per cent. None is purely forensic or purely relational. Of the 28 cases of God's righteousness 12 (i.e. 42.86 per cent) are legal, 10 of these being Palestinian, and 2 Hellenistic. Of the 84 cases of man's righteousness, only 3, all Palestinian, are legal, i.e. 3.6 per cent. Therefore, of the Palestinian cases, man's and God's, 13 out of 74, or 17.6 per cent, are legal, but of the Alexandrian, man's and God's, only 2 out of 38, or 5.26 per cent, are legal. Altogether, 15 out of 112, or 13.4 per cent, are legal. It is evident that the noun is used in a legal sense much more frequently of God than of man. Out of 84 cases of man's righteousness, all except 12 (14.3 per cent) are in relation to God. For the Palestinian books alone, the figure is lower, i.e. all but 2 out of 49 (4.1 per cent) are in relation to God, and for the Hellenistic books alone, the figure is higher, i.e. 10 out of 35 (28.6 per cent) lack this relation. This is very much what one would expect.

There are 194 instances of the adjective, of which 96 are in Hellenistic and 98 in Palestinian books. Of these 194, 26 refer to things (23.8 per cent); 28 (30 per cent) refer to God; and 140 (46.2 per cent) refer to man. Three are forensic, two being 'things' and one being 'man', together 1.5 per cent. Of the 28 cases of God as righteous, 20 are legal, i.e. 83.3 per cent, and of these 11 are Palestinian and 9 Alexandrian. Of the 140 cases of man's righteousness, only one (Palestinian) is legal, a negligible proportion. Even if we add the sole purely forensic case, the total is still only 2 out of 194, less than 1 per cent. Once again it is evident that while the word is often used of God in a legal sense, it is rarely indeed used thus of man. Even if we include the 26 cases of 'things' with man, the legal total is only 28 out of 166, 17 per cent, much lower than for God. We noted above that the Palestinian noun cases had a much higher proportion of legal cases than did the Alexandrian; for the adjective the situation is somewhat reversed. Altogether, 42 out of 194 are legal, including 'things' and the forensic case, i.e. 21.65 per cent. However for Palestinian books alone the figure is 16 out of 98, or 16.33 per cent, while for Alexandrian books alone it is 26 out of 96, or 27.08 per cent, perceptibly higher. Finally, of the 140 cases of man's being righteous, including the one purely forensic case, only 6 lack a relation to God, or 4.3 per cent. For the Palestinian books alone, the figure is lower as for the noun, 1 out of 80, or 1.25 per cent, lacking this relation, while for the Hellenistic books it is perceptibly higher, 5 out of 60, or 8.3 per cent, lacking such a relation. This again is to be expected, though as for the noun, even in Hellenistic books it is remarkably low.

The total number of instances of the adverb is too small to make an analysis, though it is worth noting that out of 8 cases of man's acting rightly, no fewer than 5 bear no discernible relation to God. This may be not significant, merely reflecting the somewhat formal and perfunctory way in which the adverb is used, in Greek as in English. The noun δικαίωσις does not occur at all, and the various compounds such as δικαιοκρισία have been included under the adjective.

Several things emerge quite plainly from this survey:

1. While the verb continues to be almost entirely forensic, the noun and adjective continue to be almost wholly ethical. There are no purely relational or forensic noun cases, and only three of the adjective, each of which is related to 'real' righteousness.

2. The tendency for righteousness to be seen in relation to God is as strong as in the canonical books, though marginally more so in Palestinian than in Hellenistic books.

3. There is a distinct tendency for God's righteousness to be legal, and for man's to be non-legal. As a complement to this, the 'gracious, saving' category as applied to God, has fallen away.

4. Particularly in the adjective, the covenant-keeping category comes into great prominence.

THE HEBREW WRITINGS OF THE INTERTESTAMENTAL PERIOD

These consist of the Qumran Scrolls and Sirach. The latter is included because of the lack of overlap with the δικαι- word-group, and in any case it is appropriately considered with the Scrolls because of the existence of fragments of it at Qumran.

One or two preliminary things must be said. The Scrolls are

often fragmentary, so that in an examination which lays stress on context, they raise a peculiar problem. There are therefore some instances of *ts-d-q* which have been omitted because there is insufficient context, or no context at all. Emendations have generally been ignored, except where they have a very high degree of probability indeed, and such cases are rare. Also ignored are instances which occur in direct quotation from canonical books; thus in the Habakkuk Commentary only those instances are dealt with which form part of the comment. However, where a canonical instance is dealt with, without the word itself being used in the comment, that fact has been noted. The cases of *tsedeq* which occur in the title מורה צדק are considered separately, in a discussion on the meaning of the title.

So far as the Scrolls' date is concerned, we follow the view of the majority of scholars, that they come from towards the end of the pre-Christian era. They are in this case valid evidence for prevailing usage leading up to St Paul.

The Verb

Of 16 instances (3 in Sirach), 7 are hiph'il, 8 qal, and 1 is hithpa'el.

Four cases of the hiph'il (CD 1. 19; 4. 7; Sir. 10. 28 (29); 42. 2) are to do with a declaratory forensic process in which man is both subject and object of the verb.[1] In 1QH 9. 9 man justifies God's judgment, and in 1QM 11. 14 God vindicates his own judgment; both are forensic, though in the latter the vindication is seen in action. The one remaining case is more difficult, viz. CD 20. 18: להצדיק איש את אחיו. Vermès renders, 'to justify each man his brother'; Rabin renders, 'to make each man his brother righteous', and Gaster, 'to bring him to righteousness'.[2] It is hard to see this as anything but 'make righteous' (cf. Dan. 12. 3), and we must conclude that while the hiph'il is mainly forensic or relational, it could, even if rarely, be used for 'make righteous'.

Of the 8 instances of the qal, 7 are in 1QH, and in all these the note of 'real' righteousness is probable, while in some it is strongly accented. In 1QH 1. 6, God is described as 'righteous in

[1] We omit the first case in Sir. 42. 2, reading משפט, not מצדיק.

[2] C. Rabin, *The Zadokite Documents* (Oxford, 1954); T. H. Gaster, *Scriptures of the Sead Sea Sect* (London, 1957); G. Vermès, *The Dead Sea Scrolls in English* (Harmondsworth, 1962).

all thy deeds' (צדקתה) and here the forensic note is weak indeed. In 7. 29, man is spoken of as 'righteous before God', but one wonders why לפניכה was thought necessary if the qal by itself was essentially forensic. Both 9. 15 cases are forensic (in God's judgment), but can hardly be merely so, for in the second case degrees of being righteous before God are allowed for, and this makes more sense if there is an ethical note as well. Moreover, in the first case, the forensic nature seems to depend not on the verb itself, but on 'in thy judgment'. In 12. 31, with God as subject, we have a more clearly forensic case, though even here it is clear that God is righteous really as well as in the context of contention, cf. the rendering of Vermès: 'there is none among them that can answer Thy rebuke; for Thou art just and none can oppose Thee'. In 1QH 13. 17 there is uncertainty because of mutilation, but it seems likely that the meaning is, with Gaster, 'it is only through Thy goodness and through Thy mercies abundant that Man can ever do right'. If so, then the forensic note is absent. 1QH 16. 11 is also hard to see as purely or even mainly forensic, cf. Vermès: 'I have chosen to keep my hands clean in accordance with (Thy) will; for the soul of Thy servant (has loathed) every work of iniquity. And I know that man is not righteous except through Thee.' The immediate context is ethical, and although a few lines later there is a reference to standing in God's presence, so that we cannot exclude all forensic meaning, yet the main stress is surely ethical. Finally, 1QS 3. 3 is plainly forensic, but firmly on the basis of character and actions.

Thus without exception the ethical note is present in the qal, and the only question is whether it is dominant over or subservient to the forensic. In only two, 1QS 3. 3. and 1QH 12. 31, can we confidently claim a predominantly forensic emphasis. One wonders indeed whether from context alone, and without reference to the qal's meaning elsewhere, we should ever have inferred a forensic meaning, except where a qualifier is present.

The sole case of the hithpa'el, Sir. 7. 5, refers to man's justifying himself, and is clearly forensic, though on the basis of the facts.

The Nouns and Adjective

Of those cases whose context and meaning are clear enough for classification, there are, apart from cases of *tsedeq* as part of the title 'Teacher of Righteousness', 51 cases of *tsedeq*, 37 of *tsedaqah*, and 21 of *tsaddiq*.

God's Righteousness

There are 14 legal cases, all of *tsedeq*, and 8 of these refer to his judgment (1QS 3. 1; 4. 4; 1QM 1. 30; 1QH 1. 23, 26; CD 20. 29, 31; Sir. 35. 17), a further 4 to his ordinances (1QS 1. 13; CD 3. 15; 20. 11, 33), while one (1QBlessings 2. 26) refers to his verdict, and one (1QH 9. 33) to his forensic rebuke.

God's righteousness also appears as his acting reliably, faithfully, within his own covenant. In 1QH 1. 27, for example, we see this clearly:

> For Thine, O God of knowledge, are all righteous deeds (מעשי הצדקה) and the counsel of truth; but to the sons of men is the work of iniquity and deeds of deceit (Vermès).

While the setting is forensic, this instance surely is not; the contrast is between man's behaviour and God's, and it is consequent that when man is before God he can say nothing. Here there is nothing particularly about God's graciousness, but rather about his constancy and uprightness, but there are some others, noted immediately below, where the dividing line between this and the 'gracious' category is thin. There are 4 cases of *tsedeq*: 1QM 4. 6 (probably – part of the title on the banner); 1QH 2. 13; 4. 40 (with a strong note of graciousness); 13. 19. There are 10 cases of *tsedaqah*: 1QS 11. 5, 6 (both with a strong note of graciousness); 1QH 1. 27; 4. 31; 7. 20; 8. 2; 14. 16; 17. 17, 20, 20 (all with a strong gracious note). There is only one case of *tsaddiq*, 1QH 14. 15.

Finally, there are the cases where God's righteousness is seen primarily as his saving, gracious activity. As we have noted, these are closely similar to the preceding group, and the difference is only one of emphasis. This two-sidedness comes out well in 1QM 18. 8 where the whole passage is covenantal, but within this, God's gracious and saving activity is in the forefront:

> Thou hast kept Thy covenant with us from of old, and hast opened to us the gates of salvation many times... Thou hast acted for the sake of Thy Name, O God of righteousness (הצדק) (Vermès).

There are 4 cases of *tsedeq*,[1] there are 13 of *tsedaqah*,[2] but none of *tsaddiq*.

Man's Righteousness

Man's righteousness involves legal activity, e.g. 1QS 9. 17, the Master 'shall impart true knowledge and righteous judgment (ומשפט צדק) to those who have chosen the way' (Vermès). In the context it is unlikely to be God's judgment, at least proximately. There are 4 cases, all of *tsedeq*: 1QS 9. 17; 10. 26 (also gracious); 1QH 6. 4; 1QBlessings 3. 24.[3]

Man's righteousness may also be ethical, but the precise nature of it be unspecified, e.g. 1QS 1. 5,

> that they may practise truth, righteousness, and justice (אמת וצדקה ומשפט) on earth (Vermès).

The context shows this to be ethical in general, rather than specifically juridical behaviour. There are 12 cases of *tsedeq*: 1QS 2. 24; 4. 9, 24; 9. 5; 11. 16; CD 4. 17; 1QH 5. 22; Triumph of Righteousness 1. 5, 6; Sir. 4. 28; 9. 16; 16. 20 (22). In 1QS 4. 9, righteousness, while still what one does, is also a power to be served. There are 4 cases of *tsedaqah*: 1QS 1. 5; 1QH 4. 30; 7. 17; Sir. 51. 30. There are also 4 cases of *tsaddiq*: 1QH 4. 38; 7. 12; 16. 10; CD 4. 7.

There are also a number of instances where it refers to the behaviour of the covenant people, the elect. The whole of the beginning of the Damascus Document shows that although the righteous are ethically upright, they are more than this, and essentially God's people, the Elect. Thus in CD 1. 19, 20, the righteous are seen over against the wicked in this sense. There are

[1] 1QS 10. 11 (cf. A. R. C. Leaney, *The Rule of Qumran and its Meaning* (London, 1966), 246); 11. 15 (both legal and gracious); 1QM 18. 8; 1QH 11. 18.

[2] 1QS 1. 21; 10. 23, 25 (also legal); 11. 3, 12, 14, 14 (all also legal); CD 20. 20; 1QH 4. 37; 11. 8, 31; 16. 9; Words of Heavenly Light 6. 3.

[3] 1QH 6. 4 is in a mutilated section, its meaning uncertain. We follow Vermès: 'those who reprove with justice', a meaning similar to Isa. 11. 4. However, Gaster takes it as a verb, 'didst vindicate my cause', and M. Mansoor, *The Thanksgiving Hymns* (Leiden, 1961), renders 'those who plead justice'.

11 cases of *tsedeq*,[1] 4 of *tsedaqah*,[2] and 15 of *tsaddiq*.[3] There are also three cases from canonical texts (4QPs37 2. 10f; 1QpHab 5. 9; 8. 3) which are important, for in each case the comment shows that the word is understood in this covenant-keeping, people of God, political sense.

We may group together graciousness, benevolence, and almsgiving connotations, for the last is really a special case of the first two. In Sir. 3. 14, for example,

> Benevolence to a father shall not be blotted out, and as a substitute for sins it shall be firmly planted.[4]

'Benevolence' is *tsedaqah*, rendered in Greek ἐλεημοσύνη. There is one case of *tsedeq*, Sir. 40. 24, rendered ἐλεημοσύνη in Greek, but another may possibly be added, 4QSl (39) 1. 18, where it is 'graciousness', but used of angels. There are also 6 cases of *tsedaqah*, all rendered ἐλεημοσύνη in Greek: Sir. 3. 14, 30 (28); 7. 10; 12. 3; 16. 14; 40. 17. There are no cases of *tsaddiq*. In some of the Sirach instances, it must be admitted that from the context alone we could not confidently put them in this category rather than in the 'Ethical, Unspecified' one. However their rendering in Greek shows that ben Sira's grandson, if not ben Sira himself, saw them thus, and while the classification must still be tentative, there is a reasonable case for it. It is rather strange that there are almost no cases from the Qumran Scrolls. The one case which occurs refers to angels rather than men. In view of its frequent occurrence in LXX, in the Rabbinic writings, and in Intertestamental literature generally, one cannot suppose the sect was not aware of it.[5]

[1] 1QS 3. 20, 22; 4. 2; CD 1. 1, 16; 1QM 3. 6; 13. 3; 17. 8; 1QH 6. 19; 16. 5; 1QBlessings 5. 26. In 1QH 6. 19 it is almost a power to be served.

[2] 1QS 5. 4; 8. 2; 1QH 7. 14; Sir. 44. 13 (which, with Sir. 51. 30, see above, Skinner classes as 'benevolence', though without full discussion, 'Righteousness in OT', 281).

[3] CD 1. 19, 20; 11. 21; 20. 20; 1QH 1. 36; 15. 15; 1Q34 (Liturgical Prayers) 3. *i*. 2, 3, 5; Sir. 11. 15 (17), 20 (22); 12. 2; 13. 17; 16. 13; 44. 17. All the Sirach cases except the last (δίκαιος) are rendered in Greek by εὐσεβής.

[4] Charles, *APOT*, 1.

[5] Professor C. F. D. Moule has suggested to me privately that as a monastic group, eschewing private property, having a common life which would render 'charity' unnecessary within the sect, and having small concern with the material welfare of outsiders, the covenanters would have little scope for almsgiving.

There is one purely forensic case, 1QH 12. 19: ואין צדיק עמכה 'Before Thee no man is just' (Vermès). This is forensic enough, but what makes it so is not really the adjective, but 'before Thee'. This meaning thus occurs only when given a clearly forensic qualifier.

The Title 'Teacher of Righteousness'

It is worth noting that the distribution of the title in the Scrolls is not as wide as might be supposed. It is found mainly in two books only, the Habakkuk Commentary and the Damascus Document. A good deal of attention has been given to identifying the Teacher and discussing the sort of figure he was, but not so much to determining what the title originally meant.[1] No doubt it came to be used unreflectively, so that we cannot use it in our analysis without great caution, but some meaning must have attached to it, which at the beginning was quite precise.

It occurs 10 times, in CD 1. 11; 20. 32; 1QpHab 1. 13; 2. 2; 5. 10; 7. 4; 8. 3; 9. 10; 11. 15; 1QpMic 2. 5. A few more may possibly be added: 4QPs37 2. 15, supplying צדק to fill the lacuna after מורה ה; in CD 20. 28 'of righteousness' is probably to be understood after 'Teacher', and in 1QpHab 5. 9 'the righteous one' is probably the Teacher. Further, there are two other expressions, each occurring once, which are related to it: 'He who teaches righteousness' in CD 6. 11 (יורה הצדק), and 'Messiah of righteousness' in 4QPatriarchalBless. 3 (משיח הצדק).

Three main explanations are given of the title's meaning. First, 'the right teacher', i.e. the orthodox one, as against other, heterodox ones.[2] Second, 'the legitimate teacher', this differing from the first in a greater stress on his status, not just his function.[3] Third, 'the one who teaches righteousness', i.e. making the genitive objective.[4] The last seems to have the strongest claim for

[1] See however G. Jeremias, *Der Lehrer der Gerechtigkeit* (Göttingen, 1963), Ch. 7, for a thorough treatment. J. Weingreen, 'The Title Moreh Sedek', *JSS*, 6 (1961), 162–74, argues not only that צדק is adjectival, and means 'true, rightful', but that מורה does not mean 'teacher', and refers rather to the exercise of juridical and political authority. We proceed on the assumption that both words may reasonably have their usual force.

[2] So Gaster, *Scriptures*, 15, 309.

[3] E.g. Milik, *Ten Years*, 76; M. Black, *The Scrolls and Christian Origins* (London, 1961), 20.

[4] Cf. G. Jeremias, *Der Lehrer*, especially 312f.

several reasons. In the first place, CD 6. 11 ('he who teaches righteousness') supports this meaning. Again, both the first two suggestions, if taken strictly, imply a 'norm' conception of righteousness, which we have not found at all a common meaning except in certain OT places where it refers to weights and measures. Thus while it is not impossible here, it is not very likely either. Thirdly, the root has in the Scrolls generally, strong covenantal associations, and we must at least allow for the possibility that it retains these when it occurs in the title.

Of course, if we follow this 'covenantal' line, and say that the title refers to the one who teaches the truths, secrets, and law of the covenant, we imply that he is also the 'right' teacher.[1] One argument used in favour of 'legitimate teacher' is the clear parallel in 4QPatriarchalBless. 3 in the expression 'Messiah of righteousness'. Now this must include the notion of true as against false Messiah,[2] but is that all? Although the text is mutilated at this point, and certainty is impossible, we may notice that the phrase is in a strongly covenantal context, so that to render 'rightful Messiah' may miss a good deal.

There is some evidence that 'Teacher of Righteousness' does mean 'covenant-teacher', which would include the idea of teaching covenant behaviour, in the Habakkuk Commentary. There, the task of the Teacher is to 'proclaim the new covenant and to interpret the words of God's servants the prophets'.[3] It comes out most clearly in 1QpHab. 1. 1 – 2. 10 and 6. 12 – 8. 3. In CD 6. 11, again, 'he who teaches righteousness' means something like 'he who teaches how to live by the law and covenant', for part of the teaching is the settling of all problems of law. Further, if M. Philonenko is correct[4] in identifying the Teacher with the 'righteous man' of Wisd. 2. 12–20 and 5. 1–7, and if our

[1] Thus Jeremias, *Der Lehrer*, 315.

[2] So F. F. Bruce, *Biblical Exegesis in the Qumran Texts* (Grand Rapids, Mich., 1959), 47.

[3] M. Burrows, J. C. Trever, and W. K. Brownlee, *The Dead Sea Scrolls of St Mark's Monastery*, 1: *The Isaiah MS and the Habakkuk Commentary* (New Haven, 1950), xix.

[4] 'Le Maître de Justice et la Sagesse de Salomon', *ThZ*, 14 (1958), 81–8. He thinks that 'the sun of righteousness' of Wisd. 5. 6*b* refers to the Teacher, who is both 'L'Illuminé' (1QH 4. 6) and 'L'Illuminateur' (1QH 4. 27). Is this, perhaps, to say he is both righteous Teacher and Teacher of covenant-righteousness?

classification of these instances is correct (see above p. 82, n. 1), our position is somewhat strengthened, for these are 'covenant' instances. The Teacher, as we should expect, is in opposition to wicked men who do not recognise the covenant.[1] However, the division is not only political or sectarian, it is also ethical, cf. CD 6. 2–11. This interpretation is similar to that of G. Jeremias, who sees *ts-d-q* as a sort of code-word for the total life of the community under God.[2] If this is correct, it means that the title instances really belong to the 'covenant-keeping' category.

Summary of Analysis

For the verb, the number of cases is too small for any generalisation, but the qal does seem to show a striking departure from the forensic pattern we now expect.

Of 109 cases of the nouns and adjective (i.e. omitting those in the title 'Teacher of Righteousness'), 46 refer to God. Of these, 14, all *tsedeq*, are legal activity (i.e. 30.4 per cent). There are no purely forensic cases. This legal use is a characteristic of *tsedeq*: it is used of God 23 times, and 14 of these are legal. In general, however, the root is strongly covenantal, for all the other cases fall into one of the two covenantal categories, i.e. 32 out of 46, or 69.6 per cent.

Of the 63 which are used of man, only 5 (including the one forensic case) are legal, i.e. 7.9 per cent. The largest category is the covenantal one, which accounts for 30 out of 63 cases, or 47.6 per cent. If we were to include the cases from the title, the figure would be higher. As in the case of God's righteousness, all the 'legal activity' instances are of *tsedeq*, but these (4) are only 13.8 per cent of the total of 29 cases of *tsedeq* used of man.

We may conclude this section with a few summary comments:

1. As in the Greek books, the 'covenantal' use is strongly represented, for God as much as for man.

2. If anything, the forensic (i.e. purely forensic) use is falling away, as even the verb in the qal has moved towards ethical meanings.

3. Although there remains in the nouns and adjective a wide

[1] Cf. Enoch as 'scribe of righteousness', 1 En. 12. 4.

[2] *Der Lehrer*, 310f. He is less convincing when he relates the title particularly to the teaching of esoteric truth; no doubt the Teacher did this, but it is unlikely to be the main import of צדק.

spectrum of use, yet specifically in the use of *tsedeq* there is a strong tendency towards employment in legal contexts when applied to God, though not when applied to man.

4. It is remarkable that all cases of man's righteousness are in some sort of relation to God.

INTERTESTAMENTAL WRITINGS – TEACHING

We do not know the extent of Paul's knowledge of these books. The date of many is uncertain, and, at least in their present form, some may be post-Pauline. We know too little about their dissemination and popularity to talk about their influence on the Apostle, although it may plausibly be maintained that he knew and used the book of Wisdom.[1] Our concern is not with direct influence; we are rather trying to lift a finger to the wind, to discover where both linguistic usage and theological understanding were heading.

Judicial Righteousness

We may begin with the tendency for God's righteousness to be judicial, but for man's not to be. Bousset long ago said that in late Judaism righteousness had become largely judicial and distributive, as against its tendency in the later OT period to be synonymous with 'graciousness', 'salvation', at least when used of God.[2] This view, however, must be corrected in two ways. First, the legal and even distributive meaning did not disappear from the OT. Second, it is too simple to say that in late Judaism righteousness in effect becomes justice. In the Greek books it is more true of God's than of man's righteousness: for the noun, 42.86 per cent in the case of God's righteousness, and 3.6 per cent in the case of man's; for the adjective, 83.3 per cent for God's, and 17 per cent for man's (including 'things'). In the Hebrew books the divergence is not so great: 30.4 per cent are legal in the case of God's righteousness – this is for both nouns and adjective together – and 7.9 per cent in the case of man's. Thus there is a

[1] Cf. Metzger, *Introduction to the Apocrypha*, 158–73; L. H. Brockington, *A Critical Introduction to the Apocrypha* (London, 1961), 61; Sanday–Headlam, *Romans*, 51f.

[2] W. Bousset, *Die Religion des Judentums* (2nd edn, Berlin, 1906), 437, 441.

tendency for both Greek and Hebrew word-groups to be much more often judicial when used of God than when used of man. Yet this must not obscure other facts, especially that we find the same varieties of meaning as in the OT. One cannot point a finger at any one thing as *the* meaning of righteousness.

Covenant-Keeping Righteousness

The increased emergence of this category has already been noted. It is present of course in the OT, but not so strongly. The 'righteous' are the sharers in the covenant, the right worshippers, those who live rightly, who are in (covenantal) relation to God, and therein obey his Law. Thus it is notable that in Wisd. 10. 4–20 the opposite of δίκαιος is ἀσεβής.[1]

The many-sidedness of this righteousness is illustrated in II (IV) Esdr. 3. 26–36, where the wicked are those who act wickedly, and who are also outside the covenant, and oppress the godly. In 7. 17f the *iusti* are those who are in relationship to God, and who are the opposite of the ungodly and evil-doers. The wicked (*impii*) are anti-God, anti-covenant, and anti-commandments (7. 22–4), but the righteous keep the commandments (7. 45, 51). The righteous in fact are those *qui vias servaverunt Altissimi* (7. 88). It seems to be taken for granted that the Law was offered to all mankind, but that only Israel accepted it, so that 'the lesser breeds without the law' are where they are culpably and by their own choice.[2] The righteous in I Enoch are thus the elect, and the Coming One is the righteous and elect One par excellence, I En. 38. 1–6; 46. 3; 47; 48; 94–105, etc. Nevertheless it is not just a matter of election, for righteousness is also obedience to the Law (I En. 93. 4; 99. 2). The stress on Law-obedience does not exclude the behaviour-in-relationship idea, for the commandments themselves aim at right relations

[1] Cf. Wisd. 3. 10; 4. 16. We have noted that in Sirach *tsaddiq* is regularly rendered by εὐσεβής. It is in line with this strong covenant emphasis that in Or. Man. 1, 8 and in Ep. Jer. 72 righteousness is set over against idolatry, and also that in Susanna 3 and TGad 3. 2 and elsewhere there is a strong emphasis on law-obedience. Cf. S–B, I, 250f, III, 164, 277. On the importance of the covenant in this period, R. Marcus, *Law in the Apocrypha* (New York, 1927), 11–14.

[2] Cf. G. H. Box, *The Ezra-Apocalypse* (London, 1912), 18.

between men,[1] and in any case are themselves an aspect of the covenant.

When 'righteous' becomes a party label, therefore, it is important to note that the two groups were differentiated both religiously and ethically, with the matter of law-obedience always in the background.[2] It is congruous with this that Noah is sometimes referred to as 'that righteous man', cf. Sir. 44. 17; Wisd. 10. 4. In part at least, it was probably due to this consciousness of themselves, either nationally or as a remnant, as the righteous, God's people, that the problem of divine justice became acute, especially in what has been called 'the literature of despair'.[3] Why did God not save them and punish their enemies? This problem partly explains the judicial tendency in the use of 'righteousness' referring to God, for when the nation's (or the sect's) salvation and vindication are in mind, so also is punitive justice against the ungodly oppressors. The judicial emphasis thus goes hand in hand with the covenantal, saving one, cf. 1QS 10. 23; 2 Macc. 1. 24f.

The men of Qumran were of course particularly aware of themselves as the righteous elect. This is most evident in the War Scroll (cf. 4. 6; 17. 8; 18. 8), but not only there (cf. 1QS 4. 5f; 1QH 7. 29f; 1QpHab 7. 10–12).[4] In the War Scroll the themes are salvation, covenant, and victory over enemies, and the terms 'righteous' and 'righteousness' are in this context. Yet 'righteous' is still an ethical, as well as an election term. The righteous are righteous because they keep God's ordinances, do his will, walk in his way.[5] Certainly, their election was apparently seen as

[1] Cf. Sir. 19. 20–4; TIss. 5. 1f; TDan 5. 1–3; TAsh. 6. 1–6; TBenj. 10. 3; Arist. 169. Also, Marcus, *Law in the Apocrypha*, 54.

[2] Cf. Gray in Charles, *APOT*, II, 628ff, and the many references there given from Pss. Sol.; Hughes, *Ethics*, 80; Ryle and James, *Psalms of the Pharisees*, xlvii–xlix. Cf. also Esth. 1. 1f (11. 7ff) where, according to Gregg in Charles, *APOT*, I, 672, 'righteous' is a 'conventional epithet for the people of God'.

[3] J. J. Lewis, 'The Ethics of Judaism in the Hellenistic Period', unpublished thesis (University of London, 1958), 318. He uses the phrase of Ass. Mos., Apoc. Abr., Life of Adam and Eve, Mart. Isa., Sib. Or. 4, II (IV) Esdr., 2 and 3 Bar.

[4] See also L. Mowry, *The Dead Sea Scrolls and the Early Church* (Chicago, 1962), 45–52.

[5] Cf. K. G. Kuhn in K. Stendahl, ed., *The Scrolls and the New Testament* (New York, 1957), 104.

stronger than any individual moral failure (1QH 7. 14–20), but one cannot sharply distinguish between ethical, liturgical, and electional elements.

Righteousness and Eschatological Figures

Like Qumran's Teacher of Righteousness, both the Son of Man and the Messiah have a special connection with righteousness. In each case, the title's bearer is sent by God, and God establishes both his mission and his character. As for the Teacher, so for the other figures, the agent of God is both righteous himself, and teaches, maintains, or establishes righteousness on earth. Thus in 1 Enoch there is a close connection between the elect and righteous ones, and the coming Elect and Righteous One.[1] Because he is at once agent and representative of God's righteousness, and the chief representative and champion of the righteous elect on earth, the coming One links God's righteousness to man's, in vindication, in salvation, and in establishing righteousness on earth.[2] Therefore, in these figures several things are held together inseparably: God's judicial righteousness in judgment and vindication; his saving righteousness; his faithfulness to the covenant; and his establishment of righteousness in the sense of good government and a good life.[3]

Forensic Righteousness

The almost complete absence of this category is striking, apart from the verb, of course. The stress on covenant righteousness does indeed involve a heavy stress on relation to God, though this does not make the words purely relational. Indeed, Sir. 35. 6 (7) suggests that it is on the basis of being δίκαιος that something

[1] Cf. 1 En. 38. 1–6; 39. 6; 46. 3; 47; 48 ('the Son of man is the support of the righteous'); 49. 1; 53. 6 (he is the righteous and elect One who vindicates the righteous and elect, cf. 61; 62; 71. 17). Also Mowinckel, *He That Cometh*, 292, on the titles for Messiah in the Targums, including 'the anointed one of righteousness'. This 'includes the idea that he will establish "righteousness", i.e. salvation and right order in religion and morals, and that he himself is therefore righteous'.

[2] 1 En. 38. 2f; 39. 5f; 46. 3; 47. 4; 49. 2; 53. 7; 58. 5; 62. 2f, 12; 71. 16, etc. Cf. TNaph. 4. 5; TLev. 8; Pss. Sol. 17. 41 (36); 18. 8 (7).

[3] Cf. Mowinckel, *He That Cometh*, 308f, 317f, 359, 366, 377ff, 383f.

becomes δεκτός, acceptable. Righteousness is still the manner of one's life, one's existence in relation to God, man, or society.

God Establishes Man's Righteousness

This idea appears often: in 1 En. 48. 7, the works of the righteous are done in dependence upon God; in Arist. 231 it is 'the gift of God to be able to do good actions'; and in 1 Bar. 5. 2, 4, 9, God's righteousness seems to be regarded as the source of man's. Thus

> v. 2 Put on the robe of the righteousness from God;
> v. 4 For your name will for ever be called by God, 'Peace of righteousness and glory of godliness'.
> v. 9 For God will lead Israel with joy...with the mercy and righteousness that come from him (RSV).

We have already referred to TDan 6. 10 (pp. 75f above) which is very likely to mean that God in his righteousness establishes man's righteousness, i.e. right living. Other places where this general notion may be found are: 1 En. 38. 2; Arist. 280, where 'crown of righteousness' probably has this meaning, also 226, 238, 248, 292; Apoc. Mos. 20. 1, where Eve was stripped of the righteousness with which she had been clothed.

The connection of wisdom with righteousness is of special interest, partly because Paul may have been influenced by some of the wisdom literature, and also because of the linking of Christ, wisdom, and righteousness in 1 Cor. 1. 30. In Sir. 45. 26, Simon's righteousness in governing comes from his wisdom, and his wisdom comes from God. In the poem on wisdom as God's special gift to Israel in 1 Bar. 3. 9 – 4. 4, 'righteousness' does not occur, but law-obedience does, 4. 1. Wisdom, as well as being identified with the Spirit of God (Wisd. 1. 7; 12. 1), with the Torah (Sir. 24. 23f; 1 Bar. 3. 36; 4. 1), or as the agent in creation (Wisd. 7. 22; 9. 9; cf. Sir. 24. 3f; 42. 21; 1 Bar. 3. 32–5; Job 28. 12–28), is also the standard and power of righteous living (Wisd. 6. 12–21; 7. 14; 1 Bar. 3. 14f). In Wisd. 8. 7, wisdom is praised as the teacher of the four cardinal virtues, and in 9. 3 God rules the world by wisdom 'in righteousness', while in 10. 4–6, 10, 13, 20, wisdom is the support, guide, and protector of the righteous.

In the Qumran Scrolls also we find God as the source of man's righteousness. Perhaps the clearest case is 1QS 10. 11:

> I will say to God, 'My righteousness' (צדקי), and 'Author of my goodness' to the Most High (Vermès).

Although there are many parallels for such a phrase's meaning 'my salvation, vindication',[1] the second half of the quotation makes it more likely that ethical righteousness from God is intended. This is confirmed by what follows: '"Fountain of knowledge" and "Source of holiness"' (Vermès). Another probable case is in the rather mutilated 1QBlessings 5. 26,[2] and 1QS 11. 6 is in its context almost certainly to be taken in the same way – God is a fountain of righteousness for the elect. In 11. 5 the word certainly means 'salvation' or 'vindication', but it need not have the same meaning in 11. 6. Even more likely is 1QS 11. 16, where 'establish all his deeds in righteousness' leads to a standing before God, but is not itself that standing. Further possible cases are the qal instances, 1QH 13. 17; 16. 11; also 1QH 4. 30f, and perhaps the places where righteousness is a power as well as what one does, especially 1QTriumph of Righteousness 1. 5, 6.

Justification

In the Greek books, justification by works of the Law is firmly stressed. Man will be acquitted at the Judgment if he has enough good works to outweigh his sins.[3] There is considerable optimism about the possibility of this in 2 Baruch 2. 2; 14. 7; 14. 12; 51. 3, 7; 63. 3, 5; 67. 6; 85. 2. Just as Abraham was justified by works (2 Bar. 57. 2; 58. 1), so also will Israel be justified, if she obeys the Law which she has received from God (2 Bar. 48. 22, 24). There is indeed a quantitative approach to works of the Law, involving treasuries of good works, which is difficult to reconcile with any view of justification or righteousness as moment by moment.[4]

[1] Cf. Leaney, *Rule of Qumran*, 246.

[2] So A. Cronbach, 'Righteousness in Jewish Literature, 200 BC – AD 100', *IDB*, IV, 85–91, at 87.

[3] Cf. S–B, I, 250; Hughes, *Ethics*, 55, 76, 80, 106, 130–43.

[4] 2 Bar. 14. 12; TLev. 13. 5; TNaph. 8. 5 (with a stress on motives as well as acts); TAsh. 2. 1–10; TGad 5. 3; II (IV) Esdr. 7. 77; 8. 33, 36; Pss. Sol. 9. 6, and other places. This is orthodox Pharisaism, cf. Charles, *APOT*, II, 478. In 1 En. 63 past unrighteousness *cannot* be obliterated by present *penitence*.

Within the literature the question arises whether, if this be the way of atonement, atonement is ever possible. Thus although the doctrine is widely taught in the literature,[1] it is in II (IV) Esdras that the problem arises. There 'Ezra' has a dialogue with God, in which he pleads for the divine compassion on those who have no wealth of good works, for as things are, few indeed may be saved (II (IV) Esdr. 7. 46ff, 65–9, 119–26; 8. 3; 9. 14f). Could not God therefore show mercy (8. 31–6)? Moreover, because of the evil seed, sinners could scarcely help sinning, so why should they be punished (3. 20ff; 4. 13–25)? But 'Ezra' gets no answer that satisfies him. In the Judgment everyone must bear his own righteousness or unrighteousness (7. 102–15), and while he may then be saved by his works *or* his faith, faith seems to be not (Pauline) saving faith, but rather fidelity to OT religion and law,[2] i.e. faithfulness in general as against fulfilment of particulars. Possibly underlying this rigorous view is the notion that the Law was offered to all men, but that Israel alone accepted it, with the consequence that those who do not fulfil it deserve no mercy.[3]

We have already referred to the doctrine of treasuries of merits upon which one may draw in the Judgment (p. 99 above). According to one line of teaching, these merits could be transferred, cf. 2 Bar. 2. 2:

> For your works are to this city as a firm pillar

though, as often in the doctrine, the reference is not to a final judgment, but to a present crisis. In 2 Bar. 14. 7; 84. 10, the people may be forgiven because of the works of others, and the latter passage explicitly refers to the merits of the fathers.[4] However, in I Bar. 2. 19, the doctrine appears to be repudiated.

In general then, the picture is of a rather uncompromising *iustitia ex lege* (an expression which usually refers to justification;

[1] A particular twist is found in Tobit and Sirach, where almsgiving leads to justification, cf. Tob. 4. 10f; 12. 8f; Sir. 3. 30; 12. 3–7; 17. 22; 29. 11–13; 40. 24; also TZeb. 5. 2.

[2] II (IV) Esdr. 9. 7, cf. 6. 5, *qui fide thesaurizaverunt*, and Box in Charles, *APOT*, II, 574, n. 5. However, Hughes, *Ethics*, 132, sees faith here as more than this.

[3] Cf. Box, *Ezra-Apocalypse*, 18, and Schechter there cited.

[4] On the merits of the fathers, see S–B, IV, 1, 5f; Marcus, *Law in the Apocrypha*, 14ff; W. D. Davies, *Paul and Rabbinic Judaism*, 269, 366; also our treatment of the Rabbis, below.

but for a Jew it is also true that righteousness consisted *in* law-obedience, e.g. TDan 6, 2 Bar. 67. 6).

A slightly different picture is presented in the Dead Sea Scrolls. The pessimistic view of II (IV) Esdras appears to be echoed in 1QH 4. 30f,[1] which in its emphasis that righteousness 'is not of man' reminds us of Rom. 3. 10, 20, and Gal. 2. 16.[2] However this passage does not say that God's righteousness is imputed to sinful men, nor anything like it. It simply says that though man is not righteous, God is, and if man is to become righteous it must be through God's creative action. We have no reason to take all this other than ethically. More relevant is 1QS 11. 3, 5, where God's righteousness wipes out man's transgression (11. 3), and effects his justification (11. 5); 'righteousness' is צדקה, and 'justification' is משפט. God's righteousness and his mercy are one, cf. also 1QS 11. 12, 14; 1QH 7. 16f, 32. This teaching and its similarity to that of Paul has often been noticed.[3] However, the parallel has not gone unchallenged. J. Jeremias has argued that the rendering of *mishpat* as equivalent to 'justification' is inadmissible, and that it refers rather to God's gracious decision to allow the suppliant to 'approach', i.e. to enter the community, and find therein the life of righteousness.[4] This, he argues, is not justification of the ungodly, but permission to enter the community and walk in the path of true obedience to the Torah. On this path he may stumble, but if he does, he will be forgiven and helped to rise and walk again, if he sincerely wants to. In other words, it is about election more than justification.

This may all be true, yet it does not remove all parallel, for even if it is about entry into the community and not into final blessedness, these two were not regarded as absolutely unrelated.

[1] 'Righteousness, I know, is not of man, nor is perfection of way of the son of man; to the Most High belong all righteous deeds. The way of man is not established except by the spirit which God created for him...' (Vermès). Cf. 1QH 1. 27.

[2] Cf. M. Burrows, *The Dead Sea Scrolls* (London, 1956), 334f.

[3] E.g. by Burrows, *Dead Sea Scrolls*, 334; W. D. Davies in Stendahl, *Scrolls and NT*, 180f; S. Schulz, 'Zur Rechtfertigung aus Gnaden in Qumran und bei Paulus', *ZThK*, 56 (1959), 155–85; Black, *Scrolls and Christian Origins*, 125f; W. Grundmann, 'Der Lehrer der Gerechtigkeit von Qumran und die Frage nach der Glaubensgerechtigkeit in der Theologie des Apostels Paulus', *RQ*, 2 (1959–60), 237–59.

[4] *Central Message of the NT*, 66–8.

Moreover, the basic principle still holds: man is accepted not by what he has done, but by the mercy and righteousness of God. Jeremias's warning is salutary, and we must not read too much into the parallel, but when he argues that nowhere else in Judaism do שפט and משפט refer to the *iustificatio impii*, he rather misses his opponents' point, which is not that they commonly do, but that, exceptionally, they do here.[1] Other passages contain the notion of man's lack of righteousness before God (1QH 7. 17, 28; probably also 4. 33f) and of God's righteousness in contrast (1QH 17. 20), and it is likely that the problem of justification is formulated also in 1QH 1. 23–6; 4. 29; 12. 27.[2]

Justification and Righteousness in 1QS 11

We have already noticed that in the Scrolls, God's righteousness may bring about man's also. It is of very great importance that in this justification passage, 1QS 11, we find God's righteousness effecting both man's forensic salvation, whether or not in a narrow, sectarian, and predestinarian fashion, and also his moral renewal. M. Burrows says that as for Paul, for whom salvation included power over sin as well as justification, so here in 11. 13ff 'we seem to have not only justification but sanctification'.[3] As we have seen, in 11. 3, 5, 12, 14, God's righteousness mercifully justifies. Yet in 11. 16 it is highly probable that 'Establish all his deeds in righteousness' (Vermès) has nothing to do with justification, at least not directly, but refers to renewal of moral life. Again, in 11. 14*a*, God's righteousness pardons; in 11. 14*b*–15 it cleanses from sin and uncleanness. Thus in 11. 12–17 we have these two strands side by side, but the final goal is perhaps expressed in 11. 17: the purpose of the whole operation is

[1] In effect, this use of משפט is like that of δικαίωμα in Rom. 5. 16. S. E. Johnson, 'Paul and the Manual of Discipline', *HTR*, 48 (1955), 157–65, especially 161–3, acknowledges unusual features, but still thinks that here God's righteousness saves sinners in the sense of forgiving them. He is less convincing when he contends that justification is vindication of the sinner against the sin which is his forensic opponent – was sin thought of thus?

[2] See also Grundmann, 'Der Lehrer', 239; Schulz, 'Rechtfertigung', 164f. On the differences from Paul, as well as Grundmann and Schulz, G. Klein, 'Rechtfertigung', [3]*RGG*, v, cols 825–8, especially 826. Differences do exist, but it would not be calamitous if they did not.

[3] *Dead Sea Scrolls*, 334f; cf. Black, *Scrolls and Christian Origins*, 126.

forensic, that man may 'stand before Thee for ever' (Vermès). It seems, then, that God not only forgives man that he may stand in the Judgment, but he also makes him righteous for the same end.

APPENDED NOTE 4

Justification by Faith in the Teacher of Righteousness?

In 1QpHab 8. 1–3, in the comment on Hab. 2. 4, stands the statement:

> This concerns all those who observe the Law in the House of Judah, whom God will deliver from the House of Judgment because of their suffering and because of their faith in the Teacher of Righteousness (Vermès).

The question is whether, with A. Dupont-Sommer,[1] the phrase ואמנתם במורה הצדק should be rendered 'faith in the Teacher of Righteousness', or 'fidelity to the Teacher of Righteousness'.[2] It could even mean 'faithfully following the Torah as interpreted by the Teacher'.[3] In the end, before we can determine the place of the Teacher in relation to the sect's faith, we must know what is meant by 'faith' in this passage. O. Cullmann says that here it has 'nothing of the sense of opposition to the works of the Law',[4] while Burrows sees three elements: fidelity to, confidence in, and belief about, the Teacher.[5] These could be parts of the whole, or they could be alternatives. The position is unsatisfactory, but as we cannot on our present evidence assign a redemptive role to the Teacher, faith in him must be considered different from Pauline saving faith in Jesus.

APPENDED NOTE 5

Genesis 15. 6 in Later Judaism

Abraham is seen as the perfectly righteous one, whose conduct was righteous and therefore pleasing to God, cf. Jub. 23. 10;

[1] *The Jewish Sect of Qumran and the Essenes*, E.Tr. (London, 1954), 55f.
[2] Johnson, 'Paul and the Manual of Discipline', 165.
[3] J. Jeremias, *Central Message of the NT*, 68.
[4] In Stendahl, *Scrolls and NT*, 23.
[5] *Dead Sea Scrolls*, 335.

Or. Man. 8; also 2 Bar. 57. 2; 58. 1, for the patriarchs as keeping the Law by anticipation. In 1 Macc. 2. 52, 'Was not Abraham found faithful when tested, and it was reckoned to him as righteousness', the latter part of Gen. 15. 6 has become attached to the event of Gen. 22. 15–18, so that it is faithfulness in the matter of offering up Isaac which is the ground of his righteousness. Thus, his faith is naturally reckoned as righteousness, for this is what it really is, viz. obedience to God's will.[1]

[1] Cf. S–B, III, 186, 204f.

CHAPTER 5

LATER JUDAISM III: PHILO AND JOSEPHUS

PHILO

About 114 instances of the noun, and 245 of the adjective and adverb, have been examined.[1] The results are such that it would be wearisome and space-consuming to list and classify them all. In the Greek tradition, the noun is either generic virtue, or one of the cardinal virtues, or sometimes, the queen of those virtues. As a virtue, it is concerned with the relations between men, and societies, and with the quality of soul out of which proper relations spring. Much the same is true of the adjective, except that it, and even more the adverb, may be used in a rather neutral manner akin to the English 'he rightly decided to go...', where to speak of a virtue is somewhat stretching the point.

One interesting fact is that the words are rarely used of God, the noun only 3 times out of 114,[2] and the adjective only 7 times out of 245 (adjective and adverb together).[3]

There is a striking absence of forensic cases, the nearest being *Flacc.* 50 where the adjective means 'deserving'. Otherwise the emphasis is heavily ethical, though often abstract. Between one-fourth and one-third of the cases of man's righteousness carry an explicit reference to God, but these figures are of small value, because in the kind of extended treatment which one finds in Philo, such a reference may very well be implicit at least as often as it is explicit. In this, Philo shows himself more Hebrew than Greek.

[1] Leisegang's Index was used: L. Cohn and P. Wendland, *Philo Judaeus, Opera* (Berlin, 1896–1915), Indices by J. Leisegang (Berlin, 1926–30). This is not entirely reliable, and it does not list δικαιοῦν at all. On its limitations, see E. R. Goodenough, *Introduction to Philo Judaeus* (Oxford, 1962), 161. Abbreviations are those of F. H. Colson and G. H. Whitaker, *Philo*, Loeb (London, 1929–65), x, xxxvf.

[2] *Quod Deus* 79; *Mos.* II 237; *Spec. Leg.* I 277.

[3] *Ebr.* 111; *Quis Her.* 163 (φιλοδίκαιος); *Somn.* II 194; *Mos.* II 100 (adverb), 279; *Spec. Leg.* II 27, 139.

Apart from compound verbal forms,[1] the verb is used much as in secular Greek, to mean 'pronounce something right' (used of the divine ordinance in the Law),[2] or 'hold something to be right'.[3] Applied to persons, it is used for doing justice or passing sentence.[4]

The Nature of Righteousness, or Justice

The classification of virtues in Philo is complex and beyond our present scope,[5] and it is often hard to tell when δικαιοσύνη is one of the cardinal virtues, when the queen of those virtues, and when it is virtue itself.[6] To be sure, it usually means the right ordering of human relations, and the quality of soul in a man or a society which produces these.[7] It is that part of a man's duty which lies towards his fellows and his society, complementing piety (ὁσιότης), holiness (εὐσέβεια), and godliness (θεοσέβεια), which are his duty towards God. Indeed, it is notable that Philo often adds one of these as a fifth cardinal virtue, and generally there is a tendency for 'justice' to be juxtaposed to one of them, to comprehend the whole duty of man.[8] Naturally, justice also often occurs in especially legal settings, and there are 37 neuter

[1] δικαιολογοῦν meaning 'plead a case' in *Leg.* 290; δικαιονομοῦν 'to judge' in *Leg. All.* III 197; δικαιοπραγοῦν 'to act rightly' in *Agr.* 123; *Ebr.* 26; *Congr.* 6, 163; *Fug.* 35.

[2] *Spec. Leg.* I 67, 109, 140; II 72, 113; III 172, 180.

[3] *Abr.* 171; *Mos.* I 44; *Migr.* 73; *Ebr.* 51; *Quod Deus* 159; so 'decide to do something', *Abr.* 142; *Quod Deus* 9, and, 'require something as right', *Mut.* 19.

[4] *Ebr.* 95. The cases cited in this and the two previous notes are from Schrenk, 'δικαιόω' in *TWNT*, II, 215, but his classification has not been followed exactly.

[5] See E. Bréhier, *Les Idées philosophiques et religieuses de Philon d'Alexandrie* (2nd edn, Paris, 1925), 250–310; H. A. Wolfson, *Philo* (2 vols., Cambridge, Mass., 1947), II, 202–8.

[6] See Goodenough, *Introduction*, 119f; Wolfson, *Philo*, II, 220.

[7] Cf. Goodenough, *Introduction*, 119.

[8] The juxtaposition with ὁσιότης is seen in *Abr.* 208; *Mos.* II 108; *Spec. Leg.* I 304; II 12, 63, 180, etc. That with εὐσέβεια in *Cher.* 96; *Det.* 73; *Virt.* 175; *Praem.* 160, 162, and elsewhere. That with θεοσέβεια is seen in *Spec. Leg.* IV 134, 170. For holiness as a fifth virtue, and sometimes their queen, ὁσιότης: *Dec.* 119; *Spec. Leg.* IV 135; εὐσέβεια: *Spec. Leg.* IV 147; *Virt.* 95; *Praem.* 53. Cf. Wolfson, *Philo*, II, 215, also J. Drummond, *Philo Judaeus* (2 vols., London, 1888), II, 316.

cases of the adjective which are 'forensic' in a broad sense, but which never refer to the standing of persons.[1]

God is the source of man's justice, and of his virtue in general. He helps man towards virtue, and so obviously approves it (*Leg. All.* III 27, 28; *Sacr.* 37; *Quod Deus* 118),[2] but there is more to it than this; virtue for Philo is 'primarily an inner state in which one lives guided by and in harmony with God and the Logos'.[3] The divine Wisdom or Logos is the source of man's virtue, which is to say that man's goodness, including his righteousness, comes from God, *Op.* 75, 81; *Leg. All.* I 63, 64, 65; *Post.* 127, 128. Generic virtue, which includes all virtues, is both an imitation of heavenly virtue (*Leg. All.* I 45–52), and also 'created after the analogy of the Logos of God' (*Leg. All.* I 65). Thus virtue is more than man's achievement, it is something God achieves in man, and the Logos is more than a model, more than a teacher, a judge, or even a mediator, he is creator of virtue.

We began by noting that 'justice' for Philo is essentially the social virtue, and the theological connections which we have just discussed must not obscure this. Indeed, it is highly important that δικαιοσύνη occurs from time to time in conjunction with φιλανθρωπία,[4] because this may be analogous to the linking of

[1] Of ordinances: *Migr.* 196; *Quis Her.* 168, 169; *Mut.* 40; *Dec.* 106; *Spec. Leg.* I 102; III 61; *Leg.* 25. Meaning 'rights': *Spec. Leg.* III 27; *Virt.* 124; *Quod Omn. Prob.* 44; *Flacc.* 53; *Leg.* 63, 180, 371, 371. A legal matter: *Post.* 59. Rules of justice: *Spec. Leg.* IV 137, 137, 138, 139, 141, 141. Decisions: *Plant.* 175; *Dec.* 140; *Flacc.* 106, 134. Arguments: *Spec. Leg.* IV 40. Prohibitions: *Spec. Leg.* IV 183. Jurisdiction: *Spec. Leg.* IV 176. Rights of a case: *Agr.* 13. Just claims, or legal pleadings: *Mos.* II 228; *Leg.* 331, 364 (all δικαιολογία), and *Leg.* 363, 366. Rightful: *Leg.* 28.

[2] See further on this Wolfson, *Philo*, II, 165–200; A. Edersheim, 'Philo' in *Dictionary of Christian Biography* (London, 1887), IV, 383, where he discusses the relation of this to election; Bréhier, *Idées*, 228ff; and C. G. Montefiore, 'Florilegium Philonis', *JQR*, 7 (1894–5), 481–545, especially 519ff.

[3] Goodenough, *Introduction*, 119. One cannot here give a survey of the meaning and importance of 'Logos' in Philo, on which the literature is extensive. See, e.g. Wolfson, *Philo*, I, 200–94; C. Bigg, *The Christian Platonists of Alexandria* (2nd edn, Oxford, 1913), 40–6; J. Daniélou, *Philon d'Alexandrie* (Paris, 1958), 153–63.

[4] *Mut.* 225; *Abr.* 232; *Mos.* II 9; *Dec.* 164; *Spec. Leg.* II 63. Cf. also *Mut.* 40; *Mos.* II 228; *Virt.* 51, 52. It is just possible that the two are complementary, so Bigg, *Christian Platonists*, 47f, but a 'benevolent' meaning for δικαιοσύνη is likely, cf. Wolfson, *Philo*, II, 218–20.

the former with ἐλεημοσύνη, and also reflect the tendency for *tsedaqah* to mean 'almsgiving' in Rabbinic writings.

The Question of Justification

Philo takes no apparent interest in any forensic approach to reconciliation with God. His concern with salvation is mystical, and justification is not an issue. Only the merest sketch of this mystical salvation is possible here.[1] His doctrine of redemption is that the soul must first master the body, and then reach up to God ecstatically. One does not, of course, start this in cold blood – conscience and penitence do matter,[2] but they lead to this, not to justification. Underlying the doctrine is a body–soul antagonism:

> Righteousness and every virtue love the soul, unrighteousness and every vice the body, and the things friendly to the one are altogether hostile to the other (*Quis Her.* 243).

Yet it is not quite true to say that for him the body is inherently evil; rather, life dominated by the sensual is bad and irrational, and must be brought under the dominion of the Logos. By asceticism, nature, instruction, renunciation of the sensual, of desire, and of passion, one struggles up to the vision of God, in ecstasy.[3] God's help is essential in all this, but when such a path is followed, then the result is righteousness, or generic virtue. That is, while the ultimate goal is release from the body, the immediate result is the subordination of the lower self to the higher, therefore subordination to the Logos, and so the nourishment of virtue, cf. *Migr.* 9.[4]

The doctrine of the merits of the fathers is changed out of recognition: the patriarchs are saviours in that they have opened

[1] See especially E. R. Goodenough, *By Light, Light* (New Haven, 1935).

[2] Cf. Montefiore, 'Florilegium Philonis', 511ff; Bréhier, *Idées*, 298–307; H. A. A. Kennedy, *Philo's Contribution to Religion* (London, 1919), 106–21.

[3] See *Quis Her.* 64–70; *Migr.* 7; *Cher.* 9. The literature is extensive, but see especially Daniélou, *Philon*, 184–99, Montefiore, 'Florilegium Philonis', 495, 503f, and of course Goodenough, *By Light, Light*.

[4] Cf. W. Fairweather, *Jesus and the Greeks* (Edinburgh, 1924), 192, and Bréhier, *Idées*, 226–37, especially on the nourishment of virtue.

a new and better mystical way of salvation, in pioneering the journey from the material to the immaterial.[1]

Genesis 15. 6 and Abraham's Faith[2]

The faith that was counted to Abraham as righteousness is generally either belief in God as first cause, or trust in God, or both: *Leg. All.* III 228; *Quod Deus* 4; *Mut.* 177, 181f, 186, 218; *Praem.* 27–30. It may be more specifically trust in God's promise (*Migr.* 44; *Quis Her.* 90–5), and frequently it is plain that faith is a virtue, that of trust or credence, which may represent the Godward side of man's duty, as righteousness represents the manward; *Quis Her.* 90–5; *Virt.* 216–18; cf. *Abr.* 270. Usually there is a strong element of distrust in man's own strength, reasonings, and conjectures: *Abr.* 262–74; cf. *Leg. All.* II 89; III 228f; *Quod Deus* 4; *Somn.* I 60. In *Quod Deus* 4 the statement of Gen. 15. 6 is applied to the offering of Isaac, and this is perhaps an application to be understood elsewhere also. As in contemporary Judaism generally, therefore, Gen. 15. 6 is probably understood in such a way that Abraham's faith is a sort of work, a form of righteousness, and indeed in *Quis Her.* 94f faith is justice towards God.

Conclusion

The Hellenism of Philo is modified, in his use of the noun and adjective, by his bringing the virtue firmly into a relation to God as its source and approver. Purely relational cases appear not to occur. We need not exaggerate Philo's importance, but there is some relevance in his attempt to construct a Jewish theology in a Hellenistic framework and in Greek terms.[3]

[1] Cf. W. L. Knox, 'Abraham and the Quest for God', *HTR*, 28 (1935), 55–60; Goodenough, *By Light, Light*, Chs V, VI; *Praem.* 49–51, and Colson's notes thereon, *Philo*, VIII, 453f.

[2] On faith in Philo, see especially Montefiore, 'Florilegium Philonis', 538; Bréhier, *Idées*, 217–25; Wolfson, *Philo*, I, 151f; II, 216ff.

[3] A recent discussion by H. Chadwick, 'St Paul and Philo of Alexandria', *BJRL*, 48 (1965–6), 286–307, argues for a common background, rather than direct dependence.

JOSEPHUS

The majority of the cases examined are without theological content.[1] This is not surprising in view of the nature of much of his writing.

The verb means 'to condemn' 4 times, 'to consider something right' twice, 'to be condemned' (passive) twice, 'to do the right thing' twice. The use is strongly forensic, and 'make righteous' does not occur. Forensic uses are also seen in the compounds δικαιοδοτεῖν (*Ant.* XVI 172), 'to administer justice', and δικαιολογεῖσθαι (6 times), 'plead a case'.

The noun δικαίωσις in *Ant.* XVIII 14, 315, means 'punishment', and the first probably has God as the source of punishment. The noun δικαιοσύνη is listed 28 times. Once it is God's punitive, legal justice, *Ant.* XI 268. Otherwise it is man's righteousness, always ethical, 20 times in relation to God, twice one of the cardinal virtues (*Ant.* VI 160; *Ap.* II 170).

The adjective may mean 'righteous, law-abiding', even 'God-obeying'. All 18 cases listed by Thackeray are ethical, and all but 5 are in relation to God, and 3 are linked with some word meaning 'kind' (*BJ* I 57; *Ant.* X 155, XI 183). It may also mean 'just, fair, reasonable': in none of the 14 cases listed by Thackeray is there explicit reference to God. In 2 further places the meaning is 'true, adequate', and in 31 it is something like 'it is right to...', 'right' varying from the perfunctory to the full sense of justice. Only 5 of these 31 have any explicit relation to God: *Ant.* I 225, III 250, VI 284, VII 332, VIII 223.

The neuter adjective with the article, either singular or plural, occurs 59 times with the meaning 'Justice'. Of these, 11 are in relation to God: *BJ* IV 362; *Ant.* VIII 126, 280, 296, 297; IX 3, 167, 169; XI 294; XV 376; XVIII 18. There are 7 cases where the adjective means 'right', followed by a genitive, and all are clearly forensic; there are also 14 where legal rights or privileges are meant, and 13 where δίκαιος εἶναι is used with a genitive or

[1] A. Schlatter, *Die Theologie des Judentums nach dem Bericht des Josefus* (Gütersloh, 1932), on *Gerechtigkeit*, 159–79, can find little basis for discussing the theological meaning of the word. For examples, we have used H. St J. Thackeray and R. Marcus, *Lexicon to Josephus* (Paris, 1930–55), though this is not exhaustive. These instances are thus only a sample, which one hopes is representative. Their abbreviations are also used.

an infinitive to mean 'deserving of'. Of all these, only one is in relation to God (*Ant.* I 232).

The adverb twice means 'righteously', in an ethical sense, but in relation to God: *Ant.* VI 87; VIII 300. It 46 times means 'justly', 'rightly', 'deservedly', 'justifiably', often quite perfunctorily; 8 of these are in relation to God, and one is used of God.

Conclusion

Both ethical and forensic meanings are found, but the latter never in the sense 'acquitted' or 'acquittal'. Only a minority are in explicit relation to God.[1]

[1] In a full treatment of Josephus, which this is not, one would have to question some of Thackeray's classifications. Here, for its limited importance, the Josephus literature has in the main been taken in accordance with his decisions.

CHAPTER 6

LATER JUDAISM IV: THE RABBINIC WRITINGS

In its recorded form, the language of the Rabbis is of course post-Pauline. It is important, however, partly as an indication of the direction in which usage was going, and partly because some of the discussions certainly go back to the first century. We are on firmer ground when talking about Rabbinic ideas, than when discussing Rabbinic vocabulary. The greatest problem is the sheer vastness of the material; therefore, while an attempt has been made to indicate the range of meanings without pretending to thoroughness, a more exhaustive analysis has been made of two samples: Genesis Rabbah and the Targum Onkelos. The influence of Rabbinic Judaism on St Paul must now surely be regarded as established. C. G. Montefiore's thesis that Paul knew only Dispersion Judaism[1] would be difficult to maintain today,[2] especially if we accept a recent argument that Paul was reared not in cosmopolitan Tarsus, but in Jerusalem itself.[3]

THE ROOT צדק[4]

The Verb

As one would expect, the forensic note dominates. Thus, the qal means 'be righteous', or 'be pronounced righteous', e.g. j. San. 22*b*. The pi'el introduces a note which is to be familiar: it

1 *Judaism and St Paul* (London, 1914), first essay, especially 58ff; similarly in recent times, Schoeps, *Paul*, 25–50.

2 See especially W. D. Davies, *Paul and Rabbinic Judaism*, 1–16; earlier, A. Lukyn Williams, *Talmudic Judaism and Christianity* (London, 1933), 35–43, 55f.

3 W. C. van Unnik, *Tarsus or Jerusalem* (London, 1962). The debate about the kind of Judaism Paul knew is discussed in Longenecker, *Paul, Apostle of Liberty*, 1–6.

4 A considerable debt is owed to M. Jastrow, *A Dictionary of the Targumim, the Talmud Babli and Yerushalmi and the Midrashic Literature* (2 vols., London, 1903), and a lesser one to G. Dalman, *Aramäisch-neuhebräisches Handwörterbuch zu Targum, Talmud, und Midrasch* (Frankfurt, 1922).

may mean 'acquit', 'declare righteous', e.g. Gen. R. XLIX 9, but it may also mean 'treat generously', 'be liberal',[1] e.g. BB 88*b*; Ḥull. 134*a*. For two reasons this is most interesting. First, it perhaps reflects the increasing use of the cognate *tsedaqah* to mean 'benevolence' or even 'almsgiving'. Second, it shows something like a parallel to Paul's apparently absurd expression, 'justify the ungodly'.

The duality in the pi'el is found also in the hiph'il, together with other uses. The meaning 'declare right, justify' is found, e.g. Gen. R. XXI 1; Ber. 19*a*; j. Soṭa 41*b*; and it is made quite clear in 'Er. 19*a* and Midr. Ps. 143. 1 that 'declaring' or 'acknowledging' the rightness of a judgment is always in accordance with the truth.[2] Yet, as in the pi'el, we find a note of graciousness or compassion, cf. Ḥull. 134*a*. The complex nature of Rabbinic usage is seen when we note that in Gen. R. XLIII 6 it means 'make righteous' in an ethical sense, and that it means 'treat with strict justice' when used (Ta'. 8*a*) in the expression הצדיק עליו את הדין. A similar expression in Ta'. 11*a* and Ber. 19*a* means 'acknowledge the justice of the (divine) judgment'. In Gen. R. XCII 9 the hithpa'el means 'justify (or excuse) oneself'. The variety of use is thus very wide, and not always forensic.

The Nouns

In the case of *tsedeq* the meaning remains much as in the OT – cf. Jastrow's listing of 'righteousness, justice, equity, virtue'. A general ethical meaning, in clear relationship to God, appears in Gen. R. XCIV 3, cf. Mak. 24*a*, where perhaps the best rendering is 'loyalty'; cf. also Gen. R. XCIII 9 for a more general meaning, and LXX 13 where 'honesty' is meant. God's righteousness is referred to in Gen. R. VIII 5 and probably in XLIII 3 (we omit discussion of places where the planet Jupiter is referred to). It refers to legal fair dealing in, e.g. San. 7*b*; Shebu. 30*a*. We have an illustration of the way in which different Rabbis could take the same OT instance quite differently, in Ta'. 8*a* on Ps. 85. 11.

[1] Cf. Dalman, 'milde handeln (nicht nach strengem Recht)'.

[2] Cf. S–B, III, 134; C. G. Montefiore and H. Loewe, *A Rabbinic Anthology* (London, 1938), 337f; also the *Zidduk ha-Din* in the Jewish Prayer Book burial service (S. Singer, *The Authorised Daily Prayer Book of the United Hebrew Congregations of the British Empire* (London, 1935), 319).

One takes it to mean 'strict justice', and another as 'working righteousness' acceptably before God, and another as (God's) mercy and benevolence. There is similar variety of interpretation of Lev. 19. 15 in Shebu. 30*a*, where in a legal context the meanings put forward are: 'strict justice', 'being merciful', 'taking the most favourable view possible', 'judging in the scale of merit'. In the use of *tsedeq* there is thus an ambivalence similar to that found in the verb.

The use of *tsedaqah* is most interesting, for as is often remarked upon, the characteristic meaning is 'charity', 'benevolence', or more specifically 'almsgiving'. Jastrow lists the meanings as 'purity, righteousness, equity, liberality, especially almsgiving'; Dalman as 'Milde, Barmherzigkeit, Mildtätigkeit, Almosen'.

God's righteousness is his mercy or love – his forensic mercy in Gen. R. XXXIII 1, cf. San. 105*b*, his graciousness in Gen. R. LXXXII 5. These are the only two places in Gen. R. where God's *tsedaqah* is mentioned, and in view of its tendency elsewhere to mean God's distributive justice, these cases are important as showing that even when used of God, the 'benevolence' meaning persists. Yet in Ab. 5. 18, God's *tsedaqah* means that he gives true, unchanging, reliable justice. A variety of meanings exist, though the first has gained more notice.[1]

Man's righteousness is his benevolence in general and his almsgiving in particular (including other acts of charity).[2] Thus, in Gen. R., apart from the cases of God's righteousness, 3 out of 9 mean 'hospitality' or 'sick-visiting' (XLIX 4; LII 1, 3), perhaps 2 mean 'kindness' (VI 6; XLIV 12), and one means 'almsgiving' XXXIII 3). The two that remain seem to have a more general meaning, but still ethical. If this sample is representative, it is too simple to identify *tsedaqah* with almsgiving or even with benevolence, but the tendency is certainly in this direction. This is not a change of meaning for the noun, for such a note is already found in the OT; besides, the more general ethical meaning still

[1] R. T. Herford, *Christianity in Talmud and Midrash* (London, 1903), 247 and 424, gives an instructive example (Pes. 87*b*) where an OT passage is reinterpreted to give *tsedaqah* a 'benevolent' meaning.

[2] R. Mach, *Der Zaddik in Talmud und Midrasch* (Leiden, 1957), in discussing 'the way to righteousness' sees it as firstly obedience (14–19), and secondly benevolence in action (19–22). His book is a very useful account of how 'the righteous' are thought of in the literature.

persists. So in Gen. R. it may mean the opposite of sin, VIII 5; LXXXVII 5, and possibly in the rather confusing XLIII 3. Nevertheless, throughout the literature the first (benevolence etc.) group of meanings is strongly represented.[1] It may take various forms, e.g. giving alms, BB 10*b*; Ab. 5. 13; or bringing up an orphan in one's own house, Ket. 50*a*; or loving deeds in general, Ḳid. 40*a*. In legal contexts, it is set over against strict justice (דין) to mean 'kindness, compassion', e.g. San. 6*b*:

> Where there is strict justice there is no charity, and where there is charity there is no justice. (Cf. San. 38*b*.)

Yet the variety of meanings remain,[2] but as long as we admit to a somewhat rash generalisation, we may say that *tsedeq* is used more for righteousness in general, and *tsedaqah* more for compassion, kindness, and charity.

More will need to be said about righteousness when we discuss the doctrine of merits, but meanwhile we must note that it is always 'before God'; this does not, of course, mean that it denotes a relationship. On the contrary it denotes activity within a relationship, as in the other literature examined. Here there is perhaps a more uniform stress on it as within the relationship to God, or as approved or demanded by him, and this is so whether we look at 'obedience' (e.g. Gen. R. XLIV 12) or 'benevolence' (e.g. *tsedeq* in Gen. R. XCIV 4) meanings. Perhaps the clearest place where we may see both elements, activity and relationship, is in the attempt to simplify and summarise the Torah in Mak. 24*a*. We begin with Moses and 613 precepts, go on to David and a reduction to 11 principles, all ethical (Ps. 15). Isaiah 33. 15f reduces them to 6, still ethical, and Micah 6. 8 to 3,

[1] Cf. Suk. 49*b*; Ber. 17*b*; Shab. 156*b*; RH 4*a*, 16*b*; Ned. 7*a*; Ḳid. 71*a*, 76*b*; BB 8*b*, 9*a*–*b*, 10*a*–*b*, 11*a*; San. 35*a*; Tos. Peah 4. 19. Cf. also S–B, IV, 1, 536–58, and other references there, also S–B, III, 525 and I, 388 and references. We remember also that LXX can render *tsedaqah* by ἐλεημοσύνη; on this, Hirsch, 'Right and Righteousness', 423; Skinner, 'Righteousness in OT', 281; Bousset, *Die Religion des Judentums*, 437.

[2] Cf. Montefiore and Loewe, *Rabbinic Anthology*, 310f: 'Sometimes it truly means righteousness, sometimes it means justice, sometimes charity, sometimes mere almsgiving. In the...paean on *Ẓeḍakah* it must have now one meaning and now another, and sometimes it is difficult to say which is the exact meaning intended' – this is amply illustrated by the long excerpt from Midr. Prov. XIV, 34 which follows.

which, whatever they meant originally, are taken to be ethical. Isaiah returns with two principles, to keep *Mishpat* and do *Tsedaqah* (the latter possibly to be understood as 'charity'). When Amos reduces the Law to one principle, 'Seek ye me and live' (5. 4), we see how intimately for the Rabbis ethics are bound up with relationship to Yahweh. The point is even clearer after R. Naḥman objects that the last could mean 'Seek me by observing the whole Torah', so that we are back where we started. Therefore lastly we have Habakkuk's one principle (2. 4), 'the righteous shall live by his faith'. Thus we see that the simplification of the Torah amounts to an emphasis on the relationship to God, from which the ethical life is inseparable.

Was righteousness purely external, or were motives and the inner self taken into account? Certainly, as Hirsch maintains,[1] philanthropy and righteousness reflect the inner life of the righteous, cf. Lev. R. XXVII 1; Ḳid. 39*b*, 40*a*, which suggest that intentions and deeds were of almost equal importance, and it has been eloquently shown by T. W. Manson that in at least some Rabbinic thought, motive was of very great moment. Yet, as Montefiore acknowledges, there was an externalist tendency in Rabbinic religion.[2]

The Adjective

In RH 17*b* צדיק referring to God means 'strictly just' in contrast to חסיד. In a more general sense, 'the Righteous of the world' is a Rabbinic synonym for God.[3]

Used of man, it is sometimes forensic, denoting one who has received the verdict from God. As R. Mach shows, this emerges most clearly in Mekh. Ex. 23. 7 where it means 'innocent'.[4] God's verdict is thus on the basis of the facts. This is nothing new, but what is important about this case is that the man may in fact be guilty, but is acquitted because of lack of evidence. Certainly this is in a human tribunal, and such a verdict would be impossible in a divine one, but while the general point is true that a verdict of acquittal is on the basis of the facts, a purely forensic

[1] 'Right and Righteousness', 423, and references there cited.

[2] See T. W. Manson, *Ethics and the Gospel* (London, 1960), 39–42, cf. S–B, IV, 1, 15, 19; Montefiore, *Judaism and St Paul*, 154.

[3] See A. Marmorstein, *The Old Rabbinic Doctrine of God* (2 vols, London, 1927–37), I, 95ff, and examples there given.

[4] *Der Zaddik in Talmud*, 9–13.

use like this can occur. Mach himself, however, observes that it is extremely rare. Normally, God's verdict is an *imprimatur* on an already existing righteousness, i.e. it is because a man is righteous that he is declared so, not vice versa, always remembering, of course, that righteousness is defined by God anyway. This is very clear in Gen. R. II 5; XXXIII 1, 3; C 2. Perhaps a good illustration is Num. R. II 12, where the forensic note is strongly sounded in the expression צדיק לפני, but earlier in the same section the adjective by itself means 'righteous' without the strong forensic connotation of the former. Usually, 'righteous' means obedient to God and his Torah, thus being both ethical and relational.[1] Jastrow lists 'virtuous, just, pious' as the meanings, which is a little to oversimplify, as is Dalman's 'gerecht; fromm'. In Gen. R. for instance, it is often covenantal, referring to the godly, the remnant, the people of God, e.g. XCIV 6; XCIX 9; also XXVIII 5; XLI 1. The description of heroes of the past as righteous perhaps belongs to this category; e.g. Abraham, XLII 8; Sarah, XLV 10; Isaac, LXXIII 8; Jacob, LXXII 3; Joseph, LXXXIV 17; David, XCVII. Sometimes 'righteous' is simply the opposite of 'wicked': Gen. R. XXXII 3; XXXIII 1; XLIX 8; LXXXVII 2; LV 2; LXIII 1; LXVI 4, etc. The double stress on ethical and relational is especially clear at Gen. R. XLI 1 and XXXIX 9, but neither element seems entirely absent anywhere. There is a stress on inward and outward together at XLV 4. As Mach observes,[2] the adjective serves as a more or less general designation of man's moral–religious character, and there are many instances of this in the literature, quite apart from Gen. R.: e.g. AZ 4*a*; Shab. 55*a*; Ta'. 18*b*; Suk. 45*b*; San. 49*a*, 111*a*, *b*; MK 28*a*; BB 75*a*; Ber. 34*b*, 58*b*; Tos. San. 13. 4, 5.

In Ḥag. 9*b* the righteous is defined as 'he that serveth God' and the wicked as 'he that serveth Him not'. This may be meant partly in liturgical terms,[3] i.e. the difference between the perfectly and the not quite perfectly righteous may lie in the recitation of one extra chapter of the Torah. Yet when further explanation of 'righteous' and 'serving God' is given, we find

[1] See Midr. Prov. XIV 34, quoted in Montefiore and Loewe, *Rabbinic Anthology*, 310.

[2] *Der Zaddik in Talmud*, 3, cf. 86–9.

[3] Cf. Montefiore in *Rabbinic Anthology*, xlv, who includes in 'righteous' liturgical as well as ethical behaviour, especially avoidance of idolatry.

ourselves concerned, somewhat obscurely, with financial fair dealing. Ḳid. 40*a* underlines heavily the view that the righteous man is he who is good to heaven, as against the good man, who is good to man, and although in RH 4*a* a man may still be wholly righteous even if his motives in charitableness are ulterior, inward and outward are generally connected. This is so when we consider the definition of the righteous as he who is 'swayed by the *Yetser ha-Tob*' and who abjures 'the evil *Yetser*', e.g. Ber. 61*b*, and cf. Gen. R. XXXIV 10. Indeed, degrees of righteousness correspond to degrees of submission to the good *Yetser*.[1] This does not really contradict righteous as 'obedient to the Torah', for God created the Torah as the antidote to the *Yetser ha-Ra'*, cf. Ḳid. 30*b*; BB 16*a*.[2]

Interesting light is thrown on the righteous as the covenant people by Num. R. VIII 2, where 'wanting to be righteous' means for a Gentile 'wanting to be a proselyte', yet allowance was made for the existence of righteous men among the nations, despite the brutality of the Romans, Tos. San. 13.

In view of all that has been said so far, we cannot accept the view that 'righteous' means 'to have received God's judicial sentence'.[3] There is some truth in it: thus when Ezekiel's definition of 'righteous' (18. 5–9) receives comment in San. 81*a*, R. Gamaliel seems to interpret 'righteous' as 'the one who lives' (although the activity meaning is not absent), and when Targum Onkelos takes 'practised righteousness before God' in Deut. 33. 21 to mean 'did meritorious things (זכוין) before God', although the note of acceptability is clear, so also is righteousness as something one *does*.[4] We cannot really draw a line between the two. Occasionally the forensic is dominant, more often the ethical, e.g. Shab. 30*b*, 104*a*, 152*b*; Ket. 104*a*; San. 38*a*, 46*a*, 47*a*, 71*b*–72*a*; 'Er. 19*a*, 21*b*, 22*a* (see above p. 116 for a rare non-ethical instance). It also seems to be a general rule that the note of acceptability is consequent to the ethical, i.e. God's approval is vital, but it is approval of an already existing

[1] On this whole matter, S. Schechter, *Some Aspects of Rabbinic Theology* (London, 1909), 264–92; Davies, *Paul and Rabbinic Judaism*, 20–3, 333; Montefiore and Loewe, *Rabbinic Anthology*, Ch. XI.

[2] Cf. S. Levy, *Original Virtue* (London, 1907), 11f.

[3] So S–B, III, 163; L. Morris, *The Apostolic Preaching of the Cross*, 242: '"Righteous" was a forensic term.'

[4] Cf. S–B, III, 29f and 163, n. 1.

righteousness, e.g. Ḳid. 40*a*, *b*; Ber. 7*a*.[1] This is a point of some importance, and not for the adjective only, for it involves the whole question of *iustitia ex lege*, or man's bringing his own righteousness to God. It is in general true that in Rabbinic literature we have to do 'not with the establishment, but with the confirmation of righteousness through God's judgment'.[2] It is difficult to reconcile this with the view that 'righteous' refers primarily to a verdict. It is nearer the truth to say that it refers secondarily to a verdict, though in fact any such reference can often be discovered only from the total, not the immediate, context. That this legalistic aspect is neither the whole story nor a fair delineation of Rabbinic doctrine will emerge when we discuss the doctrine of merits.

THE ROOT זכה

In Aramaic this largely takes over the functions of צדק, which occurs relatively seldom, and, by a sort of backlash effect, it tends to replace the verb צדק even in Hebrew.[3]

The Verb

Despite its infrequent use in the OT (qal 4 times, piʿel 3 times, hithpaʿel once), where it is essentially an ethical verb, its use both in Aramaic and in Rabbinic Hebrew is almost entirely forensic, though some ethical uses do persist, cf. Yom. 87*a*; Ab. 5. 18; Mak. 3. 16 (possibly) – all Hebrew piʿ; Targ. Ps. LXXIII 13 (Aram. paʿ). The piʿel cases mean 'make better, lead to righteousness', and the Aramaic instance, 'cleanse'. Apart from these, however, it usually means in the qal 'be acquitted, be found worthy of, obtain a right', and in the piʿel, 'acquit, obtain a privilege for', and the Aramaic is closely similar. It can also mean 'obtain a merit' (qal) or 'transfer a merit' (piʿel).

[1] The latter takes prosperity as a sign of God's approval, which only some righteous men receive, because only some righteous men are completely righteous. Cf. Hirsch, 'Right and Righteousness', 422–4, on 'righteous' as primarily an ethical term.

[2] S–B, III, 164.

[3] Cf. W. Bacher, *Die Exegetische Terminologie der Jüdischen Traditionsliteratur* (Leipzig, 1899), 50f. The verb צדק is used in Aramaic with the same range of meaning as in Hebrew, cf. Dalman and Jastrow.

The Noun זכות *(Hebrew)*, זכו, זכותא *(Aramaic)*

While this can be ethical, e.g. 'doing good' (Ta'. 29*a*), it also can mean 'acquittal, favourable judgment, plea in defence', e.g. Shab. 32*a*, and notably, 'merit' as the result of good conduct, Ab. I. 6. Its characteristic use is the forensic result of righteous behaviour, or 'merit', and we may conveniently see this in Genesis Rabbah, where its use is invariably one of the following:

(*a*) A 'right', e.g. 'a right in the land', cf. XXXIX 14, XLI.

(*b*) Reward, in the sense 'as a reward for', XLIII 8.

(*c*) Closely similar to (*b*), Merit, in the sense that something is done 'for the merit of', e.g. the Patriarchs, LXX 8; the sea divided 'for the merit of Joseph', LXXXIV 5; Israel's crossing of the Jordan was 'for the merit of Jacob', LXXVI 5.

Often, however, to state 'merit' thus is to stress it too much; the meaning is simply 'for the sake of', and this is evident where it is the Torah of whose 'merit' we read, cf. I 10; XII 2 (e.g. the world was created 'for the sake of the Torah'); also of beasts, XXXIII I. The noun זכות has the meaning (*c*), whether emphatic or simply meaning 'for the sake of', invariably except for the three cases noted for (*a*) and (*b*). What gains a merit is usually *tsedeq* or *tsedaqah*, but the merit itself is *zekuth*. This is not an absolute distinction: the latter can mean 'conduct',[1] and the former, though rarely, can mean 'merit', as in Ket. 50*a*. In Aramaic the position is more complicated, because צדק tends to be replaced by זכה anyway. In the generally literal rendering of Targum Onkelos we see the situation clearly, and this will shortly be examined.

The Adjective זכי, זכאי

This can mean 'innocent', i.e. a matching of forensic and ethical, e.g. Targ. O. Gen. 20. 4, but it also has an ordinary ethica' meaning, e.g. Targ. O. Gen. 6. 9; 7. 1; 18. 23–8.

THE RELATION BETWEEN HEBREW AND ARAMAIC IN TARGUM ONKELOS

There are 8 cases of the verb צָדַק in the MT of the Pentateuch, and all are rendered by some form of זכה with no perceptible

[1] Levy, *Original Virtue*, 16: '*zekut* means the virtue itself, and then also the reward for virtue, the claim or right to a reward for virtue, hence "merit"'.

change in meaning. The only interesting case is Gen. 38. 26, where the qal is rendered by the adjective זכי (referring to Tamar), thus perhaps confirming the view that we should understand the qal non-forensically here.

There are 12 cases of the noun צֶדֶק, none rendered by any form of זכה. All are rendered by קשוט, with one exception, Deut. 33. 19 (רעוא).

There are 9 cases of צְדָקָה, 8 rendered quite satisfactorily by זכו, and one, Gen. 18. 19, by צדקא. We cannot find any good reason for this exception, which does not appear to mean 'charity'.[1] Deut. 33. 21 is of special interest, because 'he did God's righteousness' becomes 'he did righteousness (זכו) before God', this apparently introducing the notion of merit.

There are 16 cases of צַדִּיק, of which all but 3 are rendered by זכי etc. Two (Ex. 23. 8 and Deut. 16. 19) are rendered by תריץ (straight, upright), and one (Deut. 4. 8) by קשיט (upright, straight, true).[2]

Thus, except for *tsedeq*, *ts-d-q* is represented almost solely by זכה. Also, צדיקיא is found in Gen. 49. 11, not for any exact Hebrew equivalent, but meaning 'righteous' in the sense of 'obedient to the Law'. All this suggests that the 'merit' significance usually ascribed to זכות does not carry over to other forms of the root unless the context demands it. Very often it renders *ts-d-q* satisfactorily without any apparent influence from 'merits'. One root is not necessarily more forensic than the other, though of course the number of times *zekuth* is used in a merit connection means that the forensic proportion is high. The Aramaic equivalent of δικαιοσύνη etc. is probably זכו etc.: e.g. Ps. 143. 2 and Rom. 3. 20 both have MT יִצְדַּק rendered by δικαιωθήσεται, whereas the Targum has יִזְכֵּי.[3] This, however, does not make the Greek any more or less forensic, except in a merits context. This will be important when we come to examine its use in Paul.

[1] We thus cannot agree with G. Dalman, *Jesus–Jeshua*, E.Tr. (London, 1929), 68, that *tsedaqah* meaning 'righteousness' is always rendered by זכו in the Targum.

[2] Mach, *Der Zaddik in Talmud*, 3, points out that the exceptions are where *tsaddiq* is a non-personal attribute.

[3] Cf. S–B, III, 162.

THE DOCTRINE OF MERITS

It is neither possible nor necessary to give here a full account of this doctrine. Marmorstein has done it thoroughly and with full documentation,[1] and the whole matter has been illuminatingly discussed by many other writers,[2] so that misunderstanding by Christians is unnecessary. We have already mentioned the presence of the doctrine, including the transfer of merits, in the Apocryphal and Pseudepigraphal books, especially 2 Baruch and II (IV) Esdras (above, pp. 99–100). It is in Rabbinic writings that it fully emerges.

We may begin with one's own merits. A righteous man is one whose righteous deeds – and therefore merits – outweigh his evil deeds – and therefore demerits. In a few places, the intention is equivalent to the deed, e.g. Mekh. 16*b* on Ex. 12. 28, and in Ḳid. 39*b*, 40*a*, intentions and deeds are of similar value. An unrighteous man is one whose evil deeds predominate. An 'indifferent man' is one whose righteous and unrighteous deeds balance.[3] According to one tradition, this is where God's grace comes in, and tips the balance in favour of righteousness.[4] Now all this may seem external and mechanical, and opposed to the idea of righteousness as behaviour in relationship, yet man is usually being judged as he is at any given moment, not just quantitatively.[5] Moreover, the scales are God's, and what is righteous is always by his definition, so that righteousness is still seen in relation to him.

How does one acquire merits? Marmorstein lists faith as the

[1] A. Marmorstein, *The Doctrine of Merits in Old Rabbinical Literature* (London, 1920).

[2] E.g. Levy, *Original Virtue*, 1–42; Schechter, *Aspects of Rabbinic Theology*, 170–98; C. G. Montefiore, *Rabbinic Literature and Gospel Teachings* (London, 1930), 295ff; G. F. Moore, *Judaism in the First Centuries of the Christian Era* (3 vols., Cambridge, Mass., 1927–30), I, 535–45; Davies, *Paul and Rabbinic Judaism*, 268–73.

[3] Ḳid. 40*b*; Mak. 23*a*, *b*; also S–B, I, 251f; III, 163f; IV, I, 1–22.

[4] Cf. S–B, III, 164; H. St J. Thackeray, *The Relation of St Paul to Contemporary Jewish Thought* (London, 1900), 81f, 88, sees this as 'imputed righteousness'.

[5] See Ber. 33*b*: 'There is only one treasury in heaven with God, and it is that of "fear of heaven".' Cf. Marmorstein, *Merits*, 53. The moment by moment view is upheld in Ḳid. 40*b*; Gen. R. LIII 14.

first source, i.e. trust in God, belief in God, but not as in Paul, the opposite of works, rather 'faithful work'. The second source is studying and obeying the Torah, the third is the observance of the Sabbath, circumcision, and sacrifice, and the last is charity and lovingkindness.[1] If one is truly righteous, one's merit is available not only for oneself, but for others, and there are three main ways in which this happens: the merit of the Fathers (i.e., from the recipient's point of view, of a pious ancestry); the merit of a pious contemporary, the righteous for the wicked; and even the merit of a pious posterity.[2] It is the merits of the Fathers which receive most attention. The merit of Abraham, of the other patriarchs, or the prophets, or even of one's own immediate ancestry, could be called to one's account.[3] But called to one's account for what? The first-century discussion between Shemaiah and Abtalyon sets the tone for many others,[4] and shows a division of opinion which long continued. The question was, what merit did Israel have that God should have divided the sea for them? Abtalyon's reply was, the merit of their own faith. Shemaiah answered, for the merit of Abraham's faith (Gen. 15. 6) did God do 'charity' (*tsedaqah*) with Israel at the sea (Mekh. on Ex. 14. 15). Very often this is the sort of context in which merits are discussed, i.e. not the final Judgment, but past or even present realities. Thus, 'for whose merit does the world exist?' (Lev. R. XXIII 3); 'for whose merit was the world created?' (Ber. 6*b*); 'for whose merit did Israel cross into the promised land?' (Gen. R. LXXVI 5). They are questions about the welfare of the nation, or of an individual, or sometimes of the world, cf. San. 97*b* and the thirty-six righteous men in every generation whose merits sustain the world.[5]

We notice that for both Shemaiah and Abtalyon the merit comes from faith, and that the disagreement lies in whether the act of deliverance was due to the fugitives' own merits or

[1] Marmorstein, *Merits*, 175–84. He gives full references.

[2] Cf. Schechter, *Aspects*, 171–98.

[3] Cf. Yom. 87*a*; Ab. 5. 18; MK 28*a*; Gen. R. XLIV 16; Ex. R. XV 3; Lev. R. XXIX 7, XXXVI 6. One source of merits of note is the submission of Isaac in being bound on the altar (the 'Akedah'), NB Gen. R. LVI, and cf. Levy, *Original Virtue*, 3f, 9f, 14, also Schoeps, *Paul*, 142–5.

[4] Cf. Marmorstein, *Merits*, 37f.

[5] Also Montefiore and Loewe, *Rabbinic Anthology*, 231f, and the article 'Lamed-Waw' in *JE*.

someone else's. It is this disagreement that is perhaps meant in Hillel's cryptic saying:

> If I am not for myself, who is then for me? And if I am for myself, what am I? (Ab. I. 14).

According to Marmorstein, he meant that a man must not *rely* on the Fathers in the Judgment, yet, because all his good deeds are insufficient to justify him, he *needs* the merits of the Fathers.[1]

Levy argues strongly that *Zekuth Aboth*, the merits of the Fathers, is a doctrine of grace:[2] God mercifully takes into account the merits of the righteous, in addition to one's own probably meagre merits. There is a danger that this could induce moral laxity, as some Rabbis clearly realised, for the debate continued as to whether the merits of the Fathers could be counted, i.e. whether there could be any 'transfer of merits' at all.[3] This became doubly important when the doctrine was applied to one's standing in the Judgment, and to one's entry into the world to come.[4] There was a continuing tradition against the transfer of merits, and another which maintained that the treasury of merits was by now exhausted.[5] It is possible to see the doctrine in different ways. It can be regarded as external, transactional, and therefore suspect.[6] But it is surely more correct to see in it an expression of the covenant 'as a fountain of grace on which the nation can rely at all times',[7] and an expression of the solidarity of the people of God, of the unity of one generation with another, and of one Israelite with his whole race.[8] In fact the doctrine is

[1] On Hillel, see Marmorstein, *Merits*, 38.

[2] *Original Virtue*, 17; cf. Marmorstein, *Merits*, 13ff, for how the Rabbis reserved God's gracious freedom of action. Certainly the doctrine *could* be understood as giving man a claim on God, but it is amply stressed that man has no such claim. All 'reckoning' is by God's grace. For a balanced treatment, see Montefiore, *Rabbinic Literature and Gospel Teachings*, 295–8, 361.

[3] NB Marmorstein, *Merits*, 25, 64ff, 164–71. 'Transfer of merits' is not a happy term, cf. Levy's formulation alluded to above. It is the operation of God's grace, not a commercial transaction.

[4] Cf. Marmorstein, *Merits*, 48f, 78, 80, 147–70.

[5] Shab. 55*a*. Cf. Marmorstein, *Merits*, 80f; Schechter, *Aspects*, 177f.

[6] E.g. by R. A. Stewart, *Rabbinic Theology* (Edinburgh, 1961), 127–34.

[7] Schechter, *Aspects*, 180.

[8] See R. Loewe in the Preface to Stewart, *Rabbinic Theology*, viii; Hirsch, 'Right and Righteousness', 423; Davies, *Paul and Rabbinic Judaism*, 272f; Marmorstein, *Merits*, 4, 35, 172, 187f.

continuous with the plea of Moses after the golden calf episode, where in asking for God's forgiveness he appeals to the promises made to Abraham, Isaac, and Jacob (Ex. 32. 11ff).[1] Levy sees the doctrine as the counterpart to the Christian doctrine of Original Sin, hence the title of his book, *Original Virtue*. We do in fact, he says, benefit from the good deeds of those before us, and Marmorstein also sees the solidarity of mankind as the basis of the doctrine.[2]

Merits are essentially of the righteous, i.e. what produces merits is righteousness, cf. Ḥag. 15*a*; Gen. R. XXVIII 5; XLIX 13. Yet equally, the righteous is he who has merits before God. The forensic or relational and behaviour or character sides of righteousness are inseparable. All this is of considerable importance for understanding Paul, and undoubtedly the doctrine is early enough to have been an influence on him. The elaboration of the doctrine is indeed later, and certainly not all Rabbis accepted it, nor was it the centre of Rabbinic Judaism.[3] Nonetheless it is not to be pushed right to the periphery;[4] it was certainly a point of discussion in the first century, as the debate between Shemaiah and Abtalyon shows.[5] Though their disagreement was about Israel's welfare on earth, rather than about man's standing in the Judgment, the former probably implies the latter.

We must finally relate Abraham in Gen. 15. 6 to the doctrine. Although the verse is not discussed relevantly to the doctrine in Genesis Rabbah, elsewhere the common interpretation seems to be that Abraham's faith is his faithfulness, especially in keeping the whole Torah before it was given.[6] 'Reckoned to him as...' therefore means 'accounted as meritorious' in exactly the same way as any man's good deeds or law-obedience would be counted.[7] It is certainly not a matter of faith in contradistinction from works, being reckoned as righteousness. Now, although this is markedly different from Paul's interpretation of the passage,

[1] NB Moore, *Judaism*, I, 536f, for this and the OT basis generally.

[2] *Merits*, 4.

[3] Cf. Schechter, *Aspects*, 170.

[4] Cf. Davies, *Paul and Rabbinic Judaism*, 272.

[5] See Davies, ibid. 269, and his references; Marmorstein, *Merits*, 38ff; cf. 1 En. 38. 2; Pss. Sol. 9. 6.

[6] Ḳid. 82*a*; Yom. 28*b*; j. Ḳid. 48*a*, *b*; Mekh. on Ex. 14. 31; cf. S–B, III, 186ff.

[7] See S–B, III, 201, and passages there cited.

it is not so far removed from the original meaning, if our view of the latter is right. Though here couched in the language of merits, the point is similar, that his faith was his righteousness. In the OT this is seen in terms of covenant-loyalty, here, in terms of merits, but as merits are essentially within the covenant, the Rabbis may very well have meant much the same thing.

APPENDED NOTE 6

The Merits of the Martyrs

It is a curious fact that the idea of the martyrs' deaths as atoning is very rarely indeed connected with the doctrine of merits, especially in the early Rabbinic period.[1] One clear example is where Menachem b. Zeira points out the merits of the martyrs in the Hadrianic persecution (Gen. R. XXXIV 9). This rarity is despite the clear tradition in Judaism, expressed usually in sacrificial terms, that the death of a martyr could atone for his own sins, and those of others, a tradition to be found in Apocryphal and Pseudepigraphal books, as well as in the Rabbis.[2] Naturally, the martyrs were meritorious persons, but their merit lies rather in their law-obedience than in the actual deaths, which were the consequence of their devotion to the Torah. The merits of martyrdom rank lower than those of studying the Torah (Pes. 50*a*), and Akiba is pictured as regarding the martyr death of two teachers of the Law as a disaster, because their merits had sustained their age, and would now no longer be available (Mekh. 22. 22). Sifre Deut. 6. 5 shows that a life of pious law-obedience has the merit-value of a daily martyrdom.[3]

[1] 'The merits of the martyrs were not exploited in the Judaism of the first centuries', Marmorstein, *Merits*, 57.

[2] 2 Macc. 7. 18, 32f, 37f; 4 Macc. 1. 11; 6. 28f; 10. 10; 12. 17f; 17. 10, 21f; Wisd. 3. 5f; Pss. Sol. 10. 2f; TBenj. 3. 8; MK 28*a*; Mekh. on Ex. 12. 1; 20. 6; cf. Sota 14*a*. On the tradition, H. W. Surkau, *Martyrien in jüdischer und frühchristlicher Zeit* (Göttingen, 1938), 9–33, 57–74; E. Lohse, *Märtyrer und Gottesknecht* (Göttingen, 1955), 66–78; Appendix 1 to E. Stauffer, *New Testament Theology*, E.Tr. (London, 1955); H. A. Fischel, 'Martyr and Prophet', *JQR*, 37 (1947), 265–80, 363–86, who does not, however, make a clear enough distinction between sacrificial and merit categories.

[3] Thus in San. 93*a*, it was the godliness of the three Danielic 'martyrs' rather than their suffering, which preserved the whole world from annihilation; cf. Surkau, *Martyrien*, 69, 71–3.

It seems then that the atoning effect of martyrdom was expressed almost entirely in sacrificial categories, and while it could be expressed in merit categories, this is done only rarely. In general, the merits of martyrdom cannot compare with the merits of godliness and faithfulness to the Torah.

CHAPTER 7

THE NEW TESTAMENT APART FROM THE PAULINE CORPUS

ANALYSIS OF USE: THE VERB δικαιόω

The verb occurs with two different forces, the demonstrative, where it means something like 'vindicate', and the declaratory. We prefer not to call the latter 'forensic', for both uses may be that.

As an example of the demonstrative use we may take Mt. 11. 19: καὶ ἐδικαιώθη ἡ σοφία ἀπὸ τῶν ἔργων αὐτῆς, cf. the parallel in Lk. 7. 35 (parallel passages in the Synoptics are being counted as one instance). The point of the statement is that God's wisdom is shown to be right by results, whether things done (Matthew) or persons changed (Luke).[1] In this category are: Mt. 11. 19 (and parallel); Lk. 10. 29; 16. 15; Jas 2. 21, 24, 25.

In Lk. 10. 29 the lawyer clearly wants to know, even if only for his own satisfaction, that he is in the right because he keeps the Law, and this may link with 16. 15 (οἱ δικαιοῦντες ἑαυτούς) where Luke identifies the self-justifiers with the Pharisees, who try to establish in men's eyes their own righteousness, i.e. demonstrate it.[2] The three cases in James are disputable, and raise the problem of the theologies of Paul and James. If the verb in these verses is declaratory, then James must be saying that a man is justified by faith and works together. If it is demonstrative, then the passage deals with showing the reality of an already existing faith (and therefore of salvation). Then, in v. 21, we should see the offering of Isaac as demonstrating the faith of Abraham, which was counted to him as righteousness (Gen. 15. 6). On the other hand, in all these verses, it is the person who is 'justified by works', not the faith; yet if this means 'shown to be righteous',

[1] Thus also A. Descamps, *Les Justes et la Justice dans les Évangiles et le christianisme primitif hormis la doctrine proprement paulinienne* (Louvain, 1950), 96; Hill, *Greek Words*, 138, and many others.

[2] T. W. Manson, *The Sayings of Jesus* (London, 1949), 295, and M. Black, 'The Parables as Allegory', *BJRL*, 42 (1959–60), 273–87, at 287, think it more likely that the Sadducees are meant, and that there is a play on the supposed derivation of 'Sadducee'.

the sense is quite acceptable. How else can a person's righteousness be shown but by what he does? Indeed, the most natural understanding of the passage is that if belief is genuine, it will be followed by righteous action, and the man in question will be vindicated, demonstrated as righteous.[1] If, however, one takes vv. 18–20 as introducing the later verses, then clearly we are not dealing with the problem of how man becomes accepted by God at all, and therefore not with justification in the Pauline sense.

As an example of the declaratory use we may take Mt. 12. 37: ἐκ γὰρ τῶν λόγων σου δικαιωθήσῃ καὶ ἐκ τῶν λόγων σου καταδικασθήσῃ. This is so self-evidently to do with acquittal, that one need only observe that in Matthew its context is the Last Judgment, and not justification here and now, cf. v. 36. In this category are: Mt. 12. 37; Lk. 7. 29; 18. 14; Acts 13. 39, 39.

In Lk. 18. 14 there is some disagreement whether the reference is to simple forgiveness[2] or to judicial absolution,[3] but it is usually agreed that the sense is close to Paul's 'justification'.[4] In Luk. 7. 29 the people and the tax-collectors 'justified God': this seems to be declaratory, not of course in an acquittal sense, but in that of recognising God's righteousness in the mission of John,[5] or else in that of recognising God's just demands on them.[6]

[1] So J. Murray, *The Epistle to the Romans* (2 vols in one, London, 1967), I, 351. However, C. L. Mitton, *The Epistle of James* (London, 1966), 104–6, thinks James does mean 'acquit', but at the Judgment, whereas Paul means status before God here and now – hence the seeming disagreement about the admissibility of works as evidence. In any case, it is probable that Paul and James use 'faith' differently also, cf. Reumann, in J. Reumann and W. Lazareth, *Righteousness and Society* (Philadelphia, 1967), 83; also ibid. 84, for the point that whereas for Paul works are acts to obtain justification, for James they are faith's fruit, which Paul would call 'fruits of the Spirit', cf. Gal. 5. 22; Phil. 1. 11.

[2] So Montefiore, *Rabbinic Literature and Gospel Teachings*, 370; Descamps, *Les Justes*, 97, among others.

[3] So Hill, *Greek Words*, 132f; Schrenk, *Righteousness*, 60.

[4] So Hill, *Greek Words*, 132f; T. W. Manson, *On Paul and John*, 55; G. Klein, 'Rechtfertigung im N.T.', [3]*RGG*, V, 826, points out that the man is still legally a sinner; this is therefore *iustificatio impii*.

[5] Cf. C. G. Montefiore, *The Synoptic Gospels* (2 vols, 2nd edn, London, 1927), II, 427; Hill, *Greek Words*, 138.

[6] Cf. Descamps, *Les Justes*, 95f; A. Plummer, *The Gospel According to St Luke*, ICC (Edinburgh, 1896), 206.

Although both cases in Acts 13. 39 are difficult,[1] if we take them to mean 'acquit', and do not make this too narrowly judicial, a reasonable sense is obtained. The demonstrative meaning is not possible; in theory, 'made righteous' is possible, but such a meaning is rare, and does not fit what is apparently an attempt to reproduce Pauline language. Moreover, justification from *things* fits oddly with a causative meaning. What one wants, largely because of ἀπό, is 'be quit of', 'be saved from'. Such a meaning may still be understood in relational or even forensic terms, and the reference to forgiveness in v. 38 accords with this. We can find no cases where the verb means 'make righteous' – the poorly attested δικαιωθήτω in Rev. 22. 11 probably means 'practise righteousness'.

ANALYSIS OF USE: THE NOUN δικαιοσύνη

God's Righteousness

Jas 1. 20 is dealt with below, p. 135, and we omit the two cases in the Freer Logion, the first of which combines deliverance for the righteous with punishment for the wicked, and the second of which stresses deliverance exclusively. We are then left with only two cases, Acts 17. 31 and 2 Pet. 1. 1. Acts 17. 31 is about God's activity as Judge, but does not specify further. 2 Pet. 1. 1 may refer to God's saving righteousness; if so, it is the only NT instance outside Paul's writings.[2] More plausibly, its meaning is similar to ἰσότιμον a few words earlier, and refers to God's just government of the Christian community.[3]

Christ's Righteousness

It is plainly unsatisfactory to include this with man's righteousness, in view of the NT's ascription of special honour to Jesus, but one feels equally uneasy about including it with God's righteousness, for the simple equation, Jesus is God, is not made in the NT.[4]

[1] On whether this means that the Law could justify from *some* things, F. F. Bruce, *The Acts of the Apostles* (London, 1951), 271.

[2] So Descamps, *Les Justes*, 58f, 92 n. 1.

[3] So Schrenk, *Righteousness*, 35; Hill, *Greek Words*, 159.

[4] Cf. V. Taylor, 'Does the New Testament Call Jesus God?', *ET*, 73 (1961–2), 116–18.

First, we omit the Melchizedek reference in Heb. 7. 2, which gives no real clue to the connotation, and so are left with 4 cases: Jn 16. 8, 10; Heb. 1. 9; Rev. 19. 11. The first two are notoriously difficult, but seem to refer to Christ's character as vindicated by God in his exaltation (v. 10), and this Christ-righteousness is the true righteousness, as opposed to man's erroneous ideas of righteousness.[1] In Heb. 1. 9 we are dealing with an extended quotation from Ps. 45. 6f. In LXX it is the opposite of ἀνομία, and means life in accordance with the Law, especially in government. Applied to Jesus in Hebrews, it is presumably given a Christian connotation, and means the Messiah's life of obedience to God. In Rev. 19. 11, the Messiah's righteousness is seen both in judging, and in waging war. This righteousness of the Messiah is a familiar idea, cf. Isa. 11. 3ff; 1 En. 38. 2; 39. 6; 53. 6; Pss. Sol. 17. 31, 35f, 41, etc. It occurs in a way also in Acts 17. 31 where, although God judges the world in righteousness, he does it through the Messiah.

Man's Righteousness

All the instances here refer to man's obedience to God's will and Law, and have the familiar double emphasis on activity, and on relation to God. The difficulty comes when we try to separate those cases which have a distinctively OT flavour, from those which are Christian. First, then, righteousness of the old covenant.

It is likely that even when an OT character is called 'righteous' Christian connotations are attached; our strictly historical approach cannot be read into the NT. This is exemplified in Mt. 21. 32: 'John came to you ἐν ὁδῷ δικαιοσύνης'. Probably ἐν here means 'with', and the whole phrase means 'with the message of righteousness', i.e. the message of the standard which God demands of men, the life of obedience to the divine will. There is adequate support for ὁδός as a way of life, and as the subject of preaching.[2] Some see here a double reference to John's

[1] Cf. C. K. Barrett, *The Gospel According to St John* (London, 1955), 405ff. Descamps, *Les Justes*, 89–92, sees three strands, innocence, moral righteousness, and victory over sin (i.e. Christ's righteousness is the source of Christians'), but can the text be made to bear all this?

[2] Cf. Schrenk, *Righteousness*, 36, and A. H. McNeile, *The Gospel According to St Matthew* (London, 1915), 308, and their references.

preaching and to his own exemplification of it.[1] The difficulty as to whether 'righteousness' has a Christian or a pre-Christian connotation is pointed up by the fact that the context construes John's righteousness as belonging with the Christian, rather than the other sort. In this category are: Mt. 21. 32; Lk. 1. 75; Acts 10. 35; Heb. 11. 33; Jas 2. 23; 2 Pet. 2. 5. The uncertainty just mentioned applies also to Lk. 1. 75 – did Luke understand this as Christian?

Acts 10. 35 shows that righteousness is not itself acceptability, but, in the Jewish tradition, that which leads to acceptability. In what exactly the righteousness of Cornelius consisted, is hard to say,[2] but it is certainly conduct in the fear of God. In Heb. 11. 33 there are judging and ruling aspects, and once again the righteous of old are seen as models of Christian righteousness. The same is true of 2 Pet. 2. 5, except that righteousness is ethical in a more general sense.

In view of the argument of the context, Jas 2. 23 must mean some kind of work. The 'reckoning' is possible because faith is accompanied and completed by works, as the preceding verses show, and righteousness itself is that conduct or way of life which is the prerequisite for acceptance with God. There is thus for James no element of imputation; this faith-completed-by-works *is* righteousness, and naturally is reckoned as such. Despite the actual words of 2. 23, James is really saying 'Abraham believed God, and offered up Isaac in trusting obedience, and it was reckoned to him as righteousness'. Gen. 15. 6 is quoted, but with Gen. 22 in mind.

We turn to righteousness of the new covenant, cf. Mt. 5. 6; μακάριοι οἱ πεινῶντες καὶ διψῶντες τὴν δικαιοσύνην. It has been suggested that this is God's righteousness, his eschatological salvation, his vindicating activity.[3] Others, however, see it as

[1] So G. Strecker, *Der Weg der Gerechtigkeit* (Göttingen, 1962), 187; Hill, *Greek Words*, 125.

[2] C. S. C. Williams, *The Acts of the Apostles*, Black's N.T. Commentaries (London, 1957), 136f, thinks there may be a reference to almsgiving, as does Bruce, *Acts*, 224, or to the Noachian Commandments. Descamps, *Les Justes*, 33, points out that the immediate reference is to entry into the community, not to justification.

[3] Dodd, *Bible and Greeks*, 55; Manson, *Sayings of Jesus*, 47f, sees here a double meaning.

man's life of obedience to God's will,[1] and for several reasons this latter view is more plausible. First, elsewhere in Matthew this is the word's meaning, and certainly it makes the best sense at 5. 10. Second, surely the eschatological salvation arises from God's grace, and not from man's longing for it. This assumes, of course, that 'filled' means 'filled with righteousness'. There is a third possible view, that it means 'justification',[2] but this is unlikely because of the word's usual meaning. If we are right, we have here a righteousness which is at once a demand on men, and a gift promised to them,[3] and this is of considerable importance.

The cases where 'righteousness' means Christian behaviour are: Mt. 3. 15; 5. 6, 10, 20; 6. 1, 33; Acts 13. 10; 24. 25; Heb. 5. 13; 11. 7; 12. 11; Jas 1. 20; 3. 18; 1 Pet. 2. 24; 3. 14; 2 Pet. 2. 21; 3. 13; 1 Jn 2. 29; 3. 7, 10; Rev. 22. 11. Because of scholarly disagreement at several points, a few notes must be added. Mt. 3. 15: 'Fulfil every righteous ordinance' is unlikely,[4] because the natural word for this would be δικαίωμα, and also because this is not the most natural meaning for πληροῦν either.[5] 'Acquire pardon for all' is also unlikely,[6] because it depends partly on the doubtful premise that in this passage there is a reference to Jesus as the Suffering Servant, and further because it posits an improbable sense for δικαιοσύνη.[7] Much more probably, it means righteousness of life in accordance with the divine will, a righteousness which fulfils in that it completes and finalises that of righteous men of old, and is now revealed in the

[1] So Strecker, *Der Weg*, 154ff; Descamps, *Les Justes*, 170–4; Hill, *Greek Words*, 127f; Schrenk, *Righteousness*, 35.

[2] Cf. S–B, I, 201.

[3] Cf. Strecker, *Der Weg*, 154ff; Descamps, *Les Justes*, 173; Barth, in G. Bornkamm, G. Barth, and H. J. Held, *Tradition and Interpretation in Matthew*, E.Tr. (London, 1963), 140.

[4] The view of Montefiore, *Synoptic Gospels*, II, 16f.

[5] See Hill, *Greek Words*, 125f, and especially H. Ljungman, *Das Gesetz Erfüllen, Matt. 5, 17ff und 3, 15 untersucht* (Lund, 1954), who sees πληροῦν in Matthew as expressing 'the completion and full realization of a personal relationship, involving an ethical and moral "fulfilment" of God's will' (C. F. D. Moule, 'Fulfilment-words in the New Testament', *NTS*, 14 (1968), 293–320, at 317).

[6] So O. Cullmann, *Baptism in the New Testament*, ETr. (London, 1950), 18f.

[7] Against Cullmann, cf. also Hill, *Greek Words*, 126, and Descamps, *Les Justes*, 116ff.

whole life and mission of Jesus. He is righteous in that he perfectly conforms to the will of God.[1] No doubt Matthew intends this to be exemplary, and indeed if this passage is entirely redactional, it may be argued that 'righteousness' really means right conduct as performed by the disciples.[2] It is because of this that it has been included here and not with the Messiah's righteousness, though the present classification is of course supported by the fact that it involves John as well as Jesus.

Mt. 5. 20: it is clear that the 'greater righteousness' of Christians is made specific in the ensuing antitheses. It is not in opposition to law-righteousness, but is its fulfilment, and is more inward, more thoroughgoing, more demanding.[3] There is no suggestion that it is anything but man's activity, unless one supposes that 5. 6 implies that it is also God's gift.

Mt. 6. 1: almost certainly, it is here a general word for religious, moral, and compassionate activity in general, and is inclusive of what follows in vv. 2–18, as many commentators agree.[4] The meaning 'almsgiving' is less likely,[5] despite the textual variant which in any case is poorly attested, because v. 1 reads like a general statement which is then worked out in specific cases, and because ἐλεημοσύνη in v. 2 is odd if δικαιοσύνη has the same meaning in v. 1.

Mt. 6. 33: does God's righteousness here mean his own, or that which pleases him and of which he is the standard? Some, e.g. McNeile,[6] see it as the vindication which the kingdom will bring, thus as both future and God's own. Yet if we accept that the kingdom is present as well as future in Matthew, righteousness probably is also, and consequently means that which God

[1] So many commentators, e.g. Manson, *Sayings of Jesus*, 149.

[2] Cf. Strecker, *Der Weg*, 179f.

[3] Cf. Strecker, ibid. 151f. In S–B, IV, 1, 20, it is argued that this 'better righteousness' destroys the whole basis of the Scribes' soteriology, which rested on the *letter* of the Law, cf. also S–B, I, 250ff.

[4] E.g. W. D. Davies, *The Setting of the Sermon on the Mount* (Cambridge, 1964), 307f; Barth, in *Tradition and Interpretation in Matthew*, 139.

[5] See Dodd, *Bible and Greeks*, 46n.; Hatch, *Essays*, 50f, thinks that scribes who did not know of this meaning for δικαιοσύνη altered it to ἐλεημοσύνη; W. Nagel, 'Gerechtigkeit – oder Almosen (Mt 6, 1)', *Vigiliae Christianae*, 15 (1961), 141–5.

[6] *Matthew*, 89; also Stuhlmacher, *Gottes Gerechtigkeit*, 189.

approves and wants, but which believers practise.[1] Further, προστεθήσεται points to righteousness as God's gift and not only the object of man's search; this may not make man's righteousness identical with God's, but does suggest that God is its source. Indeed, it may well be argued that 'his righteousness' here is very like 'righteousness of God' in Jas 1. 20.[2]

Heb. 5. 13: λόγου δικαιοσύνης could mean several things.[3] Something like 'a principle of righteousness' or 'moral truth' is to be preferred, because the following verse is about moral discernment.[4]

Heb. 11. 7: Noah's righteousness is ethical, and not purely forensic or relational, because of the contrast with the world's wickedness; yet it is also a righteousness which 'comes by faith' (κατὰ πίστιν), and which is God's gift to the man who believes. This of course takes Noah as a model for Christian righteousness, which also comes from faith. This undoubtedly ethical righteousness by faith (κατὰ πίστιν is equivalent to ἐκ πίστεως)[5] is important as showing that the position we adopt in the case of Paul is supported elsewhere.

Jas 1. 20: as in Mt. 6. 33, this is more likely to mean the righteousness which God demands than his own saving (or retributive) righteousness, because of the ethical context. On this commentators widely agree.[6] Schrenk remarks that this passage places man's good works under the heading of God's, and not man's, righteousness,[7] and this, like Mt. 6. 33 and Heb. 11. 7, is important for our understanding of 'righteousness in Christ'.

Jas 3. 18: δικαιοσύνης may be either a genitive of origin, or of definition. In either case, it is a manner of life that is meant, but

[1] So Hill, *Greek Words*, 129; Descamps, *Les Justes*, 178.

[2] Cf. Strecker, *Der Weg*, 155.

[3] They are listed by H. Montefiore, *The Epistle to the Hebrews*, Black's N.T. Commentaries (London, 1964), 103, and by F. F. Bruce, *The Epistle to the Hebrews* (London, 1964), 109.

[4] So both Bruce and Montefiore, ad loc.

[5] Cf. Schrenk, *Righteousness*, 37.

[6] E.g. J. H. Ropes, *The Epistle of St James*, ICC (Edinburgh, 1916), 169; Mitton, *James*, 62; S–B, III, 163; but not Bo Reicke, *The Epistles of James, Peter, and Jude*, Anchor Bible (New York, 1964), 21.

[7] *Righteousness*, 38; similarly, Stuhlmacher, *Gottes Gerechtigkeit*, 192, says that here we cannot make a strict terminological distinction between God's work and man's obedience.

in view of OT parallels to the expression καρπὸς δικαιοσύνης,[1] it is perhaps better taken as a genitive of origin.

Despite the various problems posed by these passages, two things are true of them all. First, righteousness is always 'before God'; he demands it, is its standard, and is often its source. Second, righteousness is always a way of life, a manner of behaving, thus always behavioural as well as relational.

ANALYSIS OF USE: δίκαιος AND δικαίως

Of 63 cases, 7 refer to God, 13 to Christ, and 43 to man.

God as Righteous

It refers to God as Judge in: Jn 17. 25; 1 Pet. 2. 23 (adverb); Rev. 15. 3; 16. 5, 7; 19. 2. In Jn 17. 25 it is perhaps a conventional epithet, and so is not securely in this category. 1 Pet. 2. 23 and probably all the Revelation cases have overtones of vindication.[2]

It refers to God as saving in 1 Jn 1. 9 (πιστός ἐστιν καὶ δίκαιος ἵνα ἀφῇ ἡμῖν τὰς ἁμαρτίας) though some find here notions of judgment as well as salvation.[3]

The picture is thus largely legal, but notes of vindication and salvation also occur.

Christ as Righteous

'Righteous' as a messianic designation is already familiar to us, though more as a predicate than a title (cf. e.g. 1 En. 38. 2; Wisd. 2). Something like such a formal use is found in Acts 3. 14; 7. 52; 22. 14. In 3. 14 other meanings are perhaps in the background: the innocent as distinct from the murderer,[4] and the one

[1] Cited by Ropes, *James*, 250f. Hill, *Greek Words*, 155, Mitton, *James*, 143, and Schrenk, *Righteousness*, 38f, take it as a genitive of definition.

[2] See Descamps, *Les Justes*, 279, and 295–7.

[3] E.g. Schrenk, *Righteousness*, 21, and Descamps, *Les Justes*, 139f. A. E. Brooke, *The Johannine Epistles*, ICC (Edinburgh, 1912), 19, is probably right in seeing God's faithfulness to the covenant as the primary idea, here taking the form of forgiveness.

[4] So Descamps, *Les Justes*, 59–62.

who conforms to God's will.[1] The same is true of 7. 52 and even perhaps of 22. 14.[2] This is simply to say that when it is given as a title to Jesus, it is not an empty honorific.

The adjective is applied to Christ as judge in Jn 5. 30; 7. 24. He judges truly, neither apart from the Father's word, nor by mere appearances.

The adjective is applied to Christ's ethical character in 1 Pet. 3. 18; 1 Jn 2. 1, 29; 3. 7. In the first, though the reference may be to his innocence,[3] the contrast with 'unrighteous' suggests rather an ordinary ethical sense. If the verse sees Jesus as a sin-offering,[4] then clearly δίκαιος refers to his sinlessness. In 1 Pet. 3. 18 and 1 Jn 2. 1 there is a strong soteriological note, but although Descamps sees in this the saving righteousness of God,[5] it is better to say that though this is present in the passages, it is not particularly attached to δίκαιος. In 1 Jn 2. 29 one cannot be sure whether it is God or Christ who is righteous, but we assume that the 'he' of v. 29 is the same as in v. 28, and therefore Jesus.

The adjective seems to refer to Christ as *innocent* in Mt. 27. 4, 19, 24; Lk. 23. 47. Such a view of these passages has been strongly supported by Kilpatrick,[6] who shows that in the Lukan passage, 'righteous' has less point than 'innocent', and that the legal guiltlessness of Jesus is one of Luke's interests; this is more likely than that Luke is explaining 'Son of God' to a Hellenistic audience, who would not need the explanation. In Mt. 27. 4, δίκαιον is an alternative reading for ἀθῷον, which could suggest some interchangeability; in both vv. 19 and 24 'innocent' fits the forensic setting better than 'righteous', for it is not Christ's general character that is under consideration, but his guilt or

[1] So Schrenk, *Righteousness*, 21.

[2] Schrenk, *Righteousness*, 21. In all three passages, Descamps infers the saving righteousness of God, *Les Justes*, 76–84, but its presence is not obvious.

[3] As suggested by G. D. Kilpatrick, 'A Theme of the Lucan Passion Story and Luke xxiii. 47', *JTS*, 43 (1942), 34–6, at 35.

[4] So C. Bigg, *The Epistles of St Peter and St Jude*, ICC (2nd edn, Edinburgh, 1910), 160.

[5] *Les Justes*, 67f, 142–5: Christ as the righteous intercessor saves us. *Paraklētos* occurs as a loan-word, used somewhat similarly, in Ab. 4. 11: 'he who performs one precept gets for himself one advocate'.

[6] 'A Theme of the Lucan Passion Story', 34ff; similarly Goodspeed, *Problems of New Testament Translation*, 90.

innocence at one point.[1] Yet 'innocent' carries with it the implication of ethical uprightness, at least in the specific matter. In fact, it shows the ethical controlling the forensic: Jesus is innocent because he had committed no crime, and δίκαιος is no less an ethical because it is also a forensic term. Therefore, these cases are ethical and forensic inextricably, and indeed 'innocent' well conveys this inextricability.

We note then, the distinctly forensic use of the adjective, when used of Christ in 4 out of 13 instances, and a legal use in a further 2 out of the 13. Used of God, 6 out of 7 are legal, so for God and Christ, 8 out of 20 are legal.

Man as Righteous

First, we have the adverbial or neuter cases meaning 'what is right, just, proper' (as a thing to do): Mt. 20. 4 (payment); Lk. 12. 57 (judge what is right); 23. 41 (adverb); Acts 4. 19 ('just before God', hence a forensic note); 2 Pet. 1. 13 ('I deem it right to...').

Second, we have the adjective applied to man, and meaning the pious, God-fearing, upright people of the OT: Mt. 10. 41; 13. 17; 23. 29, 35, 35; Lk. 1. 6, 17; 2. 25; 23. 50; Mk 6. 20. This is similar to the 'covenant' category we have found elsewhere. Not all are equally securely in this group. It has been argued that Mt. 23. 35 means 'innocent',[2] but more probably Abel is righteous because, in contrast to his lawless contemporaries, he did God's will.[3] Hill and Descamps think that in Lk. 1. 6, 17, 2. 25, and 23. 50, it has the special meaning 'waiting for the incarnation'.[4] Yet, though these people are depicted as waiting or preparing for the incarnation, they are in the same category as the righteous of some of the Psalms, and of Qumran; that is to say, it is more reasonable to say that they look for the Messiah

[1] So among others Hill, *Greek Words*, 121ff; Descamps, *Les Justes*, 63–6. Δίκαιος renders נקי in LXX at Job 9. 23; 17. 8; cf. Gen. 20. 5. This suggestion seems to have originated with Klostermann.

[2] Kilpatrick, 'A Theme of the Lucan Passion Story', 35.

[3] So Schrenk, *Righteousness*, 22. Descamps, *Les Justes*, 51ff, thinks this is a redactional description of Christians' suffering – Abel is viewed from the standpoint of Christ's suffering. This may be so, but the idea is in the whole passage, not particularly in δίκαιος.

[4] Hill, *Greek Words*, 123f; Descamps, *Les Justes*, 31f.

because they are righteous, than that they are righteous because they look for the Messiah. Further, in Lk. 1. 6, the righteousness of Zechariah and Elizabeth is defined by 'walking in all the commandments and ordinances of the Lord blameless'; it is 'before the Lord'. Again, in 1. 17 we have the contrast ἀπειθεῖς–δίκαιοι, which seems more decisive for the meaning of 'righteous' than the setting of the passage in the context of messianic expectation. Indeed the righteous are shown as awaiting God's salvation (see especially Lk. 2. 25; 23. 50 is less certain – 'who had not consented to their purpose and deed', v. 51, is a more natural explanation of 'good and righteous' than is 'looking for the kingdom of God'). Yet this is the consequence of their being righteous, not its definition.

In Mt. 10. 41, 13. 17, and 23. 29, it is argued, we have a conjunction of 'righteous' with 'prophets' which indicates two groups of the saints of old, the righteous being those whose witness was through teaching. Thus, when coupled with 'prophets' in the three Matthaean passages, the meaning is not just 'pious, law-abiding, covenant-keeping', as most commentators think,[1] but includes a reference to the teachers of Israel who were martyred (23. 29) and now have their Christian counterparts (10. 41), so that 'a righteous man' is 'un docteur "versé dans la science du royaume"'.[2] Now why is such a technical meaning proposed, when the natural one is 'those who live by the word of the Lord which the prophets proclaim'? It is partly because of the conjunction of prophets and wise men with *scribes* in 23. 34, which may reflect the prophetic and didactic ministries of the early Church; partly because when 'prophets' occurs with another group, viz. 'the righteous', it is suggested that the two groups, 'righteous' and 'wise men and scribes' are identical; partly because in 23. 29 the righteous are martyrs, who are witnesses, and therefore teachers; and partly because in 13. 43 there may be a reference to Dan. 12. 3, and Matthew's 'righteous' are equivalent to the συνιέντες of LXX, who are 'those who turn many to righteousness', i.e. the teachers

[1] E.g. Montefiore, *Synoptic Gospels*, II, 154f; Manson, *Sayings of Jesus*, 183; Schrenk, *Righteousness*, 22.

[2] Descamps, *Les Justes*, 41–53, 207–20; Hill, *Greek Words*, 135–8, and his earlier article, 'ΔΙΚΑΙΟΙ as a Quasi-Technical Term', *NTS*, 11 (1964), 296–302.

of Israel.[1] This outline fails to do justice to Hill's neat argument; yet we find the links too equivocal and insubstantial to justify a departure from the more usual view. Moreover, it seems likely that 'righteous', far from indicating a different group, describes the prophets, if Rabbinic literature is any guide.[2]

In all these cases, a Christian connotation was very probably given to the word, and the same is true of the group which now follows, namely 'righteous' with the meaning 'obeying the Law' – i.e. with a rather heavier ethical (and less strictly covenantal?) stress than in the preceding group. Thus, for example, Mt. 1. 19: Ἰωσὴφ δὲ ὁ ἀνὴρ αὐτῆς δίκαιος ὢν καὶ μὴ θέλων αὐτὴν δειγματίσαι. We take καί to be adversative, so that 'righteous' means 'scrupulous about the Law',[3] rather than co-ordinate, with 'righteous' meaning 'magnanimous',[4] because the adjective appears as a rule not to have this meaning; even in Rabbinic writings, the Hebrew equivalent adjective very seldom reflects the 'benevolence' meaning of the noun. In this category, then, are: Mt. 1. 19; 5. 45; 9. 13 (and parallels Mk 2. 17, Lk. 5. 32); 23. 28; Lk. 15. 7; 18. 9; 20. 20; Acts 10. 22; Heb. 11. 4; 12. 23; 2 Pet. 2. 7, 8, 8; 1 Jn 3. 12.

In some it is disputable whether righteous under the old or the new covenant is intended, e.g. Mt. 5. 45; Heb. 11. 4; 12. 23; even 2 Pet. 2. 7, 8, 8. Again, traces of the covenant party idea are also discernible, in the Hebrews and 2 Peter cases, and also in Mt. 5. 45. All are in some relation to God. It is debated whether 'righteous' in Mt. 9. 13 and parallels is 'in their own estimation',[5] or really so.[6] We have taken the view that it is not meant

[1] Hill, 'ΔΙΚΑΙΟΙ as a Quasi-Technical Term', 296–9. He goes on to produce evidence of other quasi-technical use of 'righteous' as a party in Israel, from Qumran and Enoch. But a party is not a specific function. G. D. Kilpatrick, *The Origins of the Gospel According to St Matthew* (Oxford, 1946), 126, sees prophets and teachers as the ministry of the Matthaean church, but does not connect teachers and 'righteous'.

[2] Gen. R. LXVIII 11; also Fischel, 'Martyr and Prophet', 372.

[3] With J. Lightfoot, *Horae Hebraicae et Talmudicae* (4 vols, new edition by R. Gandell, Oxford, 1859), II, 18; Hill, *Greek Words*, 124; McNeile, *Matthew*, 7, among others.

[4] So Hatch, *Essays*, 51.

[5] Thus V. Taylor, *The Gospel According to St Mark* (London, 1952), 207; Plummer, *Luke*, 161; Descamps, *Les Justes*, 98–109, and many others. The view is supported by Lk. 16. 15; 18. 9; Mt. 23. 28.

[6] Thus Hill, *Greek Words*, 130ff; Schrenk, *Righteousness*, 22; Barth in

ironically, because of the parallel with ἰσχύοντες in v. 12, which certainly does not mean 'those who erroneously think they are well'. Neither view can be regarded as completely secure, but in any case the meaning of 'righteous' is unaffected.

Finally, there are the Christian righteous, those who live in obedience to Jesus, and so receive his verdict of approval, e.g. 1 Pet. 3. 12: ὀφθαλμοὶ Κυρίου ἐπὶ δικαίους καὶ ὦτα αὐτοῦ εἰς δέησιν αὐτῶν. This illustrates not only the aspect of God's approval, but also the ethical, cf. the words that follow: 'but the face of the Lord is against them that do evil'. In this category are: Mt. 13. 43, 49; 25. 37, 46; Lk. 14. 14; Acts 14. 2; 24. 15; Heb. 10. 38; Jas 5. 6, 16; 1 Pet. 3. 12; 4. 18; 1 Jn 3. 7; Rev. 22. 11. The double note, ethical–forensic, is particularly apparent in 8 of these: Mt. 13. 43, 49; 25. 37, 46; Lk. 14. 14; Acts 24. 15; 1 Pet. 4. 18; Rev. 22. 11 – all to do with the Last Judgment. The righteous, having acted uprightly, receive God's approval. 'Righteous' is not itself the verdict. In the D reading at Acts 14. 2 'righteous' seems to be synonymous with 'brethren', recalling the saints as the righteous in the Scrolls. In Jas 5. 6, the righteous is the oppressed, faithful, obedient servant of God.

Thus, while there are no purely forensic cases of the adjective in the literature, the forensic aspect is far from missing. To take this last group alone, 'righteous' has some reference to a verdict in 9 cases out of 15 (including 1 Pet. 3. 12).

Conclusion on Analysis

In general, the verb is either declaratory or demonstrative. The noun and adjective, while having a variety of uses, always have an ethical content. 'Righteousness' is always something one *does*, though what one does is sometimes the basis of one's subsequent acceptance (cf. Mt. 5. 20; Acts 10. 35). The adjective in a substantial number of cases, both when referring to Messiah and when referring to man (though not when referring to God), has a forensic connotation, though once again this is always consequent to the ethical rightness. On the other hand, man's righteousness is never devoid of relation to God.

Tradition and Interpretation in Matthew, 139. The view is supported by Lk. 15. 7, though Lightfoot, *Horae Hebraicae*, III, 153–7, thinks the latter is ironical.

THE MEANING OF RIGHTEOUSNESS IN THE NON-PAULINE WRITINGS

We cannot adequately consider all the exegetical and theological matters raised by the passages cited, but some things must be noted.

In the Synoptic Gospels, 'righteousness' is a characteristically Matthaean term.[1] Luke uses the noun once, Mark not at all, but Matthew seven times. Thus the Synoptic use of the noun really amounts to Matthaean use. Many of the seven are probably redactional (indeed Strecker thinks they all are),[2] so righteousness is evidently a special concern of Matthew's theology. We cannot explore this, which has in any case been given a thorough examination already.[3]

We have said that righteousness in this non-Pauline literature is always something one does. Indeed, C. H. Dodd thinks it is possible that in 1 Jn 3. 7 a misconstruction of Paul's teaching is being corrected, for why else is it necessary to say that the righteous is he who does righteousness? Perhaps, Dodd suggests, it was because some wished to give 'righteous' a purely religious meaning, without moral connotations.[4] Mt. 5 shows that, though more thoroughgoing, inward, and complete, Christian righteousness is of the same order of reality as that of the Scribes,[5] and elsewhere in Matthew there are indications that righteousness largely meant loving activity, especially Mt. 25. 37, 46. It is fraternal charity which characterises the righteous.

The matter of righteousness as demand and gift is also raised by the Matthaean passages. Righteousness is to be a divine gift in the Coming Age to those who hunger and thirst for it (5. 6), but it is also something demanded of men by God (5. 20, and probably 5. 10). Indeed, a complete righteousness is required for entry into the kingdom, and not just a balance of righteous over unrighteous deeds, as for the Rabbis (cf. 5. 48, τέλειος). Righteous-

[1] See Strecker, *Der Weg*, especially 149–58, and Descamps in Cerfaux and Descamps, 'Justice, Justification', *DBS*, IV, cols 1460–71.

[2] *Der Weg*, especially 187; similarly Manson, *Sayings of Jesus*, 238.

[3] Notably by Strecker, and also Descamps, but also by Barth in *Tradition and Interpretation in Matthew*, 138f.

[4] *The Johannine Epistles*, MNTC (London, 1946), 72.

[5] Cf. Bornkamm, *Tradition and Interpretation in Matthew*, 24–32.

ness is thus both demand and eschatological gift, cf. 6. 33 as well as 5. 6.[1] This double understanding is not confined to Matthew. It may be found also in Jas 1. 20, though more probably here it is righteousness which 'vor Gott gilt', or which God demands, rather than that which God gives. In 2 Pet. 3. 13 righteousness is clearly by God's creation, but is more corporate than individual, and in a new world rather than in the present one. The Johannine literature takes us further: in 1 Jn 2. 29 'to do righteousness' is 'to be born of him', and is therefore evidence of regeneration. Descamps thinks that Jn 16. 8, 10 deal with Christ's own righteousness as the source also of the Christian's.[2] Thus, the Spirit identifies the true righteousness in Jesus, not only as a standard, but as a source. In 1 Pet. 2. 24 we have the familiar (Pauline!) theme, in the context of a Christological hymn, of dying and rising with Christ, of which the consequence is that believers live 'to righteousness'. In Hebrews there is a distinct emphasis on righteousness as proceeding from faith (we cannot use Jas 2. 23 in support, cf. above p. 132). Heb. 10. 38; 11. 4, 7; 12. 23, all relate to this in some way, but faith in 10. 38 probably means 'faithfulness', and therefore is not really to the point. In Ch. 11, while 'faith' is still not exactly Pauline, Abel's offering arises from his faith, and attests his righteousness, but there is nothing here like 'justification by faith'.[3] It is still really justification by works, yet the righteousness does arise from the faith. Noah, in 11. 7, was righteous in contrast to the world's disobedience, and this also sprang from his faith. Once again, this is not Pauline faith, yet it is important that it is the source of righteousness, cf. also 12. 23.[4]

Thus righteousness in its full ethical–relational sense is seen in the literature variously as a gift of God, as arising through Christ's righteousness, and as arising from faith.

[1] Cf. Barth, *Tradition and Interpretation in Matthew*, 140, and Bornkamm, ibid. 31.

[2] *Les Justes*, 89–92. He finds the communication of God's saving righteousness by Jesus a general theme in the literature, as the basis of man's justification, cf. 57–93, 109ff. We consider the evidence too scanty for this general conclusion.

[3] As Descamps suggests, *Les Justes*, 226ff. However, he also sees here a public proclamation of moral and religious righteousness.

[4] See H. Montefiore, *Hebrews*, 191f, 232; also J. Moffatt, *The Epistle to the Hebrews*, ICC (Edinburgh, 1924), 168.

JUSTIFICATION IN THE NON-PAULINE WRITINGS

Human righteousness as the ground of justification is rejected. Whether or not Mt. 9. 13 and Lk. 15. 7 (see p. 140 above) show this rejection, Lk. 16. 15 and 18. 9 certainly do: 'you justify yourselves before men' and 'some who had confidence in themselves that they were righteous' are both derogatory remarks. Mt. 23. 28 condemns that external righteousness which does not reflect an inward disposition,[1] and so does Mt. 5. 20. It is probably no accident that 5. 6 precedes 5. 20: human righteousness is inadequate, and what is needed is not only a more thoroughgoing kind, but one which comes as God's gift to those who long for it.

We cannot now adequately discuss the problem of justification in Paul as related to James and Matthew, for our main concern is not with the basis of justification, but with what justification is. It seems likely that James is concerned not with how a man becomes accepted by God, but with the sincerity and genuineness of faith, which must be confirmed by a subsequent life of righteousness. Matthew, especially in 5. 20 and 25. 31–46, poses a more serious question.[2] Yet to put Paul, as teaching justification by faith, in opposition to Matthew, as teaching justification by our own better righteousness, is too simple if the point just made about 5. 6 and 5. 20 is valid. The better righteousness is finally not purely human righteousness.

Other material has often been cited to show that Paul's doctrine has parallels in the Gospels and elsewhere.[3] In the parable of the Prodigal Son, and in that of the Pharisee and the Publican, we have in a nutshell what Jesus constantly showed in his ministry, God's acceptance of sinful men, e.g. Lk. 5. 29f; 15. 2, 7, 10; 19. 7. Outside the Gospels, we have already mentioned Acts 13. 38f (pp. 129f) and it is possible to take the reference to Christ's death as a sin-offering in 1 Pet. 3. 18 in

[1] Assuming, with Descamps, *Les Justes*, 201–4, that φαίνεσθε implies an external, rather than a false, righteousness.

[2] Cf. H. K. McArthur, *Understanding the Sermon on the Mount* (London, 1961), 58–79, and literature there cited.

[3] See F. F. Bruce, 'Justification by Faith in the non-Pauline Writings of the New Testament', *EQ*, 24 (1952), 66–77.

terms of justification.[1] Finally, Descamps suggests that we find, especially in Jas 5. 16; 1 Pet. 3. 12; and 1 Jn 2. 1, echoes of the doctrine of the efficacious intercession of the righteous.[2] In the last, it is the intercession of Jesus, but more because he is the exalted one, the 'Paraclete' with the Father, than because he is righteous. Indeed, no stress seems to be laid on his righteousness, but rather on who he is. In the Petrine passage, intercession appears only very allusively in v. 9, and in Jas 5. 16 it is to do with healing and not with merits or justification.

APPENDED NOTE 7

Righteousness and Eschatology in non-Pauline Writings

If we ask how far the setting of the word-group is 'futurist', or 'realised' or 'inaugurated', the position is as follows (many cases are disputable, much depending on one's definition of 'eschatological'; we take it to mean either the present fulfilment of past hope, or future fulfilment of present hope):

1. Without any perceptible eschatological reference:

Verb: Mt. 11. 19; Lk. 7. 29; 10. 29; 16. 15; 18. 14; Jas 2. 21, 24, 25.

Noun: Mt. 6. 1; Acts 10. 35; 13. 10; 24. 25; Heb. 1. 9; 5. 13; 11. 7, 33; 12. 11; Jas 1. 20; 2. 23; 3. 18; 1 Pet. 3. 14; 2 Pet. 1. 1; 1 Jn 2. 29; 3. 7, 10

(the noun δικαίωμα occurs with the meaning 'ordinance' in Lk. 1. 6; Heb. 9. 1, 10; 'judgment' in Rev. 15. 4, and 'righteous action' in Rev. 19. 8).

Adjective: Mt. 1. 19; 5. 45; 9. 13 and parallels; 10. 41, 41, 41; 13. 17; 20. 4; 23. 28, 29, 35, 35; 27. 4, 19, 24; Mk 6. 20; Lk. 1. 6, 17; 12. 57; 15. 7; 18. 9; 20. 20; 23. 41, 47, 50; Jn 7. 24; 17. 25; Acts 4. 19; 10. 22; 14. 2; Heb. 10. 38; 11. 4; Jas 5. 6, 16; 1 Pet. 2. 23; 3. 12; 2 Pet 1. 13; 2. 7, 8, 8; 1 Jn 1. 9; 2. 1, 29; 3. 7, 7, 12.

2. Realised eschatological (but future reference not necessarily absent):

Verb: Acts 13. 39, 39.

[1] So Bruce, 'Justification by Faith', 71.

[2] *Les Justes*, 142–5, 222f.

Noun: Mt. 3. 15; 5. 6, 10, 20; 6. 33; 21. 32; Lk. 1. 75; Jn 16. 8, 10; Heb. 7. 2; 1 Pet. 2. 24; 2 Pet. 2. 5, 21.

Adjective: Lk. 2. 25; Jn 5. 30; Acts 3. 14; 7. 52; 22. 14; 1 Pet. 3. 18.

3. Future eschatological (though based in the present):

Verb: Mt. 12. 37; Rev. 22. 11.

Noun: Acts 17. 31; 2 Pet. 3. 13; Rev. 19. 11; 22. 11.

Adjective: Mt. 13. 43, 49; 25. 37, 46; Lk. 14. 14; Acts 24. 15; Heb. 12. 23; 1 Pet. 4. 18; Rev. 15. 3; 16. 5, 7; 19. 2; 22. 11.

Of the 12 cases of the verb, 8 have no obvious eschatological reference, i.e. 66.6 per cent, and the figures for the noun are 17 out of 34, or 50 per cent, and for the adjective 46 out of 65, or 70.7 per cent. One must therefore hesitate to say that the word-group, the verb included, is particularly eschatological in the NT; even the theologically significant Lk. 18. 9, 14 seem to lack any eschatological reference.

CHAPTER 8

PAUL: PHILIPPIANS, COLOSSIANS, THESSALONIANS, EPHESIANS, THE PASTORALS, AND CORINTHIANS

The following examination assumes the results of the theological and especially the linguistic enquiry in the foregoing, the main points of which are:

1. The verb is predominantly declaratory, forensic, relational; or, it may denote the demonstration of an already existing righteousness. It very seldom indeed means 'make righteous', either in Greek or in the Hebrew equivalent. There is a harmony of forensic and ethical, except for the Rabbinic use of the Hebrew equivalent to mean 'treat generously'.

2. The noun and adjective are normally used to denote a way of acting, and less often to denote the character which lies behind the acting. In the OT it (or its Hebrew equivalent) may in a small minority of cases mean the consequent status of someone who acts in this way, but the minority is so small that this meaning cannot be adopted unless the context demands it. In later literature, this meaning almost totally disappears, and is not found at all in secular Greek.

3. An exception to the previous point is found in the doctrine of Merits, where 'righteousness' (*zekuth*) may be either right behaviour, or the consequent merit. Yet this is not to say that it becomes in such contexts a purely relational word, for a merit always represents something done, by oneself or by someone else, even if the thing done is simply putting trust in God.

4. If we ask what sort of activity is denoted, there is nothing in later literature to contradict, and much to confirm, the OT meaning 'loyalty to the covenant'. This, by analogy, applies even to some secular Greek literature.

While we must not exclude the possibility that Paul stretched his vocabulary beyond its usual limits, before resorting to such a solution we must try to explain his teaching within the usual meaning of the words used. Our task now, therefore, is to approach the Pauline corpus with these facts in mind, and we begin not with Galatians and Romans, where for probably polemical reasons the 'justification' vocabulary is particularly prominent, but with Philippians.[1]

PHILIPPIANS

The verb does not occur at all, but the adjective does, at 1. 7 and 4. 8. In the former, δίκαιον is unemphatic: 'It is right for me to feel thus...' as against 'It is mistaken...'. In 4. 8, δίκαια occurs in a list of things on which to fix the mind, but there is no indication of its precise meaning. As it comes in a list of qualities, it must have a broadly ethical meaning, not a relational one.

The noun is more interesting: 1. 11; 3. 6, 9, 9. In 3. 6 Paul says he was ἄμεμπτος with regard to legal righteousness, surely meaning what any Jew would mean, chiefly the fulfilment of the Law, i.e. a certain kind of behaviour. He has been showing what a good Jew he had been, and now, 3. 7–11, contrasts his wealth then with his greater wealth now, 3. 9:

> (ἵνα Χριστὸν κερδήσω) καὶ εὑρεθῶ ἐν αὐτῷ, μὴ ἔχων ἐμὴν δικαιοσύνην τὴν ἐκ νόμου, ἀλλὰ τὴν διὰ πίστεως Χριστοῦ, τὴν ἐκ θεοῦ δικαιοσύνην ἐπὶ τῇ πίστει.

Clearly this verse is to be taken with v. 6, so that the Christian's righteousness is partly to be defined by its contrast with righteousness which is ἐκ νόμου and therefore is man's achievement, 'one's own righteousness'.[2] Paul the Christian lays no claim to this.

Now grammatically, all the statements about righteousness are subordinate to the clause 'be found in him'; it is in Christ that Paul has any righteousness, and even as a Christian this is all he has or can have. It is not his, but God's, and comes through faith in Christ, διὰ πίστεως, or it meets such faith, ἐπὶ τῇ πίστει, but

[1] That there were pre-Pauline formulations of something like justification and righteousness by faith is likely, but does not really affect our study. See Reumann, *Righteousness and Society*, 23–41. In the case of Philippians, there is also a question whether it is post-Pauline: A. Q. Morton, *Paul, the Man and the Myth* (London, 1966) with J. McLeman thinks Philippians is not by Paul. His arguments are still *sub iudice*, so that any conclusions derived from Philippians must meantime be tested against other epistles. I find his view unconvincing in this case.

[2] 'Human righteousness is legal righteousness', Vincent, *Philippians*, 102.

its source is solely God (ἐκ θεοῦ). We may say, therefore, that righteousness exists in the believer only as he is in Christ – he never possesses it, but rather participates in it by faith, in so far as he is 'in Christ'. Having righteousness by faith, and having it in Christ, are identical; should he cease being in Christ his righteousness would cease, for it exists only in and through this relationship.

Further, this righteousness-in-Christ is closely linked to dying and rising with him, cf. vv. 10f. Whether τοῦ γνῶναι is final or epexegetic, being 'in him' cannot be separated from dying and rising with him, and sharing in the power of his resurrection. We have thus a doctrine of righteousness from God, through faith in Christ.[1]

So much would probably be accepted by most exegetes. Disagreement comes when we try to determine the nature of this righteousness. Is it 'acceptance', or 'justification', or 'forgiveness'? If so, the verse means that having given up the attempt to win acceptance by one's own good works, though one can scarcely call these 'righteousness' if the term means 'acceptance', one receives it by faith. That is to say, one is justified by faith, in Christ. We detect the obvious difficulty even as we state this explanation, a difficulty which has been exposed by F. W. Beare, who himself subscribes to such an interpretation: while righteousness by law is usually taken to be moral achievement, righteousness by faith is really forgiveness.[2] It not only has a different origin, it is a different species. The first is behavioural (though with overtones of relationship and acceptability), but the second is to do with relationship and acceptability with no behavioural overtones at all. Beare admits this is confusing, but is prepared to accept the confusion. We find this not plausible for two reasons. First, 'acceptability' as a meaning for 'righteousness' cannot be adequately supported from other literature. Second, such a difference of kind in the meaning of a word, in a verse where the

[1] Almost certainly not 'the faith of Christ', which would introduce a new idea. The question of the meaning of the genitive arises also in Rom. 1. 17 ('revealed from God's πίστις to man's'?); 3. 22; Gal. 2. 16, 20; 3. 22. See below, Appended Note 8.

[2] *The Epistle to the Philippians*, Black's N.T. Commentaries (London, 1959), 120; see also, among others, J. H. Ropes, '"Righteousness" and "The Righteousness of God" in the Old Testament and in St Paul', *JBL*, 22 (1903), 211–27, at 225.

two righteousnesses are contrasted for their *sources*, is unlikely. It would be better to take both as 'acceptability' did not 'blameless as to law-righteousness' in v. 6 make this impossible.

A second conceivable interpretation involves recourse to the Rabbinic doctrine of merits, with which Paul was plainly familiar.[1] One could then say that righteousness from God is real enough, and is received by faith, but for forensic purposes only – just as for the Rabbis an imputed merit was a real one, but transferred by God's grace from someone else's treasury. Yet this view has several difficulties. First, it combines the 'transfer of merits', for which only God's grace was needed, with 'merit of faith', i.e. one's own faith. This confuses the issue, and differs from the Rabbinic doctrine. Second, among the Rabbis men do not receive merits from God at all; rather God graciously counts something of one's own, or of someone else's, as a merit. Here, we cannot even say that Christ's righteousness is being laid to our account; it is clearly righteousness from God. Third, it is true that in Rom. 4 and Gal. 3, Paul appears to write against the background of the doctrine, but there it is made clear, the matter is discussed at some length, and the verb λογίʒεσθαι – obviously an appropriate one – is used. To detect the doctrine behind the very different formulation here, is quite another matter. Fourth, if this is really a statement about man's justification, why did Paul not make it plain by using the verb? Fifth, although the forensic or acceptability aspect is present in the passage,[2] and although the man who has righteousness from God is by this acceptable to God, the context shows a need for more than this. It suggests the new being in Christ, dying and rising with him, knowing the *power* of his resurrection. One wonders why all this was needed if the basic point is simply the imputation of righteousness. In this epistle as elsewhere, when a believer is in Christ he is new, radically and ethically; cf. 1. 11 – however one

[1] Rom. 11. 28 and perhaps 9. 5 surely point to this, despite Sanday–Headlam's rather odd arguments, *Romans*, 330ff; cf. Davies, *Paul and Rabbinic Judaism*, 272f. It is interesting that in 11. 28 he uses no form of δικαι-, but says διὰ τοὺς πατέρας which is a good rendering of זכות אבות. The doctrine is certainly early enough, cf. above p. 125.

[2] Cf. 'blameless' in v. 6, and 'be found', which may refer to the Last Judgment, so M. Bouttier, *Christianity According to St Paul*, E.Tr. (London, 1966), 17.

understands 'righteousness' here, ethical fruits come through Jesus Christ, cf. also 2. 1–13.

Altogether, it is greatly preferable to follow the mainly Catholic tradition of exegesis and give the word its usual meaning.[1] The righteousness is fully ethical, that of God himself communicated to us as we have faith in Jesus. By 'communicated' we do not mean the transfer of anything from God to man, but rather a participation in God's righteousness, through Christ, by believers. That this has forensic or relational implications is clear, but these implications do not exhaust the meaning, which is forensic and ethical at once – in line with the use in other literature.

There remains the occurrence of the noun in 1. 11: καρπὸν δικαιοσύνης could mean 'fruit consisting in righteousness', which would accord well with our view of 3. 9, and which would mean that as a result of our relationship to Christ we live well ethically. Perhaps the more natural meaning is that through Jesus, our righteousness bears fruit. This fruit is ethical, but this leaves unanswered the question of whether righteousness is also ethical, so that we go from the general good living to specific fruits, or whether it is purely relational, bearing ethical fruits.[2] It is probably a genitive of origin, because of the meaning of the phrase elsewhere (cf. Prov. 11. 30; Amos 6. 13; Jas 3. 18), and the usual meaning of δικαιοσύνη makes it likely that we are going from the general to the concrete. As in 3. 9, this righteousness with its concrete results is not really ours, but his, for the praise and glory are not ours, but his. Yet the results are in our lives, so that we are 'blameless at the day of Christ' (v. 10).

APPENDED NOTE 8

Faith of Christ or in Christ?

We have already alluded to the problem raised by Phil. 3. 9 and similar phrases elsewhere (above p. 149, n. 1). T. F. Torrance argues for a polarity, with Christ's faithfulness as the primary idea, and man's faithfulness as the secondary, because 'God

[1] E.g. F. Prat, *Theology of St Paul*, 1, 191–3.

[2] For the first, Vincent, *Philippians*, 14; for the second, Beare, *Philippians*, 55.

draws man into the sphere of his own faithfulness'.[1] Although such a view would suit the present argument well, it cannot, one fears, be sustained, partly because of the objections raised by C. F. D. Moule,[2] and partly because Torrance makes πίστις really indistinguishable from δικαιοσύνη, so that the verse becomes almost unintelligibly tautological, and quite so in the cases of Rom. 1. 17; Gal. 2. 16, 20. Moreover, were Torrance right, we should need another word to denote man's response. Again, the noun–verb parallel in Gal. 2. 16 makes his view very difficult indeed. He is quite right, of course, about Rom. 3. 3.[3]

COLOSSIANS AND THESSALONIANS[4]

The neuter adjective occurs once in Colossians, used adverbially with ἰσότητα (4. 1), to mean the way in which a Christian master ought to treat his servants. Clearly ethical, it must mean 'justly'. The adjective also occurs in 2 Thess. 1. 5, 6, of God's righteous judgment in v. 5, and of his 'considering it just' in v. 6. This is God's judicial righteousness in action, and vv. 6f show that δίκαιος means that God acts to afflict those who now afflict his people and to vindicate the afflicted. Both punitive and saving elements are present, directed towards different groups.[5]

In 1 Thess. 2. 10 the adverb describes the apostles' behaviour in Thessalonika (ὡς ὁσίως καὶ δικαίως καὶ ἀμέμπτως ὑμῖν τοῖς πιστεύουσιν ἐγενήθημεν). Possibly, as in secular Greek moral writing, the first adverb represents duty done to God, and the second, duty done to man, though more probably this distinction cannot be maintained, and the two words together 'describe their conduct generally as irreproachable before God and man'.[6]

[1] 'One Aspect of the Biblical Conception of Faith', *ET*, 68 (1957), 111–14, 221f; also G. Hebert, '"Faithfulness" and "Faith"', *Theology*, 58 (1955), 373–9.

[2] 'The Biblical Conception of "Faith"', *ET*, 68 (1957), 157, 222.

[3] Cf. also Murray, *Romans*, 1, Appendix B, for a thorough examination and finally rejection of the view of Torrance and Hebert. N. Turner, *Grammatical Insights into the New Testament* (Edinburgh, 1965), 110f, suggests a deliberate ambiguity, the genitive subjective and objective.

[4] These also fall under Morton's axe, but in any case their importance is negligible in the enquiry.

[5] So Descamps, *Les Justes*, 293f; also W. Neil, *The Epistles of Paul to the Thessalonians*, MNTC (London, 1950), 143f.

[6] J. B. Lightfoot, *Notes on Epistles of St Paul* (2nd edn, London, 1904), 27.

EPHESIANS

The Pauline authorship here is under such serious question that we must be cautious in using any results from our examination of the letter. The verb does not occur. The adjective is found once, in 6. 1 ('Children, obey your parents in the Lord, for this is right'). Apart from remarking that behavioural and relational elements are both present, there is nothing to be said. The ἐν Κυρίῳ belongs to the first statement, not the second. There may be a reference to the righteousness which comes in obeying the commandments.[1]

The noun occurs in 4. 24; 5. 9; 6. 14. The first has some similarity to Phil. 3. 9:

> καὶ ἐνδύσασθαι τὸν καινὸν ἄνθρωπον τὸν κατὰ θεὸν κτισθέντα ἐν δικαιοσύνῃ καὶ ὁσιότητι τῆς ἀληθείας.

The 'new man' who is 'created' is characterised by righteousness and holiness (probably 'true righteousness and holiness'), and so is created in God's image, which seems to be the meaning of κατὰ θεόν.[2] 'Righteousness' is surely ethical, in view of the context, and this verse's place in it. The similarity to Phil. 3. 9 is not verbal: faith is not mentioned, nor is 'in Christ', nor 'righteousness from God' as against law-righteousness. Nevertheless only God can create, and the new creation is in holiness and righteousness. This is then not just ordinary paraenesis, the believer being urged to lead a moral life, despite the fact that it comes in a paraenetic section,[3] and that the language of 'putting on' may indicate baptismal catechesis.[4] Yet the notion of new creation by God indicates something more – cf. 2. 8ff for good works linked to new creation in Christ. God not only indicates a path, but actually puts a man's foot upon it. Moreover, as we

and J. E. Frame, *The Epistles of St Paul to the Thessalonians*, ICC (Edinburgh, 1912), 103, take the first view; for the second, see Neil, *Thessalonians*, 42, who is quoted above.

[1] So E. F. Scott, *The Epistles of Paul to the Colossians, to Philemon, and to the Ephesians*, MNTC (London, 1930), 244.

[2] C. F. D. Moule, *An Idiom-Book of New Testament Greek* (2nd edn, Cambridge, 1959), 59, where he points to Col. 3. 10.

[3] See A. M. Hunter, *Paul and his Predecessors* (2nd edn, London, 1961), 52f.

[4] Cf. E. G. Selwyn, *The First Epistle of St Peter* (London, 1946), 391, 394, 398, also Hunter, *Paul and his Predecessors*, 129f.

shall see, one must view baptism, union with Christ, and dying and rising with him, as one whole. Therefore, despite the different formulation, the basic point is similar to that of Phil. 3. 9.

'Righteousness' in 5. 9 may be used not in a conventional ethical sense for one of the fruits of being a believer, but in something like the 'righteousness-in-Christ-by-faith' sense. The writer talks of the moral transformation of believers, who are now light ἐν Κυρίῳ; they do not *have* this light, they *are* it, yet it is not theirs, but something in which they participate. Its fruit is righteousness, holiness, and truth, which may mean that right behaviour comes through being 'in the Lord'.[1]

In 6. 14 righteousness is part of the Christian's armour; it is God's, but worn by the believer (here it differs from the strikingly similar θώρακα δικαιοσύνης of Wisd. 5. 18, where it is and remains God's breastplate). This righteousness is not the Christian's possession, any more than are truth, the gospel, salvation, the Spirit (possibly not faith, either), but is God's, worn by Christ's man when he contends against wickedness in every form. It is thus ethical, from God,[2] according well with 'righteousness-in-Christ'.

THE PASTORAL EPISTLES

It is very doubtful indeed whether these are by Paul, but they probably come from a Pauline circle or movement. We do not propose to use them as material for Pauline theology, but merely to see what happened to the word-group at the farthest limit of the Pauline corpus.

We now meet the verb for the first time in the Pauline corpus: 1 Tim. 3. 16; Tit. 3. 7. In the former, ἐδικαιώθη ἐν πνεύματι comes as the second line in a credal or hymnic statement,[3] and its meaning is not clear. It is probably in some sense demonstrative: Christ is proved right, or vindicated, at a cosmic or even celestial bar. This happens 'in the Spirit', i.e. his messiahship is

[1] Scott, *Colossians, Philemon, Ephesians*, 229, sees it as uprightness in treatment of others, the higher moral life to which fellowship with Christ leads.

[2] 'The actual rightness of character wrought by Christ', T. K. Abbott, *The Epistles to the Ephesians and to the Colossians*, ICC (Edinburgh, 1909), 185.

[3] See Hunter, *Paul and his Predecessors*, 37; J. N. D. Kelly, *The Pastoral Epistles*, Black's N.T. Commentaries (London, 1963), 89, and indeed most commentators.

confirmed by the resurrection.[1] It may even be that 'justified' is here equivalent to 'glorified'.[2] Although demonstrative, the verb is still forensic.

In Tit. 3. 7, ἵνα δικαιωθέντες τῇ ἐκείνου χάριτι... clearly means, especially in view of vv. 5f, that man cannot really claim to be righteous with his own law-righteousness, that justification is of the ungodly, and that it is purely a matter of grace. It is true that from this passage alone, a 'make righteous' meaning is possible, but a declaratory (not a demonstrative) one is equally possible, and is to be preferred as following the usual meaning in other literature. God accepts, or acquits us, purely by his grace. This justification seems to depend on baptism and the 'regeneration and renewal in the Holy Spirit' which it represents (vv. 5f). Thus, justification is not simply of the ungodly, but of the baptised or converted ungodly.[3]

The noun occurs in 1 Tim. 6. 11; 2 Tim. 2. 22; 3. 16; 4. 8; Tit. 3. 5. Every case is ethical, and one may even have *paideia* in it, 2 Tim. 3. 16. The first three refer to the Christian's righteousness, while Tit. 3. 5 denotes that human righteousness which cannot save. All are in explicit relation to God. There seems to be wide agreement that 'crown of righteousness' in 2 Tim. 4. 8 means 'crown as a reward for righteousness'. Instead of a crown which rewards athletic achievement, Paul's crown will reward achievement in righteousness when the final reckoning is made and the prizes are distributed.[4] W. Lock finds it possible that in addition the phrase means a crown consisting in righteousness,[5] but most other commentators do not. If it did mean this, righteousness would be thoroughly eschatological, referring to the life of heaven, cf. the 'crown of life' of Rev. 2. 10. While this

[1] Cf. Kelly, *Pastoral Epistles*, 90f. 'In the Spirit' may refer to vindication in the celestial, as against the earthly, 'in the flesh', sphere, cf. Rom. 1. 3f; 1 Pet. 3. 18; Isa. 31. 3, etc., and E. Schweizer, 'Two New Testament Creeds Compared', in W. Klassen and G. F. Snyder, *Current Issues in New Testament Interpretation* (London, 1962), 166–77.

[2] So Descamps, *Les Justes*, 84–9; he points also to Jn 16. 8.

[3] Cf. Kelly, *Pastoral Epistles*, 253f, who cites 1 Cor. 6. 11 to show that baptism and justification are inseparable parts of one process.

[4] So many commentators, e.g. B. S. Easton, *The Pastoral Epistles* (London, 1948), 70; C. K. Barrett, *The Pastoral Epistles* (Oxford, 1963), 119.

[5] *The Pastoral Epistles*, ICC (Edinburgh, 1924), 115; cf. Descamps, *Les Justes*, 268, who sees the righteousness of glory as the reward of the righteousness of works.

is not impossible, the athletic metaphor leads us to prefer the first view. Righteousness must then mean ethical and meritorious achievement, 'my own righteousness', not 'righteousness in Christ', and this comes very oddly indeed in a supposedly Pauline letter.

The adjective and adverb are found 4 times: 1 Tim. 1. 9; 2 Tim. 4. 8; Tit. 1. 8; 2. 12 (adverb). All are clearly ethical: the first refers to people for whom a law is really superfluous because they are morally good; in Tit. 1. 8 it is in a list of virtuous attributes required of a bishop; in Tit. 2. 12 it describes the manner of life of Christians; in 2 Tim. 4. 8 God is the 'righteous Judge', but the emphasis is rather on giving good works their deserved reward than on punishing evil deeds.

THE CORINTHIAN LETTERS

All the epistles examined so far have had their authorship questioned, more or less widely. We now turn to books universally acknowledged to be Pauline.

The Verb

It occurs in 1 Cor. 4. 4; 6. 11.

> 1 Cor. 4. 4: I am not aware of anything against myself, ἀλλ' οὐκ ἐν τούτῳ δεδικαίωμαι. It is the Lord who judges me.

This could refer to an acquittal at the Judgment,[1] or it could be demonstrative – the fact that he knows nothing against himself does not show him to be righteous. In any case he is talking about man's standing at the bar of God, but with the implication that God does acquit those who really have nothing against them. This hint of correspondence between forensic and actual righteousness is curious (could not a Rabbi have written it?) and may show that when Paul is not engaged in polemic about the way to God's favour, he uses the verb as would any Greek-speaking Jew.

> 1 Cor. 6. 11: ἀλλὰ ἀπελούσασθε, ἀλλὰ ἡγιάσθητε, ἀλλὰ ἐδικαιώθητε ἐν τῷ ὀνόματι τοῦ Κυρίου...καὶ ἐν τῷ πνεύματι...

[1] Cf. H.-D. Wendland, *Die Briefe an die Korinther*, NTD (7th edn, Göttingen, 1954), 34.

These three passives can scarcely be in an ascending time-series, i.e. first baptised, then sanctified, then justified. Nor, despite C. A. Anderson Scott,[1] can it be a descending series, first justified, then consecrated by the Spirit, then baptised. Neither sequence fits the NT teaching, and it is tremendously difficult to make any satisfactory chronological scheme. Consequently it is better to assume no sequence at all, but rather three aspects of, three different ways of seeing, the Holy Spirit's action in our redemption.[2] At least in this passage, therefore, we cannot regard sanctification as the process of which justification is the starting-point. While the two may not have exactly the same connotation, their denotation, with that of baptism, is the same.

'You were justified': does this mean simply 'you were acquitted, forgiven, brought into a right relationship'?[3] On linguistic grounds we should expect so. But could it mean an ethical putting right? Some think so.[4] The context is strongly ethical, and this verse comes as a contrast to the unethical behaviour mentioned in vv. 9f, so that one may wonder whether the three passives are not intended to be in opposition to this. Certainly at least part of the meaning must be that the Christian who is 'washed, sanctified, justified' no longer does these things. Are all three passives then ethical, with 'washed' referring to moral cleansing?[5] Yet we may still maintain the essentially forensic or relational character of 'justified' if we take the end of the verse ('in the name of the Lord Jesus Christ and in the Spirit of our God') to suggest that we are justified etc. as we are 'in the Spirit'. Thus J. B. Lightfoot said that 'justified' is 'not simply by imputation but in virtue of our incorporation into Christ'.[6] That is to say, if we see behind this verse the notion of 'righteousness-in-Christ-by-faith', which is real enough, then it is not surprising that 'justified' seems here to have a moral

[1] *Christianity According to St Paul* (Cambridge, 1927), 120.

[2] So J. Héring, *The First Epistle of Saint Paul to the Corinthians*, E.Tr. (London, 1962), 42.

[3] So H. L. Goudge, *The First Epistle to the Corinthians* (London, 1903), 45; Murray, *Romans*, I, 349f.

[4] Cf. Bultmann, *Theology*, I, 136; Wendland, *Korinther*, 45.

[5] C. K. Barrett, *The First Epistle to the Corinthians*, Black's N.T. Commentaries (London, 1968), 142, has 'sanctified' mean 'claimed by God for his own', but this does not solve the problem raised by the passage as a whole.

[6] *Notes on Epistles of St Paul*, 213.

renewal force. In fact it does not *mean* this, but it does *imply* it. We put this forward only tentatively at this stage, but it is an idea which we shall meet again, and which is not unlike that in Tit. 3. 7.

The Noun

There are 8 cases: 1 Cor. 1. 30; 2 Cor. 3. 9; 5. 21; 6. 7, 14; 9. 9, 10; 11. 15.

> 1 Cor. 1. 30: ἐξ αὐτοῦ δὲ ὑμεῖς ἐστε ἐν Χριστῷ Ἰησοῦ, ὃς ἐγενήθη σοφία ἡμῖν ἀπὸ θεοῦ, δικαιοσύνη τε καὶ ἁγιασμὸς καὶ ἀπολύτρωσις...

The Church's life is 'in Christ Jesus', and certain things are true of believers as new men in Christ, which would otherwise be true only of God. First, wisdom: ἡμῖν and ἀπὸ θεοῦ together suggest that this is not just God's own wisdom, nor simply Christ as the wisdom of God. Rather is Christ the wisdom of God for us, and this is confirmed by the contrast with the otherwise weakness and unimportance of the Church in relation to the wisdom of the world (cf. v. 26). In so far as believers are in Christ, they have wisdom, which means they do not *possess* it.[1] This accords with Jewish wisdom teaching, where wisdom is primarily God's, but becomes man's also.

Second, righteousness and sanctification: Lightfoot sees these as epexegetic of 'wisdom', because of the lack of any connecting particle between σοφία and δικαιοσύνη.[2] If he is right, we are presumably to take both these terms in the same way as wisdom, i.e. as primarily God's, but now also man's in so far as he is in Christ. 'Righteousness' can scarcely be understood here in merit terms, as the formulation involves wisdom and sanctification as well, which means that a purely forensic meaning is impossible.[3]

[1] Cf. J. Moffatt, *The First Epistle of Paul to the Corinthians*, MNTC (London, 1938), 21; J. W. Montgomery, 'Wisdom as Gift', *INTERP*, 16 (1962), 54f.

[2] *Notes on Epistles of St Paul*, 167. H. Lietzmann, *An die Korinther I, II*, *HzNT* (4th edn, Tübingen, 1949), 11, 169, apparently regards all the terms as co-ordinate, and righteousness as both justification and real freedom from sin.

[3] Barrett, *1 Corinthians*, 60f, sees righteousness here as primarily forensic, but not just a forensic 'counter', rather as 'a direct product of Christ's self-offering for men, the work of redemption'. Héring (*1 Corinthians*, 13) and others take the meaning to be 'justification'.

Moreover, ἡμῖν ἀπὸ θεοῦ must refer to these terms as well as to wisdom, so that God's righteousness, his consistently loving, gracious, loyal action, becomes ours not to possess, but to share in as we share in Christ.[1] So with sanctification: our life in Christ is marked by that holiness which comes from God in the person of Jesus, a holiness in which we can participate, but not possess.

The fourth term, 'redemption', stands rather by itself, whereas 'righteousness' and 'sanctification' are closely linked by τε καί. Is it one of the series, or is it an over-all term which sums up and includes the others? It is plainly included among the things of which we cannot boast (v. 31), because it comes from God in Christ. It may well mean deliverance from the slavery of sin, or it may refer to our final redemption, pointing to eternal life.[2] At any rate it is not exactly of a piece with the other terms, and probably is best taken quite generally, 'in Christ we have our redemption – in all its aspects'.

2 Cor. 3. 9: Here the διακονία τῆς δικαιοσύνης is an antithetic parallel to the διακονία τῆς κατακρίσεως. Yet the parallel is not exact,[3] righteousness is not simply a judicial verdict, partly because this is not a likely meaning for the noun at any time, but also because the context requires something more. In this context, 'righteousness' refers to God's whole intervention in Jesus, and resembles those places in OT where it really means 'salvation'. This includes forensic salvation, but is wider, and means God's own saving righteousness.[4]

> 2 Cor. 5. 21: τὸν μὴ γνόντα ἁμαρτίαν ὑπὲρ ἡμῶν ἁμαρτίαν ἐποίησεν, ἵνα ἡμεῖς γενώμεθα δικαιοσύνη θεοῦ ἐν αὐτῷ.

We find here the same idea as in Phil. 3. 9 and 1 Cor. 1. 30. In so far as we are in Christ, we participate in Christ's righteousness, so that we are renewed or newly created, and can act faithfully and loyally in a way analogous to God's righteousness, and derived from it. We have a sort of exchange which makes no sense apart from the notion of solidarity: he entered into our sinful situation,

[1] Cf. Tobac, *Le Problème de la Justification*, 204.

[2] So Lightfoot, *Notes on Epistles of St Paul*, 168. He cites Eph. 4. 30 and 1. 14; Rom. 8. 23.

[3] Despite many commentators, e.g. A. Plummer, *The Second Epistle of St Paul to the Corinthians*, ICC (Edinburgh, 1915), 91.

[4] Wendland, *Korinther*, 156, sees it as corresponding to 'service of Spirit' and also to 'service of reconciliation', 5. 18ff.

and thereby became our representative, the Man for us. Precisely because of this, we can now be 'in him'. His representative action was notably on the Cross, and it was there particularly that he 'became sin for us', although he did not sin.[1] While all this is not explicated, the passage makes little sense without it. He died the death of sin for us, that we might live the life of righteousness in him, cf. 5. 14f, taking 'all' to mean 'all believers'.[2] He entered our solidarity of sin, that we might enter his solidarity of righteousness, cf. Phil. 3. 9.

This interpretation requires that θεοῦ means that it is God's own righteousness, his own covenant loyalty, a loyalty which men conspicuously lack. It is unprofitable to ask whether this is *iustitia salutifera* or *distributiva*; the notion is wider than either. The meaning cannot be 'acceptability',[3] partly on linguistic grounds, and partly because the parallel suggests the opposite of 'sin', which is certainly more than 'non-acceptability',[4] partly also for the reasons adduced for Phil. 3. 9. Again, it is unlikely to mean 'the righteousness approved by God', which fits neither γενώμεθα nor ἐν αὐτῷ, and in any case is not adequate for the rich theological content of the verse. We suggest rather that it means that we are taken up into and share the covenant loyalty which hitherto has been God's alone. This is not possession: believers neither become righteous, nor have the righteousness of God, both of which would imply possession, at least of a quality. Instead, they 'become the righteousness of God in him', an expression which avoids the other and unsatisfactory formulations, and emphasises participation in, not possession of, God's righteousness.[5] The forensic note of acceptability is included, as

[1] 'Made sin for us' probably refers to the Cross as sin-offering, cf. Tannehill, *Dying and Rising with Christ*, 37, though it could refer to the incarnation, cf. Rom. 8. 3, or to the incarnation and cross together. On this whole section, see V. Taylor, *The Atonement in New Testament Teaching* (2nd edn, London, 1963), especially 60, 84, 87f, 174f, and also W. Grundmann, 'Gesetz, Rechtfertigung und Mystik bei Paulus', 65, 'In dem ὑπέρ gründet das σύν'.

[2] See E. Best, *One Body in Christ* (London, 1955), 54.

[3] Despite, among others, Lietzmann, *Korinther*, 127.

[4] For Paul's view of sin as both wrong action and wrong relationship, see W. Grundmann in G. Quell and others, *Sin*, BKW (London, 1951), 75–80. We cannot follow Stuhlmacher, *Gottes Gerechtigkeit*, 75, in seeing both sin and righteousness here as opposing powers.

[5] This is not merely individual, cf. the plurals here and in 1 Cor. 1. 30; Phil. 1. 11; Eph. 4. 24.

v. 19 makes clear, but is not the only note, cf. v. 17 and the 'new creation' note.[1]

2 Cor. 6. 7: 'Weapons of righteousness' may simply mean 'fair means, not foul', or it may mean that God in his vindicating righteousness comes to the aid and defence of his servant. It is stretching the point to say that as a man in Christ he uses the weapons of his new moral strength, for the text says nothing so precise. The first view is probably the better, as Paul is defending his record, so that the word has a general moral sense, with a reference to God as well.

2 Cor. 6. 14: this is plainly ethical, though we may note that 'righteousness' is parallel to 'believer' and 'Christ', v. 15. The use, however, is probably quite conventional.

2 Cor. 9. 9, 10: for the first time we find a hint as to what sort of activity righteousness is. Both cases here certainly mean 'benevolence', though the first, in a quotation from Ps. 112. 9, may refer to God's.[2] Whether it is God's or man's, the point is clear enough: God gives such abundance to us, that we are able to be generous in our turn (cf. v. 8). There is no sign of the righteousness-in-Christ idea. We cannot, of course, freely infer from this passage that the 'benevolence' meaning is to be assumed elsewhere.

2 Cor. 11. 15: 'servants of righteousness' refers to wicked men, acting wickedly, servants of a wicked cause, who masquerade as the opposite. Righteousness is thus undoubtedly ethical, with just possibly also present the notion of it as a power to be served.

The Adjective and Adverb

There are no cases of the adjective, but the adverb occurs once, in 1 Cor. 15. 34: ἐκνήψατε δικαίως καὶ μὴ ἁμαρτάνετε. It is tempting to take this in a full ethical sense, 'sober up morally',

[1] Cf. also Drummond, '"Righteousness of God" in the Theology of St Paul', 282f, who shows that imputative ideas will not do: God does not impute sin to Jesus, rather 'Christ descended into the realm of sin that we might ascend with him into the realm of righteousness'. We ought to mention that Stuhlmacher refers the interchange solely to the Church's mission, cf. vv. 18–20, and not to ethics at all, *Gottes Gerechtigkeit*, 76.

[2] H. L. Goudge, *The Second Epistle to the Corinthians* (London, 1927), 88f, sees both cases as 'God's approval', which is openly demonstrated; for our view, see R. H. Strachan, *The Second Epistle of Paul to the Corinthians*, MNTC (London, 1935), 143.

and to connect it closely with the knowledge of God which is mentioned in the next part of the verse, thus giving a union of moral behaviour with relationship to God. Probably, however, it simply means 'sober right up', which is adequate in the context.[1]

SUMMARY OF RESULTS

In all the letters under consideration, that is the whole Pauline corpus except Galatians and Romans, the verb occurs 4 times, the noun 20 times, the adjective or adverb 12 times, and δικαίωμα and δικαίωσις not at all.

1. The Verb: in each case the use is forensic, even 1 Tim. 3. 16 which speaks of Christ's vindication. Tit. 3. 7 and 1 Cor. 6. 11, while forensic, also hint at moral renewal in the background.

2. The Noun: it is used 3 times for law-righteousness, 'my own righteousness', Phil. 3. 6, 9; Tit. 3. 5. Twice the sense is 'benevolence', reminiscent of the Rabbinic use of *tsedaqah*, 2 Cor. 9. 9, 10. It is used 7 times of the Christian's uprightness, without any specific reference to 'in Christ': 2 Cor. 6. 7, 14; 11. 15; 1 Tim. 6. 11; 2 Tim. 2. 22; 3. 16; 4. 8. Once it is used of God's saving righteousness, 2 Cor. 3. 9. As far as man's righteousness is concerned, all the Pastorals cases are now accounted for, but less than half the rest. The remaining 7 (1 Cor. 1. 30; 2 Cor. 5. 21; Phil. 1. 11; 3. 9; Eph. 4. 24 and probably 5. 9 and 6. 14) all to some extent and in some way contain the righteousness-in-Christ-by-faith idea. This righteousness is certainly ethical, it is what man does, but equally it is from God and in Christ. The 'merits' interpretation, examined but rejected for Phil. 3. 9, is not even remotely possible for 1 Cor. 1. 30; Phil. 1. 11; Eph. 4. 24; 5. 9; or 6. 14. It is not impossible for 2 Cor. 5. 21, but the parallel with 'sin' is against it, as are the general arguments used for Phil. 3. 9. This righteousness then is not a moral quality inherent in the believer, not a possession, but exists only in the 'in Christ', faith relationship. In our examination of Jewish literature we have seen that it is a relational word, not in the sense that it denotes a relationship, but in that it denotes activity within a relationship. This is now brought to its climax and fulfilment; just as Paul has a doctrine of justification by faith, so he also has a doctrine of

[1] Cf. Barrett, *1 Corinthians*, 367. Héring, *1 Corinthians*, 173, suggests 'as is fitting'.

righteousness by faith. If faith is indivisible, it will not be surprising if we find that the two doctrines are closely associated. We have already suggested that such an association may solve the problem of 1 Cor. 6. 11, where the verb seems to have a more than forensic force. On the other hand, righteousness-in-Christ-from-God would by definition be valid before God. This connection is not elaborated in these letters, but we shall see that it is very carefully used in Galatians and Romans. Finally, it is notable that this doctrine is found in the acknowledged Paulines, in the 'deutero-Paulines', but not in the Pastorals.

3. The Adjective and Adverb: of the 12 cases, 3 refer to God as 'righteous Judge' (2 Thess. 1. 5, 6; 2 Tim. 4. 8). The other 9 are all ethical, two of them, Phil. 1. 7 and the adverb in 1 Cor. 15. 34, in an unemphatic, conventional sense. The rest are all ethical in an unspecified sense, and all are in some relation to God.

We suggest therefore, that in his use of this word-group Paul can express both man's acceptance, and his moral renewal.[1] The first attaches especially to the verb, and the second to the noun. It will have become clear that the idea of the corporate Christ is central to our argument.

[1] Regarding time: 'Justified' is clearly past in 1 Cor. 6. 11; 'righteousness-in-Christ' is surely present in 1 Cor. 1. 30; 2 Cor. 5. 21 is debatable, but v. 17 suggests the present. Phil. 1. 11 implies righteousness now, which will appear at the Judgment, cf. also 3. 9. The Ephesians cases are certainly present.

CHAPTER 9

RIGHTEOUSNESS IN CHRIST

We are now in a position to state the fundamental thesis of this book, which rests not only on the linguistic enquiry we have been undertaking, but also on the idea of 'the Corporate Christ', and to this we must now briefly turn.[1]

THE CORPORATE CHRIST

The three main places where the righteousness-in-Christ idea is found (1 Cor. 1. 30; 2 Cor. 5. 21; Phil. 3. 9) have it in common that 'righteousness' is best taken ethically, that it is God's, and that in Christ it becomes ours. Phil. 3. 9 stresses faith in Christ as the means, and associates it closely with dying and rising with him. A very similar idea is expressed in 'new creation' language in Eph. 4. 24, and in what looks like the 'putting on' language of baptismal catechesis. 1 Cor. 1. 30 is in an epistle where the two kinds of humanity are strikingly delineated (Ch. 15) and where (15. 22) 'in Christ' is contrasted with 'in Adam'. A little earlier (Ch. 12) believers are called 'the body of Christ', who belong to one another within that body. Again, in 2 Cor. 5. 14–21 we have a most important combination of juridical with what we may call incorporative elements: thus, v. 14, Christ died *for* us, and therefore we have died also (in him?). Likewise we are risen and live with him, v. 15. Therefore, being in Christ is to be a new creation (or creature, v. 17). This is possible because of Christ's ministry of reconciliation (vv. 18f) and his not reckoning our trespasses (v. 19) which amounts to justification. The reconciliation makes the new being possible. Then v. 21 recalls vv. 14f; the death of

[1] This section owes much to C. F. D. Moule, *The Phenomenon of the New Testament* (London, 1967), Ch. 2. It will be evident that I do not accept a mystical interpretation, following among many others F. Neugebauer, *In Christus* (Göttingen, 1961), and E. Best, *One Body in Christ*, who gives a useful summary of the history of interpretation, 8–19. There is no loss of personal identity or will – cf. A. R. George's crucial work, *Communion with God in the New Testament* (London, 1953), Chs. 6 and 7. Actually 'mysticism' is so ambiguous that one wishes for a moratorium on its use.

Christ is an entering into our sin, and then, by the principle of solidarity and representation, we enter his righteousness, the righteousness of God. Many of the theological connections we wish to make, are thus made in this passage by Paul himself (mission is also important in the passage, but does not control the formulation of the theology).

We may now make a brief summary of the corporate Christ idea as found in Paul, and as underlying much of what we have been saying.

To be 'in Christ' is to be in relationship with Christ, but there is more than this – Christ is seen as an inclusive figure, in whom believers are incorporate.[1] The life in Christ is the life of faith: to believe is to be in Christ.[2] As faith is indivisible, there is no distinction of that faith which is a response to God's action in Christ (i.e. justifying faith) from that which is the Christian's continuing life.[3]

To be in Christ is to be in the new Adam, in a solidarity of life, and of righteousness, as against being in 'natural' humanity, the old Adam, in a solidarity of sin and death, cf. Rom. 5. 12–21; 1 Cor. 15. 22.[4] To be in Christ is therefore both personal, because it requires personal faith and relation to Christ, and also corporate, because there is a new unity of mankind in him.

This brings us to the Church as Christ's body. Whether or not we think Paul sees the *body* of Adam as incorporating ordinary unredeemed humanity,[5] it is certain that for him to be in Christ,

[1] Cf. Moule, *Phenomenon*, 23.

[2] Cf. W. H. P. Hatch, *The Pauline Idea of Faith in Relation to Jewish and Hellenistic Religion*, Harvard Theological Studies, III (Cambridge, Mass., 1917), 38–48.

[3] Cf. Bultmann in R. Bultmann and A. Weiser, *Faith*, BKW, E.Tr. (London, 1961), 88f, 93f; also Hatch, *Pauline Faith*, 65, and Tannehill, *Dying and Rising with Christ*, 125f.

[4] Cf. Best, *One Body*, 26, and Ch. 2; A. S. Peake, 'The Quintessence of Paulinism', *BJRL*, 4 (1917–18), 303–11; R. Scroggs, *The Last Adam* (Oxford, 1966), 87f, 100ff, who stresses that in 1 Cor. 15 the point is not the sources of the two humanities, but their nature.

[5] There is some evidence that the Rabbis conceived mankind as being united in Adam's body, but the relevance of this for Paul is disputed: cf. Best, *One Body*, 35–8; Davies, *Paul and Rabbinic Judaism*, 53ff; Scroggs, *Last Adam*, 35, 49ff. For various explanations of the origin of Paul's use of 'body' for the Church, see Best, 83–93, J. A. T. Robinson, *The Body* (London, 1952), 55ff.

in the new humanity, is to be in the Church, the embodiment of that humanity, 1 Cor. 12. 12.

Being in Christ also involves dying and rising with him. This dying may refer to a previous death *in* sin (Eph. 2. 1–5) or to the death of the old self, as death *to* sin, i.e. an entering into Christ's representative action. This leads to a new life, both ethically and relationally, a risen life which is a new creation, gift as well as demand, imperative as well as indicative, cf. Col. 3. 1–17; Rom. 6. 2, 11f; Eph. 4. 17–24. This new creation may be a restoration of the image of God, dealing with a new nature, not just a new obedience.[1]

Dying and rising are expressed and enacted in baptism, the sacrament of the 'in Christ' idea, Rom. 6. 3–11; Col. 2. 12 – 3. 5. Dying and rising, however, occur outside baptismal contexts (Gal. 2. 19f; 2 Cor. 5. 14), and even in Rom. 6, baptism is secondary to it.[2] Baptism also depends on faith, cf. Gal. 3. 26f.[3]

The atonement, while there are other ways of stating it, may be expressed within, and is vital to, this circle of ideas. Christ on the Cross enters our solidarity, dying 'for us', so that we may enter his solidarity, dying and rising with him to new life.[4]

This new life, and all that goes with it, is future, but is entered now: the rising may be future, 1 Cor. 15. 20ff, or present, Rom. 6. 4, 6; 7. 4. Dying and rising may be decisive events, Col. 2. 12 – 3. 5, or continuing realities, 2 Cor. 4. 10ff; Phil. 3. 10.[5] The whole incorporative notion thus includes both the facts of our redemption, and the subsequent life of the redeemed: 'Christ is the "place" in whom believers are and in whom salvation is. The formula has these two foci about which it revolves,

[1] Cf. Scroggs, *Last Adam*, 61–71.

[2] So Tannehill, *Dying and Rising*, 7–14; cf. T. F. Glasson, 'Dying and Rising with Christ', *LQHR*, Oct. 1961, 286–91. On the alleged dependence here of Paul on the Mystery Religions see Bultmann, *Theology*, I, 139ff (proponent), and Davies, *Paul and Rabbinic Judaism*, 88ff, and Flemington, *NT Doctrine of Baptism*, 76ff (opponents).

[3] Cf. Cullmann, *Baptism in the NT*, Ch. 3.

[4] Cf. Taylor, *Atonement in NT Teaching*, 84–97 and passim; Moule, *Phenomenon*, 29; also Grundmann's remark quoted above, p. 160.

[5] Cf. E. Schweizer, 'Dying and Rising with Christ', *NTS*, 14 (1967), 1–14, at 1–3; Glasson, 'Dying and Rising'; Scroggs, *Last Adam*, 109–12, sees the new humanity as future, but partly anticipated; also on future and present aspects, Tannehill, *Dying and Rising*, 12, 47, 130.

and each of which predominates in turn but which are always connected.'[1] It is thus both forensic, and to do with moral renewal.

The incorporative circle of ideas is related to the power of a new life in several ways. First, to be in Christ is not only to know him, but also to know 'the power of his resurrection' (Phil. 3. 10). Second, though Christ and the Spirit are not thereby identified, to be in Christ is to be in the Spirit: compare 1 Cor. 1. 2 with 6. 11; 1 Cor. 6. 11 with Gal. 2. 17; Rom. 8. 9 with Gal. 2. 20; cf. also 1 Cor. 6. 17; 15. 45; Rom. 8. 9f.[2] Now the Spirit is power, δύναμις, cf. Eph. 3. 14–17.[3] Yet the more basic statement about believers and the Spirit is that he is in them (cf. Rom. 8. 9f, the reverse of the situation with Christ, where 'Christ in us' is less basic), so that power is in them, power for the Christian mission,[4] but also for love and Christian living in general.[5] Third, we are in Christ, but he is also in us, cf. Rom. 8. 10; Gal. 2. 20; Eph. 3. 17; also places where ἐν is prefixed to verbs, e.g. 2 Cor. 13. 3; Col. 1. 29. This means not the 'mere mutual interpenetration of two individuals',[6] nor two sides of one coin. It is rather that we are corporately in Christ, while he, the whole Christ, is in each part of his corporate personality.[7] Moreover, Christ in believers

[1] Best, *One Body*, 8, cf. 21, 29; see also Neugebauer, *In Christus*, 72–91, and Moule, *Phenomenon*, 27.

[2] See F. X. Durrwell, *The Resurrection*, E.Tr. (London, 1960), 103, 220. Best, *One Body*, 11f, shows that being in the Spirit and being in Christ are not interchangeable, though they overlap and each involves the other. The former is more to do with the believer's inner experience and activity, the latter with the basis of his existence.

[3] Cf. W. Grundmann, 'δύναμαι/δύναμις', *TDNT*, II, 284–317, at 311f; C. H. Powell, *The Biblical Concept of Power* (London, 1963,) 127f.

[4] Cf. Phil. 4. 13 which links Christ's strengthening power with 'in Christ', and with the apostolate, cf. also 1 Tim. 1. 12; 2 Tim. 4. 17.

[5] Cf. Gal. 5. 22f and also 5. 6. Grundmann, in 'Der Lehrer der Gerechtigkeit', 254ff, argues that to be in Christ is like being in an electro-magnetic field of force, that of Christ, the power of which is the Spirit, which comes about through baptism and dying with Christ, cf. Rom. 6. 11f. Tannehill, *Dying and Rising*, 14–20, relates dying and rising with Christ to the two dominions or aeons of Rom. 6. 20–3: in the cross and resurrection the shift of the aeons occurs, and Christians participate in (not repeat) these events. In Part II, especially 81f, he sees Christian behaviour as reflecting the new dominion, cf. Gal. 5. 19ff; Rom. 6. 18f; 8. 13. Exhortation is still needed (Rom. 6. 13) because the σῶμα is still exposed to another power, that of sin (Rom. 8. 12f).

[6] Moule, *Phenomenon*, 26. For a rare reciprocity, see Gal. 2. 20.

[7] Cf. Best, *One Body*, 9f.

means that Christ's life is in them, that he is working in them, which produces fruit both for moral renewal and for the apostolate: for moral renewal, Rom. 8. 10; perhaps Phil. 2. 13; Eph. 3. 17, 20; for the apostolate, inter alia 2 Cor. 13. 3; Col. 1. 29.

Lastly we are 'in the Lord'. While it is true that this is largely associated with exhortation and command, the imperative often implies an indicative as well as vice versa.[1]

There is no neat, logical consistency in all this, but at least it seems clear that in giving righteousness an ethical force and relating it closely to the 'in Christ' circle of ideas, we are doing no strange thing, but merely reflecting the connection between the ethical and the incorporative which is found elsewhere in Paul.

THE BASIC CONTENTION

Although the two chief sources of material have still to be examined, it may be helpful to state the basic contention in advance, and then test it by an exegetical examination of the two letters, Romans and Galatians.

1. Paul has a doctrine of justification by faith as held traditionally by the Reformed theology. This is entirely forensic or relational: God accepts us as we are, he acquits us despite our lack of deserving, he forgives us. It all rests entirely on his grace, our faith being not the ground but the means by which justification operates, though the expressions vary, cf. ἐκ πίστεως in Rom. 5. 1 and διὰ πίστεως in Gal. 2. 16. This entire dependence on grace is not only initially, at baptism or conversion, but remains. Even after a lifetime of Christian service, the believer has no works on which to rely. Justification is always by grace through faith, now, and before God's judgment throne, cf. Rom. 3. 30; 5. 1.

2. Paul has also a doctrine of righteousness through faith, in Christ. The believer enters not just a private relationship to Jesus, but a new humanity, in which he becomes a new kind of man. Thus there are not only social or corporate implications, but also ethical ones, for he now shares in the risen life of Christ,

[1] Cf. Eph. 6. 10, and Powell's comment: 'the imperative "be strong" invites him to enter into the heritage of power that is already his in the Lord', *Biblical Concept of Power*, 151; cf. Phil. 4. 2; Col. 2. 6.

which means power, including ethical power. Thus he becomes really and truly righteous. Faith is fundamental, for only as he believes is he in Christ, and therefore only as he believes is he righteous. Righteousness is thus never possessed; though it may appear to be his own, in that the observer will see righteous living, in fact it remains Christ's, in which he participates, and which is evident in his life. Thus again, even after a lifetime of Christian service, the believer cannot claim any righteousness of his own before God. It is always 'I and yet not I, but Christ lives in me' (Gal. 2. 20).[1]

3. The relation of justification to faith-righteousness is now emerging. Righteousness in Christ spells the end of law-righteousness. True righteousness does not consist in law-fulfilment, for the Christian has died to the Law both as the way to justification and as the way to righteousness.[2] Yet if God looks on believers only as they are found in Christ, he may properly declare them righteous, for in him – and only in him – they are righteous, and therefore ought to be acquitted. There is nothing fictional here.[3]

4. Yet the two conceptions are not always related in this way. Sometimes the new righteousness in Christ is possible because man has been first accepted as righteous, and being accepted, is restored to right relationship, and in that relationship may now live righteously.

This double-headed doctrine may help to explain why Paul, if meaning 'forgiveness' by justification, did not use a verb for 'forgive' or 'reconcile'. It may be partly, as V. Taylor thinks,[4] that by 'forgiveness' Paul means less than full restoration, but it is also partly that by the use of one root, verb, noun, and adjective, he can express the whole renewal of man by God, relationally, forensically, and ethically.

We may now turn to a few subsidiary points on which our

[1] Similarly, H.-H. Schrey, H. H. Walz, and W. A. Whitehouse, *The Biblical Doctrine of Justice and Law* (London, 1955), 94–108.

[2] So also Hatch, *Pauline Faith*, 59, and NB Rom. 7. 4.

[3] Cf. Peake, 'Quintessence of Paulinism', 303; 'union with Christ creates the new character which requires the new status'; also C. R. Smith, *The Bible Doctrine of Sin* (London, 1953), 133, and NB Rom. 8. 1 – for those in Christ there is no condemnation!

[4] *Forgiveness and Reconciliation*, Ch. 1; also 'Forgiveness', *ET*, 51 (1939–40), 16–21.

basic contention bears, and the first is the expression 'the Righteousness of God'. We have already given a brief discussion of this (cf. above pp. 9–14), which is sometimes called a 'formula', and said that this could be a misleading description of it. Our examination of the important pre-Pauline instances of the 'formula' has led us to no uniform meaning of it. Thus in Deut. 33. 21 it means God's legal activity, but Targum Onkelos makes it mean 'meritorious things before God'. In 1QS 11. 12 it is God's saving righteousness, leading to man's justification. In TDan 6. 10 it is either man's righteousness as required and defined by God, or God's own righteousness as opposed to man's unrighteousness, and possibly a power causing man's righteousness. Mt. 6. 33 and Jas 1. 20 probably both mean man's righteousness, but given as well as demanded by God. Therefore, in Paul's writings, each occurrence must be examined on its merits without preconceptions: it may refer to God's judicial righteousness (perhaps Rom. 3. 5), and even then may emphasise saving (2 Thess. 1. 5f) or punitive (Rom. 2. 5; 3. 5) aspects of justice. It may refer to God's saving activity apart from a judicial setting (Rom. 1. 17; 2 Cor. 3. 9). It may refer to the righteousness of which God approves, the righteousness which is valid before him (Phil. 3. 9). If we are correct, it may also mean God's righteousness, not just in itself, but as the believer participates in it (2 Cor. 5. 21; Phil. 3. 9).[1]

The second subsidiary point is the nature of righteousness as both demand and gift. Presumably nobody would dispute that in Paul's teaching righteousness is demanded of believers, cf. Rom. 6. 19. Our point is that as in Mt. 5, it is gift as well. There is nothing strange about this, for we have repeatedly seen in the background literature this idea of righteousness as God's gift or creation.[2] What must be stressed now is that for Paul the gift is inseparable from the Giver,[3] who is God in Christ. Talk of 'imparted righteousness' is therefore imprecise. Nothing is im-

[1] Especially in Deutero-Isaiah, God's saving righteousness establishes the righteousness of Israel, and this is conceived in terms of vindication, which is not merely a new *status*, but a new *life* of freedom, prosperity, and good government.

[2] Cf. above pp. 44–5 for OT; 98–9 for Intertestamental literature; 107f for Philo; 142f for the NT (non-Pauline).

[3] Käsemann's contribution is invaluable at this point, 'God's Righteousness in Paul', cf. above, p. 13.

parted, but something is lived in. Nevertheless the tangible fruits of this righteousness (Phil. 1. 11) will doubtless appear to the casual observer to be the believer's own.

The third subsidiary point is about the righteousness of the Messiah.[1] Our approach implicitly takes up the notion of the Messiah as *the* righteous one, in whom God's righteousness is evident, though of course it goes beyond it, because Jesus' righteousness is concentrated or focused in his self-giving upon the Cross (Rom. 5. 18f), and because Jesus is more than Messiah, he is the new inclusive Man.

Fourth, we have some sort of reconciliation between Protestant and Catholic traditional exegesis. While both 'imputed' and 'imparted' approaches are inadequate and inaccurate, nevertheless both preserve one part of Paul's two-sided doctrine, and their basic affirmations must stand. Justification does not mean 'make righteous', yet we do not need to make inferences from Paul's total theology in order to preserve ethical seriousness, for Paul does this in his juxtaposition of the twin doctrines of justification by faith and righteousness by faith. This is especially evident in Greek where two forms of one root are used. Our contention also helps to answer the criticism that Paul fails to take seriously repentance in the Jewish tradition,[2] that justification is an ethical cul-de-sac,[3] and that the doctrine separates justice and mercy, so distorting both.[4] It also endorses the answering of these criticisms in terms of union with Christ,[5] and suggests that the link is already there. Righteousness and justification never were separable for Paul.

Lastly, the 'mystical' and 'juridical' elements have sometimes been separated and unequally emphasised (cf. above p. 6). While we dislike the first of these terms, and much prefer to speak of 'incorporation', we should claim that the two are inseparable and need one another if distortion of either is to be avoided.

[1] On Messiah's righteousness, cf. above, pp. 41, 44f, for OT; in the Intertestamental literature, p. 97; cf. also Gen. R. XII 6.

[2] So Schoeps, *Paul*, 188.

[3] So Schweitzer, *Mysticism of Paul the Apostle*, 225ff.

[4] So J. Knox, *Chapters in a Life of Paul* (London, 1954), Ch. 9, also *The Ethic of Jesus in the Teaching of the Church*, 75–9.

[5] C. F. D. Moule, 'Obligation in the Ethic of Paul', in W. R. Farmer, C. F. D. Moule, and R. R. Niebuhr, eds, *Christian History and Interpretation* (Cambridge, 1967), 389–406, especially 400ff.

CHAPTER 10

GALATIANS

We start here rather than with Romans, simply to reserve the most complete presentation of Paul's teaching until last. Galatians' concern with justification more than righteousness is reflected in the predominance of the verb (8 times) over the noun (4 times) and the adjective (once). Although the issue initially is that of conditions of table-fellowship, 'full communion', Paul rapidly goes to the heart of the matter, acceptability with God. Every instance of the root is theologically charged, and as the argument is continuous and well-knit, we take the cases seriatim.

CHAPTER 2. 15–21

The verb occurs 4 times, thrice in v. 16, once in v. 17. The noun occurs once, v. 21. Twice in v. 16 Paul declares that man is not justified by works of the Law, and the verb plainly has its usual declaratory force. One is justified by faith in Jesus Christ;[1] this is not just faith as a general entity, but that specific faith which is man's response to God's grace in Christ. This is confirmed by 'even as we have believed in Christ Jesus'. The message of acceptance or acquittal that is undeserved, and to which man responds as the grace of God in Christ, is clearly and simply proclaimed in v. 16 as a whole. It is not clear whether Paul is thinking of a justification at the Judgment, or here and now, or even in the past, but this is not relevant to the argument anyway. The point at issue is the basis of acceptability, not the time of reckoning.

When we come to v. 17, the position is complicated. First, what does 'sinners' mean here? The most natural explanation is that since Paul is talking about works of the Law, sinners are those who do not fulfil the Law. This also fits the same word in

[1] Not 'by the faith of Jesus Christ'; 'even as we have believed in Christ Jesus' is a clarification, not an additional point. In this we follow many commentators, e.g. P. Bonnard, *L'Épître de Saint Paul aux Galates* (Neuchâtel, 1953), 53; E. D. Burton, *The Epistle to the Galatians*, ICC (Edinburgh, 1921), 121f.

v. 15, and indeed in the whole debate, which is not about the relative moral achievements of Jews and Gentiles, but about fulfilment of the Law in ritual and technical matters particularly. Paul says one is not justified by law-fulfilment; if this means that those who are justified by faith infringe the Law, is Christ therefore the agent of sin? This, v. 17, he regards as a reduction to absurdity. If we have here a statement, not a question, then it is the logical – and ridiculous – outcome of the line of thinking that Paul opposes. The real sin is not in infringing the Law, but in disloyalty to Christ and to the new way of acceptability in and through him, vv. 18f. Paul the Christian has died to the Law, both as a means of salvation and as the way of righteousness. So then, if you take the Law as your standard, Christians are sinners, but Paul does not take the Law as his standard, and thus cannot accept this definition of sinner. On the contrary, the real sin would be to revert to the way of law-righteousness, v. 18.[1]

Man is justified 'in Christ' as well as 'by faith', v. 17. But what does 'in Christ' mean here? It is possible that ἐν is instrumental,[2] but on grammatical grounds alone it is more likely that it retains its local force, so that the reference is to incorporation in Christ. Therefore, it is as men in Christ that we are justified. This is supported by the close proximity of the ideas of dying with Christ and living to God, vv. 19f, of living by faith, and of Christ's 'living in me', v. 20. Moreover, this gives sharp point to the question whether Christ becomes an agent of sin: the phrasing is not that justification by faith (a process) is such an agent, but whether Christ (a person) is. If Christians are justified in Christ, as an historical yet inclusive person, then from the legalists' point of view, he could be accused of causing sin. If we are right, then, the formulation 'justified in Christ', far from being

[1] How does reverting to legalism make one a sinner? There are three possibilities: (i) it is admitting error in abandoning the Law in the first place, cf. A. Oepke, *Der Brief des Paulus an die Galater* (3rd edn, Berlin, 1964); (ii) it is re-establishing the authority of the Law, whose demands cannot be entirely fulfilled, cf. Bonnard, *Galates*, 55; (iii) the solution suggested above, for which see also, among others, G. S. Duncan, *The Epistle of Paul to the Galatians*, MNTC (London, 1934), 68–9; this seems to fit the argument's structure best.

[2] Oepke, *Galater*, 60, and Bonnard, *Galates*, 54; however Best, *One Body*, 5, finds this impossible on linguistic grounds, cf. Tannehill, *Dying and Rising*, 19, who cites Rom. 2. 12; 3. 19, against it.

fortuitous, is a deliberate and important part of the argument. We therefore infer that while the acceptability question is in the forefront, behind it lies the Christian's being in Christ. It is as a man in Christ, and therefore righteous by faith, that he is justified. This new being is explicitly mentioned in v. 20, so that in this passage we have a fusion of the forensic–relational and the moral renewal ideas, as also of faith as both saving, and that by which the believer lives.

This interpretation is further confirmed if we take 'righteousness' in v. 21 in its usual sense, and not (as in RSV) to mean 'justification'. Those who see it here as chiefly forensic,[1] are not, of course, entirely mistaken, for the whole point is that it is acceptable to God, the righteousness valid before him. However, we suggest that it is a real righteousness which is thus valid. It is forensic, in that it has the aspect of acceptability, and ethical, in that it is essentially something one does. The main drift of the argument is indeed forensic, but at the least v. 20 shows that 'a new form of existence under a new power' is also in Paul's mind, which is reflected in 'righteousness' in v. 21.[2] Therefore, righteousness no more than justification is by the Law, and this righteousness must surely be equated with the new life of faith of v. 20. If righteousness were not in Christ, i.e. through dying and rising with him, his death would be irrelevant, v. 21. As things are, both righteousness and justification are by grace, through the Lord who dies and rises. One cannot separate the new status from the new life.

This passage then teaches that one is justified by faith, and in Christ, because in Christ one is just. It is not one's own righteousness, and there is no contradiction of 'justification of the ungodly', for the believer never has any works of his own. This exegesis means that in v. 21 there is a complete answer to the charge of v. 17.

CHAPTER 3. 6–24

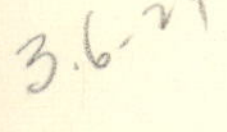

Despite N. H. Snaith's view that the whole difficulty over justification stems from an erroneous assumption that righteousness is necessary before God can accept a man,[3] the argument

[1] E.g. Burton, *Galatians*, 140.

[2] Tannehill, *Dying and Rising*, 59; cf. Oepke, *Galater*, 64.

[3] *Distinctive Ideas*, 162–5.

from Abraham's faith is pointless unless this assumption is where Paul starts from. He may not be concerned to *make* this point, but he certainly *takes* it as something assumed by his readers and opponents, then turns the tables on the latter by using their own presupposition. It could be that this is not the formulation he himself would have chosen.

Noting that the reckoning of faith as righteousness is apparently the same as justification by faith, cf. vv. 6, 8, we must first recall the Jewish exegesis of Gen. 15. 6. In Genesis itself we saw that the verse probably meant that Abraham's loyal trust was regarded as appropriate covenant behaviour, and therefore righteousness (see above, p. 43, and also on the whole question in Galatians and Romans, Appended Note 9, below). This involves taking חשב as meaning 'reckon to be', as in Gen. 38. 15; 1 Sam. 1. 13. Faith is thus not opposed to works but is a kind of work; the prevailing interpretation of the verse in later Judaism is in line with this view of it, cf. above, pp. 103f, 109, 125f. The faith of Abraham, whether understood as trust, credence, or faithfulness, was meritorious. There may even be a 'merit of Abraham's faith'. Paul's interpretation is completely opposed to this, because he sees faith not as a kind of work, but as the antithesis of works. If faith is understood thus differently, λογίζεσθαι must also be understood differently, so that it no longer means 'reckon to be', but 'take into account (as a ground of acceptance)'. This does not make δικαιοσύνη mean 'acceptance', but as to any ordinary Jew, 'ground of acceptance'. Gentiles who are justified by faith are thus the true heirs of Abraham, the man of faith (vv. 7–9), for justification by faith is the same as having faith reckoned as righteousness.

Yet this is not the whole story, for if our exegesis is correct, surely the man who has faith in Christ, who is by this fact in Christ, is therefore righteous? In terms of law-righteousness he is not, but in Christ he is, and this notion is not absent from our passage, cf. v. 5:

> Does he who supplies the Spirit to you and works miracles among you do so by works of the Law, or by hearing with faith? (RSV).

Moreover, it is likely that the quotation from Hab. 2. 4 is used in 3. 11 to show that the man with faith is in fact righteous, and we must now insert a discussion of that verse.[1] The meaning in the Hebrew Bible is undoubtedly 'the righteous will live by his fidelity', which probably means that the Israelite who keeps confidence in God will escape captivity in Babylon. Paul cannot mean anything like this, because he omits the possessive pronoun, and because he does not use 'faith' in the sense of 'fidelity'. LXX, MSS B and א, have ὁ δὲ δίκαιος ἐκ πίστεώς μου ζήσεται. Paul cannot mean this, for πίστις here is God's faithfulness. LXX, MSS A and C have ὁ δὲ δίκαιός μου ἐκ πίστεως ζήσεται, and this is how some would take it in Paul. Certainly μου is lacking, but that could be fortuitous, and in any event does not greatly affect the meaning, 'the righteous will live by faith'. That is, it is a description of the manner of life, or of the source of life, of the righteous man. J. B. Lightfoot gives a thorough defence of this rendering for both Gal. 3. 11 and Rom. 1. 17, on four grounds.[2] First, this is how the original and LXX take it (i.e. they attach 'by faith' to 'live' and not to 'righteous'). While this is true, it cannot be decisive, as we have already seen how Paul can use an OT passage, against traditional exegesis, for his own purposes. Second, Lightfoot suggests that ἐκ πίστεως in Rom. 1. 17*b* corresponds to the same phrase in 17*a*, so that there is a parallel between 'revealed by faith' and 'live by faith'. However, one may question whether there is any parallelism of thought in the verse – the double occurrence of 'by faith' could be accidental. In any case, this argument does not help in Gal. 3. 11.[3] Third, he argues that 'righteous by faith' is not a natural phrase and is unparalleled in Paul, to which we may reply that it is unparalleled for the adjective, but hardly for the noun. 'Righteousness by faith', however interpreted, is an eminently Pauline expression. Fourth, he argues that this rendering lays the stress where the context requires, both in Romans and in Galatians,

[1] In this section considerable use has been made of the earlier part of A. Feuillet, 'La citation d'Habacuc II 4 et les huit premiers chapîtres de l'épître aux Romains', *NTS*, 6 (1959–60), 52–80.

[2] *Notes on Epistles of St Paul*, 250f; cf. Kertelge, '*Rechtfertigung*', 89–95; Schlatter, *Gottes Gerechtigkeit*, 43f.

[3] If there is any parallelism there, it is between ἐν νόμῳ... δικαιοῦται and δίκαιος ἐκ πίστεως in v. 11, and also perhaps νόμος... ἐκ πίστεως in v. 12. V. 12*b* does not militate against our view, for it amounts to 'the law rests on works as a way to life'. We have assumed that Paul uses the quotation similarly in both places, but this will be checked exegetically.

but it is debatable whether one rendering does this more than another. Indeed, while certainty is impossible, I am inclined to think that 'he who is righteous-by-faith shall live' does more justice to the thought of the passage. This neatly picks up and continues the view of righteousness that we have been exploring, but of course it is not essential to that view. If we read the quotation 'the righteous shall live by faith', then we can take this to mean that the righteous man (*qua* righteous man, not *qua* man) finds the ground of his existence in faith.

We return to 3. 10. Works of the Law are not the way to righteousness; that way is doomed to failure, and indeed to curse (v. 10), because the Law is antagonistic to faith which is the God-approved way to righteousness, cf. Abraham, vv. 6–8. What then is acceptable to God? Paul uses Hab. 2. 4 in this unconventional way to show that it is the man of faith who is righteous.[1] If it is by faith that one becomes righteous, what does 'righteous' mean? Certainly it is forensic, 'acceptable to God', for this is a continuing concern of the argument. Some Protestant exegesis suggests it means only this.[2] However, if we give δίκαιος its full usual meaning, forensic and ethical, we obtain an excellent sense: the believer is really righteous because he is in Christ, though this righteousness is not and never becomes his own. This is the righteousness acceptable to God which enables the man of faith to live. This life is probably eschatological salvation, understood both forensically and in terms of eternal life, cf. Rom. 5. 17; Ezek. 18. 27.[3]

Therefore, if we are thinking of law-righteousness in v. 6, then faith is reckoned in lieu of it, as the ground of acceptance. Yet if a man has this faith, he really is righteous-in-Christ, and God may well reckon him righteous. These interpretations are not mutually contradictory, for both proclaim that we are accepted by God not on the grounds of our achievement; further while the 'faith' approach rules out one kind of righteousness, it automatically

[1] Feuillet argues, in connection with Rom. 1. 17, that only this rendering does justice to Paul's intention, which is not to establish how the righteous live, but to decide what kind of righteousness is necessary in order to live, 'La citation d'Habacuc II 4', 52. Others who hold the same view of Hab. 2. 4 include Tobac, *Justification*, 113, and Nygren, *Romans*, 81–92.

[2] E.g. Duncan, *Galatians*, 94f; Burton, *Galatians*, 166.

[3] Cf. Feuillet, 'La citation d'Habacuc II 4', 52f.

implies the other. So, from one point of view, faith is in place of righteousness, and from another, it leads to righteousness. The first is required by the faith–works antithesis, and the second by v. 5 and the Habakkuk quotation, cf. also Rom. 4. 11, 13. None of this denies that justification is by grace through faith. Man has nothing to offer, and will always have nothing to offer. It is by grace that he is in Christ, and by grace that he is justified, and the two go together.

Does this passage reflect an acquaintance with the doctrine of Merits? It is impossible to be sure, but some such idea may underlie the formulation. All the Christian's works are in Christ, and if we speak in merit language, the only merits he can claim are Christ's. On the ethical side, Christ works in him for ethical righteousness. On the forensic side, he is righteous in Christ, i.e. with Christ's merits. All this may be in the background, but is never stated. The strongest piece of evidence for its presence (apart from the logic of the argument) is that in quoting Gen. 15. 6 Paul uses a verse understood by the Rabbis in merit terms. He must have known this. In any case, whether hints of merit theology are present or not, the double-sidedness of Paul's teaching comes to very clear expression in this section of the epistle.

The three cases of the verb, in vv. 8, 11, 24, are all, then, declaratory, the last being resumptive. The adjective in v. 11 is both forensic and ethical. The noun in v. 6 is certainly referring to that righteousness which is the OT ground of acceptance with God, primarily law-righteousness, but with perhaps an allusion to or hint of that other righteousness which is not opposed to faith but the consequence of it. Paul opposes the Law both as the source of justification and as the way of righteousness, cf. the juxtaposition of being righteous by faith and justification in v. 11. Indeed this juxtaposition continues through the chapter: v. 12 opposes faith to works of the Law; vv. 13f are strikingly reminiscent of 2 Cor. 5. 21, Christ becoming a curse for us that in him we should 'receive the promise of the Spirit through faith', which seems to relate to the believer's new life in the Spirit, cf. Gal. 5. 18–24, where 'under law' is also 'in the flesh', and the contrast is between two ways of living, not two means of justification. Moreover, Gal. 3. 15–18 lack pertinence unless believers are understood to be in Christ, so that they have a new existence.

In v. 21 we must give 'righteousness' its full value;[1] righteousness by the Law is that which consists in law-fulfilment, and therefore claims a favourable verdict, though unsuccessfully according to Paul. It is not that righteousness which God wants and which is valid before him.[2] Finally, in v. 24 we are reminded of justification by faith, yet again this forensic formulation is accompanied by an emphasis on the new life, cf. v. 27 and its references to baptism and to 'putting on Christ'.

CHAPTER 5. 4–5

The verb in v. 4 is resumptive, and must be forensic–relational. What is significant for our contention is Paul's unambiguous statement in v. 4*a* that reliance on the Law for justification is to be severed from Christ, so that it is not a question of one method of justification against another, but whether or not justification is in Christ. This implies that a man is justified in Christ, and if this incorporation is lacking, it is not that we have an ineffective process instead of an effective one, but that Christ is lost, and grace abandoned.

Some consider that 'the hope of righteousness' in v. 5 means the hope of acceptance at the Judgment, i.e. final justification.[3] More probably it means either the full realisation of the new character now in Christ begun,[4] or the hope prompted by righteousness already known, the hope presumably of final acceptance. This makes righteousness an ἀρραβών. The context certainly argues for 'righteousness' in the usual, ethical sense, cf. v. 6:

> In Christ Jesus neither circumcision nor uncircumcision is of any avail, but faith working through love (RSV).

The last clause is an excellent description of righteousness in Christ, and implies a new being as well as a new standing. This is

[1] As against, e.g., Duncan, *Galatians*, 117.

[2] The law cannot make alive: this may mean that the law can point the way, but not take us there, or that the righteousness which consists in law-fulfilment does not lead to God's favourable verdict, cf. Burton, *Galatians*, 195, who thinks ζωοποιεῖν here is forensic.

[3] E.g. Bonnard, *Galates*, 104.

[4] So Drummond, '"Righteousness of God"', 285.

reinforced by the similar formulation in 6. 15, which speaks of a new creation.

Certainly the forensic cannot be excluded, because of the verb in v. 4, and because of ἰσχύει in v. 6, which most naturally refers to God's judgment, whether present or future. Therefore, perhaps the best view of the phrase is the ἀρραβών one. The hope of righteousness is then the hope of final acceptance, prompted by our present experience of righteousness in Christ, and this fits both v. 6 and 6. 15. These two also support our view of 3. 11. It is a new creation, or faith working through love, which wins God's favourable verdict. In Galatians one is justified in Christ, and by faith, and one is righteous in Christ, and by faith, and without the distinction between the two being blurred, they are closely connected. Yet it is true that the letter's main concern is forensic, and while the ethical is rather our preoccupation, it is subordinate in Paul's thinking in this debate.

The question of the time of justification is almost irrelevant, the fundamental concern being how, not when. Ch. 5. 5 may suggest it is primarily future; i.e. righteousness in Christ is present, but the verdict on it, as on law-righteousness, comes at the Judgment. Ch. 3. 6, on the other hand, shows that justification may be regarded as having already happened.

APPENDED NOTE 9

Abraham and the Reckoning of Faith

Because the meanings of חשב and λογίζεσθαι vary as widely as those of 'think', 'count', or 'reckon' in English, a linguistic examination yields only very limited results. We need to look also at Gen. 15. 6 and its interpretation in the Biblical tradition as a whole.

The Old Testament

There are 22 places where חשב ל is used, but we may exclude places where it simply means 'he thought *x* to be *y*', i.e. a matter of opinion which is either true or false, and also places where it is a simple matter of computation. There remain 13 relevant cases, including Gen. 15. 6.

i. Someone is counted as something, treated as something, though in fact he is not. Thus God counts Job as his enemy

(Job 13. 24; 19. 11; 33. 10); Job's maidservants count him as a stranger (19. 15); the crocodile counts iron as straw (Job 41. 24 (27)). These are all qal, and though the parallel with Gen. 15. 6 is in no case close, they demonstrate the possibility that the latter means 'God counted Abraham's faith as righteousness, though of course it was not'.

ii. Something is reckoned to someone's account: a sin or an evil deed, 2 Sam. 19. 20 (19) (reckoned by man, though the others are all by God), Lev. 17. 4, or it is not so imputed, Ps. 32. 2; a peace offering is not reckoned, Lev. 7. 18. All these are qal. Stopping the plague was reckoned to Phinehas as righteousness (niph.), Ps. 106. 31. Also niph. in Num. 18. 27:

> Your offering shall be reckoned to you as though it were the grain of the threshing floor, and as the fulness of the wine press (RSV).

These last two are particularly important, because they involve reckoning something *as something else* to someone's account; in Ps. 106. 31 because in fact it amounts to righteousness (covenant behaviour), but in Num. 18. 27 because it is the equivalent of something else. There is also Prov. 27. 14,

> He who blesses his neighbour with a loud voice, rising early in the morning, will be counted as cursing (RSV)

but it is doubtful whether this is 'reckoned to his account' or more simply 'considered as'. If we admit its relevance, it belongs with Num. 18. 27.

Our rather unsatisfactory conclusion is that in Gen. 15. 6 'faith reckoned as righteousness' may mean 'is reckoned to his account as being righteousness', or equally well, 'is reckoned to his account as being equivalent to righteousness (though not the same thing)'.[1]

We therefore turn to the passage, where as we saw earlier (above pp. 25, 43), the likeliest meaning is 'faith reckoned to him as being righteousness'. As loyal covenant behaviour, and therefore acceptable to God, righteousness would include such an act of loyalty as Abraham's act of confidence and trust. It is

[1] On the root as a whole, see H. W. Heidland, *Die Anrechnung des Glaubens zur Gerechtigkeit* (Stuttgart, 1936), 4–17.

naturally reckoned as righteousness, for that is what it is.[1] Heidland's stimulating interpretation that the context is about free election, of which Abraham can be only a recipient, and that 'faith is reckoned for righteousness because this is pleasing to the will of Yahweh, not because faith has this value intrinsically',[2] cannot be accepted, despite the fact that it is admirable Pauline theology. The fact is that faith does seem to have had this value intrinsically.[3]

Interpretation in Judaism

We have already noticed (pp. 125f) that in Genesis Rabbah there is no relevant discussion, but that elsewhere the faith of Abraham is reckoned to be a merit. Faith is not set over against works, but is a kind of work (cf. above pp. 103f, 109, 125f). In the discussion between Shemaiah and Abtalyon we noted (p. 123) that Abraham's faith is counted as a merit for doing *tsedaqah* (meaning 'kindness') to Abraham's children at the crossing of the sea. Generally, Abraham's faith is understood as being righteousness, i.e. it is faithfulness, especially in keeping the whole Torah before it was given. This is far removed from the Pauline exegesis, but is part of its background.

When we turn to Jewish books written in Greek, we must reckon with Heidland's contention that λογίζεσθαι predetermined a 'merit' interpretation. If we check our 13 relevant cases of חשב ל, we find that in Group I λογίζεσθαι is not used except for Job 41. 24 (27), where the construction is λογίζεσθαι ὡς. In Group II the same construction is used in Num. 18. 27, which we noted as one of the two closest parallels to Gen. 15. 6. Thus it is twice used for the reckoning of something as something else which it is not. Yet λογίζεσθαι εἰς is used, not only in Gen. 15. 6 but also in Ps. 106. 31, where the act reckoned really was an act of

[1] Cf. above p. 43, and nn. 1 and 2; also Kuss, *Römerbrief*, 181, and Lagrange, *Romains*, 84f.

[2] H. W. Heidland, 'λογίζομαι', *TDNT*, IV, 284–92, at 289.

[3] Heidland's view is set out succinctly in the article just cited, as well as in *Die Anrechnung*. He says this emphasis on pure grace was obscured in later Judaism by the less personal computing of merits, into which Gen. 15. 6 was drawn, and also by the use of Greek, for the Greek verb includes both merit and imputation ideas (art. cit., 290). Paul really restores the verse to its original meaning, after the Greek-speaking Jewish distortion which gave faith the value of righteousness.

righteousness. In the rest of Group II, the verb or a compound is used for the reckoning of something (though not as something else) in 2 Sam. 19. 20 (19); Ps. 32. 2; Lev. 7. 18; 17. 4. In Prov. 27. 14 there is a different construction. Can we really conclude from all this that the Greek verb demands an actual correspondence in value between the things reckoned? The Greek verb, like the Hebrew, may be used in almost infinitely various ways, and the meaning of any sentence must be inferred more from the things reckoned than from the verb itself. This is borne out by Paul's use, thus in Rom. 2. 26: οὐχ ἡ ἀκροβυστία αὐτοῦ εἰς περιτομὴν λογισθήσεται. Here plainly the two things are opposite, yet in Rom. 9. 8 the children of promise are reckoned as the true seed, which they are.

Nevertheless Heidland's basic contention is correct, namely that in the Greek Intertestamental literature, Abraham's faith is reckoned as righteousness because this is what it really is, cf. above pp. 103f, 109; Jub. 23. 10; Or. Man. 8; 1 Macc. 2. 52. In the last, there has been a fusion of Gen. 15. 6 with the Aqedath Isaac, Gen. 22. 15–18, which shows how thoroughly Abraham's faithfulness was what was reckoned as righteousness in later thought.[1] Philo understands faith in a variety of ways, but all are in some fashion 'works', so that faith is a form of righteousness.

The New Testament Apart from Paul

In Jas 2. 23 we really find no illumination, for the purpose of the quotation is not to explain the way of acceptance with God, but to stress the inseparability of faith and works, and the fact that faith completed by works is the true righteousness. James also connects Gen. 15. 6 with the offering of Isaac.

Paul

When we examine Rom. 4 and Gal. 3, the light must concentrate not on the meaning of 'reckon', which is very flexible, but on the relative meanings of 'faith' and 'righteousness'. First, faith is the opposite of any kind of work. This is demanded not only by the

[1] Schoeps, *Paul*, 141–8, thinks the Aqedath Isaac may provide for Paul the link between the Cross and 'counted for righteousness'. Unfortunately Paul never even adumbrates such a link; Schoeps cites e.g. Rom. 8. 32; 4. 25; 5. 8f, but these provide no link with 'counted for righteousness'.

usual meaning in Paul, but by the use of 'faith' against works of the law in both chapters. Second, need we suppose that righteousness has a different meaning from what it had in such contexts in Judaism? Does it not mean simply the ground of man's acceptance with God? Unless it does, there seems no point in quoting the verse at all, and moreover, in Rom. 4 particularly, it is quite clear that this is the meaning. It is what man has to *do* in order to be accepted. What is different is 'faith'. It is the opposite of works (Rom. 4. 2, 4; Gal. 3. 5, 10f), and the reckoning of righteousness is entirely by God's grace and not by desert (Rom. 4. 4). It is the same as justification by faith (Rom. 4. 2, 5; Gal. 3. 8) and the same as forgiveness, or the non-imputing of sin (Rom. 4. 7f). We are therefore in no doubt what faith-reckoned-as-righteousness means. What needs clarification is the meaning of righteousness. If we do not take it in the normal Jewish manner to mean the ground of acceptance, i.e. what one does to become acceptable, then how do we take it? If it means 'acceptance', then quite apart from the linguistic difficulty, what could such odd things as 'faith reckoned as acceptance' or 'faith reckoned in lieu of acceptance' possibly mean? 'Acceptability' is better, but this is really to revert to 'ground of acceptance'.

If we take 'righteousness' as this last, the argument in Rom. 4 and Gal. 3 is this: God accepts man, on no conditions at all; man need do nothing except respond to, believe in, the God who forgives and justifies the ungodly (Rom. 4. 5). Now this stands the doctrine of merits on its head. If there is a merit of faith, it means the opposite of what was traditionally meant, because faith is now the opposite of works. Paul, in using a familiar Jewish argument, turns it back on its proponents.

We have already noted (pp. 174–5, 177–8) that we may see this in two ways simultaneously. If 'righteousness' is law-righteousness, then faith is reckoned in lieu of it (cf. Rom. 4. 2–5, 9f, 21f; Gal. 3. 5–9). Yet we saw in Galatians that this would not altogether do, for 3. 5, 11 suggest something more. Not that faith is reckoned as being righteousness, but it does lead to the only righteousness that is valid before God. This righteousness is not a possession, though its fruits will be in one's life, but it remains God's. From the forensic angle one could therefore say that Christ's merits are reckoned to us – though Paul never in fact does say this.

In Rom. 4. 6 the formulation is different: 'God reckons righteousness apart from works', i.e. God reckons righteousness to one's account – but whose righteousness? It is clearly not one's own, nor does the word mean 'acceptance', for how can anyone reckon that? The whole expression denotes acceptance, not the noun by itself. This of course is an act of grace, and especially if we recall that the 'transfer' of merits is a matter of grace and mercy, it is appropriate to think in terms of forgiveness and justification (Rom. 4. 5, 7). Then in Rom. 4. 11 we find τῆς δικαιοσύνης τῆς πίστεως (cf. also v. 13). If our treatment above is correct, this should be taken as in Phil. 3. 9. The (to us) anachronism would doubtless not bother Paul.[1] The act of faith by which one is justified is the same act of faith by which one comes to live in Christ and so in his righteousness. At the moment, it is the forensic side of this that matters, as in Gal. 3, but this side does not exhaust the whole. We should therefore maintain that in his use of Gen. 15. 6 Paul combines two fundamental ideas: first, that man gains acceptance with God not by anything he does, but by faith which is the response to God's grace; second, that the believer as a man in Christ is a new and righteous creature, and this (ethical) righteousness is that which is valid before God.

[1] Cf. Kuss, *Römerbrief*, 181, and 1 Cor. 10. 4: 'the Rock was Christ'.

CHAPTER 11

ROMANS

The importance of both justification and righteousness is reflected in the number of occurrences: 14 for the verb, 7 for the adjective, 34 for δικαιοσύνη, 2 for δικαίωσις, 5 for δικαίωμα, plus one instance of δικαιοκρισία. Once again, as we have a sustained argument, we take the cases seriatim.

ROMANS I. 17

As we have already noted above (pp. 9–14, 170), the meaning of δικαιοσύνη θεοῦ here is being widely discussed at the present time. On the basis of what has been discovered in the foregoing, some things can be said at once. First, unless we are to remove Paul altogether from the Jewish tradition, we cannot talk about righteousness as an attribute of God. In the Hebrew tradition, early and late, God's righteousness is the way he acts, and notably the way he acts in maintaining the covenant. It is his activity-in-relationship, and therefore to call it an attribute is inappropriate, if by 'attribute' we mean a description of God as he is in himself. The Biblical tradition in general shows no interest in this, but in God as he acted in creation, history, and redemption. Second, we cannot accept that there is any one meaning of 'righteousness of God'. It is not a formula in the sense of a recognised phrase for a consistent notion, having a specific and unchanging content.[1] All we can do is examine a given text, trying to determine from it and its context, which interpretation, or even combination of interpretations, best fits all the facts. At the same time we do not and cannot assume that 'righteousness' has a special meaning when it occurs in the phrase, different from its usual meaning, without clear evidence.

We must begin by noting, with many others,[2] that v. 17*a* is closely parallel in structure to v. 18*a*, but antithetically parallel.

[1] Cf. above p. 170, also Kuss, *Römerbrief*, 115ff.

[2] E.g. Stuhlmacher, *Gottes Gerechtigkeit*, 78ff; Kuss, *Römerbrief*, 22f; Tobac, *Justification*, 111ff.

Now, God's wrath in v. 18 is undoubtedly his own, not as an attribute, but as an activity, cf. vv. 24–32. Working from the parallelism, we have a case for saying that God's righteousness in v. 17 is also his activity. Indeed it is widely agreed that the revelation of God's righteousness in the gospel in the verse is no static, epistemological thing, but means that it is seen at work.[1] The question then is, what sort of activity is it? Here we turn to the clear connection between vv. 16 and 17: the gospel is both the power of God leading to salvation for every believer, and also the site of revelation of God's righteousness. This surely gives us to suppose that we must be dealing with God's saving righteousness, which is for believers.

Yet there is another plausible interpretation. In v. 17*b*, ὁ δὲ δίκαιος ἐκ πίστεως is clearly about the believer's, not God's, righteousness, yet καθώς shows that this is closely related (at the least) to God's righteousness. Further, since God's righteousness is revealed ἐκ πίστεως εἰς πίστιν it must be closely related to man's response, and the similar formulation in 3. 22 suggests that it is God's righteousness which in some sense becomes man's. This view is held by Bultmann, though of course he sees righteousness as 'right standing' and 'righteousness of God' as that given by God.[2] We seem to have arrived at two opposite conclusions.[3]

Yet in the idea of righteousness by faith as already put forward, we have a framework within which these two sides fit together without paradox. God's righteousness is his own covenant loyalty, now in Paul widened beyond a covenant with Israel and made universal.[4] This righteousness is saving precisely in that man, whether Jew or Gentile, is now drawn into and lives in God's righteousness. This is gospel and power. It is power, as we shall see later especially in Rom. 6, in the two senses, power or lordship under which one lives, and power by which one lives.

[1] Cf. Murray, *Romans*, I, 29f; Nygren, *Romans*, 77f; P. Althaus, *Der Brief an die Römer*, NTD, 6 (8th edn, Göttingen, 1954), 13f.

[2] *Theology*, I, 270–80.

[3] The double-sidedness is well set out by Sanday–Headlam, *Romans*, 24f, also by Althaus, *Römerbrief*, 12f: 'Alles was Gott hat, das gibt er, und was er gibt, das ist er selbst.'

[4] Cf. Müller, *Gottes Gerechtigkeit und Gottes Volk*; Stuhlmacher, *Gottes Gerechtigkeit*, 11, 236, and passim. NB Rom. 1. 16, the two-men dialectic of Rom. 5, the stress on all men of faith as Abraham's children in Rom. 4 and Gal. 3 and 4.

The gospel is power exactly in that God's righteousness is revealed in it, and that means his activity, his powerful activity. This righteousness then is both demand and gift, as in Mt. 5;[1] it is the new life, the moral renewal of the believer, which yet remains always God's righteousness.[2] It is gospel, partly because this new life is now a gracious possibility, but perhaps primarily because it is also justification, restoration to right relationship, acquittal, purely by God's grace, and quite apart from anything man has done, will do, intends to do, or even is now beginning to do.

This double-sidedness is admirably expressed in the quotation from Hab. 2. 4 already discussed (above, pp. 175–7). We find this fitting very well into the argument if we give 'righteous' its full value as ethical and forensic at once, and render 'the righteous-by-faith will live', with 'righteous' referring to the condition and 'live' to the result. The righteous-by-faith is he who is drawn into and shares in the saving righteousness of God. The reference to faith is important, for it illuminates ἐκ πίστεως εἰς πίστιν in v. 17*a* ('as it is written' shows that Hab. 2. 4 is meant to explain or support the previous statement). This double use of the word in v. 17*a* may simply be a rhetorical way of stressing faith,[3] and not a complicated statement about two stages of faith at all. In any case, the verse as a whole makes it abundantly clear that this righteousness is for believing man.

The double-sidedness may work in two ways, according as one gives priority to the forensic or to the ethical. If the ethical is stressed, then the man in Christ is really righteous as long as he remains within the relationship, and therefore it is proper that he should be justified. This line of thought is found in Galatians. It is justification in Christ, as against by the works of the Law, and is still by grace, for the believer has no righteousness of his own. The other way is to make the forensic or relational prior. In that case, God first justifies a man, i.e. restores him to right relationship, forgives him, reconciles him, and so makes him a man in Christ, and within this relationship he is consequently righteous.

[1] Cf. Käsemann, 'God's Righteousness in Paul', 101.

[2] Ibid. 104f.

[3] So many commentators, e.g. Dodd, *Romans*, 13f. Various ways of taking the phrase are listed by F. J. Leenhardt, *The Epistle to the Romans*, E.Tr. (3rd edn, London, 1964), 55.

They are not really alternatives, for the question of chronological priority does not arise. Either way, righteousness in Christ by faith begins with the establishment of a relationship, and either way justification is by grace through faith, not by even the believer's works. What matters is that God's saving righteousness does two things for men and does them inseparably: it restores their relationship with God, and it makes them new (ethical, righteous) beings.

ROMANS 1. 32

The verse makes it quite plain that δικαίωμα has its very common meaning of 'decree, ordinance', as something declared right, or less probably, 'a sentence of judgment'. This is less likely because it usually refers to a special case, not, as here, to a general rule or decree. We give a brief discussion of this noun in Appended Note 10 below.

ROMANS 2

In v. 5 the compound δικαιοκρισία denotes God's justice in the narrower, even distributive sense, and in v. 26 δικαιώματα means the ordinances of the Law.

More important is v. 13 where δίκαιοι παρὰ τῷ θεῷ must be equivalent to δικαιωθήσονται. This seems likely to be not Paul's own theology, but an expression of the Jewish viewpoint, used to demonstrate to the Jews that their traditional way of justification is really no way, because while possessing and hearing the Law, they do not fulfil it. It would perhaps be possible to argue that this *is* Paul's own viewpoint, and shows that while justification is by faith now, it will be by works at the Judgment, but this finally makes present justification an irrelevance, and cf. 3. 20. In any case, the future tense of the verb does not necessarily imply a reference to the Judgment; it is more likely to be a logical future, thus including, but not being restricted to, the Last Judgment. This fits very well an expression of Jewish theology.[1]

The emphasis in v. 13 is forensic, as is shown by the addition of παρὰ τῷ θεῷ after the adjective, but the ethical is not excluded.

[1] Cf. Ab. 1. 17 and 3. 10, also O. Michel, *Der Brief an die Römer*, Meyer's Kommentar (12th edn, Göttingen, 1963), 77; J. Knox, *Romans*, *IB*, IX, 409, and Lyonnet, 'Justification, Jugement, Rédemption', 175f.

Men are righteous before God, in the Jewish scheme, because they have obeyed the Law. Thus the verb is forensic, but based on the realities of the situation, viz. law-fulfilment.

ROMANS 3. 4F

Since it is nonsense to speak of God's being acquitted, δικαιωθῇς in v. 4 must be demonstrative or vindicatory, i.e. either 'be shown to be right' or 'be vindicated' in the sense of 'triumph'. Indeed, the demonstrative and the vindicatory may coincide: the picture is forensic, but it is a civil case, and God wins it. The quotation is verbatim from Ps. 51. 4, LXX.[1] In v. 5, God's righteousness is opposed to man's wickedness, and thus means his own righteousness, but specifically in his activity of judging, cf. vv. 5*b*, 6. Yet there is more than this, for the basic contrast is between man's covenant disloyalty and God's covenant loyalty, cf. especially the confrontation of Jewish faithlessness with God's faithfulness in vv. 3, 4*a*. The context therefore requires both the general meaning of covenant loyalty and also that of divine justice in the narrower sense.[2] While we must generally be chary of adding significances, here the two seem to be demanded.

ROMANS 3. 10–31

In v. 10, 'none is righteous, not even one', to be righteous is the opposite of being under the power of sin, cf. v. 9 and Ch. 6, and is also the opposite of doing specific wrong things, cf. vv. 11–18, the quotation from the Psalms (a paraphrase rather than exact LXX). This catena is mainly ethical, but the relation to God is emphasised in v. 18: being righteous is not only abstaining from vicious courses of action, it is also having the fear of God. It is in fact the opposite of sin. Now this must be connected with v. 20, and the forensic statement, 'by works of the Law will no flesh be justified before him'. No one is righteous, and no one is justified by works of the Law. These statements belong together: the impossibility of justification is consequent upon the non-existence

[1] Cf. among others, Barrett, *Romans*, 63; Lagrange, *Romains*, 63f.

[2] Cf. Kertelge, '*Rechtfertigung*', 63–70; Stuhlmacher, *Gottes Gerechtigkeit*, 86.

of law-righteousness, the forensic upon the ethical. All the Law can do is to make men aware of sin, it cannot save. This is the situation in which man, and especially Jewish man, finds himself.

But now, with emphatic antithesis (Νυνὶ δέ),[1] comes the answer to the dilemma, and that is the righteousness of God, vv. 21f. It is possible that we here begin a pre-Pauline confession annotated by Paul (see Appended Note 11 below), but the exegetical task must be to make some sense of the passage as it stands. Even if Paul is glossing a formula (of an extent not universally agreed), we need to know what use he makes of it, and what he means by it.

'The righteousness of God' in vv. 21f does not seem to be simply God's saving righteousness, because of the end of v. 22: it is God's righteousness διὰ πίστεως ['Ιησοῦ] Χριστοῦ εἰς πάντας τοὺς πιστεύοντας. Once again, Χριστοῦ must be an objective genitive, because of the contrast with 'apart from the Law', and also because of 'to all who believe'. Men participate by faith in God's righteousness and so are saved.[2] This is preferable to taking righteousness to mean 'acceptance' or 'acquittal', not only on linguistic grounds, but also because the contrast is between man's sin, and consequent unacceptability, under the Law, and his righteousness, and consequent acceptability, by faith. Rather more exactly, the antithesis is between man's sin and God's righteousness for the believer. Thus a purely imputative righteousness is not the likely meaning here: the parallel between 3. 21f and 1. 17 is clear, and in 1. 17 it is certainly God's own active righteousness, whatever else it may be. Nevertheless, as the manifestation of God's righteousness is specifically in Jesus Christ, one can say that it becomes man's, both ethically and forensically. Because we stress the presence of the former, we need not exclude the latter. Man's dilemma is both forensic and ethical, cf. vv. 10–20. Indeed, vv. 23f deal with the forensic side of the dilemma. All have sinned and fallen short of the glory of God, which may well mean 'fail to be conformed to his image',

[1] 'Now' is probably not merely logical, but showing that the eschatological is present, cf. Lagrange, *Romains*, 72f.

[2] For the same view, Lightfoot, *Notes on Epistles of St Paul*, 270f. It is the opposite of law-righteousness, though ironically both Law and Prophets witness to it, cf. v. 21, Ch. 4, and Gal. 3 and 4.

i.e. an ethical failure.[1] The way out for all is the way of faith–righteousness.

However vv. 23f do not exactly follow the line of thought in which man is declared righteous because in so far as he is in Christ he really is righteous. Instead, v. 24 seems to take the obverse side: righteousness by faith is possible because of free, gracious justification. This is to take vv. 22*b*–23 as an explanatory parenthesis, and δικαιούμενοι in v. 24 as resuming the point of v. 22*a*:[2] 'the righteousness of God through faith in Jesus Christ for all believers... who are justified by his grace...'. The parenthesis about *all* falling short is brought in where it is, in vv. 22*b*–23, because of the statement about *all* believers in v. 22*a*. The passage in its finished form thus has justification restoring the relationship in which man may be righteous. This justification which is the basis of the new life in Christ is purely a gift, purely by grace. It is certainly a bold use of the verb, which usually, outside Paul and often by Paul (when the righteous-in-Christ are found justified) means the recognition or demonstration of an already existing righteousness. It is bold, but not impossible, cf. the Rabbinic use of the pi'el of the Hebrew equivalent to mean 'treat generously'.

The above view of the passage involves taking γάρ in both v. 22 and v. 23 as introducing not an explanation of what righteousness means, but an account of how it comes about. It begins with justification, which is possible because of 'redemption in Christ Jesus'. Here we see 'in Christ' embracing both man's salvation and his continuing life.

Redemption is tied inexorably to the Cross, v. 25, so that justification rests on the death of Jesus. We may take the words 'whom God set forth as a *hilastērion* through faith, in his blood', v. 25, in one of three ways, depending on our view of the meaning of ἱλαστήριον: the cross of Jesus as part of God's plan for salvation may be a propitiation,[3] or expiation,[4] or the 'place' where sins are done away and men are made new, thus taking *hilastērion* as

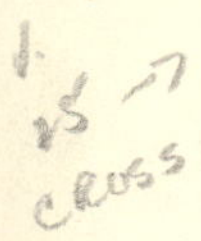

[1] Cf. Murray, *Romans*, I, 112f, who lists the possible meanings, but opts for this one.

[2] Cf. Lagrange, *Romains*, 74; Murray, *Romans*, I, 113f; Sanday–Headlam, *Romans*, 85f.

[3] Notably Morris, *Apostolic Preaching of the Cross*, Chs IV, V.

[4] Notably Dodd, *Romans*, 54f, 56–8.

'mercy-seat'.[1] Which is correct is an intricate and vexed question into which we cannot go, but whichever one we adopt, Christ's death is in some sense sacrificial and for us, and on it our redemption and justification depend.[2] It is the great reconciling act, but is not understood apart from man's response of faith;[3] the sacrificial action, however interpreted, must be accompanied by the faith-relationship between the many and the One.[4] That is, it is closely associated with and requires the notion of the corporate Christ, because faith is never separable from being in Christ, and because one cannot separate faith in Christ and his saving action, from faith which is dying and rising with him.

According to vv. 25*b*, 26, by this redemption in the Cross there is solved the problem of how God can forgive without implying that sin and righteousness do not matter.[5] In making his righteousness accessible to faith in the dying and rising Christ (the reference to Christ's blood in v. 25 is perhaps simply to Christ as dying, though sacrificial ideas are probably present), God deals with both the forensic and the ethical dilemmas. He deals with the forensic one by justifying men by grace. At the same time, and in the same formulation, Paul sees him as making men righteous, really and ethically, but only by faith and only in Christ. Thus the Cross restores the relationship, and as men die

[1] Notably Nygren, *Romans*, 156–9.

[2] Perhaps Paul himself had no precise theory, cf. M. Dibelius and W. G. Kümmel, *Paul*, E.Tr. (London, 1953), 116. It was not necessarily that there had to be some sacrifice to satisfy the demands of divine justice, though some hold this, e.g. Morris, and also Althaus, *Römerbrief*, 31. It may also be that the whole act of redemption, v. 25*a*, shows God's righteousness, his gracious covenant loyalty in coming to man's rescue and solving both forensic and ethical dilemmas. Thus προέθετο may, but need not, be a sacrificial term, cf. Barrett, *Romans*, 77; Murray, *Romans*, I, 117f. In the other NT instances (Rom. 1. 13 and Eph. 1. 9) it refers to *purpose*.

[3] 'Through faith' is probably not to be taken with 'in his blood', as faith for Paul is always in a person, cf. Taylor, 'Great Texts Reconsidered: Rom. 3. 25f', *ET*, 50 (1938–9), 295–300, at 295, 297, and Dodd, *Romans*, 56. However, if the phrase simply means 'the dying Christ', the conjunction makes good sense, cf. R. V. G. Tasker, 'The Doctrine of Justification by Faith in the Epistle to the Romans', *EQ*, 24 (1952), 37–46, at 43.

[4] Cf. Taylor, *Atonement in NT Teaching*, 59–65, 74–101.

[5] Thus Reumann, *Righteousness and Society*, 57ff, sees vv. 24–6 as a theodicy, not a soteriology, and Christ's expiatory suffering as that which prevents justification's being a legal fiction.

with Christ, it also leads to new life. God has passed over former sins, either in the sense of forgiving them, or in that of ignoring them (see Appended Note 12 below), not because he is unconcerned about righteousness, but because in righteousness-by-faith he has provided the answer.[1] We thus take 'righteousness' in v. 25*b* and 'righteous' in v. 26 to refer to God's own covenant loyalty, his own faithfulness, and therefore his concern for man's righteousness, though not without overtones that this righteousness is now set forth *for* as well as *to* men. This covenant loyalty has frequently included the dimension of coming to man's rescue, and it is therefore not at all paradoxical that he is δίκαιον καὶ δικαιοῦντα.[2] There is no contradiction with 'righteousness' in v. 25*b*: the righteousness which is concerned for the right is also that which saves, and ἔνδειξιν in both places introduces substantially the same idea. The 'righteousness of God for faith' motif comprehends the righteousness of God in himself, that righteousness as available to believers who are in the dying Christ, and also his justification of the repentant sinner. The believer who finds justification as he enters by faith into Christ's representative action, also finds therein the death of sin. In expanded form, this passage is therefore saying substantially what 1. 17 says. While 'God's righteousness' in v. 25 is more than 'saving', this does not contradict the meaning in vv. 21f. His righteousness is always concerned for right, not least when it is saving. And it is precisely God's maintenance of right, v. 25, which enables him to be 'just and justifier'. His righteousness saves by forgiving the past, and by drawing men into his own real righteousness.

Finally, this excludes boasting. Since believers never have any works of their own, justification is always by faith, never by works (vv. 28, 30). Circumcision is therefore irrelevant, all that

[1] Εἰς ἔνδειξιν and πρὸς τὴν ἔνδειξιν are probably both final, cf. C. H. Talbert, 'A non-Pauline Fragment at Romans 3. 24–6?', *JBL*, 85 (1966), 287–96, at 290; not, however, to satisfy abstract justice, rather to show God's consistent 'Bundestreue', including both his will to save, and his concern for human righteousness.

[2] C. Blackman, 'Romans 3. 26*b*: A Question of Translation', *JBL*, 87 (1968), 203f, sees καί as intensive: God is δίκαιος precisely as he is δικαιῶν. He rejects the view that the two are synonymous, the view that δίκαιον is *iustitia passiva* while δικαιοῦντα is *iustitia activa*, and finally the view that the first is *iustitia distributiva* and the second *iustitia salutifera*.

matters is faith,[1] and man can never boast. In v. 31 Paul probably means that the Law (in the form of Gen. 15. 6) teaches this very thing, so that his gospel cannot be accused of overthrowing the Law. It is just possible that he means that by the righteousness-by-faith teaching, true righteousness is now possible, and the Law's intention thus established.

ROMANS 4

As we have already discussed this (above, pp. 174f, 177f, 180–5), we cannot traverse the same ground in detail again. The problem the chapter faces is forensic rather than ethical, and it is met in terms of justification by faith, as against justification by works of the Law, vv. 2, 5. Justification of the ungodly is clearly not justification of those who refuse to have anything to do with God, but of those who can bring nothing of their own. The purely forensic or relational nature of all this is shown by its equivalence to forgiveness, or to the non-reckoning of sins, vv. 7f. Moreover, justification is also equivalent to 'faith reckoned as righteousness', since 'faith' is now opposed to works, and means man's response or even receptivity. The equivalence comes out plainly in vv. 2f, 5. This formula 'the reckoning of righteousness' apart from works, and by faith, occurs six times in the chapter, vv. 3, 5, 6, 9, 11, 22. Works of the Law, circumcision, the boast of man as against rendering glory to God (v. 22), none of these counts at all. If the whole expression is equivalent to justification, clearly 'righteousness' by itself cannot be, and we take it to mean 'ground of acceptance' as in Judaism. However, we have also seen that Paul's righteous-by-faith notion cannot be excluded at this point, partly because faith does lead to true righteousness, and partly because the full expression, τῆς δικαιοσύνης τῆς πίστεως, is connected with the forensic argument in vv. 11, 13 (the latter anarthrous). We have also seen that the

[1] With many commentators we cannot find any difference between ἐκ πίστεως and διὰ τῆς πίστεως, cf. Leenhardt, *Romans*, 112. Sanday–Headlam, *Romans*, 96, see the first as denoting source, and the second, channel, but against this see Moule, *Idiom-Book*, 195. Turner, *Grammatical Insights*, 107ff, makes the dramatic suggestion that the Gentiles' justification is by the faith of the Jews, but one could argue that Rom. 9–11 imply rather their justification because of the unbelief of the Jews.

doctrine of merits may be a secondary note: the righteousness of faith is that of Christ, which may thus be laid to our account.

Finally, we have δικαίωσις in v. 25. It is not a common word: in the whole NT it occurs only here and in 5. 18. In LXX it occurs once, for *mishpat* in Lev. 24. 22, where it means 'law'.[1] Twice in Josephus it means 'punishment', *Ant.* XVIII 14, 315. In secular Greek it is uncommon, and most of the meanings it bears have no relevance for Paul's use here. The only one that has any bearing is 'judicial vindication and justification',[2] i.e. the abstract meaning corresponding to that of the verb in Paul. Indeed, from the general drift of the chapter, and from the connection between the Cross and justification in 3. 21–31, this sense is required. Some commentators consider that the formulation is rhetorical, and the real meaning to be simply

> He died and rose for the sake of our trespasses, i.e. in order that we should be justified.[3]

They argue that it is not meaningful to try to attach 'for our trespasses' exclusively to 'delivered up', nor 'for our justification' exclusively to 'was raised'. Schrenk, however, considers the first διά to be causal, and the second to refer to the means of justification, because of the peculiar appropriateness in the context of Abraham's faith, cf. v. 17, of the connection between resurrection and justification.[4] Michel offers what is perhaps the best solution, that the first is causal and the second final.[5]

Throughout this chapter justification as past and future jostle one another, cf. vv. 7f, 22ff, so that one doubts whether we can in v. 25 make the first part retrospective and the second prospective of the Last Judgment. As in Galatians, Paul's concern is not with the *when* of justification, but with the *how*, and he apparently finds no inconsistency in moving from present or past to future.

[1] Despite Schrenk, *Righteousness*, 71, it is unlikely to mean 'right'.

[2] Schrenk, *Righteousness*, 70f, lists the meanings with references.

[3] Dodd, *Romans*, 70. There may be a pre-Pauline formula here, cf. Hunter, *Paul and his Predecessors*, 30–2; Bultmann, *Theology*, I, 46f. The question remains, however, what *Paul* meant by it.

[4] *Righteousness*, 72. However he continues: 'One single idea is presented here in parallel expressions, while the reference to Abraham lays special emphasis on "was raised".' D. S. Sharp, 'For our Justification', *ET*, 39 (1927–8), 87–90, argues for διά as retrospective both times, and Murray, *Romans*, I, 154ff, prefers both as prospective.

[5] *Römerbrief*, ad loc.

ROMANS 5

In v. 1 δικαιωθέντες clearly resumes the argument of Ch. 4, and is forensic. The relationship is restored, man is in fellowship with God. This *has* happened.

In v. 9 another resumptive instance, δικαιωθέντες νῦν, is also certainly past and certainly relational. It is important in that it again links justification with the Cross, ἐν τῷ αἵματι, and it is possible that ἐν is not simply instrumental, but incorporative,[1] so that Christ's dying for us (v. 8) is to be understood alongside our justification *in* his dying. It is certainly clear that as in 3. 24f justification and sacrificial language are put together. The point here is the connection between past justification and future salvation: justification guarantees salvation at the Judgment (ἀπὸ τῆς ὀργῆς).[2]

There is another instance of the root in this first part of the chapter, viz. v. 7, where δικαίου occurs with ἀγαθοῦ. Assuming they are both masculine and not neuter adjectives (cf. 'us' in v. 8), there are two main possibilities: either they are synonymous, or alternative.[3] In either case, 'righteous' has an ethical content, but if it is an alternative to 'good', then it presumably lacks the note of graciousness or attractiveness of character. Certainly it stands as an opposite to 'sinners', v. 8.

We come now to vv. 12–21, and the two men, or two humanities, two solidarities, cf. our discussion above, Ch. 9, of the Corporate Christ. We first note that through Adam's sin, in which all men share,[4] death comes to all men, cf. vv. 12, 14, 17 (and Gen. 2. 17). All men really are sinners, and do not merely have the status of sinners, v. 12, whatever ἐφ' ᾧ means,[5] so that

[1] Cf. Leenhardt, *Romans*, 105f. 'At the cost of' is also possible, cf. Barrett, *Romans*, 107.

[2] Thus, among others, Nygren, *Romans*, 203f, and Barrett, *Romans*, 107. However Sanday–Headlam, *Romans*, 129, see the two statements as referring to justification and sanctification.

[3] Synonymous: F. F. Bruce, *The Epistle of Paul to the Romans* (London, 1966), 124; alternative: Leenhardt, *Romans*, 136, and Lightfoot, *Notes on Epistles of St Paul*, 286f, who instances Shylock as 'righteous' but not 'good'! Cf. also the Rabbinic distinction, Ḳid. 40*a*.

[4] How this comes about is not our present concern (nor, perhaps, Paul's). The point is that the Adam-solidarity is a sin-solidarity, cf. Best, *One Body*, 34–6.

[5] A useful recent discussion is in Turner, *Grammatical Insights*, 116–18, who opts for 'in whom', i.e. in Adam.

the problem is neither simply forensic, nor simply ethical, but both together. It is relational, but it is also to do with actions in relationship. The answer, in v. 15, is not merely God's grace, but more specifically ἡ δωρεὰ ἐν χάριτι τῇ τοῦ ἑνὸς ἀνθρώπου Ἰησοῦ Χριστοῦ. The nature of this free gift is clarified in v. 17, it is the free gift of righteousness. We may say three things about this free gift of vv. 15, 17, and also v. 16 (δώρημα):

i. It leads to justification, v. 16. The word is δικαίωμα, which here cannot have its more usual meaning of 'ordinance' but must mean 'acquittal', a perfectly permissible one which is required by the parallel with κατάκριμα (see also Appended Note 10, below). So the free gift is not itself justification, but leads to it.

ii. It leads to reigning in life, v. 17, instead of being reigned over by death. This is more than justification, and includes the manner of life of the man in Christ, here and probably hereafter.[1]

iii. If we have here our familiar theme of righteousness in Christ as both ethical and forensic–relational, is it odd that for the first time it is a gift? We have repeatedly emphasised that it is not and never becomes a possession. Yet this case is not different, for it is a gift only within the total 'in Christ' theme of the passage, and in the normal sense is still therefore not a possession. We may note that 'gift of righteousness' cannot be merely a status, or v. 16 would mean that God gives us this status in order to acquit us, but acquitting us is giving us this status, and the argument becomes absurd.

What we are saying, then, is that by his Adam Christology Paul deals with man's total dilemma, ethical–relational, which is the problem of sin. It is in the grace of Jesus Christ that the free gift comes to man, and specifically to the man who receives 'the abundance of grace and the free gift of righteousness', i.e. believing man.[2] That this grace and righteousness come through Jesus is stressed in vv. 15, 17. So then, those who are in Christ receive the free gift which means, first, that they are justified, and second, that they reign, thus overcoming both ethical and relational problems.

[1] Cf. Drummond, '"Righteousness of God"', 284, who argues that righteousness and life must be as real as sin and death.

[2] 'Many' and 'all' in vv. 15, 18 can scarcely mean all men, because of v. 17 – except in so far as believers are a new humanity, and 'all' means all of this kind of men, despite K. Barth, *Christ and Adam, Man and Humanity in Romans 5*, E.Tr. (Edinburgh, 1956).

The source is clarified in v. 18 as not just Jesus, but more precisely his act of obedience, i.e. his δικαίωμα, his act of righteousness. The verse demands a meaning parallel to παράπτωμα, and this is a permissible meaning for δικαίωμα, see Appended Note 10 below.[1] The act of righteousness is of course the obedience, particularly on the Cross, so that we again find justification and new life both derived from Christ's death. Here, incorporative categories are dominant, and Christ's act *for* us must be complemented by our dying *with* him, in order to bring out the representative and corporate nature of the whole argument. These are not alternatives, but parts of the totality.

Also in v. 18 this leads to δικαίωσιν ζωῆς. The first word is obviously 'justification', as in 4. 25, and in parallel with κατάκριμα, and is therefore forensic, but what is ζωῆς? It refers to the Christian life which follows justification and is stronger than death. Here, then, justification inaugurates, rather than reflects, the new relationship in which righteousness becomes possible. This 'life' is eschatological, but begins here and now, and is unlikely to have the restricted meaning of a verdict, unless a verdict which implies that the recipient now proceeds to a life in freedom.[2] The phrase then means not just 'justification and life', but 'justification leading to life'.

Certainly something more than forensic is in v. 19. Paul has made it plain that through the disobedience of Adam (the one), the many did in fact sin; they did not merely have the status of sinners. So this verse is not just about status. The many who will be established as righteous will not merely be given the standing of righteous, but will really be righteous, through the obedience of the One.[3] In vv. 18f therefore, both justification and righteousness are the twin, inseparable results of being in Christ, the obedient, gracious Man.

Finally, in v. 21 grace reigns 'through righteousness to eternal

[1] See Barrett, *Romans*, 116 and Lagrange, *Romains*, 111. Sanday–Headlam, *Romans*, 141f, however, give it the same meaning as in v. 16.

[2] Cf. Schrenk, *Righteousness*, 62f; Hill, *Greek Words*, 189; Moule, *Idiom-Book*, 70; Bruce, *Romans*, 133.

[3] See Kuss, *Römerbrief*, 239; Scroggs, *Last Adam*, 78. Barrett, *Romans*, 117, sees both 'sinners' and 'righteous' as 'words of relationship, not character'. We cannot follow Davies, *Paul and Rabbinic Judaism*, 273, in finding a merits reference here.

life through Jesus Christ our Lord'. This is a neat summary of the preceding. All is founded on God's grace, but it comes through Christ, the New Man, by the route of the righteousness which is from God in Christ, and which means justification and righteousness for men. It leads to eternal life, i.e. it has a goal beyond itself.

ROMANS 6

Although the forensic and the ethical are inseparable, the emphasis hitherto has been more on the forensic. Now it is more on the ethical. Paul uses the idea of dying and rising with Christ, illuminated by its sacramental expression in baptism, to demonstrate that the man in Christ cannot by definition continue in sin. He is righteous in Christ, because he has died to sin.

In v. 7, ὁ γὰρ ἀποθανὼν δεδικαίωται ἀπὸ τῆς ἁμαρτίας offers several possibilities of interpretation. First, 'he who has died is freed from sin', i.e. he no longer sins. This is doubtless true, and has point if by 'sin' a power is meant, cf. v. 6, so that Paul is not talking about complete sinlessness, but about freedom from the *power* of sin, cf. Acts 13. 39. The difficulty is that this gives δικαιοῦν an unusual meaning, virtually amounting to 'make righteous'. Second, 'he who has died has his quittance from sin', supposedly based on a Rabbinic maxim, 'When a man is dead, he is free from the Law and the commandments', cf. Shab. 30*a*, 151*b*.[1] Though this is an acceptable forensic rendering of the verb, as a whole it fits Rom. 7. 1–6, where quittance from the Law is discussed, rather than here. Third, 'he who has died (with Christ) is justified from sin', i.e. acquitted, simply because the old self no longer exists, and the verdict of 'guilty' which it deserves, cannot now be passed. This really combines elements of the first two, for the believer really has died to sin (cf. vv. 2, 6), but also is justified, acquitted, forgiven, restored to right relationship.[2] This retains the normal Pauline sense for the verb, but does not tie it to a Rabbinic maxim which might not have been widely known,

[1] See Sanday–Headlam, *Romans*, 159; S–B, III, 232.

[2] R. Scroggs, 'Romans vi. 7 ὁ γὰρ ἀποθανὼν δεδικαίωται ἀπὸ τῆς ἁμαρτίας', *NTS*, 10 (1963), 104–8, sees the death as primarily that of Christ, into which the believer also enters, and this is the death that brings justification. But in what sense is Christ by his death justified from sin? It seems better to start from the believer's death-with-Christ.

and which does not refer to quite the right thing. Most commentators treat the verse something like this, within the baptismal dying-with-Christ setting.[1] Therefore, just as we found the moral renewal theme in primarily forensic contexts, so now we find the forensic in primarily ethical–renewal surroundings. The new man in Christ is also the justified man.

It is important to recall that the general purport of vv. 1–11 is 'be what you are'; you are dead to sin, you have died with him (Christ) in baptism, in order to walk in newness of life (v. 4). Very well, says Paul, then so walk (vv. 11f). You are dead to sin which no longer has dominion over you, then be free. This conjunction of indicative with imperative has often been noticed,[2] and it is important that it appears at this stage of the argument.

We may also note that the believer's future resurrection, and his already realised new life, jostle one another here, cf. vv. 4f, 8, 11. Our rising with Christ is already real, but not already complete.

In vv. 12–23 we are confronted with two powers or masters, sin and righteousness. Man lives under either one or the other. Just as sin is both what one does and a power under which he lives,[3] so also righteousness in the places where it appears as a power, vv. 13, 18–20, is at the same time what one does. Sin and righteousness are thus opposites exactly in that they are of the same kind, playing a dual role: their usual one of a certain kind of behaviour, plus the role of a power. Now there may be difficulties about the personification of sin as a power,[4] but there are few in the case of righteousness. First, we have seen that in the OT it may be more than simply something done, and be also a field of force into which one is drawn and in which one lives (cf. above p. 45). Second, there is the conjunction of righteousness with power in 1. 17. While power and lordship are different, they merge when we speak of God. Moreover, it has been strongly urged that just as gift and Giver are inseparable, so are gift and power; God's dominion accompanies his gifts. This conjunction, which is really another way of stating the gift–Giver

[1] E.g. Althaus, *Römerbrief*, 53; Barrett, *Romans*, 124f.

[2] E.g. Kertelge, '*Rechtfertigung*', 251–63; Moule, 'Obligation in the Ethic of Paul', 401.

[3] Cf. Grundmann in Quell, *Sin*, 77–83.

[4] Cf. G. Stählin, in Quell, *Sin*, 52.

conjunction, is basic to Pauline theology.[1] We see here a movement in the argument: in the previous chapter Paul spoke of righteousness as God's gift, and now we see how closely the gift is tied to the Giver, so that what is given includes power and a new dominion, replacing the old power and dominion of sin. Far from being a possession, it is that under which one lives. This dominion is of course that of Christ, in whom one is righteous, cf. v. 11.

The indicative–imperative connection, 'be what you are', of vv. 1–11, continues in the rest of the chapter. You are those who have come from death to life (v. 13), therefore 'yield your members to God as instruments of righteousness'. The imperative rests on the indicative, and is accompanied by promise: 'sin will have no more dominion...' (v. 14). This is to say that freedom from sin rests on grace; when one stops trying to erect one's own righteousness, and submits to grace, freedom from sin and obedience become possible. This verse is crucial.

The statement (v. 18) that believers, having been freed from sin, now serve righteousness, is followed by an exhortation to do this (v. 19). Probably, rather than speaking of development in righteousness, we ought to talk of submission to lordship, submission which may be of varying completeness, so that the imperatives are towards a greater submission. In observable reality, however, this will mean the believer's increasing righteousness (v. 16). Now in v. 16, instead of the expected δικαιοσύνης in parallel with ἁμαρτίας, we find ὑπακοῆς, obedience. This must be *Christian*, i.e. submission to Christ, which is the only way to Christian righteousness. It is not a clumsy formulation, but rather an extraordinarily accurate one, illuminating the nature of righteousness as founded upon such submission – the gift cannot be separated from the Giver. 'Righteousness' is also antithetically parallel to 'death', suggesting that the acceptability aspect of righteousness has not been forgotten.

What is the force of εἰς ἁγιασμόν in v. 19? Possibly righteousness is the power, and 'sanctification' the process resulting from submission to the power. This is more satisfactory than making 'righteousness' and 'sanctification' simply synonymous and parallel to τῇ ἀνομίᾳ εἰς τὴν ἀνομίαν. In fact the two nouns are not quite synonymous; certainly ἁγιασμός is ethical and describes

[1] Cf. Käsemann, 'God's Righteousness in Paul', 103ff, and Schweizer, 'Dying and Rising with Christ', 11.

a process,[1] but while righteousness for Paul is ethical, it is not really a process. It is God's righteousness into which the believer comes, in which he lives and shares, and to which he submits. Nonetheless it is real, which precludes any complete disjunction of it from sanctification. We may appropriately compare Phil. 1. 11, where we suggested taking 'the fruits of righteousness' as the concrete actualisation of righteousness, and take 'sanctification' here similarly. The same point exactly is made in v. 22, except that the believer's service there is to God, rather than to righteousness, but service to one is service to the other.[2]

ROMANS 7

We cannot here treat in detail the continuing debate about this chapter, especially about vv. 7–25, and obviously what immediately follows must be subject to question by those who believe it describes the experience of man, or of Paul himself, under the Law.[3] We take it as describing man's Christian experience, whether autobiographical or not (in any case 'man's' includes Paul's). This is largely because taken this way it admirably underlines the tension already noticed in Ch. 6, the 'be what you are', indicative–imperative tension, contained in the exhortation to submit to him who is, however, already one's Lord.[4] In practice, the believer who is righteous in Christ, who has known the exchange of dominions, who has died and lives again, still must be exhorted (Ch. 6) because he still must struggle (Ch. 7). Nevertheless there is a double deliverance from this situation, an ethical deliverance (7. 25) and a forensic one (8. 1). Because

[1] Cf. O. Procksch, 'ἁγιασμός', *TDNT*, I, 113, who stresses both these points.

[2] D. Daube, *The New Testament and Rabbinic Judaism* (London, 1956), 283f, 394f, finds 'slaves to righteousness' not only sub-Christian (cf. Dodd, *Romans*, 98), but sub-Jewish. A Jew would contemplate slavery only to God. Paul, he thinks, resorts to this desperate expedient in order to counter antinomianism, and apologises for it (v. 19*a*). Yet in our understanding, 'slavery to righteousness' is a telescoped expression for submission to God, leading to the righteousness in Christ.

[3] Among many, Dodd, *Romans*, 107f; Lagrange, *Romains*, 173ff; Sanday–Headlam, *Romans*, 184ff; Leenhardt, *Romans*, 180ff.

[4] The 'Christian' view is held, among others, by Barrett, *Romans*, 151ff; Nygren, *Romans*, 284–97. Murray, *Romans*, I, 255ff, sees vv. 7–13 as pre-Christian, and 14–25 as Christian.

believers are basically in Christ, they are acquitted, and for them there is no condemnation.

The root occurs only once in Ch. 7, δικαία in v. 12, where it describes the Law, and where three adjectives ('holy, just, and good') are used without precise differentiation to indicate that not the Law, but man, is wrong. 'Just' then is broadly ethical.

ROMANS 8

The verb occurs twice, the noun once, and δικαίωμα once. Very important also is v. 1 which makes it clear that in Christ men cannot be condemned but must be justified. In v. 4 δικαίωμα must mean 'ordinance' or, as Barrett suggests, 'requirement (that we should be righteous)',[1] and its importance for us is that it is fulfilled ἐν ἡμῖν. Even if ἐν is used for agent, not location, the verse accords well with our position. Those who fulfil it walk not according to the flesh, but according to the Spirit, which is another way of describing the Christian's new life. It is for men made new in Christ that such fulfilment is now possible. The connection between the new righteousness and life in the Spirit is made in v. 10. The body, i.e. the old self, is dead because of sin, but the new self, i.e. the spirit,[2] is alive because of righteousness. Once again sin and righteousness are linked to the old and new selves, and v. 10*a* shows that the new self depends on Christ. It is interesting that it is 'Christ in you', not vice versa, but the congruity of this with 'in Christ' is shown not only by the general principle of the whole Christ's being in each member, but also by the juxtaposition of the statement that believers are in the Spirit with the statement that the Spirit is in them, v. 9. This righteousness is therefore not man's own, but 'in Christ', and this is why it is life-giving.[3] The parallel with sin, and the setting in the context of the corporate Christ, or new life in the Spirit, makes probable an interpretation similar to that for Phil. 3. 9.

[1] *Romans*, 157. Nygren proposes the opposite of κατάκριμα, *Romans*, 317, but this does not fit the context.

[2] We take πνεῦμα to be human here, with Sanday–Headlam, *Romans*, 198. Murray, *Romans*, I, 289f, thinks it is the Holy Spirit. Either is possible, but the human reference seems to make more sense of διὰ δικαιοσύνην.

[3] Kuss, *Römerbrief*, 502–4, lists ways in which δικαιοσύνην here has been taken. Our view is supported by Nygren, *Romans*, 324f. Bruce, *Romans*, 164, takes it (with NEB) to mean 'justification'.

In v. 30 ἐδικαίωσεν is resumptive, and undoubtedly means 'justified' in a purely relational or forensic sense. In v. 33 there are many difficulties, but the meaning of δικαιῶν is not among them: the context is forensic, and the verb has its usual meaning.

ROMANS 9. 30–1

The noun occurs 4 times. The righteousness pursued by Israel was not pursued by the Gentiles, yet Israel was unfaithful to Yahweh and failed to achieve this righteousness (v. 31) which was based on law, νόμον δικαιοσύνης.[1] Yet the Gentiles who did not even attempt this righteousness have overtaken the Israelites, for they have arrived at a righteousness (v. 30), but one that is by faith. We have here, then, an antithesis of two kinds of righteousness, familiar to us from Phil. 3. 9, and emphasised in v. 32, those of works of the Law, and of faith. Now nothing in the text demands that 'righteousness' be either purely relational, or behaviour in relationship (here specifically a covenant relationship), but if on linguistic grounds we choose the latter, we find it makes perfectly good sense. The Jews thought acceptable righteousness consisted in (not just resulted from) following the Law, and so they missed it altogether. The Gentiles who were not even looking for life within the covenant, stumbled upon it when they found faith, for in finding faith they found faith-righteousness. It was tragically but exactly Israel's zeal for God's Law that prevented her from finding righteousness, because it drove her inexorably in the wrong direction.[2]

ROMANS 10. 1–10

What we have just been saying now receives confirmation, especially in v. 3:

> For, being ignorant of the righteousness that comes from God, and seeking to establish their own, they did not submit to God's righteousness (RSV – many MSS, including P46, א, and G, insert δικαιοσύνην again after 'their own').

[1] Cf. v. 32. One could take νόμον as 'principle', thus Murray, *Romans*, II, 43, for whom the whole phrase means that Israel was concerned with 'the order or institution which was concerned with justification'. We follow RSV, Leenhardt, *Romans*, 261f, and Sanday–Headlam, *Romans*, 279.

[2] Nygren, *Romans*, 375ff, also Schlatter, *Gottes Gerechtigkeit*, 308f.

We suggest that 'God's righteousness' here is to be taken in its full sense, as in 1. 17 etc., as God's outgoing, saving activity, into which man enters and in which he participates, and thus is gift, which is inseparable from the Giver. That we are not dealing with a process or method, but with God's action in Christ, with Christology, is shown by v. 4. It is thus the very opposite of one's own righteousness. Moreover, as in Rom. 6 it is a power or dominion to which one submits. There is nothing odd about all this if we take it Christologically: we are in Christ, he is our Lord, and also the power of our obedience, and so we live appropriately to this condition, i.e. righteously. Now this does not exclude all forensic meaning: it is the received, not the achieved righteousness which is acceptable, yet it is righteousness in the full sense, not just a right standing. This is clear not only on linguistic grounds, but also from v. 5: righteousness is something one practises.

In v. 4 we have the statement, τέλος γὰρ νόμου Χριστὸς εἰς δικαιοσύνην παντὶ τῷ πιστεύοντι. This is a much debated verse.[1] I think one must say that it means more than that Christ is the end of the Law as the way of winning acceptance with God, for in Paul's view it never was the way, cf. Rom. 4. Man was never meant to be, never could be, justified by works of the Law. Rather one must give 'righteousness' its full force, so that Paul is saying that Christ signals the end of the Law as the way to acceptable behaviour, as well as to acceptance. The way to this is now through believing, not believing in general, but believing in Christ. This is supported by his treatment of circumcision, which he does not reject for Gentiles only as a means of justification, but altogether, as an expression of righteousness. He is adamant that Gentiles should not be circumcised.

This does not mean he sees no good in the Law (cf. 7. 12). Nor does it deny that there is much in the Law which he continues to uphold even within this letter, nor does it reject the value of the Law in revealing sin (Ch. 7). It does deny that the Law is any longer the way to acceptable behaviour (i.e. both forensic and ethical elements), at least so far as believers are concerned. Whereas it never did have a justificatory or salvific role (cf. Rom. 4, Gal. 3), it did set the pattern of righteousness, of behaviour within the covenant. Now, for the believer, it does not do even

[1] Cf. Moule's recent discussion, 'Obligation in the Ethic of Paul', 401–4.

this, cf. Phil. 3. 9; Gal. 2. 17f; and Gal. 5. 6 for the irrelevance of circumcision, and also the supersession of the Law as the standard of righteousness in Mt. 5. However, obviously this does not mean the abrogation of everything the Law contained! It is possible that we should read Gal. 3. 23–7 in the same way: the Law had its necessary role, for how else could one know in what righteousness consisted? But now faith replaces Law, the faith that incorporates believers in Christ (Gal. 3. 26f). Therefore Christ, both the historic, redeeming, and the corporate Christ, marks the Law's end.[1]

We proceed to v. 5. We have already noted that law-righteousness is something practised, and that therefore faith-righteousness is also, but how do we take ζήσεται ἐν αὐτῇ? In Lev. 18. 5, to which it refers, the life in question is earthly life, almost well-being, which is consequent upon obedience to the statutes. Here too it is most natural to take life as consequent upon law-fulfilment, i.e. life in the widest sense, present and future.[2]

In v. 6 'the righteousness of faith' introduces what appears to be a strange piece of argumentation. First, it is clearly antithetic to the law-righteousness of v. 5, and therefore is a real righteousness, something one does, but it comes in man's receiving, participating, not in his achieving. Second, it relates to the annotated quotation from Deut. 30. 12–14. In the original the meaning is plain: what God requires of men is not to be sought out with difficulty, it is close at hand, and not obscure. Paul uses it really quite similarly. Where is the Christian's righteousness to be found? One need not search above, because the incarnation has already happened (v. 7) – but search for what? Not 'it', but him, Christ, who is the Christian's righteousness, cf. 1 Cor. 1. 30. Man needs to achieve nothing, the act of redemption and the

[1] Τέλος could mean 'fulfilment, culmination', rather than 'termination', especially in view of Gal. 3. 23–7 as taken above. C. E. B. Cranfield, 'St Paul and the Law', *SJTh*, 17 (1964), 49ff, prefers the former, and elaborates the ways in which it is such. Those who prefer the latter, usually mean *legalism* by 'the Law', cf. Moule, 'Obligation in the Ethic of Paul', 401ff. However, I am taking 'Law' to mean just that, though legalism is included, and εἰς δικαιοσύνην is construed with both 'Christ' and 'Law'. The Law no longer leads to the acceptable righteousness, but Christ does.

[2] Cf. Bultmann in R. Bultmann, G. von Rad, G. Bertram, *Life and Death*, BKW, E.Tr. (London, 1965), 72; similarly Sanday–Headlam, *Romans*, 286. On Paul's use of Lev. 18. 5, see Barrett, *Romans*, 198f; Murray, *Romans*, II, 249ff.

dawn of the new age have occurred. One finds Christ, and as a consequence righteousness, in the preaching, v. 8. It is forever at hand to be received by faith, and is as near as preaching. It is as accessible to faith as the statutes of the old covenant were to hearing. This interpretation seems to fit both the quotation, and the statements about righteousness, Christ, and faith. We may note, incidentally, that Deut. 30. 12–14 is quoted at least four times by Philo, *Mut. Nom.* 236f, *Post C.* 84f, *Virt.* 183, and *Praem.* 80. It may have been in common use in synagogue exposition.

We move on to v. 10, where faith leads to justification. Faith in (commitment to, response to) Christ as risen Lord, accompanied by confession of sin, leads to salvation, v. 9. This same believing leads to righteousness, in the full sense, and not as in RSV, 'justification', and the confession leads to salvation, v. 10. This is not to equate salvation and righteousness, or make the latter purely relational, but shows that righteousness by faith is part of salvation.

ROMANS 14. 17

'Righteousness and peace and joy in the Holy Spirit' are the marks of life in the kingdom of God, which is understood in this-worldly terms, cf. v. 18.[1] All three are gifts, and v. 18 ('he who thus serves Christ is acceptable to God and approved by men', RSV) shows that righteousness is understood in practical terms, with acceptability as consequent. This is a description of Christian life, in the Spirit.[2] 'Righteousness' is unlikely to mean God's saving righteousness which would be virtually the same as the Kingdom. In effect, 14. 17 repeats 5. 1–5.

THE TIME FACTOR

In Romans, as in Galatians, the discussion is centred on the *how* rather than the *when*. Many of the statements about justification are general, and the tenses used may well, whether present or future, be more logical than chronological. The clearest future references are 2. 13 and 3. 30; perhaps 3. 20, which may however be a logical future and understood as chronologically present in

[1] Leenhardt, *Romans*, 354f; Barrett, *Romans*, 264.

[2] So also Lagrange, *Romains*, 331; Sanday–Headlam, *Romans*, 392.

faithfulness to the source, Ps. 143. 2. On the other hand, justification is obviously already received in 3. 24, 26, 28; 4. 2–12; 5. 1, 9; 6. 7; 8. 30. While it may be true, then, that justification essentially belongs to the Judgment, the Christian has heard the verdict on him already, a verdict which he continually needs to hear until the Judgment.

If we are correct in seeing the Christian's righteousness as in Christ, it necessarily belongs to the here and now, though it too has a future dimension, cf. Gal. 5. 5.

APPENDED NOTE 10

The Noun δικαίωμα

We have given little attention to this form of the root, partly because it plays a minor role in Paul's vocabulary, and partly because it presents few problems. In LXX it renders חק 50 times, חֻקָּה 22 times, מִשְׁפָּט 40 times, other words 14 times, including צְדָקָה 3 times. The commonest meaning is thus 'ordinance', 'statute', but 'sentence of judgment' is also possible. The range of meanings outside the NT is set out in Schrenk, *Righteousness*, 66f. In 1 Maccabees it 4 times means 'ordinances', and once probably 'judgments' but possibly 'righteous deeds'; in 1 Baruch it twice means 'ordinances', once God's practice of justice, and once man's deeds of righteousness. It occurs only 5 times in NT apart from Paul, 3 times for ordinances or regulations, Lk. 1. 6; Heb. 9. 1, 10; once for righteous deeds (Rev. 19. 8), and once possibly for judgments (Rev. 15. 4). In Paul (see Schrenk, 67–70), three meanings occur: (i) ordinance, singular, perhaps hinting at the principle underlying particular ordinances; (ii) righteous act; (iii) justification, i.e. equivalent to δικαίωσις.

APPENDED NOTE 11

A Pre-Pauline Formula in Rom. 3. 21–31?

It is now widely held that in these verses Paul is glossing an earlier formulation, bending it in the direction of his theology. Thus, it is argued, in v. 25 δικαιοσύνη is God's covenant loyalty, but in v. 26 it is his saving activity. In v. 25*b*, God deals with past sins by passing them over, but in v. 26*a*, he deals with (present?) sins by saving. Again, how could Paul describe the past as the time of God's forbearance when he held that it lay under God's wrath? So, it is suggested that vv. 24f are a Jewish-Christian formula with v. 26 as the Pauline annotation, so that vv. 25, 26 describe the same saving act of God, but first from the Jewish-Christian and then from the Pauline viewpoint. See especially E. Käsemann, 'Zum Verständnis von Römer 3, 24–6', *ZNW*, 43 (1950–1), 150–4; Hunter, *Paul and his Predecessors*, 120–2; C. H. Talbert, 'A non-Pauline Fragment at Romans 3. 24–6?', *JBL*, 85 (1966), 287–96; G. Fitzer, 'Der Ort der Versöhnung nach Paulus', *ThZ*, 22 (1966), 161–83, though he thinks even the annotation is of pre-Pauline origin; Kertelge, '*Rechtfertigung*', 48–62; J. Reumann, 'The Gospel of the Righteousness of God: Pauline Reinterpretation in Romans 3. 21–31', *INTERP*, 20 (1966), 432–52, also *Righteousness and Society*, 57–62; Stuhlmacher, *Gottes Gerechtigkeit*, 88; Michel, *Römerbrief*, 103f. Against such views, Kuss, *Römerbrief*, 160f, also S. Lyonnet, 'Notes sur l'exégèse de l'Épître aux Romains', *BIB*, 38 (1957), 59. The theory is somewhat endangered by the multiplication of hypotheses: thus Talbert considers v. 24 Pauline, and vv. 25f a later interpolation, not by Paul. H. Conzelmann also disagrees with Käsemann about v. 24, 'Current Problems in Pauline Research', *INTERP*, 22 (1968), 171–86, at 177: Käsemann thinks it is from the tradition (except for 'by his grace, as a gift'), while Conzelmann thinks it is a Pauline transition.

Something like Käsemann's view is not implausible, and helps to explain the awkwardness of the passage, though our exegesis above tries to show that it can be made good sense of as it stands.

APPENDED NOTE 12

The Passing Over of Former Sins, Rom. 3. 25

It is debated whether this means forgiveness, or ignoring. Some think πάρεσις falls short of ἄφεσις, because ἐν τῇ ἀνοχῇ τοῦ θεοῦ suggests the epoch of God's patience (but what about 1. 18ff?); for further reasons, see V. Taylor, 'Great Texts Reconsidered: Rom. 3. 25f', *ET*, 50 (1938–9), 295–300, at 298. Πάρεσις is thus a sort of non-imputation rather than full forgiveness or justification, see among many others, Barrett, *Romans*, 79f; Lagrange,

Romains, 76f. In this view, it is usually taken that for πάρεσιν to mean full forgiveness, διά would have to be prospective, not causal, and this is unlikely, cf. Taylor, and H. G. Meecham, 'Romans iii 25f, iv 25 – the Meaning of διά c.acc.', *ET*, 50 (1938–9), 564. But διά could still be causal if τῶν προγεγονότων ἁμαρτημάτων refers not to past ages, but to how God regards past sins, i.e. to wiping the slate clean. Indeed, in the letter as a whole, it is better to take πάρεσις with justification *now*. In the past, God had not ignored or passed over sins (cf. 1. 18ff), but now he does, despite Acts 17. 30. Cf. W. G. Kümmel, 'Πάρεσις and Ἔνδειξις', *JThCh*, 3, 1–13, who regards the first as 'remission', 4, 9f.

CONCLUSION

I have said little about the question of how literally the forensic language ought to be taken. I must confess a natural bias towards seeing it mostly in metaphorical terms, for the restoration of relationship, but the question is not vital to my main contention.

As the basic thesis has already been stated (Ch. 9), no elaborate statement of conclusions is now necessary. The intention in the outline exegesis of the relevant parts of Galatians and Romans was to show that a quite reasonable sense is obtained if we start from the assumption that Paul uses the δικαι- word-group in the way indicated by the Hebrew and Greek background. If we take the verb as essentially relational or forensic, and the noun and adjective as describing behaviour within relationship, and if we also make full use of the corporate Christ idea, we arrive at an exegesis which satisfies the concerns of both traditional Catholicism and traditional Protestantism. Nothing is lost: justification is entirely by grace through faith, it is declaratory, yet on the other hand, Paul's ethical seriousness is fully allowed for, *within the one section of vocabulary*.

The relation between justification and righteousness is not uniform. Sometimes, especially in forensic passages, it seems that justification depends on righteousness in Christ by faith. Sometimes, justification initiates the relationship in which righteousness becomes a possibility. Always, solely by God's grace is man forgiven, acquitted, restored to right relationship, but also made a new creature whose life is now righteous in Christ, really and observably.

These two moments of man's salvation are interdependent and inseparable.

APPENDIX I: ANTONYMS

ἀδικεῖν occurs 26 times in the NT and invariably means 'do wrong to, injure, harm' someone or something: Mt. 20. 13; Lk. 10. 19; Acts 7. 24, 26, 27; 25. 10, 11; 1 Cor. 6. 7 (passive), 8; 2 Cor. 7. 2, 12, 12 (passive); Gal. 4. 12; Col. 3. 25, 25; Philem. 18; 2 Pet. 2. 13 (passive); Rev. 2. 11 (passive); 6. 6; 7. 2, 3; 9. 4, 10, 19; 11. 5; 22. 11. It occurs with δίκαιος and δικαιοσύνη in Rev. 22. 11, where the ill-attested alternative reading δικαιωθήτω must mean 'be righteous', ethically.

ἀδικία occurs 25 times, all ethical: Lk. 13. 27; 16. 8, 9; 18. 6; Jn 7. 18; Acts 1. 18; 8. 23; Rom. 1. 18, 18, 29; 2. 8; 3. 5; 6. 13; 9. 14; 1 Cor. 13. 6; 2 Cor. 12. 13; 2 Thess. 2. 10, 12; 2 Tim. 2. 19; Heb. 8. 12; Jas 3. 6; 2 Pet. 2. 13, 15; 1 Jn 1. 9; 5. 17. Of these, 5 are in conjunction with δικαιοσύνη: Rom. 1. 18, 18; 3. 5; 6. 13; 1 Jn 1. 9. As well as being ethical, 16 are in clear (but of course wrong) relation to God, that is all except Lk. 16. 8, 9; 18. 6; Rom. 9. 14; 1 Cor. 13. 6; 2 Cor. 12. 13; Jas 3. 6; 2 Pet. 2. 13, 15.

ἄδικος occurs 12 times, all ethical: Mt. 5. 45; Lk. 16. 10, 10, 11; 18. 11; Acts 24. 15; Rom. 3. 5; 1 Cor. 6. 1, 9; Heb. 6. 10; 1 Pet. 3. 18; 2 Pet. 2. 9. Of these 4 occur in conjunction with δίκαιος: Mt. 5. 45; Acts 24. 15; 1 Pet. 3. 18; 2 Pet. 2. 9. Certainly 4 (Acts 24. 15; 1 Cor. 6. 9; 1 Pet. 3. 18; 2 Pet. 2. 9) are in wrong relation to God, plus possibly another 4 (Mt. 5. 45; Lk. 16. 10, 10, 11). As in the case of the noun, some which lack this relation do so because the reference is to God (as being not unjust), and not man (ἀδικία: Rom. 9. 14; ἄδικος: Rom. 3. 5; Heb. 6. 10). The adverb occurs only once, and means 'unjustly' (1 Pet. 2. 19).

ἀδίκημα occurs 3 times, all ethical: Acts 18. 14; 24. 20; Rev. 18. 5. Only one of these (Rev. 18. 5) is in clear relation (wrong, of course) to God.

In the cases of ἀδικία and ἄδικος, they occur often enough together with δικαιοσύνη and δίκαιος to indicate that they are true antonyms. It is therefore important that both the negative noun and the negative adjective have clearly ethical meanings, and that they are commonly in (a wrong) relation to God as well. This corroborates (though in itself, of course, not conclusively) the view that δικαιοσύνη and δίκαιος are behaviour-in-relationship words.

The verb is used so differently from its formal antonym that it gives us no illumination.

APPENDIX II: THE APOSTOLIC FATHERS

These writings are worth examining to discover what has happened both linguistically and theologically in the sub-Apostolic Church, although we cannot draw hasty conclusions from them. They may not only have used words differently, but also have misunderstood Paul. The term 'Apostolic Fathers' here covers: 1 and 2 Clement, Barnabas, the Didache, the Shepherd of Hermes, Diognetus, Ignatius, Polycarp to the Philippians, and the Martyrdom of Polycarp.

LINGUISTIC FACTS

Rather than go in detail through all the occurrences of δικαι- in the literature, we may select only those cases where there is some special interest. Thus, in the verb, while it means 'acquit' in the majority of cases, it 4 times means 'make righteous' (Barn. 15. 7; HVis 3. 9. 1; HMan. 5. 1. 7; HSim. 5. 7. 1) with a possible fifth (Diog. 9. 5 – the problem of Diog. 9 is discussed below). The existence of this meaning may point to a development beyond Paul in a moralistic direction.

Whenever the noun is used of man, it is always for conduct in relation to God, and similarly the adjective is always in some sense ethical, with nearly always an explicit relation to God. The exceptions are: 1 Clem. 44. 3 (adverb); HSim. 1. 4 (adverb); Mart. 11. 1. Thus, as in earlier literature, adjective and noun are used for behaviour in relationship – the behavioural note is never absent, and the relational seldom.

TEACHING ON JUSTIFICATION

That the Apostolic Fathers have small understanding of justification by faith has been shown by T. F. Torrance, *The Doctrine of Grace in the Apostolic Fathers* (Grand Rapids, 1959), 133–9 and passim. We have already seen that the verb can sometimes mean 'make righteous', and that this may be due to the moralistic concern generally present in the literature. Justification is by works as well as by faith: in 2 Clem. 6. 7–9, the doctrine of the merits of the patriarchs is expressly rejected, but is replaced not by justification by faith, but by our own righteousness. This is not an isolated instance, cf. 1 Clem. 10. 7; 12. 1; 31. 2; 50. 5; HVis. 3. 2. 1; 3. 5. 3; also 2. 2. 7 and 2. 3. 3, and cf. K. Hörmann, *Leben in Christus* (Vienna, 1952), 258f. Probably, however, this idea of justification by works is not attached to the verb δικαιοῦν. Yet, even if it lacks the Pauline splendour, the doctrine of justification by grace through faith is found, cf. Polyc. 1. 3; Diog. 9. 4, and Stuhlmacher, *Gottes Gerechtigkeit*, 12.

Stuhlmacher maintains that justification is now future rather than present, because the eschatology is now wholly futurist, and on the whole the texts support this view (Barn. 4. 10; Ign. Rom. 5. 1; Philad. 8. 2. Diog. 5. 14 is ambiguous).

TEACHING ON RIGHTEOUSNESS

Apart from an emphasis on its expression in love (1 Clem. 48. 2, 2; Polyc. 3. 3; perhaps Barn. 1. 6), righteousness is a matter of choosing the way of the angel of righteousness rather than that of the angel of wickedness (HMan. 6. 2. 1–9; cf. HMan. 5. 1), or more simply of choosing the righteous way (Barn. 19. 6, 11; 20. 2, 2; Did. 3. 9; 4. 3; 5. 2, 2).

In Polyc. 8. 1 Christ is the ἀρραβών of our righteousness, and though this is understood partly in exemplarist terms (8. 2), it is also connected with redemption. Christ thus appears to be both the pattern and the means of our righteousness, cf. 1 Clem. 48. 2, 4. Righteousness is God's gift (cf. 1 Clem. 35. 2) and the fruit of the Spirit (HSim. 9. 25. 2).

DIOGNETUS 9

The 'time of righteousness' in 9. 1 must refer to man's ethical righteousness now made possible by God, because of the context, which is a contrast between wickedness until now, and goodness now, through God's power. How does God deal with our former wickedness? The righteous Jesus (this is a description, not a title, in 9. 2, cf. ἀδίκων, also 9. 5, and H. G. Meecham, *The Epistle to Diognetus* (Manchester, 1949), 129) takes our sin upon himself, and obliterates it by his own righteousness (9. 2, 3). This must be understood in expiatory or even substitutionary terms, but 'righteousness' in v. 3 and 'righteous' in v. 2 are both ethical, because of the righteousness–wickedness parallel. This substitution amounts, of course, to forgiveness (cf. Meecham, *Diognetus*, 129f). In 9. 4, if we take the verb to be declaratory, the understanding of justification is similar to that of Gal. 2. 17, i.e. it is 'in Christ'. In our wickedness, we can be justified only in him. Then comes the crucial passage:

> O the sweet exchange... that the wickedness of many should be concealed in the one righteous, and the righteousness of the one should make righteous (or justify?) many wicked (9. 5 – the translation of K. Lake, *The Apostolic Fathers* (2nd edn, London, 1965) in Loeb).

The verb could be declaratory, as Meecham thinks (*Diognetus*, 130), but this has the disadvantage of not reflecting the contrast between man's wickedness and Christ's righteousness before the exchange, and man's righteousness after it. It is tempting to conclude, therefore, that in however unclear a fashion, the Pauline double-sidedness of justification and righteousness as twin gifts of God to man, is reflected here. We have justification, and have it in Christ, but the time of righteousness does not simply mean the time of acquittal. It means the time of *ethical* righteousness, the opposite of wickedness. It is thus not necessary to say with Stuhlmacher (*Gottes Gerechtigkeit*, 12) that Diognetus alters Paul. Indeed Diog. 9 can best be explained against the background of Paul's thought.

SELECT BIBLIOGRAPHY

Abbott, T. K. *The Epistles to the Ephesians and to the Colossians* (ICC), Edinburgh, 1909.

Achtemeier, E. R. 'Righteousness in the O.T.', *IDB*, IV, 80–5.

Achtemeier, P. J. 'Righteousness in the N.T.', *IDB*, IV, 91–9.

Allegro, J. M. 'Fragment of a Commentary on Ps. XXXVII from Qumran', *Palestine Exploration Quarterly*, 86 (1954), 69–75.

'Further Light on the History of the Qumran Sect', *JBL*, 75 (1956), 89–95.

'Further Messianic References in Qumran Literature', *JBL*, 75 (1956), 174–86.

'Fragments of a Qumran Scroll of Eschatological Midrāšîm', *JBL*, 77 (1958), 350–4.

'Commentary on Hosea from Qumran's Fourth Cave', *JBL*, 78 (1959), 142–7.

'An Unpublished Fragment of Essene Halakhah (4Q Ordinances)', *JSS*, 6 (1961), 71–3.

Althaus, P. *Der Brief an die Römer* (NTD), 6, 8th edn, Göttingen, 1954.

Amiot, F. *The Key Concepts of St Paul* (E.Tr.), Freiburg, 1962.

Arndt, W. F. and Gingrich, F. W. *A Greek–English Lexicon of the New Testament and other Early Christian Literature*, Cambridge, 1957.

Avigad, N. and Yadin, Y. *A Genesis Apocryphon*, Jerusalem, 1956.

Bacher, W. *Die exegetische Terminologie der jüdischen Traditionsliteratur*, Leipzig, 1899–1905.

Bailey, C. *Epicurus, the Extant Remains*, Oxford, 1926.

Baillet, M. 'Les Paroles des Luminaires', *RB*, 68 (1961), 195–250.

Barr, J. *The Semantics of Biblical Language*, Oxford, 1961.

Barrett, C. K. *The Gospel According to St John*, London, 1955.

The Epistle to the Romans (Black's N.T. Commentaries), London, 1957.

From First Adam to Last, London, 1962.

The Pastoral Epistles, Oxford, 1963.

The First Epistle to the Corinthians (Black's N.T. Commentaries), London, 1968.

Barth, K. *The Epistle to the Romans* (E.Tr.), Oxford, 1933.

Christ and Adam. Man and Humanity in Romans 5 (E.Tr.), *SJTh* Occasional Papers, 5, Edinburgh, 1956.

Barth, M. 'The Challenge of the Apostle Paul', *Journal of Ecumenical Studies*, 1 (1964), 58–81.

Barthélemy, D. and Milik, J. T. *Discoveries in the Judaean Desert I: Qumran Cave I*, Oxford, 1955.

Baumgarten, J. and Mansoor, M. 'Studies in the New Hodayot (Thanksgiving Hymns)', *JBL*, 74 (1955), 115–24, 188–95; 75 (1956), 107–13; 76 (1957), 139–48.

Beare, F. W. *The First Epistle of Peter*, Oxford, 1947.

The Epistle to the Philippians (Black's N.T. Commentaries), London, 1959.

Bekker, I. *Aristoteles. Opera*, 11 vols., Oxford, 1837.

Benz, K. 'Δικαιοσύνη Θεοῦ beim Apostel Paulus', *ThQ*, 94 (1912), 590–2.

Berliner, A. *Targum Onkelos*, Berlin, 1884.

Best, E. *One Body in Christ*, London, 1955.

Bickerman, E. J. 'The Date of the Testaments of the Twelve Patriarchs', *JBL*, 69 (1950), 245–60.

Bigg, C. *The Epistles of St Peter and St Jude* (ICC), 2nd edn, Edinburgh, 1910.

The Christian Platonists of Alexandria, 2nd edn, Oxford, 1913.

Bihlmeyer, K. *Die apostolischen Väter* (*Neubearbeitung der Funkschen Ausgabe*), vol. 1, Tübingen, 1956.

Black, M. *The Scrolls and Christian Origins*, London, 1961.

'The Parables as Allegory', *BJRL*, 42 (1959–60), 273–87.

Black, M. and Rowley, H. H. *Peake's Commentary on the Bible*, new edn, London, 1962.

Blackman, C. 'Romans 3 26*b*: A Question of Translation', *JBL*, 87 (1968), 203f

Blackman, P. (ed.). *Mishnayoth*, 7 vols, London–New York, 1951–63.

Bollier, J. A. 'The Righteousness of God', *INTERP*, 8 (1954), 404–13.

Bonnard, P. *L'Épître de Saint Paul aux Galates*, Neuchâtel, 1953.

Bornkamm, G., Barth, G. and Held, H. J. *Tradition and Interpretation in Matthew* (E.Tr.), London, 1963.

Bousset, W. *Die Religion des Judentums*, 2nd edn, Berlin, 1906.

Bouttier, M. *Christianity According to Paul* (E.Tr.), London, 1966.

Box, G. H. *The Ezra-Apocalypse*, London, 1912.

Bréhier, E. *Les Idées philosophiques et religieuses de Philon d'Alexandrie*, 2nd edn, Paris, 1925.

Briggs, C. A. *Psalms* (ICC), 2 vols, Edinburgh, 1906.

Brockington, L. H. *A Critical Introduction to the Apocrypha*, London, 1961.

Bromiley, G. W. 'The Doctrine of Justification in Luther', *EQ*, 24 (1952), 91–100.

Brooke, A. E. *The Johannine Epistles* (ICC), Edinburgh, 1912.

Bruce, F. F. *The Acts of the Apostles*, London, 1951.

Biblical Exegesis in the Qumran Texts, Grand Rapids, 1959.
The Epistle to the Hebrews, London, 1964.
The Epistle of Paul to the Romans (Tyndale), London, 1966.
'Justification by Faith in the non-Pauline Writings of the New Testament', *EQ*, 24 (1952), 66–77.
Bultmann, R. *Theology of the New Testament* (E.Tr.), 2 vols, London, 1952–5.
'Ignatius and Paul', in S. M. Ogden (ed.), *Existence and Faith*, London, 1961.
'Adam and Christ According to Romans 5', in W. Klassen and G. F. Snyder (eds), *Current Issues in New Testament Interpretation*, London, 1962, 143–65.
'ΔΙΚΑΙΟΣΥΝΗ ΘΕΟΥ', *JBL*, 83 (1964), 12–16.
Bultmann, R. and Weiser, A. *Faith* (BKW, E.Tr.), London, 1961.
Bultmann, R., von Rad, G. and Bertram, G. *Life and Death* (BKW, E.Tr.), London, 1965.
Burrows, M. *The Dead Sea Scrolls*, London, 1956.
Burrows, M., Trever, J. C. and Brownlee, W. K. *The Dead Sea Scrolls of St Mark's Monastery*, I *The Isaiah MS and the Habakkuk Commentary*, New Haven, 1950; II fasc. ii, *The Manual of Discipline*, New Haven, 1951.
Burton, E. D. *The Epistle to the Galatians* (ICC), Edinburgh, 1921.
Calvin, J. *Institutes of the Christian Religion*, ed. J. T. McNeill, London, 1961.
Cambier, J. 'Justice de Dieu, salut de tous les hommes et foi', *RB*, 71 (1964), 537–83.
'Péchés des hommes et péché d'Adam en Rom. v. 12', *NTS*, 11 (1964–5), 217–55.
Carmignac, J. *La Règle de la Guerre des Fils de Lumière contre les Fils de Ténèbres*, Paris, 1958.
Cazelles, H. 'À propos de quelques textes difficiles relatifs à la Justice de Dieu dans l'Ancien Testament', *RB*, 58 (1951), 169–88.
Cerfaux, L. *Christ in the Theology of St Paul* (E.Tr.), 2nd edn, New York–Edinburgh, 1959.
The Christian in the Theology of St Paul (E.Tr.), London, 1967.
Cerfaux, L. and Descamps, A. 'Justice, Justification', *DBS*, IV, cols 1417–510.
Chadwick, H. 'St Paul and Philo of Alexandria', *BJRL*, 48 (1965–6), 286–307.
Charles, R. H. *The Greek Versions of the Testaments of the Twelve Patriarchs*, Oxford, 1908.
The Ethiopic Version of the Book of Enoch, 2nd edn, Oxford, 1912.

Charles, R. H. *The Apocrypha and Pseudepigrapha of the Old Testament*, 2 vols, Oxford, 1913.
Commentary on Daniel, Oxford, 1929.
Clements, R. E. *Prophecy and Covenant*, London, 1965.
Cohn, L. and Wendland, P. *Philo Judaeus, Opera*, Berlin, 1896–1915; Indices by J. Leisegang, Berlin, 1926–30.
Colson, F. H. and Whitaker, G. H. *Philo* (Loeb), London, 1929–65.
Conzelmann, H. 'Current Problems in Pauline Research', *INTERP*, 22 (1968), 171–86.
Cooke, G. A. *Ezekiel* (ICC), Edinburgh, 1936.
Cranfield, C. E. B. 'St Paul and the Law', *SJTh*, 17 (1964), 43–68.
Creed, J. M. *The Gospel According to St Luke*, London, 1930.
Cremer, H. *Die paulinische Rechtfertigungslehre im Zusammenhange ihrer geschichtlichen Voraussetzungen*, Gütersloh, 1899.
Cremer, H. and Kögel, J. *Biblisch-theologisches Wörterbuch der Neutestamentlichen Gräzität*, 10th edn, Gotha, 1911–15.
Cronbach, A. 'Righteousness in Jewish Literature, 200 BC – AD 100', *IDB*, IV, 85–91.
Cullmann, O. *Baptism in the New Testament* (E.Tr.), London, 1950.
Dalman, G. *Die richterliche Gerechtigkeit im Alten Testament*, Berlin, 1897.
Aramäisch–neuhebräisches Handwörterbuch zu Targum, Talmud, und Midrasch, 2nd edn, Frankfurt-am-Main, 1922.
Jesus–Jeshua (E.Tr.), London, 1929.
Danby, H. (trans.). *The Mishnah*, Oxford, 1933.
Daniélou, J. *Philon d'Alexandrie*, Paris, 1958.
Dantine, W. 'Verheissung der Lehre von der Rechtfertigung in der Gegenwart', *ThZ*, 22 (1966), 279–91.
Daube, D. *The New Testament and Rabbinic Judaism*, London, 1956.
Davidson, A. B. *The Theology of the Old Testament*, Edinburgh, 1904.
Davidson, R. *The Old Testament*, London, 1964.
Davies, W. D. *Paul and Rabbinic Judaism*, London, 1948.
The Setting of the Sermon on the Mount, Cambridge, 1964.
Deane, W. J. *The Book of Wisdom*, Oxford, 1881.
Deissmann, A. *Paul. A Study in Social and Religious History* (E.Tr.), new edn, New York, 1957.
Denney, J. 'Righteousness (in St Paul's Teaching)', *ERE*, x, 786–90.
Denzinger, H. *Enchiridion Symbolorum et Definitionum*, Freiburg, 1922.
Descamps, A. *Les Justes et la Justice dans les évangiles et le christianisme primitif hormis la doctrine proprement paulinienne*, Louvain, 1950.
'La Justice de Dieu dans la Bible grecque', *Studia Hellenistica*, 5 (1948), 69–92.
De Witt, N. W. *Epicurus and his Philosophy*, Minneapolis, 1954.
Dibelius, M. and Kümmel, W. G. *Paul* (E.Tr.), London, 1953.

Dobschütz, E. von. 'Die Rechtfertigung bei Paulus, eine Rechtfertigung des Paulus', *ThStKr*, 85 (1912), 38–67.

Dodd, C. H. *The Epistle to the Romans* (MNTC), London, 1932.

The Bible and the Greeks, London, 1935.

The Johannine Epistles (MNTC), London, 1946.

Drummond, J. *Philo Judaeus*, 2 vols, London, 1888.

'On the Meaning of "Righteousness of God" in the Theology of St Paul', *HJ*, 1 (1902), 83–95, 272–93.

Duncan, G. S. *The Epistle of Paul to the Galatians* (MNTC), London, 1934.

Dupont, J. *La réconciliation dans la théologie de Saint Paul*, Bruges, 1953.

Dupont-Sommer, A. *The Jewish Sect of Qumran and the Essenes* (E.Tr.), London, 1954.

The Essene Writings from Qumran (E.Tr.), Oxford, 1961.

Durrwell, F. X. *The Resurrection* (E.Tr.), London, 1960.

Easton, B. S. *The Pastoral Epistles*, London, 1948.

Edersheim, A. 'Philo', *Dictionary of Christian Biography*, vol. IV, London, 1887.

Eichrodt, W. *Theology of the Old Testament* (E.Tr.), 2 vols, London, 1961–7.

Eissfeldt, O. *The Old Testament, an Introduction* (E.Tr.), Oxford, 1965.

Ellis, E. E. *Paul's Use of the Old Testament*, Edinburgh, 1957.

Paul and his Recent Interpreters, Grand Rapids, 1961.

Epictetus, *Discourses* (with E.Tr. by W. A. Oldfather), Loeb, 2 vols, London, 1926–8.

Epstein, I. (ed.). *The Babylonian Talmud*, 35 vols, London, 1935–52.

Etheridge, J. W. *The Targums of Onkelos and Jonathan ben Uzziel on the Pentateuch*, 2 vols, London, 1862–5.

Fahlgren, K. Hj. *Sedāḳā, nahestehende und entgegengesetzte Begriffe im Alten Testament*, Uppsala, 1932.

Fairweather, W. *Jesus and the Greeks*, Edinburgh, 1924.

Feuillet, A. 'La citation d'Habacuc II 4 et les huit premiers chapîtres de l'Épître aux Romains', *NTS*, 6 (1959–60), 52–80.

Fischel, H. A. 'Martyr and Prophet', *JQR*, 37 (1947), 265–80, 363–86.

Fitzer, G. 'Der Ort der Versöhnung nach Paulus', *ThZ*, 22 (1966), 161–83.

Flemington, W. F. *The New Testament Doctrine of Baptism*, London, 1948.

Frame, J. E. *The Epistles of St Paul to the Thessalonians* (ICC), Edinburgh, 1912.

Freedman, M. and Simon, M. (eds). *Midrash Rabbah*, 10 vols, London, 1939.

Furnish, V. P. *Theology and Ethics in Paul*, Nashville–New York, 1968.

Gaster, T. H. *Scriptures of the Dead Sea Sect*, London, 1957.
Geffcken, J. (ed.). *Die Oracula Sibyllina*, Leipzig, 1902.
George, A. R. *Communion with God in the New Testament*, London, 1953.
Glasson, T. F. 'Dying and Rising with Christ', *LQHR*, Oct. 1961, 286–91.
Goodenough, E. R. *By Light, Light*, New Haven, 1935.
An Introduction to Philo Judaeus, 2nd edn, Oxford, 1962.
Goodrick, A. T. S. *The Book of Wisdom*, London, 1913.
Goodspeed, E. J. *Problems of New Testament Translation*, Chicago, 1945.
'Some Greek Notes', *JBL*, 73 (1954), 86–91.
Goudge, H. L. *The First Epistle to the Corinthians*, London, 1903.
The Second Epistle to the Corinthians, London, 1927.
Grundmann, W. 'δύναμαι/δύναμις', *TDNT*, II, 284–317.
'Gesetz, Rechtfertigung, und Mystik bei Paulus', *ZNW*, 32 (1933), 52–65.
'Der Lehrer der Gerechtigkeit von Qumran und die Frage nach der Glaubensgerechtigkeit in der Theologie des Apostels Paulus', *RQ*, 2 (1959–60), 237–59.
Häring, Th. ΔΙΚΑΙΟΣΥΝΗ ΘΕΟΥ *bei Paulus*, Tübingen, 1896.
Halevy, A. A. מדרש רבה, 8 vols, Tel Aviv, 1956–63.
Harrison, E. *Studies in Theognis*, Cambridge, 1902.
Hatch, E. *Essays in Biblical Greek*, Oxford, 1889.
Hatch, W. H. P. *The Pauline Idea of Faith* (Harvard Theological Studies, III), Cambridge, Mass., 1917.
Hebert, A. G. '"Faithfulness" and "Faith"', *Theology*, 58 (1955), 373–9.
Heidland, H. W. *Die Anrechnung des Glaubens zur Gerechtigkeit*, Stuttgart, 1936.
'λογίζομαι', *TDNT*, IV, 284–92.
Henshaw, T. *The Writings*, London, 1963.
Herford, R. T. *Christianity in Talmud and Midrash*, London, 1903.
Héring, J. *The First Epistle of Saint Paul to the Corinthians* (E.Tr.), London, 1962.
Hill, D. *Greek Words and Hebrew Meanings*, Cambridge, 1967.
'ΔΙΚΑΙΟΙ as a Quasi-Technical Term', *NTS*, 11 (1964–5), 296–302.
Hirsch, E. G. 'Right and Righteousness', *JE*, x, 420–4.
Hörmann, K. *Leben in Christus*, Vienna, 1952.
Horst, F. *Gottes Recht: gesammelte Studien zum Recht im Alten Testament*, Munich, 1961.
Hughes, H. M. *The Ethics of Jewish Apocryphal Literature*, London, 1909.

Hunter, A. M. *Paul and his Predecessors*, 2nd edn, London, 1961.
Hyatt, J. P. *Jeremiah*, *IB*, v.
Jacob, E. *Theology of the Old Testament* (E.Tr.), London, 1958.
Jaeger, W. *Paideia: the Ideals of Greek Culture* (E.Tr.), 3 vols, Oxford, 1939–47.
Jastrow, M. *A Dictionary of the Targumim, the Talmud Babli and Yerushalmi, and the Midrashic Literature*, 2 vols, London, 1903.
Jeremias, G. *Der Lehrer der Gerechtigkeit*, Göttingen, 1963.
Jeremias, J. *The Central Message of the New Testament*, London, 1965.
Johnson, A. R. *Sacral Kingship in Ancient Israel*, Cardiff, 1955.
Johnson, S. E. 'Paul and the Manual of Discipline', *HTR*, 48 (1955), 157–65.
de Jonge, M. *The Testaments of the Twelve Patriarchs*, Assen, 1953.
'Christian Influence in the Testaments of the Twelve Patriarchs', *NT*, 4 (1960), 182–235.
Jowett, B. *The Dialogues of Plato* (5 vols), 3rd edn, Oxford, 1892.
Jüngel, E. *Paulus und Jesus*, 2nd edn, Tübingen, 1964.
Käsemann, E. 'Zum Verständnis von Römer 3, 24–26', *ZNW*, 43 (1950–1), 150–4.
'God's Righteousness in Paul', *JThCh*, 1 (1965), 100–10.
Kautzsch, E. *Über die Derivate des Stammes* צדק *im alttestamentlichen Sprachgebrauch*, Tübingen, 1881.
Kelly, J. N. D. *The Pastoral Epistles* (Black's N.T. Commentaries), London, 1963.
Kennedy, H. A. A. *Philo's Contribution to Religion*, London, 1919.
Kertelge, K. '*Rechtfertigung*' *bei Paulus*, Münster, 1967.
Kilpatrick, G. D. *The Origins of the Gospel According to St Matthew*, Oxford, 1946.
'A Theme of the Lucan Passion Story and Luke xxiii 47', *JTS*, 43 (1942), 34–6.
Klaar, E. 'Rm 6. 7: ῾Ὁ γὰρ ἀποθανὼν δεδικαίωται ἀπὸ τῆς ἁμαρτίας', *ZNW*, 59 (1968), 131–4.
Klein, G. 'Rechtfertigung', [3]*RGG*, v, cols 825–8.
Knight, G. A. F. *A Christian Theology of the Old Testament*, London, 1959.
Deutero-Isaiah, New York, 1965.
Knox, J. *Chapters in a Life of Paul*, London, 1954.
The Ethic of Jesus in the Teaching of the Church, London, 1962.
The Epistle to the Romans, *IB*, ix.
Knox, W. L. 'Abraham and the Quest for God', *HTR*, 28 (1935), 55–60.
Köhler, L. *Hebrew Man* (E.Tr.), London, 1956.
Kölbing, P. 'Δικαιοσύνη Θεοῦ in Röm. 1, 17', *ThStKr*, 68 (1895), 7–17.

Kümmel, W. G. 'Πάρεσις and Ἔνδειξις', *JThCh*, 3, pp. 1–13.
Küng, H. *Justification* (E.Tr.), London, 1966.
Kuss, O. *Der Römerbrief*, Regensburg, 1957.
Lagrange, M. J. *Saint Paul: Épître aux Romains*, Paris, 1931.
Lake, K. *The Apostolic Fathers* (Loeb, 2 vols), 2nd edn, London, 1965.
Leaney, A. R. C. *The Rule of Qumran and its Meaning*, London, 1966.
Lee, E. K. *A Study in Romans*, London, 1962.
Leenhardt, F. J. *The Epistle to the Romans* (E.Tr.), 3rd edn, London, 1964.
Lévi, I. *The Hebrew Text of the Book of Ecclesiasticus* (Semitic Study Series, III), Leiden, 1904.
Levy, S. *Original Virtue*, London, 1907.
Lewis, J. J. 'The Ethics of Judaism in the Hellenistic Period', Unpublished dissertation, London University (1958).
Licht, J. *The Thanksgiving Scroll*, Jerusalem, 1957.
Liddon, H. P. *Explanatory Analysis of St Paul's Epistle to the Romans*, 4th edn, London, 1899.
Lietzmann, H. *An die Römer* (*HzNT*, 8), 4th edn, Tübingen, 1933.
An die Korinther I, II (*HzNT*, 9), 4th edn, Tübingen, 1949.
Lightfoot, J. *Horae Hebraicae et Talmudicae* (4 vols), new edn by R. Gandell, Oxford, 1859.
Lightfoot, J. B. *Notes on Epistles of St Paul*, 2nd edn, London, 1904.
Ljungman, H. *Das Gesetz Erfüllen, Matt. 5, 17ff und 3, 15 untersucht*, Lund, 1954.
Lock, W. *The Pastoral Epistles* (ICC), Edinburgh, 1924.
Lofthouse, W. F. 'The Righteousness of Jahveh', *ET*, 50 (1938–9), 341–5, and 'The Righteousness of God', ibid. 441–5.
Lohse, E. *Märtyer und Gottesknecht*, Göttingen, 1955.
Longenecker, R. N. *Paul, Apostle of Liberty*, New York, 1964.
Lüdemann, H. *Die Anthropologie des Apostels Paulus*, Kiel, 1872.
Lyonnet, S. 'Notes sur l'exégèse de l'Épître aux Romains', *BIB*, 38 (1957), 35–61.
'Justification, Jugement, Rédemption, principalement dans l'épître aux Romains', *Recherches Bibliques*, 5 (1960), 166–84.
'Pauline Soteriology', in A. Robert and A. Feuillet (eds), *Introduction to the New Testament* (E.Tr.), New York–Rome–Paris–Tournai, 1965, 820–65.
McArthur, H. K. *Understanding the Sermon on the Mount*, London, 1961.
Mach, R. *Der Zaddik in Talmud und Midrasch*, Leiden, 1957.
McNeile, A. H. *The Gospel According to St Matthew*, London, 1915.
Manson, T. W. *The Sayings of Jesus*, London, 1949.
Ethics and the Gospel, London, 1960.
On Paul and John, London, 1963.

Mansoor, M. (ed.). *The Thanksgiving Hymns*, Leiden, 1961.
Marcus, R. *Law in the Apocrypha*, New York, 1927.
Marmorstein, A. *The Doctrine of Merits in Old Rabbinical Literature*, London, 1920.
The Old Rabbinic Doctrine of God, 2 vols, London, 1927–37.
May, H. G. *Ezekiel*, *IB*, VI.
Meecham, H. G. *The Letter of Aristeas*, Manchester, 1935.
The Epistle to Diognetus, Manchester, 1949.
'Romans iii. 25f, iv. 25 – the Meaning of διά c.acc.', *ET*, 50 (1938–9), 564.
Metzger, B. M. *An Introduction to the Apocrypha*, New York, 1957.
Michel, O. *Der Brief an die Römer* (Meyer's Kommentar), 12th edn, Göttingen, 1963.
Milik, J. T. *Ten Years of Discovery in the Judaean Desert* (E.Tr.), London, 1959.
'Le Testament de Lévi en Araméen', *RB*, 62 (1955), 392–406.
'Prière de Nabonide', *RB*, 63 (1956), 407–11.
Mitton, C. L. *The Epistle of James*, London, 1966.
Moffatt, J. *The Epistle to the Hebrews* (ICC), Edinburgh, 1924.
The First Epistle of Paul to the Corinthians (MNTC), London, 1938.
Montefiore, C. G. *Judaism and St Paul*, London, 1914.
The Synoptic Gospels (2 vols), 2nd edn, London, 1927.
Rabbinic Literature and Gospel Teachings, London, 1930.
'Florilegium Philonis', *JQR*, 7 (1894–5), 481–545.
Montefiore, C. G. and Loewe, H. *A Rabbinic Anthology*, London, 1938.
Montefiore, H. W. *The Epistle to the Hebrews* (Black's N.T. Commentaries), London, 1964.
Montgomery, J. W. 'Wisdom as Gift', *INTERP*, 16 (1962), 43–57.
Moore, G. F. *Judaism in the First Centuries of the Christian Era*, 3 vols, Cambridge, Mass., 1927–30.
Morris, L. *The Apostolic Preaching of the Cross*, London, 1955.
Morton, A. Q. and McLeman, J. *Paul, the Man and the Myth*, London, 1966.
Moule, C. F. D. *An Idiom-Book of New Testament Greek*, 2nd edn, Cambridge, 1959.
The Phenomenon of the New Testament, London, 1967.
'The Biblical Conception of "Faith"', *ET*, 68 (1956–7), 157, 222.
'Obligation in the Ethic of Paul', in W. R. Farmer, C. F. D. Moule, and R. R. Niebuhr (eds), *Christian History and Interpretation*, Cambridge, 1967, 389–406.
'Fulfilment-words in the New Testament', *NTS*, 14 (1968), 293–320.
Moulton, J. H. and Howard, W. F. *Grammar of New Testament Greek*, vol. 2, Edinburgh, 1913.

Moulton, J. H. and Milligan, G. *The Vocabulary of the Greek Testament*, London, 1914–29.

Mowinckel, S. *He That Cometh* (E.Tr.), Oxford, 1956.

The Psalms in Israel's Worship (E.Tr.), 2 vols, Oxford, 1962.

Mowry, L. *The Dead Sea Scrolls and the Early Church*, Chicago, 1962.

Müller, C. *Gottes Gerechtigkeit und Gottes Volk*, Göttingen, 1964.

Muilenburg, J. *The Way of Israel*, London, 1962.

Isaiah, *IB*, v.

Murray, J. *The Epistle to the Romans* (2 vols in 1), London, 1967.

Nagel, W. 'Gerechtigkeit – oder Almosen?', *Vigiliae Christianae*, 15 (1961), 141–5.

Neil, W. *The Epistle of Paul to the Thessalonians* (MNTC), London, 1950.

Neugebauer, F. *In Christus*, Göttingen, 1961.

Newman, J. H. *Lectures on the Doctrine of Justification*, 4th edn, London, 1885.

North, C. R. *The Second Isaiah*, Oxford, 1964.

Nygren, A. *A Commentary on Romans* (E.Tr.), London, 1952.

Oepke, A. *Der Brief des Paulus an die Galater*, 3rd edn, Berlin, 1964.

'ΔΙΚΑΙΟΣΥΝΗ ΘΕΟΥ bei Paulus in neuer Beleuchtung', *ThLZ*, 78 (1953), 257–64.

Oesterley, W. O. E. *The Psalms*, 2 vols, London, 1939.

Ottley, R. R. *The Book of Isaiah According to the Septuagint*, London, 1904.

Peake, A. S. 'The Quintessence of Paulinism', *BJRL*, 4 (1917–18), 285–311.

Pedersen, J. *Israel, Its Life and Culture* (4 parts in 2 vols), London–Copenhagen, 1926–40.

Philonenko, M. 'Le Maître de Justice et la Sagesse de Salomon', *ThZ*, 14 (1958), 81–8.

Plummer, A. *The Gospel According to St Luke* (ICC), Edinburgh, 1896.

The Second Epistle of St Paul to the Corinthians (ICC), Edinburgh, 1915.

Polybius, *The Histories* (Loeb, E.Tr. by W. R. Paton), 6 vols, London, 1922–7.

Porteous, N. W. *Daniel, A Commentary*, London, 1965.

Powell, C. H. *The Biblical Concept of Power*, London, 1963.

Prat, F. *The Theology of Saint Paul* (E.Tr.), 2 vols, London, 1926–7.

Procksch, O. 'ἁγιασμός', *TDNT*, I, 113.

Quell, G. *Sin* (BKW, E.Tr.), London, 1951.

Quell, G. and Schrenk, G. *Righteousness* (BKW, E.Tr.), London, 1951.

Rabin, C. *The Zadokite Documents*, Oxford, 1954.

von Rad, G. *Old Testament Theology* (E.Tr.), 2 vols, Edinburgh, 1962–5.

The Problem of the Hexateuch and Other Essays (E.Tr.), London, 1966.
Rahlfs, A. (ed.). *Septuaginta*, 2 vols, Stuttgart, 1935.
Ranston, H. *The Old Testament Wisdom Books*, London, 1930.
Reicke, B. *The Epistles of James, Peter, and Jude*, New York, 1964.
Reumann, J. and Lazareth, W. *Righteousness and Society, Ecumenical Dialog in a Revolutionary Age*, Philadelphia, 1967.
Richardson, A. *An Introduction to the Theology of the New Testament*, London, 1958.
Ringgren, H. *The Faith of the Psalmists*, London, 1963.
Ritschl, A. *Die christliche Lehre von der Rechtfertigung und Versöhnung dargestellt*, vol. 2, 2nd edn, Bonn, 1882.
Roberts, B. J. *The Old Testament Text and Versions* (Cardiff, 1951).
Robinson, H. W. *The Religious Ideas of the Old Testament*, London, 1913.
Inspiration and Revelation in the Old Testament, ed. L. H. Brockington and E. A. Payne, Oxford, 1946.
Robinson, J. A. T. *The Body*, London, 1952.
Ropes, J. H. *The Epistle of St James* (ICC), Edinburgh, 1916.
'"Righteousness" and "The Righteousness of God" in the Old Testament and in St Paul', *JBL*, 22 (1903), 211–27.
Rosenberg, R. A. 'Jesus, Isaac, and the Suffering Servant', *JBL*, 84 (1965), 381–8.
Rowley, H. H. *From Moses to Qumran*, London, 1964.
Rupp, E. G. *The Righteousness of God*, London, 1953.
Ryle, H. E. and James, M. R. (eds). *Psalms of the Pharisees*, Cambridge, 1891.
Sabatier, A. *The Apostle Paul* (E.Tr.), London, 1891.
Sanday, W. and Headlam, A. C. *The Epistle to the Romans* (ICC), Edinburgh, 1902.
Schechter, S. *Some Aspects of Rabbinic Theology*, London, 1909.
Schlatter, A. *Die Theologie des Judentums nach dem Bericht des Josefus*, Gütersloh, 1932.
Gottes Gerechtigkeit; ein Kommentar zum Römerbrief, 4th edn, Stuttgart, 1965.
Schlier, H. *Der Brief an die Galater* (Meyer's Kommentar), 12th edn, Göttingen, 1962.
Schmid, H. *Gerechtigkeit als Weltordnung*, Tübingen, 1968.
Schnackenburg, R. *Baptism in the Thought of St Paul* (E.Tr.), Oxford, 1964.
The Moral Teaching of the New Testament (E.Tr.), Freiburg, 1965.
Schoeps, H. J. *Paul. The Theology of the Apostle in the Light of Jewish Religious History* (E.Tr.), London, 1961.
Schrey, H.-H., Walz, H. H. and Whitehouse, W. A. *The Biblical Doctrine of Justice and Law*, London, 1955.

Schürer, E. *A History of the Jewish People in the Time of Jesus Christ* (E.Tr.), Edinburgh, 1890–8.

Schulz, S. 'Zur Rechtfertigung aus Gnaden in Qumran und bei Paulus', *ZThK*, 56 (1959), 155–85.

Schwab, M. (trans.). *Talmud Yerushalmi* (*Le Talmud de Jérusalem*), new edn, 11 vols in 6, Paris, 1960.

Schweitzer, A. *Paul and his Interpreters* (E.Tr.), London, 1912.

The Mysticism of Paul the Apostle (E.Tr.), London, 1931.

Schweizer, E. 'Gerechtigkeit Gottes im N.T.', ³*RGG*, II, cols 1406f.

'Two New Testament Creeds Compared. 1 Corinthians 15. 3–5 and 1 Timothy 3. 16' in W. Klassen and G. F. Snyder (eds), *Current Issues in New Testament Interpretation*, London, 1962, 166–77.

'Dying and Rising with Christ', *NTS*, 14 (1967), 1–14.

Scott, C. A. A. *Christianity According to St Paul*, Cambridge, 1927.

Scott, E. F. *The Epistles of Paul to the Colossians, to Philemon, and to the Ephesians* (MNTC), London, 1930.

The Pastoral Epistles (MNTC), London, 1936.

Paul's Epistle to the Romans, London, 1947.

Scroggs, R. *The Last Adam. A Study in Pauline Anthropology*, Oxford, 1966.

'Romans vi. 7 ὁγ ἀρ ἀποθανὼν δεδικαίωται ἀπὸ τῆς ἁμαρτίας', *NTS*, 10 (1963), 104–8.

Selwyn, E. G. *The First Epistle of St Peter*, London, 1946.

Sharp, D. S. 'For our Justification', *ET*, 39 (1927–8), 87–90.

Singer, S. (trans. and ed.). *The Authorized Daily Prayer Book of the United Hebrew Congregations of the British Empire*, London, 1935.

Skemp, J. B. *The Greeks and the Gospel*, London, 1964.

Skinner, J. 'Righteousness in O.T.', *HDB*, IV, 272–81.

Smith, C. R. *The Bible Doctrine of Salvation*, London, 1941.

The Bible Doctrine of Sin, London, 1953.

Smith, W. R. *Lectures on the Religion of the Semites*, 3rd edn by S. A. Cook, London, 1927.

Snaith, N. H. *The Distinctive Ideas of the Old Testament*, London, 1944.

Stalder, K. *Das Werk des Geistes in der Heiligung bei Paulus*, Zürich, 1962.

Stauffer, E. *New Testament Theology* (E.Tr.), London, 1955.

Stendahl, K. (ed.). *The Scrolls and the New Testament*, New York, 1957.

Stevens, G. B. 'Righteousness in N.T.', *HDB*, IV, 281–4.

Stevens, W. A. 'The Forensic Meaning of δικαιοσύνη', *AJT*, 1 (1897), 443–50.

Stewart, R. A. *Rabbinic Theology*, Edinburgh, 1961.

Strachan, R. H. *The Second Epistle of Paul to the Corinthians* (MNTC), London, 1935.

Strack, H. L. *Introduction to the Talmud and Midrash*, New York, 1965.

Strack, H. L. and Billerbeck, P. *Kommentar zum Neuen Testament aus Talmud und Midrasch* (5 vols in 6), Munich, 1922–56.

Strecker, G. *Der Weg der Gerechtigkeit*, Göttingen, 1962.

Strugnell, J. 'The Angelic Liturgy at Qumran', Supplements to *VT*, vii (Oxford Congress Volume), Leiden, 1960, 318–45.

Stuhlmacher, P. *Gottes Gerechtigkeit bei Paulus*, Göttingen, 1965.

Surkau, H. W. *Martyrien in jüdischer und frühchristlicher Zeit*, Göttingen, 1938.

Swete, H. B. *An Introduction to the Old Testament in Greek*, 2nd edn, Cambridge, 1914.

Talbert, C. H. 'A non-Pauline Fragment at Romans 3. 24–6?', *JBL*, 85 (1966), 287–96.

Tannehill, R. C. *Dying and Rising with Christ* (Beiheft zur *ZNW*), Berlin, 1967.

Tasker, R. V. G. 'The Doctrine of Justification by Faith in the Epistle to the Romans', *EQ*, 24 (1952), 37–46.

Taylor, V. *Forgiveness and Reconciliation*, London, 1941.

The Gospel According to St Mark, London, 1952.

The Epistle to the Romans, London, 1955.

The Atonement in New Testament Teaching, 2nd edn, London, 1963.

'Great Texts Reconsidered: Rom. 3. 25f', *ET*, 50 (1938–9), 295–300.

'Forgiveness', *ET*, 51 (1939–40), 16–21.

'Does the New Testament Call Jesus God?', *ET*, 73 (1961–2), 116–18.

Thackeray, H. St J. *The Relation of St Paul to Contemporary Jewish Thought*, London, 1900.

Thackeray, H. St J. and Marcus, R. *Lexicon to Josephus*, Paris, 1930–55.

Thackeray, H. St J. and others. *Josephus* (Loeb, 9 vols), London, 1926–65.

Tobac, E. *Le Problème de la Justification dans St Paul*, Louvain, 1941.

Torrance, T. F. *The Doctrine of Grace in the Apostolic Fathers*, Grand Rapids, 1959.

'One Aspect of the Biblical Conception of Faith', *ET*, 68 (1956–7), 111–14, 221f.

Turner, N. *Grammatical Insights into the New Testament*, Edinburgh, 1965.

van Unnik, W. C. *Tarsus or Jerusalem*, London, 1962.

Vermès, G. *The Dead Sea Scrolls in English*, Harmondsworth, 1962.

Vincent, M. R. *The Epistles to the Philippians and to Philemon* (ICC), Edinburgh, 1902.

Watson, N. M. 'Some Observations on the Use of ΔΙΚΑΙΟω in the Septuagint', *JBL*, 79 (1960), 255–66.

Weber, M. *Ancient Judaism*, Glencoe, Ill., 1952 (E.Tr. of *Religionssoziologie III: Das antike Judentum*).

Weingreen, J. 'The Title Moreh Sedek', *JSS*, 6 (1961), 162–74.

Weiser, A. *The Psalms, A Commentary* (E.Tr.), London, 1962.

Wendland, H.-D. *Die Mitte der paulinische Botschaft*, Göttingen, 1935.

Die Briefe an die Korinther (NTD, 7), 7th edn, Göttingen, 1954.

Whiteley, D. E. H. *The Theology of St Paul*, Oxford, 1964.

Williams, A. L. *Talmudic Judaism and Christianity*, London, 1933.

Williams, C. S. C. *The Acts of the Apostles* (Black's N.T. Commentaries), London, 1957.

Winter, J. and Wünsche, A. *Mechilta: Ein tannaitischer Midrasch zu Exodus*, Leipzig, 1909.

Wolfson, H. A. *Philo*, 2 vols, Cambridge, Mass., 1947.

Wrede, W. *Paul* (E.Tr.), London, 1907.

Zänker, O. 'Δικαιοσύνη Θεοῦ bei Paulus', *ZSystTh*, 9 (1931–2), 398–420.

Zahn, Th. *Der Brief des Paulus an die Galater*, Leipzig, 1905.

Der Brief des Paulus an die Römer, Leipzig, 1910.

Zimmerman, F. *The Book of Tobit*, New York, 1958.

Zuckermandel, M. S. (ed.). *Tosephta*, 2nd edn, Jerusalem, 1937.

I. INDEX OF PASSAGES CITED

A. THE OLD TESTAMENT

INDEX OF PASSAGES CITED

B. THE APOCRYPHA AND PSEUDEPIGRAPHA OF THE OLD TESTAMENT

C. THE NEW TESTAMENT

D. THE DEAD SEA SCROLLS

E. RABBINICAL LITERATURE

(Tractates are arranged alphabetically)

(*i*) *The Mishnah*

(*ii*) *The Babylonian Talmud*

F. CLASSICAL AND HELLENISTIC AUTHORS AND EXTRA-CANONICAL CHRISTIAN WRITINGS

II. INDEX OF AUTHORS

Alexandria Still

PRINCETON ESSAYS IN LITERATURE

(For a list of the other titles in this series, see page following index.)

Alexandria Still

FORSTER, DURRELL, AND CAVAFY

Jane Lagoudis Pinchin

PRINCETON UNIVERSITY PRESS

PRINCETON, NEW JERSEY

PUBLISHED BY PRINCETON UNIVERSITY PRESS, PRINCETON, NEW JERSEY
IN THE UNITED KINGDOM: PRINCETON UNIVERSITY PRESS,
GUILDFORD, SURREY

LIBRARY OF CONGRESS CATALOGING IN PUBLICATION DATA WILL
BE FOUND ON THE LAST PRINTED PAGE OF THIS BOOK

PUBLICATION OF THIS BOOK HAS BEEN AIDED BY A GRANT FROM THE
ANDREW W. MELLON FOUNDATION

THIS BOOK HAS BEEN COMPOSED IN LINOTYPE CALEDONIA

PRINTED IN THE UNITED STATES OF AMERICA
BY PRINCETON UNIVERSITY PRESS, PRINCETON, NEW JERSEY

for Hugh

WITH WHOM I SHARE THE MARVELOUS JOURNEY

Table of Contents

Acknowledgments

When, in the summer of 1971, my husband and I traveled from Cairo to Alexandria, Athens, Thessalonika, and then to Cambridge, following the trail of Cavafy, Forster, and Lawrence Durrell, we met an extraordinary number of generous, helpful people. Since then I have had the same good fortune. I would like to thank Robert Liddell, Lawrence Durrell, George Savidis, Rae Dalven, Stratis Tsirkas, Magdi Wahba, Dinos Koutsomis, Mrs. Zelita, George Thomson, and Basil Lagoudis, as well as those in charge of the Cavafy papers at the Benaki Museum in Athens, and Elizabeth Ellem and Penelope Bulloch, Archivists of the Twentieth-century Manuscripts at King's College, Cambridge, and the Trustees and Fellows of King's for permission to quote from unpublished material by Forster.

For a careful reading of this manuscript, I am grateful to Helen Regueiro, Robert Maguire, Joan Ferrante, Herman Ausubel, Jerry Sherwood, and, particularly, to Edmund Keeley and Peter Bien, who gave me the benefit of their immense knowledge of Cavafy.

My special thanks to five people: to my parents, Sarah and Emanuel Lagoudis—in whom I first saw that strange, fine bonding of Greek and English-speaking worlds—for traveling around the libraries of New York when I couldn't; to John Unterecker, the best of teachers, my E. M. Forster; and finally to Hugh and Sarah Eleni, the one for all the right help, the other for the right interruptions.

I am indebted to the Colgate University Research Council for financing my trip to Austin, Texas.

List of Abbreviations

THE following works are used frequently in the text and have been abbreviated as follows:

BY E. M. FORSTER:

(AH) *Abinger Harvest*
(AE) *Albergo Empedocle and Other Writings*
(A) *Alexandria: A History and a Guide*
(AN) *Aspects of the Novel*
(E) *Egypt*
(GLD) *Goldsworthy Lowes Dickinson*
(HD) *The Hill of Devi*
(HE) *Howards End*
(LC) *The Life to Come and Other Stories*
(LJ) *The Longest Journey*
(MT) *Marianne Thornton*
(M) *Maurice*
(PI) *A Passage to India*
(PP) *Pharos and Pharillon*
(RV) *A Room with a View*
(TCD) *Two Cheers for Democracy*
(WAFT) *Where Angels Fear to Tread*

BY LAWRENCE DURRELL:

(CP) *Collected Poems*
(B) *Balthazar*
(C) *Clea*
(J) *Justine*
(M) *Mountolive*
(SP) *Spirit of Place*

A full reference for each of these works is given in the Selected Bibliography.

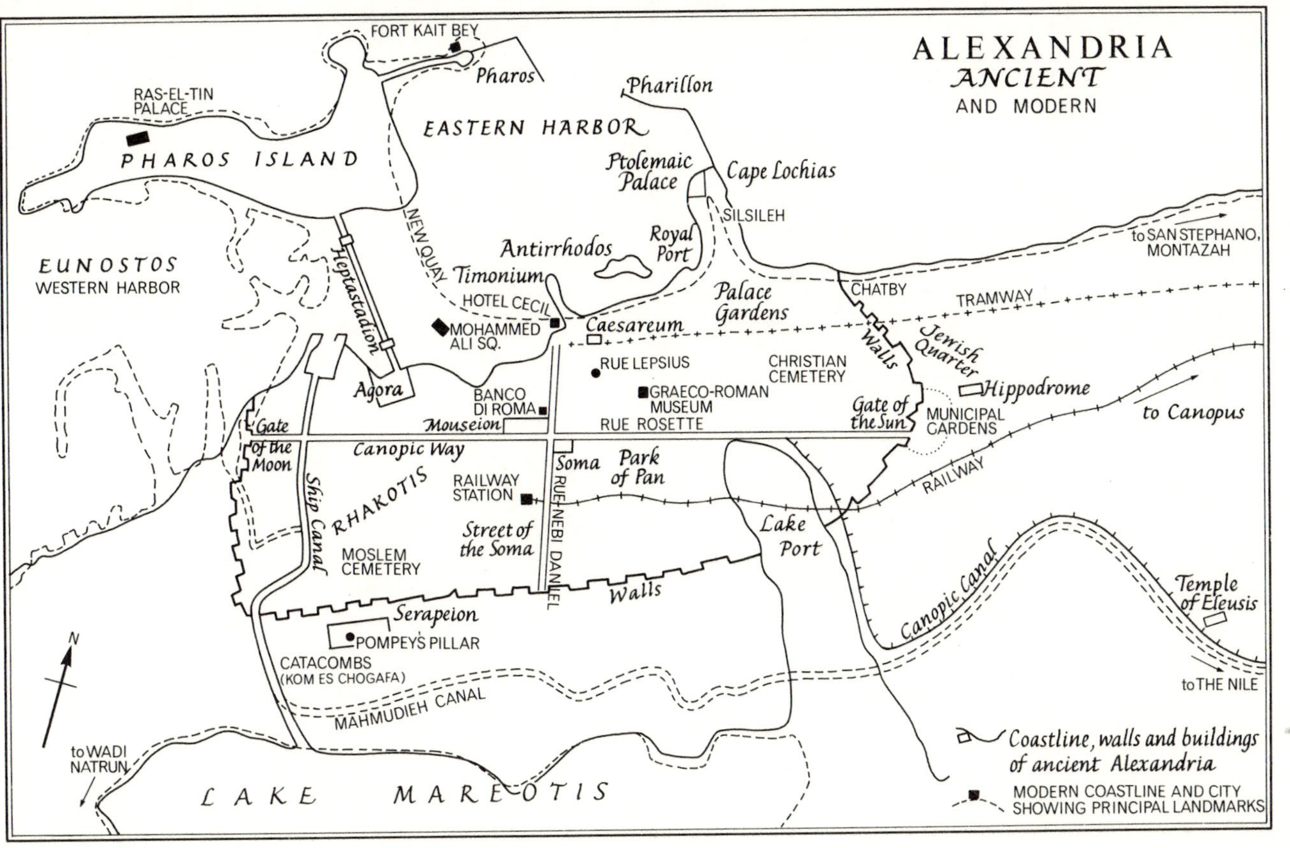
ALEXANDRIA
ANCIENT
AND MODERN
FORT KAIT BEY
Pharos
Pharillon
RAS-EL-TIN PALACE
PHAROS ISLAND
EASTERN HARBOR
Ptolemaic Palace
Cape Lochias
SILSILEH
Royal Port
Antirrhodos
Timonium
NEW QUAY
HOTEL CECIL
MOHAMMED ALI SQ.
Heptastadion
EUNOSTOS
WESTERN HARBOR
Caesareum
Palace Gardens
CHATBY
TRAMWAY
to SAN STEPHANO, MONTAZAH
Walls
Jewish Quarter
Hippodrome
to Canopus
RUE LEPSIUS
CHRISTIAN CEMETERY
GRAECO-ROMAN MUSEUM
RUE ROSETTE
Agora
BANCO DI ROMA
Mouseion
Gate of the Moon
Canopic Way
Gate of the Sun
MUNICIPAL GARDENS
RAILWAY
Soma
Park of Pan
RAILWAY STATION
RUE NEBI DANIEL
Ship Canal
RHAKOTIS
Street of the Soma
Lake Port
MOSLEM CEMETERY
Walls
Serapeion
POMPEY'S PILLAR
CATACOMBS (KOM ES CHOGAFA)
MAHMUDIEH CANAL
Canopic Canal
Temple of Eleusis
to THE NILE
N
to WADI NATRUN
LAKE MAREOTIS
Coastline, walls and buildings of ancient Alexandria
MODERN COASTLINE AND CITY SHOWING PRINCIPAL LANDMARKS

Alexandria Still

As you set out for Ithaka
hope your road is a long one,
full of adventure, full of discovery.
. . . .
May there be many summer mornings when,
with what pleasure, what joy,
you enter harbors you're seeing for the first time;
may you stop at Phoenician trading stations
to buy fine things,
mother of pearl and coral, amber and ebony,
sensual perfume of every kind—
as many sensual perfumes as you can;
and may you visit many Egyptian cities
to learn and go on learning. . . .

· 1 ·

THE CITY

. . . the important determinant of any culture is after all—the spirit of place. Just as one particular vineyard will always give you a special wine with discernible characteristics so a Spain, an Italy, a Greece will always give you the same type of culture—will express itself through the human being just as it does through its wild flowers. . . . Yes, human beings are expressions of their landscape . . . I think that not enough attention is paid to [the sense of place] . . . as a purely literary criterion. What makes "big" books is surely as much to do with their site as their characters and incidents. . . . They are tuned in to the sense of place. You could not transplant them without totally damaging their ambience and mood; . . . this has nothing I think to do with the manners and habits of the human beings who populate them; for they exist in nature, as a function of place.

(SP, 156-163)

LAWRENCE DURRELL is right, of course. And one feels foolish when mentioning Homer, Dickens, or Tolstoy as proof of what he says. Most "big" books are thoroughly grounded as, perhaps less obviously, are most "big" poems. Ireland shapes Yeats as much as it does Joyce. Curiously, Twain and Eliot were equally moved by that "great brown god" the Mississippi. And for all his weddings of Imagination and Reality, Wallace Stevens places "A Dish of Peaches in Russia" and Crispin in Carolina. After the free-flying human condition, we, like Durrell, like Forster and Cavafy before him, seem only to touch it when turning a corner onto the windy corniche in, say, Alexandria.

Few places have had as passionate a character. Few have shaped as many sensibilities; for, like a handful of other world-cities, Alexandria was the center of cultural, political, and religious life for many long centuries. Contemporary readers often think of antiquity in terms of Athens and then Rome, losing a sense of Greater Greece and its core Alexandria. But perhaps this loss is not out of keeping with the spirit of that exotic city.

Alexandria produced many strange figures: Alexander, who gave the city its name but was drawn to a remoter east; Theocritos, Euclid, Callimachus; its philosophers and theologians, Plotinus, Hypatia, the rivals Athanasios and Arios; conquerors and leaders, Ptolemy Sotir, Amr, Mohammed Ali;[1] and of course Cleopatra and her Antony, that Roman Alexandrian who heard the music of the god Hercules, fading as the god left the city, and recognized it as an omen of his own defeat.[2]

But Alexandria, with its rich past, is at present out of the world's eye, noted, if at all, as a town where Egyptian presidents on occasion entertain heads of state. The contempo-

[1] Greek or Latin spelling? I have generally adopted the method used by the translators Edmund Keeley and Philip Sherrard in C. P. Cavafy, *Collected Poems*, ed. George Savidis (Princeton: Princeton University Press, 1975) approximating the sound of modern Greek when dealing with Greek names, except when other usage is already well-known and firmly established. The line is a fine one: if Theocritos why not Kallimachos? There are no happy solutions, and the problem is compounded when quoting from secondary sources or different translators. Inevitably the reader will draw his own boundary and disagree with individual choices made here, even when agreeing that we should, in the main, no longer use latinized forms of Greek names. Names given, when citing sources, will be spelled as they are in each source and will, therefore, sometimes differ from the spelling in my text.

[2] See Shakespeare's *Antony and Cleopatra*, IV, iii. In Plutarch, Shakespeare's source, the god is Bacchus. Cavafy saw the god as Dionysus. His poem, "The God Abandons Antony," is on pp. 142-143.

rary city might have been easy to forget, except that the spirit of this particular place shaped the fiction of three major twentieth-century writers and through them the imaginations of us all.

For the modern city produced one of Alexandria's strangest figures: C. P. Cavafy, the Greek poet who made her a mythical land, linking an outpost of contemporary European culture to its Hellenistic past. Thanks to the incredible energy of E. M. Forster and of fine scholars and translators who followed, Cavafy's work is now becoming well-known to an English-speaking audience. New translations of the collected poems, a new biography, and a new book-length study of the Cavafian imagination will all be available in English within the course of this year.[3]

Less widely known, and the subject of this study, is the profound influence the spirit of Alexandria and of the city's poet had on two English-speaking writers—E. M. Forster and Lawrence Durrell—whom world war brought to Alexandria, where they confronted the city's history and ambience, the legendary Cavafy, and themselves. Both wrote about the poet and Alexandria and, in different ways, sought what Cavafy had sought: to capture the spirit of an extraordinary place.

E. M. Forster came to Egypt during the First World War, and it is here that Cavafy's and Alexandria's influence on the

[3] I have used Keeley and Sherrard's translations of the *Collected Poems* throughout, except when the work of another translator is clearly indicated. They are excellent, as is Robert Liddell's *Cavafy: a Critical Biography* (London: Duckworth, 1974) from which the English-speaking reader can get a good, if opinionated, notion of the controversies in Cavafian criticism, as well as a sense of the man whose person shaped so many fictive visions. Universal praise pales, as anyone writing recommendations or reviews soon discovers, but I must add that along with those new works is one equally fine: Edmund Keeley's *Cavafy's Alexandria: Study of a Myth in Progress,* soon to be published by Harvard University Press—tracing the chronological development of Cavafy's imaginative vision—the manuscript of which the author kindly lent me while I was revising my own piece. I am clearly indebted to this exciting work.

contemporary English-speaking world had its start. For Forster, Alexandria was a passage to India, a bridge, a link, teaching him to come to terms with history and with love. As we shall see, the direction of Forster's fiction changed as a result; it finally encompassed loss.

The Second World War found Lawrence Durrell almost literally washed upon Alexandrian shores. Durrell could not, like Forster, know Cavafy, but he still felt the Greek poet's presence—an unseen mentor—and, like Forster, wrote about young Englishmen and older, wiser Easterners, and about The City, for Durrell a metaphor for modern life, the battleground upon which man, the artist, must struggle to survive. He too uses Cavafy as his guide, although only at times can he follow his mentor's whispers of defeat. Clearly, as it had for others before him, Alexandria triggered the best in Durrell's imagination.

In attempting to discover the influence of Cavafy and Alexandria on these English Alexandrians, we begin with our own examination of the city's history and landscape, knowing from the start what the *Alexandria Quartet* would have us see: that there are more than four sides to any story. Although momentarily digressing twice, to angle our vision at Macedonia and Selefkia and later at Byzantium—because these places were for many, including Cavafy and Durrell, extensions of the Alexandrian spirit—we will follow Alexandria's history chronologically: from its formation and its periods of Ptolemaic splendor through Roman and Moslem conquests, finally, to the city that sprang from its own ashes two centuries ago, and, now faded, "goes on being Alexandria still."[4]

Our study cannot encompass the city's history; an objective or complete history is of course as illusory as an objective photograph. Durrell's *Quartet* begins with a note: "The characters in this story . . . bear no resemblance to living

[4] A Cavafy poem, "Exiles," set in Alexandria after the Moslem conquest, opens with the line, "It goes on being Alexandria still."

persons. Only the city is real." (J, 7) "Real," the only word, as Nabokov has said, that requires quotation marks. Durrell's city is a mythic land, as is Forster's and Cavafy's. But Alexandria, her landscape and her peoples, the spirit of place, had, perhaps more than any other city of this century, the power to excite mythic visions, and in order to know those visions fully we must examine the spot on which they grew. Our study cannot encompass the city's history, but it can help the reader hear the sounds of Alexandrian life, the din that surrounded, and shaped, all these writers, so that he can better note the particular strains each chose to stress, the music each of these Antonys claimed as his own.

Even Alexandria's geography is extraordinary. Flying over the Greek Islands toward Cairo, I was astonished to see sudden unrelenting yellow sands. Alexandria is only a short distance from the Libyan Desert, which has had its role in shaping her spirit, but most of the city is surrounded by water. The promontory of Ras-el-Tin, once the island Pharos of which Homer speaks but now connected to the mainland by the accumulation of silt, thrusts its hourglass form into the Mediterranean, an ancient harbor on either side. The city, formed on alluvial soil, is bordered on the south by Lake Mareotis—its harbor connected during Alexandria's earliest history with a canal that led to the "Canopic Mouth" of the Nile and thus to Africa. E. M. Forster captured some of the sense of the city's proximity to and yet detachment from that continent:

> There is a certain little bird—I forget its name but its destiny is to accompany the rhinoceros about and to perform for him various duties that he is too unwieldy to perform for himself. Well, coastal Egypt is just such a little bird, perched lively and alert upon the hide of that huge pachyderm Africa. It may not be an eagle or

a swan. But unlike the rhinoceros, its host, it can flit through the blue air. And now and then it sings.[5]

Ἀλεξάνδρεια πρὸς Αἰγύπτωι, Alexandria ad Ægyptum. Like her poet, she has always been adjacent to Egypt, never quite part of that land.

> Among the happy advantages of the city, the greatest is the fact that this is the only place in all Ægypt which is by nature well situated with reference to both things—both to commerce by sea, on account of the good harbours, and to commerce by land, because the river easily conveys and brings together everything into a place so situated—the greatest emporium in the inhabited world.[6]

Thus the Roman visitor Strabo described Alexandria after the fall of Cleopatra. Harbors providing access to three continents. A link to Macedonia and Greece and the riches of the African Nile. A base leading to Asia and conquest of the Persian Empire. In 331 B.C., having conquered Syria and Egypt, Alexander ordered the construction of a city on this strategic spot where only the small town of Rhakotis stood, housing fishermen, goatherds, and coast guards.

The flat enclosed land didn't inspire the architectural inventiveness of an ethereal, spiraling Pergamum.[7] But the city's planning did become a part of the mythology of Alexandria. Plutarch tells us that, lacking chalk, the builders marked out streets with barley meal—which the birds

[5] "A Musician in Egypt," *The Egyptian Mail*, 21 October 1917, p. 2.

[6] Strabo, *The Geography of Strabo*, trans. Horace Leonard Jones (London: Wm. Heinemann, 1959), VIII, 53.

[7] The Rhodian Dinocratis, Alexandria's architect, used a common Hippodamian plan producing regular parallel streets with two wide main avenues intersecting one another at right angles. Traveling one, from west to east, an Alexandrian could go from the Eunostos Harbor to the Canopic canal; traveling the other, from north to south, would lead one from the Eastern harbor to the harbor of Lake Mareotis. A causeway—the Heptastadion—linked Pharos with the mainland.

promptly ate. Disturbed, Alexander consulted his seers, who assured him that this was a good omen, indicating abundance. Alexandria would be "nursing mother for men of every nation."[8] Greek, Jew, Egyptian, Armenian, Italian, Syrian, French, English—with names that take on the repetitive magic of litany in Durrell's city—clearly proved the prophecy true over and over again.

Alexander was to have little else to do with his city. Journeying from it into the desert, he met the prophet Ammon, who addressed Alexander as a god, equivocally. And like a young god, Alexander dreamed of conquering Asia, and of bringing harmony to the world. "That way lies madness," E. M. Forster was to write of these dreams of India. (PP, 27) More than eight years later Alexander's body was brought back to Alexandria, but he never saw the city again.

Out of Alexander's conquests, after much struggling over the spoils, three great dynasties emerged—separate but linked by language and culture. The leaders of each shared the idea that, above all else, they were Greeks, these Macedonians, Selefkians, and Ptolemies.

Greater Greece

With their capital at Pella, the Macedonian heirs of Antigonos Gonatas spent generations fighting to maintain control of much of the Greek mainland. Defending Hellenism from Roman as well as from Northern and Celtic forces, they often discovered that Greece preferred Roman to Macedonian rule. Final defeat came with the battle of Pydna in 168 B.C., a battle, like many Cavafy focused upon, through which Roman power controlled a large part of the Hellenic world.

In Asia the division of Alexander's empire went to a long line of men called Selefkos or Antiochos. These generally weak kings controlled a huge area—from Afghanistan to the

[8] *Plutarch's Lives,* trans. Benadotte Perrin (London: Wm. Heinemann, 1958), VII, 301.

Straits, from the Pontus to Syria—which began to erode almost immediately. Feeling themselves Greek, they wanted to live near the Mediterranean, and as a consequence Syria became the real center of their empire, with Antioch on the Orontes their capital. The great Persian kings had ruled from an Iranian center which was better suited for keeping their vast kingdom united. By the first century before Christ the Selefkid empire had dwindled to include only Syria.

Still Antioch, like Alexandria, remained an important city until the Arab conquest in A.D. 638. Antioch had a population of nearly 250,000 in the fourth century A.D. and a reputation—shared or caused by the neighboring resort Daphne—as a beautifully and infamously dissolute city. She was, at the same time, an important center of Christianity—the setting for some of the early works of Peter, Paul, and Barnabas—famous for her conflict with the Emperor Julian the Apostate and as the place from which the fifth century hermit Simeon Stylite came. A remarkable city, a city in which—particularly in the later poems—many Cavafian characters find their home, Antioch was, in temperament and in fate, closest to Alexandria in the Hellenic world.

Alexandria was of course the capital of the third part of Alexander's world: the Ptolemaic Empire.

> Egypt is the very home of the goddess; for all that exists and is produced in the world is in Egypt; wealth, wrestling grounds, might, peace, renown, shows, philosophers, money, young men, the domain of the θεοί ἀδελφοί, the king a good one, the museum, wine, all good things one can desire, women more in number. . . .[9]

Through the fictive voice of an old matchmaker, the poet Herodas creates a feeling for abundant Alexandria in the days of Ptolemy II, Philadelphos (285-247 B.C.).

Philadelphos' most noteworthy accomplishment was, as

[9] Herodas, "Mime I," *The Mimes and Fragments,* ed. A. D. Knox (Cambridge: Cambridge University Press, 1966), p. 5.

Forster puts it, "domestic." Like the Egyptian god Osiris, he married his sister. "It was the pride of race carried to an extreme degree." (A, 16) Durrell sees the union as more basic—sexuality carried to an extreme degree, to root-knowledge—the incestuous spirit that haunts his city and its citizens. This mating, certainly alien to Greek practice, became a precedent for a long chain of Ptolemies, Arsinoes, and Cleopatras. The line was to decline—Athenaios describes Cleopatra's unpopular father as "not a man but a flute player and a juggler"[10]—but the first three Ptolemies built an outstanding, if over-planned, city, holding sway in courts that were celebrated throughout the world.

Ptolemaic Alexandria

The architectural sites of Alexandria included the Pharos, that huge ancient lighthouse built by Sortratos of Knidos and one of the seven wonders of the ancient world. The Soma, the temple-tomb, was said to have housed the golden coffin of Alexander and was, for Durrell, the axis from which the ancient city radiated, "like the arms of a starfish." (C, 55) In the southwest corner of the city the first Ptolemy placed another temple, dedicated to the new god Serapis, a fine truly Alexandrian creation, combining features of the Egyptian gods Osiris and Apis with the Greek deities Zeus, Pluto, and Aesculapius, the god of healing, and thus embodying what Forster, in particular, saw as the essential character of the city, its ability to act as a bridge between cultures and ideas.

Pharos, the Soma, the temple to Serapis: all are clearly linked in our visions with the Mouseion and its Library, justifiably the best-known wonder of Ptolemaic Alexandria. By 250 B.C. the Library contained 400,000 volumes, including Aristotle's collection; the chief librarian ruled as the most important official in the Mouseion, a vast center of learning

[10] Athenaeus, *The Deipnosophists,* trans. Charles Burton Gulick (London: Wm. Heinemann, 1928), II, 433.

in which scholars could write, do research, or teach under the patronage of the state.

As is perhaps obvious, the intellectual climate did not produce memorable historians or philosophers. But mathematics and natural science fared well,[11] as did literary scholarship. Editing became important: the Alexandrians sifted through the variants that had come down through an oral tradition to give the Greek world definitive editions of its major writers.[12] This was an age in which poet-grammarians often taught royal princes in return for courtly patronage. But Hellenistic Alexandria lacked the freedom and conflict alive in the fifth-century city-state.

The effects on literature were telling. Poetry was no longer recited to large groups as a vivid part of national life, and drama declined in importance.

> I hate your hackneyed epic; have no taste
> For roads where crowds hither and thither haste.
> Loathe vagrant loves; and from the public springs
> I drink not; I detest all common things.[13]

Even through the translation, Callimachus' epigram gives one some sense of the mood of his period, a mood that brings to mind Cavafy who, though seldom loathing vagrant loves, hated the ordinary and the overblown. Scholasticism, elegance, often ennui, dominated the short, precious poems of the Alexandrians with extraordinary attention paid to

[11] On the works of the mathematicians Euclid and Apollonios of Perga, the geographer Eratosthenis, the astronomer Aristarchos of Samos, the medical researchers Erasistratos and Eudemos, an astounding amount of our current scientific achievement rests.

[12] See Leslie Dunlap, *Alexandria, the Capital of Memory, Bulletin of Information,* Kansas State Teachers College of Emporia, 43, No. 3 (March 1963), 21.

[13] "Odi profanum vulgus," translated by R. A. Furness, *The Oxford Book of Greek Verse in Translation,* ed. T. F. Higham and C. M. Bowra (Oxford: Clarendon Press, 1950), p. 586. Furness was a friend of both Forster and Cavafy, in Alexandria.

technique—to genre and its associated dialect—to literary and scientific allusions, emphasizing art for its own sake, and the use of old forms in startling, original ways.

The most important Alexandrian genre was the elegiac epigram. Centuries old, it was no longer used only as it had once been in Greece, on tombs or as commemorative song. Its central figures were now often imaginary, and, more importantly, the scope of the epigram was enlarged. It began to talk about how men live.

> Who art thou, shipwrecked stranger? Leontichus found thee here dead on the beach, and buried thee in this tomb, weeping for his own uncertain life; for he also rests not, but travels over the sea like a gull.[14]

The form came to epitomize Alexandrian style. Later it survived the transfer of Greek life to Byzantium and centuries later found a central place in the poetry of C. P. Cavafy.

Along with an attention to forms and subjects from the classical past, Ptolemaic Alexandria developed a reaction against the idealization of the classical period. Portraits were painted. Sculpture became more realistic, its subjects often drawn from the city's poor and even from its deformed. In Callimachus' writings the gods become almost one with men. Theocritos and Herodas—in idylls or "little pictures" —focus their attention on the commonplace. On Gyllis the matchmaker, on Gorgo and Praxinoa, who prattle about traffic and crime in the streets.[15] Theocritos' attention to details of life about him led to the start of a new form, the pastoral, which had not yet taken on the saccharine quality with which it was later to be associated. We recognize the

[14] Callimachus, Book VII, 277, *The Greek Anthology*, W. R. Paton (London: Wm. Heinemann, 1919), II, 153.

[15] Herodas, p. 5; Theocritus, "Idyll XV," *Theocritus*, ed. A.S.F. Gow (Cambridge: Cambridge University Press, 1950), I, 108-121.

scent of late summer, move among tangled blackberry thorns.[16]

Erotic love, central forever after to fictive visions of the city, became an important, and surprisingly new, poetic concern. Generally homosexual, Alexandrian love poetry pleads for the consummation of attractions, sometimes with open, pained emotion. This is anecdotal, realistic, often graphically physical verse. Small, personal, very Alexandrian, it produced a long line of tersely moving poems.

> Just now, as I was passing the place where they make garlands, I saw a boy interweaving flowers with a bunch of berries. Nor did I pass by unwounded, but standing by him I said quietly, "For how much will you sell me your garland?" He grew redder than his roses, and turning down his head said, "Go right away in case my father sees you." I bought some wreaths as a pretence, and when I reached home crowned the gods, beseeching them to grant me him.[17]

Courtly patronage was responsible for much in the tone of Alexandrian verse, but it was also to produce an almost antithetical spirit: the love of gross ceremonies, huge canvases on which sweetmeats, frankincense and myrrh, pigeons, captive Indian princesses, lions and elephants, gold, were all paraded. Ptolemaic spectaculars involved casts of thousands. A tiny part of a contemporary description—by Kalleixinos of Rhodes—conveys some of the flavor of a procession under Ptolemy Philadelphos.

> After these women came a four-wheeled cart twelve feet wide and drawn by sixty men, in which was seated an image of Nysa, twelve feet high . . . [which] could rise up automatically without anyone putting his hand to it, and after pouring a libation of milk from a gold

[16] "Late Summer in the Country," trans. Walter Pater, *The Oxford Book of Greek Verse,* p. 555.

[17] Strato, Book xii, 8, *The Greek Anthology,* iv, 287.

> saucer it would sit down again. . . . Next came a four-wheeled cart . . . drawn by six hundred men; in it was a wine skin holding thirty thousand gallons, stitched together from leopards' pelts; . . . Following the skin came a hundred and twenty crowned Satyrs and Sileni. . . .[18]

The spirit of pageantry—so much a part of Durrell's vision of the city and, perhaps more strangely, of Cavafy's as well—degenerated after the third century, Ptolemaic rulers from Philopator on coming to be known as base and licentious, even by their own people.[19] And a strange people they were, in almost every account labeled cruel, unruly, quarrelsome, sarcastic, turbulent. Passionate and sensuous, "the crowd of revellers who go down from Alexandria by the canal to the public festivals . . . who play the flute and dance without restraint and with extreme licentiousness, both men and women."[20] Strabo's Roman Puritanism colors his portrait of the suburb Canopus and of Egypt's "drunken," "violent" leaders. But one does sense a feverish mood in Alexandria in the second and first centuries B.C., during which Rome grew to become the controlling force in the Greek world.

Roman Rule

Actual Roman power came to Alexandria in the second century, official control in 80 B.C., but the world's metaphor for the loss of passionate Greek-Egypt to austere Roman strength did not emerge until 31 B.C. Alexander with all his victories never quite embodied the spirit of his city. Cleopatra and Antony, in the moment of their dying, did. Images of the pair are a part of our collective imagination, too nu-

[18] Quoted in Athenaeus, *The Deipnosophists*, pp. 400-401.

[19] Ptolemies VI and VII fought for the throne—the latter called Kakergetis (Evil-doer) by the Alexandrians who imposed Ptolemy VIII in their stead. The tenth Ptolemy was massacred by the populace.

[20] Strabo, p. 65.

merous to follow here, and now clearly more important than a factual telling, were that possible.[21] It is enough that for us they seem to have lived in a careless sensuous decadence and to have died, not bravely, but with dignity, in full knowledge of their loss. Cavafy, Forster, and Durrell were all drawn to their story, yet how differently each told the tale.

Under Octavian Alexandria managed to become an important source of the grain supplied to Rome, and thus regained its economic prosperity. A Roman prefect ruled Egypt, but because of Alexandria's strategic and economic importance no Roman of senatorial rank could enter the city without permission. The times were unstable; the Alexandrian mob given to riots. Thus, like their superiors in imperial Rome, the prefects moved in and out of office in swift succession.

Under Roman rule the conflict that Flavius Josephus says existed from the time of Alexander on, the antagonism between Greeks and Jews, erupted over and over again. One should remember that in Alexandria, the greatest city of the Jewish as well as of the Greek world, Jews occupied one of the largest quarters and held equal privileges with the Greeks—with whom they shared language and culture. It is the tension that Jews in the diaspora felt, between loyalty to their faith and the attractions of assimilation, that fasci-

[21] Many have attempted to discover the "real" Cleopatra ("She was like all the Ptolemies proud, cruel, domineering, and unscrupulous, but lacked the vices of the male Ptolemies of drunkenness and lust. Like all the women of the line she had no especial interest in love-intrigue . . ." [Grace M. Macurdy, *Hellenistic Queens* (Chicago: Argonaut, 1967), p. 221]). But the most delicious attempt at judging Cleopatra comes in *Schindler's Guide to Alexandria* ([Cairo: K. Schindler, 1943], p. 36), written for British servicemen: "The last of a glorious succession, she is Egypt's parallel to Henry VIII, for she married her brothers Ptolemy XIV and XV and at the same time became mistress to Julius Caesar! Later, she became mistress to Mark Antony. . . . Realizing her youth was past and that defeat had come, she killed herself with an Asp."

nated Cavafy. Forster, on the other hand, was to write about the genius of Alexandrian unity—the works of Philo, combining Semitic theology with Greek philosophy, and the third-century Septuagint—the translation of the Old Testament into Greek. But, even with assimilation, coexistence was not peaceful.[22]

The violence that seems to have burned through Alexandrian history during this period—finding its way into the mood of Durrell's *Quartet*—produced a cleared ground for the making and unmaking of emperors and queens. In Alexandria's encounter with Caracalla we can most clearly sense the spirit of the time and of the city. In 215 the emperor came to Alexandria and met the satirizing mockery of its populace. The consequences of their caricatures were devastating. After an exchange of pleasantries, Caracalla outwitted the Alexandrians, who thought that he had gathered their young men to make them soldiers. They were surrounded and charged instead.

The Spiritual City

It may seem strange that against this backdrop of violence Alexandria bred some of the world's most subtle and spiritually absorbing religious and philosophical movements. But Roman control had muted civic responsibility and patriotism in the Greek mind and perhaps had shaken a belief in the workings of this world. Hastened by the decreasing importance of the Mouseion, the result was that an interest in nature, in science, and objective knowledge declined, while introspective spiritual involvements grew.

It can hardly be stressed strongly enough: Alexandria was the center of religious development and controversy,

[22] In A.D. 38 under Caligula there was serious rioting in Alexandria, and less than twenty years later 50,000 people were killed in renewed fighting during Nero's reign. Under Trajan, in 116, the Jews revolted and, although massacres occurred on both sides, the large Jewish population in Alexandria was all but annihilated.

both outside and inside the Christian church, during the Roman period. From the first through the fifth centuries, neo-Pythagoreanism, neo-Platonism, Gnosticism, and Christianity established themselves and vied for the minds and souls of Alexandrians. Like the Judaism that had preceded them, most were linked with Greek traditions carried through their classical and Ptolemaic past.

In the first century, neo-Pythagoreanism interjected a religious element into pagan philosophy. Platonic ideas were linked with Pythagorean numbers, the Good with the One; the material world became the realm of evil from which the soul must be freed. Neo-Pythagoreanism paved the way for another, more important, Alexandrian spiritual movement: neo-Platonism, which was to grow during the third century and find its chief spokesmen in Ammonios Sakkas—in whose school one of Cavafy's fictive, and beautiful, youths finds only boredom[23]—and his most famous pupil Plotinus, a figure to whom E. M. Forster was surely drawn. Divorced from the corporeal world by moral and intellectual discipline, but aided by the contemplation of beauty, Plotinus and his followers strove to find their way back to the One, the Good, the eternal primeval supreme being from which all comes. There, for a moment in time, through a mystic vision, the neo-Platonist would arrive, would *be* God.

Alexandrian neo-Platonism was an important force in the world of Greater Greece and Rome, but Christianity, reputedly established in Alexandria by St. Mark, gradually became more and more powerful. By the fifth century, Alexandrian church fanaticism would no longer tolerate the heathen. Defenders of Serapis were killed in their temple. Philosophers were forced to leave Alexandria. Wealthy Jews were attacked. Hypatia, the city's leading neo-Platonist and an eloquent lecturer, was dragged from her chariot, stripped naked, and butchered by a Christian mob that included a large force of Egyptian monks anxious to destroy the Greek

[23] "From the School of the Renowned Philosopher."

elements that dominated Alexandria.[24] Neo-Platonism had lost to a force that assimilated much from that movement, lost in part, as St. Augustine suggests, because it was too speculative to hold the mass of men.

Mystic Gnosticism had waned two centuries earlier. Spiritual ancestors to many of the characters in Durrell's *Quartet,* and now to almost the whole cast in his newest novel *Monsieur,* the Gnostics believed that our world was the unfortunate creation not of God, but of a lower demiurge, and that the unconscious spirit of man, thrown into this alien world, sleeps until awakened by the Savior. Much from this religion of revelation had also been encompassed within Christianity.

Alexandria was indeed a city of assimilation, producing schools like that of the second-century Christian Clement of Alexandria and his pupil Origens. These two Alexandrians saw knowledge as evolutionary—Greek philosophy prepared men for the yet greater truth of Christianity and shared its desire to obtain a noble life. It was not simply an antithetical force. The dividing line between the heathen and the Christian, between the orthodox and the heretical, was less rigidly maintained in their catechetical school than in other parts of the Christian world.

As is easily evident, philosophical assimilation does not necessitate brotherly union. Much has been written about the persecution of Christians by pagan Greeks, the leveling of churches, the enslavement of servants, the destruction of scriptures, before the edict of toleration and Constantine's conversion. We have already spoken of Christians persecuting heathens once the tides of power turned. Conflict with the church hierarchy drove Origens himself from Alexandria. But perhaps of even greater interest to the study of that city and the development of Christianity is the conflict that began in the fourth century in Alexandria and proceeded to divide the whole Christian world against itself.

[24] The subject of Charles Kingsley's novel *Hypatia,* first published in 1853.

Was the Son "of the same substance" as the Father, or was he created by the Father and therefore not equally divine? On this question, and those consequences reverberating from it, the Alexandrians, Athanasios, and Arios—subjects of Forster's study—were passionately and irrevocably divided, as were emperors, patriarchs, priests, and their followers. After a century of conflict the consubstantiality of Father and Son was firmly established as the orthodox Christian position. What Gibbon sees as Arios' "profane and absurd" reasoning, what many have called a move toward polytheism, failed.[25] But not before creating painful divisions between factions in the Alexandrian clergy, between Constantinople and Alexandria, ultimately between East and West.

Still we should remember that fourth-century Christianity and the remarkable Athanasios were responsible for unity within the church as well. For Coptic monasticism, beginning with figures like St. Anthony and Pachomios, had grown. Its numbers were composed of uneducated, poor Egyptians whose natural enemies were the landowning Greek neo-Platonists and, potentially, the leaders of the highly organized Greek Alexandrian church. Athanasios kept the monks united with the church organization and also succeeded in introducing monasticism to the West, in itself an act that altered history. In Anatole France's delicate novel *Thais* one gets a fine portrait of fourth-century Alexandria and of the monks who surrounded that city. They lacked the subtlety of the Alexandrian mind, but not its passion. And in their strange, wild approach to asceticism, these desert-dwellers were akin to the sensuous city from which many of their number had come. It is from these monks that Durrell's Narouz Hosnani descends.

The monks kept their loyalty to the powerful Alexandrian patriarchy, an office which they came to control, and soon

[25] *The History of the Decline and Fall of the Roman Empire* (London: J. M. Dent and Sons, 1925), II, 274. Early in the fourth century the Council of Nicaea condemned Arianism.

the Egyptian church as a whole found itself in conflict with Constantinople. Relations between the two cities were unfriendly from the start. Constantine had ignored Alexandria when establishing a new capital. The Arian controversy hadn't helped matters, and now division came over a new theological subject, or excuse, the Monophysite heresy.[26] The long-term results were a schism permanently dividing the Coptic and Eastern Orthodox churches and a lack of unity when, in the seventh century, the Moslem world conquered the city that had preserved Hellenism and made Constantinople possible.

The Moslem Conquest

Constantinople, of course, became the new Greek city, woven into that fabric of Hellenism which had joined Alexandria to Athens. By the close of the fourth century the Roman Empire had split in two.

> Within the Empire the culture of the Hellenistic world which had arisen in the kingdoms of the successors of Alexander the Great lives on and moulds the achievement of East Rome. For the Byzantines are Christian Alexandrians. In art they still follow Hellenistic models; they inherit the rhetorical tradition, the scholarship, the admiration for the Great Age of classical Greece which characterized the students of the kingdom of the Ptolemies.[27]

[26] The question debated was whether Christ had two natures, as the Council of Chalcedon (in 451) contended, or one nature in which the human was subsumed in the divine. The Alexandrian patriarch Dioskoros was deposed for proclaiming the Monophysite position. Riots broke out when the emperor attempted to place his "Melekite" nominee Proterios in the patriarchy, resulting in the murder of Proterios and, in reaction, the punishment and sacking of Alexandria—all of which simply led to a new round of religious warfare, in which the monks' choice and the emperor's chased one another in and out of the patriarchy.

[27] Norman Baynes, *Byzantium* (Oxford: Clarendon Press, 1953), p. xix.

From the reign of Justinian on, on the very eve of Alexandria's fall, the Eastern Romans abandoned Latin to return to Greek. Through these Byzantines, the Komninoi and Kantakuzinoi who talk of their troubles in Cavafy's poems, Greater Greece lived, always tenuously, for another eight hundred years.

The year 616 saw Egypt fall to the Persians, but in twelve years, due to the brilliant campaigns of Heraklios, it was back in Byzantine hands. The emperor tried to heal the wounds between the Orthodox and the Monophysite, between Constantinople and Alexandria, by creating a new theology.[28] But unfortunately his agent of reconciliation, the very tyrannical Patriarch Kyros, proceeded to persecute all those Monophysites who would not follow him. By the time the Moslems arrived, Alexandria was ripe to fall. Greek culture had long since decayed; loyalty to the Orthodox Church and the Eastern Empire was completely severed. In 641 Kyros handed the city over, without a real struggle, to the Arab general Amr, an extraordinary man, through whose initiative the Arabs moved into Egypt and North Africa. Strategically there seemed no reason for defeat. No reason except that given by Forster: "One is almost driven to say that she fell because she had no soul." (A, 61)

In a guidebook written shortly before Forster's, Alexander R. Khoori tells us that Moslems "destroyed by fire [Alexandria's] famous library":

> "If the books confirm the Koran, destroy them, as their service is rendered superfluous. If they contradict our Holy book, burn them, as their teachings are to our detriment", thus wrote Omar, the Caliph, to his general Amr. The burning of such a large number of books was a wearisome task, which required six months for carrying out. The books sufficed to feed the fires of Alexan-

[28] "Monothelism," in which an attempt was made to reconcile the two positions—Christ still has two natures, but here he has only one will.

dria's 4,000 baths for 183 days. History, Science and Literature would have much benefited if that precious library had not been destroyed.

Khoori is recounting an old—and erroneous—tale.[29] Centuries earlier, with much more venom against the Greek world, Christians had completed the burning. The Moslems were clearly tolerant rulers. Still, they neither understood nor liked Alexandria. Their interest lay elsewhere, inland, in Fustat (Misr)—one of the camp cities that the caliph had built in order to protect his troops from the distressing softening of places like Alexandria—and later on Cairo's solidly Arabic soil.

For more than a thousand years Alexandria languished, a colorless town. Even her geography reflected the change, for in the twelfth century the Canopic mouth of the Nile silted up and Lake Mareotis was no longer navigable. "The greatest emporium in the inhabited world" was cut off from Africa, its cosmopolitan flavor lost; its culture, language, and religion, in general, that of Arabic conquerors.[30]

In 1517 the Ottomans captured Egypt, but for Alexandria the change seemed unimportant. The city continued to decrease in stature and size under Turkish rule. One finds, in the sixteenth-century journal of John Evesham, Gentleman, "The said citie of Alexandria is an old thing decayed or ruinated. . . ."[31] When in 1798 Napoleon's troops rediscovered Alexandria, with a population down to four or five thousand,

[29] *Alexandria: How to See It* (London: Anglo-Egyptian Supply Association, 1926), p. 15. The guide was first published in 1917.

[30] The Coptic population was at first left free to practice its own religion on payment of a tribute of money and clothes, but once the Arabs began to see themselves as colonizers rather than conquerors, taxation and extortion increased, as did conversion. There were various rebellions of Copts, including one in the ninth century which resulted in the massacre and enslavement of many and the further dwindling of Coptic Christianity in Egypt.

[31] Quoted in Leslie Greener, *The Discovery of Egypt* (London: Cassell and Company, 1966), p. 43.

the comments of one of his party were not so far from Evesham's: "In this short journey I saw enough to disabuse me of the idea I had formed of this superb Alexandria: tumbledown houses falling into ruin, irregular walls, streets of bazaars where the air barely circulated."[32] Perhaps the most telling remarks about the long centuries between the seventh and the nineteenth come from a poet, Robin Fedden, stationed in Egypt during the Second World War:

> Not the least curious thing about a country with so much "past", is that the stranger finds no historical continuity. . . . What is missing is the middle distance: where there should be an eighteenth century, there is the Turkish hiatus. Saladin is juxtaposed to cinemas. . . . For the average cultured European with his seventeenth and eighteenth centuries, from which his taste may wander but to which it inevitably returns, a recent historical continuity is the very ground he stands on . . . the innocent exile coming to the "cradle of civilization" is taken aback.[33]

The City That Mohammed Ali Built

The French were in Egypt for three years—most of this time spent warring with England off Alexandria's shores—but following a British victory both sides went home, leaving the task of revitalizing Alexandria to the Turkish Sultan's Viceroy in Egypt, the Albanian Mohammed Ali. Mohammed Ali loved modernization and Napoleonic splendor and, while selfishly mismanaging Egypt, he certainly re-created Alexandria.

> The development of Alexandria during Mohamed Ali's reign was indicative of the growth of trade connections

[32] *Ibid.*, p. 89.

[33] "An Anatomy of Exile," *Personal Landscape, An Anthology of Exile* (London: Editions Poetry London, 1945), pp. 9-10. Saladin ruled Egypt in the twelfth century.

> with Europe. The construction of the Mahmudieh Canal concentrated all the import and export trade, which had previously been shared with Damietta and Rosetta, on Alexandria, now connected by water with the markets of Cairo and the villages of Upper Egypt and the Delta. A large proportion of the increased population consisted of foreigners of all nationalities, but mostly Greeks and Italians, who settled in Alexandria as a result of their connection with the foreign trade of the port. By the end of Mohamed Ali's reign about 6,000 of the permanent residents of Alexandria consisted of foreigners. Their wealth and importance was out of all proportion to their numbers, and before Mohamed Ali died Alexandria was well on the way to becoming a European city, more akin to Marseilles, Genoa, or Barcelona than to Cairo.[34]

Foreign capital and foreign control poured into Egypt and dominated Alexandria particularly. It was during this period that families like Cavafy's entered the city and that foreign travelers—at first on their way to India or the interior of Africa, later to explore the newly fashionable taste for Egyptian relics—visited Alexandria. At the "Hotel d'Europe" English ladies and their beaux could holiday almost in the manner to which they had become accustomed in Paris or Rome.[35] Visitors included the famous, such as Flaubert—"Alexandrie d'ailleurs est presque un pays européen, tant il y a d'européens"[36]—and William Makepeace Thackeray.

> I had been preparing myself overnight, by the help of a cigar and a moonlight contemplation on deck, for sensations on landing in Egypt. I was ready to yield

[34] John Marlowe, *Anglo-Egyptian Relations: 1800-1956* (London: Frank Cass and Company, 1965), p. 56.

[35] See Rashad Rushdi, *English Travellers in Egypt during the Reign of Mohammed Ali* (Cairo: Fouad I University Press, 1952), p. 36.

[36] *Les Lettres d'Egypte de Gustave Flaubert*, ed. Antoine Youssef Naaman (Paris: A. G. Mizet, 1965), p. 119.

myself up with solemnity to the mystic grandeur of the scene of initiation. . . .

The landing quay at Alexandria is like the dockyard quay at Portsmouth: with a few score of brown faces scattered among the population. There are slop-sellers, dealers in marine-stores, bottled-porter shops, seamen lolling about; flies and cabs are plying for hire: and a yelling chorus of donkey-boys, shrieking, "Ride, sir!—donkey, sir!—I say, sir!" in excellent English, dispel all romantic notions. The placid sphinxes brooding o'er the Nile disappeared with that shriek of donkey-boys. You might be as well impressed with Wapping as with your first step on Egyptian soil.

Clearly Thackeray's description tells us as much about the country from which he comes, as about the city in which, in 1844, he finds himself. But an artist has angled his eye on Alexandria, and in his account the nineteenth-century city takes on life.

The character of the houses by which you pass is scarcely Eastern at all. The streets are busy with a motley population of Jews and Armenians, slave-driving-looking Europeans, large-breeched Greeks, and well-shaven buxom merchants, looking as trim and fat as those on the Bourse or on 'Change; only among the natives, the stranger can't fail to remark (as the Caliph did of the Calendars, in the "Arabian Nights") that so many of them have only one eye. It is the horrid ophthalmia which has played such frightful ravages with them. You see children sitting in the doorways, their ravages feeding on them.

We are startled, for Durrell meets the same natives, a century later, unchanged. Thackeray finds the broad street where hotels, shops, and consulates are to be found handsome and reminiscent of Marseilles. But he is not generally impressed.

> The curiosities of Alexandria are few, and easily seen. We went into the bazaars, which have a much more Eastern look than the European quarter, with its Anglo-Gallic-Italian inhabitants, and Babel-like civilization. Here and there a large hotel, clumsy and white-washed, with Oriental trellised windows, and a couple of slouching sentinels at the doors, in the ugliest composite uniform that ever was seen, was pointed out as the residence of some great officer of the Pasha's court. . . .
>
> We went the round of the coffee-houses in the evening, both the polite European places of resort, where you get ices and the French papers, and those in the town, where Greeks, Turks, and general company resort, to sit upon uncomfortable chairs, and drink wretched muddy coffee, and to listen to two or three miserable musicians, who keep up a variation of howling for hours together.[37]

For most English tourists Alexandria was odd, but neither odd enough to be very interesting nor filled with a sense of antiquity easily seen. Of ruins she could boast few, "Pompey's" pillar arousing, as Forster says, "few emotions in the modern breast" (PP, 60), and "Cleopatra's Needles" heading for new lives in other lands.

Nor was the city Mohammed Ali built—with no encompassing plan and sadly little use of its natural surroundings—itself architecturally beautiful. She grew quickly, but haphazardly, and even a champion, a citizen of the city, in a 1914 guidebook full of praise for her tolerant, hospitable peoples, must admit that the city's modern architects hadn't equalled Dinocratis. "Indeed we are almost obliged to confess that the greater number of the public and private buildings are of mediocre taste."[38] The critic and Cavafian

[37] *Notes of a Journey from Cornhill to Cairo*, in *The Works of William Makepeace Thackeray* (London: Smith, Elder, 1869), xiv, 480-485.

[38] E. Breccia, *Alexandrea ad Aegyptum: a Guide to the Ancient and Modern Town, and to its Graeco-Roman Museum* (Bergamo: Istituto

biographer Robert Liddell, in his fine novel *Unreal City*, portrays a fictionalized Alexandria thirty years later: a city with a seafront "on which several cultures had done their worst," whose architecture resembles "bad wallpaper, as it were, overlaid with bands of vulgar jewellery," a city "anciently vulgar, like Pompeii." But Liddell clearly agrees with his own Christo Eugenides, a character who closely resembles Cavafy, "I think that is a comfort. I should be less happy in Birmingham, I daresay, or in Pittsburgh."[39] For this visitor, the city that grew up under Mohammed Ali's influence, though hardly beautiful, seemed to have a strange and pleasant spirit: European—especially Greek and French—and Oriental. Walking the streets of Alexandria, you are struck by the eclectic. You look up to note the mosaic ornamentation on a building, then, moments later, bump into the Italian Renaissance, built as the Banco di Roma. The elegance of a Beardsley drawing shapes a cafe, just off the sea, where, even now, stooped waiters in soiled white jackets speak in four or five languages with ease.

As the home of the foreign community, with its special privileges that included the business advantages of exemption from taxation and the legal advantages of special courts, Alexandria became the fitting site for confrontation between nationalism and outside control. In 1882 it came. Riots, the massacre of foreigners, the British bombardment of the city, more riots and fire. The result was that Great Britain controlled Egypt and, by unilateral declaration, made it a British protectorate from 1914 until 1922, when it nominally became an independent state, although Britain still controlled Egypt's defenses and determined the rights of its foreign community. After much bitter conflict, control weakened and tension produced change. Nineteen thirty-seven saw the adoption of plans for the gradual end of special privilege:

Italiano d'Arti Grafiche, 1922), p. 5. Breccia's guide was first published in French in 1914.

[39] *Unreal City* (London: Jonathan Cape, 1952), pp. 9-10 and 66.

foreigners were to become subject to Egyptian law. But it was not until a military junta ousted King Farouk seventy years after the famous bombardment of Alexandria that Egyptian rather than foreign interest fully controlled the country.

It was of course in Alexandria that the great majority of foreigners in Egypt lived. By 1917, she had a population of 435,000—which nearly equalled that of Cleopatra's city—70,000 of whom were foreign, and of those 30,000 Greek and 20,000 Italian. And in Alexandria during the first half of this century, for the rich among the Greek, English, French, Armenian, Syrian, and Italian populations life held some of the Ptolemaic luxury seen by Herodas. Witness one of their number's description of the thirties:

> Alexandria was the foremost port of Egypt, and a hive of activity for the country's cotton brokers . . . with wide streets flanked by palms and flame trees, large gardens, stylish villas, neat new buildings, and above all, room to breathe. Life was easy. Labour was cheap. Nothing was impossible, especially when it involved one's comfort.[40]

She was a social city. Forster makes fun of fashionable Alexandria's attempts at Parisian smartness: "Eternally well-dressed people driving infinitely in either direction—that is its ideal." (PP, 87) Mirroring the men and women he met in the 1940s, Robert Liddell sketches a whole cast of anciently vulgar, comforting, and humorous Alexandrians. But the interesting thing about Liddell's Alexandrians is that they link social and intellectual pretensions. In *Unreal City* the fashionable vote on the immortality of Proust! It is a chord that the poet and novelist D. J. Enright, who lived in and wrote about Alexandria just after the Second World

[40] Jacqueline Carol, *Cocktails and Camels* (New York: Appleton-Century-Crofts, 1960), p. 16. Mrs. Carol was an Armenian Alexandrian.

War, also hears. In Enright's novel *Academic Year*, fashionable Alexandrians are constantly giving "causeries," "conversaziones," or "conferences," intellectual fashion shows where hats and -isms are on view, where desert is really a "gateau existentialiste."[41]

In a short article on the intelligentsia of Alexandria, Enright notes that in Alexandria "The one great disease is an excess of 'taste': a nervous, enervating concentration on some niggling, precious excellence, carried to a degree unheard of in any of our native Ivory Towers."[42] One remembers ancient poet-grammarians. For their modern counterparts the results were often twofold, encompassing a fear of the innovative (abstract art "smelt of the engine rooms which had no part in their myth of Europe") and a refusal to note poverty and despair, or the mundane, in life around them (to write without once alluding to "beggars, dust, dirt, desert, palm trees, lizards, policemen, diseases of the eye, illiteracy, education, gallabiehs or automobiles").[43] It is this side of Alexandrian life that evoked her death-knell.

'I speak from the port—your friend—do you remember
The tortuously maimed, who bobbed along on buttocks,
  begging at your side?
Outside the marbled bank, the idiot with a giant's
  breasts, suckling a human frog?
Does it still haunt your nights—Authority's bland
  looming wooden face?
The thumb-stained permits and the tear-stained cheeks?
The naked boy, the falling house, the child who hugged
  a dead kid like a teddy bear?
Fat royal thighs in night-clubs, the private royal room?
. . . .

41 *Academic Year* (London: Secker and Warburg, 1955).

42 "The Cultural War: A Note on the Intelligentsia of Alexandria," *World Review*, New Series No. 35 (January 1952), p. 66.

43 D. J. Enright, *Academic Year*, pp. 52-53.

Come back, young friend, grow bored and lose your
conscience here.'

In Enright's poem "Foreign Correspondent"[44] we meet the spirit of an imprisoning city whose whispers are all the more haunting because, like Enright and Liddell, Forster and Durrell lived in a country in which, as Englishmen, they were thought of as part of the foreign community and, more particularly, part of a colonizing group as well. Much of their writing is shaped by this fact, although their attitudes toward the Egyptians who hover on the edges of Alexandrian life vary greatly.

The focus was to shift, for Egypt became Egyptian. The Greek, French, and Italian hospitals of Alexandria were replaced by Egyptian hospitals, as were the schools. Arabic street signs replaced the French—"10 rue Lepsius"—the address on all those envelopes passed between Forster and Cavafy—is no more. In a letter Robert Liddell wrote me, he echoed the sentiments of many who had lived in Alexandria: "I shan't go there again—I loved and hated Alexandria, and there is nothing left to love."[45] Even when we had gotten as far as Cairo and were about to set off on the short train-ride to Alexandria, an Egyptian professor viewed the venture with much scepticism. "Why bother to go there? It's only a provincial Egyptian town now, cleaner than most perhaps."[46]

D. J. Enright, as one of the last witnesses to Alexandria ad Ægyptum addressed a poem about the city's dying "To Cavafy, of Alexandria":

[44] *Laughing Hyena and Other Poems* (London: Routledge and Kegan Paul, 1953), pp. 46-47.

[45] Dated 19 October 1971.

[46] Harry Hopkins has given a different view: "Egyptian voices lift as they pronounce its name Iskanderia is always an exclamation with them. . . . An Egyptian said to me: 'If I have an enemy and I meet him in Alexandria, I cannot be his enemy. In Cairo it is different. . . .' So, despite post-war Egypt's Arabism, the long love affair with Alexandria goes on. . . ." *Egypt the Crucible* (London: Secker and Warburg, 1969), p. 59.

THE CITY

Greece, in this city, has faded since your death:
  though your compatriots still sway
The *salons de thé*, live on pashas' paunches and
  sweet teeth,
Whose pendulous women catch cake crumbs on
  their bosom—
In the city of someone called Iskander.

In the blind Greek's bookshop, your old
  acquaintances still meet,
Out of the heat, in a litter of cellophane, where
Forever Amber giggles in the Arab tongue.
        They mention you often—
'Our T. S. Eliot'—and write unpublished essays
  on you.
They know, they must know, their Cavafy (whom,
  living, it was better not to know)—
In Alexandria, 'where', you said, 'it is difficult
  to impress'.

Society, you complained, was puritan: it made
  the other love so hard,
Your reputation marred. Poor sinner! Far greater
  scandals titillate the city now:
A higher highness, with every new convenience,
  outdoes you
In 'closed and scented rooms' along the guarded
  coast.
And naked feet, unheard of in your verses, pad
Soter's shuttered streets: the blinded, angry Arab
Stabs for a right reason the wrong, the merely
  'foreign' man—
In the land of Alexander, a soldier, called the Great.

Greeks, Romans, French and British—
  we all have helped to lose your city.
Her life is hanging by a cotton thread.[47]

[47] *Laughing Hyena,* p. 28.

By the time we got to see her, twenty years later, Greece in this city had all but faded away. The building in which Cavafy had lived was marked by two signs, one in Greek and Arabic commemorating the poet, the other advertising the Pension Amir. We came away from our visit to his rooms with a clear image of the Arab children who had stared at their strange visitors, and a vague feeling of admiration for Cavafy's protagonist in "The Afternoon Sun" who revisits a room, now part of an office building, and tentatively, with difficulty, succeeds in piecing together its past life, from the sense of space, the slant of light. Alexandria seemed gray, full of peeling paint and broken glass.

But the Hotel Cecil still stood on the waterfront, even if closed while under repair. And several floors up, in a grim, dirty building, we entered the apartment of Mrs. Zelita—wife of the publisher of *Ta Grammata*, in whose pages many of Cavafy's poems were first seen—where sunlight, a jungle of friendly plants, and sketches of Greek intellectuals covering the walls seemed to bring us back to the early years of this century, when, in rooms which she had not left in almost forty years, this handsome gentle woman entertained ὁ καϊμένος Καβάφης, the poor soul, Cavafy, and even his friend Mr. Forster.

The life of the back streets has paled too. But a few men still meet to play backgammon and smoke water pipes in the coffee houses. And in an almost empty taverna, Greek men even now dance to the bouzouki. We came upon a narrow, crowded shop poorly lit and in disarray but full of old books, where a nervous Greek sold me a first edition of Cavafy's poems. His frail father sat on a chair in the rear and, when he had heard our purpose, began to recite "Waiting for the Barbarians" slowly, without missing a line, in the 1970s, among those yellowed books in Alexandria.

· 2 ·

CAVAFY'S CAPITAL OF MEMORY

IN the *Alexandria Quartet* Lawrence Durrell writes about "the city's exemplars—Cavafy, Alexander, Cleopatra and the rest," (B, 156) placing the Greek Alexandrian in exalted company, where he belongs. For Constantine P. Cavafy comes to represent a moment in the city's life, while, at the same time, his poems bring Alexandria's past into the present. It is a perfect match. Cavafy gave the city a new mythology, and Alexandria gave the poet a history and a setting in which he could ground his poems and hear his voice.

Echoing sentiments Durrell has also expressed about wartime Alexandria, Robert Liddell writes of his stay in the city, "Cavafy seemed the *genius loci*."[1]

> Many people in Alexandria have known him, more have known friends of his. They have drawn caricatures of him for his posthumous admirers on the backs of envelopes, they have tried to imitate for us that unique and extraordinary voice; they have told us stories about him, and a little scandal.[2]

He adds a personal note that seems in any case true for many who worked in and wrote about the city: "It is no affectation to say that only the great past of Alexandria made it tolerable to live there—and only Cavafy connected the great past with the contemporary world."[3]

[1] Robert Liddell, *Cavafy: a Critical Biography* (London: Duckworth, 1974), p. 210.

[2] Liddell, "Studies in Genius: VII—Cavafy," *Horizon* 18, No. 105 (1948), 187.

[3] Liddell, *Cavafy*, p. 210.

In order to understand the importance of Alexandria and her history in Cavafy's work one must have a sense of Cavafy's own history. He was born in 1863, the last child of Peter and Hariclia Cavafy, both of whom came from well-established families in Constantinople. The Cavafys had seven surviving children, all sons. Cavafy's father and uncle ran an exporting firm that sent Egyptian cotton to England and had offices in Liverpool, Manchester, London, Constantinople, and Cairo. In the prosperous Greek community of Alexandria, theirs was one of the leading families, and among its earliest settlers. But family fortunes changed when, in 1870, Cavafy's father died, leaving a relatively small estate that was further depleted by mismanagement. As a result, Cavafy, who had known wealth only as a small child, was to spend much of his life combatting real, though genteel, poverty.

Two years after her husband's death, Hariclia and her children settled in England, where Cavafy spent seven of his formative years: from the age of nine to sixteen. This Alexandrian poet, who is reputed to have spoken Greek with a slight English accent, who had had an English nanny in Egypt, whose conversations with his brothers were often in English, who wrote his first verse in that language, was certainly very basically influenced by his years in London and Liverpool.

Writings in English—diaries, letters to friends like Pericles Anastasiadis, prose essays like "Give Back the Elgin Marbles," and reading notes, like those Cavafy made about Hardy's *Jude the Obscure*—attest to his comfort with the English language,[4] and although we can believe his English superior at the government Ministry of Irrigation, where

[4] See M. Perides, *'Ανέκδοτα πεζά κείμενα* (Athens: Phexis, 1963); G. Papoutsakis, *Πεζά* (Athens: Phexis, 1963); P. M. Fraser, "Cavafy and the Elgin Marbles," *Modern Language Review*, 58 (1963), 66-68. I am grateful to those in charge of the Cavafy papers at the Benaki Museum in Athens for allowing me to see and photograph original copies of notes and letters in English.

he worked for thirty years, could on occasion find fault with a phrase or idiom—"A tall man, Mr Cavafy, not a long man"—it is equally easy to imagine Cavafy and his brothers making fun of English officers and their inelegant speech, or to hear echoes of those fine convoluted Cavafian sentences about which Forster speaks. Even his sketchy library clearly indicates that Cavafy was well-grounded in English literature.[5] In the early poem "King Claudius" we see Cavafy bouncing off Shakespeare as he was often to bounce off Plutarch or Gibbon. In this tale told by an ordinary citizen praising a gentle king needlessly killed by his crazy nephew, we are far from Alexandria, but we nevertheless begin to hear the peculiar voice. Cavafy's work shows an affinity with that of several nineteenth-century English writers, particularly Browning, although, as Arnold Toynbee reminded Forster—who had just introduced him to Cavafy's poetry—"He is adept at the dramatic monologue, without Browning's over-emphasis and elaboration."[6]

Many have noted the influence of the Romantics and also of the French Symbolists and the Decadent movement in England and France on Cavafy's writing. All the early poems are derivative. Those like "Artificial Flowers" show Cavafy drawn to the search for exotic sensation, for an art separated from nature and the workaday world. This sympathy nurtured important strains in his work, but it was dangerous too, for it might have trapped Cavafy in the mainstream, where he would most likely have remained an imitative poet.[7]

[5] Liddell, pp. 127 and 37. For a partial review of the contents of Cavafy's library see pp. 121-122.

[6] Unpublished letter, dated 12 June 1924, among the Forster papers at King's College, Cambridge.

[7] Edmund Keeley's unpublished doctoral dissertation—"Constantine Cavafy and George Seferis: A Study of Their Poetry and Its Relation to the Modern English Tradition," Oxford University, 1952—deals with English writers who may have influenced Cavafy, particularly with Shakespeare, Wilde, and Browning. Keeley's *Cavafy's Alexandria* (1976) includes a review of rejected traditions.

But for Alexandria. In 1879 Cavafy and his family returned to the city, where they were to feel the history of Egypt and their personal destinies collide, for three years later, with the bombardment of Alexandria, antagonisms between the Egyptian and the foreign communities came to a head. For Cavafy the immediate result was another leave-taking—with the European exodus that immediately preceded the bombardment—and three important years in Constantinople, where it is likely that he had his first homosexual relationship and wrote his first poetry.

The long-range results have been debated, for it can be argued that the bombardment of Alexandria marked the beginning of the end of the Greek community's foothold in Egypt and that the community's deterioration, during Cavafy's lifetime, influenced his poetry—paralleling the decline in the importance of the Cavafy family, and the period when Cavafy became aware of the barriers homosexuality created between himself and parts of his world. We should note the reverse side of this coin: that the Greek population increased steadily during the poet's lifetime and, more importantly, that many Greek family fortunes were made after the British occupation.[8]

Still one hears Cavafy as he talks to Forster in 1918. He is comparing the Greeks and the English, noting their glaring similarities. " 'But there is one unfortunate difference between us, one little difference. We Greeks have lost our capital—and the results are what you see. Pray, my dear Forster,

[8] The former position is held by the Cavafian critic Stratis Tsirkas, author of Ὁ Καβάφης καὶ ἡ ἐποχή του [Cavafy and his Epoch] (Athens: Kedros, 1958) and Ὁ πολιτικὸς Καβάφης [the Political Cavafy] (Athens: Kedros, 1971), the latter by Robert Liddell, in his *Cavafy*, who reviews Tsirkas' arguments in detail but with scorn, outrage or anger. Tsirkas, a novelist whose trilogy *Drifting Cities*—trans. Kay Cicellis (New York: Knopf, 1974)—takes the reader on another fictional journey through Alexandria, suggests that Cavafy's early poems reflect the poet's concern for the Greek-Alexandrian issues of his day, but that this concern died out after 1911, with Cavafy's disillusionment over British domination in Egypt.

oh pray, that you never lose your capital.'" (TC, 248) The economic position of Hellenes all over the twentieth-century world was surely in marked contrast to their past, and one must finally agree that Cavafy's Greek sense of resignation, which, as Peter Bien suggests, is so close to contemporary *ennui*, was shaped by that fact, as it was by his own family's decline.[9]

Cavafy seemed, for a period, obsessed with past family glory, writing *My Genealogy* with less than the ironic eye he would later turn to others. ("'Aristocracy in modern Greece? . . . To be an aristocrat there is to have made a corner in coffee in the Peiraeus in 1849,'" he told Forster.) Luckily Cavafy could link the personal and the communal —which is why we cannot draw a line between the historical and the love poems—and the concern for family history broadened to a concern for Alexandrian history, in a sense an extension of that genealogy: the study of a glorious and dying race.

This obsession proved the poet's salvation, for it provided Cavafy with a coherent mythology, a stage upon which he could set his cast of characters, his petty princes, haberdashers' assistants, hawkers, and clerks. This was not the shopworn classical kingdom, nor was it a private world. Many have compared Cavafy with the early Eliot, and with Yeats as well. As Edmund Keeley reminds us, Cavafy began to build his mythical city earlier than, and without benefit of, the mythical kingdoms that grew up during the first half of this century in the works of these writers, as well as others —Joyce, Pound, Faulkner, and Proust. C. M. Bowra has made a particularly important point here:

> What Yeats found for a time in old Irish legends, what Eliot found for *The Waste Land* in figures and events from anthropology, Cavafy found much less laboriously in the Hellenistic past. His system has advantages which

[9] Peter Bien, *Constantine Cavafy* (New York: Columbia University Press, 1964), p. 33.

neither Yeats's nor Eliot's has . . . it is really a homogeneous body of material, with its own life and its own plan, and . . . it is sufficiently familiar to most educated people and has already some meaning for them.[10]

The success of Cavafy's mythical world is certainly built upon our sense of Hellenistic history, but it is built upon something else as well, which can perhaps be best illustrated by looking at Cavafy's "Tomb of Lanis":

The Lanis you loved, Markos, isn't here
in this tomb you come to weep by, lingering hours
  on end.
The Lanis you loved you've still got close to you
in your room at home when you look at his portrait—
the portrait that still keeps something of what was
  valuable in him,
something of what you used to love.

Remember, Markos, that time you brought in
the famous Kyrenian painted from the Proconsul's
  palace?
What artistic subtlety he used trying to persuade
  you both,
the minute he saw your friend,
that he absolutely must do him as Hyacinth—
in that way his portrait would come to be better
  known.

But your Lanis didn't hire out his beauty like that;
reacting strongly, he told him to paint
neither Hyacinth nor anyone else,
but Lanis, son of Rametichos, an Alexandrian.[11]

[10] *The Creative Experiment* (London: Macmillan, 1949), p. 33. Also see George Seferis "Cavafy and Eliot—A Comparison," *On Greek Style,* trans. Rex Warner and Th. Frangopoulos (Boston: Little Brown, 1966).

[11] I have, as noted earlier, in the main used Edmund Keeley and Philip Sherrard's translations in the *Collected Poems* (Princeton:

We believe in History. We believe in names like Lanis, son of Rametichos, an Alexandrian, even when they are the products of a poet's imagination. Cavafy tells us he will substitute the mythical Hyacinth with the "real" Lanis and in doing so builds his own mythology, carrying us with him. The one long poem that is his work gives us a sense of being encompassed within accurate fact. When we read the account his Ptolemaic man-in-the-street gives us of the Battle of Actium, our collective memories are jolted, and in remembering Antony and Cleopatra's defeat we ourselves engage in the act that is, for Cavafy, the genesis of poetry. But even when we have only the fuzziest image of John Kantakuzinos or Alexander Jannaios, even when we meet a purely fictive Lanis, we feel grounded in a sense of history, and, believing we touch that elusive god, the real, accept Cavafy's vision, willingly entering his kingdom.

It is a kingdom that must be looked at as a whole, for Cavafy's historical ancestors, who actually bore no relation to the nineteenth-century Greeks who settled in Alexandria, were spiritually linked to contemporary Alexandrians in his poems, just as his ancient Alexandrians were one with the Hellenes who peopled Antioch, Beirut and even—especially—the farthest points in the diaspora. It was as if he would extend the citizens of his city through space and time, and through them, through this host of minor officials, allow a provisional clerk in the Third Circle of the Ministry of Irrigation to dream, linking the past to the view from his balcony.

The Historical Poems

Cavafy's historical poems span twenty centuries of Greek life—from the classical period to the fall of Byzantium. But

---

Princeton University Press, 1975). The reader can assume the translation is theirs unless another translator is named. See Appendix A for a review of Cavafy and his English translators.

they also cluster around certain moments in time; in order to know him well one must have a sense of those events he chose to focus upon and, just as surely, those he would ignore.

It should seem obvious that the classical perfection of fifth-century Greece did not interest him.[12] More surprising perhaps is the fact that the high points in early Hellenistic history receive little attention in Cavafy's poems. The poet of Greater Greece, of pan-Hellenism, meets Alexander only once, and in a poem focusing upon the Lacedaimonians who refused to join Alexander's pan-Hellenic campaign. A Greek meditates upon their independent but foolish choice and, with grandiose flourish concludes:

> We the Alexandrians, the Antiochians,
> the Selefkians, and the countless
> other Greeks of Egypt and Syria,
> and those in Media, and Persia,
>   and all the rest:
> with our far-flung supremacy,
> our flexible policy of judicious integration,
> and our Common Greek Language
> which we carried as far as Bactria,
>   as far as the Indians.
>
> How can one talk about Lacedaimonians now!

In spite of the focus and the tone, a sense of inspired achievement, even elation, seems to sweep through the poem. Then we remember its title and realize that this Greek speaks "In the Year 200 B.C." just as Alexander's world begins to fall to Rome.

The splendor of third-century Egypt, also all but ignored, does find itself praised in "The Glory of the Ptolemies."[13]

[12] Except when standing on the edge of defeat, as in the poem "Thermopylae," or when seen through the eyes of an unsuccessful traitor in "Dimaratos." For a period, before he had focused on Alexandria, Cavafy wrote several poems about pre-classical Greece.

[13] The other third-century ruler Cavafy concerns himself with is

Here Lagides, Ptolemy I Sotir, while speaking of his own power, recognizes a greater force: Alexandria "The greatest preceptor, queen of the Greek world, / genius of all knowledge, of every art." By doing so he shows his own wisdom and shares the exultation of a love the author never undercuts with irony.

But Cavafy has little empathy for the grandeur and size Ptolemy and his immediate heirs embodied. He leaves them, although he never leaves their poets. For even a cursory glance at the Greek Anthology makes evident Cavafy's link to the poetic tradition rooted in the third century Mouseion with its use of the dramatic monologue and elegiac epigram. One has only to remember the exotic love poem examined earlier—Strato's narrator and his seller of garlands, making furtive gestures of love, afraid of onlooking eyes—to be reminded of Cavafy's late poem "He Asked about the Quality."

> They kept on talking about the merchandise—
> but the only purpose: that their hands might touch
> over the handkerchiefs, that their faces, their lips,
> might move close together as though by chance—
> a moment's meeting of limb against limb.
>
> Quickly, secretly, so the shopowner sitting at the back
> wouldn't realize what was going on.

There are other poems that can be specifically compared,[14] but it is of course a general similarity in tone, scope, and

---

Alexander's stepbrother Dimitrios, a particularly appealing character to Cavafy, who gives him the ability to lose fittingly and to live as gods and artists should: as if life were a creative act. See "King Dimitrios."

[14] Note, for instance, Callimachus' poem about conformity (see chapter one) and Cavafy's "And I Leaned and Lay on Their Beds" as well as "Artificial Flowers," or the use of men as gods and gods as men in Boethius' poem about Dionysus (Book IX, 248 in *The Greek Anthology,* trans. W. R. Paton [London: Wm. Heinemann, 1919] III, 131) and in Cavafy's "One of Their Gods."

subject matter that makes the comparison important. As many have noted, except for its lack of concern with nature, Cavafy's verse is remarkably like those educated small personal, often homosexual, poems of his predecessors. Callimachus' pained pleasure matches Cavafy's.

> If I came to thee in revel, Archinus, willingly, load me with ten thousand reproaches; but if I am here against my will, consider the vehemence of the cause. Strong wine and love compelled me one of them pulled me and the other would not let me be sober-minded. But when I came I did not cry who I was or whose, but kissed the door-post: if that be a sin, I sinned.[15]

For all his reliance on the great Hellenistic tradition, Cavafy wrote few poems honoring his literary forebears. Still "The First Step" is truly a celebration of union, for in it a fictional Theocritos admonishes a young poet, a third-century Cavafy, who is discouraged by his small output, saying that they are both part of a sacred brotherhood, a special city, "And it is a hard, unusual thing / to be enrolled as a citizen of that city." Poets celebrate beauty:

> To have reached this point is no small achievement:
> what you've done already is a wonderful thing.
> Even this first step
> is a long way above the ordinary world.

But successes, even those of his own people, even of the Alexandrians, hardly excite Cavafy; they are victories of the actual rather than the imaginative. Thus Cavafy's energy and curiosity are drawn to the centuries that follow the third, the years when Greater Greece fell to Roman power and its own family wrangling. Cavafy is concerned with Roman victors only when, in the fever of triumph, they refuse to recognize personal disaster lying around the corner.[16] His focus is upon the sophisticated, decadent souls

[15] Book XII, 118, *The Greek Anthology*, IV, 341.

[16] Cavafy's "Roman" poems—about Caesar, Pompey, and Nero—

who inhabited the crumbling Macedonian, Selefkid, and Ptolemaic kingdoms. And because he gives a touch of triumph to their loss, because he sees the most unprincipled men as having unfulfilled—never-to-be-fulfilled—dreams of being true to their Greek past, Cavafy writes patriotic verse.

Like the Achaian in "Those Who Fought for the Achaian League," Cavafy occasionally praises the valiant, fearless troops who resisted the likes of Mummius and fell in noble defeat. "When Greeks are in a mood to boast, they'll say, / 'It's men like those our nation breeds.' " But the edge of irony—a soft, human irony—is always near; the protagonist writes his epigram from the sad but safe distance separating Alexandria from Corinth. The edge is sharper in another poem about Rome's rape of that city. In it Kimos, a wealthy young Greek-Italian, "devotes his life to amusing himself," but "On an Italian Shore" he watches men unload the spoils from Greece and, momentarily depressed, determines to forego a day's pleasure. That is all. Cavafy portrays Kimos' act as pitiful and inconsequential, but he does not leave it open to scorn for, in a small, human, contemplative way, Kimos has affirmed man's sympathy with the best in himself—even when it is hardly recognizable.

The actual moment of loss, both personal and political, becomes the focus of Cavafy's imaginative creations. And so, for this subtle and delicate poet, wars, and the battles that mark them, oddly enough, take on extreme importance. Sometimes, as in "Craftsman of Wine Bowls," they provide the occasion for a love poem—the artist-lover's personal celebration of beauty, fixed forever by the death of a young soldier at the Battle of Magnesia in 100 B.C.

> . . . O memory, I begged
> for you to help me most in making
> the young face I loved appear the way it was.

---

are all about unheeded signs of catastrophe. See "Footsteps," "Nero's Term," "The Ides of March," and "Theodotos."

This proved very difficult because
some fifteen years have gone by since the day
he died as a soldier in the defeat of Magnesia.

More often they give Cavafy a dramatic moment through which his protagonists can view their own lives and that of their race, in full knowledge, with illusion no longer possible.

Cavafy's bias is clear. He does not choose to portray the second and first centuries in terms of the disruption and warfare that set Macedonians, Ptolemies, and Selefkians against one another. The possession of Coele-Syria (Palestine) was not his concern.

The historian Edwyn Bevan, whose *House of Seleucus* numbered among the works in Cavafy's library, stresses Rome's waning influence during the centuries that preceded the reign of Caesars, declaring that, from the middle of the second century on: "The eastern powers are once more left for the most part to their own devices. The family quarrels of the houses of Seleucus and Ptolemy are fought out with no interference from Rome. . . ." Bevan later goes on to say: "If there is one characteristic of this final period of decline in the kingdoms of the Near East which were formed out of the breakup of Alexander's Empire it is the universal domestic quarrels."[17] Smaller pan-Hellenic states seem often to have preferred the distant, loosening control of Rome to the reign of their powerful Greek neighbors.

But Cavafy's eye rests at a different angle. He wishes to look at these years in light of the corrosion of Hellenism and its fall at the hands of an alien enemy. The Ptolemaic brothers quarrel and, in Cavafy's poem, appeal to Delphi, but their "Envoys from Alexandria" suddenly leave the magical spot, for "the 'oracle' was pronounced in Rome; the dispute was settled there."

Cavafy does not ignore conflicts between leaders of Alex-

[17] Edwyn Bevan, *The House of Seleucus* (New York: Barnes and Noble, 1966), II, 197 and 204.

ander's empire—but his focus in these conflicts is on a failure of heart, an inability to live up to the call of brotherhood that Hellenism implies. Cavafy is not moralizing. He recognizes and notes the failure, and judges it human. Man's action will not improve, but, like his protagonists, the poet has the wistful fleeting hope that life could be otherwise.

Thus in "The Battle of Magnesia" Philip V of Macedonia broods on Antiochos III's devastating defeat. The two are now enemies: Antiochos hesitated and failed to support Philip seven years earlier when at Cynoscephalae the Macedonians were crushed by Rome, and Philip as a consequence sided with Rome during the Selefkians' march to control Greece. But for a moment, hardly a moment, Cavafy has a tired, defeated Philip sit amid dice and roses, the pleasures allowed a puppet king, and think about the news he has just heard.

> . . . What if Antiochos
> was defeated at Magnesia? They say
> the bulk of his brilliant army was totally crushed.
> Maybe they're stretching it a bit; it can't all be true.
> Let's hope so anyway. Because though enemies,
> they do belong to our race.

The note of brotherhood is tenuous, but it has been struck, and it hangs in the air, nowhere more strongly perhaps than in the Macedonian's response. "Of course Philip won't put off the festivities":

> He recalls how much they mourned in Syria,
> the kind of sorrow they felt,
> when Macedonia, their motherland, was smashed
> to pieces.
> Let the banquet begin. Slaves! The music, the lights!

Memory, Philip's one remaining blessing, by returning him to images of the Selefkid failure of heart, has momentarily restored the vigor of this world-weary man, a vigor born of an intensity that seems to link hate with love.

Cavafy carries the story one generation further and gives us a protagonist on the other side. Again we see the failure, and the wistful wish, but here we feel that it is made even more poignant for Cavafy, because the call to brotherhood —the appeal for union with the Macedonians in their final battle with Rome—is evoked by a young man, one of those rare beauties whom the ancient world honored with what the poet felt were perfection's rightful rewards. Most of Cavafy's beautiful youths are apolitical, concerned with a little learning perhaps, or art. But in "To Antiochos Epiphanis" we meet a young Antiochian who has the power to command riches, but will give them up in loyalty to the Hellenic world.

> The young Antiochian said to the king:
> "My heart pulses with a precious hope.
> The Macedonians, Antiochos Epiphanis,
> the Macedonians are back in the great fight.
> Let them only win, and I'll give anyone
> who wants them
> the lion and horses, the coral Pan,
> the elegant palace, the gardens of Tyre,
> and everything else you've given me,
> Antiochos Epiphanis."

Even if the speaker hardly believes he will be called upon to make these sacrifices, the appeal is somewhat grand, standing in sharp and sad contrast to what follows, to the caution and fears of man and the indifference of fate.

> The king may have been moved a little,
> but then he remembered his father, his brother,
> and said nothing: an eavesdropper
> might repeat something they'd said.—
> In any case, as was to be expected,
> the terrible defeat came swiftly, at Pydna.

Cavafy wrote two poems about Antiochos' nephew and successor. The first, "The Displeasure of Selefkidis," is another fine sketch portraying a triangle, one of whose sides is Rome. Here the two Greek powers are the Selefkians and the Ptolemies, and the question is not of union but of style. The Selefkid Dimitrios Sotir—educated in Rome and therefore acquainted with many of the most sophisticated contemporary Greeks—is quite disturbed when seeing his cousin Ptolemy Philomitor enter Rome dressed as a pauper:

> Selefkidis of course knows
> that basically even now they've become
> something like servants
> to the Romans; . . .
>
> . . . .
>
> But they should maintain a certain dignity
> at least in their appearance;
> they shouldn't forget that they are still kings,
> are still (alas) called kings.

As we shall see later, Cavafy is as obsessed with the reality of appearances as Dimitrios, but so is Ptolemy VI who rejects his cousin's robes, "in order to make his begging more effective." History proved Philomitor the wiser man; the Romans judged him powerless and let him rule.

Dimitrios—the subject of one of Cavafy's many wonderful character sketches, poems that climb from a man's soul—is seen more fully in "Of Dimitrios Sotir (162-150 B.C.)"

> Everything he'd hoped for turned out wrong.

The stark, isolated line opens the poem, setting the tone for our vision of the youthful Dimitrios. Quickly Cavafy introduces us to the complexity of the man, his desire to overturn the defeat at Magnesia, his wounded pride at the subtle, patronizing of Roman youth, and his dreams.

> Only to be in Syria!
> He was so young when he left his country
> he hardly remembered what it looked like.
> But in his mind he'd always thought of it
> as something sacred that you approach reverently,

as a beautiful place unveiled, a vision
of Greek cities and Greek ports.

Suddenly Cavafy compresses the time dimension and takes us back to the opening line. He has shaped history, ignoring Dimitrios's daring, youthful escape from Rome and his reign in Syria—these moments of triumph hardly excite him, except as they reflect upon Dimitrios's final disillusionment.

And now?
Now despair and sorrow.
They were right, the young men in Rome.
The dynasties resulting from the
Macedonian Conquest
can't be kept going any longer.

Cavafy's Dimitrios has been defeated by a failure of brotherhood, in this case among the people of his own kingdom. But in spite of this, a disillusioned, morose figure still maintains one aspect of his youthful self, and is thus a fitting Cavafian hero.

And in his bleak disillusion
there's only one thing in which he still takes pride:
that even in failure
he shows the world his same indomitable courage.

The rest: they were dreams and wasted energy.
This Syria—it almost seems it isn't his country—
this Syria is the land of Valas and Herakleidis.

Like the defeated Spartans who had preceded him, like Philip, even like Kimos, Dimitrios still holds on to a vestige of the privileges and responsibilities of Hellenism, in his pride, in the face he shows the world.

Cavafy wrote many poems in which fictive ancient artists themselves shape history or myth. Usually their art is visual or tactile, their subjects the objects of homosexual love. But in "Dareios" Cavafy creates the poet Phernazis, a somewhat comical figure, yet very like Cavafy himself. The setting is Cappadocia in 88 B.C. With dreams of fame and fortune, Phernazis gets down to work on his epic, to the deep thought required in order to analyze the feelings with which the legendary Dareios entered battle: "Arrogance, maybe, and intoxication? No—more likely / a certain insight into the vanities of greatness." Then the news of real war intervenes, leaving Phernazis, ironically, with little insight into his own vanities. He is dumbfounded, almost overwhelmed by the way life has invaded art. What are his chances of destroying his critics now? Will the king bother about his poetry? "In the middle of war—just think, Greek poems!" He grows frightened; after all, the Romans are terrible enemies. Can the Cappadocians compete? "Great gods, protectors of Asia, help us."

> But through all his nervousness, all the turmoil,
> the poetic idea comes and goes insistently:
> arrogance and intoxication—that's the
> most likely, of course:
> arrogance and intoxication are what Dareios
> must have felt.

Cavafy has slowed the tempo and, with these last lines, exonerated a silly, pompous man. Now Dareios is less noble than before, but we feel that Phernazis has got him right after all and, more importantly, shown himself to be a poet at last, consumed, finally, neither by the war that threatens nor by the more insidious politics of poetry and patronage but by the poetic act.[18] Here is the passion that held Cavafy

[18] D. N. Maronitis, in "Arrogance and Intoxication: The Poet and History in Cavafy," *Eighteen Texts: Writings by Contemporary Greek Authors,* ed. Willis Barnstone (Cambridge, Mass.: Harvard University Press, 1972), pp. 117-134, suggests that it is precisely the confrontation with history that changes Phernazis' vision, permitting him to get things right at last.

as well. Histories, inscriptions, and coins led him to imagine, to capture exactly, what each of his Dareioses, his Dimitrioses, and Phernazises "must have felt."

He studies the face of Orophernis, Dimitrios's Cappadocian protégé, on a four-drachma coin and around it builds a myth. The face is too lovely, too delicate to allow the historian's tale—Orophernis as the worst of leaders, a violent extortionist who, after taking refuge in Dimitrios's court, attempts a plot against that king when he finds Dimitrios weakest. Cavafy's Orophernis is a different youth:

> . . . one day unfamiliar thoughts
> broke in on his completely idle life:
> he remembered how through his mother Antiochis
> and that old grandmother Stratoniki
> he too was connected with the Syrian crown,
> he too almost a Selefkid.
> For a while he gave up lechery and drink,
> and ineptly, half dazed,
> tried to start an intrigue,
> do something, come up with a plan;
> but he failed pitifully and that was that.

A taste of nobility in the midst of the ridiculous, a taste of inept heroism, Hellenism. Just as Cavafy was most interested in an age in which the Greek ideals were themselves distorted and dying, he was particularly fascinated by those Asian princes and peoples who stood farthest from the central Hellenic powers, by those like Orophernis, or those who lived "In a Town of Osroini," Cappadocia, Libya, or Kommagini and still felt a touch of kinship with a Greek past, perhaps because they were most clearly kin to the twentieth-century Alexandrians, living in a city on the periphery of all her cultures.

> We're a mixture here: Syrians, migrated
> Greeks, Armenians, Medes.
> Remon is one of these too. But last night,

when the moon shone on his sensual face,
our thoughts went back to Plato's Charmidis.

Cavafy was one of those souls (perhaps Forster was too) born exactly where they should have been, but we should not forget that he was born in a city of exiles. He came from Egypt not Europe, and like his fictive ancient traveler in "Returning from Greece" had to come to terms with that fact.

Well, we're nearly there, Hermippos.
Day after tomorrow, it seems—that's what
  the captain said.
At least we're sailing our seas,
the waters of our own countries—Cyprus,
  Syria, Egypt—
waters we know and love.
Why so silent? Ask your heart:
didn't you too feel happier
the further we got from Greece?
What's the point of fooling ourselves?
That wouldn't be properly Greek, would it?

It's time we admitted the truth:
we're Greeks also—what else are we?—
but with Asiatic tastes and feelings,
tastes and feelings
sometimes alien to Hellenism.

We simply can't be ashamed
of the Syrian and Egyptian blood in our veins;
we should really honor it, delight in it.

Cavafy makes fun of the philosophers and petty princes who are un-Hellenic because they try to hide their dual natures—the "Philhellene" or the "Prince from Western Libya"—who adhere to the outer markings of a culture they don't understand. Still in sketching even "a piddling, laughable man" like Aristomenis, who speaks few Greek words in order to avoid barbarisms, Cavafy climbs inside his skin, knowing that "he was driven almost out of his mind, having / so much talk bottled up inside him." " 'Exactly what I feel in England,' " a Greek friend told Forster. (TC, 247) Language is probably the primary source of access to any culture, but nowhere was this more true, nowhere was it more clearly the sole mark of entrance, than in the Hellenic diaspora, and Cavafy has compassion for those ancient Poseidonians—Greek in origin but assimilated into Latin Sicily —"living and speaking like barbarians, / cut off so disastrously from the Greek way of life." But his highest praise goes to those like Antiochos of Kommangini, who rest on the circumference of Magna Graecia, where one could most easily go the way of Poseidonians, who yet preserve their Hellenism:

"He was a provident ruler of the country.
He was just, wise, courageous.
In addition he was that best of all things, Hellenic—
mankind has no quality more precious:
everything beyond that belongs to the gods."

Macedonia, Selefkia, the satellite states that came under Roman control—Cavafy's imagination seldom went where others had been. And yet his final metaphor for the triumphant defeat of Greek values in a Roman world was one that Shakespeare, Spenser, and innumerable others had used before him: the events of 31 B.C.

He was haunted by the Battle of Actium—in which Octavius won control of Egypt—writing six poems about it over a period of almost twenty years. The reasons are in part obvious; battles at Corinth, Magnesia, Cynoscephalae, and Pydna came earlier and did not involve his beloved city and the Ptolemies who ruled her. And Antony is, after all, an intriguing figure.

Still the choice is puzzling. For Antony is a Roman, from a people upon whom Cavafy hardly looks with warmth, and the love affair that captured the world's attention is of no interest to Cavafy, who all but ignores Cleopatra. It is not that as a homosexual he avoids poems about women. His poems include many startling women, but they are all mothers, like Anna Dalassini ("Those cold words 'mine' and 'yours' were never spoken"), most of whom mourn the loss of their beautiful sons, or, like another Anna—that "arrogant Greek woman" Anna Komnina—figures consumed by a desire for power their sex only thwarts. In Cleopatra heterosexual passion and power were one; she is not a figure Cavafy would enjoy, and, as a result, he writes around her, picturing her lover, sons, and subjects, entering the thoughts of each. Innumerable writers have dealt with Actium, but scarcely in this way.

Cavafy's first poem in the 31 B.C. cycle, written in 1907, is "Antony's Ending," a poem Cavafy did not include in his collected work. Edmund Keeley and George Savidis write:

> There is no other poem in the Cavafy corpus that treats a Roman subject with this degree of sympathy. Here, instead of diminishing Antony, as in "Alexandrian Kings," or admonishing him to rise up with courage so as to be worthy of the Greek city he has known so well, as in "The God Abandons Antony" (1911), we find Cavafy portraying Antony almost as though he were a Greek . . . ready to face defeat with the knowledge of who he is, and with full pride in this knowledge.[19]

Part of what they say is certainly true. There is honor in defeat here: "he hadn't fallen humbly, / but as a Roman vanquished by a Roman." In "Antony's Ending" Cavafy's

[19] "Introduction," C. P. Cavafy, *Passions and Ancient Days,* trans. Edmund Keeley and George Savidis (New York: The Dial Press, 1971), p. xviii. Elsewhere, in the notes to the *Collected Poems,* Savidis tells us that this poem is based on Act IV Scene v of Shakespeare's *Antony and Cleopatra.*

protagonist feels that "all he'd worshipped blindly till then — / his wild Alexandrian life / now seemed dull and alien." By disdaining "madam with her oriental gestures," by abandoning the city, he regains his dignity.

But my thoughts return to Phernazis. Antony must have felt. . . . Between 1907 and 1911 Cavafy changed his mind. While finding his own voice, he again came to Antony, heard him anew—a larger figure, no longer deserting oriental Hellenism in disgust, no longer deserting his city, but now a true Greek, with the courage to watch Alexandria abandon him, and the knowledge that nothing that beautiful would ever appear again. *This* Antony could move Cavafy to write "The God Abandons Antony," one of his finest poems, a poem which was so to impress both Forster and Durrell that it became a refrain in both their works.

The next poem in the Antony cycle, "Alexandrian Kings," focuses on Cavafy's belief in the joy, the truth of imaginative fictions, particularly those that stand beside a thorough awareness of life's greys and browns. He chose for the poem a persona that was to become a haunting one for him: the mob of onlookers who participate almost vicariously in an event. Like world-weary Syrian princes, Cavafy's crowds vaguely wish for a better world, always avoiding the risk necessary to obtain it. But although Cavafy's poems about individual Asian Greeks stress the moment of indecision—the temporary communion with a lost Hellenic spirit—poems centering on communities usually focus on the defeat and complacency inaction breeds.

Thus we have men rationalizing "In a Large Greek Colony, 200 B.C."—"Let's not be too hasty: haste is a dangerous thing. / Untimely measures bring repentance"—while others assemble in the public squares "Waiting for the Barbarians." Although the second group is at least redeemed by awareness ("Now what's going to happen to us without barbarians? / Those people were a kind of solution"), it is the Greek, Egyptian, and Hebrew crowd in "Alexandrian Kings" that receives Cavafy's strongest approval precisely because, three years after Actium, it celebrates the coronation of Cleopatra's pretty sons as a gorgeous spectacle.

> The Alexandrians knew of course
> that this was all just words, all theatre.
>
> But the day was warm and poetic,
> the sky a pale blue,
> the Alexandrian Gymnasium
> a complete artistic triumph,
> the courtiers wonderfully sumptuous,
> Kaisarion all grace and beauty
> (Cleopatra's son, blood of the Lagids):
> and the Alexandrians thronged to the festival
> full of enthusiasm, and shouted acclamations
> in Greek, and Egyptian, and some in Hebrew,
> charmed by the lovely spectacle—
> though they knew of course what all this
>   was worth,
> what empty words they really were,
>   these kingships.

We are reminded of a later work, "Of Colored Glass," in which Cavafy celebrates the impoverished Byzantines John Kantakuzinos and his wife Irini because, having no precious stones with which to decorate their crowns, they fittingly used bits of colored glass.

The last two poems in the cycle also deal with the psychology of crowds. "In a Township of Asia Minor," Greeks adjust complacently to the unexpected outcome of Actium: Octavius is substituted for Antony; there is no need to write a new address. Except for their persistent pride in the Greek language, these Greeks are indifferent to the change. The other poem "In Alexandria, 31 B.C." confronts the problem of perspective and its relationship to time, so interesting to Cavafy the poet and Cavafy the historian. Centuries later we view Actium with an awareness of its outcome and importance, but what of the common people, the traders in olive oil, gum, and incense who live through the event? Jostled about and befuddled, might they not believe "the huge palace lie: / that Antony is winning in Greece"?

This sense of seeing history from an odd angle is precisely where Forster and others, like W. H. Auden, are most indebted to Cavafy.[20] But it is also precisely where the poet engages all his readers. For Cavafy requires that we bring our communal past to the poem, our remembrances. Forced to look from a new point of view, we do what we must do when an event or object reinfects memory—we chip away, combining elements of the old and new; we ourselves create, ourselves take part in the imaginative act that is the poem.

In "Kaisarion" (1918) the angle of vision, the voice is Cavafy's own. Like "Alexandrian Kings," this work portrays Cleopatra's son. In the earlier poem he is a boy splendidly dressed in rose-colored silk, wearing jewels and flowers. His youthful masculine beauty is enough to make artists out of onlookers, to make Alexandrians participate in an imaginative event. In "Kaisarion" as in "Orophernis" Cavafy lets an image from the past shape a personality. But here the subject of the poem actually is the process, the link between history and memory. The poem begins rather prosaically: the poet is whiling away some time, doing a bit of casual research, only peripherally engaged by the benevolent Ptolemies and their marvelous Berenices. Then suddenly a name catches his eye—and with it an image.

[20] This sense of the exclusion of ordinary men from great events is also found in "But Wise Men Perceive Approaching Things." Both of Cavafy's poems bring to mind W. H. Auden's "Musée des Beaux Arts." In his "Introduction," *The Complete Poems of Cavafy,* trans. Rae Dalven (New York: Harcourt, Brace and World, 1961), p. vii, Auden tells us: ". . . C. P. Cavafy has remained an influence on my own writing; that is to say, I can think of poems which, if Cavafy were unknown to me, I should have written quite differently or perhaps not written at all." Among those poems should be numbered "Atlantis," indebted to "Ithaca," an observation for which I am indebted to the poet Alan Ansen, who was at one time Auden's secretary.

There you stood with your indefinable charm.
Because so little
is known about you from history,
I could fashion you more freely in my mind.

Art creates a face, a dreamy beauty. But the process does not stop there. Once blown into life, the subject takes on a reality of its own, compelling the artist to discover what it thinks and feels. The poet must blow out his lamp and meet Kaisarion in the dark.

Cavafy wrote another "cycle" of poems, was obsessed by one other historical figure, one other moment in time. The character is Julian, the date 362—when the emperor visited Antioch and found himself in conflict with its citizens' religious views and an object of their satire. Again the choice seems strange. Some have pictured Julian as a sensitive Hellenic spirit and savior—the last leader to believe in the pagan gods. There are notes among E. M. Forster's papers, almost certainly attributable to George Valassopoulo, Cavafy's friend and translator, and even he speaks of Julian as one of the "two solitary instances of perfection in man," a man who could have saved the world from Hun, Goth, and innumerable others including Hitler.[21] The list clearly outdates Cavafy as well as Julian, whose passionate adherent tries, with much wishful thinking, to maintain that the poet was neutral about the emperor. It seems clear to this reader that Cavafy can't stand the fellow or his Hellenism. Instead he sides with Antioch's Christians, even though his own ties with Christianity were not demonstrably strong.

Why then did he write these poems and so many others about religion? Certainly the history of Magna Graecia dur-

[21] Among Forster's papers at King's College, Cambridge, are sheets commenting on Cavafy's poetry, on the back of which Forster has written "Valassopoulo?" The handwriting clearly matches that elsewhere attributable to Valassopoulo.

ing the early centuries of this epoch was religious history. But what in it evoked the passionate concern that produced such fine poems? It is worth pausing to look at religion in Cavafy's poetry, for the nature of his concern is not obvious. Cavafy did not, like Hopkins or Eliot, address God or faith, and he was certainly not interested in men like Arios and Athanasios.

He did celebrate the Greek Orthodox Church in a poem that honors without irony—quite unlike Lawrence Durrell's "Greek Church: Alexandria," where incense and majesty become at times "a fearful pomp for peasants" (CP, 84-85) —but one feels Cavafy's poem honors the pageantry, the sense of high drama, that he felt characteristic of his people, whether in a stadium in Alexandria, 34 B.C. or in Agia Sophia.

> I love the church: its labara,
> its silver vessels and candleholders,
> the lights, the ikon, the pulpit.
>
> When I go there, into a church of the Greeks,
> with its aroma of incense,
> its liturgical chanting and harmony,
> the majestic presence of the priests,
> dazzling in their ornate vestments,
> the solemn rhythm of their gestures—
> my thoughts turn to the great glories of our race,
> to the splendor of our Byzantine heritage.

The praise is for continuity with the past, no mean praise, but not in any sense theological. We are reminded of Robert Liddell's *Unreal City*, for in that novel the cultured and shabby Greek homosexual Eugenides, who writes articles that "brilliantly illuminate a little piece of the past," introduces his young English friend to Greek church music, confessing that it fills him with a nostalgia for the greatness of the Byzantine empire.

> Yes, thought Charles, in this strange outpost of Hellenism there were two authentic pieces of the Greek heritage—the church which they had just left, and the little old man beside him.[22]

"In Church" and its adherence to ritual does provide a part of the answer. But a more important vision of why Cavafy was engaged by religion can be gained from examining his erotic poetry. Much like Callimachus, Cavafy could write, in "To Sensual Pleasure":

> My life's joy and incense: recollection of those hours
> when I found and captured pleasure as I wanted it.
> My life's joy and incense: that I refused
> all indulgence in routine love affairs.

At the same time the protagonist in the 1915 poem "He Swears" does not seem far from Cavafy's vision of his youthful self:

> He swears every now and then to begin
> a better life.
> But when night comes with its own counsel,
> its own compromises and prospects—
> when night comes with its own power
> of a body that needs and demands,
> he returns, lost, to the same fatal pleasure.

It is likely that ambivalent feelings about those sensual pleasures that society condemned helped to shape his poetry, particularly the earlier poems about religion—for they focus upon one central battle: a battle between the sensualist and the ascetic.

Passion and austerity constantly war. Cavafy's fictive third-century student believes that he can yield his body to Alexandrian sensuality while "when I wish, at critical moments I'll recover / my ascetic spirit as it was before." The

[22] *Unreal City*, pp. 74 and 176.

poem's title—"Dangerous Thoughts"—belies his faith and links him with Cavafy's beautiful young Hebrew Ianthis who, in "Of the Jews (A.D. 50)," willing deserts "the elegant and severe cult of Hellenism" for the holiness of religion "'. . . to remain forever / a son of Jews, the holy Jews.'"

> But he didn't remain anything of the kind.
> The Hedonism and Art of Alexandria
> kept him as their dedicated son.

Often these conflicting impulses are seen at the death or funeral of a young homosexual, an image that brings the elegiac epigrams of the Greek Anthology to mind, an image that constantly recurs in Cavafy's verse, appearing as the central simile in "Longings" and again, with wonderful delicacy, in "Lovely White Flowers," as well as in many historical poems.[23]

The erotic quest can be quite literally killing, as it is for the morally exhausted Kleitos or for the beautiful Iasis:[24]

> But from being considered so often a Narcissus
> and Hermes,
> excess wore me out, killed me. Traveler,
> if you're an Alexandrian, you won't blame me.
> You know the pace of our life—its fever, its
> absolute devotion to pleasure.

Cavafy takes pride in the risk that living the sensuous passionate life brings, but he also understands and sympathizes with the ascetic, who is of course also living at risk and passionately, and out of the range of the routine. The battle takes place because, in the poet's vision, the two warring principles are almost equally matched, are major forces.

[23] See "The Battle of Magnesia," "In the Month of Athyr," "Tomb of Evrion," "Aimilianos Monai, Alexandrian, A.D. 628-655," and "For Ammonis, who died at 29 in 610" in addition to the poems mentioned below. Also note the very early poem "Our Dearest White Youth" in which the abstractions youth, purity, and death merge.

[24] "Kleitos' Illness" and "Tomb of Iasis."

As we shall see, it is here that Cavafy's sensibility comes close to that of Lawrence Durrell, with which it is in many other ways antithetical. For Durrell sexuality is, more than humorously, "root-knowledge." He too believes that one must, as Cavafy suggests in "Growing in Spirit," "mostly violate / both law and custom, and go beyond / the established, inadequate norm." Whereas both would take the path of the sensualist, each sees a connection between the need to push beyond limits of the normal in the realm of the physical and that need in the realm of the spiritual. "Where sense verges into spirit," Forster wrote of the arts that Cleopatra taught Antony, although temperamentally he was himself less anxious to explore extremes. The impulse to visit the depths of the erotic and the spiritual led Durrell to become fascinated by Gnostics like Carpocrates ("unsavory charlatans," says Forster), who were "prepared to founder in the senses as deeply and truly as any desert father in the mind," (J, 87) who made of sexuality itself a religion. It also caused him to become interested in the monks who had, for centuries, dwelt outside Alexandria.

A similar impulse drew Cavafy, like his pagan protagonist, to honor Simeon Stylites:

> Please don't smile; for thirty-five years—think of it—
> winter and summer, night and day, for thirty-five years
> he's been living, suffering, on top of a pillar.

In a marginal note Cavafy wrote eighteen years before he wrote "Simeon," and inserted in his copy of Gibbon—a note that brings to mind the poem "As Much As You Can" with its plea not to cheapen life "by too much activity and talk" —Cavafy discusses Simeon, while criticizing Tennyson's interpretation of the man:

> This great, this wonderful saint is surely an object to be singled out in ecclesiastical history for admiration and study. He has been, perhaps, the only man who has dared to be really *alone*. . . . It was a very difficult task

—a task reserved, perhaps, for some mighty king of art
—to find fitting language for so great a saint, so wonderful a man.[25]

Anatole France, a contemporary whom Cavafy greatly admired, could love his Thais as prostitute and as madonna. For Cavafy the fascination with purity, with ascesticism, was almost equally strong, and, although his objects of interest were beautiful young men, he could write as sympathetically about the commitment to asceticism one youth followed, as about another's devotion to pleasure. Thus the "Tomb of Ignatios" mirrors the "Tomb of Iasis":

> Here I'm not the Kleon famous in Alexandria
> (where they're not easily dazzled)
> for my marvelous houses and gardens,
> my horses and chariots,
> the jewels and silks I wore.
> Far from it—here I'm not that Kleon:
> his twenty-eight years are to be wiped out.
> I'm Ignatios, lector, who came to his senses
> very late;
> but even so, in that way I lived ten months
> in the peace, the security of Christ.

In the glimpse of fourth-century life Cavafy gives us, asceticism is usually associated with Christianity—except in the Julian cycle. There it is the emperor, intent on returning his world from Christianity to its pagan past, who withdraws from the artistic and sensuous joy of pleasure-seeking Antioch. In his own writings the often witty and clearly intelligent emperor declares himself part of a great past: "I myself, though my family is Thracian, am Greek in my habits."[26] His Hellenic tradition—derived from Plato and

[25] Quoted in Keeley and Savidis, pp. 67-68, and in Peridis, pp. 70-74.

[26] *Misopôgôn, The Works of the Emperor Julian,* trans. Wilmer Cave Wright (London: Wm. Heinemann, 1954), II, 501.

Aristotle, abhorring acting, dancing, feasts, warm beds, and homosexual love; honoring "dignity," "sobriety," and a "manliness" obtained through the denial of desire and happiness —sees the ascetic as Puritan judge, not solitary singer. Here we have solid, sensible austerity. Clearly not Cavafy's heritage! But perhaps that is the point. Cavafy hated Julian so fervently because the emperor had the audacity to deny the necessary connection between Cavafy's own night-life and that Hellenic past the poet used to give it a form and justification he seems to have needed. Many others had honored all the wrong things, but Cavafy saw Julian as evil, for he called them Greek.

Rage fires the Julian cycle, poems giving Cavafy yet another focus around which he can examine multiple points of view, reality not in the event but in the eye. One aspect of the compelling power religion held for Cavafy rests in the knowledge that, even more than death, it could divide men, isolate them in their vision, making loved ones strangers. His pagan lover attends the funeral of Myris but, gradually aware of the widening gulf between them, leaves "quickly before it was snatched away and altered / By their Christianity—the memory of Myris."[27] Taught to despise pagans, a young Christian still cannot deal with his father's death:

> I grieve, O Christ, for my father
> even though he was—terrible as it is to say it—
> priest at that cursed Serapeion.[28]

Cavafy doesn't care which god one chooses. In fact, many of his poems take on their special brilliance because he allows for truth in all, conflicting visions. He pictures a young

[27] "Myris: Alexandria, A.D. 340," translated by Robert Liddell. See "Studies in Genius," p. 201, and *Cavafy*, p. 201.

[28] "Priest at the Serapeion." Cavafy of course also deals with those for whom choice is irrelevant, an alternative to boredom. Christianity is of passing interest to the young man in "From the School of the Renowned Philosopher," resembling the political choices open to Cavafy's persona in "To Have Taken the Trouble."

man ill, his aged servant praying to a pagan god whom she had almost forgotten during years of service to Christians. We know that her kind but pitiful efforts will not succeed, and feel a patronizing sympathy for her and her false idol. But Cavafy startles us, destroying our complacency. Suddenly we are one with the poor soul, the poor fool who "doesn't realize that the black demon couldn't care less / whether a Christian gets well or not."

Like Queequeg's, the black idol has grown real. He is as arrogant and believable as are the gods in Cavafy's earliest poem about Julian. Written in 1896, more than twenty years before Cavafy returned to his subject, "Julian at the Mysteries" is in some ways his most complicated examination of point of view. Here we see a young Julian, reverting to habit and crossing himself in fright when figures of Greek gods appear before him at the famous pagan initiation at Eleusis. The gods vanish. When Julian's reaction is to believe they did so because of the power of the cross, the Greeks laugh in scorn, suggesting that the gods left in disgust. A Christian, mocking both Julian and the Greeks, tells us the story. Cavafy greets the situation with an irony he conveys by making all the opposing possibilities momentarily real (he is in this way unlike Gibbon—his source—whose declared scepticism makes all alternatives suspect from the start). Cavafy's poem gives us a series of shifting voices: now Julian's, now the Greeks', now the gods', and finally the Christian's. Cavafy probably intended to approach all the Julian poems in like manner, showing the irony inherent in the separate truths of opposing visions, in Christians and in black demons. But the character of Julian got in the way, unbalancing objectivity, creating different, angry, but equally successful poems.

In each of the six Julian poems that followed, between 1923 and 1933, Cavafy chose to stay close to one voice. But the cycle, like the poems about Antony, becomes a series of reverberating echoes. In "Julian Seeing Contempt" the mocking voice is Greek ("Nothing in excess, Augustus"). In

"Julian in Nicomedeia" Cavafy comes closest to letting the emperor speak for himself, but the weight of the piece is on Julian's hypocrisy. The central character in an unrelated poem "If Actually Dead" is a sixth-century figure, "one of the few pagans, / one of the very few still left," who must also face the world as a Christian. But Cavafy seems to excuse his pretense, because this pagan lives in a period in which the church has become inflexible and frightening, and because he is "a trivial and cowardly man" from whom life cannot expect courage. Cavafy never condemns the urge to survive. Julian, on the other hand, is primarily a political pragmatist ("the rumor must be killed at all cost") who greets the need for deception with smug flourish:

> . . . with deep reverence he reads out loud
> passages from the Holy Scripture,
> and everyone marvels at his Christian piety.

Cavafy gave his readers two more poems about Julian. Ignoring the side of the emperor seen in the *Misopôgôn*—the man who is fully aware of the criticism leveled at him and chooses to satirize it—in "Julian and the Antiochians" Cavafy allows us to see his character through the eyes of elegant, sophisticated lovers and artists, advocates of "the notorious life of Antioch, / delectable, in absolute good taste" for whom Julian is a boring, graceless prude. The other work, "A Great Procession of Priests and Laymen," like the poems that follow, focuses on a Christian point of view. The procession celebrating Julian's death is engulfed in an aura of magical beauty, perhaps because it is led by "a handsome white-clad boy" carrying the cross. "You Didn't Understand" and Cavafy's last poem "On the Outskirts of Antioch" are angrier pieces. As with much in Cavafy, their special strength is the immediacy they give to history. The conflict becomes real: the gloating (when Apollo's statue burns without a word from that god, "Ashes the idol: to be thrown out with the garbage"); the sarcasm; the colloquial speech; the hatred. Finally the hatred.

> Julian blew up, and he spread it around—
> what else could he do?—that we, the Christians,
> had set the fire. Let him say so.
> The essential thing is: he blew up.

Cavafy wrote three poems set in the year 400. Pagans had long since lost their last hope with Julian's sudden death, and Magna Graecia itself stood on the edge of disaster. Although these, like all of Cavafy's poems about the period between the fifth and ninth centuries, deal essentially with art and sexuality, the dates they wear in their titles remind us that the values the poet and his ancient world honored, the respect given to the imaginative word and the inventive act, were frail and now lived on the edge of disaster, just as they were to live even more tenuously in modern Alexandria.

In "Temethos, Antiochian, A.D. 400" Cavafy gives us a lovesick poet who, in his poem within a poem, has disguised his lover, making him an historical personage.

> . . . We the initiated—
> his intimate friends—we the initiated
> know about whom those lines were written.

The unsuspecting Antiochians read simply "Emonidis." Cavafy does just what Temethos has done. The "Young Men of Sidon (A.D. 400)," the young men of that ancient city-state, are also the youths of contemporary Alexandria. The son of a notable family who composes daring homosexual verse that he circulates furtively in "Theatre of Sidon A.D. 400" is of course also Cavafy.

> Son of an honorable citizen—most important of all,
> a good-looking
> young man of the theatre, amiable in many ways,
> I sometimes write highly audacious verses in Greek
> and these I circulate—surreptitiously, of course.

O gods, may the gray ones who prattle about morals
never see those verses: all about a special kind of
  sexual pleasure,
the kind that leads toward a condemned, a
  barren love.

What is perhaps more interesting is that Cavafy can breathe life into an abstract, potentially deadening poem about the power of the "Art of Poetry," "Language," and "Imagination" by giving it the outrageous title: "Melancholy of Jason Kleander, Poet in Kommagini, A.D. 595." Suddenly generalizations are shaped by a human soul. Thus Cavafy finds a ninth-century framework within which he can talk about extremes, expressing an idea shared by many contemporaries raised in the Decadent and Symbolist movements of the 1890's—the belief that "a sensual pleasure achieved morbidly, corruptingly—" has "an erotic intensity health cannot know. . . ." He speaks not for himself but for "young Imenos (from a patrician family) / notorious in Syracuse for his debauchery / in the debauched times of Michael the Third."[29]

Cavafy wrote nothing about the actual fall of Alexandria to the Arabs, nothing, that is, except a poem set, two centuries later, in the 870's.

It goes on being Alexandria still. Just walk a bit
along the straight road that ends at the Hippodrome
and you'll see palaces and monuments that will
  amaze you.
Whatever war-damage it's suffered,
however much smaller it's become,
it's still a wonderful city.

The restrained optimism of these opening lines makes the poem all the more painful, because we soon see that they are spoken by "Exiles" desperately attempting to endure, to gather together some false hopes and some shreds of Hel-

[29] "Imenos."

lenism when banished from Constantinople to Alexandria, where few Greeks remain. We are reminded of that old man in the bookstore and of Mrs. Zelita and Mr. Koutsoumis, who, one thousand one hundred years later, wait in a faded city.[30]

When he came to write of "the lords and ladies of Byzantium," Cavafy proved no more interested in the likes of Justinian and Theodora than he had been in Alexander or Ptolemy Sotir. His eye wandered from the high points of that civilization to the eleventh century where for a brief moment the Komninoi made a dying Hellenism shine. Even here he is not interested in Alexios, the king who set things right for a very short while, but focuses on those around him, two gentle souls—his mother Anna Dalassini and his wise and successful grandson Manuel Komninos—and one fiery one: Anna Komnina, always frustrated in her all-consuming desire "to gain the throne, / virtually snatched out of her hands by impudent John." Cavafy allows us to see power as a personal, psychological force. Like Anna, the fourteenth-century persona in "John Kantakuzinos Triumphs," having chosen a losing team, is consumed by its gnawing, cancerous need. But the times are bad; now even triumphant Greeks wear crowns "Of Colored Glass."

Central to every Greek's conception of history is the year 1453, the year that means dignity and defeat. Ancient history ends abruptly; the thread is finally broken. Cavafy writes about the fall of Constantinople with the patriotism common to all Hellenes, but in focusing on a kinsman of the last Byzantine emperor, he gives another poem, "Theophilos Palaiologos," its peculiar angle of vision and allows

[30] Dinos Koutsoumis publishes a newspaper for the four or five thousand Greeks remaining in Alexandria today.

himself an expression of patriotism that might otherwise have seemed excessive but here rings true.

> This is the last year, this the last
> of the Greek emperors. And, alas,
> how sadly those around him talk.
> Kyr Theophilos Palaiologos
> in his grief, in his despair, says:
> "I would rather die than live."
>
> Ah, Kyr Theophilos Palaiologos,
> how much of the pathos, the yearning
>   of our race,
> how much weariness—
> such exhaustion from injustice and
>   persecution—
> your six tragic words contained.

The Love Poems

Cavafy ignores the centuries between 1453 and his own, just as he all but ignores Egyptians in Egypt. And when he deals with his own period it is mostly to talk about love. But it would be foolish, impossible, to divide the ancient historical verse neatly from the modern erotic poems, for, as we have already seen, history often provides a mythic mask enabling Cavafy to talk about the beauty of the god-like male form or his feelings about sensuality. The historical poems are often love poems.

And the love poems are often history. Robert Liddell gives us a sense of this when he says of Cavafy:

> His poems are set in his own past (real or imagined) which is itself a period of Greek history like any other. Some of them (not necessarily autobiographical) bear such titles as: "In his twenty-fifth year," or "Days of 1896," or of 1901, 1908, 1909, 1910 and 1911. For all their passionate intensity, few are in the present tense.

> Moreover, he is almost pedantically accurate in telling us how much their heroes earn at their work, at cards, or trictrac, or prostitution. No doubt he could have told us what they gave for their pink or mauve shirts—he knew (though he only revealed it in private conversation) how much a yard would have been paid in 31 B.C. for the rose-silk chiton of Caesarion.
>
> And the mood is like that of ancient poetry.[31]

Sometimes when Cavafy's lamp is lit at nine o'clock it evokes images of Kaisarion; at other times it brings back the unrecognizable streets, theatres, and cafés of the poet's youth or the faces of those from whom death or circumstances have separated him.

> Half past twelve: how the time has gone by.
> Half past twelve: how the years have gone by.[32]

A watercolor "In an Old Book" inspires a poem, just as the face of Orophernis on a tetradrachm had. A book, a sketch, a memento from the past causes Cavafy to ask himself the question Hart Crane does in "My Grandmother's Love Letters":

> "Are your fingers long enough to play
> Old keys that are but echoes:
> Is the silence strong enough
> To carry back the music to its source
> And back to you again
> As though to her?"[33]

Bringing the past, alive and safe, into the present is Cavafy's task: difficult and delicate work, and sometimes more

[31] Liddell, "Studies in Genius," p. 197.

[32] "Since Nine O'Clock."

[33] *The Complete Poems and Selected Letters and Prose of Hart Crane*, ed. Brom Weber (Garden City, New York: Doubleday, 1966), p. 6.

difficult when the past is near, when the din of daily events keeps us from hearing the music and the silence.

Or so it seems with Cavafy. His poems grounded in ancient Alexandria never miss their mark. A few of those set in his own past do, either because, like "Comes to Rest," they seem a bit self-indulgent, or because they lose the sense of the actual—the ragged, precious moments upon which we dream—that shapes the best of Cavafy's erotic poetry. A few poems, like "I've Looked So Much . . ." are almost ruined by "The body's lines. Red lips. Sensual limbs. / Hair as though stolen from Greek statues"; most of the love poems are not.

Still, there is one way in which these poems differ dramatically from those set in an historical context. For the latter Cavafy could count on our collective memory, the history we share, however indistinctly, our sense of history. He could count on snatches of memory reappearing, combining with the particular new perception of an event he would give us and himself: process became a part of the poem; the past, in again becoming ours, came alive. The history Cavafy used for his love poems was not collective, and, if shared at all, shared only by a few. Cavafy had to discover ways of grounding these poems for his readers. He did so by making them one with the historical poems, and he did so by creating a persona: that of an old man remembering—Edmund Keeley's point is important here: the poet used an old voice before he was himself old.[34] The voice makes the process of remembering part of the poetry, a process that we are again, in a new sense, called upon to share.

In the historical poems, while immortalizing "the feelings of my own people, / of the dead so little recognized"—to borrow from "Since Nine O'Clock" a poem set in contemporary Alexandria—Cavafy ironically makes his historical

[34] *Cavafy's Alexandria.* Keeley also helps us to see how Cavafy worked to make sure that his readers moved from the historical to the love poems, and back again.

personages seem fragile, tangible human beings, not the immortal dead. Frailty, loss, the sense of the temporary, are always essential to his vision of life.

In the contemporary poems he captures this same sense by making the process of snatching moments from the past part of his poems. Thus he gives us "Long Ago":

I'd like to speak of this memory,
but it's so faded now—as though nothing's left—
because it was so long ago, in my adolescent years.

A skin as though of jasmine . . .
that August evening—was it August?—
I can still just recall the eyes: blue,
  I think they were . . .
Ah yes, blue: a sapphire blue.

The triumph in this poem comes in its final line precisely because the memory has finally been captured. Elsewhere the poet recreates a room as it had been:

The couch was here, near the door,
a Turkish carpet in front of it.
Close by, the shelf with two yellow vases.
On the right—no, opposite—a wardrobe
  with a mirror.[35]

It is not that Cavafy has an imperfect memory, nor that he would hide what memory reveals, but that through his hesitant conversational tone he makes us remember remembering, relive that act.

Here too the clues, the details that lure us into the past, seem fragile and tangible, real precisely because they are themselves neither momentous nor symbols of a greater reality—not "my green, my fluent mundo"[36] but a soiled

[35] "The Afternoon Sun."

[36] From Wallace Stevens' "Notes toward a Supreme Fiction," *The Collected Poems* (New York: Knopf, 1961), p. 407.

bandage, a cinnamon-colored suit. This is what Lawrence Durrell calls "Cavafian actuality," a quality that is to find its way into the *Quartet*, shaping some of its best moments. "Indeed all the grandeur of Cavafy lies in this patient, loving, miserly way of looking at objects and events—reinfecting memory time and time again with the passionate actuality of something that has disturbed him. . . ."[37] Even in some of the earliest verse, like "My Friends, When I Was in Love," which Durrell has translated, where much is conventional in form and metaphor, where the beloved is safely female, we hear Cavafy's passionate actuality in images of a cheap cretonne dress or mountain flowers.

Cavafy's love poems build a twentieth-century mythological kingdom that has much in common with the crumbling world of ancient days. Here lovers meet "On the Stairs" of wretched brothels, "At the Theatre," "At the Café Door," in front of "The Window of the Tobacco Shop," across counters in ugly little stores, or, again and again, "In the Tavernas." They inhabit the seedy reaches of their city, sleeping on shaky beds between dirty sheets. We as readers get a sense of moving "In the Same Space."

> The setting of houses, cafes, the neighborhood
> that I've seen and walked through years on end:
>
> I created you while I was happy, while I was sad,
> with so many incidents, so many details.
>
> And, for me, the whole of you has been transformed
> into feeling.

Cavafy's lovers work in dull offices, or for tailors, ironmongers, or small shopkeepers. Like Ptolemy Philomiter, they are often forced to beg. Like Antiochos Epiphanis' beloved, they give their perfect bodies for the rewards of this world. The mood is the same, but Greater Greece is so

[37] "A Cavafy Find," *London Magazine* 3, No. 7 (1956), 11-14. Durrell translates three of Cavafy's earliest poems: "My Friends, When I Was in Love," "Flowers of May," and "Douya Gouzeli."

much smaller than it once was. A coral Pan, the gardens of Tyre: beauty was once rewarded openly, by leaders of state, with gifts the poet felt befit its majesty. Now, in secret, young men win cognacs and coffee, an expensive tie, a blue shirt.

Love is temporary, fleeting, gone with "The Afternoon Sun":

> . . . One afternoon at four o'clock we separated
> for a week only . . . And then—
> that week became forever.

The beloved is always off to places "far away—New York or Canada."[38]

> We were lovers for a month.
> Then he went away to work, I think in Smyrna,
> and we never met again.
>
> Those gray eyes will have lost their charm—
>   if he's still alive;
> that lovely face will have spoiled.[39]

Loss follows love, no matter how much the lover would wish it otherwise. Still there is a type of salvation.

> At least let me now deceive myself with illusions
> so as not to feel my empty life.
>
> And yet I came so close so many times.
> And yet how paralyzed I was, how cowardly;
> why did I keep my lips sealed
> while my empty life wept inside me,
> my desires wore robes of mourning?
>
> To have been so close so many times
> to those sensual eyes, those lips,
> to that body I dreamed of, loved—
> so close so many times.

[38] "Before Time Altered Them."

[39] "Gray."

Salvation does not come as the speaker would have it in "September, 1903." The poem is in fact a denial of illusions —made more obvious to us because of its opening line—an honest appraisal of failure, and in its honesty a celebration of emotions that actually did exist, and still exist in memory: a pride in the face of loss that is comparable to Cavafy's Hellenism.

The erotic poems are characterized by muted but distinct affirmation, one of the reasons perhaps for their particular appeal in times when the momentary physical encounters Cavafy describes seem closer and closer to heterosexual as well as homosexual love. Though the image of the Cavafian figure as an old man with his young sailor or actor or mechanic appears in fictional caricatures of the poet, and, it would seem, in life, we should not forget: in the poetry the old persona meets his double. He remembers *himself* as young and beautiful, as twenty-five or twenty-nine. Cavafy's lovers are young—although remembered by that old voice—and often deeply and mutually in love. More often than not they are equals, educated, sensitive youths who live on the edge of scandal, like the "Two Young Men, 23 to 24 Years Old" who share sixty pounds won at cards:

> Now all joy and vitality, feeling and charm,
> they went—not to the homes of their
> respectable families
> (where they were no longer wanted anyway)—
> they went to a familiar and very special
> house of debauchery . . .
>
> . . . .
>
> happy, they gave themselves to love.

Nor is there in these poems the terrible split between the intellectual and the sensuous, earthy man, between Cambridge and game-keepers, with which Forster and so many of his fellow Englishmen had to contend. The artist will immortalize the moment, turning even an encounter in a shabby, frightening room into poetry. And when W. H. Auden asks, "But what, one cannot help wondering, will be the future of the artist's companion?"[40] we hear Cavafy answering: he too has "something of the artist in the way he dresses / —the color of his tie, shape of his collar—"[41] he too will shape life.

Like Antony, Cavafy's lovers willfully tempt disaster. They are after intensity, not security, and court defeat.

> In the small room, radiantly lit
> by the chandelier's hot fire,
> no ordinary light breaks out.
> Not for timid bodies
> the lust of this heat.[42]

Permanence comes only through memory, essentially through the historical act, itself a risky business because memory is fragile, ageing, mortal. Cavafy's persona—an old man sitting before a dim light or gazing from his balcony; holding a letter, a coin, or photograph; listening in the silence to whispers that bridge twenty-two, twenty-six, a thousand years—lives with loneliness and the danger that they will no longer come, these images, these companions from the past.

> Memory, keep them the way they were.
> And, memory, whatever you can, bring back of that love.[43]
> Whatever you can, bring back tonight.

Although Cavafy was also a gregarious man whose love of good conversation delighted his visitors and the numerous

[40] W. H. Auden, "Introduction," *The Complete Poems of Cavafy,* p. x.

[41] "Sensual Pleasure."

[42] "Chandelier."

[43] "Gray."

Boswells with whom he frequented Alexandrian cafes,[44] the persona was clearly close to the poet.

Cavafy died of cancer of the throat in 1933, and many have noted that he had difficulty coming to terms with death. But there was a kind of salvation here too, for in his last years the voices from his past did not fail him. The poems of this period, often dangerously close to the sentimental, succeed, because they are touched by the passionate actuality found in the cheap colored handkerchiefs that frame "He Asked about the Quality" and, more importantly, by the deft sense of the dramatic which had always characterized the best of his poetry. Death, poverty of the spirit, and loneliness are at hand. But one hears celebration too, a quiet, ironic celebration.

D. J. Enright has hit upon some of the appeal inherent in this affirmation when he compares Cavafy and his world to spanking clean, efficiently sterile contemporary society. "How health-giving, in this degenerate context, is the presence of a 'decadent' poet! . . . In short, and taking the one adjective with the other, a civilized human being. He is willing to settle, not triumphantly, for the second best, although he knows what the first best would be. . . . It is not that Cavafy reminds us we are merely human. He reminds us that we *are* human."[45] Enright says very similar things

[44] One of these visitors, the British critic Bonamy Dobrée, speaks of Cavafy's conversation in tones that, we shall see, come close to Forster's: "I have met an Alexandrian—with all that implies. Implication, that word is important when thinking of Mr. Cavafy, for his poems are like his conversation, his conversation like Alexandria, and Alexandria is all implication. . . . He may talk of the Alexandrian tram-service, of the Ptolemies, of the use of a certain word in seventeenth-century English: one scarcely knows what it is that one has talked to Mr. Cavafy about . . . both his talk and his poems leave you with a flavour, something you have never quite met before, a sound that remains in the ear. . . ." "C. P. Cavafy, Alexandrian," *La semaine égyptienne: numéro spécial consacré au poète Alexandrin C. P. Cavafy* (April 1929), p. 13.

[45] "Too Many Caesars: The Poems of C. P. Cavafy," *Conspirators and Poets* (London: Chatto and Windus, 1966), p. 161.

in a poem in his collection, *The Old Adam*, a fine tribute "To Old Cavafy, From a New Country."

> 'Imperfect? Does anything human escape
> That sentence? And after all, we get along.'
>
> But now we have fallen on evil times,
> Ours is the age of goody-goodiness.
>
> They are planning to kill the old Adam,
> Perhaps at this moment the blade is entering.
>
> And when the old Adam has ceased to live,
> What part of us but suffers a death?
>
> The body still walks and talks,
> The mind performs its mental movements.
>
> There is no lack of younger generation
> To meet the nation's needs. Skills shall abound.
>
> They inherit all we have to offer.
> Only the dead Adam is not transmissive.
>
> They will spread their narrowness into space,
> The yellow moon their whitewashed suburbs.
>
> He died in our generation, the old Adam.
> Are our children ours, who did not know him?
>
> We go to a nearby country, for juke-boxes and
> Irony. The natives mutter, 'Dirty old tourists!'
>
> We return, and our children wrinkle their noses.
> Were we as they wish, few of them would be here!
>
> Too good for us, the evil times we have fallen on.
> Our old age shall be spent in disgrace
> and museums.[46]

[46] *The Old Adam* (London: Chatto and Windus, 1965), p. 45.

But Enright is wrong too, for the times have caught up with C. P. Cavafy. Ours is an age in which not only the old and sensitive are frightened by expansive, easy optimism, or projects of scale, an age that looks for celebration but only as it is found in poems like "Lovely White Flowers."

There a shoddy world of venality and deception is made even more meaningless by death. Yet set in this world, never denying its shabby reality, one finds grace in the simple gesture of a rejected lover:

> Sunday they buried him, at ten in the morning.
> Sunday they buried him, almost a week ago.
>
> He laid flowers on his cheap coffin,
> lovely white flowers, very much in keeping
> with his beauty, his twenty-two years.

It is as if Cavafy became that "Mirror in the Front Hall" he speaks of in one of his last poems. A delivery boy, "a tailor's assistant / (on Sundays an amateur athlete)," enters a house of wealth, waits for his receipt, straightens his tie as he looks in the mirror, and leaves. That is all.

> But the old mirror that had seen so much
> in its long life—
> thousands of objects, faces—
> the old mirror was full of joy now,
> proud to have embraced
> total beauty for a few moments.

One final biographical detail comes insistently to mind. When he was about to leave home to enter hospital for the last time, Cavafy looked at his suitcase and wept, writing on the block of paper he had always to hand (he could no longer speak): "I bought this suitcase 30 years ago, in a hurry one evening, to go to Cairo for pleasure. Then I was young and strong, and not ugly."[47] The ragged object evok-

[47] Liddell, p. 205.

ing memories, that double—the old and young selves, continuity based on a series of fleeting moments, love on the run. The story does not mirror Antony's end, although there are those who report that he heard life leave him like one worthy of such a city. But it is a fitting Cavafian tale.

· 3 ·

THE BRIDGE: E. M. FORSTER IN ALEXANDRIA

E. M. Forster arrived in Alexandria in 1915. He was thirty-six and already an established writer, with four novels and a collection of short stories behind him and a fifth novel written but unseen. Forster's was a unique voice, even from the start, large and marked by a generous humanism that has not found its equal in contemporary British fiction. He had already toured Greece, Italy, and India, and his early fiction reflects this contact with worlds that call into question the values of upper-middle-class England, the values of home, just as it reflects the special perception a homosexual brings to a heterosexual, and alien, world.

But the questioning, as we shall see in a moment, is ultimately not pushed beyond the point of comfort and retreat. Forster is deeply concerned with the historical process in his early novels, but he also shows a certain antagonism toward history. The only truth to be told is that of a happy ending. The Wonhams, the Emersons, the Schlegels, the Halls, and the Scudders will inherit England. Because they must. And in love Ansell and Stephen, Helen and Margaret and Maurice and Alec will live happily ever after, whether in the greenwood or at Howards End. Of Forster's novels only *A Passage to India* comes to terms with loss, with the potential chaos that lurks behind a meeting of cultures, a chaos that has become central to the reality of modern man.

E. M. Forster needed a bridge to his India. He needed to do more than visit; he had to live and work in a spot where East and West would touch. Alexandria was that place, "a maritime gate-way to India and the remoter east." (A, 10)

But in order to know this city Forster had first to find a guide.

"I often think of my good fortune and the opportunity which the chance of a horrible war gave me, to meet one of the great poets of our time,"[1] the novelist once wrote to a friend. He was fortunate. For in Cavafy Forster met a writer whose work had many of the strengths Forster's lacked, and in that Greek poet he found a temperament close enough to his own for there to be easy understanding between them.

Most critics have spoken of a "dry spell" in Forster's career—a period between the quick succession of early novels leading up to the publication of *Howards End* in 1910 and the 1924 publication of *A Passage to India*. Although we now know that Forster completed *Maurice* between 1913 and 1914, many are still left wondering about a decade in which Forster produced no new fiction. Too little attention has been given to those years, and particularly to the First World War period in Alexandria, for they were responsible for two important books: *Pharos and Pharillon*, Forster's new venture in form, a Cavafian attempt to turn anecdotal history into fiction, and *Alexandria*, a full-scale study of history which focused upon concerns that were to become central to Forster's last novel—religion, love, and the relationship between East and West. With Cavafy's help Forster could discover Alexandria and make it his own private passage to India. The "dry spell" was perhaps the most fertile period in Forster's long life.

Forster Before the War Years

Love between Comrades

Before we can examine the effects of the war years in Alexandria on Forster, we must briefly look at his life and art before 1915 and on the forces that shaped it.

[1] Quoted in *The Complete Poems of Cavafy*, trans. Rae Dalven (New York: Harcourt, Brace and World, 1961), p. 216.

Forster was left fatherless at an even earlier age than Cavafy had been. Eddie Forster died less than two years after his son's birth, leaving his wife, "a beautiful young widow" (MT, 270) of twenty-five, dependent on the support of her husband's relatives, one of whom—Marianne Thornton—proved a generous and yet manipulating benefactress. Mrs. Forster lived with her son until her death, which occurred when Forster was himself sixty-six. In *Marianne Thornton*, Forster writes about growing up in their beautiful Hertfordshire home, the prototype for Howards End and so unlike Miss Thornton's Clapham, where one "seemed never to see the sun." (MT, 269)

From this home that was as feminine as Helen declares the Schlegels' to be, Forster went on to become a day student in the masculine world of Tonbridge, one of the many public schools that prepared young men for the "great world" of "telegrams and anger," a setting in which Forster felt brutalized, unhappy, and alone.

Opposed to the public school stood Good Cambridge (not just university, for Tibby's Oxford also seems to leave one with an "undeveloped" heart) where Forster's subjects were, significantly, classics and history. Here intellectual and artistic interests and kind, gentle treatment could foster comradeship and love. Edward Carpenter, speaking about a slightly earlier Cambridge than Forster's, touches on the unacknowledged nature of the sexuality around him:

> What a curious romance ran through all that life; and yet on the whole, with few exceptions, how strangely unspoken it was and unexpressed! This succession of athletic and even beautiful faces and figures, what a strange magnetism they had for me, and yet, all the while how unsurmountable for the most part was the barrier between.[2]

[2] Quoted in *Edward Carpenter: In Appreciation* (London: George Allen and Unwin, 1931). There were of course overtly homosexual groups at Cambridge during Forster's time as a student there, like that of Lytton Strachey and his friends. Strachey was to become

A. Alvarez called Cambridge "Forster's Fatal Cleopatra."[3] The phrase is apt, for whereas D. H. Lawrence's social and psychic needs made him lash out at the intellectual—and for him sterile—conversations of Clifford Chatterley and his Cambridge friends, Forster's made him fall prey to the seduction of an environment that was to become, in much of his early fiction and in his life, the perfect home. It is, after all, an adolescent world, one that brings well-being by avoiding rather than encompassing the goblins Helen Schlegel hears in Beethoven's Fifth Symphony.

Sexuality was not, for Forster, always to remain the muted force it had been at Cambridge, although it is most likely that Forster's first love relationship did not occur until his days in Alexandria. P. N. Furbank has said of Forster:

> He achieved physical sex very late and found it easier with people outside his own social class, and it remained a kind of private magic for him—an almost unobtainable blessing, for which another person was mainly a pretext. He valued sex for its power to release his own capacities for tenderness and devotion, but he never expected an *equal* sexual relationship. His chief feeling towards anyone who let him make love to them was gratitude. Intense gratitude led him to romanticize them, at least with one part of his mind, and by romanticizing them he managed to keep them at a distance. He was infinitely attentive and thoughtful and exacting. Always determined to keep his lover "up to the mark" —not be slack or idle, write proper letters and so on— but he never showed any wish to set up house with him.[4]

---

the Risley of *Maurice*, a homosexual whose style differed completely from that of the main Cambridge characters and the author of that novel.

[3] A. Alvarez, "E. M. Forster: From Snobbery to Love," *Saturday Review*, 16 October 1971, p. 42.

[4] "The Personality of E. M. Forster," *Encounter*, 35 (November 1970), 62. Furbank is writing Forster's biography.

We have become terribly suspicious of "the liberal imagination" and are often more frightened of patronizing social relations than of openly hostile ones. And Forster was too. Miss Lavish condescends to love Italians and be a nonconformist, and succeeds in being a hateful snob. The Schlegels, for all their generosity, are partners in the murder of Leonard Bast. Forster's conscious mind understood it all. Still, one doesn't live—or write—under the clear direction of one's conscious mind. And it is just, humanly necessary, to be suspicious of love relationships that are built upon the importance of class distinction.

As we shall see shortly, in much of Forster's early fiction the beloved is split into two selves: one spiritual and intellectual, and one sensuous. The latter is of the earth and from the lower classes. The parallels between life and fiction are real. But in looking at both, we must be careful not to lie through exaggeration. The tone of Colin Wilson's remarks does that, when he writes: "There was also this amusing complication that, as a shy, subtle, withdrawn man, he had a sexual preference for stupid and extroverted males. (This later developed into a preference for policemen, says my informant—a taste he shared with Hugh Walpole and James Agate)."[5] Wilson offends his readers, as well as those about whom he speaks. George Savidis, the Greek scholar and translator of Cavafy, whom I met in 1971 in Thessalonika, knew Forster well, and chuckled at the idea that anyone could think his friend stupid. Nor could one think that of Stephen Wonham or Alec Scudder.

The Early Novels

Cavafy made his homosexuality central to his poetry. But what about Forster? In a review of the posthumously published novel *Maurice*, Joseph Epstein writes:

> Now that Forster is known to have been a homosexual

[5] "A Man's Man," *Spectator*, 9 October 1971, p. 512.

> others, heterosexual and homosexual alike, will no doubt wish to return to his other works to rake them over for homosexual strains and allusions. Already the players are beginning to line up. Biographical criticism carried to this extreme is finally an insult to the richness of the human imagination: it assumes that an American can only write about Americans, a Jew about Jews . . . the very basis of the novelist's art is his ability to slip into hundreds of other skins besides his own. The homosexual influence in Forster's other novels, if it exists at all, is so negligible as scarcely to be worthy of notice.[6]

Epstein's admonition frightened me. The slap that Lawrence Durrell's Clea gave Darley when he said he'd write criticism still rings in the ear. But Epstein is wrong about the raking. E. M. Forster's homosexuality shaped his writing—I'd venture to say, more than any other force did. And it influenced those works that do not explicitly deal with homosexuals every bit as much as it affected *Maurice* and the stories in *The Life to Come.*

"The facts" about Forster's life as a homosexual were carefully guarded from public knowledge during his lifetime. Fiction that described homosexual love went unpublished until after his death; even when writing about figures like Goldsworthy Lowes Dickinson, Edward Carpenter, and Cavafy, Forster does not mention homosexuality.

One can easily, and for the most part correctly, argue that even if the biographical pieces suffer from their lack of candor, we now have *Maurice* and *The Life to Come* and, what is more important, we have fiction in which Forster created masks, enabling him to talk about love as he felt it most deeply, producing a tension between the fictive and the real that resulted in fine novels.

Still Wallace Stevens' mouse nibbles in the wall. Forster preached love and truth. And yet the *Times Literary Sup-*

[6] "*Maurice*, by E. M. Forster," *The New York Times Book Review*, 10 October 1971, p. 1.

plement is not wrong when it notes that Forster's "desire to remain in that world [of marriage and marriage novels] was stronger than his desire to tell the truth about himself —he made out of self-deprecation, transference, and evasion a personal and functioning style."[7] Passion and truth sometimes seem sacrificed to convention in the early novels —in Ansell's reaction to Rickie's marriage or in Maurice's jealousy toward Ada—because of Forster's fear that if he really struck at the core of these relationships, he might not be able to come back to Sawston, or to Howards End. So he muddles just a bit. Mr. Emerson tells Lucy: "Take an old man's word; there's nothing worse than a muddle in all the world." (RV, 236)

THE EARLY NOVELS AND HISTORY

> . . . Between life and books there is one great difference —a difference that is too often neglected. . . . It is simply this. The *end* is of supreme importance in a book. The *end* is not of supreme importance in life. . . . I think one cannot be too emphatic over this question of the end. . . . A man today, if he writes a novel, how will he end it? "Happily, of course," the optimist hums and haws. . . . And sooner or later, he will give the old, old answer, *marriage*. . . . A hundred years ago, or fifty years ago, this would have seemed a very good answer. But our social feelings are altering very rapidly. We of today know that whatever marriage is, it is not an end . . . we turn to that despised creature the pessimist, and say "How would *you* end a book?" And the pessimist replies, quite simply and satisfactorily, "By some scene of separation." It seems to me that the modern author, if he is conscientious and artistic, is bound to listen to this advice. . . . He has not merely been taught that all things change. He has breathed it in, as men have breathed it in at no other age. . . . Where shall

[7] "A Chalice for Youth," *The Times Literary Supplement*, 8 October 1971, pp. 1215-1216.

> such a man find rest with honour? Scarcely in a happy ending. . . . Separation—that is the end that really satisfies him—not simply the separation that comes through death, but the more tragic separation of people who part before they need, or who part because they have seen each other too closely. Here is something that does last—the note of permanence on which his soul was set. He has laboured sincerely, he has told a story not untrue to life. . . .

So said E. M. Forster when lecturing to the Working Men's College Old Students' Club in December, 1906 on "Pessimism in Literature." (AE, 134-137) Four years later he made a similarly wise statement about Beethoven: "He brought back the gusts of splendor, the heroism, the youth, the magnificence of life and death, and amid vast roarings of a superhuman joy, he led his Fifth Symphony to its conclusion. But the goblins were there. They could return. He had said so bravely, and that is why one can trust Beethoven when he says other things." (HE, 34)

Despite his stage goblins, can one trust Forster? Were the deep-seated forces that produced his fiction in harmony with a critical faculty that called for the truth of separation and flux? Many have attacked *Maurice*, suggesting that it differs from other novels because in writing directly about homosexuality Forster lost his objectivity and demanded that the novel have a happy ending. "I shouldn't have bothered to write otherwise." (M, 25) But what of the other early novels? Maurice and Alec go off to the greenwood and inherit England, but so do the other fictive characters whom Forster loves.

Forster's desire for continuity was incredibly strong. Before the First World War, before Alexandria, he could not look on his country's history—seen in its landscape and in its class structure—he could not look at art, without dwelling on permanence, on continuity. And when he turned to love, his desire for undying comradeship held his early fiction, not quite permitting it to tell a story of separation "not untrue to life."

In Forster's early novels history and art are always unifying forces. In *Howards End,* Forster writes: "Margaret realized the chaotic nature of our daily life, and its difference from the orderly sequence that has been fabricated by historians. Actual life is full of false clues and signposts that lead nowhere." (HE, 106) Even though he might wish it otherwise, history and art could not mirror chaos in Forster's work, because Forster could not yet accept what in *Room with a View* he called "the sadness of the incomplete—the sadness that is often life, but should never be Art." (RV, 140)

Perhaps this is why his early work is dominated by images of ancient Greece. Lionel Trilling is only partially correct when he writes: "We know of Forster that he is a Hellenist but not a 'classicist,' that he loves Greece in its mythical and naturalistic aspects, that Plato never meant much to him, perhaps because he mistrusts the Platonic drive to the absolute and the Platonic judgement of the body and the senses."[8] Greece and Greek art certainly symbolize the mythical and the sensual for Forster—"A Gothic statue implies celibacy, just as a Greek statue implies fruition." (RV, 99) It also, of course, implies homosexual love. Alec's features are yet more beautiful than the Greek statuary that surround and enhance them. Stephen breaks the statue of Hermes of Praxiteles, because he is the real thing. In "Albergo Empedocle," amid ancient ruins, Harold awakens from his public-school lethargy to the knowledge that he had loved "better" and "differently" in a former Greek life.

This connection between the Hellenic and the sensual is of extreme and lasting importance to Forster, but we should also note the link Forster makes in the early novels between his idea of Greece and his belief in the absolute necessity for continuity and unity. When truth finally reveals itself to Maurice, he is looking at a replica of the Acropolis, mur-

[8] *E. M. Forster* (London: Hogarth Press, 1967), p. 19.

muring, "I see, I see, I see." (M, 222) We are reminded of Rickie Elliot's musing, "on the Acropolis at Athens beauty and truth do exist, really exist as external powers." (LJ, 176) Sometimes, despite his better judgment, Forster, like Plato, strove for the absolute. But he had not yet met Cavafy, who reacted against the neat perfection of what Forster was to call "Public School Greece": "Pericles and Aspasia and Themistocles and all those bores." (PP, 94)

Still, even before the First World War, Forster confronted forces attempting to destroy his faith in continuity and order. Unlike Cavafy, who wrote almost exclusively about his city, Forster distrusted cities; they brought with them "odours from the abyss," odors of chaos. Forster very seriously noted that "we are reverting to the civilization of luggages, and historians of the future will note how the middle classes accreted possessions without taking root in the earth, and may find in this the secret of their imaginative poverty." (HE, 150) Ruth Wilcox, who joins Failing in the list of Forster's magical characters, understands many of life's mysteries:

> One knew that she worshipped the past and that the instinctive wisdom the past can alone bestow had descended upon her—that wisdom to which we give the clumsy name of aristocracy. High-born she might not be. But assuredly she cared about her ancestors, and let them help her. (HE, 22)

For Yeats the aristocracy and the peasantry shared in a special grandeur that was denied the middle class. They were connected to their past and to the land. They had continuity. How strangely like him the liberal Forster sometimes seems. Gino and Stephen Wonham, Robert and Flea Thompson are unlike Leonard Bast—for they are equal, superior, to most rich people, even those with umbrellas. They will inherit the earth. Because for Forster they must.

Forster wishes us to make no mistake about it. If chaos rules the world, urban middle-class values will dominate.

If the world moves in directions he applauds, there will be a new order—in which the best values of his past are perpetuated and all the peoples of his land "connect." Thus intellectual Schlegels and capitalist Wilcoxes are at center stage in *Howards End*, along with those victims of urban poverty Leonard and Jackie Bast, and with the Averys, keepers of the eternal wisdom of the British peasantry.

The new order in Forster's early fiction seeks to unite these classes as it hopes to unite two other divergent communities in English society—men and women. Forster's novels seem to sympathize with the attitude of Goldsworthy Lowes Dickinson, who, while believing in women's rights, wasn't happy in wartime Cambridge where he found himself lecturing to women. (GLD, 163) The affable classicist Mr. Jackson, echoing the tone of *The Longest Journey*, says: "Go away, dear ladies. . . . You think you see life because you see the chasms in it. Yet all the chasms are filled with female skeletons." (LJ, 199) Forster showed a distaste for feminists who "agitate and scream," (RV, 226) who, like Helen's companion Monica, are persons "whom one respects but avoids." (HE, 294) Still, as a homosexual Forster knew the horrors of a sexually polarized society in which the Eternal Woman and her white knight erase the values of the individual soul, (RV, 47) and understood how deeply urban middle-class values are based on sexual inequality, creating Charles Wilcoxes who believe in temptresses, "the strong man's necessary compliment." (HE, 216) Forster saw a chasm between men and women, a failure to communicate, and envisioned a society in which unity would be coupled with continuity, in which men and women of all classes lived on the land and let their ancestors help them.

THE EARLY NOVELS AND LOVE

Communication, comradeship is the goal of the best heterosexual relationships in Forster's fiction, "where man and woman, having lost themselves in sex, desire to lose sex itself in comradeship." (HE, 311) "Not until we are comrades shall we enter the garden," says the wise and wonderful Mr. Emerson. (RV, 146) Still, for all his emphasis on marriage and manners, Forster's writing is not primarily about heterosexual love. In art, as in life, he was haunted by the image of undying affection between members of the same sex, which is precisely why comradeship, indeed the very word, was so important to Forster, almost permitting the unity of two irreconcilable forces: the respectability of home and the lawlessness of love. A particularly English virtue—"comradeship, not passionate, that is our highest gift as a nation" (HE, 268)—it nevertheless encompassed what Englishmen hatefully called "the unspeakable vice of the Greeks." (M, 51)

Affection between members of the same sex is obviously the central concern of stories like "Ansell," "Dr. Woolacott," "The Point of It," and "Mr. Andrews," and the novels *The Longest Journey* and *Maurice*, but what is surprising is that it is central to the ostensibly heterosexual love stories *Where Angels Fear to Tread* and *Howards End.*[9]

Caroline Abbott is in love with Gino and is loved by Philip, but, I would contend, the most vital side of that triangle is the relationship between the two men. In that powerful scene in which Italian nearly kills Englishman, physical violence disrobes civility, ultimately binding the men "by ties of almost alarming intimacy." (WAFT, 174) In *Where Angels Fear to Tread*, published in 1905, gentle Mr. Forster showed the links between violence and sexuality as vibrantly as did the temperamentally antithetical D. H.

[9] Even in *A Room with a View*, Forster's frothy boy-meets-girl novel —and the first novel he wrote, although not the first to be published —the central image is a bathing scene in which the "good" men— Forster's pagan hero, honest clergyman, and typically weak younger brother—shed clothes and inhibitions and play until cut short by the call of "Hi! hi! Ladies" and the medieval chivalry of the dominant male. Still they have shared "a passing benediction whose influence did not pass, a holiness, a spell, a momentary chalice for youth"; (RV, 153) they have reinforced our belief in the power of friendship.

Lawrence when portraying the battle between Paul Morel and Baxter Dawes. The death of Gino's English and Italian child generates this violence. Gino fondles the infant in life; Philip cradles it in death. And after the violence, Gino's reaction to Philip is no longer surprising—"a vision of perfect friendship . . . you would have thought it was my son who had died" (WAFT, 174)—for these two are united in an act of creation, destruction, and rebirth around which the novel pivots, giving *Where Angels Fear to Tread* its special strength.

> Howards End is the weak novel it is because it has heterosexual relationships at its centre—an engagement, a marriage, and a fornication move the plot—and Forster could not handle any of them convincingly.[10]

The *Times Literary Supplement* is wrong, for what moves the plot, quite obviously, need not be at the center of a novel. *Howards End* (1910) is a fine book precisely because heterosexual relationships are not at its core; a rare work, written by a man, in which the central consciousness is a warmly intelligent female and the central concern the love of two sisters and their struggle to maintain the principles upon which that love rests.

> She was not going to say: "I love my sister; I must be near her at this crisis of her life." The affections are more reticent than the passions, and their expression more subtle. If she herself should ever fall in love with a man, she, like Helen, would proclaim it from the house-tops, but as she only loved a sister she used the voiceless language of sympathy. (HE, 9)

In the course of the novel Margaret—one of the most sensitive female figures in British fiction—is made to choose between the officially sanctioned virtues of marriage and the subtle expression of affection shared by sisters, friends.

[10] "A Chalice for Youth," p. 1215.

Again and again Forster shakes with anger because comradeship goes "unlabelled," almost unnoted in our society; often, like Rickie Elliot, Forster seems to want "a friendship office, where the marriage of true minds could be registered." (LJ, 78) In Margaret Schlegel Forster creates an answer to society's snubs, a character who would willingly sacrifice legal heterosexual love to "the voiceless language of sympathy."

Is comradeship sexual in Forster's fiction? It is, clearly, in the fiction published since his death, like the surprisingly similar works "Albergo Empedocle" and *Maurice*. But there are sexual dimensions to friendship and, especially, to sibling affection in Forster's other works as well. Forster wrote in a world in which he could not, and would not, speak directly about his own sexual life. Images of comrades and siblings gave him the necessary fictive mask through which he could deal with homosexuality, and often allowed him to dig to the roots of sexuality in familial and friendship relationships. They sometimes produced the tension we see in Cavafy's historical-love poems. I do not mean to suggest that the mask was always conscious. Nor do I feel that Forster was always courageous enough to face the sexuality he had created. But in the brotherhood of figures like Stephen Wonham and Rickie Elliot, Forster found a permissible way of describing unpermissible impulses. The bond of flesh and blood serves well as a mirror for the bond of physical contact. Through it Forster could reach to some of the narcissistic links between lover and beloved and the patterns by which they reenact the roles of mother and child.[11]

Rickie and Stephen are linked to another young man in a pattern that is common in Forster's early fiction, where

[11] The brothers take turns serving in the parental role. What is more, like so much of Forster's fiction, *The Longest Journey* (1907) uses childbirth as its central symbol. Early in the novel heterosexual love is associated with a train wreck and the death of a child; at its close Rickie gives new life to his brother-son Stephen, sacrificing himself in another encounter with that train and thus spawning Stephen's child—a girl named after their beautiful, sensual mother.

love usually takes place in groups of three. Stephen Spender has defined two distinct types of homosexual relationships, one based on "identity and the other on 'otherness.'" In the latter "differences of class almost replace differences of sex."[12] But Forster's central characters are torn. Like Rickie, they are always faced with two beloveds, one spiritual and one physical, and in all cases their most successful relationship is with a Mediterranean man or British peasant, with an earthy mate. In *The Longest Journey* and in *Maurice* the spiritual beloved is another student. His relationship with the protagonist moves toward physical consummation, and is marked by very similar idyllic scenes in which the boys stroke each other's hair and tussle in the grass, only partly aware of their sexual play, until evil forces—women, conventions, a lack of courage—intervene. Paul Morel could not face the interweaving of the spiritual and the physical in his mother or in himself and so, in seeking a surrogate mother-lover, found two persons—the spiritual Miriam and the sensual Clara. Like this Lawrence hero, Forster's protagonists search for a beloved and for themselves but find that they and their doubles are split. Although Rickie and Maurice attempt love with Ansell and Clive, consummation can only come through the peasant beauty of a Stephen or an Alec.

In *The Longest Journey* this division causes little pain—the fight with evil lies elsewhere and the two halves of Rickie's other self are happily united in the end. But in the raw, flamed, and honest *Maurice*, Forster ends with a scene in which author and protagonist seem out of control. The focus is wrong. When he should be loving Alec, Maurice is out chastising Clive. "You'll do anything for me except see me. That's been it for this whole year of Hell. . . . I was yours once till death if you'd cared to keep me, but I'm someone else's now. . . ." (M, 245) We get a sense of anger, the desire to punish. The division should not have been

[12] "Forster's Queer Novel," *Partisan Review* (Summer 1972), p. 116.

necessary. But until Forster learned to love "better" and "differently," he and his heroes would have to live in this way.

HISTORY AND LOVE UNITE

No one who admires Forster's fiction can miss its sadnesses. A stranger bends toward Lucy "as if he had an important message for her." (RV, 44) The message is blood. As in life, death is everywhere and a surprise. Gino's baby, Leonard Bast, Mrs. Wilcox, and, most painful of all, Forster's second self Rickie, thinking himself alone. Death causes those like George Emerson to doubt, and affirm, life. For Helen Schlegel it stamps all who are really alive. "We *know* that there's poetry. We *know* that there's death. They can only take them on hearsay." (HE, 301-302) There are also sadnesses more wearying than death. There is Leonard Bast's evening with Ruskin. Mrs. Wilcox, dying, is carted away from her home. About such things Forster tells his reader what Rickie tells Agnes, when her lover dies: "I did not come to comfort you. I came to see that you mind." (LJ, 67)

But Forster minded so much that he could not resist giving those fictive selves he loved eternal comfort. The contest is on in most of Forster's early novels. The prize is the direction of human destiny. The prize is England. The problem, a very poignant one for Forster and perhaps for most homosexuals, is that continuity and a type of unity are promised to most heterosexual couples. The Wilcoxes breed like rabbits and, as Maurice realizes with immense sadness, even his ineffectual mother can create the mystery of human life. Comrades do not have "this divine hope of immortality." (WAFT, 67) Clive's answer—indeed art's answer—that love can link eternity and the moment, is not enough for Forster. He wants true comrades to possess the land, his island. He wants this so much that he will make it happen in the world he controls most fully, even if, in the process, he has to be a bit untrue to history, and even to love.

And so Forster bears children in his fiction. They are never children of individual souls; they always carry with them the weight of history and human destiny. Stephen's child vies with Agnes' baby. The question is, who will inherit the earth? And the answer is plain. The good will inherit the earth. Time will stand still. Homosexual lovers will leave heirs.

Thus, in spite of the admission that "London's creeping," *Howards End* closes with all its divergent classes entwined and planted firmly on the English countryside. Because Helen won't marry and Margaret won't have children, these dearest friends will live on, surrounded by Margaret's husband and Helen's son, who is her sister's and England's heir. The infant will also have a lifelong comrade, Miss Avery's grandson Tom, and in the union of these boys life joyfully comes full circle, for they link classes which might have united two generations earlier, had Miss Avery married Tom Howard, owner of Howards End. The boys will be like Maurice and Alec: ". . . England belonged to them. That, besides companionship, was their reward. Her air and sky were theirs, not the timorous millions' who own stuffy little boxes, but never their own souls." (M, 239)

The sisters are equally successful, for they have defied what we must all face in our parents' houses, what Forster all but defied in life: the necessity of separation. "They could never be parted . . . there would after all be a future, with laughter and the voices of children. . . . They looked into each other's eyes. The inner life had paid." (HE, 299)

Forster almost makes us believe it all possible, because he, and perhaps we, cannot yet face the words "that despised creature the pessimist" must speak.

The War Years and Cavafy

Forster's fiction was to change. Lecturing on "English Prose between 1918 and 1939" in the midst of the second great war, Forster remembered the first:

> The French lady, Madame de Sevigné, writing letters during the wars of the late seventeenth century, can feel tranquil. The English lady, Jane Austen, writing novels in the Napoleonic wars, can feel tranquil. Those wars were not total. But no one can write during or between our wars and escape their influence. There, then, is one obvious characteristic of our prose. It is the product of people who have war on their mind. They need not be gloomy or hysterical—often they are gay and sane and brave—but if they have any sensitiveness they must realize what a mess the world is in. . . . (TC, 277)

In a 1917 letter to Bertrand Russell, Forster reveals a bit of the emotions that accompanied his personal response to his first encounter with total war:

> Here I have been for nearly two years. Harmless and unharmed. Here is Egyptian hospitals. I live in their wards, questioning survivors. It has been a comfortable life. How unreal I shan't know till I compare it with the lives others have been leading in the period. I don't write, but feel I think and think I feel. Sometimes I make notes on human nature under war conditions. . . . I love people and want to understand them and help them more than I did, but this is oddly accompanied by a growth of contempt. Be like them? God, no.[13]

The great war marked the beginning of the modern world, altering the relationships between nations and man's relation to the land, producing writers who were influenced by new economic and psychological awareness and new visions of relativity. Marx, Freud, Einstein, airplanes, movies, suburban sprawl. *Be* like it? God, no.

Thirteen years later Forster told Cavafy: "I wish I was inventing something. Novels and stories no longer form in my mind and I suppose that, at my age, if that process once

[13] Letter in Forster's unpublished papers at King's College, Cambridge, dated 28 July 1917.

ceases it will never recommence."[14] In the main, the process did not recommence, and we may in part hold the war and the world it produced responsible, for life's differences seemed too great, there was no longer a meeting of cultures, even within Forster's own. But for a period between that letter to Russell and the other to Cavafy Forster produced his best work. Tension was in the air. The old complacencies would not hold. World War I made it impossible to avoid loss, and it also introduced Forster to Cavafy, who helped make it possible to face personal and political defeat with the dignity he summons forth in "The God Abandons Antony," one of Forster's favorite poems:

When at the hour of midnight
an invisible choir is suddenly heard passing
with exquisite music, with voices—
Do not lament your fortune that at last subsides,
your life's work that has failed, your schemes that
  have proved illusions.
But like a man prepared, like a brave man,
bid farewell to her, to Alexandria who is departing.
Above all, do not delude yourself, do not say that
  it is a dream,
that your ear was mistaken.
Do not condescend to such empty hopes.
Like a man for long prepared, like a brave man,
like the man who was worthy of such a city,
go to the window firmly,
and listen with emotion
but not with the prayers and complaints of the coward
(Ah! supreme rapture!)
listen to the notes, to the exquisite instruments
  of the mystic choir,
and bid farewell to her, to Alexandria whom you
  are losing.[15]

[14] Letter in Forster's unpublished papers at King's, dated 24 August 1930.

[15] The translation is by Forster's and Cavafy's mutual friend George Valassopoulo. (PP, 55) and (A, 104)

Richard Howard has captured something of the enormous magnetism of Cavafy, when he writes:

> He is the first Greek poet since Euripides we read with that kind of demonic self-recognition. He has influenced any poet who reads him, indeed it is correct to say he influences any reader, for Cavafy is among the few, the very few writers who return us to the true meaning of "influence": an astrological implication, the pressure of a fatality upon our lives. . . . Cavafy is one of the great writers we turn to . . . not because he delights us or because he demands our attention (though he does these things as well as they have ever been done), but because he comes to terms, answerable terms, with that relation to our own lives we most mistrust and evade—the relation to loss.[16]

When we examine the work Forster wrote during and after his stay in Alexandria, we will see this influence make itself felt. But in order to understand Cavafy's effect upon Forster, we must, for a moment, look at a friendship between two gregarious and yet deeply solitary men from vastly different cultures, who met through the accidents of war and continued their friendship in a correspondence which lasted until Cavafy's death.

The two are in many ways similar and, as others have noted, one of Forster's portraits of Cavafy captures some of the delightful oddity that is Forster himself. He describes Alexandrians who have the good fortune of meeting their poet:

> They hear their own name proclaimed in firm yet meditative accents—accents that seem not so much to expect an answer as to pay homage to the fact of individuality. They turn and see a Greek gentleman in a straw hat,

[16] Quoted in Edmund Keeley, " 'Latest' Poems Increase Cavafy's Appeal to Students," *University: A Princeton Quarterly*, No. 48 (Spring 1971), pp. 25-26.

standing absolutely motionless at a slight angle to the universe. His arms are extended, possibly. "Oh, Cavafy . . . !" Yes, it is Mr. Cavafy, and he is going either from his flat to the office, or from his office to the flat. If the former, he vanishes when seen, with a slight gesture of despair. If the latter, he may be prevailed upon to begin a sentence—an immense complicated yet shapely sentence, full of parentheses that never get mixed and of reservations that really do reserve; a sentence that moves with logic to its foreseen end, yet to an end that is always more vivid and thrilling than one foresaw. Sometimes the sentence is finished in the street, sometimes the traffic murders it, sometimes it lasts into the flat. It deals with the tricky behaviour of the Emperor Alexius Commenus in 1096, or with olives, their possibilities and price, or with the fortunes of friends, or George Eliot, or the dialects of the interior of Asia Minor. It is delivered with equal ease in Greek, English, or French. And despite its intellectual richness and human outlook, despite the matured charity of its judgments, one feels that it too stands at a slight angle to the universe: it is the sentence of a poet.

(PP, 96)

The sketch brings to mind P. N. Furbanks' remarks about Forster:

Again, both as a critic and a creator, he was the master of *angle*. As all his friends remarked, nobody came at things from queerer angles. It was not whimsicality; it arose from his seeing things more concretely than other people. . . . His great strength as a novelist was his sense for the angles at which people stood to one another and to the universe surrounding them and the constant dance of changing angles from which he makes us view them. For him, the art of fiction, like the art of life, lay in finding one's bearings. "One must face facts," a friend once said to him. "How can I," he replied, "when they're all around me."[17]

Cavafy and Forster have similar sensibilities; a delicate irony encompasses both men's works. Forster's "non-conforming" Lady Novelist, Miss Lavish, views Mr. Emerson as a crude, working-class countryman. When he speaks wisely and sensitively: "Miss Lavish frowned. It is hard when a person you have classed as typically British speaks out of his character." (RV, 74). As we have seen, in Cavafy's poetry, the irony is not so frequently humorous, but it is pervasive, and responsible for the work's dominant tone. In "Waiting for the Barbarians," the civilized ceremoniously await the arrival of their conquerors. But they do not come: "Now what's going to happen to us without barbarians? / Those people were a kind of solution."

We cannot speak of similar sensibilities without discussing a sense of scope in the writings of Forster and Cavafy. When looking at the famous statue next to the Suez Canal, Forster wrote: "May I never resemble M. de Lesseps . . . may no achievement on an imposing scale be mine." (AH, 257) For Forster, just as for Ernst Schlegel, "It is the vice of a vulgar mind to be thrilled by bigness." (HE, 29)

Cavafy agreed. He ignored Ancient Egypt, except to say: "I don't understand those big immobile things."[18] The poet saw history as brief, private moments in the lives of persons like Aimilianos Monai, or Jason, son of Kleander, or Anna Komnina. Forster, who worked tirelessly to get a book of translations of Cavafy's poems in print, remembers that Cavafy didn't favor the project: "peut-être sent-il, avec son ancêtre littéraire Callimachus, qu'un grand livre est un grand mal."[19] Lawrence Durrell's poem "Cavafy" touches

[17] "The Personality of E. M. Forster," p. 62.

[18] Quoted in Robert Liddell, *Cavafy: a Critical Biography* (London: Duckworth, 1974), p. 208.

[19] "Dans la rue Lepsius," *La semaine egyptienne*, Numéro spécial consacré au poète Alexandrin C. P. Cavafy (April, 1929), p. 18. Forster's words come to us only in this translation by C. Mauron, for

the essence of why we appreciate Cavafy's use of scale, although the lines that follow comment strangely on Durrell's own work.

> And here I find him great. Never
> To attempt a masterpiece of size—
> You must leave life for that. No
> But always to preserve the adventive
> Minute, never to destroy the truth
> Admit the coarse manipulations of the lie.
> (CP, 157)

Cavafy *is* a miniaturist. Each poem is a small, finely etched portrait. But that is of course only part of the story, for Cavafy is a miniaturist who chose to depict the entire history of Hellenism, to chronicle a race! Although the figures he portrays are hardly the stuff of which ordinary heroes are made, they do build a mythology. It is difficult to imagine a grander task. Forster also wrote with passionate concern about his people, as they lived on his beloved island and, chronicling their clash with others, as they moved in the world. At times the broad sweep fails—in the operatic conclusion to *Howards End* for example, where we feel the strain of an attempt to reconcile all the major forces in the English social structure—but at its best we hardly notice the immensity of Forster's scheme, perhaps because he, like Cavafy, wears the mask of a little man, certainly because he has the poet's uncanny ability to make larger historical and social pulls seem truly subordinate to the personal.

The men were alike. And Forster, who wrote constantly about friendship between men of different classes or different races, was, with Cavafy, to live a friendship between an Anglo-Saxon and an Easterner. But it was not easy. Forster brought to Alexandria predispositions he could share

---

although he has written another, entitled "In the Rue Lepsius"—*The Listener*, 5 July 1951, pp. 28-29—much of the piece in French does not appear elsewhere.

most comfortably only with those at home, as a letter to R. C. Trevelyan about Cavafy makes clear:

> I am very well, and as an escape from the war Alexandria is matchless; or rather escapes; I went to see a Greek poet yesterday whose mind overflowed on the subject of a school at Volo. This school has been the butt of mistaken or malignant criticism. . . . The school triumphed. . . . But in triumphing it has expired. Its young ladies—for it was a female school—have returned unsmirched but unfinished to their homes.
>
> There are other escapes—the Syrian, the Italian, the Bedouin and etc—but I prefer the Greek, for the Greeks are the only community here that attempt to understand what they are talking about, and to be with them is to re-enter, however imperfectly, the Academic world. They are the only important people east of Ventimiglia—dirty, dishonest, unaristocratic, roving, and warped by Hellenic and Byzantine dreams—but they do effervesce intellectually, they do have creative desires, and one comes round to them in the end. I wonder if you will ever hear of the poet I have just mentioned—he is a great name in the Eastern Mediterranean and discussed in the little magazines that spring up and die without ceasing in its creeks. C. P. Cavafy. He writes short things in Romaic: with much help I have read one or two and thought them beautiful.
>
> The Syrians dance.
> The Bedouins lay eggs.
> The French give lectures on Kultur to the French
> The Italians build il nostro Consolato, . . .
> The English have witnessed 'Candida' or
> 'Vice Detected'.
>
> I send my love.
>
> MORGAN SMITH[20]

[20] Quoted in *A Garland for E. M. Forster*, ed. by H. H. Anniah Gowda (Mysore, India: The Literary Half-Yearly, 1969), pp. 131-132. The letter is dated 6 August 1917.

The unguarded letter gives us a sense of Forster's reservations about Cavafy and his friends that pieces written for publication would not.

Still, in the introduction to *The Hill of Devi* Forster speaks about how we often deprecate our subject untruthfully in letters home, and the essays on Cavafy, like those in *Pharos and Pharillon* and in *Two Cheers for Democracy*, tell us another kind of truth, pointing to an intimacy that the exchange between Forster and his English friend would belie. Some notes Forster wrote on Cavafy allow us a glimpse of that friendship:

> It never occurred to him that I might like his work or even understand it . . . and I remember the delight to us both, one dusky evening in his flat, when it appeared that I was 'following'. When he was pleased he['d] jump and light a candle, and then another candle and he would cut cigarettes in half and light them and bring offerings of mastica with little bits of bread and cheese, and his talk would sway over the Mediterranean world and over much of the world within.[21]

[21] In Forster's papers at King's College. Written in pencil, these are notes for a lecture, or more likely, the first draft of the piece that is now in *Two Cheers*. Much in the two is identical, although this opening has been replaced by the less idiosyncratic:

> The first English translation of Cavafy was made by Cavafy. The occasion is over thirty years ago now, in his flat, 10 Rue Lepsius, Alexandria; his dusky family-furnished flat. He is back from his work in a government office; the Third Circle of the Irrigation employs him as it might have employed many of his heroes. I am back from my work, costumed in khaki; the British Red Cross employs me. We have been introduced by an English friend, our meetings are rather dim, and Cavafy is now saying with his usual gentleness, 'You could never understand my poetry, my dear Forster, never.' A poem is produced—"The God Abandons Antony"—and I detect some coincidences between its Greek and public school Greek. Cavafy is amazed. 'Oh, but this is good, my dear Forster, this is very good indeed,' and he raises his hand, takes over, and leads me through. (TCD, 243-244)

The passage, as well as the final essay of which it is a draft, gives one a sense of the magic that kept Forster writing to Cavafy for fifteen years. They are often chatty letters introducing a friend who is to arrive in Alexandria ("I have indicated your address, and 7.0. P.M. as your most favourable hour"),[22] asking Cavafy to write to a young admirer, William Plomer,[23] or describing his journey to India: " 'Cavafy's bit of the Mediterranean' I said to myself when I saw the white ridge of Ida [on Crete] . . . we are running to Port Said, and this is as near as I can hope to get to the Rue Lepsius for the present." In that same letter, dated 15 March 1921, Forster tells Cavafy that he has given up on his history and guide of Alexandria.

> As for my book on Alexandria, I have lost all interest in it. The MS remains in Clarif Pacha Street and for ever will remain as far as I can see. . . . What is the use of map and plans in a state of proof? What is the use of any MS? And what, above all, is the use of Clarif Pacha Street? I would wish, next time you walk down it, you would ask, in those tones of yours, that question.

This seems to have been a time of some doubt for Forster, but it preceded a period of great productivity. He completed *Alexandria* after a trip there on his way home from India the following year (he was to visit the city once again, for the last time, in 1929).

[22] Letter in Forster's unpublished papers at King's College, Cambridge, dated 16 July 1919.

[23] Letter dated 14 May 1931. Plomer's admiration for Cavafy led him to write "To the Greek Poet C. P. Cavafy on his Poimata (1908-1914)," *The Fivefold Screen* (London: Hogarth Press, 1932), p. 57. The poem concludes:

> Voices of Asia and of Europe fuse
> In the mad Russians and the vigorous Jews,
> But you, Cavafy, more divinely speak
> As your own blood spoke long ago, in Greek,
> Wisdom and tears and tenderness and style
> Blent in a subtle and nostalgic smile.

Most of Forster's letters do not deal with his own work, however. They deal with Cavafy's, and with the monumental job Forster did of getting the Valassopoulo translations and finally, thirty years later, the Mavrogordato book to the English-speaking public. When we think of the energy Forster expended as an unofficial agent-editor-occasional translator, meeting with gratitude but little encouragement, we are left with the rare conviction that the image of generosity we had formed of a public man befits his private self. Forster was constantly coaxing for more translations from Alexandria—"It is important to keep your name before the public, now that interest has been aroused"[24]—and when they arrived, if need be revising them, with the help of Arnold Toynbee or T. E. Lawrence. At the same time he corresponded with the editors of the *Athenaeum*, the *Oxford Outlook*, *Chapbook*, the *Criterion*—anyone who would publish Cavafy in English or give the poet two guineas instead of one for a poem.[25] Forster introduced Cavafy's work to T. S. Eliot, Robert Graves, and Siegfried Sassoon; he encouraged the Woolfs' interest in publishing a book of Cavafy's poetry and tackled Heinemann and Chatto and Windus on the subject as well. Meeting with countless frustrations—"I quite agree with you that Valassopoulo is your ideal translator if he would but translate! The British public won't know you as I wish, if he only sends a poem a year"[26]—Forster plugged on, despite the fact that a book of translations never seemed to emerge from Alexandria (nor could Cavafy support Forster's suggestion that a new translator be found).

Forster of course also wrote about Cavafy, first in a 1919

[24] Unpublished letter at King's College, Cambridge, dated 1 August 1923.

[25] Unpublished letter to Harold Munro, dated 13 August 1925, at the Humanities Research Center, University of Texas, Austin, Texas. There are four notes to Munro about Cavafy's poem and payment.

[26] Unpublished letter at King's College, Cambridge, dated 14 April 1924.

essay for the *Athenaeum*, reprinted that year in the English Alexandrian newspaper the *Egyptian Gazette* and in the Greek Alexandrian *Grammata*, and later included in *Pharos and Pharillon.* Cavafy liked this work very much indeed and, in answer to a question from Forster, said that the novelist had a good sense of his poetry. Although often a poor correspondent who had to be joked and cajoled into writing, Cavafy was clearly grateful for help from his well-known friend. We sense that both men knew that Forster stood at the center of a literary empire while Cavafy remained in a diaspora, but each also held what was more important: a belief in his own art and in his friend's. With characteristic modesty Forster once said of Cavafy, I "did a little to spread his fame. It was about the best thing I did."[27]

Forster's essays tell us much about both men. *Pharos and Pharillon, Alexandria,* and *A Passage to India* show the poet's influence on Forster. But it is an early letter, at which we shall look in a moment, that gives us the richest sense of the flavor of their friendship. Forster clearly did not share Cavafy's vision of a link between past and present Alexandria based upon a refined decadence. His city is fairly free from "sin" and, in some sense, at least in his formal works, from sexuality. But Forster had an important love affair in Alexandria. Probably his first. Evert Barger, whose mother was an intimate friend of Forster, speaks of letters discussing "an agonized relationship with a young man in Alexandria . . . over which his biographer must decide whether or not to draw the veil of discretion."[28] Edward Carpenter, to whom Mrs. Barger lent a photograph of Forster's lover, writes "But what a pleasure to see a real face after the milk & water mongrelly things one sees here! It was a literal refreshment to me. Those eyes—I know so

[27] "C. P. Cavafy: 1863-1933," *Umbrella*, 1 (October 1958), 5-7.

[28] "Memories of Morgan," *The New York Times Book Review*, 16 August 1970, p. 32.

well what they mean, and I think you do too, *now*! . . . I really believe you don't want to come home. . . ."[29] With more reserve Lytton Strachey wonders whether Forster exaggerates the romance, adding: "But I don't know: Romance can hardly be exaggerated."[30] The relationship to which they all refer was clearly important to Forster, as was his contact with Cavafy, in whose life and work homosexuality was openly viewed.

Forster's letter seems to deal with a time when he had found some sexual fulfillment, although this is not stated explicitly and is certainly less important than the affection and seriousness which permeates the whole. Forster's jolly mask is down. He is sharing with a friend, who is depressed and plagued by doubts he connects with depravity, the friend who was to become Forster's guide through Alexandria.

British Red Cross Convalescent
Hospital No 7
Montazah
1-7-17 *Alexandria*

Dear Cavafy,

Valassopoulo was over this afternoon and told me that since I saw you something has occurred that has made you very unhappy; that you believed [the artist (?)] must be depraved: and that you were willing he should tell the above to your friends. It made me want to write to you at once. . . .

Of late I have been happier than usual myself. And have accepted my good luck with thankfulness and without reservation. But I suspect that at the bottom of one's soul one craves not happiness but peace. I seem to see this when the tide is flowing strongly neither way—I mean when I am disturbed by no great pre-

[29] Letter dated 13 March 1918, among the unpublished Forster papers at King's.

[30] Unpublished letter, dated 24 May 1917, at King's.

dominance of either joy or sorrow. I don't write this to console you—consolation is a very inferior article which can only be exchanged between people who are not being quite straight with one another. Only there does seem something fundamental in man that is unhappy perhaps, but not with these surface unhap[p]inesses, and that finds its repose not in fruition but in creation. The peace that passeth all understanding is the peace at the heart of a storm. In other words—in extreme other words!—you will go on writing, I believe.

V. and I discussed depravity a little, but not to much effect. He seemed to connect it with passion to which it is (for me) the absolute antithesis. I am not even sure that I connect it with curiosity even, though if it exists at all it exists as something *solid*—and would consequently not be a particularly useful ingredient to the artist. That is the only thing I can tell you about depravity—its temperature. It has nothing to do with material. No action, no thought is per se depraved.

These two paragraphs are very muddleheaded and I shall hardly clear them by telling you that in each I have thought of Dante: first of his remarks that the Herald Angels promised not happiness but peace; secondly of the centre of his Hell, which was ice, not fire.

. . . I shall come and see you as soon as I return. This letter does not—then or now—expect an answer. It is only to remind you that among your many friends you have one on the edge of your life in me.

E.M. FORSTER

The Passage to India: Forster's Alexandria

E. M. Forster worked with the Red Cross in Alexandria from November 1915 until January 1919.

I arrived there in the autumn of 1915 in a slightly heroic mood. A Turkish invasion was threatened, and although

> a civilian I might find myself in the battle line. The threat passed and my mood changed. What had begun as an outpost turned into something suspiciously like a funk-hole, and I stuck in it for over three years, visiting hospitals, collecting information, and writing reports. "You are such a wonderful sticker," a detestable Red Cross colonel once said to me scathingly. I was; and I dared not retort that it takes both stickers and climbers to make a world. (A, xv)

Forster works hard to convince us that he is a little man. We forget that his friendships were scattered among the major talents of his day and remember that he was said to look like the man who came to wind the clocks. His sticker sounds awfully like the historians Forster describes in "Consolations of History," an essay written in 1920.

> It is pleasant to be transferred from an office where one is afraid of a sergeant-major into an office where one can intimidate generals, and perhaps this is why History is so attractive to the more timid amongst us. We can recover self-confidence by snubbing the dead. The captains and the kings depart at our slightest censure, while as for the "host of minor officials" who cumber court and camp, we heed them not, although in actual life they entirely block our social horizon. . . . Difficult to realize that the past was once the present, and that, transferred to it, one would be just the same little worm as today, unimportant, parasitic, nervous, occupied with trifles, unable to go anywhere or alter anything, friendly only with the obscure, and only at ease with the dead.
>
> If only the sense of actuality can be lulled—and it sleeps forever in most historians—there is no passion that cannot be gratified in the past. (AH, 167)

Cavafy, whose historical sense Forster so greatly admired, clearly never lulled his "sense of actuality." In his poems the past *is* the present. Perhaps because he was one of them, his vision rests precisely on that "host of minor officials" who themselves view the events of history at a peculiar slant. But what of Forster?

Lionel Trilling feels that the "persistent fault of taste" which Forster characterizes so accurately in "Consolations of History" is exactly what's wrong with almost all Forster's historical sketches. *Alexandria* is given minor praise as "scholarly, attractive and efficient," but the history collected in *Abinger Harvest* and *Pharos and Pharillon* has for Trilling an "archness," a "lofty whimsicality" that destroys. "Under Forster's implacable gentleness, the past becomes what it should never be, quaint, harmless and ridiculous."[31] This is certainly true of moments in Forster's essays—in the description of powerful members of Ptolemy V's court, "Œanthe, . . . an elderly but accomplished woman who knew how to shampoo" and "the wife of a forage contractor who would say to the King: 'Here, Daddy, drink this' "; (PP, 29) or in the portrait of Jews traveling First in "Philo's Little Trip," a piece that almost offends as much as Lytton Strachey's "Dizzy."[32]

Forster *can* become coy in his historical essays. But the lofty whimsicality, the preciousness, is also present at times in essays set in contemporary situations (the hashish den in Alexandria is antiseptic and amusing but as much of a lie as Durrell's overactive brothels), and in his early fiction the classical world is more often than not divorced from a "sense of actuality."

Trilling is, on the whole, wrong about the historical es-

[31] *E. M. Forster*, pp. 118-119. In a footnote Trilling adds: "The historical part of the book is a model of popularization without condescension. Especially notable are the lucid pages on the Alexandrian mystics; the exposition of Plotinus has the quality of creative insight into mystical thought that makes *A Passage to India* so remarkable."

[32] In *Biographical Essays* (London: Chatto and Windus, 1960), p. 264. "The absurd Jew-boy, who set out to conquer the world, reached his destination. . . . After a lifetime of relentless egotism, he found himself at last old, hideous, battered, widowed, solitary, diseased, but Prime Minister of England."

says. Many are strange and wonderful tales peering at us around corners we had not noticed. It is important to see that peculiar angle of vision Forster assumes in viewing history, to note how it moves at different points in Forster's life. Important not only because this enhances our enjoyment of the essays themselves but because it helps us understand how history gave Forster's fiction a substance and an attention to detail from which it benefited immeasurably.

The Early Historical Essays

Between 1903 and 1905 Forster wrote several historical pieces that show the influence of his interest and travels in Italy and Greece. Even in the first—"Malconia Shops" (1903)—we can see why Forster and Cavafy must become friends if they should meet. How close to the poet who blows out his lamp to meet Kaisarion in the dark Forster is here, in spite of the comic tone! Cavafy reads inscriptions, studies coins, and lets his imagination surround them, creating personalities and poems. Forster sees the Cista Ficoroniana in Rome's Kirchner Museum, reads its inscription, and around it builds a tale about Dindia Malconia, an Etruscan lady who bought a bronze toilet case for her daughter. Next he examines the figures on the piece. "Two —the most beautiful figures of the whole composition— are standing together, leaning on their spears, with the knowledge that they have passed through one more labour in company." We see, almost with the eye of Cavafy's sculptors, lovers.

Forster shares Cavafy's interest in little-known ancient places like "Cnidus," and scarcely remembered historical figures like Girolamo Cardano ("we are concerned with Cardan's character, rather than with his achievements" [AH, 197]). But it is in the subject of another sketch, "Gemistus Pletho," that we are most clearly reminded of the poet for, like Cavafy, Forster is fascinated by a Byzantine who rejects contemporary faiths, seeking "his religion among the half-forgotten rites of ancient Greece." (AH,

180) Like Cavafy, Forster is drawn to a man who, while thoroughly muddling Plato, Aristotle, and the classical household of gods, hears strains of an ancient spirit.

G. D. Klingopulos, in an important essay, "E. M. Forster's Sense of History: and Cavafy,"[33] writes about the essential change in Forster's Hellenism that develops as a result of his contact with Cavafy, a movement from an earlier "idealising sort in which the ancient world is invoked as a standard to set off the deficiencies of modern civilization," "a nostalgia for blessed simplicity," to a fallibly human, peculiar Hellenism, a Cavafian Hellenism. Certainly, as we have seen earlier, the "Public School Greece" that Forster himself belittles in an essay on Cavafy (PP, 94) was very much a part of his early fiction, whether in the dreams of Mr. Lucas or of Maurice.

I'm not sure that I agree with Klingopulos when he says that "the vision of the classical world which Mr. Forster attributes to George Gemistus is the vision of the earlier Forster," for I feel that even the early historical essays set in antiquity are grounded in the actual in a way that the fiction is not. But I do know that there was a change in the Hellenism of Forster's historical essays, a change profoundly influenced by Cavafy and Alexandria—affecting the form of these essays as much as their content, creating *Pharos and Pharillon.*

Alexandria Vignettes

Forster wrote nothing in 1916, but in August of 1917, two years after his last published piece, he began writing articles for *The Egyptian Mail,* signing them "Pharos." Several went under the title "Alexandria Vignettes." Many of the best—and most Cavafian—vignettes written for the Anglo-Egyptian newspaper and later, when Forster had returned to England, for the *Athenaeum* were collected and published in 1923 as *Pharos and Pharillon.* Before looking at those essays we should examine some of the articles never

[33] *Essays in Criticism,* VIII (1958), 156-165.

republished, for many are very fine indeed, telling us much about Forster and, in themselves, a pleasure to read. They are unfortunately all but hidden in the newspaper collection of the British Library.[34]

Pharos roamed widely, tasting wonders of the modern world, the world of the machine. "Personally I hate it," Forster said years later. (TC, 278) Here we see his initial reactions to new sights, like a map come alive: "And this was flying, this was what scientists had aimed at and poets dreamed of for centuries. Even Shelley never flew." He is impressed with the beauty of the earth and describes the journey in great and amusing detail ("I was exactly frightened now") but comes back in the end to those who had once guessed at the view, those with whom, one suspects, he would have liked to share the ride: "Dante guessed better than Shelley, I find—no doubt because he had a saner conception of space."

Pharos looks at photographs, bemoaning the fact that he is never shown studies of "the little muddles and messes of the modern street" instead of false visions: harems and pyramids, or pictures "in a second album from under the

[34] The order of the articles that were written for *The Egyptian Mail* and *not* included in *Pharos and Pharillon* is: "Diana's Dilemma" (26 August 1917), about films; "Sunday Music" (2 September 1917); "A Musician in Egypt" (21 October 1917); "The Scallies" (18 November 1917), reprinted in *Abinger Harvest*; "XXth Century Alexandria: the New Quay" (2 December 1917); "Gippo English" (16 December 1917); "Handel in Egypt" (6 January 1918); "Photographic Egypt" (13 January 1918); "John McNeill has Come: Impressions of a Meeting" (10 February 1918), about a preacher with no historical imagination addressing the troops; "Higher Aspects" (5 May 1918), on flying; "The Modern Sons of the Pharaohs: Second Notice" (18 August 1918), a review of a work by S. H. Leeder (the review is, I believe, unavailable, copies of the newspaper for that date seem to have been lost); "Canopus, Menouthis, Aboukir" (29 December 1918), the review of a work by J. Faivre; "Army English" (12 January 1919); "England's Honour (Being Extracts from the Diary of Mme. Kyriakidis, Ramleh)" (26 January 1919). All articles are on page 2 of the Sunday edition of *The Egyptian Mail.*

counter" (where he might have seen the photograph in Cavafy's poem). Off to the movies, he is once again disappointed by technology's application to art, although unwilling, it seems, to imagine the form's possibilities. Where film is concerned, he is as he proclaims himself, "irredeemably a prig." Before his eyes floats the face of Diana, Myra, or Soava—"the same light woman among the same heavy furniture"—"like some big pale whale." Again he seeks solace in the street and, just as surely, in the mystic dimensions of prose:

> A fruit shop was opposite; it rose from the darkness as a square of light, no larger than a cinema-screen, but oranges, and cucumbers, bananas and apricots glowed in it, like jewels, or piled in the foreground stood in black relief against the radiance, where an Arab moved like a magician. The name of this shop in Greek, is "The Garden of the Hesperides," and the fruiterer, his grasp of French not being equal to mine, has translated it as "Le Jardin des Soirées." He may call it what he will, he has reminded one customer that life can be more beautiful and amusing than art—an agreeable reminder. Diana's dilemma is so dull. That is its greatest defeat. It is duller than life. It is incidentally false but fundamentally dull. A fruit shop beats it as poetry. . . .

Language shaped even the odd corners of life. But a new force was in the air. War brought technology, bureaucracy, and "Army English." Pharos listens. When remembering direct speech and hospitality, he says wistfully, "That's the way we used to write and behave before the war purged us." Now language reflects the "edict of the Immanent Will," even more sublime than the imperative: "The numerous convalescent officers at present to be seen perambulating Cherif Pacha St. in blue bands will thus be obviated."

Pharos meets another new language as well: "Gippo English" on shop signs—"Whose for a feed at the old Angleterre. / A fee you know will carry you fare"—or spoken by those around him—"Yes, yes come here Bulkeley and Glymenopoulo," said the old man indicating the tram stops. He notes that this innocent, exuberant language, the result of a contact between peoples, was slowly destroyed by the condescension accompanying war. Egyptians knew they were being laughed at and stopped trying. Nouns were reduced to "Johnny" and verbs to "finish." "Gippo English has lost the spring of its youth for ever. As the cabman remarked of his horse, 'No finish, but yes finish moving.' "

Pharos listens to music as well as to speech. Or he tries to listen. He goes to an inaudible concert of "Sunday Music" at San Stephano, Beethoven accompanied by the chatter that so deeply offends Harriet in *Where Angels Fear to Tread.*

He *does* hear the new composition of a "Musician in Egypt" and, in this important essay, comments on Levantine Egypt—"a civilisation of eclecticism and of exiles"—and its art.

> It is not a heroic talent, but we do not live on heroic soil, nor, with all respect to the great war, in a heroic age. We are exiled here in Egypt for the purpose of doing various little job[b]s—eggs cotton, onions, administration and so on—and out of a population of exiled little jobbers it is impossible that a heroic art should be raised. Michelangelo, Shakespeare, Beethoven, Tolstoy—they must in the nature of things spring from a less cosmopolitan society. But what coastal Egypt can do and what from time to time it has done is to produce eclectic artists, who look for their inspiration to Europe. In the days of the Ptolemies they looked to Sicily and Greece, in the days of St. Athanasius to Byzantium, in the 19th century it seemed they would look to France. But there was always this straining of the eyes beyond the sea, always this turning away from Africa, the vast, the formless, the helpless and unhelpful, the pachyderm.

Forster might have been describing Cavafy instead of the composer Enrico Terni, except that the poet made eclecticism indigenous to his landscape; he let the spirit of place take over, grounding his art in its narrow strip of soil. His cosmopolitan world, peopled by exiled little jobbers is, as Forster suggests, a mirror of its age, of our age. But Cavafy created a whole larger than its parts: his eyes strained beyond the sea and then came home again, to Alexandria.

Pharos listens to Handel's Messiah as well, hearing as he does the problems, the characteristics of the English voice and, we might add, of Forster's own. When Forster wrote to Cavafy about the *Athenaeum*, the *Criterion*, or the Hogarth Press, it was to suggest that the poet would, in their pages, be read "by those who are capable of appreciating you." All sorts of men and women picked up *The Egyptian Mail* on a Sunday afternoon in 1918, and it is to Forster's credit that, although the subjects of his articles are directed to a wide audience, he never condescends, nor does he placate the officers and soldiers, the ladies and the nannies in whose company war placed him. The obverse is true. Complacency is pricked on all counts, which is why these pieces seem queer amidst the fluid, pleasant prose that, in the pages of the *Egyptian Mail*, surround them.

Of all these little-known articles, "Handel in Egypt" is the queerest and most beautiful. Rhythm, expansion: music was the other art that Forster loved most and found closest to the novel. Like the repetitive "little phrase" he much admires in Proust, music haunts his novels, whether it is Lucy's piano-playing, Beethoven's Fifth, or Tchaikovsky's "Pathetique." No wonder, then, that here he uses the "Messiah" to describe the Englishman's engaging—and dangerous—optimism.

"Few Englishmen can listen to Handel's music unmoved" he begins. "We forget that Handel was not an Englishman, and indeed yielded to the temptation to belong to quite another nation. . . . And we remember how in our childhood the village choir did 'an anthem out of Handel' at Christmas, or how Uncle James and Aunt Margaret took us up to London to hear 'Handel done really properly' at the Albert Hall. What expeditions those were! What a crush and how the mackintoshes and umbrellas smelt!" Forster goes on to describe the expedition and the music as it soared "to the heights not of the Albert Hall but of Heaven."

> 'But thou didst not leave his soul in Hell' came the voice, 'neither suffer thy Holy One to see corruption. But thou didst not leave his soul in Hell.' It was sentimental and middle class, but when did middle class sentimentality come nearer to great art than in the Messiah.

But Handel is in Egypt now, a fish out of water. Pharos wonders what the clever Levantines in this Alexandrian church audience think of his song. "It must have seemed to them so formless and provincial."

> As the Oriental grows thoughtful he grows sad. . . . But as the Englishman grows thoughtful he grows hopeful—it is the main source of his strength. And Handel . . . expresses as no other musician can an Englishman's hopefulness and his sentimental belief in an eternal home.

The Englishman finds in Handel "a balm for the incurable wound of the world," a balm that is particularly poignant "in Egypt and at the close of another year of war." Forster does not view his countryman as an outsider. He cannot, for he too has, at times, risked truth for hope, for the truly appealing comforts of home. But Forster has also noticed those musical, intelligent Levantines whose "clever dark heads . . . showed up here and there in the acquiescent audience like notes of interrogation," and unlike some of the countrymen about whom he writes, he will hear new sounds.

Pharos and Pharillon: *Cavafian Tales*

Those essays that Forster wished to reach a wider audience were collected as *Pharos and Pharillon.* The book—divided into two parts: *Pharos* ancient, and *Pharillon*, modern history—travels through Alexandria chronologically and, like Cavafy's poetry, although composed of autonomous sketches, forms a whole. Forster sets the geographical scene and then moves on to tales about Alexander, the Ptolemies, and the religious leaders of the city from Philo through "Timothy Whitebonnet." In *Pharillon* he begins again where Alexandria did, at the end of the eighteenth century. Here we meet the "somewhat spiteful Mrs. Eliza Fay." We are introduced to contemporary Alexandria and her surroundings, and finally to her poet Cavafy.[35]

The straightforward chronology is balanced by Cavafy's "The God Abandons Antony," which divides the book,[36] and the differing moods and subject matter of the separate anecdotes, now about political power, now bigotry and religion, now about gossip, the evils of industrialization, or poetry. That strange mixture, as D. J. Enright notes, is characteristic of the city around which the essays grew.[37]

[35] The order of the essays as they were written and published in *The Egyptian Mail* is "The Den" (30 December 1917), "Cotton from the Outside" (3 February 1918); "Solitary Place" (10 March 1918); "The Return from Siwa" (14 July 1918); "Lunch at the Bishops" (31 July 1918: this was to become Part I of "St. Athanasius"), "Epiphany" (6 October 1918). And in *The Athenaeum*: "The Poetry of C. P. Cavafy" (23 April 1919); "St. Athanasius II" (23 May 1919); "Timothy Cat and Timothy Whitebonnet" (25 July 1919); "Clement of Alexandria" (8 August 1919); and "Pharos" (12 December 1919).

[36] In a letter to Cavafy (dated 31 December 1922, in the unpublished papers at King's) Forster excitedly tells his friend about the organization of his book and about how it, like *Alexandria*, will be divided by Cavafy's poem. After giving Cavafy the chronology of essays, he writes: "—I didn't mean to inflict all of this on you when I started. Don't mention it (i.e., the details) to anyone, for the chief point of my tiring work goes to if it ceases to be a surprise."

[37] "A Passage to Alexandria," *A Garland for E. M. Forster*, ed. H. H. Anniah Gowda (Mysore, India: The Literary Half-Yearly, 1969), p. 49.

There are those who would agree with Trilling's evaluation of *Pharos and Pharillon.* Others, like Rose Macaulay, seem to enjoy the essays just where this reader finds them irritating—"we like the gay, caressing and titillating candles of comedy to light for us the sawdusty antic by-ways of history."[38] D. H. Lawrence's comments, given to Forster in a letter, are as usual egocentric, and perceptive: "Thank you for Pharos and Pharillon, which I have read. Sad as ever, like a lost soul calling Icabod. But I prefer the sadness to the Stracheyism. To me you are the last Englishman. And I am the one after that."[39]

But there is one review, a 1923 review in the *Times Literary Supplement*, that captures much of the "shimmering magic that dances" on the pages of *Pharos and Pharillon:*

> The fortune of war cast Mr. Forster upon Alexandria, and Alexandria cast her spell upon him. We know this, because he has been able to communicate it to us, and to make us feel what in our minds we know, that only this debatable ground, where Greece and Asia strove for harmony and the human sought to include the infinite, could contain the music by which the god Hercules bade farewell to Antony. . . . So the story of Alexandria, seen (or it may be refracted) through Mr. Forster's mind, becomes a manifestation of himself. Here is a world of events that he can comfortably inhabit; in this garment the very tricks of his mind can be accommodated. He was made for it and it for him—for his friend the Alexandrian poet, Cavafy, also, in whose diaphanous verses, as in Mr. Forster's prose, the outward incoherence of Alexandria that is and was seems refracted into unity.

[38] *The Writings of E. M. Forster* (London: Hogarth Press, 1938), p. 148.

[39] Letter dated 19 February 1924, among the Forster papers at King's. Copies of the unpublished Forster-Lawrence correspondence are also available at The Humanities Research Center, Austin, Texas.

The reviewer goes on to note the strange angle from which both writers view the world, a vision, he feels, that will be deplored by right-minded, straight-thinking people.

> . . . they will never understand how much of the new and true these crooked people see. . . . To this dubious race Mr. Forster indisputably belongs. Being a dubious character, he goes off to a dubious city, to that portion of the inhabited world where there is most obviously a bend in the spiritual dimension . . . to a tense and exciting "field" (as the physicists would call it) where the atmosphere is preternaturally keen and there is a lucid confusion of the categories. At this point a spinning eddy marks the convergence of two worlds, and in the vortex contradictions are reconciled. It is nothing less than a crack in the human universe. Mr. Forster wanders off to put his ear to it. He finds Mr. Cavafy already engaged in the enterprise. So they listen together. . . .

Answering the objection that any spot might have excited Forster's crooked vision and that in fact Forster has listened and looked oddly before, the reviewer remarks:

> Certainly he has shown an inclination that way before. That is why we remember his former books. They were not exactly good books, sometimes they were almost childish books, but they were in parts peculiar. But "Pharos and Pharillon"—except for one essay which recalls Mr. Strachey—is wholly peculiar and wholly good. Therefore we conclude that in Alexandria Mr. Forster found a spiritual home; the queer fish found it easier to breathe in those suspiciously crystalline waters. Whether he knew what had befallen him the moment he arrived there, or whether it was his encounter with Mr. Cavafy and his recognition of him as a fellow-exile from the world of things which simply are what they are called—no matter which of these encouraged him

to expand his own idiosyncrasy in the favouring air, it is certain that Mr. Forster has never yet been so convincingly himself or so manifestly different from his fellow writers.

Yes, we must look for the cause in Alexandria. . . . In that same curious city, we feel, Mr. Forster first gained the courage of his own vision, and first dared to venture himself wholly into "a field" that is by right his own. . . .[40]

It is a fine review, and we take particular pleasure in reading a happy letter Forster wrote to Cavafy about it and about *Pharos and Pharillon:*

My Dear Cavafy

You are a bad poet. I have written to you and sent you, two copies of the book and a message via Valassapoulo. Do I get a word in reply? Not one word. You really must answer this. For things are rather exciting. The book has had a great success for a book of its type, 900 copies have been sold in 6 weeks, we are rushing out a second edition; a review of over a column in the Times Literary Supplement, long reviews in the Nation, the New Statesman, The Daily Telegraph and so on. And the things that have attracted most attention in it are your poems. The reviewers have in some [cases?] quoted them in full, and I have had private letters—e.g. from Siegfried Sassoon—for more of them and for more about you. And now I come to the exciting point. I was at Chatto and Windus' the other day—they are one of our leading publishers—and they began asking me about you, and what's more if your poems couldn't be translated. . . .

Forster goes on to discuss the possibility of getting Cavafy's poems published in England and then concludes his letter:

[40] The *Times Literary Supplement,* 31 May 1923, p. 369.

Do you want to see some of the reviews? If you will be a good poet instead of a bad one I will lend you them. The Times (by Middleton Murry I fancy, tho its unsigned) is really rather beautiful—semi mystic, semi humorous, and [illegible word] has 'got' us rather well.
It sold any how like hot cakes.

Your expectant friend
E. M. FORSTER[41]

The book that sold like hot cakes was peculiar. Some have said the essays are all like those of Strachey, others that Forster is imitating Theocritos, but I think D. J. Enright has at least half the story when he writes: "Forster shows himself in this book a sort of genteel Cavafy, a sweeter-natured observer of the scene, though some of the sweetness may be connected with the fact that he is not really involved, a Cavafy applying himself to a *Times* third leader, . . .[42] Enright doesn't elaborate, and Forster is remote only in essays like "Timothy the Cat and Timothy Whitebonnet" or "Cotton from the Outside." Still, "a sort of genteel Cavafy." Cavafy turns history into poetry, and, as we shall see when we look at individual tales, in *Pharos and Pharillon* Forster uses many Cavafian techniques to create a form that moves between the short story and the historical sketch.

In a letter to the editor of the *Athenaeum*, written in 1920, Forster answered a critic of Herbert Read's "Beyle and Byron"—a sketch written in dialogue imagining a conversation between the two men.

Sir, —In his comments on Mr. Herbert Read's article has not Mr. del Re mistaken its aim? Mr. Read was surely not attempting history, but an imaginative sketch, and, whatever be the value of this type of composition, it is a type that follows its own artistic laws.

[41] Letter dated 6 July 1923. In the unpublished Forster papers at King's.

[42] "A Passage to Alexandria," p. 49.

> To acknowledge one's sources—imperative in history—would be pedantry here. And though accuracy of fact remains important, it does become of secondary importance. Of primary importance is the internal life; the sketch must be alive within itself, and here it seemed to me, Mr. Read was entirely successful. . . .[43]

Forster might have been describing his own work, for he too moves beyond accuracy of fact in capturing the internal life of Alexander, Clement of Alexandria, or St. Athanasios, just as Cavafy captures his Antony or Julian. Strachey and other biographical essayists work in a similar genre. But Forster, in his very best sketches, is closer to the poet Cavafy, because both are interested in more than characterization. Both glimpse life through the very particular eyes of one human soul grounded in his own soil, at a peculiar —although not necessarily spectacular—moment in time. They see the irony that is the distance between that soul's vision and ours. A moment in time and space. History as fiction.

"Epiphany," (PP, 29-32) told almost as if it were a grim fairy tale—with the characters identified historically only in the last sentence—has one vibrant Cavafian character. The queen, like Anna Komnina, is a strong woman who craves power. At her husband's death:

> She knew what to do quite well. She was now Regent, and her first act was to dismiss the ministry. Moreover, since he was now four years old, her son no longer required a nurse. The old heroic feelings came back to her. Life seemed worth living again. She returned to her apartments full of exaltation. She entered them. As she did so, the curtains, which had been soaked with inflammable oil in her absence, burst into flame. She

[43] *The Athenaeum*, No. 4717, 24 September 1920, p. 419.

> tried to retire. The doors had been locked behind her, and she was burnt to death.

"The old heroic feelings came back to her." "Epiphany" fails because, although short, it lacks focus, and because it is often cute. But still we have this momentary glance at an Alexandrian, and the Cavafian line.

"That afternoon was one of comparative calm for the infant Church." With this sentence Forster begins "St. Athanasius,"[44] and in the first part of the essay we can most clearly see the Cavafian vision Forster adopts and makes his own. The tale will concern the destiny of Christianity and, more importantly, the loss of harmony and continuity that had characterized Alexandria and made her a spiritual city. The essay preceding "St. Athanasius" in *Pharos* is about Clement of Alexandria, an earlier church father. It closes magically:

> He lived in a period of transition, and in Alexandria. And in that curious city, which had never been young and hoped never to grow old, conciliation must have seemed more possible than elsewhere, and the graciousness of Greece not quite incompatible with the Grace of God. (PP, 42)

All this is to be shattered. But the seeds of that monumental destruction shoot up unnoticed, on an ordinary summer day. "What lovely weather! The month was June, and the beacon of smoke that rose from the summit of the *Pharos* was inclined over Alexandria by a northerly wind."

We enter the thoughts of Alexander, Bishop of Alexan-

[44] The essay, the fifth in the collection, is divided into two parts in *Pharos*. The first appeared in *The Egyptian Mail* in July 1918 as "Lunch at the Bishops." It is on pages 43-46 in *Pharos and Pharillon*. Part II was first published in *The Athenaeum* the following year (23 May 1919).

dria, as he waits for some clergymen whom he has invited to lunch and absent-mindedly watches a few poor boys play on the beach. His thoughts return to the direction of Christianity, to his successor, and to Constantine who "so easily got mixed." Suddenly: "Stop! Stop! Boys will be boys, but there are limits. They were playing at Baptism now, and the sportive youth [their leader] was in the act of pouring some of the harbour water over two other Gippoes." The Bishop is diverted, and alarmed, for he has seen the boy "performing accurately what he had no right to perform . . . and Heaven alone knew the theological consequences."

But the skinny little heathen, summoned by the great man, wins the cleric's favor. "Taken into the Bishop's house, he became his pupil, his deacon, his coadjutor, his successor in the see, and finally a saint and a doctor of the Church: he is St. Athanasius." The end of tolerance, the death of a city, wait in the wings, while an old man smiles on a lovely morning in June, in Alexandria.

The secret sense of loss, the tension between the earth-shaking and the ordinary, the irony inherent in that tension, all are of course basic to Cavafy's historical poems, as is the dramatic frame, the situation grounded in time and space, and the impressionistic point of view, the third-person–first person narration that allows us to be, at the same time, both in and outside a character. All these forces come together for Forster, and nowhere more beautifully than in the second essay in *Pharos*: "The Return from Siwa." (PP, 25-29)

Forster begins with a picture of Alexander the Great as he founds his city, full of a desire to spread the Hellenism he had adopted. We are being given some straight historical background, when suddenly the action starts. Alexander leaves his city, setting off into the desert with a few friends.

> It was summer. The waters of Lake Mariout, more copious then than now, spread fertility for a space. Leaving their zone, he struck south, over the limestone hills,

> and lost sight of civilization whether of the Hellenic or non-Hellenic type. Around him little flat pebbles shimmered and danced in the heat, gazelles stared, and pieces of sky slopped into the sand. . . .

At the oasis of Siwa he meets the priest whose bad Greek may have been responsible for a salute in which Alexander was called the Son of God. But even if an ignorant mistake, "A scare he did get—a fright, a psychic experience, a vision, a 'turn' " which altered his focus moving it from Greece to the whole. He

> flung himself again, but in new spirit, against the might of Persia. He fought her as a lover now. He wanted not to convert but to harmonize, and conceived himself as the divine and impartial ruler beneath whom harmony shall proceed. That way lies madness. Persia fell. Then it was the turn of India. . . .

But for Forster the madness makes Alexander "more lovable now than before. He has caught, by the unintellectual way, a glimpse of something great, if dangerous, and that glimpse came to him first in the recesses of the Siwan Oasis." Forster's imagination is held by the man. And in a passage that immediately brings his last novel to mind Forster wanders on to witness Alexander face death in the summerhouse at Babylon:

> . . . did it seem to him as after all but the crown of his smaller quests? He had tried to lead Greece, then he had tried to lead mankind. He had succeeded in both. But was the universe also friendly, was it also in trouble, was it calling on him, on him, for his help and his love? The priest of Amen had addressed him as "Son of God". What exactly did the compliment mean? Was it explicable this side of the grave?

Writing almost ten years later, Forster hears echoes of that questioning. He distinguishes between the two mythological aspects of the novel: fantasy, which invokes "all that is medieval this side of the grave" and prophecy, an unuttered invocation "to whatever transcends our abilities, even when it is human passion that transcends them, to the deities of India, Greece, Scandinavia and Judea, to all that is medieval beyond the grave and to Lucifer son of the morning." (AN, 110)

Alexandria: *A Passage, a Bridge*

> That the question has ever been not only asked but seriously debated, whether History was an art, is certainly one of the curiosities of human ineptitude. What else can it possibly be? . . . Facts relating to the past, when they are collected without art, are compilations; and compilations, no doubt, may be useful; but they are no more History than butter, eggs, salt and herbs are an omelette. . . .[45]

Alexandria: A History and a Guide is Forster's single attempt at writing an extended history. It is certainly not a compilation. In the Conclusion to *Pharos and Pharillon*, Forster notes that "A serious history of Alexandria has yet to be written. . . . After the fashion of a pageant it might marshal the activities of two thousand two hundred and fifty years." The Preface to *Alexandria* suggests that he is writing just such a work.[46] In *Pharos* Forster goes on to say "But unlike a pageant it would have to conclude dully. Alas! The modern city calls for no enthusiastic comment. . . . Menelaus accordingly leads the Alexandrian pageant with solid tread, cottonbrokers conclude it; the intermediate space is thronged with phantoms, noiseless, insubstantial,

[45] Lytton Strachey, "Gibbon," *Portraits in Miniature and Other Essays* (London: Chatto and Windus, 1931), p. 160.

[46] "The 'History' attempts (after the fashion of a pageant) to marshal the activities of Alexandria during the two thousand two hundred and fifty years of her existence." The dates of publication for *Pharos and Pharillon* and *Alexandria* do not clearly indicate when either of these statements were written.

innumerable, but not without interest for the historian." (PP, 99) How lucky that the author of *Maurice*, the author of *Howards End*, became fascinated by a city whose story ends "dully." Alexandria's history moves toward shiftless, muted defeat again and again.

Like *Pharos, Alexandria* is full of wonderful character sketches. Forster is typically less interested in facts than in internal life ("Ptolemy was no soaring idealist. He desired neither to Hellenise nor to harmonise it. But he was no cynic either." [A, 13] "The second Ptolemy . . . was a more pretentious person than his father." [A, 16]). And, like Cavafy, Forster seems always caught by those individuals whom one does not quite expect.

Alexandria's heroes, Menelaus, "Immortal, yet somehow or other unsatisfactory," (PP, 99) the Ptolemies, or Alexander do not stay with us as forcefully as do her "heavies," the emperor who lost Egypt, Heraklios—an able, sensitive leader, often overwhelmed by depression—and Amr, the general who won Alexandria and thereby caused the destruction of the city. Forster likes Amr. "He was an administrator, a delightful companion, and a poet—one of the ablest and most charming men that Islam ever produced." (A, 60) And telling us of Amr's dying words, like the imagined thoughts of a dying Alexander in *Pharos*, he involves us in some of the magic we are again to meet in *Passage to India.*

But *Alexandria* is not only an impressionistic account of character. Although grounded in generalized theories about human nature and the Alexandrian soul—"no impartial book but an Intelligent Tourist's Guide to Humanism"[47]—it is also astoundingly thorough. Like Cavafy, who could tell you the probable cost of Kaisarion's pink silk, Forster combines the patience of the "sticker" with the artist's love for the texture of detail.

[47] Wilfred Stone, *The Cave and the Mountain: A Study of E. M. Forster* (Stanford, California: Stanford University Press, 1966), p. 293.

He forces us to look hard at old maps, to understand that "less is more," to see that Eratosthenes built and Claudius Ptolemy defied the scientific spirit. Forster makes us understand, a little, the importance of science in third-century B.C. Alexandria:

> (from this point of view) the greatest period that civilization has ever known—greater even than the nineteenth century A.D. It did not bring happiness or wisdom: science never does. But it explored the physical universe and harnessed many powers for our use.
>
> (A, 41)

And here too he surprises—for, caught in the excitement of discovery, he makes us relive the achievements of Eratosthenes, of Euclid, Aristarchos of Samos, and Erasistratos, as imaginative acts.

Forster is thorough in still another odd way. One of the major concerns in this book, and indeed in all Forster's work, is with the question of what effect war and bureaucracy have upon civilizations and their art. Military machinery produces Army English and stifles Gippo English. It gets in the way of the beautiful. Forster is quick to remind us that "History is too much an affair of armies and kings," showing us how in Theocritos' Fifteenth Idyll his two gossips, "evoked an entire city from the dead and filled its streets with men." (A, 37-38) And yet Forster is fascinated by battles, describing them endlessly. Caesar's little war, Actium, the "Battle of the Nile," the bombardment of Alexandria. We learn every maneuver and think back to the battle of Magnesia, the Achaian League—the surprising importance of war in Cavafy's poetry.

Forster's Alexandria is characterized in many ways—it does not appreciate the pastoral, is not tragic, loves scientific toys and games—but amid the vivid detail one can see that, for Forster, Alexandria has three essential concerns: love; the theological question of how man and God are united; and the physical—and mystical—reality that makes the city a passage to India. The three are irrevocably bound. Emotionally, physically, and spiritually Forster's Alexandria is a bridge, a link.

The form of *Alexandria* is itself concerned with bridges.

> The "History" is written in short sections, and at the end of each section are references to the second part—the "Guide." On these references the chief utility of the book depends, so the reader is begged to take special note of them: they are to help him to link the present and the past. (A, xx)

Thus the reader can move from past to present, learn of the monks who murdered Hypatia and then, touching ground at Wadi Natrun, let spirit of place invade him. Past and present are bridged in yet another way in *Alexandria.* Just as in *Pharos and Pharillon,* Cavafy's "The God Abandons Antony" unites the two sections of this book.

The poem is particularly important here because the story of the lovers is central to *Alexandria.* Forster does not quite give us his own version of the tale, but Cleopatra interests him. (In his detailed guide of the Greco-Roman Museum, we have Forster's comment: "Cabinet D: Alleged portrait in marble of Cleopatra in her declining years. Thin, firmly compressed lips and general expression of severity discredit the theory." [A, 126]). She becomes one of the ways he can show us that Alexandria has always been a city of love.

In an appendix he gives us versions—by Plutarch, Shakespeare, and Dryden—of the famous death scene. He is fascinated by an historical personage who turned living and love into art.

> Voluptuous but watchful, she treated her new lover as she had treated her old. She never bored him, and since grossness means monotony she sharpened his mind to those more delicate delights, where sense verges into

> spirit. Her infinite variety lay in that. She was the last of a secluded and subtle race, she was a flower that Alexandria had taken three hundred years to produce and that eternity cannot wither, and she unfolded herself to a simple but intelligent Roman soldier.
>
> (A, 28)

As we have seen earlier, this beautiful passage captures much that Cavafy and Durrell, as well as Cleopatra, were to bless in Alexandrian love.

In discussing Ptolemaic literature, Forster again touches upon the importance of love. "Darts and hearts, sighs and eyes, breasts and chests, all originated in Alexandria. . . ." "Love as a cruel and wanton boy flits through the literature of Alexandria . . . one tires of him, but it is appropriate that he should have been born under a dynasty that culminates in Cleopatra." (A, 33) Forster avoids the homosexual nature of most of this love poetry. Although he uses Theocritos in *The Longest Journey*, here he does not seem moved by the Anthologists and is, in general, flippant about their work.

In contrast he is drawn to a figure who saw love tragically united to religion, Valentios, the Gnostic whose doctrine held "Sophia" responsible for the world. One of many offshoots of God, she was "least perfect of all. She showed her imperfection not, like Lucifer, by rebelling from God, but by desiring too ardently to be united to him. She fell through love . . . and the universe is formed out of her agony and remorse." (A, 76) This story captures Forster's imagination, as do others revolving around what he saw to be the central Alexandrian love story—the relation between God and man. "How can the human be linked to the divine?" (A, 83) is for Forster *the* Alexandrian question.

> It occurs to those who require God to be loving as well as powerful, . . . and it is the weakness and the strength of Alexandria to have solved it by the conception of a

> link. Her weakness: because she had always to be shifting the link up and down—if she got it too near God it was too far from man, and *vice versa*. Her strength: because she did cling to the idea of love, and much philosophical absurdity, much theological aridity, must be pardoned to those who maintain that the best thing on earth is likely to be the best in heaven.

Islam, with its all-powerful God, did not ask the question and could not be assimilated into the Alexandrian soul. As he lay on a couch in his inland city of Fustat, Amr was asked how an intelligent man felt approaching death. " 'I feel as if the heaven lay close upon the earth and I between the two breathing through the eye of a needle.' " The comparative dimensions of the simile are moving, and, as Forster tells us, the conversation "could never have taken place between two Alexandrians." (A, 63)

All the other religions to reach her shores could be molded by Alexandria. "She did cling to the idea of love." She was a sophisticated city able to add new dimensions—new links—to the more primitive versions of the religions she met. The Alexandrian Jew, unsatisfied with an inaccessible god, created Sophia or Wisdom and then his Logos or Word, the messenger who bridges the gulf between Jehovah and man, just as the Ptolemies had created Serapis from Greek and Egyptian ingredients.

Christianity too changed when it reached Alexandria. Frederick Crews is in part right when, in writing about *Pharos and Pharillon*, he says of Forster:

> Like Gibbon, he looks upon the advent of Christianity as a major catastrophe for civilization, a senseless and small-minded vengeance against the Greek ideal. . . . He repeatedly asserts that Christianity barbarized the areas it conquered . . . and the emphasis is laid in every case upon the triumph of monomania, hypocrisy and antihumanism. As for Christianity's persistent influence

in the modern world, this, says Forster elsewhere, must be "due to the money behind it, rather than its spiritual appeal."[48]

Forster hated a certain kind of Christianity. But it is most interesting that this type of Christianity is what he would have labeled (had he been an American) un-Alexandrian. Alexandria was a growing, fluid, imaginative city. In the "Introduction" to the 1960 edition, Forster wrote of his book: "there are scarcely any national susceptibilities it does not offend. The only locality it shouldn't offend is Alexandria herself, who in the 2,000 years of her life has never taken national susceptibilities too seriously." (A, xvii) And so with religious distinctions.

Hateful Christianity calls other gods false; it is the hard Christianity of the centuries that followed the fourth, of the Egyptian monks who hated Alexandria and would substitute superstition for inquiry. It has a corner on truth.

In sophisticated Alexandria, Forster suggests, Christianity in its earliest stages took a philosophical turn. Christian Alexandrians asked the old question—what is the link? And found the answer in Christ. But for Clement of Alexandria there was another link: "the graciousness of Greece seems in his pages not incompatible with the Grace of God. . . . Only in Alexandria could such a theologian have arisen." (A, 78)

Yes, Christianity could be honored as a religion of love. But it is Plotinus and his neo-Platonism with which Forster really becomes engrossed—and, as we shall see later, here he is embarking on his passage to India. Wilfred Stone has said that *Alexandria* is filled with humor in order to overcome the Miltonic horror of death.[49] And, in a less dramatic tone, Crews has similarly suggested that Forster may be using wit as "a means of coping with dissatisfaction, a com-

[48] *E. M. Forster: The Perils of Humanism* (Princeton: Princeton University Press, 1962), p. 17.

[49] Stone, p. 291.

promise with misgivings that refuse to vanish," with religious misgivings that "lurk behind each of his novels and finally step forward to assume control in *A Passage to India*."[50]

Clearly Forster, who can be so funny, so cutting, about religious righteousness, was captivated by his study of various Alexandrian theologies. And, although one may question his theory of the Alexandrian link—asking whether Judaism and Islam can be best divided on that ground—it is most interesting that the author of *A Passage to India* was involved with such a thesis. Clearly an impulse toward a mystic vision also held its appeal. Not ignorant Coptic mysticism (which was really superstition), but the thoughtful mysticism that held the likes of Plotinus.

The *Enneads* ("Alexandria produced nothing greater" [A, 70]) is of special emotional interest for Forster, who explains its philosophy:

> Not only do all things flow from God; they also strive to return to him; in other words, the whole Universe has an inclination towards good. We are all parts of God, even the stones, though we cannot realise it; and man's goal is to become actually, as he is potentially, divine. Therefore rebirth is permitted . . . and therefore the Mystic Vision is permitted, in order that, even in this existence we may have a glimpse of God. God is oneself, our true self. . . . (A, 71)

Forster goes on to quote directly from a long and wonderful passage, one like Clement's description of the grasshopper, (PP, 40) in which theology becomes art. Plotinus urges his listener to

> Withdraw into yourself and look. And if you do not find yourself beautiful yet, act as does the creator of a statue that is to be made beautiful, he cuts away here,

[50] Crews, p. 18.

> he smooths there, he makes this line lighter, that purer, until a lovely face has grown upon his work. . . . You are now become very vision; now call up all your confidence, strike forward yet a step—you need a guide no longer—forward yet a step—you need a guide no longer —strain and see.[51]

Forster is haunted by the idea that "each individual *is* God, if he only knew it." Each individual is God and, as a consequence, the whole universe has an inclination toward good. Godbole and the third part of *A Passage to India* of course come to mind. Forster reinforces the connection when he says,

> The Christian promise is that man shall see God, the Neo-Platonic—like the Indian—that he shall be God. Perhaps, on the quays of Alexandria, Plotinus talked with Hindu merchants who came to town. At all events his system can be paralleled in the religious writings of India. He comes nearer than any other Greek philosopher to the thoughts of the East. (A, 72)

Plotinus is himself a bridge between theologies. He and his city, like the images of Ganpati, are "emblems of passage; a passage not easy, not now, not here, not to be apprehended except when it is unattainable." (PI, 314-315) A passage between East and West.

Alexandria, like *Pharos and Pharillon* and *A Passage to India*, begins with geography. The sense of place is all-important. Early on, Forster tells us that ancient Alexandria "stood in the position of Port Said to-day; a maritime gateway to India and the remoter east." (A, 10) The image is reinforced, not only with Plotinus, but with those who came to visit, or to conquer, as well.

Forster had created one necklace: between Alexander and Cleopatra was "suspended, like a rare and fragile chain,

[51] Forster tells us this is S. McKenna's translation. (A, 71-72)

the dynasty of the Ptolemies." (A, 30) Now he is to create another. When describing the "modern period" of Alexandrian history, he speaks of Napoleon:

> The romance of the Nile valley had touched his imagination, and he knew that it was the road to an even greater romance—India. At war with England, he saw himself gaining at England's expense an Oriental realm and reviving the power of Alexander the Great. In him, as in Mark Antony, Alexandria nourished imperial dreams. The expedition failed but its memory remained with him: he had touched the East, the nursery of kings. (A, 91)

Napoleon fails, as does another leader with whom Forster is engaged, Mohammed Ali.

> A kingdom, comparable in extent to the Ptolemaic, had come into existence with Alexandria as its centre, and it seemed that the dreams of Napoleon would be realised by this Albanian adventurer, and that the English would be cut off from India. (A, 95)

The British curtailed the plan. But the dream of passage is more important than its achievement, and in it Forster has created a chain of those who would follow Alexander in his "madness." The links include some, like Eliza Fay—that vicious but lively British woman—and Forster, who do not lead men (except the likes of poor Mr. Fay) but who are irrevocably touched by their own private passage to India—their glimpse of something great, if dangerous—and others, who have altered history—Antony, Napoleon, Mohammed Ali.

And this is primarily *why* Forster is fascinated by battles, by conquests. Cavafy saw in them the destruction of Magna Graecia, and used them as metaphors for individual defeat and hopeless hope. Forster is not really concerned with imperial Rome; he hurries over discord between Greeks and

Jews and in general views the imperial period as one that brought happiness to Alexandria. For him, conquest provides a form of knowledge, a strange kind of passage, the touch of two cultures. But as with his fictionalized marriage contracts, what binds threatens to destroy. The countryside must pay the penalty of Octavian and the British; "history repeats herself." (A, 180)

In 1882 Britain left its mark on Alexandria. "Fort Kait Bey was also shattered and the minaret of its 15th century Mosque was seen 'melting away like ice in the sun.'" (A, 101) The passage that is not easy, not now, not here, is often badly muddled, and the sadnesses that result were to become central to Forster's greatest work.

Echoes from Egypt: Forster's India

A Passage to India is, as we shall see, Alexandrian. Praise of the novel from The Alexandrian is therefore all the more pleasing. Cavafy had praised before, giving *Pharos and Pharillon* high marks on all counts, but the compliments were, however sincere, too all-encompassing to be interesting.[52] Cavafy likes everything here as well ("I like the style, I like the characters, I like the presentation of the environment, I like the attitude") but his response to *A Passage* is clearly personal. In 1925 he tells Forster "I was *charmed* by this book. I keep it by me. Very often I take up and read over again now this part of it, now that."[53] Four years later, after Forster's brief visit to Alexandria, Cavafy writes about the novel once again:

> Your stay here was too short, and I am glad to read you contemplate coming to Alexandria again. The hours we were together were too few: our friendship required more. At least, during these few hours I had the oppor-

[52] A draft of a letter in Cavafy's hand, dated: "10 July '23 (or maybe 11 July)." King's College, Cambridge.

[53] Letter dated 16 January 1925, at King's.

> tunity to express to you fully my admiration for that beautiful book "A Passage to India," to explain the reasons for my admiration. They have become, ever since 1924, companions of mine: Mrs. Moore, Fielding, Aziz, Adela, Heaslop, McBryde. I walk into the club, and get much agitated by the "women and children" ρήματα [clichés] I am in Heaslop's house and listen, knowingly, to "red nine on black ten", which of course pertains to the patience, but is also indicative of a firm decision to keep out of the inane mess.[54]

It is the kind of letter one would like to receive about one's work, not because it praises but because it speaks of images that have infected another imagination, from which they can no longer be removed.

Mrs. Moore, Fielding, Aziz, Adela, Heaslop, and McBryde, in one way or another, as this name or that, had been Forster's companions for over a decade before they were known to his friend, for the first seven chapters, as well as bits of Chapters VIII, XII, and XIV, date from before the First World War. But the manuscript of *A Passage to India,* as well as Forster's own commentary, makes clear that the rest of the novel's thirty-eight chapters were written ten years later, while Forster put together his two books on Alexandria.[55] So it is not surprising to find Alexandrian concerns central to *A Passage to India.* Forster focused his study of Alexandria on the metaphors of the bridge and the necklace: the link between man and God; the love that binds men to one another; and geography, history, politics—the

[54] Letter dated 15 October 1929, at King's. Interestingly the Forster letter to which this is an answer reads: "I wish I could have stopped longer. There was so much to say, and I quite forgot to tell you that I have written a novel and some short stories which cannot be published, and which I should like you to have seen. But you would have to come to England to see them and this you will never do!" In brackets, in the margin, Forster has written: "Private, this." Letter dated 26 July 1926.

[55] See Appendix B for a discussion of chronology in the creation of *A Passage.*

gateway between East and West. These links reappear in *A Passage*, touching Forster's last novel with a refracted light, with colors that are absent in his earlier works.

Man and God

The study of comparative theology that fascinated Forster in *Pharos* and to an even greater extent in *Alexandria* again becomes central in *A Passage to India.* In these three works the rational atheist confronts a side of religion and of himself that he had not approached before, and that he cannot ignore. In "cracks in the human universe" it is not only Ronny's suburban Christianity that goes by the board.

Forster is a man who has rejected religion but is drawn to and perplexed by it, especially when put into a situation in which religion takes on new dimensions. Like Cavafy he is fascinated by the clean lines of the religious life. Forster, hating "snobbery, the desire for possessions, creditable appendages," suggests that it is to escape these "rather than the lusts of the flesh that the saints retreat into the Himalayas." (PI, 241) "I'm a holy man minus the holiness," says Fielding. (PI, 121) It is easy to see goodness without mystery here, to see "loving-kindness" (that word Durrell would justly have us celebrate) without a sense of the extremes, the sensuous and ascetic doubles, that Durrell and Cavafy find so compelling, or Cavafy's interest in the ways religions separate men.

Forster could almost be dismissed, or applauded, as a man concerned with a warm but not passionate unity of love. But in Alexandria unity of love was of necessity linked with passion *and* theology, underscoring mystical chords that had always existed in Forster's imaginative world. In going after a harmonizing spirit in the east, in attempting to understand death and life and capture the whole, Forster, like Alexander, like Mrs. Moore, had to confront madness and its echoes; he had to confront the prophetical. The enlightened intellect of a Fielding, Quested, Schlegel, or Forster would no longer do.

The religious visions Forster confronts in *A Passage* are essentially the same as those in *Alexandria* and, as many have noted, the three-part structure of the novel moves us through Moslem, Christian, and finally Hindu answers to the nihilistic "Boum" of the caves.

As in *Alexandria*, Islam provides no real answers, although here at least we find it linked to the Persian expression for God: The Friend, "who never comes yet is not entirely disproved." (PI, 106) In *A Passage to India* Islam is connected with brotherhood—when they head off for the caves, Mrs. Moore says, "We shall be all Moslems together now, as you promised" (PI, 131)—but it does not confront the real theological question, the Alexandrian question of how God and man are linked, how man relates to the creative force of the universe. In the novel its festival is the Mohurran, associated with death, with unrelenting drums and near-riots, with the chaos that marks the caves.

Islam is a religion of poets and good men, but like Fielding and his rationalism, it misses the mystery:

> Like himself, those shallow arcades provided but a limited asylum. "There is no God but God" doesn't carry us far through the complexities of matter and spirit; it is only a game with words, really, a religious pun, not a religious truth. (PI, 276)

Amr cannot understand Alexandria, nor can Aziz know India. They can be gracious hosts but never guides.

"Poor little talkative Christianity" (PI, 150) seems at first to fare worse than Islam. It is a religion that is not taken seriously even by its adherents.

> Ronny's religion was of the sterilized Public School brand, which never goes bad, even in the tropics. Wherever he entered, mosque, cave or temple, he retained the spiritual outlook of the Fifth Form, and condemned as 'weakening' any attempt to understand them.
> (PI, 257)

This is the religion to which Adela returns before the trial. "God who saves the King will surely support the police." (PI, 211) It is the religion of those, like Athanasios, who would honor justice rather than love.

But one must remember that, as in *Alexandria*, there is a mysterious, as well as a parochial side to Christianity. The missionaries, old Mr. Graysford and young Mr. Sorley—not unlike Godbole—are foolish men, live among Indians, avoid the Club, and attempt to understand the link between man and his god. It is sadly fitting that Major Callendar, the character who, more than any other, embodies division and hate, has, in operating on her without Aziz, killed Mr. Grayford's wife.

Mr. Sorley and Mr. Grayford teach that in God's many mansions there is room for black and white, and even for animals, "the mercy of God, being infinite, may embrace all mammals. And the wasps?" But the progressive Mr. Sorley "became uneasy during the descent to wasps. . . . We must exclude someone from our gathering, or we shall be left with nothing." (PI, 38) The missionaries fail, but they have tried to love all things.

Hinduism is left to silence the echo of the caves, to attempt "to embrace the whole of India." (PI, 145) But like Cavafy's Hellenism, this is not a narrow Hinduism. Its great festival, Gokul Ashtami, associated with flood and fertility, is undramatic and unartistic; it muddles its motto, "God si love," (PI, 316) but still it encompasses Godbole, Ralph, Stella, and Mrs. Moore, all who, like Forster's Alexandrians, know that "God . . . is . . . love."[56]

[56] (PI, 51) Certainly Forster's attitude toward the specific festival he witnessed in 1921, upon which he based the imagery of Part III of the novel, is much more skeptical and critical in his letters than in *A Passage*. In his letters he emphasizes the inelegance and fatuous bad taste of the decorations. (HD, 106) He writes, "But by now you will have heard enough of religions of sorts. I have, and am ashamed that the good people here should have felt I was so sympathetic. The mere fact that I did not hold aloof seemed enough—they did not the least mind my saying that it all meant nothing to me." (HD, 113)

In the earlier chapters, Mrs. Moore admired the wasp, Mr. Sorley rejected it. Now during the Hindu ceremony of rebirth, Godbole has a mystic vision; he becomes one with God and with the parts of God that enter his sensibility—the images of Mrs. Moore and of a wasp. Mr. Sorley could not do it, but Godbole "loved the wasp equally, he impelled it likewise, he was imitating God." We think of Forster's description of Plotinus: "The whole Universe has an inclination toward good. We are all parts of God, even the stones, though we cannot realise it; and man's goal is to become actually, as he is potentially divine." (A, 71) "And the stone where the wasp clung—could he . . . no, he could not, he had been wrong to attempt the stone, logic and conscious effort had seduced." (PI, 286) Like Mr. Sorley, Godbole has his limitations; still he calls "Come, come" and strikes forward yet a step to strain and see.

Confronting oneself, confronting the mysteries of life, involves facing horrors—meeting one's ghosts and echoes, uncanny doubles or evil let loose. In a 1921 letter from India Forster wrote, "I tap about over this place and wonder whether I grow deaf or whether there really is no echo." (HD, 121) He goes on to express fear that no important thought goes on in India. In *A Passage*, just *before* the party reaches the Marabar Hills, "a new quality occurred, a spiritual silence which invaded more senses than the ear. Life went on as usual, but had no consequences, that is to say, sounds did not echo or thoughts develop." (PI, 140)

Those like Major Callendar never hear echoes, and dismiss them as fancy. (PI, 213) Fielding and Aziz move beyond spiritual silence, but even for them the echo lies on the verge of the mind; (PI, 276) they are unmoved by the caves. Only those, like Godbole, who understands dark mirrors, who, like Valentios, face the evil and meaningless in us all, can go beyond them—can face separation and death and still find peace. Forster, when taking a serious look at the religions of the Near and Far East, seems to have listened, not to Handel, nor to Lucy's piano or the "Pathetique," not to music even, but to noise, an echoing "Boum" that threatens to destroy, that is, for those like Mrs. Moore, as it was perhaps for Alexander, not "explicable this side of the grave."

Love

Most of us cannot see theology in a grasshopper, as Clement of Alexandria did, (PP, 40) or in Mr. Godbole's wasp, or Plotinus' stone. For Cavafy, for Cleopatra, and sometimes for Forster, the mystery of the divine, the religion of love, sings forth in the human form—where sense verges into spirit. Even dry, honest Adela realizes the limits of her suburban Jehovah when faced with a vision of the humblest man in the courtroom:

> Almost naked, and splendidly formed. . . . He had the strength and beauty that sometimes come to flower in Indians of low birth. When that strange race nears the dust and is condemned as untouchable, then nature remembers the physical perfection that she accomplished elsewhere, and throws out a god—not many, but one here and there . . . he seemed apart from human destinies, a male fate, a winnower of souls.
>
> (PI, 217)

Like the Bedouin in "Solitary Places" who sings "tunes to the camel that he can only sing to the camel, because in his mind the tune and the camel are the same thing," (PP, 86) the punkah wallah does not understand the world in the same way the educated do; he "didn't even know he worked a fan, though he thought he pulled a rope." (PI, 218) But unlike those Englishmen whom Mrs. Moore feels only pose as gods, (PI, 50) "He stood out as divine, yet he was of the city," (PI, 217) real, although living among rubbish heaps, touched by eternity.

We see the origins of this central image in a diary entry from Forster's first trip to India, written 25 March 1913.

Forster and a friend visited a court: ". . . civil surgeon giving evidence in murder case. Punkah boy, seated at end of table, had the impassivity of Atropos."[57]

Taking the image ten years later Forster expanded it, and produced a Cavafian beloved, very like the figure who appears in one of Forster's favorite poems, "One of Their Gods," a poem he knew exceedingly well. The following is a Valassopoulo translation, revised by Forster with the help of T. E. Lawrence:

> When one of them used to pass by
> the market-place
> of Seleucia, about the time of nightfall,
> a tall young man of perfect beauty,
> with the joy of immortality in his eyes
> and perfumed black hair,
> the people used to watch him
> and ask one another whether they knew him,
> whether he was a Syrian Greek or a stranger.
> But some
> who looked with greater attention
> understood and made way;
> and while he disappeared under archways
> among the evening lights and shadows
> on his way to the place that lives only at night
> with orgies and drunkenness
> and every kind of lust and debauchery,
> they wondered which of them it was
> and, for what unavowed pleasure
> he had come down to the streets of Seleucia
> from the Sacred and Hallowed Dwellings.[58]

[57] "Indian Entries," *Encounter*, 18 (January 1962), 25.

[58] In 1922 Cavafy gave Forster two copies of both his 1908-1914 and his 1915-1922 poems. One copy of the latter shows Forster's attempt to read this poem, written in 1917, in the original. He has underlined words and by "ὥρα" has correctly put "hour." In all his collections of translations, which are now among the Forster papers at King's

In Robert Liddell's Alexandrian novel, *Unreal City*, the Cavafian Christo Eugenides loves a Canadian Air Force corporal whom he envisions as Antinous. When the young man dies Christo almost deifies him, as Hadrian deified his Bithynian lover. Cavafy would have enjoyed the parallel with an emperor who made a religious cult of his lover's beauty, immortalized in works of art that celebrate a new, less conventionally heroic ideal. But what Cavafy does in "One of their Gods," like what he did earlier in an equally extraordinary poem "Ionic," is even more magical than the making of a god. He *believes* in a god and asks us to believe in him, to recognize his presence in our midst, a Greek god.

> That we've broken their statues,
> that we've driven them out of their temples,
> doesn't mean at all that the gods are dead.
> O land of Ionia, they're still in love with you,
> their souls still keep your memory.
> When an August dawn wakes over you,
> your atmosphere is potent with their life,
> and sometimes a young ethereal figure
> indistinct, in rapid flight,
> wings across your hills.

Here is the acceptance of mystery, of magic to which the poet is privileged, what Cavafy called "the hidden sound / of things approaching" that the wise perceive, what Forster

---

College, he has this poem marked off and has, among his papers, in his own hand, several variations of a Valassopoulo translation of the poem, which he "very carefully revised" with the help of T. E. Lawrence for publication in "Chapbook" (see a letter to Harold Munro, 13 August 1925, in the Humanities Research Centre, Austin, and a letter to Cavafy, 27 September 1925, at King's). He writes about the poem, quoting it in its entirety, in *Two Cheers for Democracy*, using the Mavrogordato translation, which he liked less than Valassopoulo's, because his article was about Mavrogordato's "The Complete Poems of C. P. Cavafy." (pp. 247-248)

in *Aspects of the Novel* called a "tone of voice," a "sensation of song or sound": prophecy. (AN, 125-136)

When Aziz's trial ends, a rumor runs through the Indian crowd declaring that Adela "had been stricken by the Deity in the middle of her lies." (PI, 233) She had. His aloofness caused her to "rebuke the narrowness of her suffering." (PI, 218) His beauty exorcised the ghost—the very old, very small echo of nihilism that first appeared to mark a betrothal without love and reappeared in the "Boum" of the caves—just as another kind of beauty, an unknown name on a map and thousands of coconut palms may have released Mrs. Moore. In Adela's moment of truth "the airs from the punkah behind her wafted her on. . . ." (PI, 228)

A figure of perfect beauty, a stranger, a male fate, winnower of souls, the punkah wallah in all his Greekness dominates the courtroom. Once its partisans have left, the Indians joyful, the English in numbed defeat, "no one remained on the scene of the fantasy but the beautiful, naked god." (PI, 231)

The servitor who appears at the height of the Gokul Ashtami festival, when the boats bump, is a similar figure, an echo of the punkah wallah, "naked, broad shouldered, thin-waisted" with "his beautiful dark face expressionless." (PI, 315) The triumphant male form of these hidden gods stands in significant contrast to the physical symbol the English adopt, Mrs. Blakiston, "with her abundant figure and masses of corngold hair," English womanhood, "all that is worth fighting and dying for." (PI, 181)

In later overtly homosexual stories admiration of the physical no longer has the understatement, the whisper so central to Cavafy's poetry. Forster was right to fear them as "positively dangerous" to his career as a writer. (LC, xii) Oliver Stallybrass sees Forster's gradual acceptance of himself as a homosexual as responsible for a change of heart, for the decision to stop writing for publication, and calls *A Passage* "a magnificent rearguard action," "completed with the aid of a theme that relegated sex to a minor role." (LC, xiv)

But homosexual concerns *are* there in *A Passage*—more vibrantly and with greater truth than they were in earlier works—and so is an artistic tension that was shortly to break, causing Forster to write essays and unpublishable "sexy stories."

Forster had to pull away, to move beyond comfort when looking at his island, his people. He had to know an alien world and the tension it produced, in order to write his best fiction. Later, we may suspect, when the world became too strange, he could listen but no longer write. In examining love, Forster had also to move beyond comfort, and possibly here too the necessity to tell the truth as he saw it, while producing his finest novel, insured that it would be his last.

The event around which *A Passage* moves is an alleged assault on a white woman by a dark man. "The darker races are physically attracted to the fairer, but not vice versa," (PI, 219) is McBryde's scientific law. Like the heat, sexuality threatens. The senses are jarred. We hear drums and riots, feel the needles that stick in Adela's skin, her fever, her body as it shrinks from touch. Madness shines on the faces of English men and women incited by an unspoken vision of the ultimate fear: racial union.

But a real crime is going on as the trial approaches, a major crime, more important than Aziz's advances, had they occurred—Mrs. Moore, although at her most cynical, says of what happened in the cave, "there are worse evils than love." (PI, 208) It is a crime more important than the other scandal in the air, McBryde's adultery with Miss Derek, or even her theft of an Indian's car.

Earlier in the novel we were introduced to Nureddin, "an effeminate youth" from whom Aziz evoked a promise to disavow the ghost that hit his grandfather's car: " 'not to believe in Evil Spirits, and if I die . . . to bring up my three children to disbelieve it them too.' " "Nureddin smiled, and a suitable answer rose to his pretty lips." (PI, 99-100) But chance intervened before he could reply. Later, while Anglo-India waits for justice, a second minor car accident puts Nurredin in the hospital, where he finds himself in Major Callendar's hands. The white doctor hates Indians, thinks the boy is homosexual, and knows that he is beautiful. He mutilates Nureddin's face.

> His beauty's gone, five upper teeth, two lower and a nostril. . . . Old Panna Lal brought him the looking-glass yesterday and he blubbered. . . . I laughed; I laughed, I tell you, and so would you; that used to be one of these buck niggers, I thought, now he's all septic; damn him, blast his soul—er—I believe he was unspeakably immoral—er— . . . nothing's too bad for these people. (PI, 216)

One thinks of many who would condemn the "unspeakable vice of the Greeks," but of none in Forster's fiction who have performed a more evil, a more depraved act.

In the closing sections of the novel we meet Ralph Moore, one of Forster's many younger brothers. "Not a type that is often exported imperially. The doctor in Aziz thought, 'Born of too old a mother,' the poet found him rather beautiful." (PI, 309) Aziz has the chance to hurt Ralph as Callendar did Nureddin. He does not, and Ralph goes on to become his mother's surrogate, the odd embodiment of a spirit, a delicate chant that defeats an all-but-encompassing "Boum" to become the Indian goddess Emiss Esmoor. Acting as guide, he leads Aziz and Fielding out of chaos and back into one another's love.

It is this friendship between Aziz and Fielding, Easterner and Westerner, that stands at the center of the novel. Here the beloved is no longer split into a sensual dark man or peasant and an intellectual friend. Forster now knew Easterners, knew them as poets, like Aziz and Cavafy, as lawyers, doctors, lovers, friends. The going is not smooth, the tension one finds in the letter to Trevelyan about Greeks and Cavafy, or in *The Hill of Devi*, often surfaces—"something racial intruded—not bitterly, but inevitably, like the colour of their skins. . . ." (PI, 260) Their sense of proportion differs, their sense of scale. "Your emotions never seem in proportion to their objects, Aziz." "Is emotion a sack of potatoes. . . ? I shall be told I can use up my emotions by using them, next." "I should have thought you would." (PI, 254) They end up saying inappropriate things and must work hard to avoid devils of their cultures—the Oriental's suspicion, the Westerner's hypocrisy. (PI, 280)

In the end love has its grand moment. But as with spiritual triumph, it is a victory intertwined with loss. "Separation . . . not simply the separation that comes through death, but the more tragic separation of people who part before they need, or who part because they have seen each other too closely," wrote Forster in that 1906 essay on pessimism. (AE, 137)

> . . . One afternoon at four o'clock we separated
> for a week only. . . . And then—
> that week became forever.[59]

Like Cavafy's lovers, Forster's friends finally, quietly part:

> 'If I don't make you go, Ahmed will . . . we shall get rid of you, yes, we shall drive every blasted Englishman into the sea, and then'—and he rode against him furiously—'and then,' he concluded, half kissing him, 'you and I shall be friends.'
>
> 'Why can't we be friends now?' said the other, holding him affectionately. 'It's what I want. It's what you want.'
>
> But the horses didn't want it—they swerved apart; the earth didn't want it . . . the temples, the tank, the jail, the palace, the birds, the carrion, the Guest House,

[59] "The Afternoon Sun."

> . . . they didn't want it, they said in their hundred voices, 'No, not yet,' and the sky said, 'No, not there.' (PI, 322)

Geography, History, Politics

Love was central to Forster's vision of Alexandria and India. But it was love grounded in geography and history. Like Cavafy, he was interested in the fates of peoples as they affect individual men, he would chronicle his race. Like Lawrence Durrell he understood how the land shapes people. Alexandria was a geographic as well as a spiritual gateway to India, and he who was always fond of guidebooks captured the spirit of place in what Bonamy Dobrée called "surely the best guide-book ever written"[60] and in *Pharos and Pharillon*, where he makes geography spiritual and full of magic, sketching the short-lived desert spring, the flowers "come all of a rush" in solitary places where "the spirit of place, without being savage, is singularly austere," but "however austere, the primaeval softness persists." (PP, 82-86)

It is not surprising that *A Passage to India* has such a strong sense of geography and often the flavor of a guidebook. Nor that it uses the metaphor of the guide that Aziz always fails to be and Ralph so easily becomes. The land, the weather veers toward chaos, only to be replenished by rain. But always there is a tension now, nothing so easy as the hayfields of Howard's End. "Presently the ground opened into full sunlight and they saw a grassy slope bright

[60] *The Lamp and the Lute* (New York: Russell and Russell, 1963), p. 79. Forster's vision was, of course, always odd, resting on "a tiger, a siren, and a very large melon" (A, 186) painted on a peasant's house, as easily as on the unattainable Parisian smartness of the Rue Rosette. (PP, 88) D. H. Lawrence said of *Alexandria*, "But what a funny task to set yourself—though I always remember the thrill you got out of that National Gallery catalogue." (In a note to Forster, from Mexico City, 11 April [1923], at King's College, Cambridge.)

with butterflies, also a cobra. . . . The scene was as park-like as England, but did not cease being queer." (PI, 317)

Forster captures much of the Indian landscape—and a sense of her history as well. This he does by peopling her with Hindus, Moslems, and Englishmen; by giving us her festivals and her sights; and, most importantly, by making Aziz a poet with an historical sense. The six Mogul emperors ride through the book—Alamgir, the pious; Babur, who never betrayed a friend; Akbar, mad like Alexander, wishing to embrace the whole of India. Like Cavafy, Aziz lives with his history, allowing it to heighten his contemporary world. In his despair he asks, "Of what help, in this latitude and hour, are the glories of Cordova and Samarcand?" (PI, 268) When frightened by the British he begins to write modern patriotic verse. But Godbole—who like Plotinus has imitated God and known His triumph—funny old Godbole likes only one poem, the one that moves beyond motherland to internationality. We remember how much Forster admired the breath of Cavafy's Hellenism.

> . . . Greece for him was not territorial. It was rather the influence that has flowed from his race this way and that through the ages, and that (since Alexander the Great) has never disdained to mix with barbarism. . . . Racial purity bored him, so did political idealism. . . . If the strain died out—never mind: it had done its work, and it would have left, far away upon some Asian upland, a coin of silver, stamped with the exquisite head of a Hellenizing King. Pericles, Aristides, Themistocles, schoolroom tyrants: what did they know of this extension which is still extending, and which sometimes seemed (while he spoke) to connote the human race? (TCD, 248)

This is what Godbole, a fitting, if odd, Minister of Education, would wish for Aziz's poetry: Cavafy's scattered, extended Greece, which is of course close to Forster's India.

It is not a vision that appealed to Indian nationalists any more than it does to British imperialists, and Forster's novel has been attacked in both camps.

Forster is clearly uneasy about men who "kick and scream on committees," (PI, 292) but he has much less sympathy for those who have ruled others with staleness and ungenerosity, and in the imperative mood. Forster paints a painful and devastating picture of Heaslop, Lesley, and Turton, who "retained a contemptuous affection for the pawns he had moved about for so many years, they must be worth his pains." (PI, 214) These people give bridge parties at which no one ever connects. Caught in a rapidly changing age, they are so quickly ossified.

Here too Alexandria played her part, for in the city Forster witnessed the problems of British imperialism at first hand, and with the particular intensity war provides. Cavafy saw personal relations within the framework of history, but except on one occasion—in a poem that mourns a young fellahin unjustly hung to avenge an Englishman's death[61] —he was not concerned with the contemporary problems of Egypt. Durrell, while drawn out of Alexandria toward the landscape and peoples of Egypt, while creating highly political characters, paid little attention to the relations between England and the people she ruled. But Forster, because he identified so firmly with his country, was particularly pained by the problems of empire, whether in Egypt or India. In 1920 he wrote a pamphlet, *Egypt*, prepared for the Labour Research Department. The piece was obviously helpful to Forster as novelist; its tone is devoid of all that is precious and, like *Alexandria*, it is again grappling with the concrete and with history. Indeed Forster begins by saying, "the following notes attempt to state facts rather than a case." (E, 3) The attempt does not succeed. Forster

[61] "27 June 1906, 2 p.m." Robert Liddell has translated this poem in his *Cavafy* (London: Duckworth, 1974), p. 91. For the original see: *Cavafy's Unpublished Poems: (1882-1923)*, ed. George Savidis (Athens: Ikaros, 1968), p. 149.

is clearly a biased observer. But in writing the pamphlet he had to confront, with as little sentimentality as he could, the effects of British rule on an Oriental environment.

Written in the midst of growing tension between the Nationalists and Egypt's British "advisors," the paper covertly agrees with the Labour Research Department's recommendations that precede it, to the extent that they favor Egyptian independence accompanied by the withdrawal of the British garrison.[62]

Forster blames English unconscious deceit for his favorite ill: muddleheadedness. (AH, 20) Casting his ironic eye on situations that are all too reminiscent of the American involvement in Vietnam, he writes: "We assert that it has been necessary for us to 'advise' Egypt from 1883 to the present moment, and to enforce at times her adoption of our advice by dismissing her Ministers. . . ." (E, 4) He saw World War I and its aftermath bring conscription, commandeering of food, reprisals that wiped out whole villages. "Before the war was over the countryside had experienced, under British auspices, many of the exactions of Oriental despotism. . . . During the winter of 1918-19 the natives, including the peasantry, became definitely anti-British: I noticed the change." (E, 6)

In signed letters in the *Manchester Guardian* and *The Times* Forster spoke about the secret enlistment of "volunteers," his second-hand knowledge that they were treated brutally when they were well, and his certainty that they were treated disgracefully when ill. Hospitals were centers

[62] Egypt was later given nominal independence by the Conservative Government, but Britain retained control of the defense of Egypt and the protection of foreign interests and national minorities—who, while controlling most of the country's industry and business, were exempt from taxation and Egyptian courts, a situation Forster deplored.

Forster clearly sympathized with Zaboul and the Wafd nationalists; he spoke of the 1882 Bombardment of Alexandria and the defeat of Arabi with sadness, "Thus perished a moment which, if treated sympathetically, might have set Egypt upon the path of constitutional liberty." (E, 4)

of infection, typhus was rampant. "And just at the time of our victories a plaintive little popular song was born and sung to a minor tune about the streets—'My native town, oh my native town. / The military authorities have taken my boy.' "[63]

The country was ruled by men like Lord Cromer, a successful administrator, reformer, financier—but, Forster adds in *Egypt*, "he had a profound distrust of Orientals" (E, 4) —and Lord Milner, "a militant Imperialist, who sincerely believed that the world would be happier if it were ruled by the British upper-middle classes." (E, 7) They brought with them an ever-increasing body of bureaucrats. A footnote brings the screams of Mrs. Turton to mind: "Some of the officials have served previously in India; such may be useful for their administrative qualities, but they, and still more their women-folk, introduce a racial arrogance from which the regular Anglo-Egyptian officials are free." (E, 4) They are like the British division, the Colonials, "who ought never to be quartered amongst friendly Oriental peoples." (E, 5) We think of the stray subaltern, who might have been Aziz' friend.

Forster touches the same chords in his last piece for *The Egyptian Mail*, "England's Honour (Being extracts from the diary of Mme. Kyriakidis, Ramleh)," a failed comic piece about the racial snobbery of English nannies as told by a Greek-Egyptian lady. For more than three years Forster watched the English witness the likes of "Vice Detected" or "Cousin Kate." He watched his countrymen "do justice and keep the peace." (PI, 50) And he learned about all Orientals what Fielding says of Indians: they "know whether they are liked or not—they cannot be fooled here. Justice never satisfies them, and that is why the British Empire rests on sand." (PI, 260)

Egypt and India taught Forster that Aziz and Fielding

[63] Trouble in Egypt: Treatment of the Fellahin," *The Manchester Guardian*, 29 March 1919, p. 8, and "The Egyptian Labour Corps," *The Times*, 13 November 1919, p. 8.

must part. They would remain proud of each other, but they would be drawn into the ever-widening circles their camps produced. They would not touch again. Here we *do* hear Beethoven's Goblins. And we think of Forster's letter to Cavafy:

> Only there does seem something fundamental in man that is unhappy perhaps, but not with these surface unhap[p]inesses, and that finds repose not in fruition but in creation. The peace that passeth understanding is the peace at the heart of the storm.

This note of separation, the pessimist's note, has finally been struck in Forster's fiction. But it brings with it its own affirmation.

> Ithaka gave you the marvelous journey.
> Without her you wouldn't have set out.
> She has nothing left to give you now.[64]

Cavafy's Ulysses must learn that it is not home he seeks but the journey home. In Forster's earlier fiction the triumph of process had to be matched by the triumph of results. In *A Passage* Aziz and Fielding honor a moment of love, without illusion. Like the music surrounding Antony, "Here is something that does last—the note of permanence on which his soul was set. He has laboured sincerely, he has told a story not untrue to life." (AE, 137)

[64] "Ithaka."

· 4 ·

DURRELL AND A MASTERPIECE OF SIZE

All indeed whom war or time threw up
On this littoral and tides could not move
Were objects for my study and my love.

LAWRENCE DURRELL, "*Alexandria*"
(CP, 72)

WORLD war brought Lawrence Durrell to Alexandria, as, thirty years earlier, it had brought E. M. Forster. Fleeing the Nazi invasion of Greece, Durrell found himself in Egypt in 1941, supporting himself initially by writing for a newspaper, as Forster had—here the Alexandrian *Egyptian Gazette*—and then by working as Foreign Press Officer for the British Embassy in Cairo.[1] In 1944 he was posted as Press Attache to Alexandria.

Letters and poems like "Alexandria" show the pain Durrell felt.

Here at the last cold Pharos between Greece
And all I love, the lights confide
A deeper darkness to the rubbing tide;

[1] He was given the job by Sir Walter Smart, Oriental Counselor, an "artist-cherisher" with a wonderful chuckle, who told Durrell an anecdote about his own breach of Foreign Service etiquette—he didn't show up for duty for several days. "The reason for this lapse was that someone had given him an introduction to a then completely unknown Greek poet called C. P. Cavafy who lived over a brothel in Alexandria. Smart had been impelled to visit him and spend several days talking literature with him. It was well worth the reprimand, he added." (SP, 72) It was Smart who told Liddell that, if he wrote a novel about Alexandria, it would have to center on Cavafy.

Doors shut, and we the living are locked inside
Between the shadows and the thoughts of peace: . . .

In a dramatic way the city marked the end of innocence. The writer of the travel book, the writer for whom poetry is landscape, found in Greece the perfect place to work and live. A change of scene changed everything. "The loss of Greece has been an amputation," he writes in the "Epilogue in Alexandria" that closes *Prospero's Cell.* His marriage did not survive the transfer to Egypt. Like his "Conon in Alexandria" Durrell fell on a "coast of torn-out lighthouses."

Ash-heap of four cultures,
Bound by Mareotis, a salt lake,
On which the winter rain rings and whitens,
In the waters, stiffens like eyes.

I have been four years bound here:
A time for sentences by the tripod:
Prophecies by those who were born dead,
Or who lost their character but kept their taste.

A solitary presumed quite happy,
Writing those interminable whining letters,
On the long beaches dimpled by the rain,
Tasting the island wind

Blown against wet lips and shutters out of Rhodes.
I say 'presumed', but would not have it otherwise.

* * *

Steps go down to the port
Beyond the Pharos. O my friends,
Surely these nightly visitations
Of islands in one's sleep must soon be over?

. . . .

The moon's cold seething fires over this white city,
Through four Februaries have not forgotten.

(CP, 137-138)

The pain was obvious, but there were consolations in this new life as well. Durrell lived among many young writers stationed in Egypt[2] and, with Robin Fedden, edited a magazine of their work: *Personal Landscape, A Magazine of Exile*, 1942-1945. He was, as always, playful, enjoying some of the games Forster had. We think of "Gippo English" when reading "We have also collected a number of shop signs and wall-notices. For example 'THE OXFORD IRONY' (Cairo Laundry Sign)." (SP, 76) Still, in letters written while he lived in Alexandria, Durrell paints the city with even less enthusiasm than Forster did when writing home. It is something of a "funk-hole," but unredeemed. To Henry Miller he writes,

> No, I don't think you would like it. . . . this smashed up broken down shabby Neapolitan town, with its Levantine mounds of houses peeling in the sun. A sea flat, dirty brown and waveless rubbing the port. Arabic, Coptic, Greek, Levant French; no music, no art, no real gaiety. A saturated middle European boredom laced with drink and Packards and beach-cabins. NO SUBJECT OF CONVERSATION EXCEPT MONEY. Even love is thought of in money terms. . . . No, if one could write a single line of anything that had a human smell to it here, one would be a genius.[3]

To another friend, the dancer Diana Gould, he again complains about the city, calling it a "flesh-pot, sink-pot, melting-pot of dullness."

Melting-pot of dullness!

Durrell quite obviously altered his vision of the city, or added new layers to the first image on the screen, because

[2] G. S. Fraser, Bernard Spencer, Keith Douglas, Gwyn Williams, Patrick Leigh Fermor, Xan Fielding, and Lord Kinross were among those whom Durrell knew in Egypt.

[3] *Lawrence Durrell and Henry Miller, A Private Correspondence*, ed. George Wickes (New York: E. P. Dutton and Co., Inc., 1963), p. 195.

the city changed him. He fought with and conquered the spirit of a peculiar, dangerous place, learning to love again and, as he suggests in "Alexandria," "to suffer and not condemn":

> As for me I now move
> Through many negatives to what I am.
>
> (CP, 72)

Like Darley, Durrell moved through negatives, through sadnesses but also images, through the frames of Alexandria to get to his *Quartet*. It took twelve years. Durrell spent much of the intervening period in Greece, Argentina, and Yugoslavia. In 1946 he wrote T. S. Eliot, telling him of a "big book" begun and germinating in his mind "involving the attitude of the near-Levant to sex." (SP, 83) In 1952 Durrell decided he had to leave the Foreign Service in order finally to get at that book. With his infant daughter Sappho-Jane—born of a second faltering marriage, to the Alexandrian Eve Cohen—he set off alone for Cyprus, where at 4:30 each morning he worked on *Justine*, before leaving at dawn to teach school. On Cyprus he met Claude, a French novelist from Alexandria, who was to become his third wife. The parallels with Darley are obvious, as are those with Pursewarden when, later in his stay on the island, during the crisis of Enosis, Durrell was again working for the Foreign Office, fighting the severely conflicting loyalties of Greek friendships and service to the Crown. By 1956, when he left Cyprus, Durrell had finished *Justine*; the other three quarters, written in France, came more quickly and by 1960, fifteen years after his stay in Alexandria, the completed *Quartet* was in print. More fertile finally than the Greek sun, the winds that move through all his Alexandrian poems, like ghosts demanding to be exorcised, had breathed life into a shabby Neapolitan town, turning a promising writer into a major figure of his day.

Alexandria

At the doors of Africa so many towns founded
Upon a parting could become Alexandria, like
The wife of Lot—a metaphor for tears;
"*Alexandria*" (CP, 73)

For Forster, Alexandria was a bridge between his early novels and *Passage to India.* A meeting-ground for East and West, for lovers and theologians who concerned themselves with links. It was a subtle mind, that city, and, with its poet, taught Forster to live with loss, to understand—paradoxically—just how fragile those links could be, to harbor Alexander's dream of harmony and Antony's music with the full knowledge that they were unobtainable.

Durrell paints a different town. A fevered city, a dying city, a prodigal, stranger-loving, leaf-veined city.[4] A city of deep resignation, of spiritual lassitude and self-indulgence, of jealousy and retribution.[5] "The shining city of the disinherited"—a city of exiles, the capital of Asiatic Europe.[6] Elegant, and as sexual as Justine, stylishly wicked, hybrid, and proud, and yet "Alexander's shabby capital," "clinging to the minds of old men like traces of perfume upon a sleeve: Alexandria, the capital of Memory."[7] Durrell's Alexandria is a place where one comes to expect kidnapping, child prostitution, murder, international intrigue, poisoning, and suicide; where marriage is a business venture; where people are generous with friends; a place some suspect of having strong flavor without any real character. Like Justine.

How do all these divergent images add up? They are dramatic, erotic, anything but peaceful; they cannot be easily summarized, for Alexandria is like the recurring palms that appear in the mirrored walls of the ballroom at the Cecil, fractured and prismatic. She is to be discovered.

[4] See (J, 166), (J, 161), (M, 132), (M, 20).
[5] (B, 171), (M, 132), (B, 158).
[6] (C, 79), (C, 78), (M, 132). [7] (M, 145), (J, 166).

> Capitally, what is this city of ours? What is resumed in the word Alexandria? In a flash my mind's eye shows me a thousand dust-tormented streets. . . .
>
> Five races, five languages, a dozen creeds: five fleets turning through their greasy reflections behind the harbour bar. But there are more than five sexes and only demotic Greek seems to distinguish among them. . . . You would never mistake it for a happy place.
>
> (J, 11-12)

A city of many languages and peoples, "The very names of the train stops echoed the poetry of these journeys: Chatby, Camp de Cesar, Laurens, Mazarita, Glymenopoulos, Sidi Bishr. . . ." (J, 46) A city whose diversity of sounds fascinates Durrell. He asks us over and over to listen to the very names of Alexandrians: "Pia dei Tolomei, Benedict Dangeau, Dante Borromeo, Colonel Neguib. . . ."[8]

The diversity Durrell chose to emphasize was certainly a dominant feature of Alexandrian life, but it could be viewed in many ways and became the source of humor for writers like D. J. Enright and Robert Liddell, who saw an Alexandria very different from Durrell's fictive city. In describing the *Quartet* Enright has written:

> Alexandria *is* a rather melodramatic city, and not only by British-provincial standards. Its extremes of wealth and poverty are staggering. . . . Its beggars are the most horrifying in the world. Its population ranges from a simple fellahin through a cartoonist's cotton-pashas to the ultra-sophisticated society of Baudrot, *L'Atelier* and the big houses. Its sea is bluer than the most unlikely Mediterranean postcard. In the khamseen . . . the city honestly looks like the end of the world. Why, then, did Durrell feel obliged to paint the lily and throw an extra stench on the putrescence?[9]

[8] (B, 185). See also (J, 55) and (B, 37) for the listing, the music of Alexandrian names.

[9] "Alexandrian Nights' Entertainments: Lawrence Durrell's 'Quar-

Enright never paints the lily. He is a fine writer graced with wit, compassion, and good sense, and seldom subject to the excess that mars Durrell's work. The diversity in Alexandrian life, when it is not simply funny, seems in his writing to touch a saddened social conscience. It is never romanticized. In "To an Alexandrian Poet," he ponders about the difference between himself and the tasteful Alexandrians around him, telling us much about the city:

'Poetry is truth, but truth wrapped round with words.
The wrappings matter more.' So, *mon ami*—
You'd shudder at the gross word 'friend'—
I failed to write it.
The wrappings slipped and always slipped again
Between my clumsy fingers, whirled away, away,
Away with that Janus-mouthed Egyptian wind.
For then I saw—
Believe me, by no will of mine—the beggar's
red smashed leg,
He prying slowly at his filthy wrappings:
the wrappings matter—
And all the more along a public street.

The long fingering sea, like the rippling back
of some blue persian:
Snow-blinding sands, like splintered pearls, at Abousir:
The happy cleanly dolphins, and the comic stilted crabs
Scampering along damp sands, like some new
pavement toy—
away,
Whirled away in that double-edged Egyptian wind,
and lost.

And so it seems I'm poorer, in the end, than you—
Have lost what you have found, and nothing
gained beside

---

tet,'" *Conspirators and Poets* (London: Chatto and Windus, 1966), p. 111. Baudrot was an elegant café; *L'Atelier* the society for the arts.

(The beggar fidgets at his rags and eyes me sullenly)
—neither a cure for beggars' legs,
Nor your large graceful house and manners.[10]

Durrell is certainly enamored of fashionably artistic Alexandria, with its graceful houses and manners. Wearing a Scott Fitzgerald mask, the boy staring at inaccessible sweets, he is often drawn to just those whom Enright, for reasons more important than delicacy, will not call friends. But above all else, Durrell envisions the artist unwrapping truth. Not because he is touched by the beggar (in some essential way he seems unmoved by the poor). Because he is sure truth lies beyond the barriers, Durrell will risk our cries of excess to take us on a magical journey where the battle lies, to his Alexandria, city of extremes, of smashed legs *and* palaces. This isn't the Alexandria Durrell wrote letters about any more than Cavafy's mythic land is the city he saw from the windows of the Third Circle of Irrigation, or even the balcony of 10 Rue Lepsius.

Extreme sensuality and intellectual asceticism, "the two deepest psychological traits" of which man is conscious, meet in Durrell's Alexandria: "That is why we are hysterics and extremists." (J, 87) The passionate intensity of the desert father and the hetaira, Thais, or Cavafy's Simeon Stylite, and Forster's Cleopatra. "The only city left where every extreme of race and habit can meet and marry," (B, 19) this is how Durrell would see Alexandria. Sacred and profane, loving and obscene, (B, 155) she is "Alexandria, princess and whore. The royal city and the *anus mundi*," (C, 55) the contemporary wasteland, over which broods a regal, decadent poet.

This Alexandria is home of the medieval quest—a quest that, as John Unterecker suggests—lies at the core of most of Durrell's important work.[11] The hero must take a ritual

[10] In *The Laughing Hyena and Other Poems* (London: Routledge and Kegan Paul, 1953), p. 30.

[11] John Unterecker, *Lawrence Durrell* (New York: Columbia Uni-

journey across water entering a sick land. There he seeks balms to cure his own wounds and those of his city: there he does battle with all the forces that would destroy.

But, ironically, the city that he would save, that he does save, is the dangerous power he must fight. In a letter about the island of Rhodes, Durrell once called it "the great dark abdominal FEMALE PRINCIPLE! !" (SP, 87) Princess and whore. For Durrell Alexandria is, even more, dark femininity. We are not now dealing with Forsterian visions of a subtle mind, a unifying principle. The image moves closer to the chasm than the bridge. No, Durrell's city is like his women, passive and yet dangerously malevolent. She courts the Lord of Misrule and the many faces of Mephistopheles. She is reality, a force to be feared.

> The characters in this story . . . are all inventions. . . .
> Only the city is real. (J, 7)

> The characters . . . are entirely imaginary, . . .
> Nor could the city be less unreal. (B, 7)

We shall see just how "unreal" Durrell's characters can be, how much they are, not only themselves, but the embodiment of several selves, the reincarnation of outlooks and actions seen throughout history, the echo of Antony or of a forgotten clerk. Only the city is real, for she is life itself, the sum of all divergent parts, the continuous flow from which no man can escape, which man—the artist—must confront on her own ground.

> You tell yourself: I'll be gone
> To some other land, some other sea,
> To a city lovelier far than this
> Could ever have been or hoped to be—
> Where every step now tightens the noose:
> A heart in a body buried and out of use:

versity Press, 1964), pp. 30-31. Unterecker acknowledges his indebtedness to the observations of Eve Zarin.

How long, how long must I be here
Confined among these dreary purlieus
Of the common mind? Wherever now I look
Black ruins of my life rise into view.
So many years have I been here
Spending and squandering, and nothing gained.
There's no new land, my friend, no
New sea; for the city will follow you,
In the same mental suburbs slip from youth to age,
In the same house go white at last—
The city is a cage.
No other places, always this
Your earthly landfall, and no ship exists
To take you from yourself. Ah! don't you see
Just as you've ruined your life in this
One plot of ground you've ruined its worth
Everywhere now—over the whole earth?

(J, 221)

Reading Durrell's translation of Cavafy's sad tribute "The City" brings to mind Durrell's letters and his own poems about Alexandria, about the loneliness and pain of men caught and held by war in that hybrid city of exiles. "The City" haunts *Justine*, where it sets the stage for Durrell's tales of Alexandria. At the very opening Darley writes, "I had to come here in order completely to rebuild this city in my brain—melancholy provinces which the old man* saw as full of the 'black ruins' of his life." The asterisk sends us to a translation, as it will again when Nessim, near madness, thinks of asking Justine " 'Why don't we leave this city,' " and recalls Cavafy's poem. (J, 160) Pursewarden recites the poem (J, 79) and Darley himself writes: "If one were to go away, I catch myself thinking, to Italy perhaps or to France: to start a new sort of life: not a city life this time. . . ." (J, 202)

The poem becomes an emblem of despair. In the *Quartet* this is an early, temporary despair the hero-artist must go through before he can conquer the female, life, Alexandria, the city, before he can stand tall, take his glasses off, write, and reign. For Durrell's heroes the poem is a kind of lesson, not primarily that acceptance of failure is a part of living—an accent stronger in Cavafy than in Durrell—but that the battle must be fought now, "Here at the last cold Pharos between Greece / And all I love," that one can go back to the islands in one's sleep, to the "plate of olives and the glass of wine" (CP, 137) only after facing Alexandria.

The City: a History

It is no wonder Durrell asked that Forster's *Alexandria* be sent on with his notes, when he sat down to grapple with *Justine*. He would make specific references to the *History and Guide* when looking at Amr or Valentios' Sophia, but, more importantly, the whole *Quartet* is steeped in history—a history that provides the backdrop for actions of contemporary Alexandrians. We think of Cavafy, and Forster. But for one difference: Cavafy's imagination was held by certain moments in time; his poems cluster around periods and peoples. He avoids much of Alexandrian history almost entirely. He avoids the glories of Alexander and Ptolemy Sotir, of Athanasios and Arios. In his poems we meet neither Amr nor, with one exception, other Moslems. Dying Alexandrians, dying Byzantines—Kaisarion or Anna Komnina—catch Cavafy's eye. Forster also focuses—particularly on the periods of religious conflict—and ignores, even when his purpose is to scan 2,500 years.

Durrell covers the whole canvas. Like Scobie's friend, scheming to sell fragments of the Pharos as paperweights, he leaves no historical stone unturned. Durrell does not give us a chronological look at Alexandria and its surroundings down through the ages, Darley writes, "what I most need to do is to record experiences, not in the order in which they took place—for that is history—but in the order in which they first became significant for me," (J, 102) but Durrell does give us a *complete* picture. Because for Durrell the novel is a tale of quest, the hero must fight against all the dangers that are life, all its adventures extended through time and space.

Egypt under the Pharaohs is invoked with the Sphinx and Petesouchos, the crocodile goddess. We meet young men who look like Rameses II (M, 110) and, in Pursewarden and Liza, people who would imitate Osiris and Isis. (C, 167) In the Ptolemaic period this theme of incest, central to so many of the love relationships in the *Quartet*, is again reinforced by reference to the marriage of Ptolemy and Arsinoe.

Durrell spends much time with Alexander and his heirs. Darley walks the city's streets much as Forster had, trying to visualize how it all must have looked—the Park of Pan, Pharos, the Mouseion, the Soma: the ancient city "radiating out like the arms of a starfish from the axis of its founder's tomb."[12] Mnemjian's barber shop is a "Ptolemaic parlour"; (B, 20) Justine keeps the universe according to Claudius Ptolemy above her bed. All this in modern Alexandria, "the Hellenistic capital of the bankers and cotton-visionaries—all those European bagmen whose enterprise had re-ignited and ratified Alexander's dream of conquest after the centuries of dust and silence which Amr had imposed upon it." (C, 29)

Durrell plays with history. In doing so he borrows from the best history and guidebook around. Justine's Gnosticism, Nessim's attraction to Plotinus, references to Petesouchos and the ankh—all find their origins in *Alexandria*.[13]

[12] (C, 55) Ambrose Gordon, Jr.—"Time, Space, and Eros: The *Alexandria Quartet* Rehearsed," in *Six Contemporary Novels*, ed. William O. S. Sutherland, Jr. (Austin: University of Texas, 1962), p. 8—makes an interesting parallel between Alexandria and the *Quartet*. The city spirals out from the Soma and the mysterious, mythic dead body of Alexander, and Durrell's work also "spirals from the dead body of a young man": Pursewarden, whose suicide Gordon sees as the central act in the novels.

[13] William Leigh Godshalk notes many of the details from Forster's

But it is *Pharos and Pharillon* from which Durrell the writer of historical fiction has really learned. For Durrell has Nessim near madness, consumed by historical dreams. In one of these Justine and Balthazar, under marble colonnades, are linked to the Mouseion. In another, which in tone and imagery comes so close to Forster, Nessim, in his memory's memory, sees Macedonian soldiers attempting to conquer this strange alluvial coast. "They were hungry. The march had driven them all to extremities. . . . The wild asses, loitering just out of bowshot, maddened them with the promise of meat. . . ."

> The brave plumed helmets with which they had been issued were too hot to wear at midday. Africa, which they had somehow visualized as an extension of Europe —an extension of terms, of references to a definite past —had already asserted itself as something different: a forbidding darkness where the croaking ravens matched the dry exclamations of spiritless men. . . .
>
> (J, 157-158)

We hear echoes of "The Return from Siwa"—a note Durrell will pick up again in a march across the desert in *Monsieur* —and then, in a moment, the Cavafian irony of "Envoys from Alexandria."

> Where the paths had crossed they had sacrificed to Heracles (and in the same breath murdered the two

---

Alexandria found in the *Quartet*. See "Some Sources of Durrell's *Alexandria Quartet*," *Modern Fiction Studies*, 13, No. 3 (Autumn 1967), 362-363. Godshalk says that Durrell's debt to Forster is "greater than acknowledged." But Forster himself insisted, quite correctly, that the rules of fiction are not the rules of history. Actually, Durrell acknowledges this source quite explicitly, and much more thoroughly than might be expected. Here is a novel with footnotes, like other historical-mythical works of the imagination with which it can be compared, such as "The Waste Land" or Cavafy's poems as they reach a modern audience. Durrell's real debt is to Forster's Cavafian vision rather than to the details Godshalk mentions.

guides, just to be on the safe side); but from that moment everything had begun to go wrong. Secretly they knew they would never reach the city and invest it. And God! Never let that winter bivouac in the hills be repeated. . . . (J, 159)

Durrell adds further irony: these dreams may have been fictitious, created to fool Darley, but they help to set the tone of a novel in which one constantly feels the weight and mythic grandeur of history behind the acts of ordinary men. Clea says of Justine, "'. . . our friend is only a shallow twentieth-century reproduction of the great *hetairae* of the past, the type to which she belongs without knowing it, Lais, Charis and the rest . . . she is truly Alexandrian.'" (J, 67-68) Like Cavafy's twentieth-century Alexandrians, Durrell's characters are the reincarnations of historical figures, particularly of the Ptolemys. Edmund Keeley speaks of Cavafy's "'two-plane' image of Alexandria" using Joyce's phrase.[14] The choice is apt, and applies to Durrell as well as Cavafy, for Durrell's Alexandria is a kind of *Finnegans Wake*: everything equals everything else.

In Durrell's city Justine is clearly one "of that race of terrific queens . . . The giant man-eating cats like Arsinoe were her true siblings." (J, 18) By the end of the *Quartet*, Alexandria herself is "like the sad history of some great queen whose fortunes have foundered among the ruins of armies and the sands of time!" (C, 240) And it is the most famous queen in history, princess and whore, to which she and all of her women are compared. Fatima, the black Ethiopian maid, draws the rings off Justine's long finger as Charmian might have. Like Cleopatra, like all Oriental women, Justine "is not a sensualist in the European sense; there is nothing mawkish in her constitution. Her true obsessions are power, politics and possessions. . . ." (M, 181) Balthazar says of Arnauti and Justine, "she preyed upon all that he might have kept separate—his artist-hood if you

[14] *Cavafy's Alexandria*, in manuscript.

like. He is when all is said and done a sort of minor Antony, and she is a Cleo." (J, 86)

They are not the only Alexandrians to reenact the famous pair. Mountolive, shaken by Nessim's treachery, dreams of being on a lake with the two brothers armed and stalking him in another boat: "Soon he would be overtaken; but warm in the circle of Leila's arms, as if he were Antony at Actium, he could hardly bring himself to feel fear." (M, 224) Even the mild Melissa unrolls herself into Darley's life like the dangerous queen (J, 50) and Clea, her complement, her double, is a Cleo too. When, on their imagined Timonium, Darley saves Clea from death—as he had Melissa—he tells us, "softly we baled her up like Cleopatra." (C, 219) Clea is a reincarnation of her friend as well as the mythic queen. Everything equals everything else.[15]

In fact, all of Durrell's women are Cleopatras, all of his men Antonys.

> 'You can read all about it in Shakespeare. And then as far as Alexandria is concerned, you can understand why this is really a city of incest—I mean that here the cult of Serapis was founded. For this etiolation of the heart and reins in love-making must make one turn inwards upon one's sister. The lover mirrors himself like Narcissus in his own family: There is no exit from the predicament.' (J, 86)

Durrell is interested in Cleopatra's story for the same reason he feels compelled to write about sexuality—"the root-knowledge" (C, 121)—for it allows the artist to remove the codpiece, to discover himself. Homosexuality, infidelity, voyeurism, infant sexuality, prostitution, all help the lover to strip bare. But doubles and incestuous pairs hold a special

[15] Parallels between the women are strong. Darley begins his love affair with Clea at a cafe in the "exact station in place and time where I had once found Melissa." (C, 66) Over an interval of years both women even appear in the same dress with its leaf-veined pattern.

fascination for Durrell;[16] they throw mirrors back on the self, in a novel of mirrors, of splintered glass.

> The symbolic lovers of the free Hellenic world are replaced here by something different, something subtly androgynous, inverted upon itself. . . . Alexandria was the great wine-press of love; those who emerged from it were the sick men, the solitaries, the prophets—I mean all who have been deeply wounded in their sex. (J, 12)

Why does Durrell see Cleopatra and Antony as an incestuous pair? Partly because they have, in every telling, in every age, touched the quick of love, impelling us to believe in emotions as frightening as they are exhilarating. They touch bottom where we all fear some treasures of our familial ties lie. One does not come back from this battle unscarred. Then too Antony and Cleopatra loved even unto evil, and in suggesting the incestuous in their relationship and in that of their many contemporary heirs, Durrell makes us witness a break with the last taboo. Like Cavafy, Durrell believes in evil—because he believes that the artist must revel in blackness in order to know the whole of life. The battle may, in wounding, heal.

Cleopatra was, for Durrell, the blackness that consumes, the earth, Alexandria, Justine—the feminine principle with which the artist must contend—and reality, the alternately passive and treacherous queen each Antony must love and fight to the death. The vision is of enemy and Adam's rib. Forster saw her as a rare flower opening before a simple Roman soldier; Cavafy focused on those around her, sons and lovers. How intriguing that only Durrell, the high priest

[16] Nessim and Narouz, as well as Pursewarden and Liza find their parallels in *Tunc* and *Nunquam*. Piers, Sylvie, and Bruce in *Monsieur* melt doubles and siblings. In the *Quartet* Justine speaks of incestuous love for Pursewarden, Leila for Mountolive and, in the same way, Nessim and Melissa are described as being like doomed brother and sister.

of heterosexual love, finds her a terrifying creature whom man must ultimately conquer.

Like Forster's, Durrell's ancient Alexandria is a city of God as well as a city of love. Here too Durrell's quest requires that he cover the whole canvas, that he seek the healing balms wherever they may be found. His interest in the Ptolemies extends to their spectacles (the Hellenistic parades Kallixeinos of Rhodes describes were surely models for Scobie's religious festivals) and to those religious wonders, like the Serapis and the Septuagint, that developed during their reign.

Hypatia, Plotinus—whom Nessim hears beckoning him to moral courage: "'Look into yourself,'" (J, 160)—even the interreligious burial ground at Kom El Shugafa, all find their way into the *Quartet*. "Alexandria is a city of sects— . . . Steinerites, Christian Scientists, Ouspenskyists, Adventists. . . ." (B, 24) Moslem, Greek Orthodox, Jew, Copt move through the novels.

> Alexandria is a town of sects and gospels. And for every ascetic she has always thrown up one religious libertine—Carpocrates, Anthony—who was prepared to founder in the senses as deeply and truly as any desert father in the mind. . . . 'extreme sensuality and intellectual asceticism. Historians always present syncretism as something which grew out of a mixture of warring intellectual principles; that hardly states the problem. It is not even a question of mixed races and tongues. It is a national peculiarity of the Alexandrians to seek a reconciliation between the two deepest psychological traits of which they are conscious. That is why we are hysterics and extremists. That is why we are the incomparable lovers we are.' (J, 87)

Because, for Durrell, extremes exemplify Alexandria, and life, his primary religious interests are with Gnosticism and the Cabal—"*indulge but refine*" (J, 89)—and with figures like the sixteenth-century German Paracelsus who preach a magical and maniacal sympathy between the universe and the individual soul, who avoid the "tramlines of empirical fact." (C, 177) The frequent images of incest in Durrell's work link intensity of love with danger, and with evil. A similar fascination focuses on the Gnostic Valentios' Sophia who wanted too ardently to be one with God, who "fell through love." These forces hold Durrell, for they, and Alexandria (even Pursewarden's *Essays*) are back again in his latest novel, *Monsieur,* where the usurping God of Evil rules. Gnosticism has an intense and irrational power, as Piers' struggle with the snake Ophis makes clear, but that power is linked with the intellect and with a delicate sensibility open only to those who make every act an art. In the *Quartet* Gnosticism engages readers and protagonists alike, as does the unrefined intensity of creatures who seem to have emerged from the desert in *Thais*, who may hold the answer to the question that is the quest, to the meaning of Alexandria. Durrell gives us his fictive Magzub, a holy and evil desert father, Taor at Wadi Natrun, and Narouz, whose preaching could awaken the coiled poetic consciousness in the Coptic spirit.

Like the Moslem chant of the blind muezzin, these strains of Alexandrian theology echo throughout the novels; they are often melodramatic, sometimes ludicrous. But, I should add, Durrell balances against them a sense of the tolerance that created Serapis, the blending of Coptic and Moslem strains in the birth of that jolly new saint El Scob, " 'a student of harmlessness,' " (C, 71) and a sense of humor. Jesus the great Ironist just saves the day.

Durrell is as interested in Alexandria after the Moslem conquest as he is in the Ptolemaic city or in the periods of religious fervor. The epic journey takes us to Amr. We hear his dying words (J, 77) and talk of the burning library. (J, 106) And Durrell follows the Hellenic spirit as Cavafy had, watching it flee from Alexandria to Constantinople. It is Justine and Nessim whom he makes the inheritors of Byzantium: Nessim with his "Byzantine face such as one might find among the frescoes of Ravenna—almond-shaped, dark-eyed, clear-featured"; (M, 16) Justine, whose "smouldering eyes, were those of some ancient Byzantine painting," (J, 198) who wears a dangerous ring that Cavafy might have loved, "the ivory intaglio taken from the tomb of a dead Byzantine youth." (B, 162)

". . . symbols of Alexandria, a dead brackish lake surrounded by the silent, unjudging, wide-eyed desert which stretches away into Africa under a dead moon." (B, 171) Just as Cavafy had to place his figures at the farthest reaches of the Greek diaspora, Durrell must move his characters through space as well as time. But unlike Cavafy, Durrell gives his readers a sense of the alien land surrounding Alexandria—the land that the city found difficult to ignore after the seventh century—a sense of Egypt. At times he sounds like the Forster of "Solitary Places":

> Ancient lands, in all their prehistoric intactness: lake-solitudes hardly brushed by the hurrying feet of the centuries where the uninterrupted pedigrees of pelican and ibis and heron evolve their slow destinies in complete seclusion. Cloverpatches of green baize swarming with snakes and clouds of mosquitoes. A landscape devoid of songbirds yet full of owls. . . . Egypt! The goose-winged sails scurrying among the freshets with perhaps a human voice singing a trailing snatch of song.
> (C, 40)

But like D. J. Enright, Durrell knew a harsher land than did Forster: ". . . the whole countryside of Egypt shares this melancholy feeling of having been abandoned, allowed to run to seed, to bake and crack and moulder under the brazen sun." (C, 41)

True, Durrell's Egypt is to a large extent a Copt's country. It is Karm Abu Girg, where Mountolive learns the full history of *genus Pharaonicus* "the true marrow of Egypt." (M, 38) But, as we hear from old Hosnani, who, like Cavafy's prince from Western Libya, has "this conversation stacked up inside him," (M, 37) the Copts are integrated into the Moslem state. Narouz' problems and pleasures are those of an Egyptian, not an Alexandrian. At Karm Abu Girg one eats without implements and then listens to the old Arab singer praise the Prophet, and when one works it is to fight the desert.

Narouz himself becomes the vehicle through which we meet Arabian herdsmen—"four tall lean men, made of brown paper" (B, 73)—whom Durrell calls automata. "The fierce banality of their lives was so narrow, so regulated." (B, 73) Elsewhere he is to suggest that "nobody can think or feel only in the dimensionless obsolescence of Arabic." (M, 23) But Durrell, in part, romanticizes here too. For his blank men are dramatic counterparts to the desert through which the Hosnanis run: "the nakedness of space, pure as theorem."[17]

Certainly there are few Moslem characters in the *Quartet* and, we might add, the most important of these is not introduced until the end of the third book. But in his portrait of Memlik one can again see that Durrell, like Cavafy, could not leave history alone. How close the Minister of the Interior comes to Mohammed Ali, with his Armenian father and love of things European. Memlik's reception-room—"a cross between an abandoned geological museum and a corner of the old Crystal Palace" (M, 233)—and the architecture that bears his name—"a sort of travesty of an Egyptian

[17] (B, 71) The silence of the herdsmen is balanced against another sense of the Moslem that runs through the *Quartet:* "the strangely captivating lilt of Arabic with its heavy damascened imagery, the thick brocade of alliterative repetitions . . . the epic contours" (C, 128) of the story of Yuna and Aziz, heard by an audience that believes in its mythology, making Pursewarden jealous for the poor Englishman, whose literature hasn't provided a similar experience since Chaucer.

tomb, adapted by a pupil of Corbusier!" (M, 228)—give us some of the flavor of the soul that rebuilt Alexandria in the nineteenth century and still touches its spirit today.

In the figure of Memlik we see an important way in which Durrell's attitude toward nineteenth- and twentieth-century Alexandrian history differs from Forster's, and get another glimpse of Durrell's vision of life, Alexandria, as battleground. Both Forster and Durrell wrote about the British presence in Egypt and about the conflict between a growing nationalism and the interests of a large foreign community. Both wrote about the ways in which the East can free the Englishman from a damning rigidity and complacency. No one is harder on his countrymen than Durrell, who has Pursewarden speak of "the long slow toothache of English life," (B, 104) of the "suicidal boredom" (C, 37) of a country in which one is educated "not to wish to feel," (M, 17) in which one loves judicially and associates happiness with guilt. "A nation of mental grannies" (C, 108) with a "tea-cosy over reality" (C, 117) is Pursewarden's cry, and we feel the echo of Durrell's approval.

No English Alexandrian could be more fascinated by the desert than Durrell or by the Arab quarters of the city, where men sell pornography as if they were medieval pardoners, (M, 257) where Scobie roams, nor feel the necessary connection with the Oriental world—with extreme differences, with the other. The image is of mating and murder, an incestuous union with "the perfect submissiveness of the oriental spirit—the absolute feminine submissiveness which is one of the strongest forces in the world." (M, 181)

Like Forster, Durrell recounts the history of the British presence in Alexandria. He shows us a photograph of Maskelyne's grandfather, clearly the Brigadier-bureaucrat's spiritual ancestor, wearing a medal from the 1882 battle of Tel-el-Kebir (C, 201)—the battle in which the British finally defeated the Nationalist leader Arabi. He gives us a sense of the power of the High Commission and its gradual defeat.

And, like Forster, Durrell writes about a friendship between Englishman and Oriental, that, for the former, defies race. He too knew the civil service and found himself drawn to those intrigues that entangle public and private selves, that involve all who have an historical imagination. Fielding promises Turton he'll resign and leave India if his faith in Aziz proves ill-founded, as does Pursewarden when Maskelyne uncovers Nessim's plans. The difference is that Fielding's judgment is right, Pursewarden's wrong, and Pursewarden's error proves fatal: "the man happens to be my friend. Therefore . . . a quietus." (M, 165)

Durrell certainly doesn't want us to feel that Pursewarden should have acted differently. We join in Mountolive's embarrassment and shame when he tells Leila: " 'I cannot discuss an official matter with a private person.' " (M, 254) Nor does Durrell applaud Maskelyne's narrow patriotism. But the necessary union with and love of the Oriental, like the love of woman, is tangled with treachery in the *Quartet*.

Forster did not devote much of his attention to Egyptians; he found the Arab world "static and incomprehensible,"[18] but when he did turn his eye on the British High Commission or the courts and taxation of the foreign communities, his sympathies were clearly with the Egyptian nationalists, who he felt represented the exploited majority.

Durrell, on the other hand, must meet Egypt and her harsh dry land and men, but, ironically, the magnetic pull of the country surrounding Alexandria does not insure the same sympathy. Nessim and Pursewarden risk death because of political affiliations that put them in opposite camps. But they really agree about the political and economic answer for Egypt. Power should be placed in the hands of the foreign community. Durrell invites identification with both L. G. Darley and Pursewarden, but we would have no reason to identify Pursewarden's black vision of nationalism with Durrell were it not for the likes of Memlik. Forster

[18] "A Musician in Egypt," *The Egyptian Mail*, 21 October 1917, p. 2.

deplores the special privilege the courts of the foreign community provide. Durrell applauds them as a necessary alternative to Egyptian corruption:

> Europeans had still the right, by treaty, to submit their judicial problems or answer charges against them at Les Tribunaux Mixtes, European courts with European lawyers to prosecute or defend. But the Egyptian judicial system (if one could dare to call it that) was run directly by men of Memlik's stamp, the anachronistic survivals of a feudalism as terrible as it was meaningless. (M, 229)

For Durrell, we must meet our doubles, our mates, our second selves, and in that meeting touch the bone: love, fight, manipulate or submit, but never trust them.[19]

The *Quartet* carries the history of Alexandria and Egypt through to the end of the Second World War. In *Mountolive* we first hear reports of a "new Attila" (M, 72) and visit an hysterical Berlin cabaret. In *Clea* we see Alexandria locked in war: Pombal with the Free French, Mountolive frozen in Egypt, Maskelyne fighting and dying as he had always wished he could.

[19] One might add that Durrell makes Memlik stupid as well as corrupt. When Memlik's European barber plants an idea in his master's mind, Durrell writes: "He proceeded slowly, for to register an idea in a Moslem mind is like trying to paint a wall: one must wait for the first coat to dry (the first idea) before applying a second." (M, 245)

Mahmoud Manzalaoui's article—"Curate's Egg: An Alexandrian Opinion of Durrell's *Quartet*," *Etudes Anglaises*, 15, No. 3 (1962), 248-260—is a particularly interesting study of Durrell's attitude toward the Arab, for as a Moslem Manzalaoui finds the *Quartet* offensive and inaccurate. He speaks about Durrell's misuse of Arabic and about "pseudo orientalism," and he shows us many of the religious and geographical errors in the *Quartet*. "Curate's Egg" is often extremely pedantic, but it does point to an aspect of Durrell's work that is very troubling.

War was sobering, saddening—numbing, for Forster. He would have agreed with Clea when she said, "Curiously, what I hate most about it all is the sentimentality which spells violence in the end!" (C, 89) Or with Darley—"If the war did not mean a way of dying, it meant a way of ageing, of tasting the true staleness in human things, and of learning to confront change bravely." (C, 89)

But Durrell's vision of war takes another turn as well. Although it obliterates grace—"The city was always perverse, but it took its pleasures with style at an old-fashioned tempo, even in rented beds: never up against a wall or a tree or a truck! And now at times the town seems to be like some great public urinal" (C, 88)—it also leads to a confrontation with life and death that can make full human beings out of one-dimensional men. It is the tournament, the final test. John Keats is transformed by it. A second-rate journalist becomes a man of god-like beauty, capable of leaving us with that wonderful line: "Even the dead are overwhelming us all the time with kindnesses." (C, 163) For Durrell, war heightens our sensibilities. Clea and Darley first make love while the sirens blare.

> So it was that love-making itself became a kind of challenge to the whirlwind outside which beat and pounded like a thunderstorm of guns and sirens, igniting the pale skies of the city with the magnificence of its lightning-flashes. And kisses themselves became changed with the deliberate affirmation which can come only from the foreknowledge and presence of death. It would have been good to die at any moment then, for love and death had somewhere joined hands. (C, 84)

By the end of the *Quartet*, the war and the city have been won; Durrell's Alexandrians, urbane, contemporary folk challenging life on every front, have run through a spectrum of experiences of almost inconceivable breadth. More important: they have relived all those experiences from which time would have seemed to bar them, those adventures we call history, and in doing so have rediscovered, recovered, themselves.

> Walking those streets again in my imagination I knew once more that they spanned, not merely human history, but the whole biological scale of the heart's affections—from the painted ecstasies of Cleopatra (strange that the vine should be discovered here, near Taposiris) to the bigotry of Hypatia (withered vine-leaves, martyr's kisses). And stranger visitors: Rimbaud, student of the Abrupt Path, walked here with a belt full of gold coins. And all those other swarthy dream-interpreters and politicians and eunuchs were like a flock of birds of brilliant plumage. (C, 12)

The city that Darley and Nessim, like Cavafy's protagonist, contemplate leaving, encompasses history and, more than history, "the whole biological scale of the heart's affections": life itself. It cannot be avoided, nor can Durrell's Alexandrians avoid reinacting life's crucial events. They are Antonys. They are Cleopatras. The present and the past are one.

The parallels with Cavafy are strong, but there is an important difference as well. Linking modern and ancient days, the Greek poet creates a mythology in which the great are, like the rest of us, subject to small acts of courage and recurrent failure. Chance, not an ennobling stature, creates one man a shopkeeper's assistant, the other an emperor's lover, and the latter is as likely as the former to be driven by petty desires, petty frustrations. The historical parallels reduce the famous to the size of contemporaries, whom we can know. The dialogue between past and present moves in the opposite direction in Durrell's *Quartet*. The contest between man and life, between the artist and Alexandria, takes on epic scope, enlarging all who touch it.

We live in an age, as George Steiner suggests, that distrusts "the grand motion, the orchestral, the 'copious,'" militating against even major talents, like Durrell's, that are not given to sparse constraint.[20] This seems the likely reason for much of the strangely hateful criticism of Durrell's recent work. His talent *is* a large one, and in the *Quartet* the epic, historical sweep engulfs us in its magic, partly because it is so grand, partly because Durrell, a most un-Cavafian temperament, creates the old Greek poet as a presence in his work, a figure who adds a welcome tension to the quest, who can undercut pomposity and even the Passions of Justine.

Cavafy: a Guide

If only the brown fingers franking his love
Could once be fixed in art, the immortal
Episode be recorded—there he would awake
On a fine day to shed his acts like scabs . . .
"CAVAFY" (CP, 157-158)

History and landscape—reality itself—must be interpreted to be felt, to be understood. And for Durrell relativity is the key; there *seem*, at least, to be a thousand truths. The reader works, piecing the *Quartet* together with the light refracted from Darley's books, Balthazar's interlinear, Arnauti's novel, and everyone's diaries, letters, notebooks, stories, poems, photographs, and paintings. He tries to catch the peculiar intonations of Alexandria through records, impersonations, radios, dictaphones, even a parrot, through the whispers of echoes. The devices are all there, the mirrors and movements, but they tell us no more than do the macabre blow-ups that give evidence but no solution to the murder at the Cervonis' ball. (B, 184) Only the artist, frail and often wounded, can walk through the maze and return with Ariadne and the gold, only "one of us, one

[20] "The Problem of Powys," *The Times Literary Supplement*, 16 May 1975, p. 541. Steiner cites artists like John Cowper Powys, Sir Michael Tippett, David Jones, and Durrell as examples of those who are neglected because they are not in tune with the normative habits of our day.

of the tribe," (C, 101) can know and heal the self and Alexandria.

In the *Quartet* they, the "Real Ones," (C, 243) encompass not only the fictive Darley, Pursewarden, Arnauti, Keats, Clea, Nessim, Carlo Montenegro, and Scobie, but also those real artists whom one suspects Durrell, as well as Pursewarden, loves best.

In *Clea* we even get the fictive poet and novelist's history of English literature: Byron, Donne—"Truth should make one wince"—Shakespeare, Pope, Eliot—"but where is the smile?"—Blake, Whitman, Longfellow who invented the mechanical piano—"You pedal, it recites"—Auden, and Lawrence, "a limb of the genuine oak-tree, with the needed girth and span." (C, 114-115) Elsewhere we hear the echoes of a line from Coleridge[21] and, in my favorite moment in the *Quartet*, join in celebrating "the birthday of Codger Blake." (M, 59)

Cavafy set his imaginative figures in amongst his historical characters. In "Temethos, Antiochian, A.D. 400," he has his fictive protagonist write a poem in which he substitutes an historical name for that of his lover: "The title: 'Emonidis' —the favorite / of Antiochos Epiphanis;" but as it turns out Emonidis is as much a figment of Cavafy's imagination as is Temethos. Only Antiochos Epiphanis is real. Like the "unsuspecting Antiochians" we have been fooled, willingly suspending disbelief because one historical character lent credibility to the rest. In the same way, the historical poems ground and encompass those poems that have no base in history.

Durrell manipulates his readers just as Cavafy did—perhaps with more audacity, for he uses figures from our own recent past. D. H. Lawrence is Pursewarden's beloved friend! Rimbaud, Claudel, and Joyce are added to the tribe, but fittingly no historical personage, no artist—not even Lawrence—takes on the importance of C. P. Cavafy who,

[21] On "reliques of sensation." See (B, 192) and (C, 38).

like the city herself, actually becomes a character in the novels. Durrell gives us more than a Cavafian character—although he does that too: he gives us Cavafy. Along with Cleopatra and Alexander the poet becomes an exemplar of the city. (B, 156) His thoughts and even his voice frame and haunt the whole; his poems encompass it.

Robert Liddell, who also spent the war in Alexandria, said of the city "—built on a narrow limestone ridge, cut off from Egypt by salt lakes, from Europe by the sea—there is every temptation to occasional claustrophobia."[22] The sense of waiting, of gradually learning, permeates Liddell's *Unreal City* and, paradoxically, Durrell's novel of conquest as well, and is one of the reasons why both have as central characters a young literary figure—a teacher or writer—who absorbs the wisdom of mentors more vital than he. The other reason, I believe, is Cavafy, that decadent and wise old man with his coterie of young admirers who, even forty years later, keep tales of their mentor alive, tales that shape the spirit of Alexandria. Durrell's Darley, like Liddell's persona, like Fielding, is a character who bears witness and, only in the end, is able to leave and enter other worlds. He learns from foolish older men, brothers to Godbole, men who are privy to the wisdom of maturity and the Orient, and finally to the wisdom of death, who have accepted the chaos of violence and disorder with a measure of dignity—like Scobie and Pursewarden, like Cavafy and his friend Balthazar.

When, in March of 1970, John Unterecker, a woman named Fiddle, and I spent an evening with Durrell at the Algonquin in New York, Durrell said about himself and Cavafy: of course I didn't get to Alexandria until after his death, but I knew many of his friends and through them felt his presence in the city.[23]

[22] "Studies in Genius: VII—Cavafy," *Horizon*, 18, No. 105 (1948), 190.

[23] This is the spirit—but certainly not the letter—of what he said. In a review of Keeley and Sherrard's *C. P. Cavafy: Selected Poems*, Dur-

In the homosexual physician—the healer—Balthazar, Durrell paints a fictive vision of one of these friends, and, in part, of Cavafy himself.

As the *Quartet* opens, against the backdrop of snatches from "The City" and "The God Abandons Antony," Durrell takes us to cafés, like Al Aktar, where we are to meet over and over again boys who play backgammon hunting for a stranger's touch, "where Balthazar went so often with the old poet of the city." (J, 12) Darley, the young artist lost in the womb, the grave of Alexandria, needs a mentor to help him find his way, to enable his vision to move beyond Justine, beyond *Justine*. And his first crucial, painful help comes from Cavafy's fictive friend.

Balthazar, whose room, like the fictive Arnauti's, like the real Cavafy's, is in Rue Lepsius, looks like Cavafy—"His pale face with its gleaming goat-eyes"—and speaks as Forster would have us believe Cavafy did. "In an English not the less faultless for having been learned." (J, 83)

> . . . Balthazar talked discursively (half asleep) of the Vineyard of Ammon, the Kings of the Harpoon Kingdom and their battles, or of the Mareotic wine to which, not history, but the gossiping Horace once attributed Cleopatra's distempers of mind. . . . ('History sanctions everything, pardons everything—even what we do not pardon ourselves.') (C, 213)

And like Cavafy, whose love affairs Durrell describes as "Egregious if you like and often shabby," (CP, 157) Balthazar sometimes finds himself abused and demeaned by his love.

---

rell also spoke of Cavafy's presence in the city, adding: "So I felt my way into the Alexandrian scene through him, in a manner of speaking; I already knew his work well, but here I was able to situate it clearly in its demographic context. It helped me to estimate his greatness." "C. P. Cavafy," *The New York Times Book Review*, 21 January 1973, pp. 2-3.

> But the object of my choice, a Greek actor, was the most disastrous that anyone could hit upon. To look like a god, to have a charm like a shower of silver arrows—and yet to be simply a small-spirited, dirty, venal and empty personage: that was Panagiotis! I knew it. It seemed to make no difference whatsoever. I saw in him the personage of Seleucia on whom Cavafy based his poem. (C, 59)

Balthazar is clearly like Cavafy. He becomes one of the many prisms through which we get to know the old poet of the city—who will help us, in turn, to understand Alexandria herself. "If Mnemjian is the archives of the City, Balthazar is its Platonic *daimon*—the mediator between its Gods and its men." (J, 81) Certainly one of those Gods is C. P. Cavafy.

When he wanders back through the war-torn city, through the sounds of Arab quarter-tones and the screams of the Bourse, Darley finds his footsteps leading him to the doctor's flat, "to the narrow opening of the Rue Lepsius, to the worm-eaten room with the cane chair which creaked all night, and where once the old poet of the city had recited 'The Barbarians'." (C, 57-58) Years earlier he was similarly compelled to discover the poet behind the poems, to hear Cavafy's voice:

> . . . our footsteps lead us to Balthazar's door, and seeing his light on, we knocked. The same night, on the old horn gramophone (with an emotion so deep that it was almost horror) I hear some amateur's recording of the old poet . . . (J, 125)

Ironically the poem Darley, Balthazar, and Pursewarden hear Cavafy recite is "Voices," from which Durrell gives us a stanza:

> Ideal voices and much beloved
> Of those who died, of those who are
> Now lost for us like the very dead;

Sometimes within a dream they speak
Or in the ticking brain a thought revives them. . . .
(J, 125)

The record, the poet's voice within a voice, and Balthazar's "deep croaking voice of great beauty, particularly when he quotes or recites," (J, 81) help Darley to understand Cavafy better. They provide clues, clues that he again seeks when unsuccessfully attempting to see Cervoni's new Cavafy manuscript, to "get a look at the handwriting of the old poet." (B, 177)

Darley had certainly known much about Cavafy from the start, had seen the image before he'd heard the voice: "I was haunted by his face—the horrifyingly sad gentle face of the last photograph." Indeed he'd lectured on Cavafy, on "the antinomian nature of irony," and had met Justine in doing so.

> . . . it was painful to me feeling the old man all around me, so to speak, impregnating the gloomy streets around the lecture-room with the odour of those verses distilled from the shabby but rewarding loves he had experienced—loves perhaps bought with money, and lasting a few moments, yet living on now in his verse—so deliberately and tenderly had he captured the adventive minute and made all its colours fast.

"But always to preserve the adventive / Minute, never to destroy the truth / Admit the coarse manipulations of the lie." (CP, 157) Darley sounds like the Durrell who wrote the poem "Cavafy." And with his thoughts, if not his acts, he certainly understands the irony upon which Cavafy's poems rest.

> What an impertinence to lecture upon an ironist who so naturally, and with such fineness of instinct took his subject-matter from the streets and brothels of Alexandria! And to be talking, moreover, not to an audience of

> haberdashers' assistants and small clerks—his immortals —but to a dignified semi-circle of society ladies for whom the culture he represented was a sort of blood-bank: they had come along for a transfusion. (J, 26)

We may suspect that Cavafy would have not only seen but enjoyed the impertinence Darley describes. But the Darley who writes *Justine*—like Justine and Liza—is almost devoid of humor. Old "Lineaments of Gratified Desire," as Pursewarden calls him, (B, 92) he's really a sentimentalist at heart.

And so he must learn from mentors like Pursewarden and Balthazar the truths Cavafy held all along: the truths of irony and tenderness that *do* order the world for Durrell—that defy relativity. Balthazar, a fellow-student as well as a close friend of Cavafy, begins the lesson, saying of Cavafy:

> I sometimes think that I learned more from studying him than I did from studying philosophy. His exquisite balance of irony and tenderness would have put him among the saints had he been a religious man. He was by divine choice only a poet and often unhappy but with him one had the feeling that he was catching every minute as it flew and turning it upside down to expose its happy side. He was really using himself up, his inner self, in living. Most people lie and let life play upon them like the tepid discharges of a douche-bag. To the Cartesian proposition: "I think, therefore I am", he opposed his own, which must have gone something like this: "I imagine, therefore I belong and am free". (J, 83)

A balance of irony and tenderness, the words echo through the *Quartet* and mark no character more than they do Pursewarden, whose "ironic chuckle" sounds again and again—even moments before his death—and joins a choir of chuckles: from Keats, Nimrod, Clea, little Justine, and even from sober Darley who finally emerges as an artist when he too can chuckle reading a notebook Pursewarden addressed to Brother Ass. "Truth disappears with the telling of it. It can only be conveyed, not stated; irony alone is the weapon for such a task." (C, 124)

Pursewarden embodies another aspect of the poet that Balthazar touched upon in speaking of Cavafy: "I imagine, therefore I belong and am free," for he demands of himself, "Outface, defy, disprove the Oracle in order to become the poet, the darer!" (C, 133) Living in a seedy hotel that later becomes a brothel, Pursewarden again reminds us of Cavafy. His sister, when told about Mount Vulture, says "So much the better" (C, 190) for she believes what Cavafy tells us in "Growing in Spirit":

> He who hopes to grow in spirit
> will have to transcend obedience and respect.
> . . . .
> He won't be afraid of the destructive act:
> half the house will have to come down.

But Pursewarden himself tells Darley something about Cavafy that echoes Balthazar's "he was catching every minute . . . and turning it upside down to expose its happy side."

> . . . I am full of hope. For always, at every moment of time, there is a chance that the artist will stumble upon what I can only call The Great Inkling! . . . Yes, I believe in this miracle. Our very existence as artists affirms it! It is the act of yea-saying about which the old poet of the city speaks in a poem you once showed me in translation.* (C, 120)

The asterisk then leads us to Darley—Durrell's free translation of "Che Fece . . . Il Gran Rifiuto," on the very last page of the *Quartet*. And here again we get a sense of the important differences in tone that separate Durrell and Cavafy.

Both believe in the tribe, in the chain of artists encompassing Theocritos and those on "The First Step" like Cavafy's fictive Evmenis, as well as Lawrence, Auden, and Ludwig Pursewarden. Both see in that chain, in that city in which "it's a hard, unusual thing / to be enrolled as a citizen," life's real affirmation. But for Cavafy that affirmation is tempered by, is based upon, a sense of loss. Although he never quite sees himself as the free man Balthazar declares him to be, Cavafy sometimes has hope. Speaking of "Hidden Things" that have shaped his life, he says:

> Later, in a more perfect society,
> someone else made just like me
> is certain to appear and act freely.

But what one ultimately does feel when reading Cavafy is a sense of loss. It is *not* the act of yea-saying about which the old poet speaks. He is, as always, interested in the loser, in the right No, in the man who could give up his office as Pope to return to monastic life.

I like Durrell's renderings of Cavafy poems. They are inaccurate, but they don't aim for accuracy—they "transplant rather than translate" (J, 221)—and in them I feel the energy of a giant imagination. They are poems in English—"The City," "The God Abandons Antony," "The Afternoon Sun," "Far Away," "One of Their Gods," and "Che Fece . . . Il Gran Rifiuto"—and, given to us in *Justine* and then *Clea*, they serve to frame the *Quartet*. When they do seem flawed it is because they miss the subtle sense of dignity bonded to loss that marks Cavafy's work, and this is nowhere more true than in "Che Fece." Pursewarden's remarks about the act of yea-saying lead us to the following poem:

> To some among us comes that implacable day
> Demanding that we stand our ground and utter
> By choice of will the great Yea or Nay.
> And whosoever has in him the affirming word

Will straightway then be heard.
The pathways of his life will clear at once
And all rewards will crown his way.
But he, the other who denies,
No-one can say he lies; he would repeat
His Nay in louder tones if pressed again.
It is his right—yet by such little trifles,
A 'No' instead of 'Yes' his whole life sinks and stifles.
(C, 255)

There is a consolation in Cavafy's poem, resulting in part from its perfect prosody and rhyme, and encompassing its pessimistic vision.[24] Durrell's translation admirably mirrors that affirmative quality. But his rendering misses an essential point. Keeley and Sherrard's translation, like Dalven's and Mavrogordato's, comes closer to the spirit as well as the letter of the original, for Cavafy's poem is about the right answer, about an admired act of nay-saying:

For some people the day comes
when they have to declare the great Yes
or the great No. It's clear at once who has the Yes
ready within him; and saying it,

he goes from honor to honor, strong in his conviction.
He who refuses does not repent. Asked again,
he'd still say no. Yet that no—the right no—
drags him down all his life.

There is a triumphant chord in Durrell's translation that doesn't ring true, and that finds its parallel in other aspects of the *Quartet* as a whole. It can best be seen by looking at a poem that Durrell runs through the novels and uses to unify the *Quartet*: "The God Abandons Antony."

At the very opening of *Justine* we are given "Notes for landscape-tones," sketches of the city:

[24] See Appendix A for the original and the other translations, as well as for a discussion of the various English translators of Cavafy.

> A drunken whore walks in a dark street at night, shedding snatches of song like petals. Was it in this that Antony heard the heart-numbing strains of the great music which persuaded him to surrender for ever to the city he loved? (J, 12)

So we have our first entrance, our first surrender to the music that is Alexandria. The musical motif, so essential to Cavafy's poem and to Forster's vision, is repeated by another Alexandrian. As the novel moves on we accompany Darley while he visits the dying old furrier Cohen:

> He sighed once more and then to my surprise, in a small gnome's tenor muffled almost to inaudibility sang a few bars of a popular song which had once been the rage of Alexandria, *Jamais de la vie*, and to which Melissa still danced at the cabaret. 'Listen to the music!' he said, and I thought suddenly of the dying Antony in the poem of Cavafy—a poem he had never read, would never read. . . . How different from the great heart-sundering choir that Antony heard—the rich poignance of strings and voices which in the dark street welled up —Alexandria's last bequest to those who are her exemplars. Each man goes out to his own music, I thought, and remembered with shame and pain the clumsy movements that Melissa made when she danced. (J, 99)

From this point on entrances and exits are marked by music, often strains of "Jamais de la vie," a name that also invades the senses as Justine's perfume. Narouz attends a carnival where the crowd with its banners and torches "poured on with its own wild music (perhaps the very music that the dying Antony in Cavafy's poem heard)." (B, 131) The image is again reinforced when Darley speaks of Justine's kisses, "Unique and unfading as the memories of the city they exemplified and evoked: a plume of music from a forgotten carnival-guitar echoing on in the dark streets of Alexandria for as long as silence lasts. . . ." (B, 192)

Death and departure are marked by music. At the Cervonis' ball, while Toto's body lies undiscovered, Da Capo stands with Darley watching the dancers: "Well, this is where to quote Cavafy the God abandons Antony. Good night. . . ." (B, 178) The end comes for Pursewarden when he casually chooses to dance with Melissa, moving "lightly round the floor, humming to himself the tune of *Jamais de la vie*." (M, 150)

Mountolive's entrance into and exit from Alexandria is very clearly framed by Antony's music. As he drives into the city to meet his Cleopatra after so many years, Mountolive find himself humming an old song, "Jamais de la vie." "Even the hateful song helped him to recover the lost image of an Alexandria he had once found charming." (M, 248) He enters the city in the midst of a thunderstorm and sees it anew. "It was the ancient city again; he felt its pervading melancholy under the rain. . . . The brilliant unfamiliar lightning of the thunder-storm recreated it, giving it a spectral, story-book air—broken pavements made of tinfoil—the lovers wandering in Mohammed Ali Square. . . ."

But, true to his name, Mountolive betrays the city. The meeting with Leila is horrifying, and for this reader the most painful moment in the *Quartet*—"she smelt like some old Arab lady!" (M, 251) ". . . the skin of an elephant. *He did not recognize her at all*!"[25]—for unlike Pursewarden, Mountolive deserts affection, retreating into his official self. Following their meeting Mountolive is attacked by a troop of child prostitutes; the city has become a nightmare, and this Antony leaves it "hurriedly like a common thief." (M, 264)

[25] (M, 252) The portrait of Leila—cheap perfume, shrill voice, exaggerated make-up, and unkempt hands—is later mirrored by Darley's portrait of the new Justine. It is as if each Antony must pull his Cleopatra from her pedestal, must both affirm and reverse history, save and desert his queen.

> . . . he looked back once, with a shudder of disgust at the pearly mirage of minarets rising from the smoke of the lake, the dawn mist. . . . He turned on the radio of the car at full blast to drown his thoughts. . . . He heard the soft hushing of strings and the familiar voice of the city breaking in upon him once again with its perverted languors, its ancient wisdoms and terrors.
>
> *Jamais de la vie,*
>
> . . . .
>
> With an oath he snapped the radio shut, choked the voice, and drove frowning into the sunlight as it ebbed along the shadowy flanks of the dunes. (M, 264-265)

We think of Darley's line: "Each man goes out to his own music."

The *Quartet* is of course a *Bildungsroman*, the story of Darley's coming of age, and so it is particularly interesting to note how this next Antony—with his Three Graces, his three Cleopatras—hears his own music. When Darley and the child, the little Justine, cross the water and return to Alexandria they hear strains of "some dog-eared jazz." "To her it must have seemed appropriate music for a triumphal entry into the city of childhood. 'Jamais de la vie' I caught myself humming softly in my own mind. . . ." (C, 24)

Darley is to hear other music—"Snatches of a quartet squirted from a cafe . . . reminded me of Clea once saying: 'Music was invented to confirm human loneliness.' " (C, 56) —but his own particular exit from the city is marked by a grandeur that mirrors "the great heart-sundering choir that Antony heard." It is foreshadowed by Clea's accident on the island she insists must be Timonium.

> 'They've never found the site, you know . . . When Antony came back defeated from Actium—where Cleopatra fled with her fleet in panic and tore open his battle-line, leaving him at the mercy of Octavian; when

he came back after that unaccountable failure of nerve, and when there was nothing for them to do but to wait for the certain death which would follow upon Octavian's arrival—why he built himself a cell on an islet. . . . And here he must have spent his leisure—*here*, Darley, going over the whole thing again and again in his mind. That woman with the extraordinary spells she was able to cast. His life in ruins! And then the passing of the God, and all that, bidding him to say goodbye to her, to Alexandria—a whole world!' (C, 196-197)

The accent is, of course, on feminine treachery. But having himself rejected Justine, Darley is strong. Like Beowulf, he triumphs in an underwater world; like Arthur he must pull his Excalibur from a stone. Free from woman's spell, he can now rescue her, his last Cleopatra, on a Timonium that touches death but lives with rebirth instead.

Just before he leaves Alexandria Darley hears Antony's music, "Alexandria's last bequest to those who are her exemplars." It comes from Scobie's celebration, that great Hellenistic parade, and echoes the wild music Narouz heard at an almost identical carnival, music that reminded Darley of Cavafy's poem. (B, 131) Acrobats, tumblers, street-preachers, male prostitutes:

> And to all this queer discontinuous and yet somehow congruent mass of humanity the music lent a sort of homogeneity; it bound it and confined it within the heart-beats of the drums, the piercing skirl of the flutes, the gnashing of the cymbals. (C, 234)

The siren from a distant ship reminds Darley that he must go, and with Balthazar, who bids him farewell, he leaves Alexandria: "We found a gharry and sat silent in it, hearing the music and drumming gradually receding as we traversed the long rolling line of the marine parade." (C, 235)

Darley is not alone. "'Leave-takings are in the air'"

(C, 243) and extend to Clea, Mountolive and Liza, Amaril and Semira, possibly Justine and Nessim, and even Balthazar, who, as the first Alexandrian, leaves only for a visit. The use of the Cavafy poem seems fitting, a leitmotif binding, lending a sort of homogeneity to, the *Quartet*. And in a way it is. As in Forster's vision, music holds together what relativity or even logic would pull apart. But Durrell has turned the poem on its head. Cavafy's poem is about endings, about the dignity that comes when we face loss without deception.

The leave-takings with which the *Quartet* closes do not encompass loss; the war is over and all good lovers are united, almost as neatly as if "happily ever after" accompanied the "once upon a time" that Darley can finally write. The wounds have been healed. Boy gets girl in every case —plus art and position. Pursewarden told Clea he wanted his last volume to encompass an act of tenderness—but the "utterly merciless" tenderness that irony alone can convey. (B, 204) Somehow sentimentality seems to prevent Durrell from writing a similar work.

Anthony Burgess joins a chorus of critics when he writes about the *Quartet*: "many are ashamed of having been taken in by those waxwork lay-figures. . . . clever *maquillage* and cunning arrangement of shadows."[26] Burgess is arrogantly wrong. Leila, Scobie, Pursewarden: the colors hold fast. The *Quartet* is a large work, not one about which anyone need feel ashamed.

Still Burgess—and others like Enright and Bonamy Dobrée—strike a raw nerve when they complain of the violence in the *Quartet*, the sensationalism that, with the blink of an eye, does away with arms, noses, and eyes themselves.[27] Certainly much of this criticism rings true, but it

[26] "Durrell and the Homunculi," *Saturday Review*, 21 March 1970, p. 30.

[27] Enright, "Alexandrian Nights' Entertainments," pp. 111-126 and Bonamy Dobrée, "Durrell's Alexandrian Series," *Sewanee Review*, 69,

also brings Pursewarden's complaint about Darley's work to mind:

> These books have a curious and rather forbidding streak of cruelty—a lack of humanity which puzzled me at first. But it is simply the way a sentimentalist would disguise his weakness. Cruelty here is the obverse of sentimentality. He wounds because he is afraid of going all squashy. (B, 91)

We think of Pursewarden's nickname for Darley. But there of course is the final joke, the final irony. It is a touch that Cavafy would have thoroughly enjoyed. L.G.D. Old Lineaments of Gratified Desire knew his weakness all along—and made sure he would have the first chuckle. He even allows Pursewarden to parody Darley's prose—the prose of *Justine*. The *Quartet* becomes an ironic comment on itself, on its very style.

His readers get angry with Durrell—for overblown action, for a patronizing vision of the female and the oriental, for the need to write a masterpiece of size that would all but destroy the understated truth upon which poetry like Cavafy's is based. Then they hear echoes of another popular song that Durrell, the self-taught jazz pianist, brings into the *Quartet*. "Tiresias." Tiresias, master of masculine and feminine knowledge, with whom Cavafy has been aptly compared.[28] Tiresias, who like Esmiss Esmoor becomes an oriental patron-saint, embodied as El Scob, at whose

No. 1 (1961), 61-79. Dobrée is particularly troubled by what he feels to be the lack of values in the *Quartet*.

[28] In a review of Cavafy's poetry, Horace Gregory talks about how much the last photograph of the poet—a picture that has held so many imaginations—brings Tiresias to mind: "A 20th Century Alexandrian," *Poetry*, 81 (March 1953), 383; Robert Liddell's "Studies in Genius," p. 196 also speaks of the parallels with Tiresias.

shrine men and women talk and laugh. Like Pursewarden's chuckle, here is a tune that encompasses loving-kindness and undercuts excess, just as, at Mountolive's initiation as Ambassador to Egypt, Scobie's odd anthem ironically alters the scene.

And if Durrell did not hear all the chords of "The God Abandons Antony," he does hear Cavafy in other poems and lets the old man's voice help him find the phrases of tenderness—and loss as well—that *are* in the *Quartet*, that become its magic, a magic of repetition as well as fragmentation.

It is difficult to include poetry within prose, for as when music is added to drama, the two forms must intertwine or the addition interrupts. C. P. Cavafy was the spirit of his city, and nothing makes that clearer than the realization that four Englishmen lived in and wrote about Alexandria in this century, and each one of them used Cavafy's poems within the body of his prose Forster brought Valassopoulo's translations into both books about the city: "The God Abandons Antony" links *A History* with *A Guide* as well as with *Pharos* and *Pharillon*. D. J. Enright placed an old Greek man in the middle of his novel *Academic Year*, a Mr. Papadopoulo who waits, in the period following the Second World War, behind bolted doors, fearing an Arab attack. Mr. Papadopoulo "delivered himself of something which Packet took to be verse. Turning to his visitor he added in English, somberly, 'Cavafy, our own poet—Waiting for the Barbarians—he complains that they do not come, that there are no Barbarians anymore! Poetry, poetry.' "[29] Mavrogordato's translation of "Ithaca" is also in *Academic Year*. Both poems work, but neither is so organically tied to the prose as are the poems Robert Liddell uses in *Unreal City*, a novel that teaches us much about why Cavafy's poems add such texture to the *Alexandria Quartet*.

[29] *Academic Year* (London: Secker and Warburg, 1955), p. 144.

In *Unreal City* the Cavafy poems—"He Asked about the Quality" and "Myris: Alexandria, A.D. 340"[30]—are not given in translation, although Liddell is himself a fine translator of Cavafy. Instead they become stories from Christo Eugenides' youth, musings that this Cavafy, this Wasteland figure, shares with his young English friend and his Antinous. The poems, because they are conversational, easily lend themselves to a prose adaptation. Liddell has changed some details. In his embarrassment, Christo tampers with the gender of his pronouns when describing the shop assistant with whom he touched hands while asking "Can you show me anything of a better quality?"

Cavafy's Christian Myris becomes Isaac, a young Jew, but he is still the beloved of a speaker from whom he is separated in death because of a strange religion. Cavafy's poem works so well because he has created as his pagan lover a persona in whom we can believe. The confusion, the asides, the conversational tone add to the poignancy of the separation and to the sense of a memory at work, a fragile salvaging hope. Liddell has captured this elsewhere, in a direct translation of the poem:

> Some old women near me began talking softly
> About the last day of his life—
> The name of Chirst continually on his lips,
> His hands held a cross—
> Then there came into the room four Christian priests
> And they made prayers and fervent supplications
> to Jesus,
> Or to Mary (I don't know their religion well).[31]

In *Unreal City* the pull is not between pagan and Christian but between Christian and Jew, where in fact it may have

[30] *Unreal City* (London: Jonathan Cape, 1952), pp. 154 and 218.

[31] "Studies in Genius," pp. 200-201. See *Cavafy*, p. 201, for a fragment of "Myris" in which Liddell has slightly altered the translation.

been in Cavafy's life. The details are also different. But Liddell's prose imitates Cavafy's tone:

> He lay in a room, prepared for burial: you know how quickly everything is done here? And it was the sabbath, or something, next day. I have a confused memory of prayers . . . and old men in hats who turned around and glared at me.

"I felt so cut off from Isaac . . . I ran out of that horrible house." Christo speaks just as Cavafy would wish us to believe Myris' lover did, sixteen hundred years earlier:

> I rushed out of their frightful house,
> I ran quickly before it was snatched away and altered
> By their Christianity—the memory of Myris.

Some essence of the poems—what Auden calls Cavafy's sensibility—is captured in Christo's tales, and made real because we believe that they could come from their speaker. It is as if we were in a café with Cavafy, as if we too were friends, listening to incidents that were later to become magnificent poems.

"Voices," "In the Evening," "The City," "The Barbarians," "One of Their Gods," "Che Fece," "In Alexandria, 31 B.C.," "The Afternoon Sun," "Far Away," and "The God Abandons Antony." Strains of the ten Cavafian poems that weave through the *Quartet* sometimes come to us as musical motif, or the introduction of an odd Cavafian point of view, sometimes in direct translation or, like Liddell's "Myris," as a prose telling of a Cavafian tale. Durrell uses every possibility available to him, every technique; he covers the whole canvas once again.

Numerous images of tired men on balconies merge when we hear Justine

> sitting up in bed . . . reciting slowly, wryly, those marvellous lines of the old Greek poet about a love-affair long since past—they are lost in English. . . . touching every syllable of the thoughtful ironic Greek with tenderness. . . .
>
> And with what feeling she reached the passage where the old man throws aside the ancient love-letter which had so moved him and exclaims: "I go sadly out on to the balcony; anything to change this train of thought, even if only to see some little movement in the city I love, in its streets and shops!" Herself pushing open the shutters to stand on the dark balcony above a city of coloured lights: feeling the evening wind stir from the confines of Asia: her body for an instant forgotten.
>
> (J, 24)

Here Durrell has given us the last stanza of "In the Evening"—a poem, like many in the *Quartet*, linking visions of personal disappointment to images of Alexandria, just as those visions are linked in "The City," one of several poems woven into the novels through conversational prose lines hauntingly repeated.

Sometimes the poems are only suggested. We hear faint traces of "The Barbarians"—which Cavafy recited in Balthazar's room—when Pursewarden gets his evening paper from boys who "ran howling through the thoroughfares like winged messengers from the underworld, proclaiming . . . the fall of Byzantium." (M, 147) A central incident, the death of Fosca, brings Breugel, Auden, and of course Cavafy to mind. Darley, Balthazar, and Clea watch the accident from the shore:

> And yet, all the time, outside the centre-piece of the picture, so to speak, with its small tragic anecdote, normal life goes on unheeded. (We did not even hear the bullets, for example. Their sullen twang was carried away on the wind.) . . . everywhere people bustled, the

> chandlers cried. . . . A water-carrier clashed his brass mugs, crying: "Come, ye thirsty ones." And unobtrusively in the background, as if travelling on silk, a liner stole noiselessly down the green thoroughfare towards the open sea. (C, 180-181)

We think of course of the peddler in "In Alexandria, 31 B.C." hawking his perfume, olive oil, and gum through the streets of Alexandria, unaware that the Hellenic world stood on the edge of disaster.

But it is the Cavafian love poem, hesitant and melancholy, that Durrell integrates into the *Quartet* so beautifully, adding much to the texture of his work. He does not use these poems in fictive relationships among homosexuals. There are, in fact, few homosexual loves in the *Quartet*, although Scobie has "tendencies" and Balthazar and Nimrod vie for the favor of the likes of Panagiotis and Socrates Pittakakis.[32] The homosexual in the *Quartet* is a loner, a wise old man, a Tiresias—an ironic observer of the scene.

Love relationships in the *Quartet* are not homosexual; they are heterosexual and in some ways strangely whole. By the end of *Clea* all those Alexandrians who have been in love are either linked with their perfect mates or, it would seem, equally neatly dead. Pursewarden, Leila, and Melissa are the major casualties. But memory and relativity make even the boundary of death ambiguous—witness DaCapo's reappearance—and so love lives on. It is *here* that Cavafy's voice is heard. It is here that we get a sense of those events

[32] Clea's love for Justine is the one exception. Durrell's attitude toward this love is really quite conventional, for although he enjoys new visions of scandalous sexuality, he is sure that a good woman like Clea grows by discovering her heterosexual self. She must be cured of her homosexuality and her virginity by men, by lovers like Amaril and Darley, who ultimately reverse the sexuality of birth, giving Clea new life and, with a new hand, new art. Clea is the only female artist in the *Quartet*, and Durrell seems to be insisting that because of this she too must encounter woman, must love the deadly Justine, before she can truly become the creator.

that, unmarked and barely noticed, stand at the center of our lives.

Two poems, "The Afternoon Sun" and "Far Away" (or "Long Ago"), are linked and used as a kind of refrain for the quiet and touching affection that binds Melissa to Darley, and for the loss of all precious moments. In "The Afternoon Sun"—echoed in Durrell's own poem "Episode" (CP, 77)—Cavafy's persona reenters a room which has now become part of an office building but where once he had been in love. In Durrell's translation:

> Once here, by the door, stood a sofa,
> And before it a little Turkish carpet,
> Exactly here. Then the shelf with the two
> Yellow vases, and on the right of them:
> No. Wait. Opposite them (how time passes)
> The shabby wardrobe and the little mirror.
> And here in the middle the table.
>
> Somewhere all these old sticks of furniture
> Must still be knocking about. . . .
>
> And beside the window, yes, that bed.
> The afternoon sun climbed half way up it.
> We parted at four o'clock one afternoon,
> Just for a week, on just such an afternoon.
> I would have never
> Believed those seven days could last forever.
>
> (C, 253)

The poem echoes throughout the *Quartet*. Darley talks generally about "Particular rooms in which I have made love, particular café tables where the pressure of fingers upon a wrist held me spellbound." (J, 201) Justine says of the furniture and tenement in which her daughter died, a child-prostitute: " 'In my memory I have become attached to that old divan. It must be knocking about somewhere.' " (C, 125)

But the poem is used especially to describe the tentative,

frail, and yet poignant love that Melissa and Darley share for a moment in time, a metaphorical afternoon. The first note is struck in *Justine*, when Darley sends Melissa off to a sanitarium: "She is going for a week, but in the panic, half-asleep I can see that she may never come back." (J, 91) Later Darley revisits the room he had often shared with Melissa, now redecorated by Pombal's latest mistress. He looks for the old furniture. " 'Somewhere' I thought in quotation from a poem by the old poet, 'somewhere those wretched old things must still be knocking about.' " (J, 153)

In *Clea* the poem reappears and is interwoven with images from "Far Away," in which Cavafy's persona is again tentative, groping, searching through memory for visions of an old love. From Durrell's free translation:

> A skin made of jasmine-petals on a night . . .
> An August evening . . . but *was* it August?
> I can barely reach it now, barely remember . . .
> Those eyes, the magnificent eyes . . .
> Or was it perhaps in September . . .
>   in the dog days . . .
> Irrevocably blue, yes, bluer than
> A sapphire's mineral gaze. (C, 254)

In his notes Durrell-Darley gives us complete translations of both poems, but they appear and mingle in the text when, during the war, Darley once again enters the same flat to find old furniture and the Cavafian lines still knocking about in his mind. The servant Hamid gives him a crumpled photograph of Melissa and Darley walking arm in arm on a forgotten "winter afternoon around the hour of four." (C, 34) "Yes, it was winter, at four o'clock. She was wearing her tatty sealskin. . . . 'Sometime in August—*was* it August?' I mentally quoted to myself again." (C, 35)

Like Durrell's portrait of Cavafy, Melissa is pieced together through images from the past. We remember what Durrell wrote about Cavafian "passionate actuality," when he was translating some of Cavafy's earliest poems.[33] We see the poet allowing a simple, shop-worn object to reinfect his memory. But for Darley the experience is too wearying, and in a sense too real. Melissa had "*utterly vanished,*" could not be evoked—even "with that lying self-deception so natural to sentimentalists" (C, 35)—for the poems will not allow the prose to exaggerate, to lie. It is fitting that Melissa is Greek and, although everyone's mistress, Darley's innocence.

Here is the sense of loss, of personal disappointment and ironic tenderness that Cavafy brings to the *Quartet.* At its best it is a small and subtle force, but like its poet, "standing at a slight angle to the universe," it does much to shape our vision of the whole.

[33] "A Cavafy Find," *London Magazine*, 3, No. 7 (1956), 11.

APPENDIX

·A·

CAVAFY AND HIS ENGLISH TRANSLATORS

In 1919, through the efforts of E. M. Forster, the English-speaking world was fortunate enough to be introduced to C. P. Cavafy and to his translator George Valassopoulo. At the close of the twenties, just over a dozen poems had found their way into journals like the *Oxford Outlook, The Nation and the Athenaeum*, and *The Criterion*. In 1976 the Engilsh reader finds five collections of Cavafy's poetry available to him in English and well over a dozen translators trying to capture the flavor of Cavafy's verse.

A major study of these translators should be undertaken, but that is not possible here. Nor is it possible to speak of the problems of translation in general and of modern Greek translation in particular.[1] This appendix will instead review the history of Cavafian translation, in order that the reader may be better aware of the variety of translations available in English.

W. H. Auden speaks of the surprise he felt when realizing that a poet writing in a completely foreign tongue had influenced him. He had previously thought that poetry, unlike prose, couldn't be translated.

> What, then, is it in Cavafy's poems that survives translation and excites? Something I can only call, most in-

[1] Two works are helpful in this regard: "Problems of Poetic Translation in Modern Greek," *The Times Literary Supplement*, 2 April 1970, pp. 349-350, and Kimon Friar, "On Translation," *Modern Greek Poetry: From Cavafis to Elytis* (New York: Simon and Schuster, 1973), pp. 647-678.

> adequately, a tone of voice, a personal speech. I have read translations of Cavafy made by many different hands, but every one of them was immediately recognizable as a poem by Cavafy; nobody else could possibly have written it.[2]

Cavafy's tone of voice *is* eminently translatable. His magic moves into English in almost every translation. But, as we have already seen in the body of this text, different personalities have attempted this work, and temperamentally some have been much closer to the poet than others.

"The first English translation of Cavafy was made by Cavafy." (TCD, 243) So Forster begins an essay on Cavafy, describing the poet's leading him through the Greek poems. We could almost take Forster more literally, for we do have one strong English prose translation of "The Satrapy" in Cavafy's hand which, as Michales Perides contends, could only be the poet's own—and was probably written for an English friend.

> What a disaster, whilst you are made for beautiful and great acts, this iniquitous fate of yours ever to refuse you encouragement and success; always do littlenesses and base customs, and indifferences stand in your way. And how terrible the day on which you yield (the day on which you abandon yourself, and yield), and you leave, a wayfarer for Susa, and you go to the monarch Artaxerxes who admits you with favour in his court, and offers you satrapies, and the like. And you, you accept these things in despair; these things which you do not desire. Other things does your soul demand, for other things is your soul weeping—the praise of the Demos and of the Sophists; the difficult and invaluable "Euges"; the Agora, the theatre, the crown of laurel. These things Artaxerxes cannot give you; these things you will not

[2] "Introduction," *The Complete Poems of Cavafy*, trans. Rae Dalven (New York: Harcourt, Brace and World, 1961), p. viii.

find in the satrapy; and what sort of life will be yours without them.[3]

Actually the earliest translations of Cavafy were neither by the poet himself nor by Valassopoulo. They were done by Cavafy's brother John, who himself wrote poetry in English: romantic, sentimental, overblown pieces that are clearly imitative.[4] The brothers were very different, and John translated only the earliest poems, those written before Cavafy's unique voice was clearly heard. Still even translations like "In the Soul's House," with its formal, correct English, give us some of the flavor of what is to come. Here we have the Passions dancing in the inner rooms of the Soul's house, while:

> Out of the house the Virtues badly dressed
> pale-visaged,—conscious of their being clad
> in things disused, disvalued past recall,—
> hear the carousal and the wild unrest
> of the depraved Hetairae and are sad.
> Up to the lighted windows they advance
> in pensive silence and, their foreheads pressed
> against the glass, they contemplate the hall
> and stare at jewels, flowers, and lights, and all
> the wonder of the dance.[5]

Valassopoulo's translations were clearly those favored by Forster, and by Cavafy, who was to tell his English friend how faithful to the originals he felt these translations to be.[6]

[3] See *'Ανέκδοτα πεζά κείμενα* [Unpublished Prose Texts], ed. Michales Perides (Athens: Phexis, 1963), pp. 86-88. The date of the original poem is 1910.

[4] Some of John's poems, along with his translations, are among the Cavafy papers in the Benaki museum. There one can find a handsomely printed flyleaf of both the original "*Τείχη*" and John's translation, "My Walls"—most likely prepared as a gift for friends.

[5] A photograph of the translation in John Cavafy's handwriting, dated 5 October 1899, is in *Πεζά* [Prose], ed. G. A. Papoutsakis (Athens: Phexis, 1963), p. 249.

[6] Letter dated 1 October 1919 in the Forster-Cavafy correspondence at King's College, Cambridge.

Valassopoulo translated many of the historical poems.[7] He brought poems like "Ithaca" to the English public, in language marked by grace:

When you start on the way to Ithaca,
Wish that the way be long,
Full of adventure, full of knowledge.
The Laestrygones and the Cyclopes
And Angry Poseidon, do not fear:
Such, on your way, you shall never meet
If your thoughts are lofty, if a noble
Emotion touch your mind, your body.
The Laestrygones and the Cyclopes
And angry Poseidon you shall not meet
If you carry them not in your soul,
If your soul sets them not up before you.

Wish that the way be long,
That on many summer mornings,
With great pleasure, great delight,
You enter harbours for the first time seen;
That you stop at Phoenician marts,
And procure the goodly merchandise,
Mother-of-pearl and corals, amber and ebony,
And sensual perfumes of all kinds,
Plenty of sensual perfumes especially;
To wend your way to many Egyptian cities,
To learn and yet to learn from the wise.

[7] "Ionicon," "The Ides of March," "Manuel Comnenus," and "Come Back," in *The Oxford Outlook*, 6, No. 26 (1924), 94-95; in *The Nation and the Athenaeum*, "Darius" (6 October 1923, p. 14), "The City" (5 April 1924, p. 16) and "Theodotus" (21 June 1924); and in *The Criterion*, 8, No. 30 (1928), 33-34: "For Ammones Who Died at the Age of 29 in the Year 610" and "If He Did Die." Forster's essay on Cavafy appeared in *The Athenaeum* on 23 April 1919, four years before it was reprinted in *Pharos and Pharillon.* Included in it were Valassopoulo translations of "In the Month of Athyr," "Morning Sea," "Alexandrian Kings" and "The God Abandons Antony." There are also copies of "Aristobulos," "The Meaning," "When They Wake Up," "Caesarion," and "The End," translated by Valassopoulo, among the Forster papers at King's.

Ever keep Ithaca in your mind,
Your return thither is your goal.
But do not hasten at all your voyage,
Better that it last for many years;
And full of years at length you anchor at your isle
Rich with all that you gained on the way;
Do not expect Ithaca to give you riches.

Ithaca gave you your fair voyage.
Without her you would not have ventured
  on the way.
But she has no more to give you.

And if you find Ithaca a poor place,
  She has not mocked you.
You have become so wise, so full of experience
That you should understand already what
  These Ithacas mean.[8]

But, as he told Forster in a surprising letter written during the Second World War, Valassopoulo felt incapable of translating the "lurid" love poem and felt Cavafy's reputation as a poet would be enhanced by their omission.[9]

He also dawdled, and so the job of doing the first English translation of the poems Cavafy considered to be his complete work went to John Mavrogordato in 1951.[10]

I must count myself among those who would agree with Edouard Roditi when he objects to "the awkward and pedantic English of John Mavrogordato,"[11] although D. J. Enright makes a good case for its strong points and charm.[12] Mavrogordato is faithful to the rhyme schemes in Cavafy's

[8] *The Criterion*, 2, No. 8 (1924), 431-432.

[9] Letter dated 2 February 1944, among the Forster papers at King's.

[10] *Poems of C. P. Cavafy*, trans. John Mavrogordato (London: Chatto and Windus, 1951).

[11] "Cavafis and the Permanence of Greek History," *Poetry*, 81 (March 1953), 389.

[12] "Tales of Alexandria," *The New Statesman*, 25 August 1961, pp. 244-245.

poetry, as none of the other translators are. Witness Cavafy's "Che Fece . . . Il Gran Rifiuto":

Σὲ μερικοὺς ἀνθρώπους ἔρχεται μιὰ μέρα
που πρέπει τὸ μεγάλο Ναὶ ἢ τὸ μεγάλο τὸ Ὄχι
νὰ ποῦνε. Φανερώνεται ἀμέσως ὅποιος τὄχει
ἕτοιμο μέσα του τὸ Ναὶ, καὶ λέγοντάς το πέρα

πηγαίνει στὴν τιμὴ καὶ στὴν πεποίθησί του.
Ὁ ἀρνηθεὶς δὲν μετανοιώνει. Ἂν ρωτιοῦνταν πάλι,
ὄχι θὰ ξαναέλεγε. Κι ὅμως τὸν καταβάλλει
ἐκεῖνο τ'ὄχι—τὸ σωστὸ—εἰς ὅλην τὴν ζωή του.

And Mavrogordato's:

To certain men when there comes a day
They must say the great Yes or the great No.
Whoever he is will straightway show,
Who has Yes within him ready to say;

And on he goes and honour ensues him.
He never repents who has once denied;
He would say No again, if he were tried.
Yet that proper No all his life subdues him.

It is an admirable attempt, but one that is often costly. Durrell uses rhyme in his version of "The City," but he does not use the exact patterning Cavafy has. Mavrogordato does, and the result is a weakened poem:

"You'll find no other places, no new seas in all
your wanderings,
The town will follow you about. You'll range
In the same streets. In the same suburbs change
From youth to age; in this same house grow white.
No hope of another town; this is where you'll
always alight.
There is no road to another, there is no ship
To take you there. As here in this small strip
You spoiled your life, the whole earth felt your
squanderings."

Still, Enright is right when he suggests that Mavrogordato's translations have certain advantages over those of the American Rae Dalven.

> . . . Miss Dalven invariably uses the horrid word "deviate" to render Cavafy's description of the nature of his eroticism, where Mavrogordato always uses "lawless." If "lawless intoxication" is a bit romantic, then "deviate erotic drunkenness" sounds like a rather grave police charge.[13]

And he is correct when he suggests that Mavrogordato's "Ithaca" closes more successful than Dalven's, although I would add that I prefer the looser Valassopoulo line. Mavrogordato:

> Ithaka has given you your lovely journey.
> Without Ithaka you would not have set out.
> Ithaka has no more to give you now.
>
> Poor though you find it, Ithaka has not cheated you.
> Wise as you have become, with all your experience,
> You will have understood the meaning of an Ithaka.

And Dalven:

> Ithaca has given you the beautiful voyage.
> Without her you would never have taken the road.
> But she has nothing more to give you.
>
> And if you find her poor, Ithaca has not defrauded you.
> With the great wisdom you have gained, with so
> much experience,
> You must surely have understood by then what
> Ithacas mean.

[13] "Tales of Alexandria," p. 245. As we have seen earlier, Dalven's translations are collected as *The Complete Poems of Cavafy* (New York: Harcourt, Brace and World, 1961).

Dalven *does* sound a bit impatient with her dim voyager.

Dalven's translations are seldom extraordinary, but they are unobtrusive, and they generally allow the Cavafian voice to come through.

> To certain people there comes a day
> when they must say the great Yes or the great No.
> He who has the Yes ready within him
> reveals himself at once, and saying it he crosses over
>
> to the path of honor and his own conviction.
> He who refuses does not repent. Should he be
>   asked again,
> he would say No again. And yet that No—
> the right No—crushes him for the rest of his life.

There are moments when I like Dalven's translations best. We have already met Keeley and Sherrard's version of the lines with which "On the Outskirts of Antioch" close. Their Julian "blew up," Dalven's emperor is "bursting with rage." Keeley and Sherrard close "The Mirror in the Front Hall" with "the old mirror was full of joy now, / proud to have embraced / total beauty for a few moments." In Dalven, although the lines are cluttered with pronouns and conjunctions, they do shine:

> but this time the old mirror was delighted,
> and it felt proud that it had received unto itself
> for a few moments an image of flawless beauty.

Dalven's book brought Cavafy to a still wider audience, but the best translations were yet to come. In 1971 Edmund Keeley and George Savidis produced a new volume of Cavafy's poetry in translation. *Passion and Ancient Days*[14] brought those poems that Cavafy had not included in his canon to the English-speaking public. The book is a fine work, sensitively translated with the Greek text placed op-

[14] *Passion and Ancient Days*, trans. Edmund Keeley and George Savidis (New York: Dial Press, 1971).

posite each translation, and it includes many of Cavafy's most candid poems, poems we are lucky to have like "Half an Hour," "Hidden Things," "Strengthening the Spirit," and the raw and moving "The Bandaged Shoulder."

. . . .
I did it up again, taking my time
over the binding; he wasn't in pain
and I liked looking at the blood.
It was a thing of my love, that blood.

When he left, I found, in front of his chair,
a bloody rag, part of the dressing,
a rag to be thrown straight into the garbage;
I put it to my lips
and kept it there a long while—
the blood of love against my lips.

Keeley had earlier joined with Philip Sherrard in putting together a collection of modern Greek verse that included some of Cavafy's poems.[15] In 1972 they collaborated again. The Result was *C. P. Cavafy: Selected Poems*, a volume that Durrell praised highly:

> The arrival of Edmund Keeley and Philip Sherrard on the modern Greek translation scene marks quite a definite and definitive stage of process. . . . Thanks to them we can now say that we "have" Seferis and Cavafy in English, and in versions not likely to be superseded.[16]

There are poems in this collection that Keeley had translated with Savidis the preceding year. In this volume Keeley

[15] *Six Poets of Modern Greece* (New York: Alfred Knopf, 1961).

[16] "C. P. Cavafy," *The New York Times Book Review*, 21 January 1973, p. 2. Several weeks later Auden wrote a letter to the editor attacking Durrell's piece and praising Rae Dalven's translations. *The New York Times Book Review*, 11 March 1973, p. 51. Keeley and Sherrard's *Selected Poems* was published by Princeton University Press, as was the 1975 *Collected Poems*.

and Sherrard hear Cavafy's voice as an extremely colloquial modern one. Mavrogordato closes "Caesarion" with

still hoping that they would have mercy on you,
the baser sort—chattering their "Too many Caesars."

Dalven gives us less interesting lines:

still hoping that they would pity you,
the wicked—who murmured "Too many Caesars."

And Keeley and Sherrard stretch the meaning of "*οἱ φαῦλοι*" and render the lines:

still hoping they might take pity on you,
those bastards who whispered: "Too many Caesars."

Sometimes these translations give Cavafy an immediacy that serves the poetry well. At other times, in lines like "The Alexandrians knew of course / that this was just talk and show-business" the language jars.

But because Keeley and Sherrard have been constantly reconceiving even their own translations, because, like Cavafy, they seem less anxious to "have" a definitive version of a poem than to watch it change and grow, they looked at the poetry once again and, in 1975, produced the *Collected Poems*, a volume that could have resulted only from years lived with Cavafy's work. Often a whole translation is altered. Sometimes nothing is changed, sometimes only the shape of a line, or a mark of punctuation. But anyone who has worked with their earlier translations knows how thoroughly every line, every word has been heard anew. The Keeley and Savidis translation of "September, 1903" includes the following:

why did I keep my lips sealed
while my empty life wept inside me,
my desires dressed in black?

In Keeley and Sherrard's new translations, the final line has become "my desires wore robes of mourning?" "Those bastards" in "Kaisarion" are now "the scum" who whispered. "Talk and show-business," in "Alexandrian Kings" has become: "The Alexandrians knew of course / that this was all just words, all theatre." The language is still conversational, but it seems to be conversation closer to Cavafy's own. Keeley and Sherrard's collection, with the Greek included side by side with the translations, and with George Savidis' notes, is a large and fluid work, a major event for those who love Cavafy and for those who have yet to discover him.

Keeley and Sherrard give us a different "Ithaka" from Valassopoulo's, Mavrogordato's, Dalven's, or even from their earlier version,[17] but it is a fine translation.

As you set out for Ithaka
hope your road is a long one,
full of adventure, full of discovery.
Laistrygonians, Cyclops,
angry Poseidon—don't be afraid of them:
you'll never find things like that on your way
as long as you keep your thoughts raised high,
as long as a rare excitement
stirs your spirit and your body.
Laistrygonians, Cyclops,
wild Poseidon—you won't encounter them
unless you bring them along inside your soul,
unless your soul sets them up in front of you.

Hope your road is a long one.
May there be many summer mornings when,
with what pleasure, what joy,
you enter harbors you're seeing for the first time;

[17] Also see Edward Fenton's translation of "Ithaca" in *A Little Treasury of World Poetry*, ed. Hubert Creekmore (New York: Scribner and Sons, 1952), pp. 256-257; Kimon Friar's in *Modern Greek Poetry*, pp. 142-143; and Robert Liddell's in *Cavafy: a Critical Biography* (London: Duckworth, 1974), p. 154.

may you stop at Phoenician trading stations
to buy fine things,
mother of pearl and coral, amber and ebony,
sensual perfume of every kind—
as many sensual perfumes as you can;
and may you visit many Egyptian cities
to learn and go on learning from their scholars.

Keep Ithaka always in your mind.
Arriving there is what you're destined for.
But don't hurry the journey at all.
Better if it lasts for years,
so you're old by the time you reach the island,
wealthy with all you've gained on the way,
not expecting Ithaka to make you rich.

Ithaka gave you the marvelous journey.
Without her you wouldn't have set out.
She has nothing left to give you now.

And if you find her poor, Ithaka won't have
  fooled you.
Wise as you will have become, so full of experience,
you'll have understood by then what these
  Ithakas mean.

Other translators have attempted various poems. Kimon Friar, in his impressive study of modern Greek poetry, has chosen an interesting selection of "new" poems and poems from the established canon, although I prefer Keeley and Savidis' translation of poems like "The Bandaged Shoulder" to Friar's:

> Then I rebound his shoulder, but in so doing
> took my time, because it didn't hurt him,
> and I liked seeing the blood. It was
> but part and parcel of my love for him.[18]

[18] *Modern Greek Poetry: From Cavafis to Elytis*, p. 151.

Earlier we examined the selection Durrell used in the *Quartet*. Robert Liddell has translated over a dozen poems in his *Cavafy: a Critical Biography*. One wishes he had translated more, for they are fine translations, as we see when reading "Of Coloured Glass":

A detail much moves me
At the coronation of Vlachernae of John Cantacuzene
And Irene, daughter of Andronicus Asan.
As they had only a few precious stones
(The poverty of our empire was great)
They wore artificial ones. A lot of little bits of glass,
Red, green or blue. In my eyes
They have nothing humble or undignified
About them, these little bits
Of coloured glass. Rather they are like
A sorrowful protest
Against the unjust misfortune of the crowned.
They are symbols of what should have been,
Of what on all accounts should have been
At the coronation of a Lord John Cantacuzene
And a Lady Irene, daughter of Andronicus Asan.[19]

Still others have tried, and more will continue to try to touch the Cavafian line. Occasionally they will meet with the success Nikos Stangos and Stephen Spender did when translating "He Enquired after the Quality," one of the love poems that their translations and David Hockney's drawings attempt to capture.

He enquired after the quality of the handkerchiefs
and what they cost, in a low voice
almost stifled by desire.
And the answers that came followed suit
abstracted, in a choking voice
implying willingness.

[19] Liddell, *Cavafy*, p. 199. An earlier version of Liddell's translation of this poem can be found in "Cavafy," *Personal Landscape, An Anthology of Exile* (London: Editions Poetry London, 1945), p. 108.

They kept on murmuring things about the goods—but
their sole intent: to touch each other's hands
across the handkerchiefs; to bring their faces
and their lips close together, as if by chance;
a momentary contact of their limbs.
Quickly and stealthily so that the owner of the shop
sitting at the far end should not notice.[20]

[20] *Fourteen Poems by C. P. Cavafy: Chosen and Illustrated with Twelve Etchings by David Hockney*, trans. Nikos Stangos and Stephen Spender (London: Editions Alecto, 1966).

APPENDIX

· B ·

THE CHRONOLOGY OF *A PASSAGE TO INDIA*

> *Let me tell you a little more about* A Passage to India. *I had a great deal of difficulty with the novel, and thought I would never finish it. I began it in 1912, and then came the war. I took it with me when I returned to India in 1921, but found what I had written wasn't India at all. It was like sticking a photograph on a picture. However, I couldn't* write *it when I was in India. When I got away, I could get on with it. . . .*[1]

In an interview with P. N. Furbank and F. J. H. Haskell, Forster talked about the long interruption in the composition of his last novel, as he did again in *The Hill of Devi.*[2] Nineteen-twelve to January 21, 1924—the date on the last page of Forster's manuscript—a long span. It is particularly important for our study that we have a clear notion of what was written in 1912-1913 and

[1] "The Art of Fiction: I, E. M. Forster," *Paris Review*, 1, No. 1 (1953), 28-41.

[2] "I began this novel before my 1921 visit [to India], and took out the opening chapters with me, with the intention of continuing them. But as soon as they were confronted with the country they purported to describe, they seemed to wilt and go dead and I could do nothing with them. I used to look at them of an evening in my room at Dewas, and felt only distaste and despair. The gap between India remembered and India experienced was too wide. When I got back to England the gap narrowed, and I was able to resume. But I still thought the book bad, and probably should not have completed it without the encouragement of Leonard Woolf. . . ." (HD, 155)

what came after the war. Forster's generosity helps us here, for in 1960 he allowed the original manuscript of *A Passage* to be auctioned off to aid the London Library. It was purchased by the University of Texas—worlds away from that other repository of Forster material, the comfortable library almost hidden in the midst of King's College, Cambridge—and is now housed in its Humanities Research Center, modern and temperature-controlled, where I went to have a look in March, 1974.

Forster once suggested "Green ink chapters written c. 1913 [chapters I-VII]. Adela as Edith or Janet. Ronnie [*sic*] as Gerald. Rest written 1922-1923." But Oliver Stallybrass, who got the manuscript ready for auction, and was in touch with Forster, suggests that

> it would be more correct to say "Chapters I-VII and subsequent green-ink leaves written c. 1913, rest written 1922 or 1923 to 1924." In this case, eleven leaves are all that remain of the earlier version for Chapters VII-XIV; though it is possible that Chapters IX-XI, which are not essential from a structural point of view, had no existence until the later period.[3]

Actually the task of dating is much easier than one would suppose, for the divisions are quite obvious to the eye. The earlier work is not only written in green ink but is also on yellower, watermarked paper.[4] Consequently we can say

[3] "Forster's Wobblings: The Manuscripts of *A Passage to India*," *Aspects of E. M. Forster*, by Oliver Stallybrass (London: Edward Arnold, 1969), p. 149.

[4] Except for a few leaves from chapter two, that seem also to be from the early period and are on much smaller paper than all the rest and in black ink, but penned with a broader tip than the later writing in black. The manuscript has been the subject of several studies. See R. L. Harrison's paper, "The Manuscript of *A Passage to India*" (unpublished Ph.D. dissertation, University of Texas, 1964), as well as accounts in June Perry Levine's, *Creation and Criticism: A Passage to India* (Lincoln: University of Nebraska, 1971) and Appendix B of George Thomson's, *The Fiction of E. M. Forster* (Detroit: Wayne State University Press, 1967).

with assurance that what dates from before the war is the following:

1. Chapters I-VII except for some minor additions, notably the description of Islam (PI, 19), in the book but not in the original manuscript, and the Persian inscription which, Cavafy-like, Aziz wants to put on his tomb, as well as a few references to the malice of English women, and English womanhood's distaste for missionaries, which were added later. The few omissions seem simply to have tightened the prose and removed sentimentality.

2. The opening of Chapter VIII, about Ronny's new "official" character, Miss Quested's decision not to marry him, Aziz's stud pin, and Ronny's distaste for the trip to the caves, but without the couple's dialogue or her announcement of her decision, and of course without the reconciliation that follows. The incident of the animal charging the car in chapter VIII, so central to the image of ghosts running through the novel, is, as Forster's letters reveal, based on an event that occurred in 1921.

3. The description of the Ganges and the hills with which Chapter XII opens, but not the description of the caves.

4. A very much altered version of a bit of chapter XIV, including the description of the false dawn and its comparison with the sunrise at Grasmere, and the description of getting the elephant which leads Aziz to call the east a place where friends of friends really do count.

We do not know if other parts of chapters VIII through XIV were written and destroyed. It seems more than likely that chapters IX-XI were not. But, clearly, from its inception Forster had at least projected the novel to the Marabar Caves.[5] Stallybrass suggests that the central incident in the caves caused Forster great trouble, and much rewriting—and that this is why, and where, he was forced to stop in

[5] "When I began *A Passage to India* I knew that something important happened in the Marabar Caves, and that it would have a central place in the novel—but I didn't know what it would be." Interview with Furbank and Haskell.

1913: a draft of the first seven chapters, and at least sketches of the book up to chapter XIV.

It is interesting that when Forster got stuck, he seems to have turned to another manuscript: *Maurice*, written between 1913 and 1914, a work in which all troubling echoes are lovingly resolved. *Then* came the war and Forster's involvement with Cavafy and Alexandria, and with the two books on Alexandria he was putting together, in 1922-1923, when writing *A Passage to India*.

Selected Bibliography

Annan, Noel. "Morgan Forster remembered by Lord Annan." *The Listener*, 18 June 1970, p. 826.

Anon. "A Chalice for Youth." Review of *Maurice* by E. M. Forster and *E. M. Forster* by J. R. Ackerley. *The Times Literary Supplement*, 8 October 1971, pp. 1215-1216.

———. "Problems of Poetic Translation in Modern Greek." *Times Literary Supplement*, 2 April 1970, pp. 349-350.

———. "A Vision of Alexandria." Review of *Pharos and Pharillon* by E. M. Forster. *The Times Literary Supplement*, 31 May 1923, p. 369.

Alvarez, A. "E. M. Forster: From Snobbery to Love." Review of *Maurice* and *Albergo Empedocle and Other Writings* by E. M. Forster. *Saturday Review*, 16 October 1971, pp. 39-43.

Athenaeus. *The Deipnosophists*. Trans. Charles Burton Gulick. Vol. II. London: Wm. Heinemann, 1928.

Auden, W. H. "Introduction." *The Complete Poems of Cavafy*. Trans. Rae Dalven. New York: Harcourt, Brace and World, 1961.

Barger, Evert. "Memories of Morgan." *The New York Times Book Review*, 16 August 1970, pp. 2-35.

Baynes, Norman. "Introduction." *Byzantium*. Ed. Norman Baynes. Oxford: Clarendon Press, 1953.

Beer, J. B. *The Achievement of E. M. Forster*. London: Chatto and Windus, 1963.

Beith, Gilbert, ed. *Edward Carpenter: In Appreciation*. London: George Allen and Unwin, 1931.

Berque, Jacques. *L'egypte: imperialisme et revolution*. Paris: Gallimard, 1967.

Bevan, Edwyn R. *The House of Ptolemy: A History of Egypt under the Ptolemaic Dynasty*. Chicago: Argonaut, 1968.

———. *The House of Seleucus*. New York: Barnes and Noble, 1966.

Bien, Peter. *Constantine Cavafy*. New York: Columbia University Press, 1964.

Blunt, Wilfred Scawen. *Secret History of the English Occupation of Egypt*. New York: Howard Fertig, 1967.

Bowra, C. M. "Constantine Cavafy and the Greek Past." *The Creative Experiment*. London: Macmillan, 1949. Pp. 29-60.

Bradbury, Malcolm. *Forster: A Collection of Critical Essays*. Englewood Cliffs, N.J.: Prentice-Hall, 1966.

Brander, Lawrence. *E. M. Forster: A Critical Study*. London: Rupert Hart-Davis, 1968.

Breccia, E. *Alexandrea ad Aegyptum: a Guide to the Ancient and Modern Town, and to its Graeco-Roman Museum*. Bergamo: Istituto Italiano d'Arti Grafiche, 1922.

Burgess, A. "Durrell and the Homunculi." *Saturday Review*, 21 March 1970, pp. 29-41.

Carol, Jacqueline. *Cocktails and Camels*. New York: Appleton-Century-Crofts, 1960.

Cavafy, C. P. *'Ανέκδοτα πεζά κείμενα* [Unpublished Prose Texts.] Ed. Michales Perides. Athens: Phexis, 1963.

———. *'Ανέκδοτα ποίηματα* (1882-1923). [Unpublished Poetry.]

———. *Πεζά*. [Prose.] Ed. G. A. Papoutsakis. Athens: Phexis, 1963.

———. *Ποίηματα*. [Poetry.] Ed. George Savidis. Athens: Ikaros, 1963.

———. " 'Alexander Jannai' and 'One of the Jews.' " Trans. Simon Chasen. *Treasury of Jewish Poetry*. Ed. N. Ausubel and M. Ausubel. New York: Crown Publishers, 1957, p. 93.

———. Cavafy Papers. Benaki Museum, Athens.

———. "The City." Trans. G. Valassopoulo. *The Nation and the Athenaeum*, 5 April 1924, p. 16.

———. *C. P. Cavafy: Collected Poems*. Trans. Edmund Keeley and Philip Sherrard. Princeton: Princeton University Press, 1975.

———. *C. P. Cavafy: Selected Poems*. Trans. Edmund Keeley and Philip Sherrard. Princeton: Princeton University Press, 1972.

———. *The Complete Poems of Cavafy*. Trans. Rae Dalven. New York: Harcourt, Brace and World, 1961.

———. "Darius." Trans. G. Valassopoulo. *The Nation and the Athenaeum*, 6 October 1923, p. 14.

———. *Fourteen Poems by C. P. Cavafy: Chosen and Illustrated with Twelve Etchings by David Hockney.* Trans. Nikos Stangos and Stephen Spender. London: Editions Alecto, 1966.

———. "'Ionicon,' 'The Ideas of March,' 'Manuel Comnenus,' and 'Come Back.'" Trans. G. Valassopoulo. *The Oxford Outlook*, 6, No. 26 (1924), 94-95.

———. "Ithaca." Trans. Edward Fenton. *A Little Treasury of World Poetry*. Ed. Hubert Creekmore. New York: Scribner, 1952.

———. "Ithaca." Trans. G. Valassopoulo. *The Criterion*, 2, No. 8 (1924), pp. 431-432.

———. *Passions and Ancient Days*. Trans. Edmund Keeley and George Savidis. New York: Dial Press, 1971.

———. *Poems of C. P. Cavafy*. Trans. John Mavrogordato. London: Chatto and Windus, 1951.

———. "Theodotus." Trans. G. Valassopoulo. *The Nation and the Athenaeum*, 21 June 1924, p. 380.

———. "Three Poems by C. P. Cavafy: 'The Pawn,' 'The Mimiambi of Herodas,' 'The Enemies,'" Trans. Rae Dalven. *Poetry*, 120, No. 5 (1972), 257-259.

———. "Two Poems by C. P. Cavafy: 'For Ammones Who Died at the Age of 29 in the Year 610' and 'If He Did Die.'" Trans. G. Valassopoulo. *The Criterion*, 8, No. 30 (1928), 33-34.

———. "Waiting for the Barbarians." Trans. Richard Lattimore. *The Kenyon Review* (Spring 1955), pp. 291-292.

Crews, Frederick C. *E. M. Forster: The Perils of Humanism*. Princeton: Princeton University Press, 1962.

Davis, Harold T. *Alexandria, The Golden City*. 2 vols. The Principia Press of Illinois, 1957.

Dobrée, Bonamy. "Durrell's Alexandrian Series." *Sewanee Review*, 69, No. 1 (1961), 61-79.

———. *The Lamp and the Lute*. New York: Russell and Russell, 1963.

Duff-Gordon, Lucie. *Letters from Egypt (1862-1869)*. Ed. Gordon Waterfield. London: Routledge and Kegan Paul, 1969.

Dunlap, Leslie. *Alexandria, The Capital of Memory*. In *Bulletin of Information*. Kansas State Teachers College of Emporia, 43, No. 3 (March 1963), 1-25.

Durrell, Gerald. *My Family and Other Animals*. London: Penguin Books, 1971.

Durrell, Lawrence. *Balthazar*. London: Faber and Faber, 1968.

———. *The Black Book*. New York: E. P. Dutton, 1963.

———. "A Cavafy Find." *London Magazine*, 3, No. 7 (1956), 11-14.

———. *Clea*. London: Faber and Faber, 1969.

———. *Collected Poems*. New York: E. P. Dutton, 1960.

———. "C. P. Cavafy." Review of *Selected Poems*, trans. E. Keeley and P. Sherrard. *The New York Times Book Review*, 21 January 1973, pp. 2-3.

———. *Justine*. London: Faber and Faber, 1969.

———. *A Key to Modern British Poetry*. Norman: University of Oklahoma Press, 1952.

———. *Mountolive*. London: Faber and Faber, 1971.

———. *Monsieur or The Prince of Darkness*. London: Faber and Faber, 1974.

———. *Nunquam*. New York: E. P. Dutton, 1970.

———. *Prospero's Cell and Reflections on a Marine Venus*. New York: Dutton, 1962.

———. *Spirit of Place: Letters and Essays on Travel*. Ed. Alan G. Thomas. New York: E. P. Dutton, 1969.

———. *Tunc*. New York: E. P. Dutton, 1968.

Enright, D. J. *Academic Year*. London: Secker and Warburg, 1955.

———. "Alexandrian Nights' Entertainments: Lawrence Durrell's 'Quartet.'" *Conspirators and Poets*. London: Chatto and Windus, 1966. Pp. 111-120.

———. "A Passage to Alexandria." *A Garland for E. M. Forster*. Ed. H. H. Anniah Gowda. Mysore, India: The Literary Half-Yearly, 1969. Pp. 49-50.

———. "The Cultural War: A note on the Intelligentsia of Alexandria." *World Review*, New Series No. 35 (January 1952), 66-67.

———. *The Laughing Hyena and Other Poems*. London: Routledge and Kegan Paul, 1953.

———. *The Old Adam*. London: Chatto and Windus, 1965.

———. "Too Many Caesars: The Poems of C. P. Cavafy." *Conspirators and Poets*. London: Chatto and Windus, 1966. Pp. 160-166.

———. "The Poet-Historian." *The New Statesman*, 29 January 1971, pp. 156-157.

———. "Tales of Alexandria." *The New Statesman*, 25 August 1961, pp. 244-245.

Epstein, Joseph. "E. M. Forster's Posthumous Novel—More Important to the Man than to Literature." Review of *Maurice*. *The New York Times Book Review*, 10 October 1971, pp. 1-29.

Fedden, Robin. "An Anatomy of Exile." *Personal Landscape, An Anthology of Exile*. Ed. R. Fedden *et al.* London: Editions Poetry London, 1945, pp. 7-15.

Forster, E. M. *Abinger Harvest*. New York: Harcourt, Brace and World, 1964.

———. *Albergo Empedocle and Other Writings*. New York: Liveright, 1971.

———. *Alexandria: A History and a Guide*. New York: Doubleday, 1961.

———. "Alexandria Vignettes: Army English." *The Egyptian Mail*. 12 January 1919, p. 2.

———. "Alexandria Vignettes: Canopus, Menouthis, Aboukir." *The Egyptian Mail*. 29 December 1918, p. [2].

———. "Alexandria Vignettes: England's Honour (Being Extracts from the Diary of Mme. Kyriakidis, Ramleh)." *The Egyptian Mail*. 26 January 1919, p. [2].

———. "Alexandria Vignettes: Handel in Egypt." *The Egyptian Mail*. 6 January 1918, p. 2.

———. "Alexandria Vignettes: Higher Aspects." *The Egyptian Mail*, 5 May 1918, p. [2].

———. "Alexandria Vignettes: Photographic Egypt." *The Egyptian Mail*. 13 January 1918, p. 2.

———. *Aspects of the Novel*. New York: Harcourt, Brace and World, 1954.

———. *The Celestial Omnibus and Other Stories*. New York: Knopf, 1923.

———. "C. P. Cavafy: 1863-1933." *Umbrella*, 1 (October 1958), 5-7.

———. *Egypt*. London: Labour Research Department, 1920.

———. "The Egyptian Labour Corps." *The Times*, 13 November 1919, p. 8.

———. *The Eternal Moment and Other Stories*. New York: Harcourt, Brace and Co., 1928.

———. "A First Flight." *National Review*, 73 (March 1919), 118-119.

Forster, E. M. Forster-Cavafy Correspondence. Forster Papers, King's College, Cambridge.

———. "Gippo English." *The Egyptian Mail*, 16 December 1919, p. 2.

———. *Goldsworthy Lowes Dickinson*. New York: Harcourt, Brace and Co., 1934.

———. *The Hill of Devi*. London: Edward Arnold, 1953.

———. *Howards End*. New York: Vintage Books, n.d.

———. "Indian Entries." *Encounter*, 18 (January 1962), 20-27.

———. "In the Rue Lepsius." *The Listener*, 5 July 1951, pp. 28-29.

———. "John McNeill Has Come." *The Egyptian Mail*, 10 February 1918, p. 2.

———. Letter to Robert Trevelyan. *A Garland for E. M. Forster*. Ed. H. H. Anniah Gowda. Mysore, India: The Literary Half-Yearly, 1969. Pp. 131-132.

———. *The Life to Come and Other Stories*. New York: W. W. Norton, 1972.

———. "Literature and History." *The Athenaeum*, No. 4679, 2 January 1920, pp. 26-27.

———. *The Longest Journey*. Norfolk, Connecticut: New Directions, n.d.

———. *Marianne Thornton*. London: Edward Arnold, 1956.

———. *Maurice*. New York: W. W. Norton, 1971.

———. "A Musician in Egypt." *The Egyptian Mail*, 21 October 1917, p. [2].

———. "Our Diversions, [1]: Diana's Dilemma." *The Egyptian Mail*, 26 August 1917, p. [2].

———. "Our Diversions, 2: Sunday Music." *The Egyptian Mail*, 2 September 1917, p. [2].

———. *A Passage to India*. New York: Harcourt, Brace and World, 1952.

———. *Pharos and Pharillon*. New York: Alfred A. Knopf, 1962.

———. *A Room with a View*. New York: Vintage Books, n.d.

———. "To the Editor of the Athenaeum." *The Athenaeum*, No. 4717, 24 September 1920, p. 419.

———. "The Trouble in Egypt: Treatment of the Fellahin." *The Manchester Guardian*, 29 March 1919, p. 8.

———. "XXth Century Alexandria: the New Quay." *The Egyptian Mail*, 5 December 1917, p. 2.

———. *Two Cheers for Democracy.* London: Penguin Books, 1965.

———. *Where Angels Fear to Tread.* New York: Vintage Books, n.d.

France, Anatole. *Thais.* Trans. Robert B. Douglas. London: Lane, 1926.

Fraser, P. M. "Cavafy and the Elgin Marbles." *Modern Language Review,* 58 (1963), 66-68.

Friar, Kimon. *Modern Greek Poetry: From Cavafis to Elytis.* Trans. Kimon Friar. New York: Simon and Schuster, 1973.

Furbank, P. N. and F.J.H. Haskell. "The Art of Fiction: I, E. M. Forster." *Paris Review,* 1, No. 1 (1953), 28-41.

Furbank, P. N. "The Personality of E. M. Forster." *Encounter,* 35 (November 1970), 61-68.

Gibbon, Edward. *The History of the Decline and Fall of the Roman Empire.* 2 vols. London: J. M. Dent, 1925.

Godshalk, William Leigh. "Some Sources of Durrell's *Alexandria Quartet.*" *Modern Fiction Studies,* 13, No. 3 (1967), 361-374.

Golffing, Francis. "The Alexandrian Mind: Notes toward a Definition." *Partisan Review,* 22 (1955), 73-82.

Gordon, Ambrose. "Time, Space, and Eros: *The Alexandria Quartet* Rehearsed." *Six Contemporary Novels.* Ed. William O. S. Sutherland, Jr. Austin: University of Texas, 1962. Pp. 6-21.

Greener, Leslie. *The Discovery of Egypt.* London: Cassell, 1966.

Gregory, Horace. "A 20th Century Alexandrian." *Poetry,* 81 (March 1953), 383-388.

Grimal, Pierre. *Hellenism and the Rise of Rome.* London: Weidenfeld and Nicolson, 1968.

Higham, T. F. and C. M. Bowra, eds. *Oxford Book of Greek Verse in Translation.* Oxford: Clarendon Press, 1950.

Hopkins, Harry. *Egypt the Crucible.* London: Secker and Warburg, 1969.

Josephus, Flavius. *The Works of Flavius Josephus.* Trans. William Whiston. Philadelphia: David McKay, n.d.

Julian. *The Works of Emperor Julian.* Trans. Wilmer Cave Wright. 2 vols. London: Wm. Heinemann, 1954.

Keeley, Edmund. *Cavafy's Alexandria: Study of a Myth in Progress.* In manuscript.

———. "Constantine Cavafy and George Seferis: A Study of Their Poetry and Its Relation to the Modern English Tradition." Unpublished Ph.D. dissertation, Oxford University, 1952.

———. " 'Latest' Poems Increases Cavafy's Appeal to Students." *University: A Princeton Quarterly*, No. 48 (Spring 1971), pp. 25-29.

———. "The 'New' Poems of Cavafy." *Modern Greek Writers.* Ed. Edmund Keeley and Peter Bien. Princeton: Princeton University Press, 1972. Pp. 123-143.

Keeley, Edmund, and Philip Sherrard, trans. *Six Poets of Modern Greece.* New York: Alfred Knopf, 1961.

Kelvin, Norman. *E. M. Forster.* Carbondale and Edwardsville: Southern Illinois University Press, 1967.

Khoori, Alexander R. *Alexandria: How to See It.* London: The Anglo-Egyptian Supply Association, 1926.

Kingsley, Charles. *Hypatia. The Works of Charles Kingsley.* Vol. VI. Philadelphia: Morris and Co., 1898-1899.

Kirkpatrick, B. J. *A Bibliography of E. M. Forster.* London: Rupert Hart-Davis, 1968.

Klingopulos, G. D. "E. M. Forster's Sense of History: and Cavafy." *Essays in Criticism*, 8 (1958), 156-165.

Leveque, Pierre. *The Greek Adventure.* Trans. Miriam Kochan. London: Weidenfeld and Nicolson, 1968.

Levine, June Perry. *Creation and Criticism: A Passage to India.* Lincoln: University of Nebraska, 1971.

Liddell, Robert. *Cavafy: a Critical Biography.* London: Duckworth, 1974.

———. "Cavafy." *Personal Landscape, An Anthology of Exile.* London: Editions Poetry London, 1945. Pp. 100-110.

———. "Studies in Genius: VII—Cavafy." *Horizon*, 18, No. 105 (1948), 187-202.

———. *Unreal City.* London: Jonathan Cape, 1952.

Macaulay, Rose. *The Writings of E. M. Forster.* London: Hogarth Press, 1938.

McDowell, Frederick P. W. *E. M. Forster.* New York: Twayne, 1967.

Macurdy, Grace M. *Hellenistic Queens.* Chicago: Argonaut, 1967.

Malanos, Timos. Ἡ *μυθολογία τῆς Καβαφικῆς πολιτείας* [The Mythology of the Cavafian City.] Alexandria: N.p., 1943.

Mallalieu, H. B. " 'Variations on a Theme of Cavafy' and 'Portrait.' " *Poetry*, 120, No. 5 (1972), 272-273.

Mannin, Ethel. *Aspects of Egypt*. London: Hutchinson, 1964.

Manzalaoui, Mahmoud. "Curate's Egg: An Alexandrian Opinion of Durrell's *Quartet*." *Études anglaises*, 15, No. 3 (1962), 248-260.

Marlowe, John. *Anglo-Egyptian Relations: 1800-1956*. London: Frank Cass and Co., 1965.

———. *The Golden Age of Alexandria*. London: Victor Gollancz, 1971.

Maronitis, D. N. "Arrogance and Intoxication: The Poet and History in Cavafy." In *Eighteen Texts: Writings by Contemporary Greek Authors*. Ed. Willis Barnstone. Cambridge: Harvard University Press, 1972. Pp. 117-134.

Milne, J. Grafton. *A History of Egypt*. 6 vols. London: Methuen, 1898.

Moore, Harry T. *E. M. Forster*. New York: Columbia University Press, 1965.

Morcos, Mona Louis. "Elements of the Autobiographical in *The Alexandria Quartet*." *Modern Fiction Studies*, 13, No. 3 (1967), 343-359.

Paton, W. R., trans. *The Greek Anthology*. 5 vols. London: Wm. Heinemann, 1919.

Plomer, William. *The Fivefold Screen*. London: Hogarth Press, 1932.

Plutarch. *Plutarch's Lives*. Trans. Benadotte Perrin. Vol. VII. London: Wm. Heinemann, 1958.

Potter, Robert and Brooke Whiting. *Lawrence Durrell: A Checklist*. Los Angeles: University of California Library, 1961.

Roditi, Edouard. "Cavafis and the Permanence of Greek History." *Poetry*, 81 (March 1953), 389-392.

Rostovtzeff, M. *The Social and Economic History of the Hellenistic World*. 3 vols. Oxford: Clarendon Press, 1941.

Ruehlen, Petroula Kephala. "Constantine Cavafy: A European Poet." *Nine Essays in Modern Literature*. Ed. Donald E. Stanford. Baton Rouge: Louisiana State University Press, 1965. Pp. 36-62.

Rushdi, Rashad. *English Travellers in Egypt during the Reign of Mohammed Ali*. Cairo: Fouad I University Press, 1952.

Rutherford, Andrew, ed. *Twentieth-Century Interpretations of A Passage to India*. Englewood Cliffs, N.J.: Prentice-Hall, 1970.

Schindler's Guide to Alexandria. Cairo: K. Schindler, 1943.

Seferis, George. "Cavafy and Eliot—A Comparison." *On the Greek Style*. Trans. Rex Warner and Th. Frangopoulos. Boston: Little, Brown and Co., 1966. Pp. 119-163.

La semaine egyptienne. Numéro spécial consacré au poète Alexandrin C. P. Cavafy, Avril 1929.

Sherrard, Philip. "Constantine Cavafis (1863-1933)." *The Marble Threshing Floor*. London: Vallentine, Mitchell, 1956. Pp. 83-123.

Spender, Steven. "Forster's Queer Novel." Review of *Maurice* by E. M. Forster. *Partisan Review*, 39 (1972), pp. 113-117.

Stallybrass, Oliver, ed. *Aspects of E. M. Forster*. London: Edward Arnold, 1969.

———. "Forster's 'Wobblings': The Manuscripts of *A Passage to India*." *Aspects of E. M. Forster*. Ed. Oliver Stallybrass. London: Edward Arnold, 1969. Pp. 143-154.

———. "Introduction." *The Life to Come and Other Stories*. E. M. Forster. New York: W. W. Norton, 1972. Pp. vii-xxi.

Stewart, Desmond. *Young Egypt*. London: Allan Wingate, 1958.

Stone, Wilfred. *The Cave and the Mountain: A Study of E. M. Forster*. Stanford, California: Stanford University Press, 1966.

Strabo. *The Geography of Strabo*. Trans. Horace Leonard Jones. Vol. VIII. London: Wm. Heinemann, 1959.

Strachey, Lytton. *Biographical Essays*. London: Chatto and Windus, 1960.

———. *Portraits in Miniature and Other Essays*. London: Chatto and Windus, 1931.

Thackeray, William Makepeace. *Notes of a Journey from Cornhill to Cairo*. In *The Works of William Makepeace Thackeray*. Vol. XIV. London: Smith, Elder, 1869.

Theocritus. *Theocritus*. Ed. A.S.F. Gow. Vol. I. Cambridge: Cambridge University Press, 1950.

Thompson, George H. *The Fiction of E. M. Forster*. Detroit: Wayne State University Press, 1967.

Thomson, George. "A Forster Miscellany: Thoughts on the Uncollected Writings." *Aspects of E. M. Forster*. Ed. Oliver Stallybrass. London: Edward Arnold, 1969. Pp. 155-175.

Trilling, Lionel. *E. M. Forster*. London: Hogarth Press, 1967.

Tsirkas, Stratis. *Drifting Cities*. Trans. Kay Cicellis. New York: Knopf, 1974.

Unterecker, John. *Lawrence Durrell*. New York: Columbia University Press, 1964.

Vryonis, Speros. *Byzantium and Europe*. London: Thames and Hudson, 1967.

Waller, John. "Cavafy." *Poetry* [London], No. 23 (Winter 1951), p. 33.

Warner, Rex. "Introduction." *Poems of C. P. Cavafy*. Trans. John Mavrogordato. London: Chatto and Windus, 1951. Pp. 1-9.

Weigel, John A. *Lawrence Durrell*. New York: Twayne, 1965.

Wescott, Glenway. "A Dinner, a Talk, a Walk with Forster." *The New York Times Book Review*, 10 October 1971, pp. 2-22.

Wickes, George, ed. *Lawrence Durrell and Henry Miller: A Private Correspondence*. New York: Dutton, 1963.

Wilson, Colin. "A Man's Man." Review of *Maurice* by E. M. Forster. *Spectator*, 9 October 1971, pp. 512-513.

Index

PRINCETON ESSAYS IN LITERATURE

The Orbit of Thomas Mann. By Erich Kahler

On Four Modern Humanists: Hofmannsthal, Gundolf, Curtius, Kantorowicz. Edited by Arthur R. Evans, Jr.

Flaubert and Joyce: The Rite of Fiction. By Richard Cross

A Stage for Poets: Studies in the Theatre of Hugo and Musset. By Charles Affron

Hofmannsthal's Novel "Andreas." By David Miles

On Gide's "Prométhée": Private Myth and Public Mystification. By Kurt Weinberg

Kazantzakis and the Linguistic Revolution in Greek Literature. By Peter Bien

Modern Greek Writers. Edited by Edmund Keeley and Peter Bien

Wallace Stevens and the Symbolist Imagination. By Michel Benamou

The Inner Theatre of Recent French Poetry. By Mary Ann Caws

Cervantes' Christian Romance: A Study of "Persiles y Sigismunda." By Alban K. Forcione

The Prison-House of Language: A Critical Account of Structuralism and Russian Formalism. By Fredric Jameson

Ezra Pound and the Troubadour Tradition. By Stuart Y. McDougal

The Poetic World of Boris Pasternak. By Olga Raevsky Hughes

Wallace Stevens: Imagination and Faith. By Adalaide Kirby Morris

On the Art of Medieval Arabic Literature. By Andras Hamori

The Aesthetics of György Lukács. By Bela Kiralyfalvi

Achilles' Choice: Examples of Modern Tragedy. By David Lenson

Library of Congress Cataloging in Publication Data

Pinchin, Jane Lagoudis, 1942-
Alexandria still.

(Princeton essays in literature)
Bibliography: p.
Includes index.
1. Kabaphès, Kōnstantinos Petrou, 1863-1933—Criticism and interpretation. 2. Forster, Edward Morgan, 1879-1970—Criticism and interpretation. 3. Durrell, Lawrence Wood, 1888- —Criticism and interpretation. 4. Alexandria, Egypt. I. Title.
PA5610.K2Z85 809′.933′2 76-3014
ISBN 0-691-06283-8